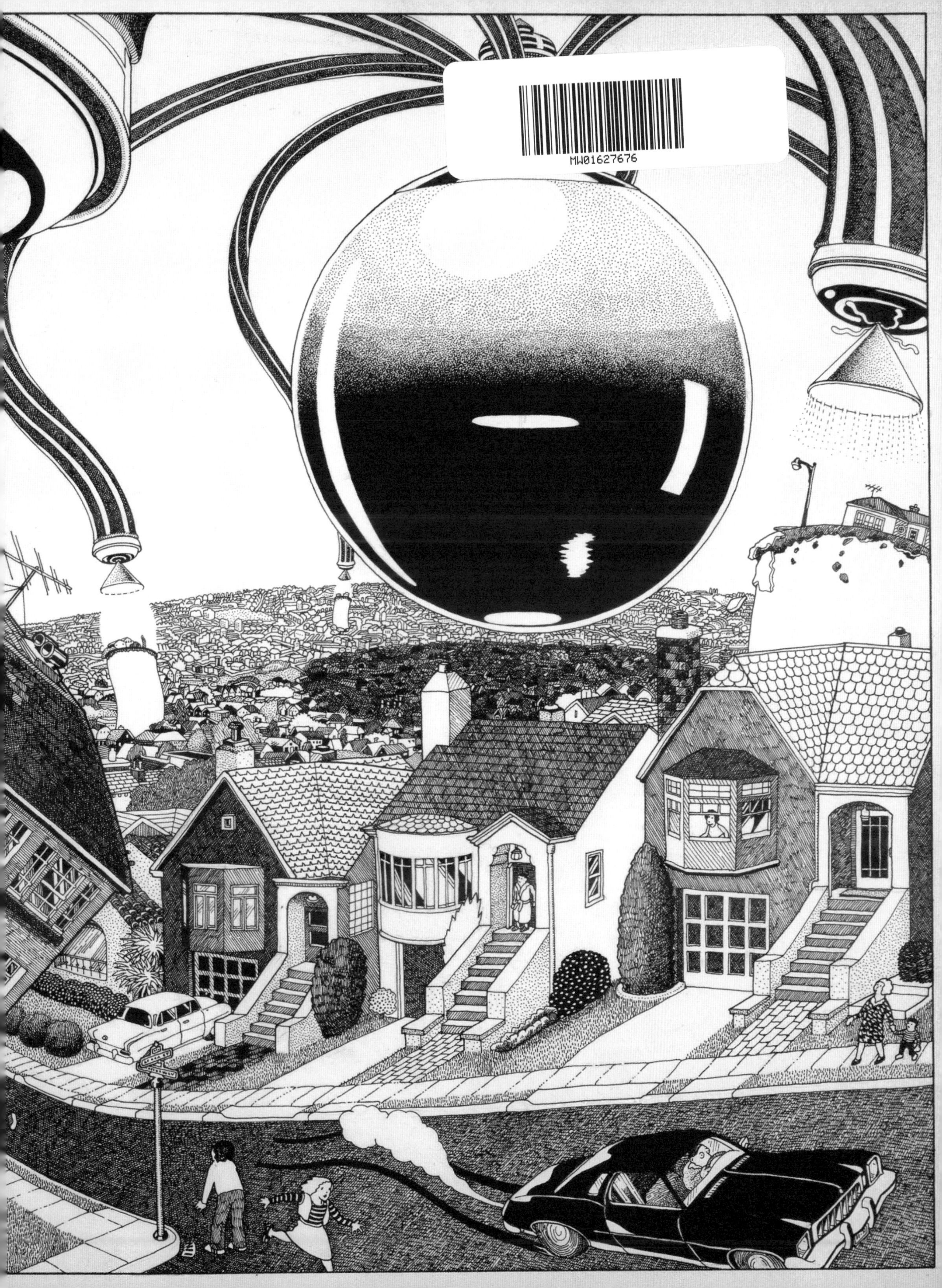

TERMINAL EXPOSURE

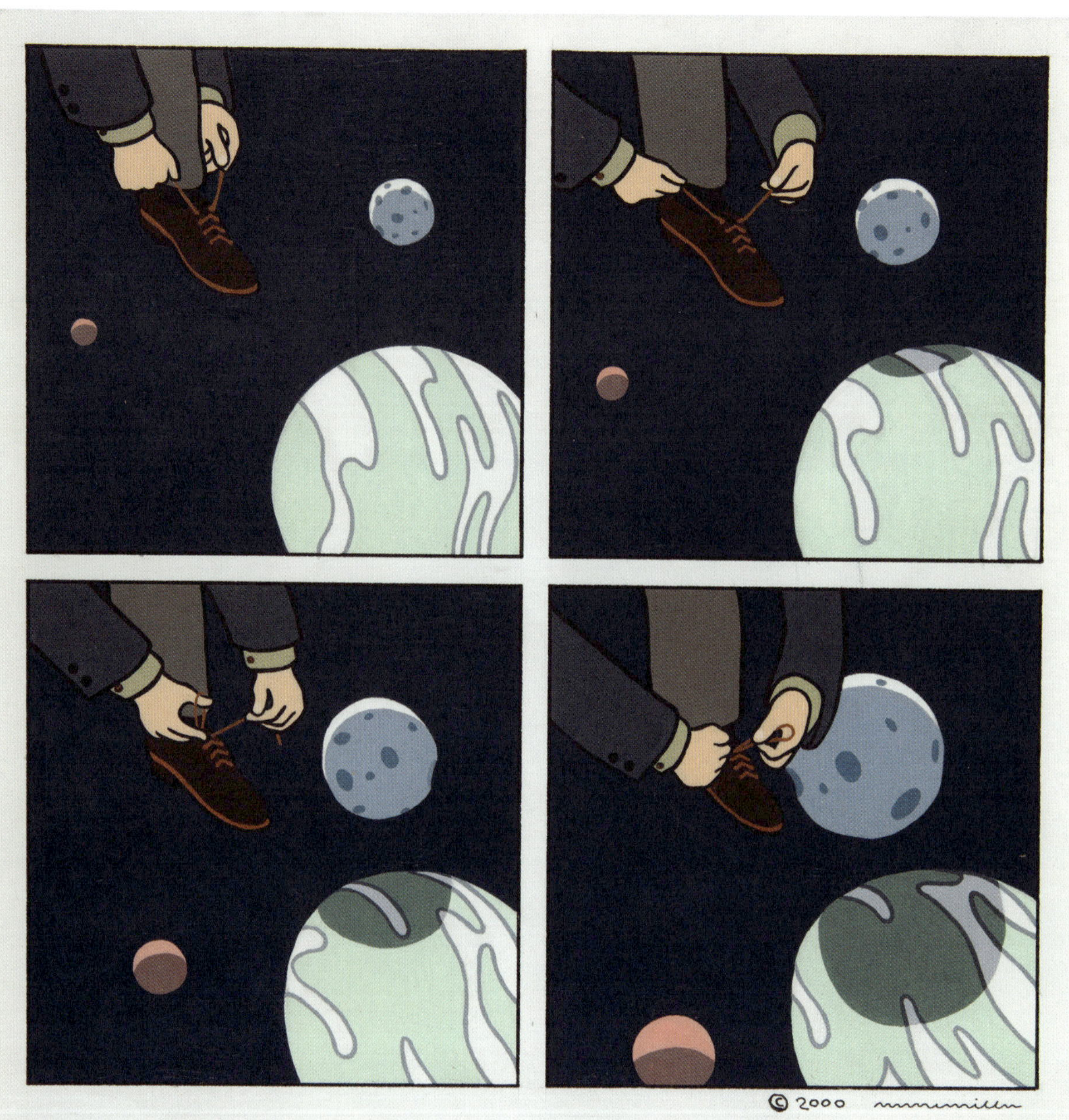

He stops to tie his shoe while distant moons roll forever through eccentric orbits

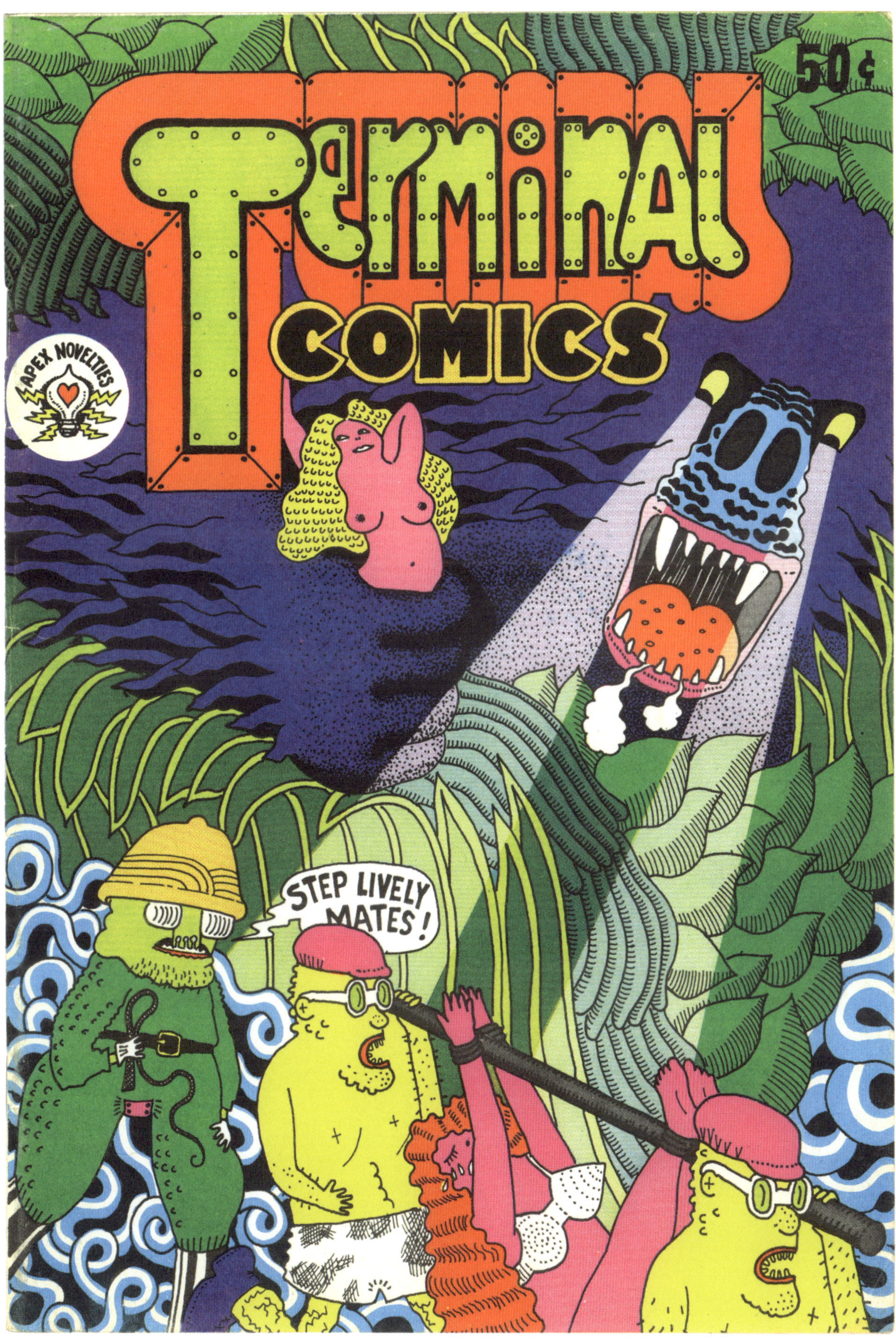
50¢
Terminal
COMICS
APEX NOVELTIES
STEP LIVELY MATES!

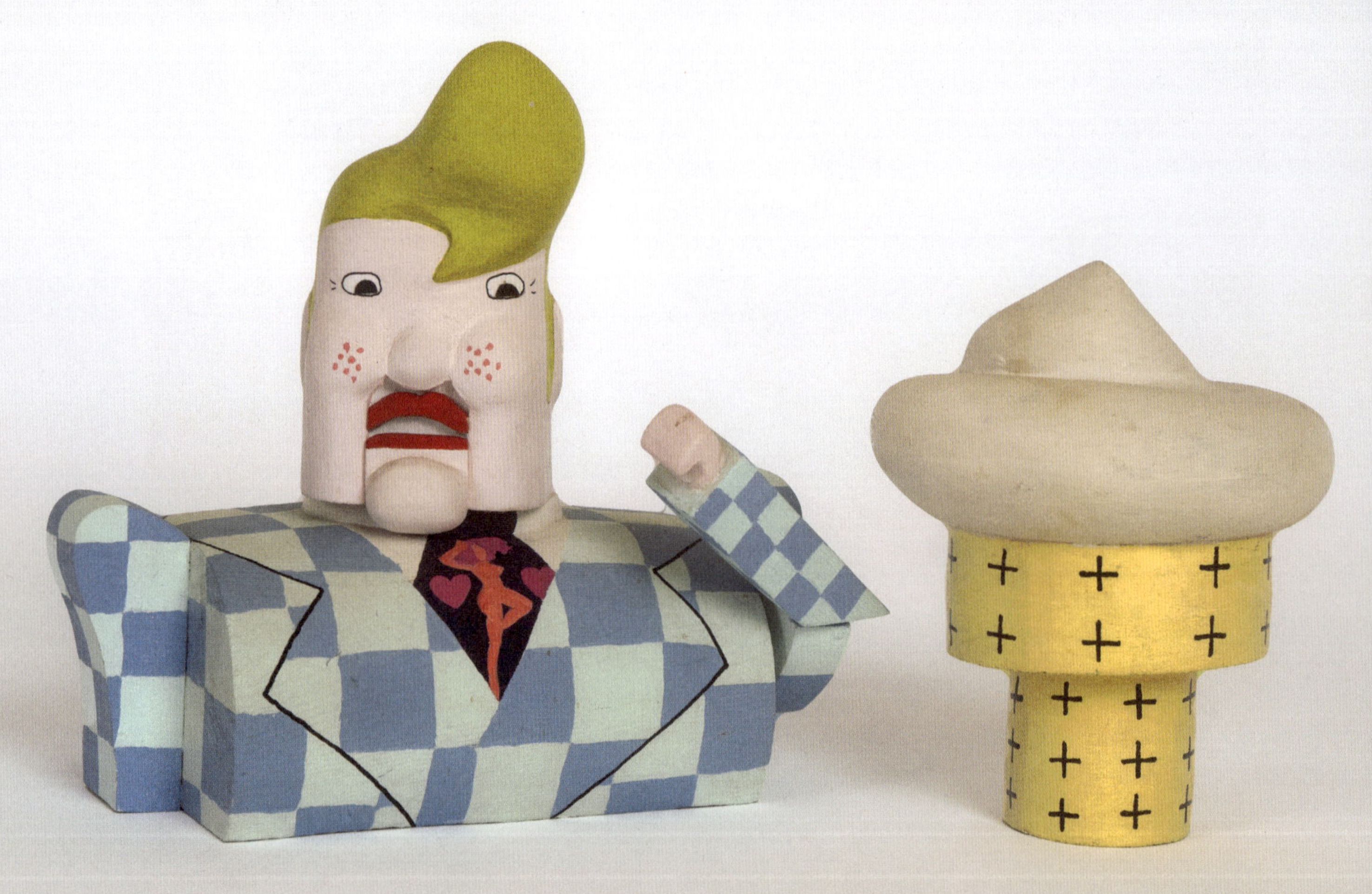

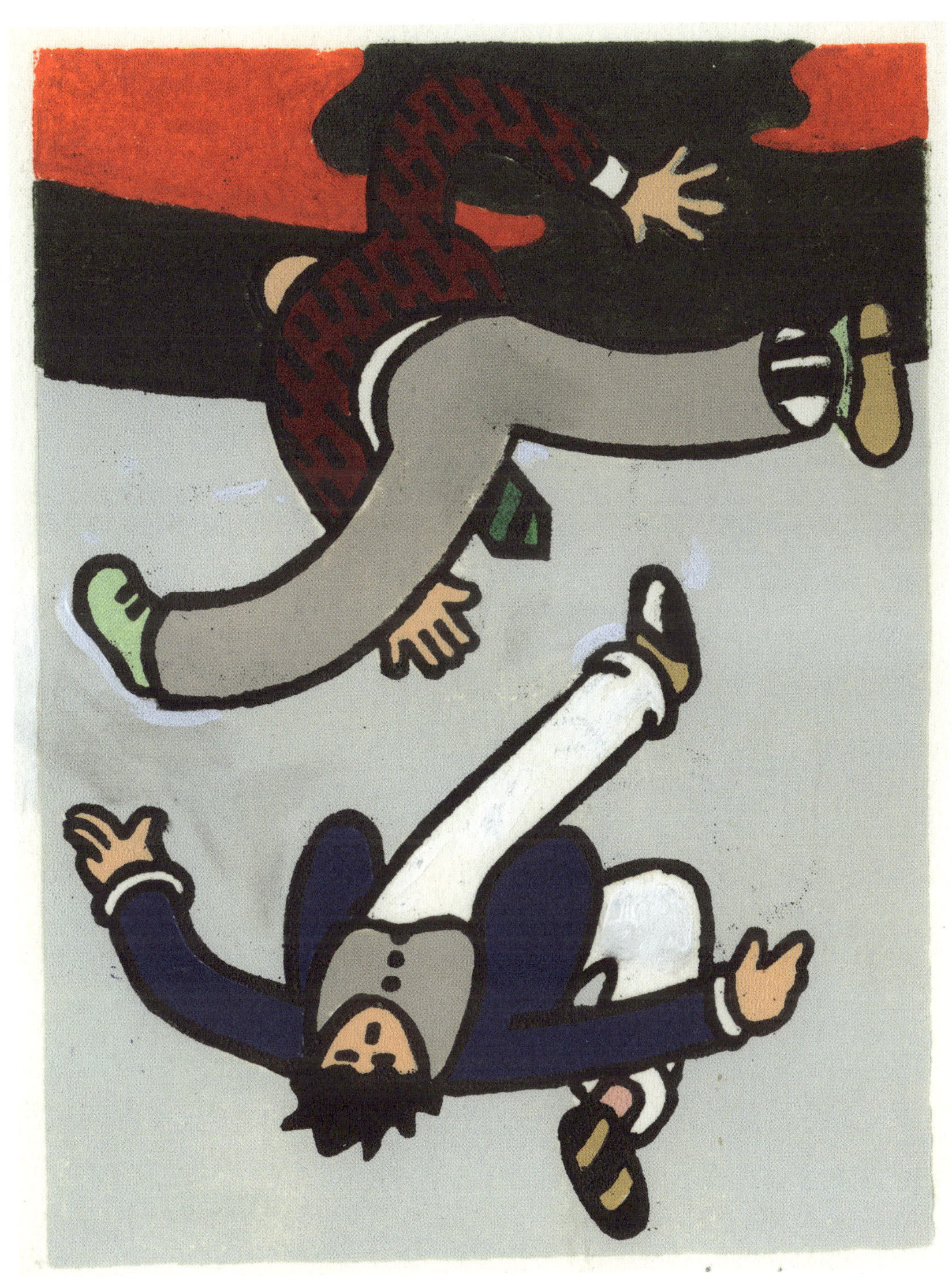

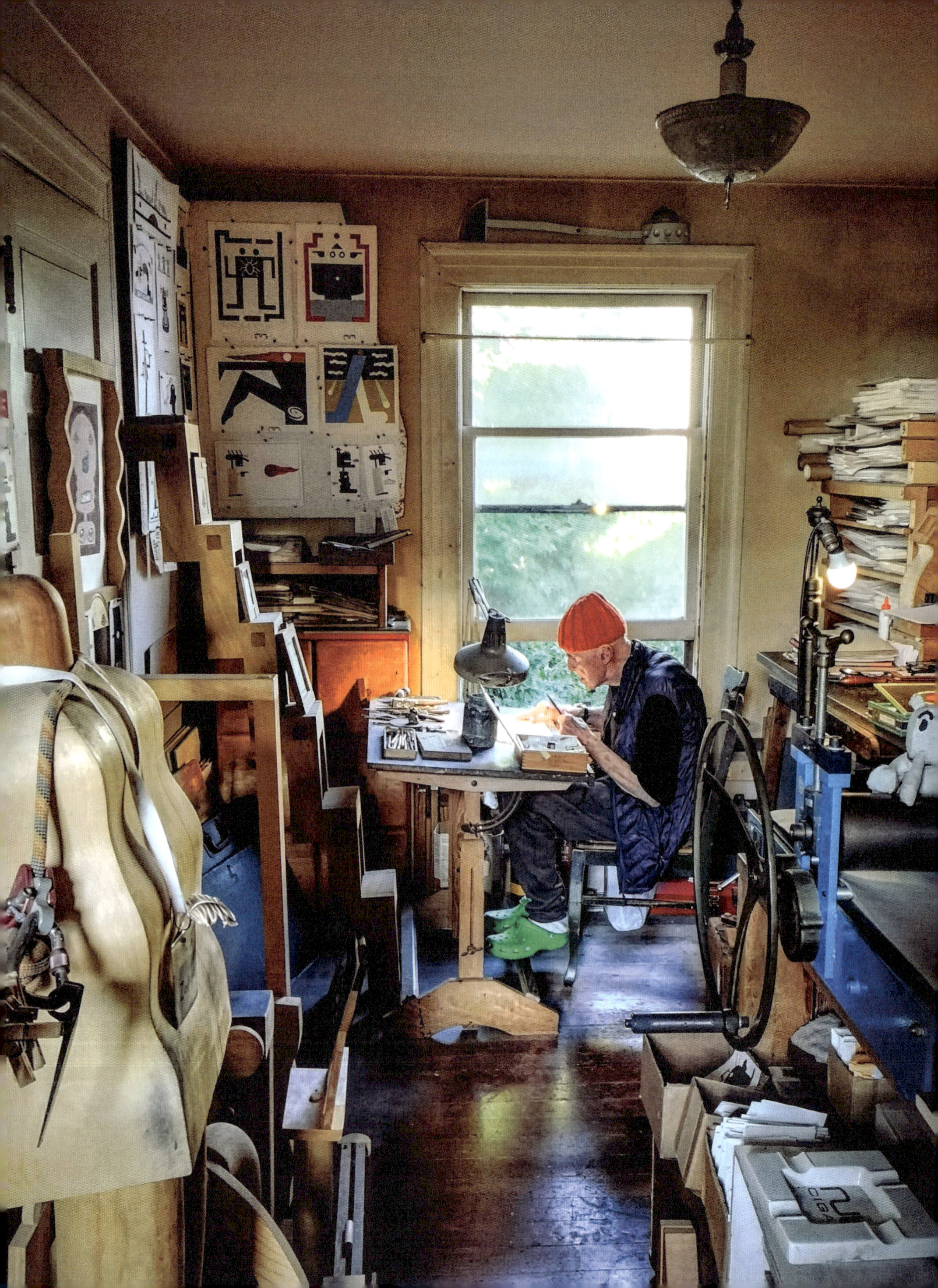

TERMINAL EXPOSURE

COMICS, SCULPTURE & RISKY BEHAVIOR

MICHAEL McMILLAN

INTRODUCTION BY DAN NADEL

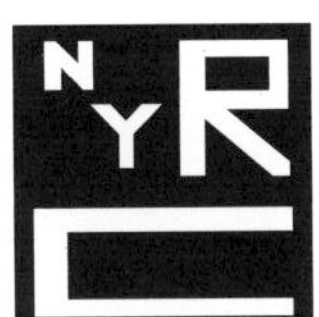

NEW YORK REVIEW COMICS
NEW YORK

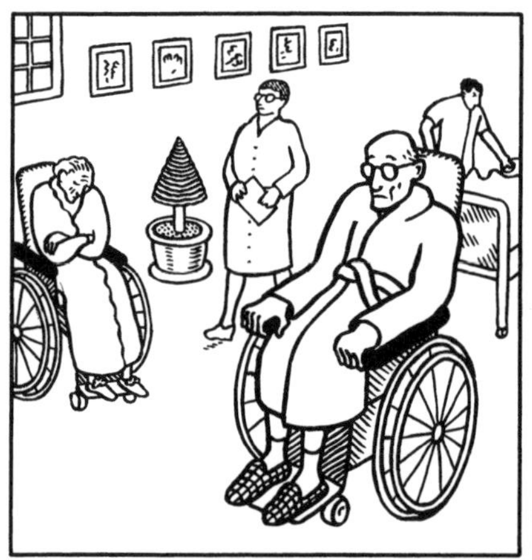

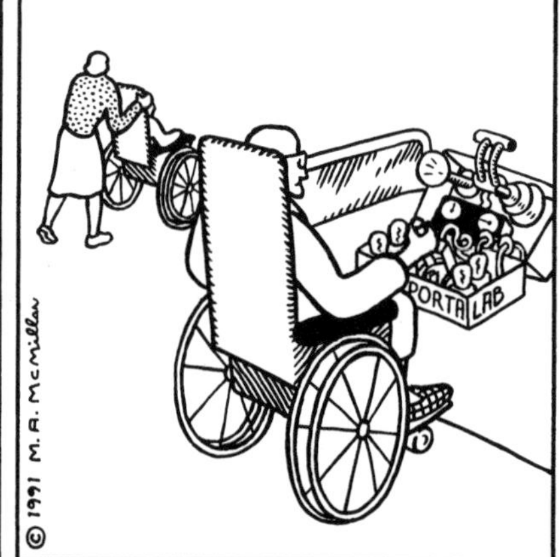

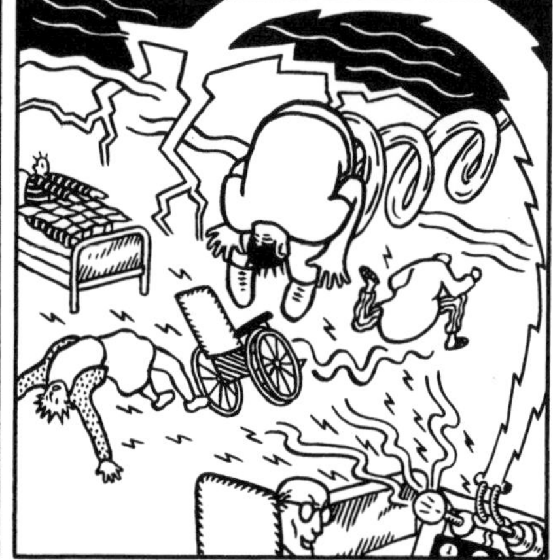

THIS IS A NEW YORK REVIEW COMIC
PUBLISHED BY THE NEW YORK REVIEW OF BOOKS
207 East 32nd Street, New York, NY 10016
www.nyrb.com/comics

Cover design by Ella Gold
Typesetting by Anika Banister

New York Review Comics would like to thank Electric Works, Patrick Kroboth, Dan Nadel, and George Olsen for their assistance on this book.

A catalog record for this book is available from the Library of Congress.

ISBN 978-1-68137-931-9

The authorized representative in the EU for product safety and compliance is eucomply OÜ, Pärnu mnt 139b-14, 11317 Tallinn, Estonia, hello@eucompliancepartner.com, +33 757690241.

Printed in Italy.
10 9 8 7 6 5 4 3 2 1

Michael McMillan was born in Pasadena, California. While attending San Francisco State University for a master's degree in sculpture in the late 1960s, he saw an exhibition by the Hairy Who at the San Francisco Art Institute. That exhibition, together with R. Crumb's *Zap Comix*, spurred his career as a comic book artist. He went on to produce his debut book, *Terminal Comics*, and contributed to publications such as *Young Lust*, *Arcade*, *Weirdo*, and *Lemme Outa Here!* throughout the 1970s. A fine artist as well as a cartoonist, McMillan has worked in many mediums over the course of his career, including film, animation, sculpture, and printmaking, which he currently pursues full-time. McMillan lives in the Bay Area.

Dan Nadel is the Curator-at-Large for the Lucas Museum of Narrative Art. He is the author and editor of several books, including *Crumb: A Cartoonist's Life*; *R. Crumb: Existential Comics*; *Peter Saul: Professional Artist Correspondence, 1945–1976*; *Gertrude Abercrombie; The Collected Hairy Who: Publications, 1966–1969; Art out of Time: Unknown Comics Visionaries, 1900–1969; Gary Panter; Art in Time: Unknown Comic Book Adventures, 1940–1980*; and the New York Review Comics collections *Return to Romance: The Strange Love Stories of Ogden Whitney* and *It's Life as I See It: Black Cartoonists in Chicago, 1940–1980*. He lives in Brooklyn, New York.

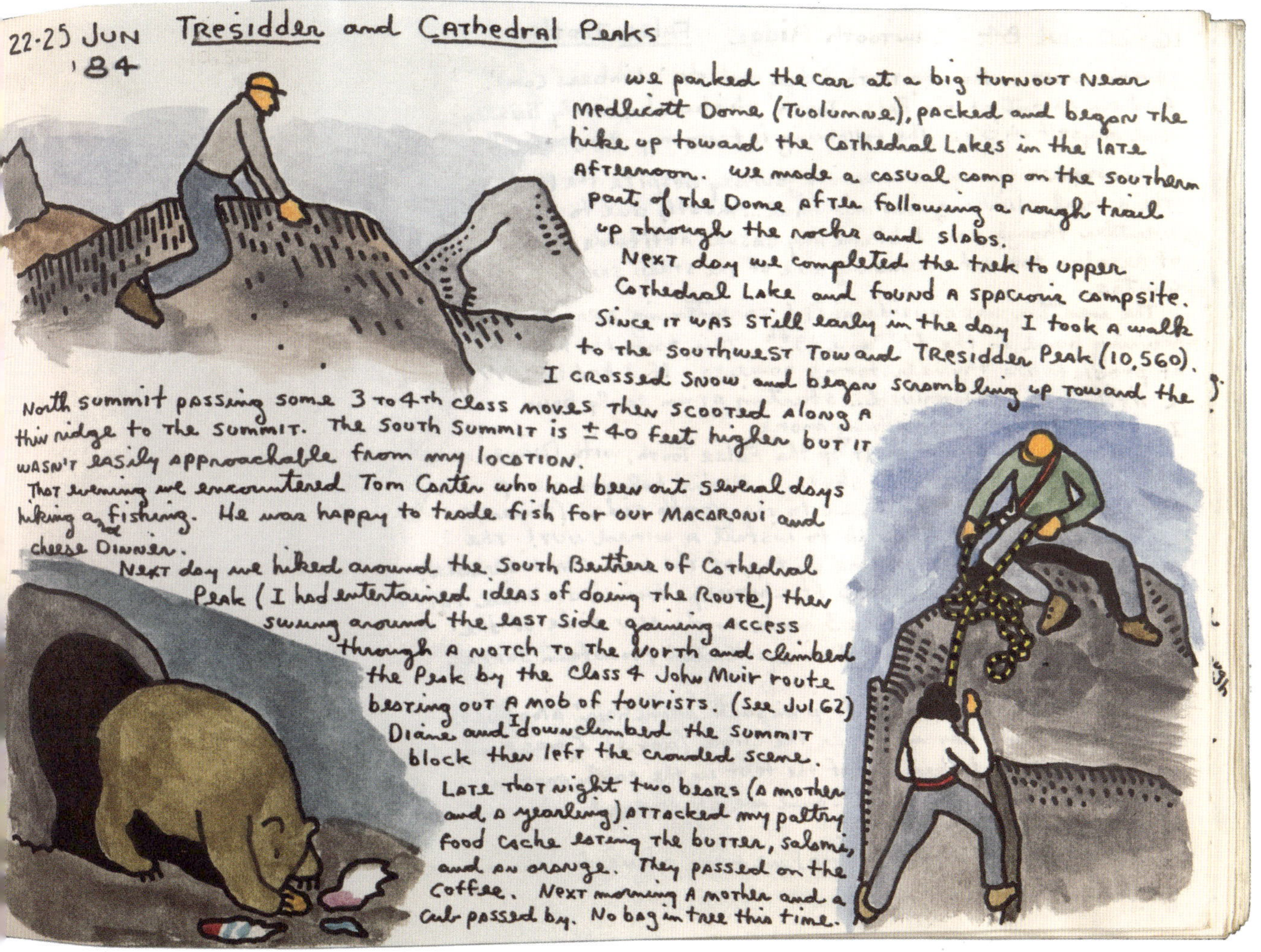

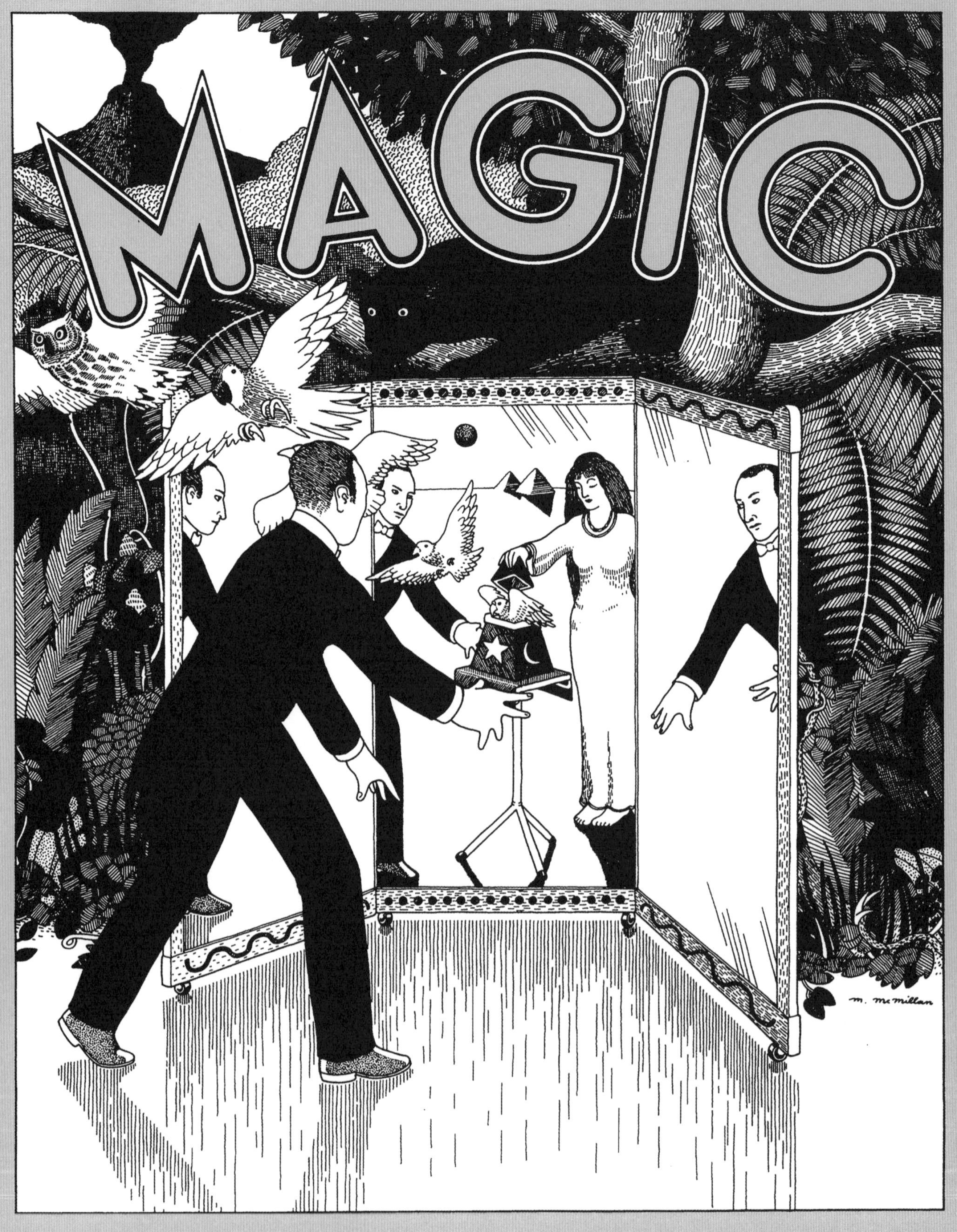

MAGIC DECEMBER 19, 1979 – FEBRUARY 29, 1980

THE FINE ARTS MUSEUMS OF SAN FRANCISCO DOWNTOWN CENTER
THREE EMBARCADERO CENTER / PODIUM LEVEL, SAN FRANCISCO, CA (415) 434-1407

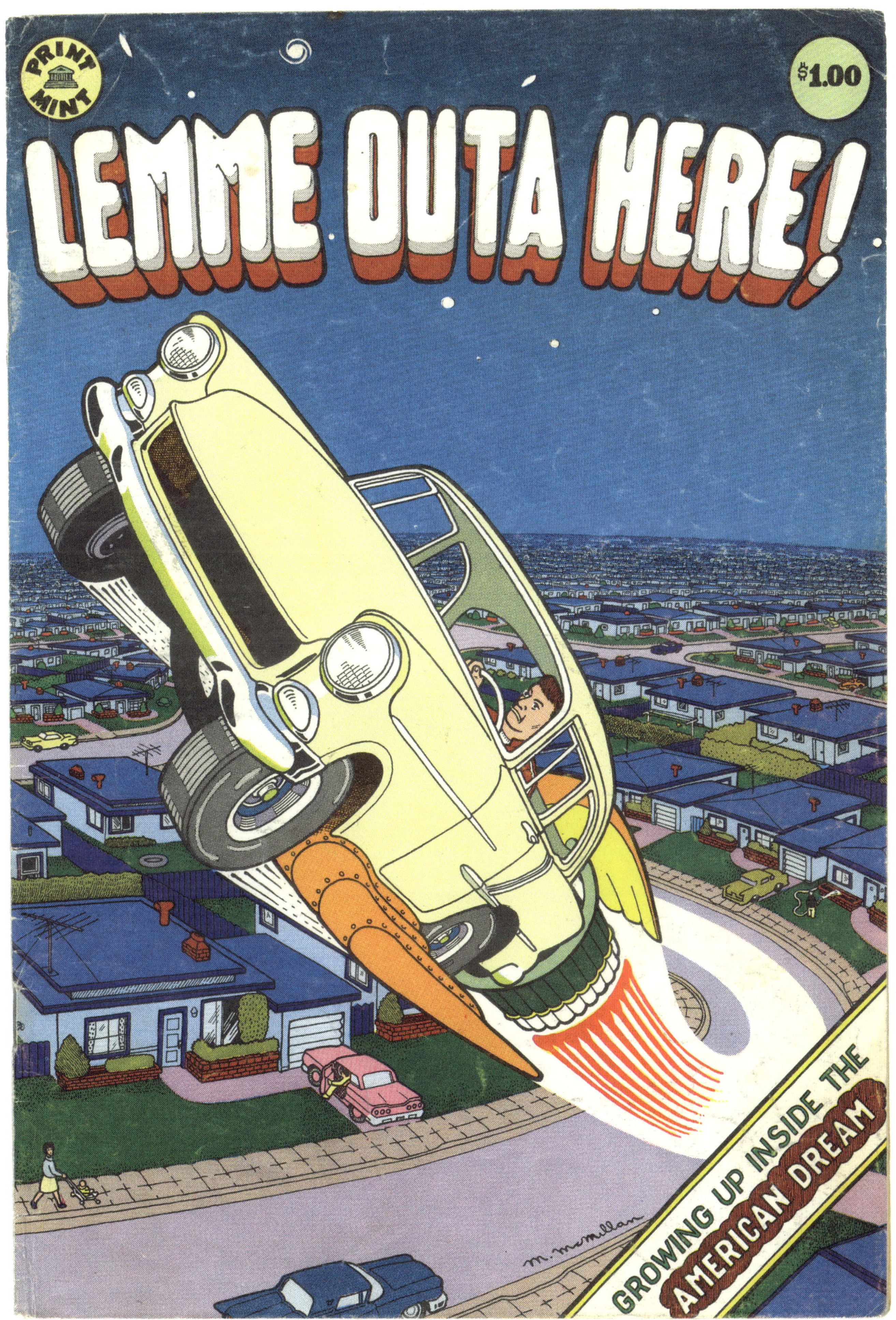
PRINT MINT
$1.00
LEMME OUTA HERE!
m. mcmillan
GROWING UP INSIDE THE
AMERICAN DREAM

WESTERN MAN

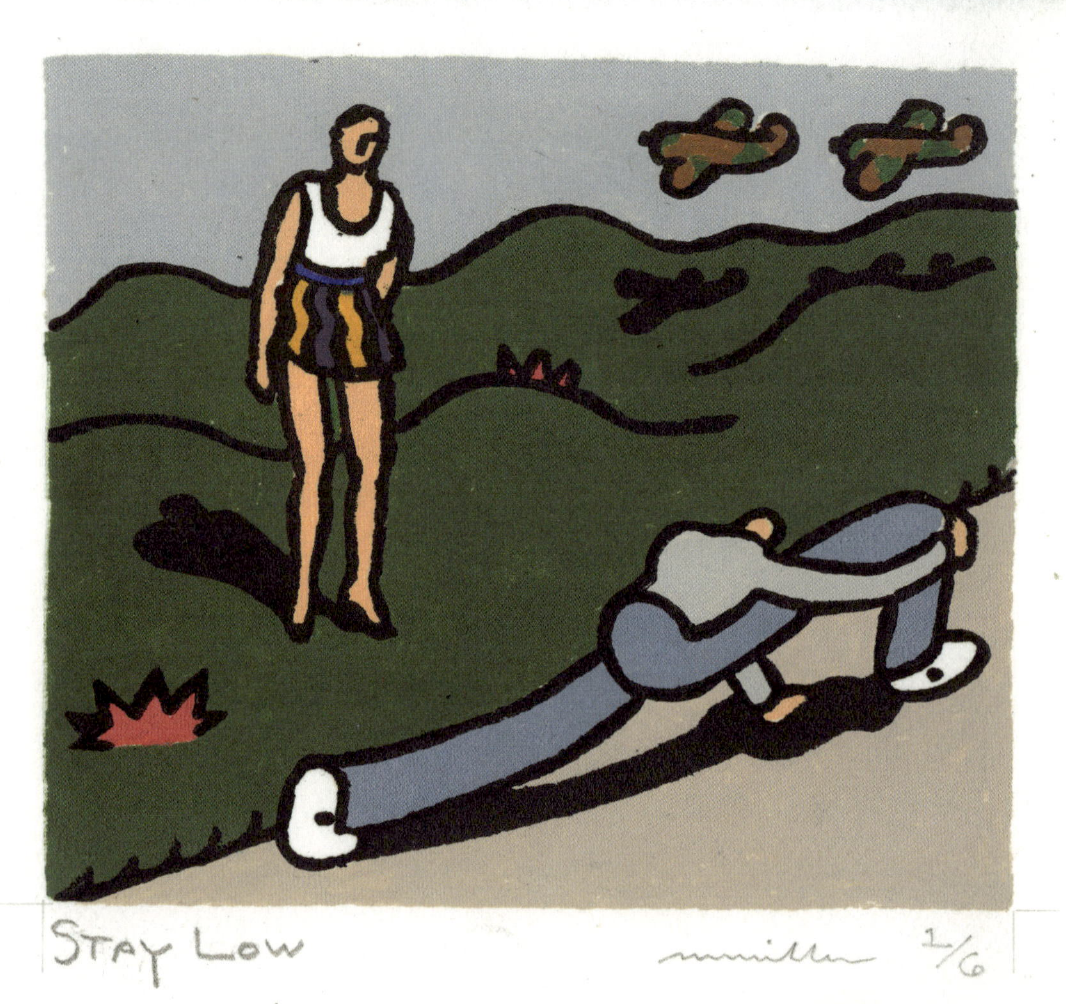

"My life," Michael McMillan says, "is like geographical strata. Climbing is the base stratum. It generates my energy and defines my attitude to everything. The next stratum is craft—sculpture and printmaking. And the final stratum is drawing comics and painting." A more Californian opening statement would be difficult to find. Michael is a Westerner, born in Pasadena in 1933. He is rarely to be found east of the Mississippi, and is forever asserting the primacy of life outside, and moving up and over terrain. Art is another activity, one as intuitive as a ramble across boulders and down into a pebbly cove. It is not, he emphasizes, a job. "Mountain wandering" (as Michael calls it) and climbing, like art, necessitates problem solving (how to get to that next point) and in return offer a reward of perspectives (look at that down there) otherwise strictly for the birds. Those views—above, around, and sideways—inspire the work within the present volume.

And what a lot of work! Guided by patient and steady mind and hand, here are paintings, three-panel autofiction comics, conceptual photography, underground comics, sculpture, comics reconciling art and reality, a strip for *Climbing* magazine, excerpts from Michael's climbing journals, single-panel cartoons, koan-like two-panel comics, three-panel comics about bodies moving through space, woodblock prints at the intersection of fantasy and memory; and Sunday–page style strips. Most of them have never been published because, as Michael has told me more than once in the last twenty years, he was not interested in putting his work out there. He likes the idea of making something and not gaining from it. Put Michael's way, he likes making "useless objects." This is an attitude specific not just to Northern California art but to a particular kind of artist quietly searching for peace on the worktable in front of him.

Michael tells us much of what we to know about him in the stillness of his untitled autobiographical comic strips (pages 19–24). Fittingly for a climber, one of Michael's earliest memories is a ride with his father up in an airplane, feeling the wind and noticing the curiously small buildings down below. His approach to making comics and sculptures is one way to achieve that view. In his final autofiction strip, he writes that his stand-in "persisted in maintaining a link to objective reality." Michael is a fantasist grounded in the real, possessed of a clean line and crisp spatial ability, so he can begin with a truth, like a runway, and take off from there, soaring into unexpected space. Everything in his thematic and visual field is experienced at angles only possible when hanging or flying or zooming or moving.

This path was gifted to Michael by his father, who was an office worker for the Santa Fe Railroad. When Michael was a boy, he and his mother, an art teacher, moved over two hundred miles northeast to Fresno, California. Fresno is in the Central Valley, where the Okies came fleeing the Dust Bowl to start over in the hundreds of miles of agriculture that stretched across the region. As a boy of the 1930s and '40s, Michael was transfixed by comics and film. In the newspapers it was *Dick Tracy*, *Little Orphan Annie*, *Buck Rogers*, and *Terry and the Pirates*. On the newsstand it was *Superman*, *Batman*, and *Detective Comics*. James Whale's Frankenstein films "traumatized" young Michael, though those visions were leavened by endless B-movie double features experienced alone in dark, air-conditioned theaters. Far from any city and left mostly on his own, Michael stowed away in a screened-in porch on the second floor of his home, developing projects rooted in the culture he was absorbing. He constructed model airplanes and railroads, built a wearable gorilla suit head with a movable jaw, and made a head of Frankenstein, domesticating the monster and soothing his fears in the process. The painting of the screened-in porch on page 16 is an emotional memory strongly rooted in fact.

Outside of Michael's workshop, orchards and creeks led into the foothills of the Sierra Nevada, where he discovered his love of climbing. It was as impractical a passion as art was for a working-class kid, but climbing with new tools and techniques, out there in the great wide open, was a way to practice nonconformity while keeping the body fit and the mind sharp. Michael, always drawing, published cartoons in his high school newspaper and took up producing abstract canvases. For an education, though, he was more practical, earning a degree in Industrial Design at the University of Southern California School of Architecture in 1955. Just out of school, not yet a professional, Michael was drafted into the army, serving from 1955 to 1957 in North Carolina as a photography lab technician.

After his time in the service, he moved to San Francisco, where by the end of the 1950s countless other dreaming men and women took up residence in spindly, rundown Victorians, enticed by the cheap rent and proximity to glorious scenery. Michael plied his trade as a draftsman for the Otis Elevator Company, various electronics firms, and all manner of packaging concerns. Somewhere along the way—like many others of that era—Michael got fed up with the square life. He thought teaching might be a better choice than being chained to a drafting table. In 1967 he enrolled at San Francisco State University on the GI Bill to pursue a teaching degree. After seeing his portfolio, the wise SFSU administrators suggested he study art, specifically sculpture under Stephen De Staebler. De Staebler had (like his mentor Peter Voulkos) helped shift ceramics out of craft and into the realm of art by insisting on foregrounding its earthy lumps and using it not for function but as a way to explore the human figure, indicating weight and motion through attention to form and detail.

In the art that Michael was tracking in magazines and galleries, a certain mode of well-crafted, high-spirited, surrealist-inflected painting and sculpture was popping up around the country. In the Bay Area, William T. Wiley and Bruce Nauman, antic artists obsessed with wordplay and the idea of communicating through multiple mediums, decided that a simple green linoleum-covered footstool bought at a junk store in Mill Valley would be called the Slant Step. They made the footstool the subject of multiple artworks and a 1966 exhibition in San Francisco, with several artists reinterpreting it. To this day, the Slant Step remains an inspiration for art that revels in its uncanny uselessness. Like these artists, Michael had a healthy interest in Dada, in which he found a strategy, or at least an example, for pushing his work to the edge of absurdity. He began making useless objects, like fins he attached to his calves. These were gestures that meant more to the artist than anyone else, gestures at an art for oneself.

As the Slant Step slouched into view, hundreds of miles east, in Chicago, six artists began putting on exhibitions as the Hairy Who, one of which occurred in 1968 at the San Francisco Art Institute. Visiting this exhibition inspired Michael to broaden his graphic approach to encompass humor and linear grotesqueries. The Hairy Who artists Jim Nutt and Karl Wirsum distilled the commercial imagery of the century into lines and colors that displayed ecstatic bodies, punning wordplay, and 1940s references and were made with exquisite attention to detail. Faced with a teeming but bland urban expanse, and with no trees or slopes to soothe them, the Hairy Who labored to sear their bright colors into eyeballs, defiant to be seen. Both crews, and Michael, too, shared a love for the acrobat, sculptor, printmaker, and veteran H. C. Westermann, who traversed the country showing art-goers terrible truths about war and America in a vernacular sculpture language polished to seemingly impossible levels of craft perfection. In Westermann, Michael found an example of a fellow athlete who moved fluidly between disciplines with humor and dignity.

Add to that mix Robert Crumb's *Zap Comix*, which Michael discovered at City Lights, where a climbing buddy worked. In 1968, Crumb's comic book, released with an upstart publisher named Don Donahue, was viewed as much a part of the up-for-grabs non–New York art world as any of the above. Crumb took the old medium of the comic book and turned it to exclusively personal, radical use. This was a conceptual and material breakthrough that allowed comics to take in any kind of content.

Crumb's breakthrough brought a flood of underground comic books. From 1970 to 1973, floppy publications—in envy-inducing print runs of ten thousand or more—poured into head shops and bookstores across the country, to be bought alongside roach clips and incense. During that time, the medium became capacious enough to hold nearly every kind of idea, no matter how serious or absurd. Most underground cartoonists were coming from EC Comics and *MAD*, and they were either antagonistic or indifferent to gallery art. It was usually popular, not "high," culture that fed the underground dream. But Michael, a decade older than most of them, was grounded in contemporary art and Depression-era entertainment. His drawings from that period have the spiky grotesque lines of Jim Nutt but plots torn from James Whale films. It says a lot about both the popularity of underground comics and the looseness of the times that in 1971 Michael could simply walk over to Don Donahue's place in the Mission District with the artwork for his first and only comic book, *Terminal Comics*, and walk out with a publishing agreement.

In a sea of comics that looked like 1950s takeoffs, Crumb knockoffs, or psychedelic sludge, Michael's crisp work and aesthetic sophistication stood out, and other cartoonists with ambitions for the medium to grow in scope, sophistication, and intensity took notice, among them Bill Griffith, Diane Noomin, Jay Kinney, Justin Green, Rory Hayes, and Art Spiegelman, all of whom asked him to contribute to anthologies in the ensuing years. For a young artist like Gary Panter in Texas, seeing *Terminal Comics* was a signal that the visual culture he was absorbing in magazines, museums, and head shops needn't be parsed into bins labeled "art" and "comics" but rather that art could be comics and comics could be art.

But then the underground comics world took a serious hit by the end of 1973. Inflation, spiking fuel costs, and new obscenity rules drove retailers away from the nascent scene. Publishers shut down, artists got older and needed steadier income, and the culture veered rightward, kicking out against the liberal stew of the "Sixties." Happily, Michael wasn't looking to make a living from comics, and he bounced to commercial work, designing and producing several short animated films, including *Be My Gas* (page 78), and TV spots. He also worked on the poster artist and cartoonist Victor Moscoso's TV spots for KMEL radio.

In the late 1980s, two of Michael's Otto strips appeared in Aline Kominsky-Crumb's *Weirdo* anthology, but otherwise Michael worked as he always did—for himself. If no one was going to ask, he wasn't going to suggest it. So Michael continued making comics that tested the style and form of the medium. In the following pages he adapts the curvilinear bodies of the Fleischer brothers' cartoons in the late 1970s strips, the curlicues of Memphis-era postmodernism for Otto, and then the thick strokes and trunk-like forms of Harold Gray's *Little Orphan Annie* for the contemplative strips of daily life.

All along he'd made sculptures and paintings, and soon he started making prints on his home printing press. He is, in his studio, the still-dreaming child clutching The Phantom and The Shadow. Those are memories as real as climbing Mount Shasta in a snowstorm. His sculptures appear with the same solidity as his 1980s comic strips—sturdy things that often have a foot or a wedge forward, that could inhabit one of his pages or take a step down the alley, rooted in some of the same sources as Westermann's work—the allure of a block of wood, the finish of a fine tool, a smoothly carved toy. Accompanying the allusive sculptures, linoleum cuts, and paintings are precision images of memories and dreams. Michael-the-narrator seems ever present in these images, telling a story, whispering a communication. Like the sculptures, their clarity does not yield obvious interpretations. Rather, as with the best surrealism, the clarity of their disjunctions—why is The Shadow in the living room? Who is in bed smoking that cigarette?—make them even more beguiling.

Happily, our artist isn't above letting us in on the trick. As much as he might do it all for himself, the self wants to chat about the enchantment of making art, perhaps to share that delirious moment of invention. If there is a secret to Michael's world, it's in a few lines from "Otto Comic Strip 17, The Enigmas of the Identity" (page 99): "Now this you might call art. I don't call it anything! In that way I don't have to become an artist like everyone else. / Once you call yourself something... there you go! Into the dumper! You start getting mail from the society of serious whose-its! / If you are really serious you've gotta sneak up on yourself. Then presto!..."

—DAN NADEL

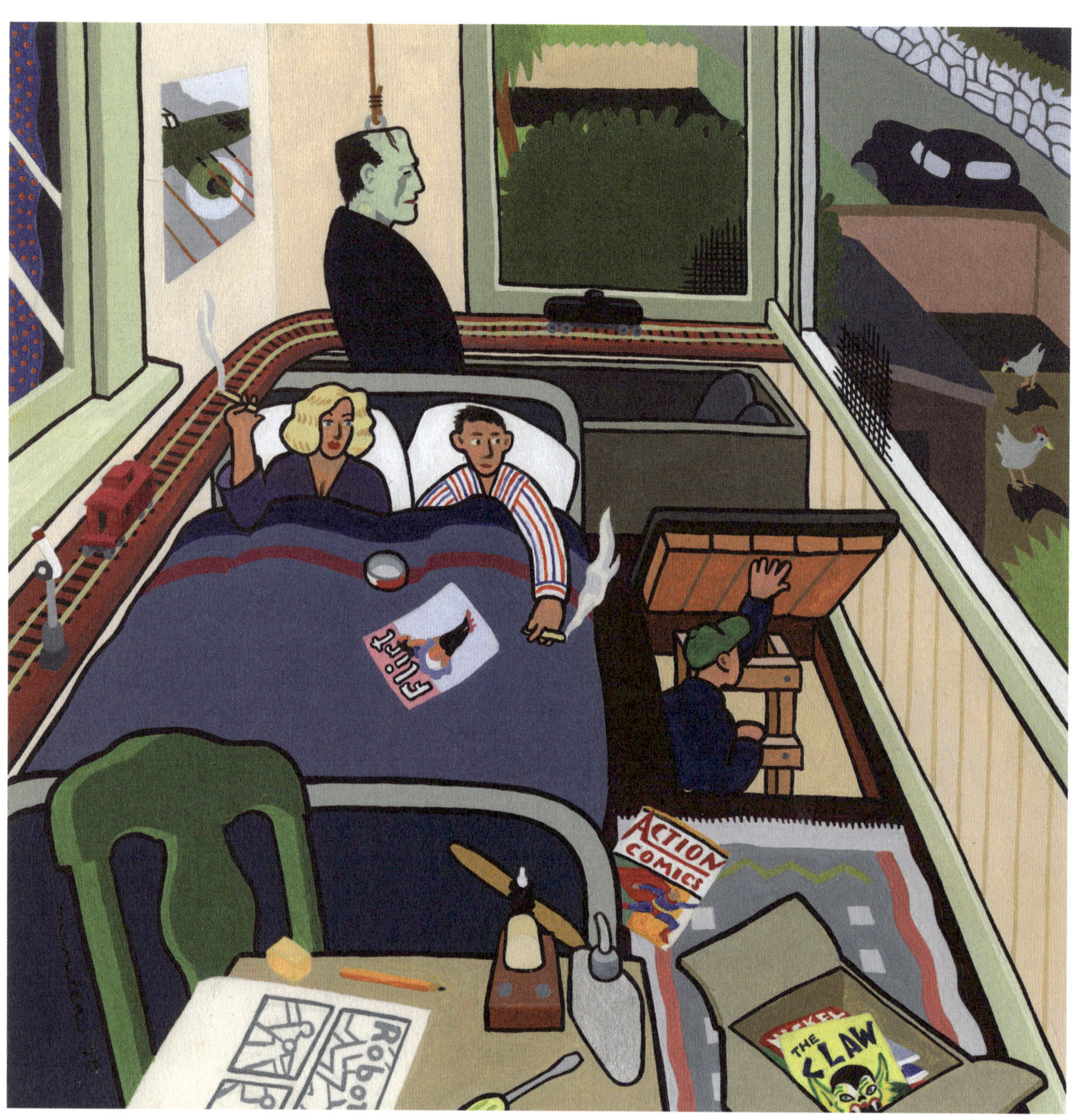

By 1945 my parents had separated. I was temporarily deposited in the upper back room of my uncle's house in Dinuba, California. It was the right locale for engaging all my activities. My friends could visit through a trap door. All an accurate depiction except for the blonde in bed. Wishful thinking for a twelve-year-old.

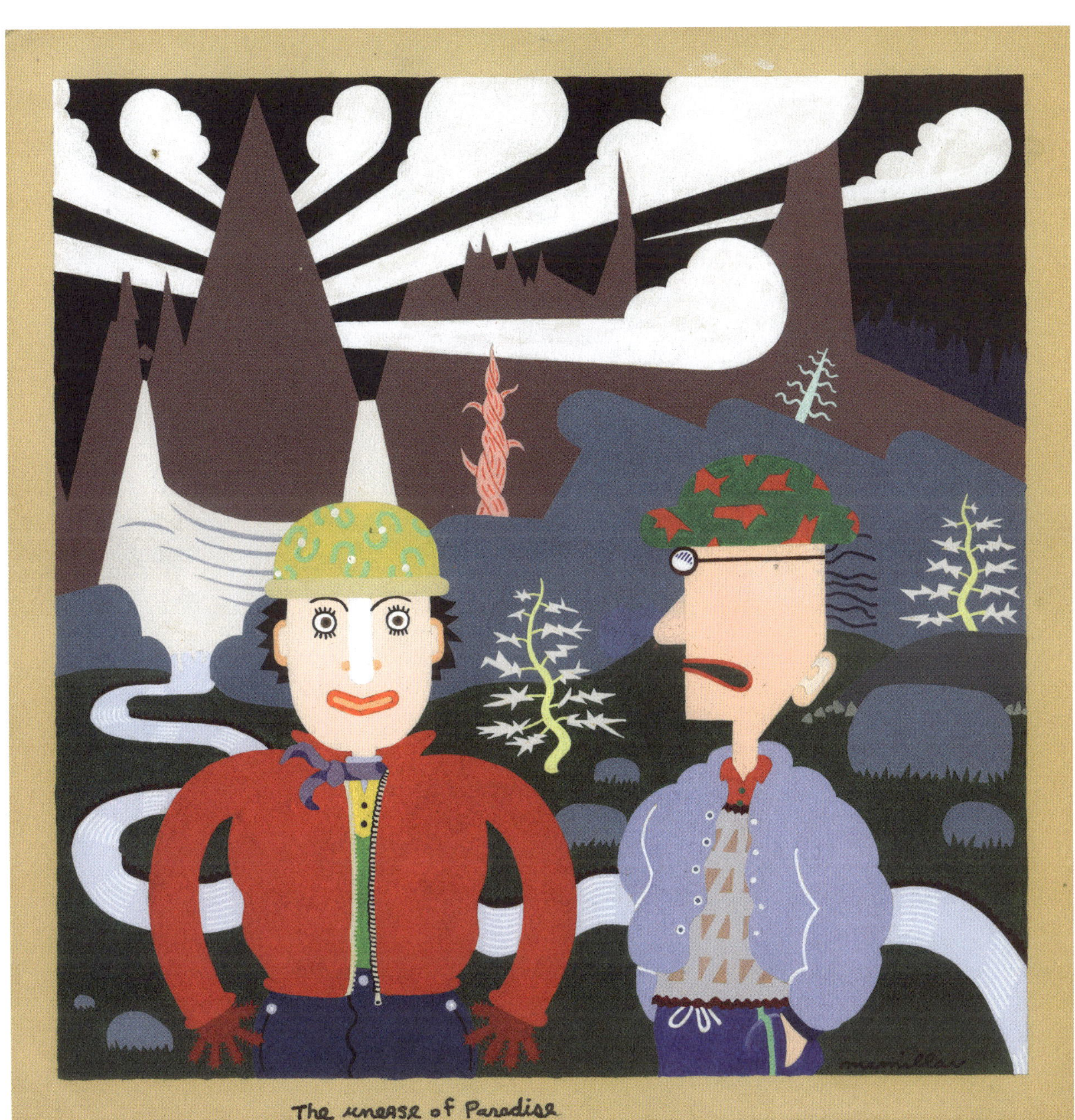
mcmillan
The unease of Paradise

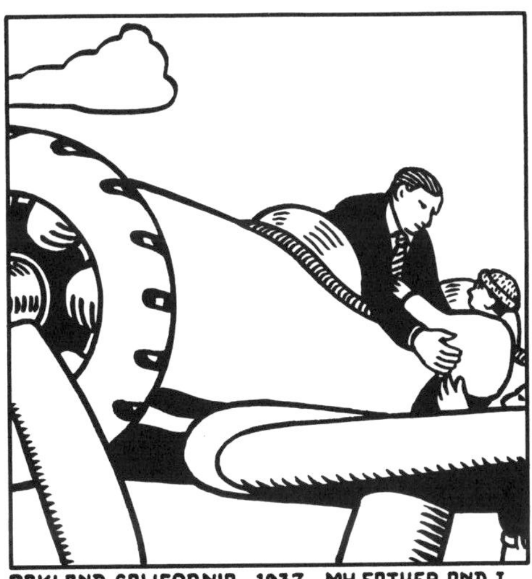

OAKLAND CALIFORNIA 1937. MY FATHER AND I WENT FOR A THIRTY MINUTE "AEROPLANE" RIDE.

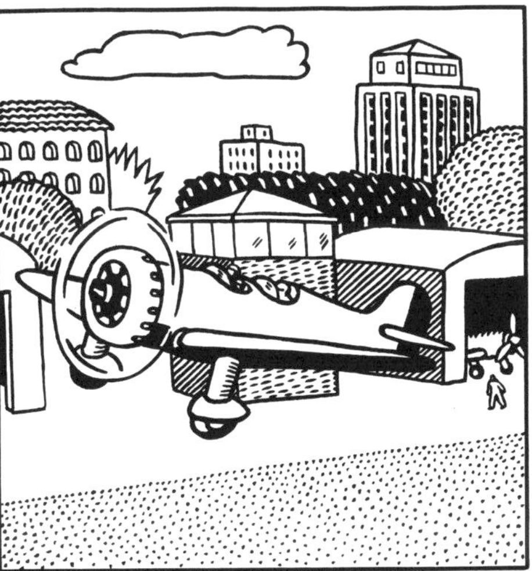

WHEN WE TOOK OFF, WE LEFT THE CONVENTIONAL "BIG" WORLD....

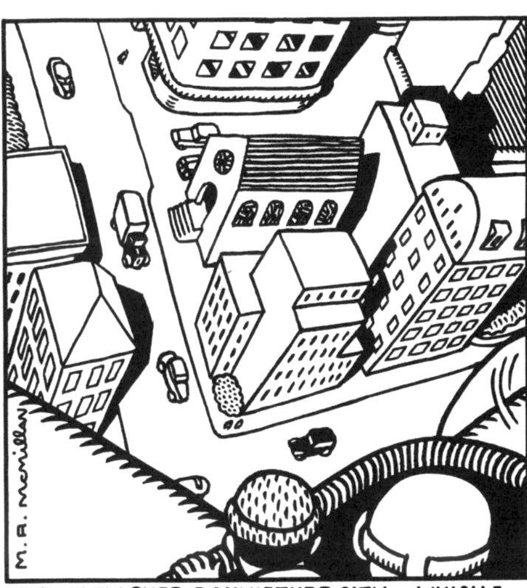

THEN FLEW OVER A MINIATURE CITY...WHICH I HAVE SINCE NEVER BEEN ABLE TO LOCATE.

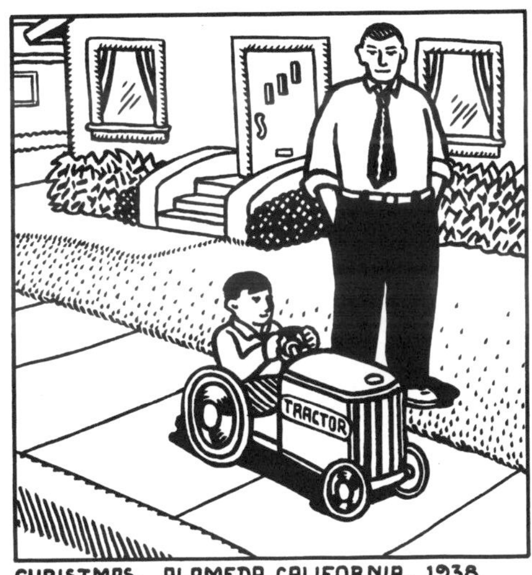

CHRISTMAS. ALAMEDA CALIFORNIA. 1938. THE YEAR OF THE PEDAL-CAR TRACTOR.

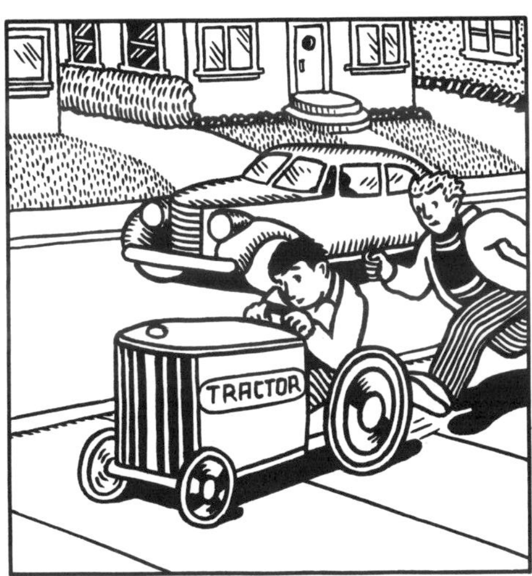

THERE WAS NO ASSOCIATION WITH FARMING. THE LARGE REAR WHEELS ADDED UNUSUAL SPEED.

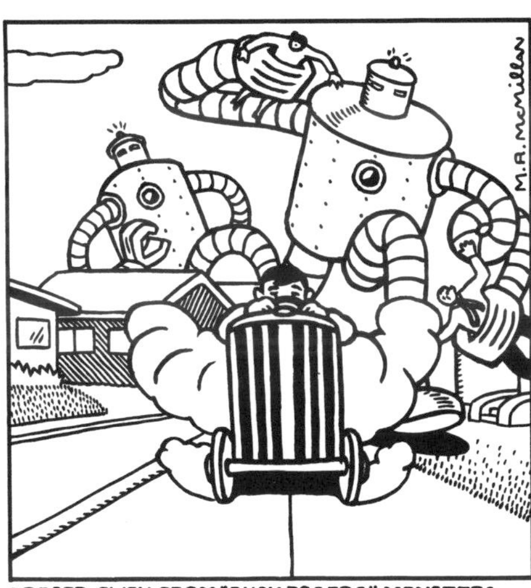

I RACED AWAY FROM "BUCK ROGERS" MONSTERS. IF THESE WERE THE DEPRESSION THEY SNARED MY PARENTS.

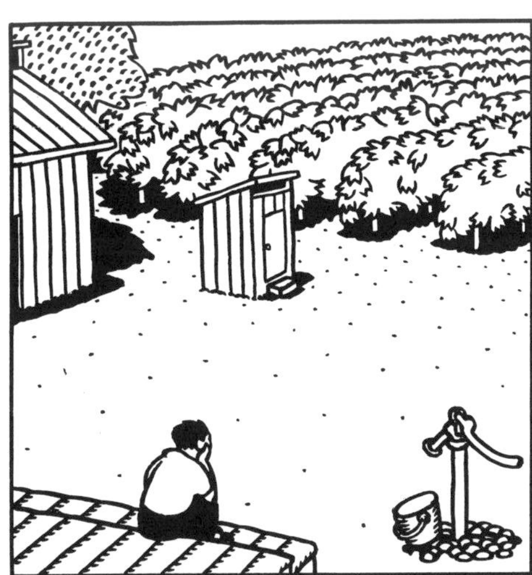

1939. WE MOVED TO THE SAN JOAQUIN VALLEY WHERE MY GRANDFATHER MANAGED A SMALL VINEYARD.

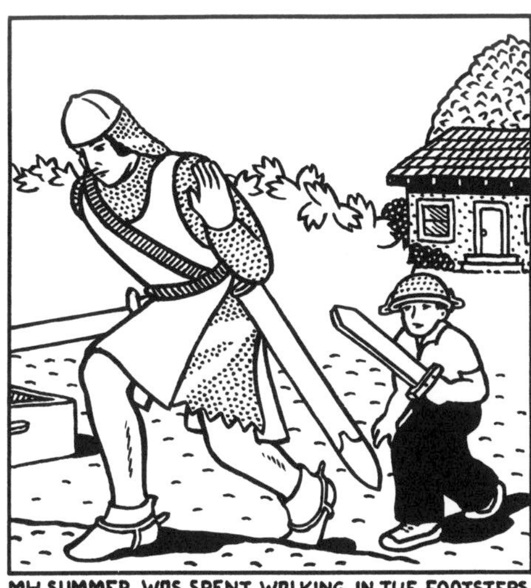

MY SUMMER WAS SPENT WALKING IN THE FOOTSTEPS OF "PRINCE VALIANT."

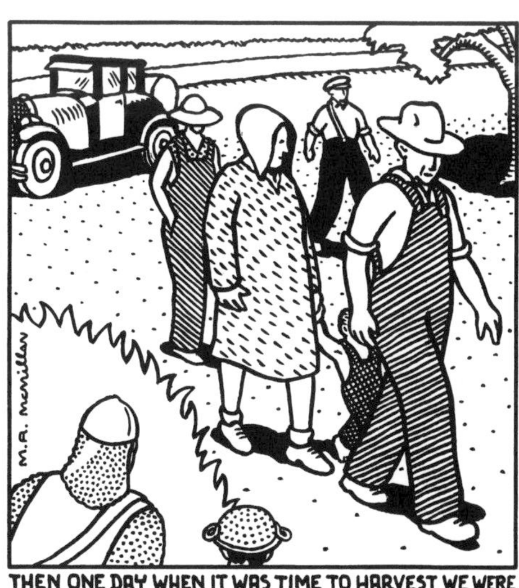

THEN ONE DAY WHEN IT WAS TIME TO HARVEST WE WERE VISITED BY A PEOPLE UNKNOWN TO MY IMAGINATION.

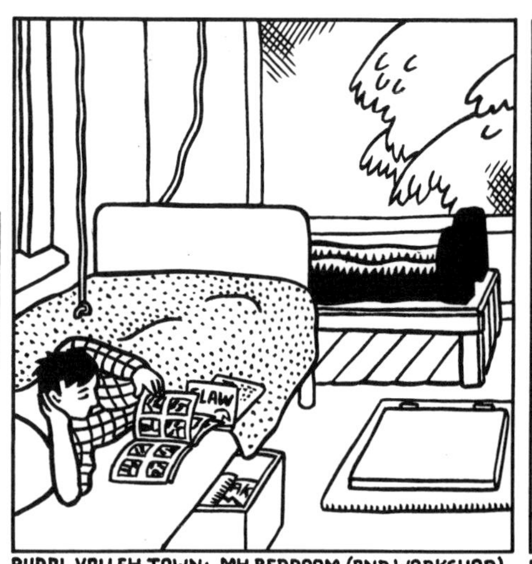

RURAL VALLEY TOWN: MY BEDROOM (AND WORKSHOP) WAS AT THE UPPER LEVEL OF A SCREENED PORCH.

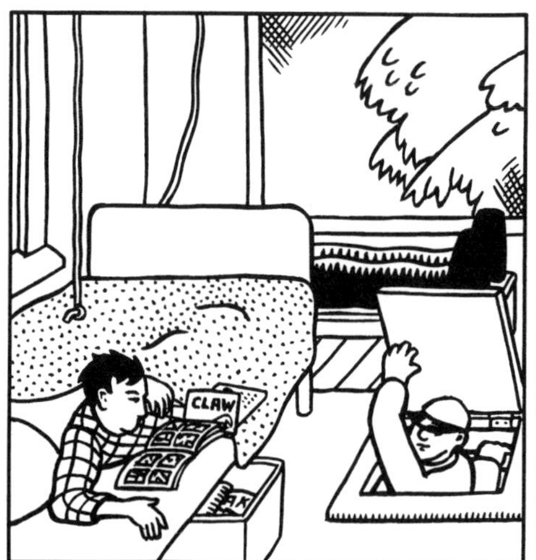

MY FRIENDS COULD CONVENIENTLY VISIT BY USING A FIRE ESCAPE LADDER AND TRAP DOOR.

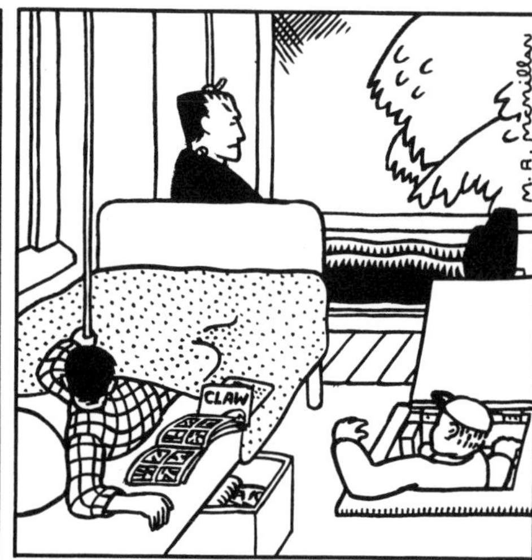

BY THIS TIME I HAD LEARNED ENOUGH SKILLS TO FABRICATE A BOGEYMAN GUARDIAN.

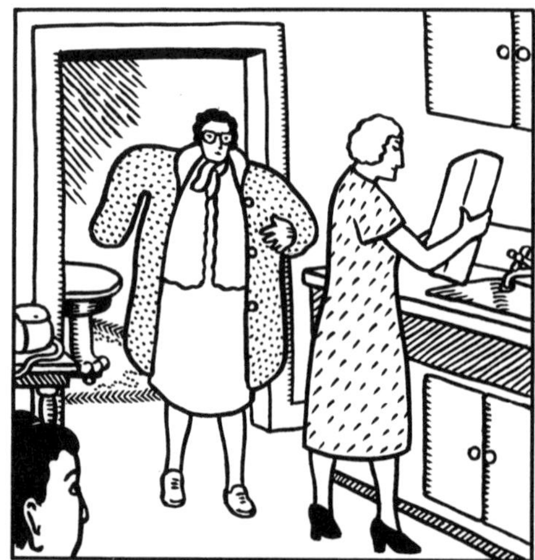

IT WAS PROBABLE THAT WOMEN HAD EARS... BUT NAVELS?! MY MOTHER? MY GRANDMOTHER?! HARD TO VISUALIZE.

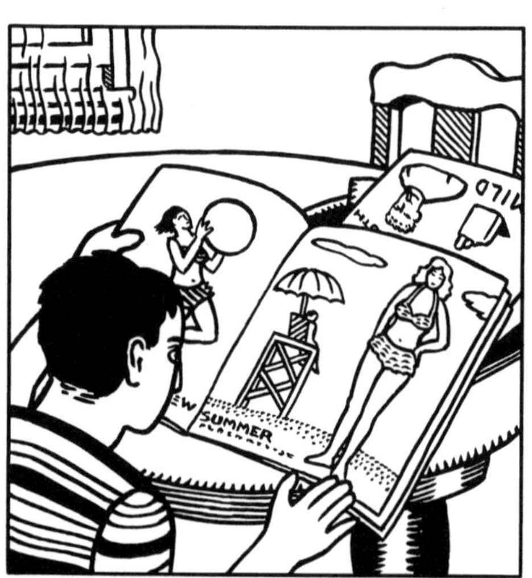

POPULAR MAGAZINES WERE STARTING TO SHOW THAT AT LEAST SOME WOMEN IN FACT DID HAVE THEM.

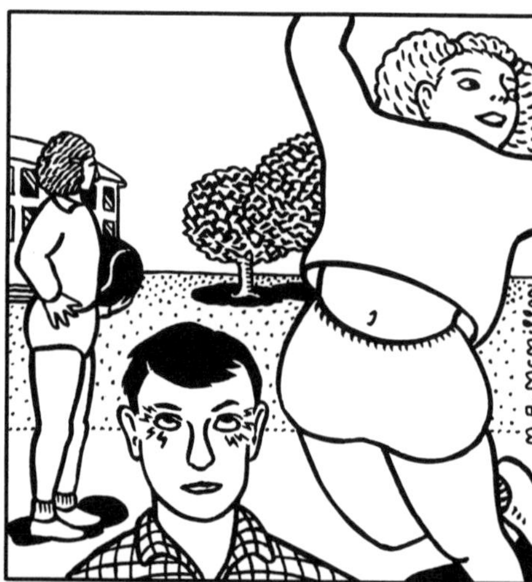

WHEN AT SCHOOL BRENDA BAKER FLAUNTED HERS... I BECAME MEZMERIZED BY THE UNDENIABLE EVIDENCE.

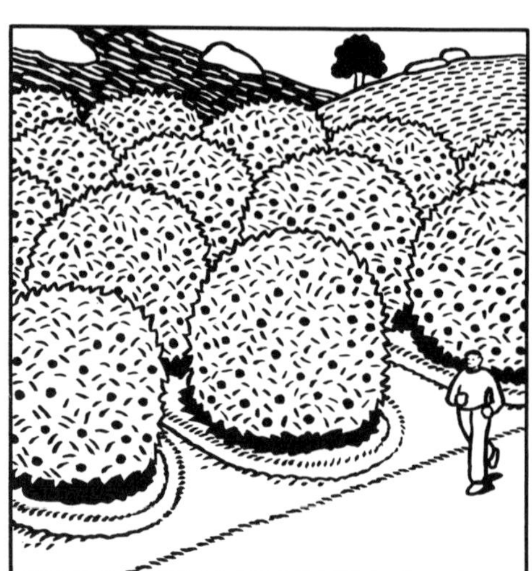

1949. I BEGAN TRAINING AT A TIME WHEN RUNNING ON ROADS WAS AS COMMON AS WALKING ON WATER.

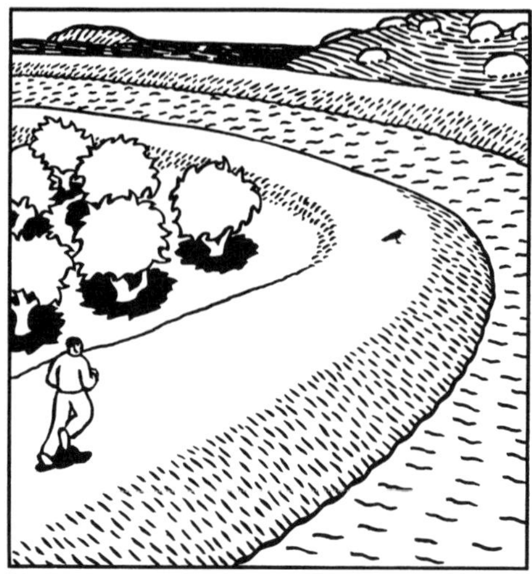

MY TERRAIN WAS THE SIERRA FOOTHILLS. I HAD GOOD RAPPOR WITH THE WILDLIFE AND THE SALIENT FEATURES.

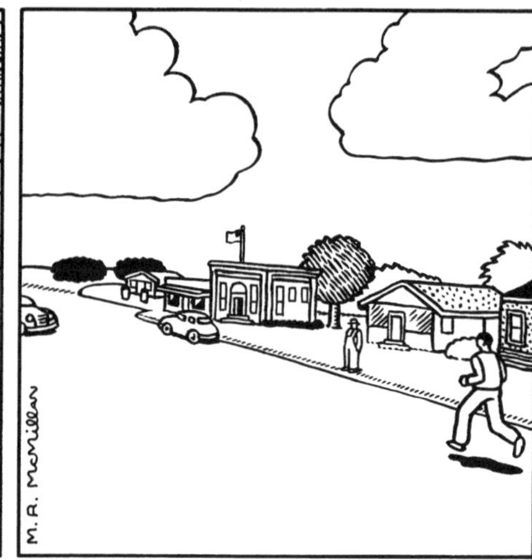

IT WAS ONLY AT THE ENCOUNTER WITH OTHER HUMANS THAT I WAS OBLIGED TO EXPLAIN MYSELF.

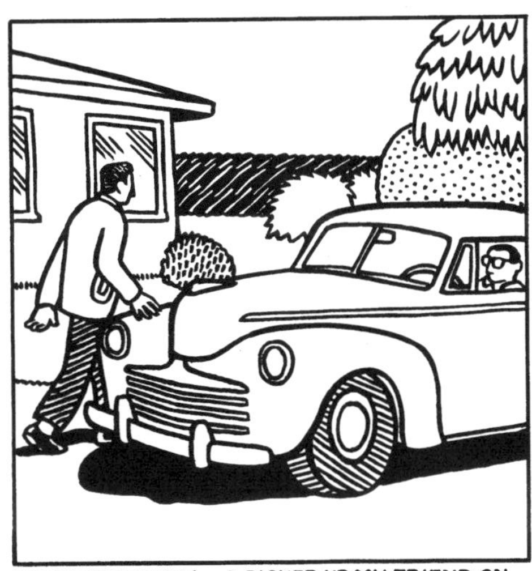

DOUBLE DATE 1951: I PICKED UP MY FRIEND ON OUR WAY TO THE GIRL'S HOMES.

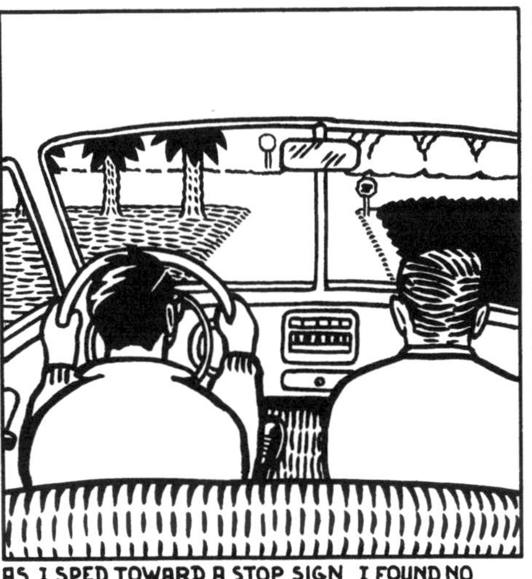

AS I SPED TOWARD A STOP SIGN I FOUND NO RESPONSE WHEN I POUNDED THE BRAKE PEDAL!!

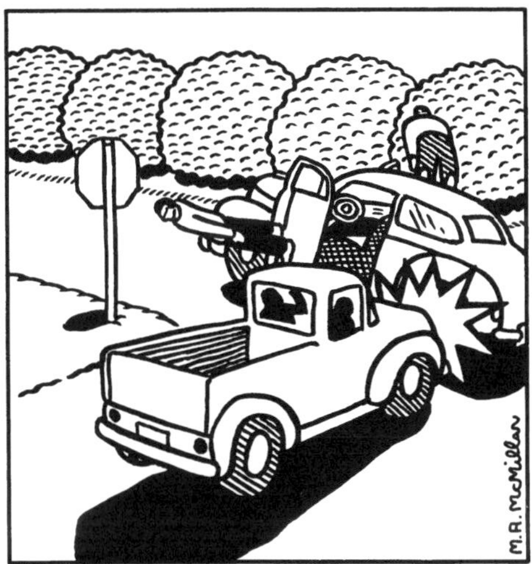

PREFERRING THE POSSIBILITY OF DEATH TO EMBARRASSMENT I KEPT QUIET AND HOPED FOR THE BEST.

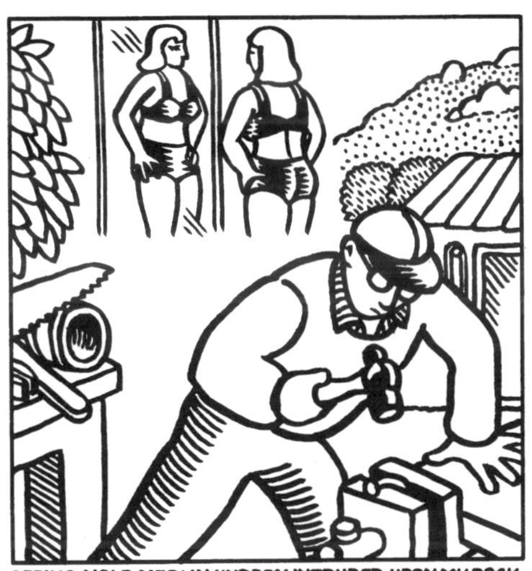

SEEING NOLA MERLIN UNDRESS INTRUDED UPON MY ROCK CLIMBING VISIONS. I BENT A LARGE NAIL INTO A "PITON".

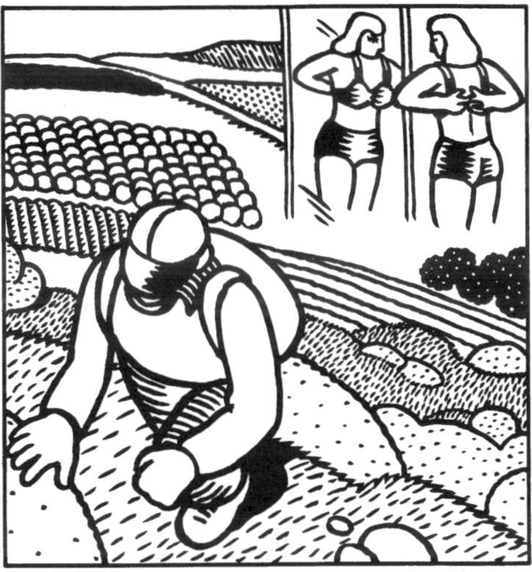

AS I ASCENDED A NEARBY HILL TO TRY MY EQUIPMENT NOLA BEGAN TO UNHOOK HER BRA.

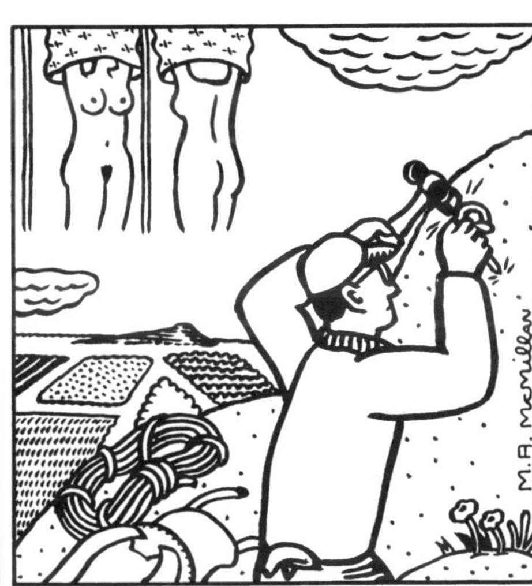

JUST AS I REPLAYED THE KEY MOMENT I LEARNED THAT PITONS CANNOT BE DRIVEN INTO SOLID ROCK.

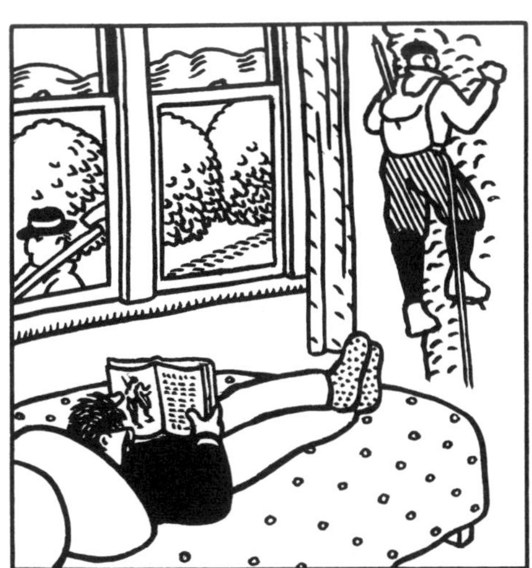

1950'S: CALIFORNIA VALLEY FARM. HE WAS SOMEWHERE ELSE;

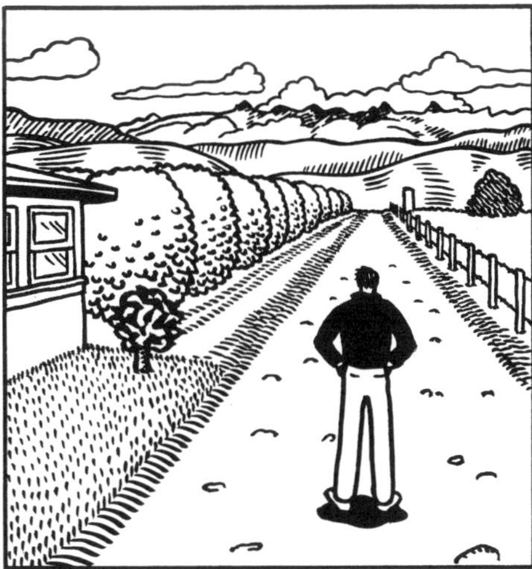

ANSWERING THE CALL TO ADVENTURE;

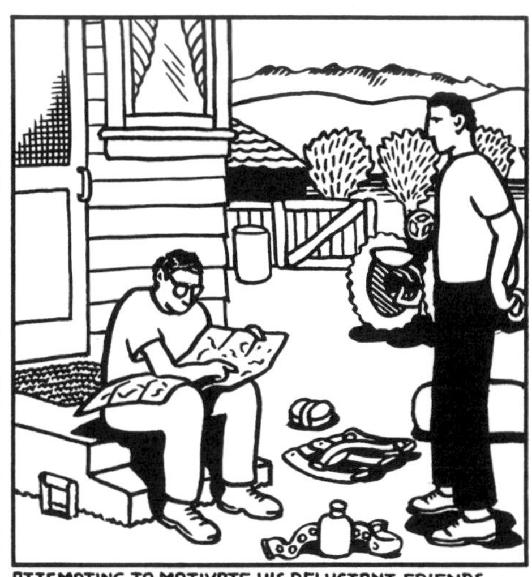

ATTEMPTING TO MOTIVATE HIS RELUCTANT FRIENDS.

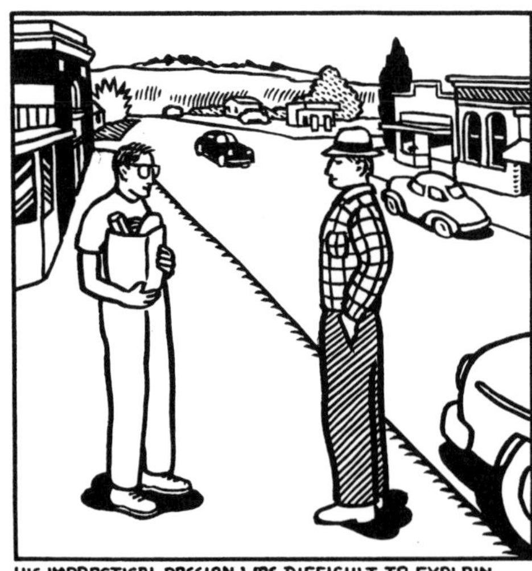
HIS IMPRACTICAL PASSION WAS DIFFICULT TO EXPLAIN.

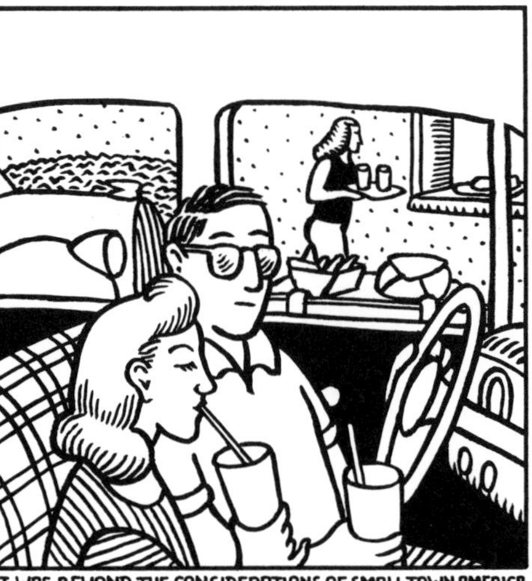
IT WAS BEYOND THE CONSIDERATIONS OF SMALL TOWN AMERICA.

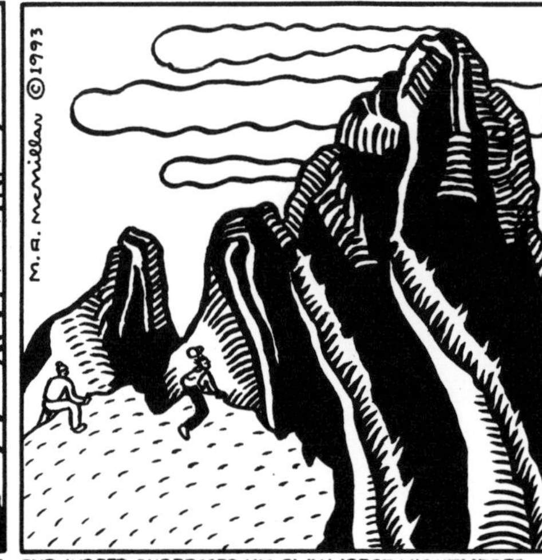

AND INDEED SURPASSED HIS OWN WORST NIGHTMARES.

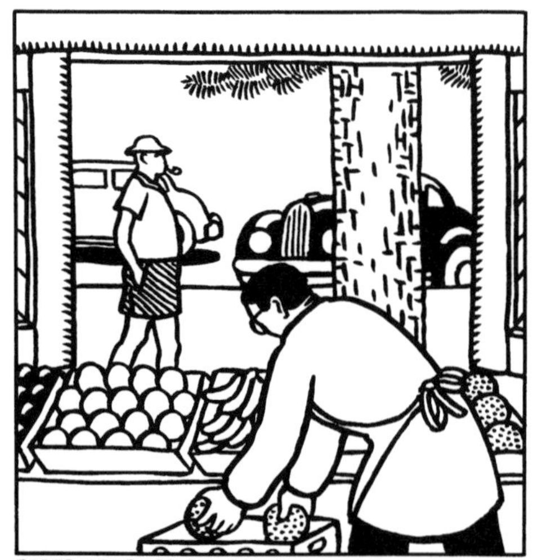
AFTER GRADUATION FROM HIGH SCHOOL I WORKED IN A MARKET AT A NATIONAL PARK RESORT.

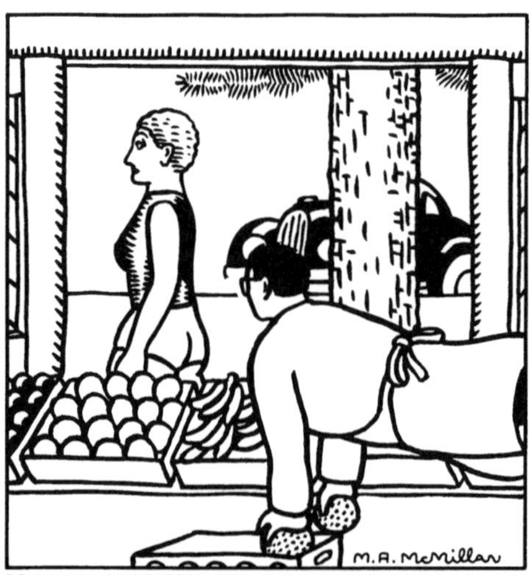

AS I UNPACKED FRUIT THE GIRL WHO WORKED AT THE GIFT SHOP PASSED BY ON HER DAY OFF.

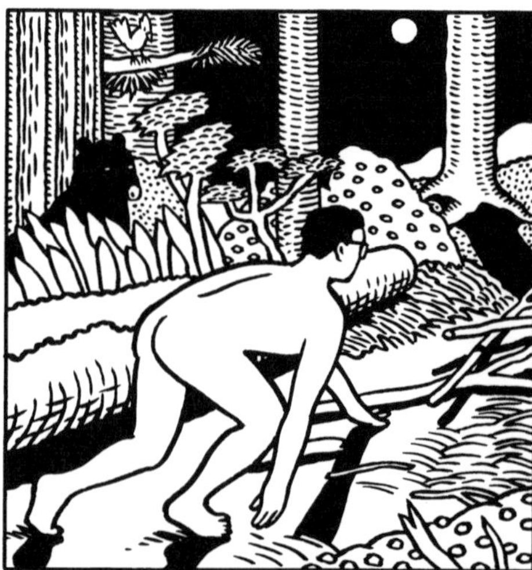
CAUSING ME TO SPEND THE EVENING ACHIEVING A MYSTICAL COMMUNION WITH THE PRIMEVAL FORCES.

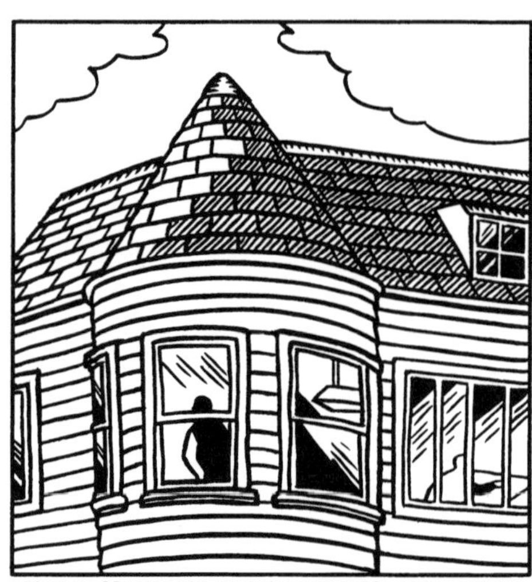
WHILE IN COLLEGE AT MY ARCHITECTURAL FRATERNITY HOUSE I OCCUPIED THE ATTIC SPACE INSIDE THE "CONE".

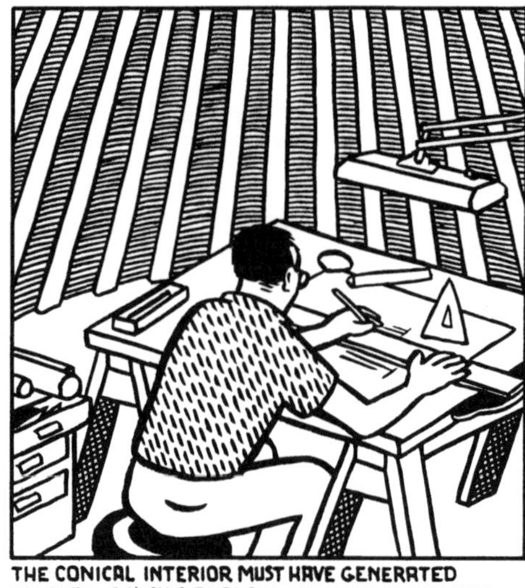
THE CONICAL INTERIOR MUST HAVE GENERATED POWERFUL PSYCHIC ENERGY. DURING MY STAY I....

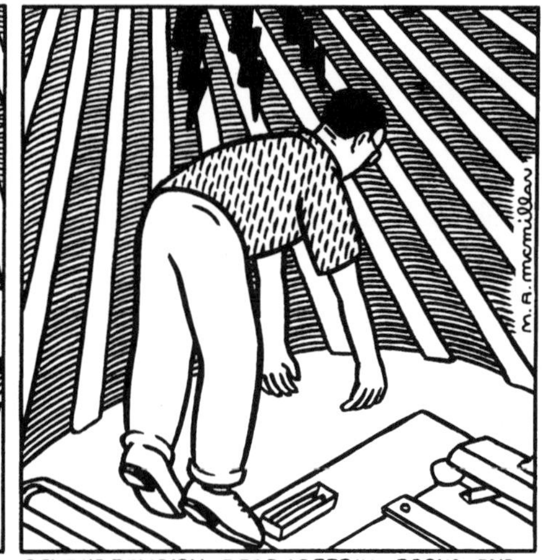

GAVE UP RELIGION, BEGAN READING BOOKS, AND PERCEIVED MY CULTURE AS A BIG SCALE CON GAME.

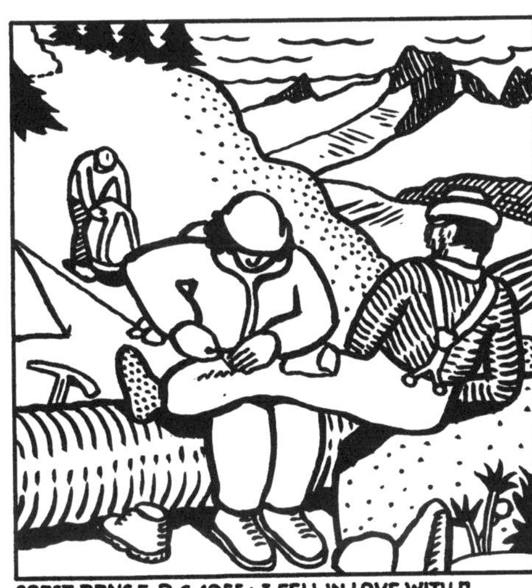

COAST RANGE, B.C. 1955: I FELL IN LOVE WITH A MARRIED WOMAN AS SHE SEWED A RIP IN MY PANTS.

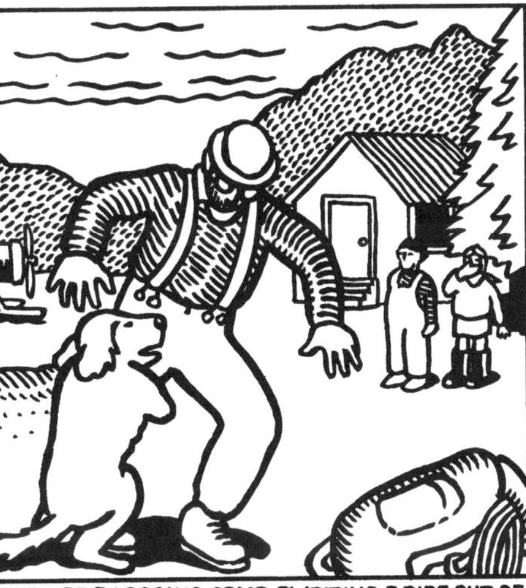

LATER, AT A LOGGING CAMP, AWAITING A RIDE OUT OF THE MOUNTAINS ... A DOG FELL IN LOVE WITH ME.

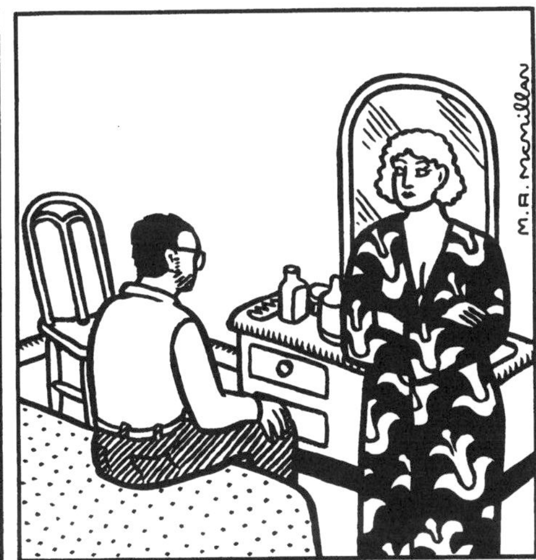

AS SOON AS I RETURNED TO THE CITY I DECIDED TO SEEK PROFESSIONAL GUIDANCE.

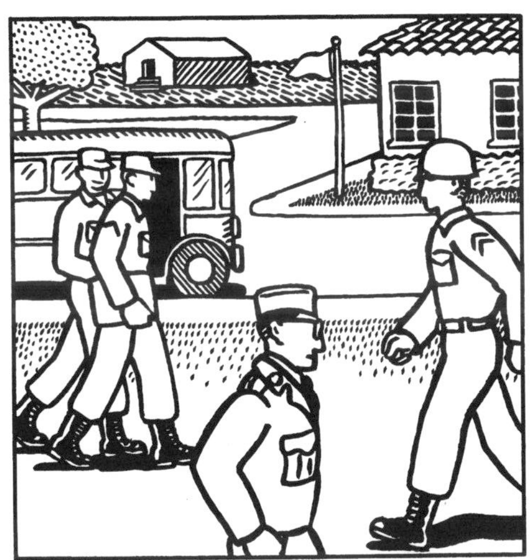

U.S. ARMY, N. CAROLINA, 1956. WITH A WEEKEND PASS I ENTERTAINED ONLY ONE IDEA: GETTING LOST!

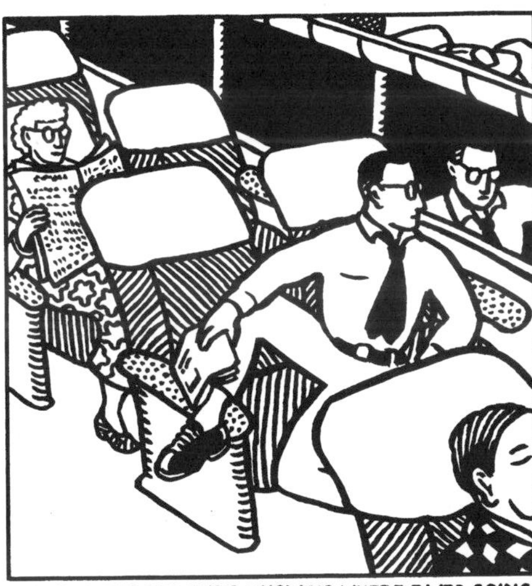

TO PICK A BUS AND AVOID KNOWING WHERE I WAS GOING OR WHICH DIRECTION: INTENTIONAL DISORIENTATION.

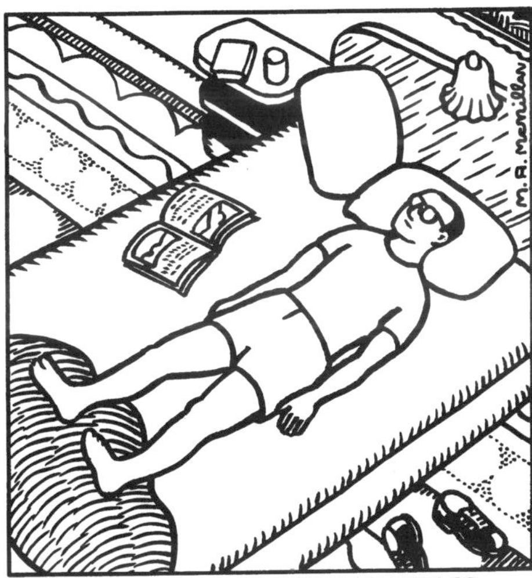

THE ABSOLUTE PLEASURE OF MY FEW HOURS OF EXISTENTIAL FOG ESTABLISHED A LIFELONG PRIORITY.

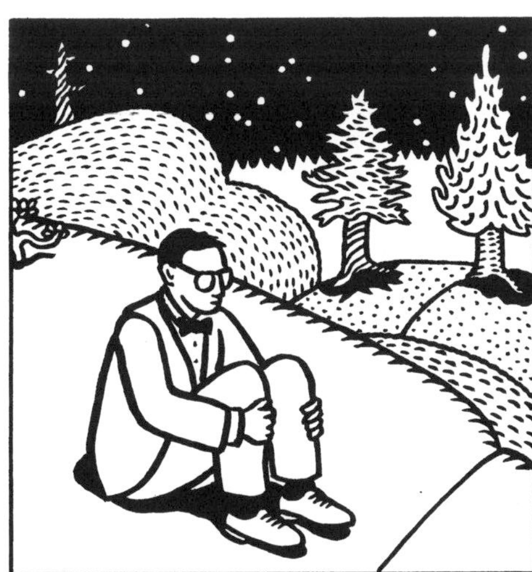

COSMIC DIALOGUE 1953: "SCHOOL! JOB! CAR! MARRIAGE! HOUSE! KIDS! ... PREDICTABLE BOREDOM!!

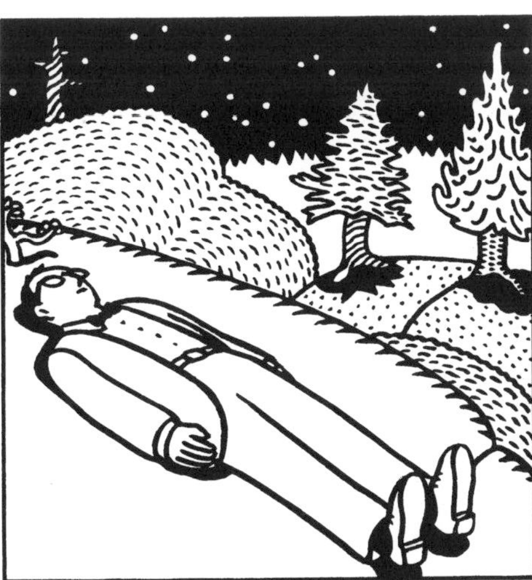

I'LL JUST LOOK UP AND REMEMBER MRS. WOLF'S LEGS AS SHE WALKED AMONG OUR PRONE BODIES DURING SPEECH THERAPY.

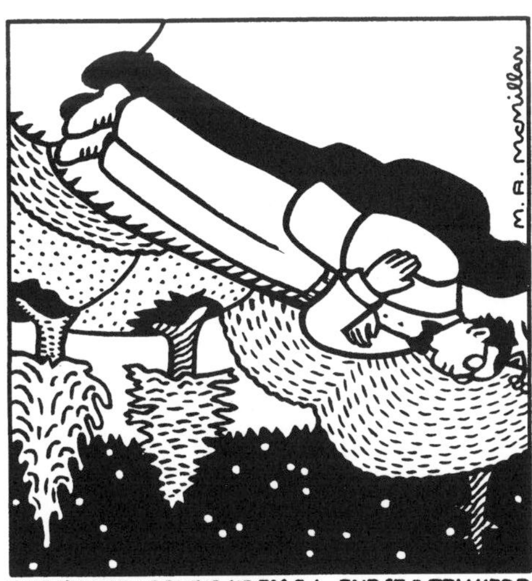

BUT I'M NOT LOOKING UP AM I! ... AND IF I TRY HARD I SHOULD JUST FLOAT RIGHT OFF THE EARTH!"

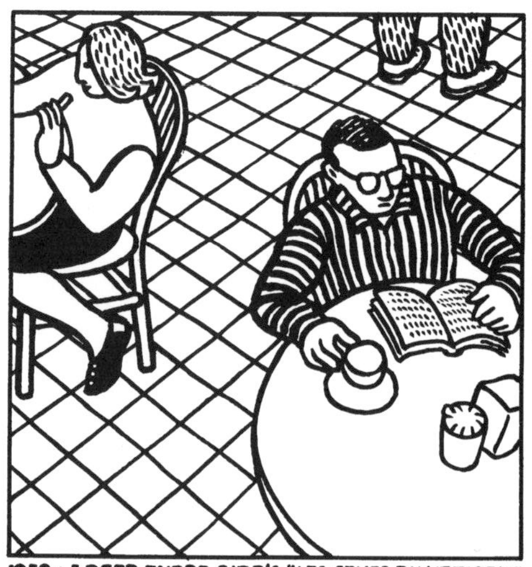
1958: I READ ANDRE GIDE'S "LES CAVES DU VATICAN" ABOUT THE GRATUITOUS ACT.. THE UNMOTIVATED CRIME.

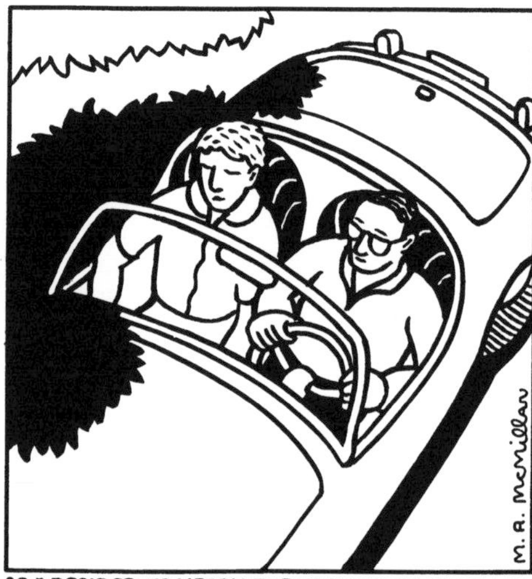

SO I DECIDED TO MARRY THE VERY NEXT WOMAN WHO CAME INTO MY LIFE. WHY NOT?

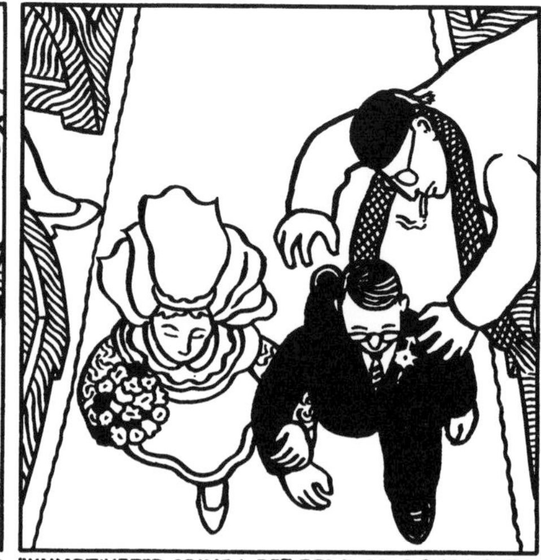
"UNMOTIVATED CRIME! EET EES A GOOD ONE! BUT ZE CRIMINAL FLY EN ZE SPIDER'S WEB. YES?"

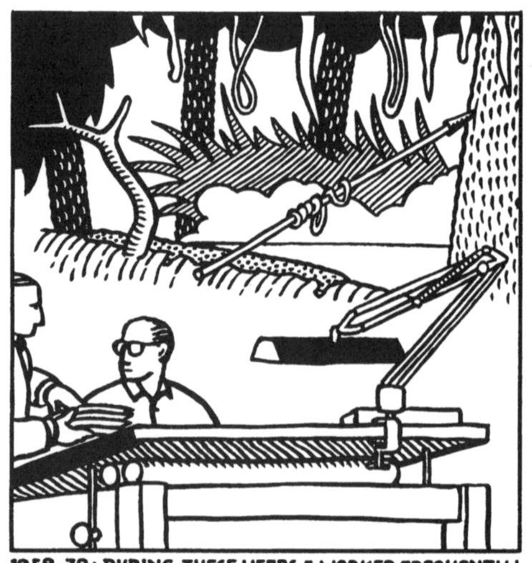
1958-70: DURING THESE YEARS I WORKED FREQUENTLY AS A DRAFTSMAN IN VARIOUS ENGINEERING OFFICES.

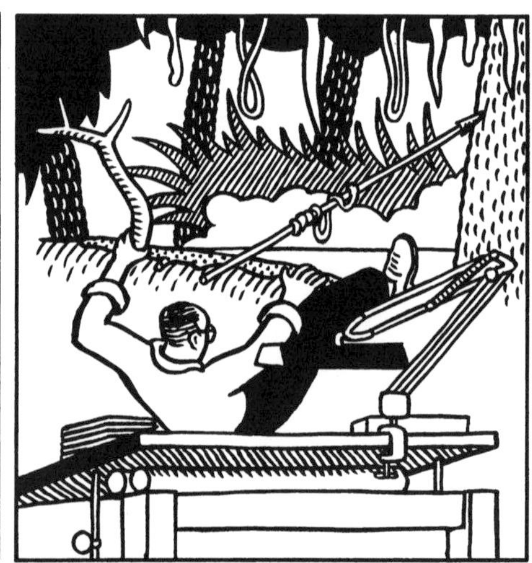
THOUGH I WAS ALWAYS CONSCIENTIOUS AND HIGHLY REGARDED, I FOUND MYSELF PERPETUALLY BORED.

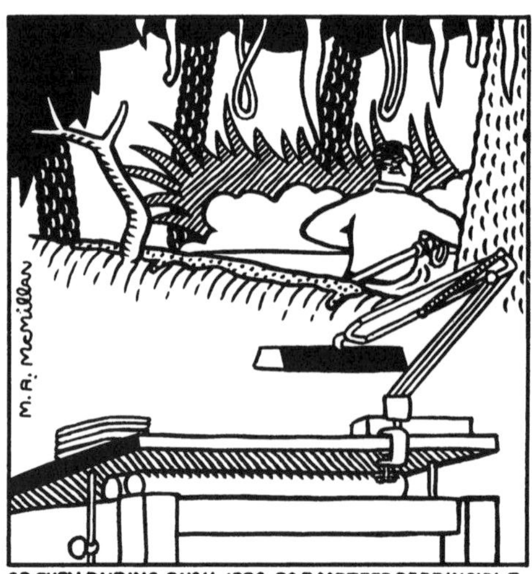

SO EVEN DURING RUSH JOBS, AS A MATTER OF PRINCIPLE, I REMAINED LOYAL TO A PARALLEL REALITY.

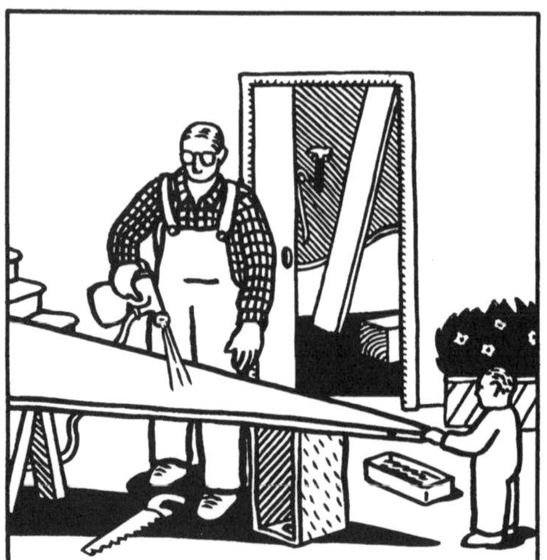
WHILE THE STREAM OF EVENTS FLOWED I PERSISTED IN MAINTAINING A LINK TO OBJECTIVE REALITY:

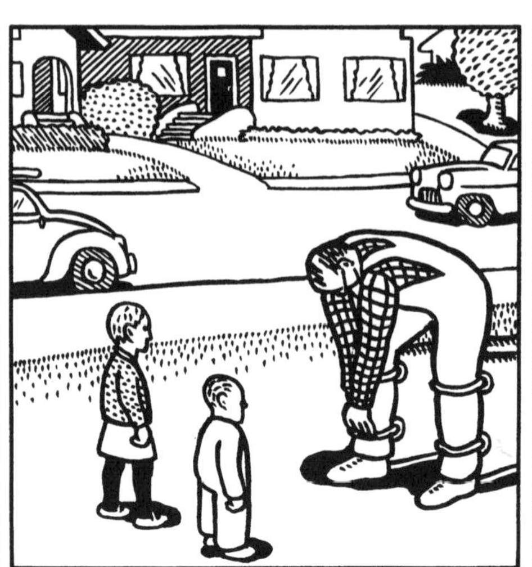
CONSTRUCTION THAT HAS, THROUGH THE YEARS, RELIABLY RESCUED MY FLOUNDERING PSYCHE.

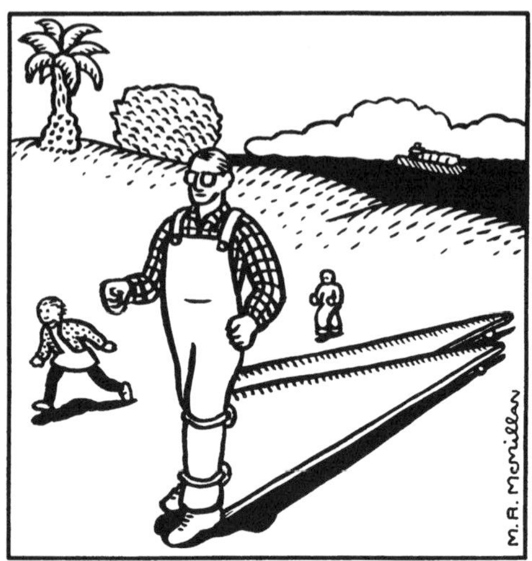

TO ACHIEVE THIS IT IS NECESSARY TO AVOID CONVENTIONAL ASSUMPTIONS.

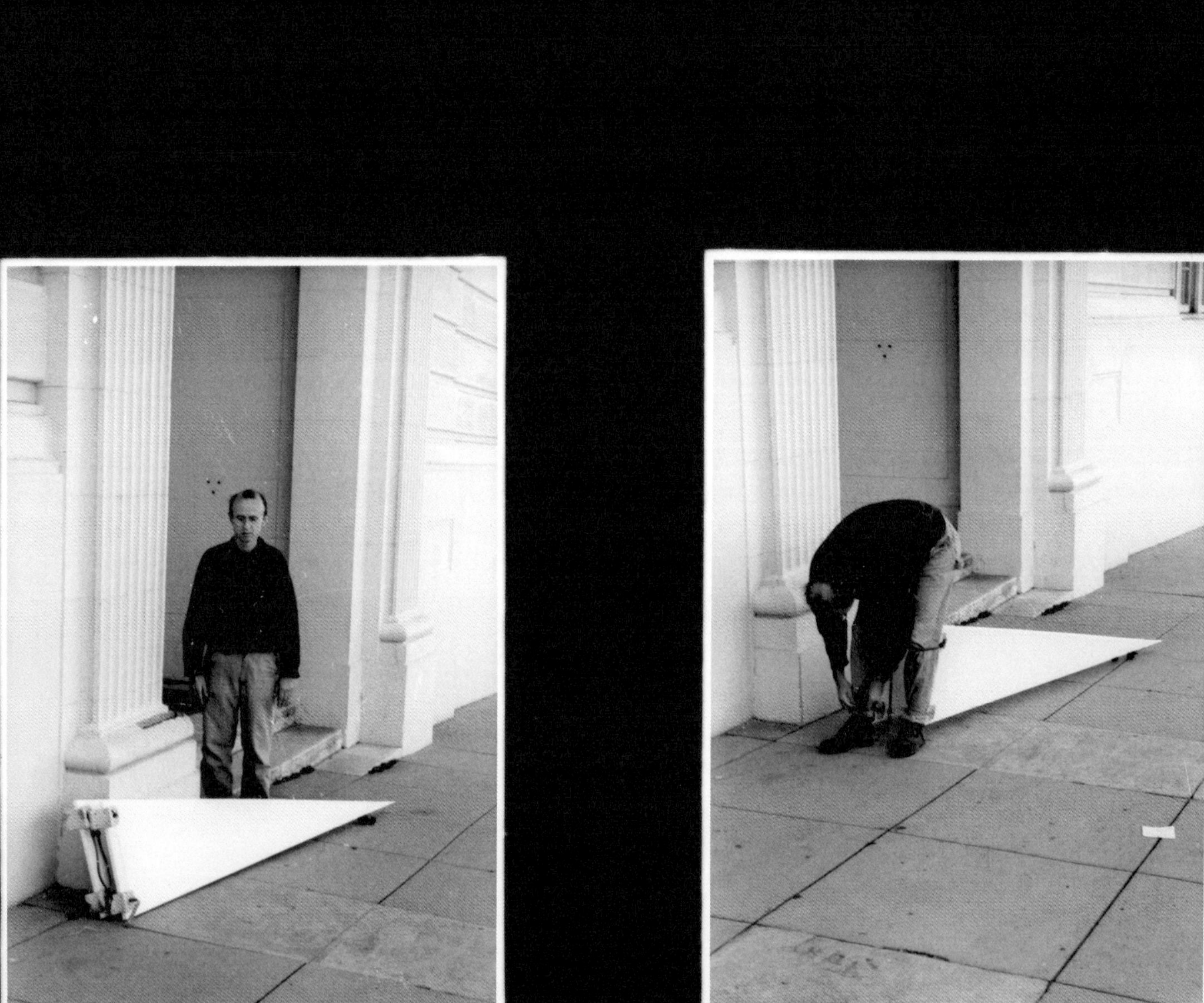

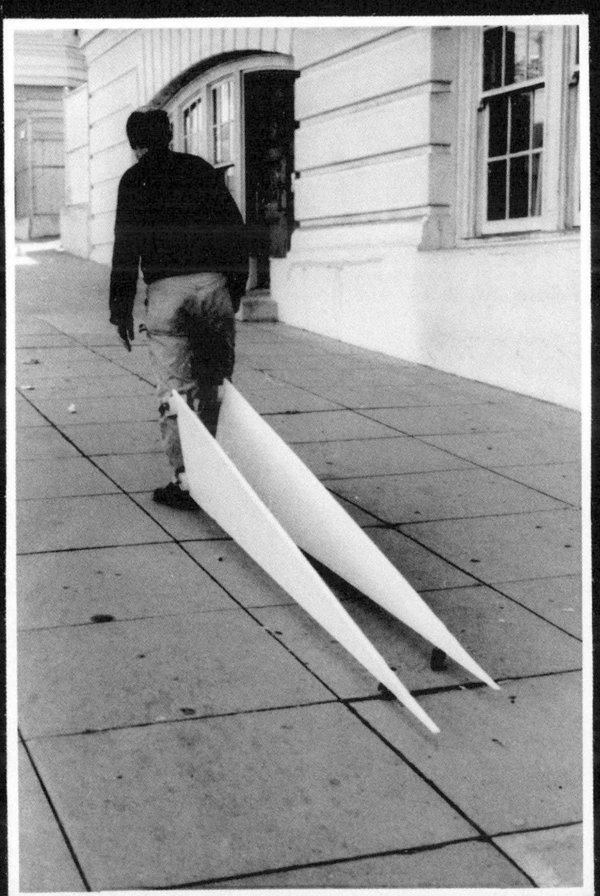

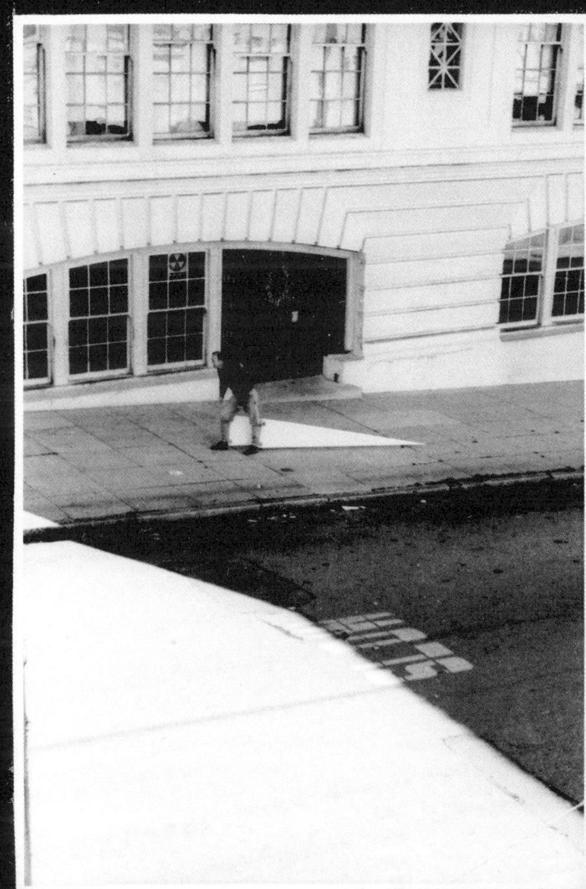

Sculpture as a body extension. No symbolism intended. Think of Abe Lincoln's stovepipe hat. What's that all about?

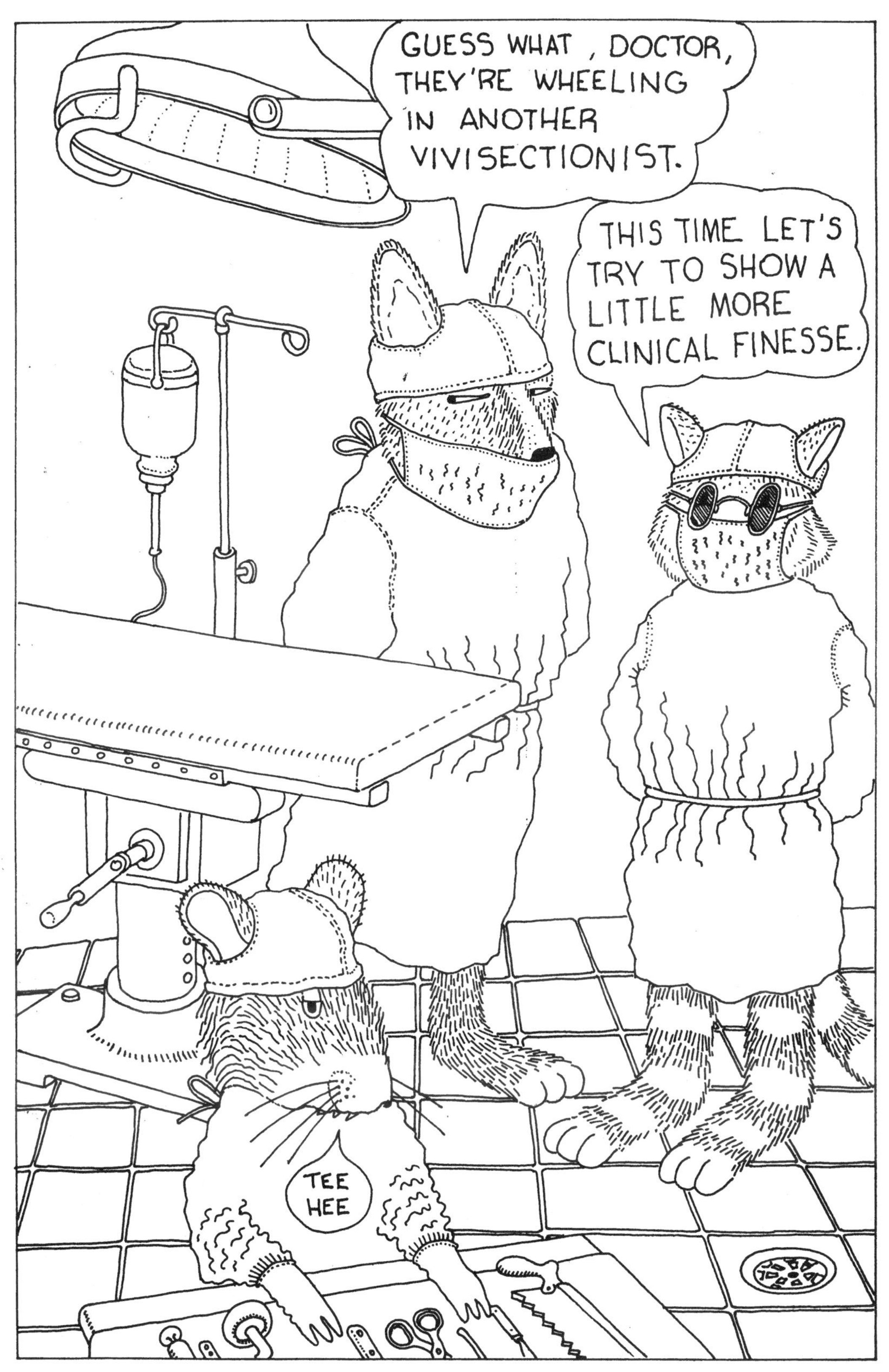
GUESS WHAT , DOCTOR, THEY'RE WHEELING IN ANOTHER VIVISECTIONIST.
THIS TIME LET'S TRY TO SHOW A LITTLE MORE CLINICAL FINESSE.
TEE HEE

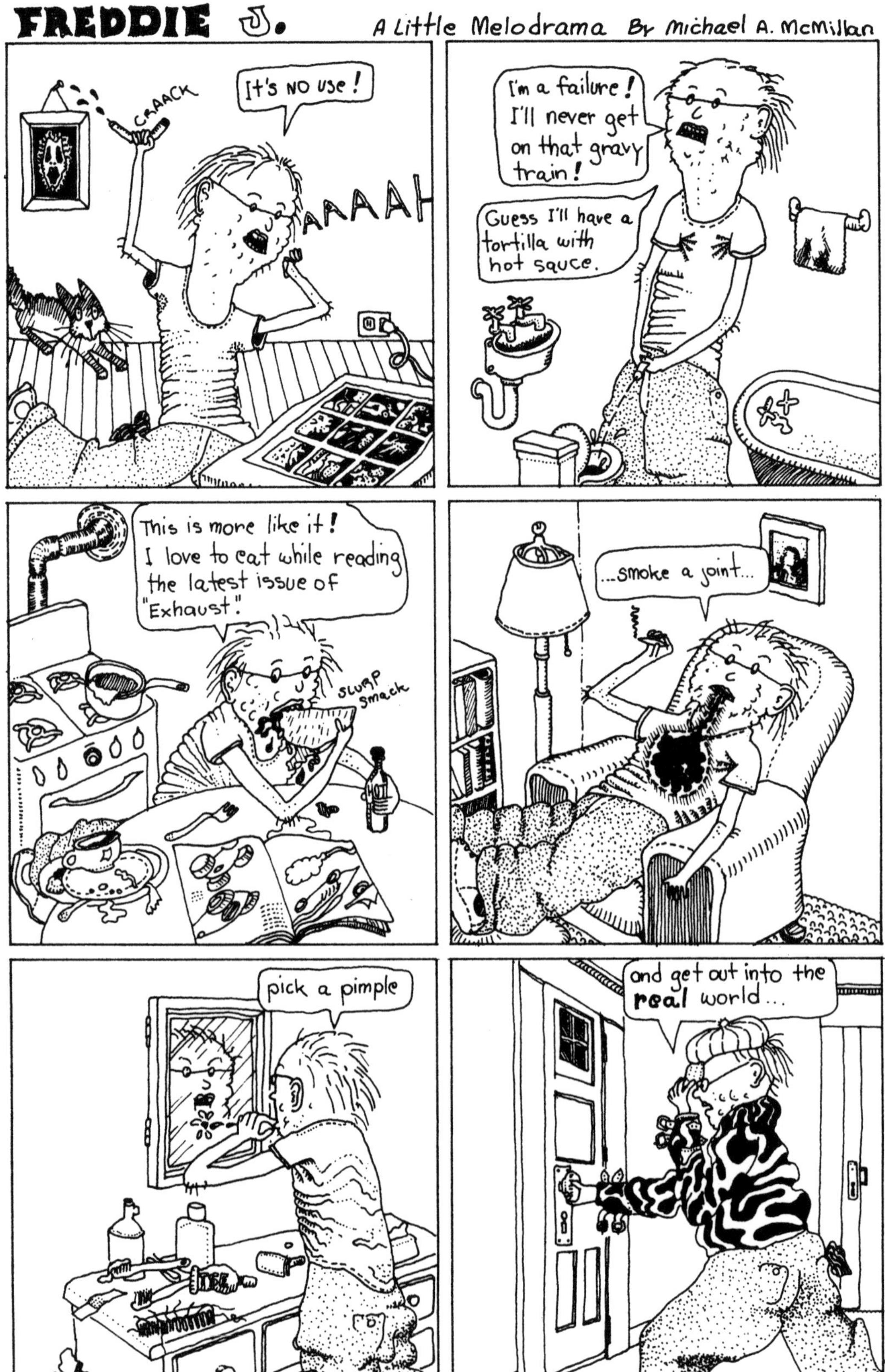
FREDDIE J.
A Little Melodrama By Michael A. McMillan
It's NO use!
CRAACK
AAAAH
I'm a failure! I'll never get on that gravy train!
Guess I'll have a tortilla with hot sauce.
This is more like it! I love to eat while reading the latest issue of "Exhaust."
SLURP smack
...smoke a joint...
pick a pimple
and get out into the real world...

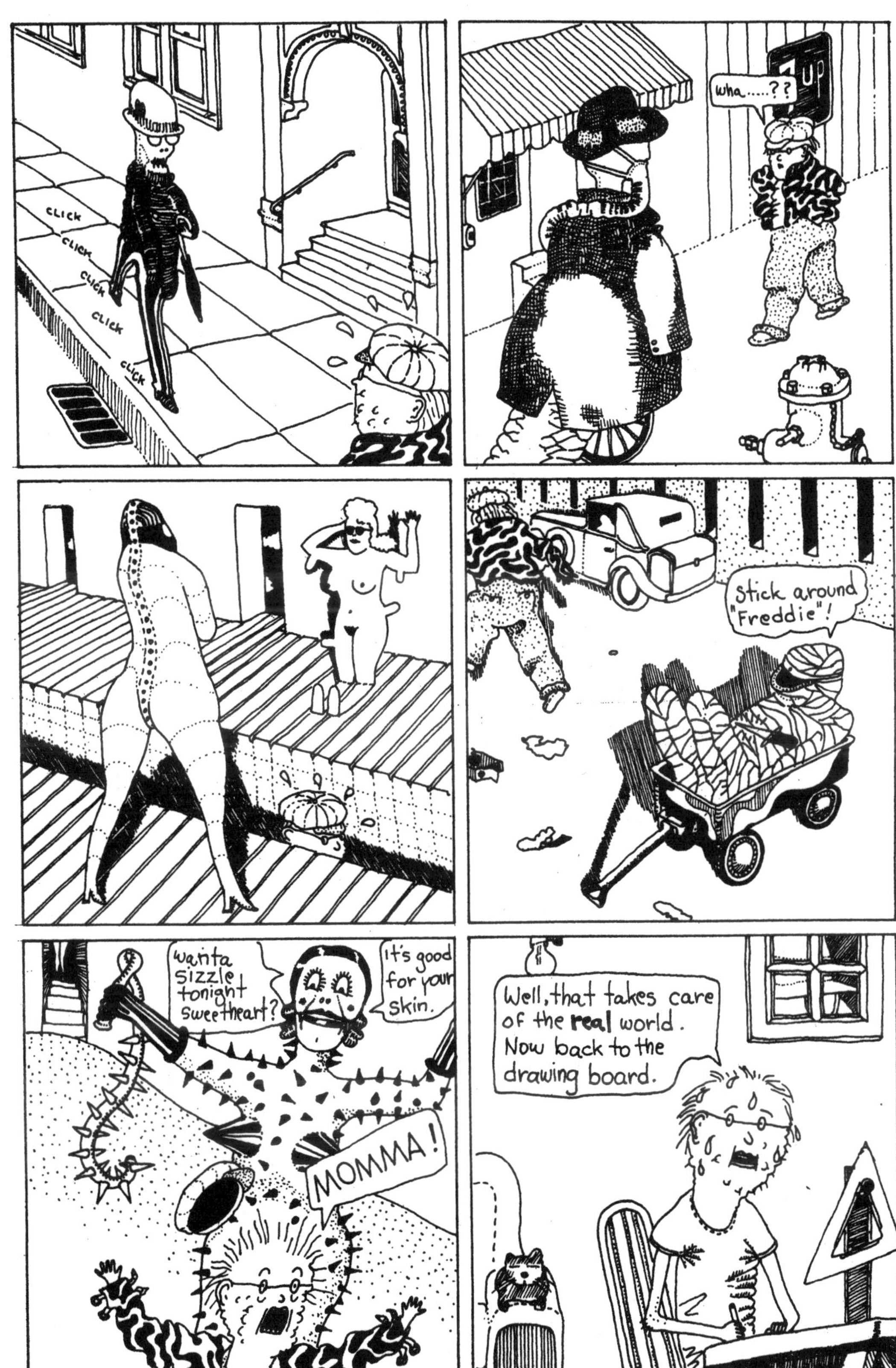
CLICK
CLICK
CLICK
CLICK
CLICK
wha.....??
UP
Stick around "Freddie"!
wanta sizzle tonight sweetheart?
It's good for your skin.
MOMMA!
Well, that takes care of the **real** world. Now back to the drawing board.

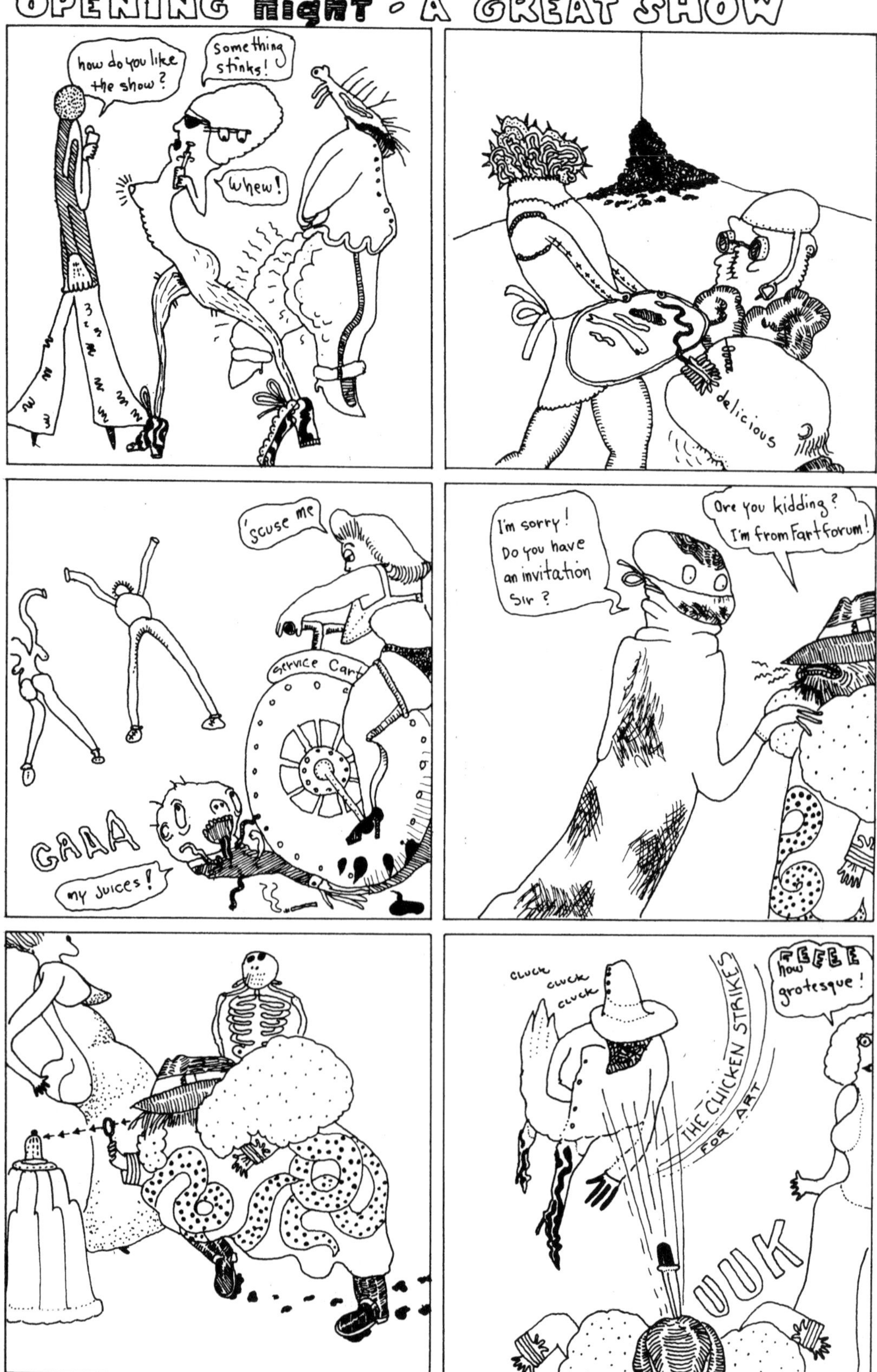
OPENING Night - A GREAT SHOW
how do you like the show?
Something stinks!
Whew!
delicious
'scuse me
Service Cart
GAAA
my juices!
I'm sorry! Do you have an invitation Sir?
Are you kidding? I'm from Fartforum!
cluck cluck cluck
THE CHICKEN STRIKES FOR ART
EEEEE how grotesque!
UUK

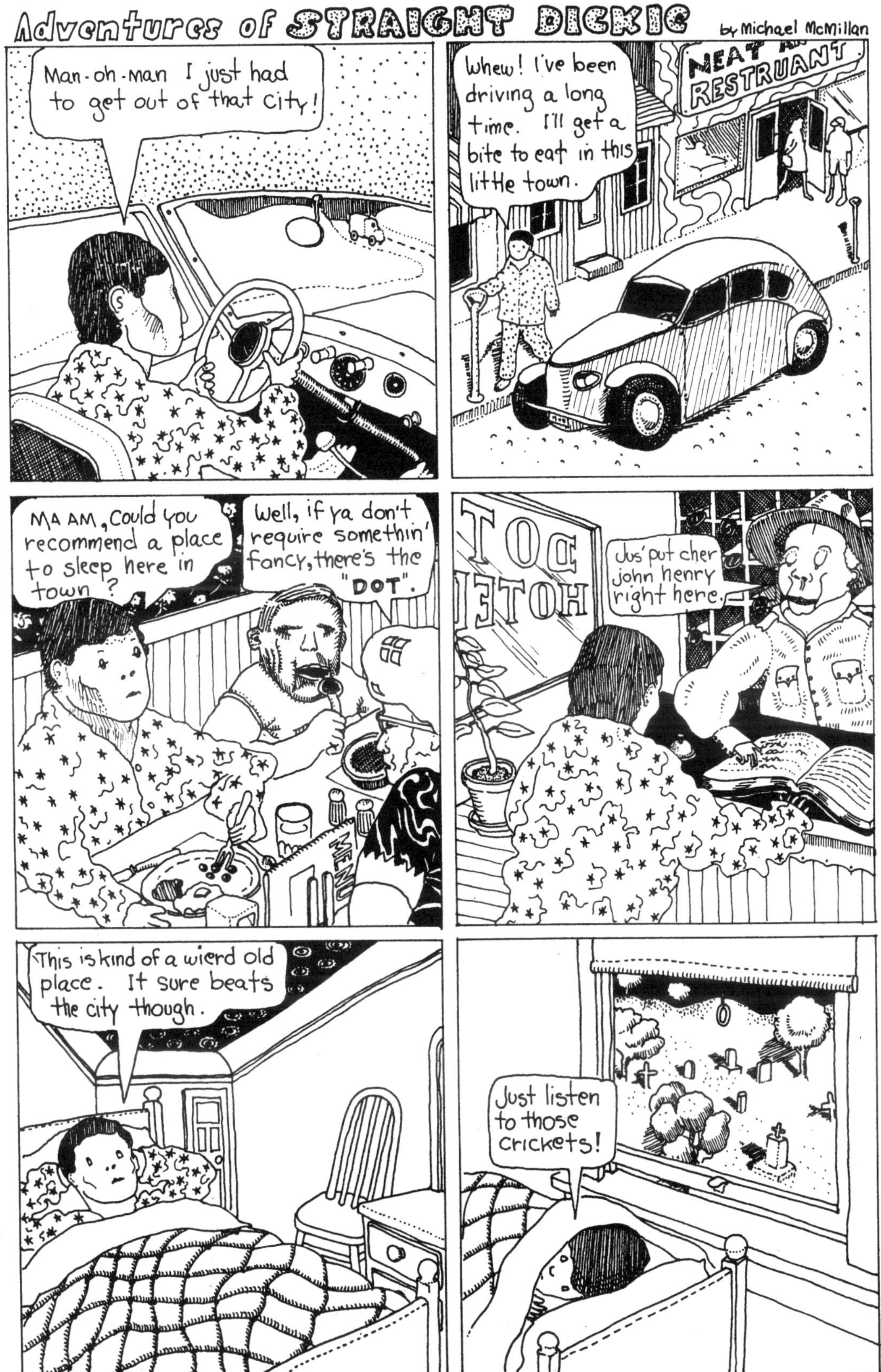
Adventures of STRAIGHT DICKIE
by Michael McMillan
Man-oh-man I just had to get out of that city!
Whew! I've been driving a long time. I'll get a bite to eat in this little town.
NEAT
RESTRUANT
MA AM, Could you recommend a place to sleep here in town?
Well, if ya don't require somethin' fancy, there's the "DOT".
MENU
DOT
HOTEL
Jus' put cher john henry right here.
This is kind of a wierd old place. It sure beats the city though.
Just listen to those crickets!

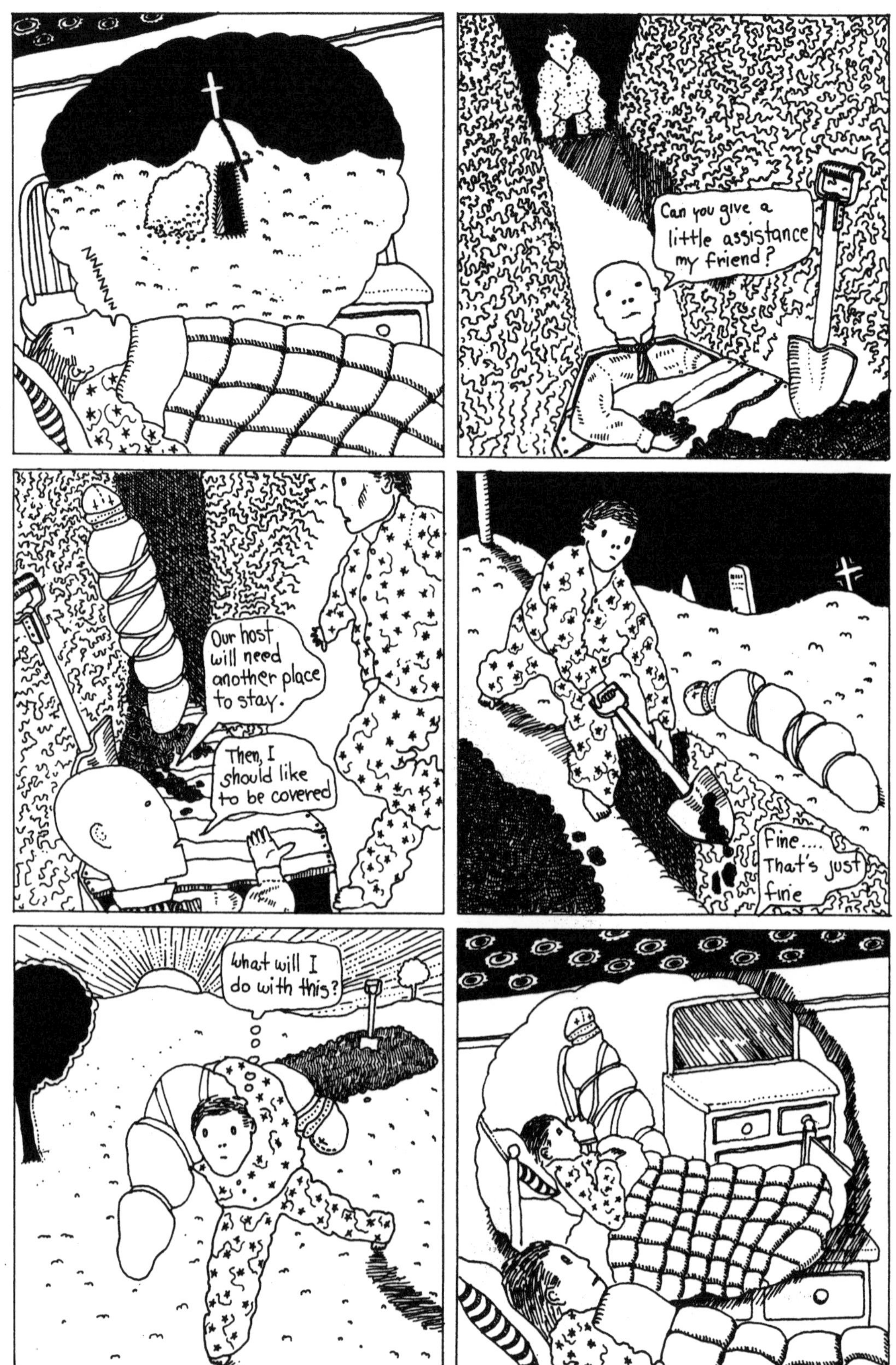

ZZZZZZ
Can you give a little assistance my friend?
Our host will need another place to stay.
Then, I should like to be covered
Fine.... That's just fine
What will I do with this?

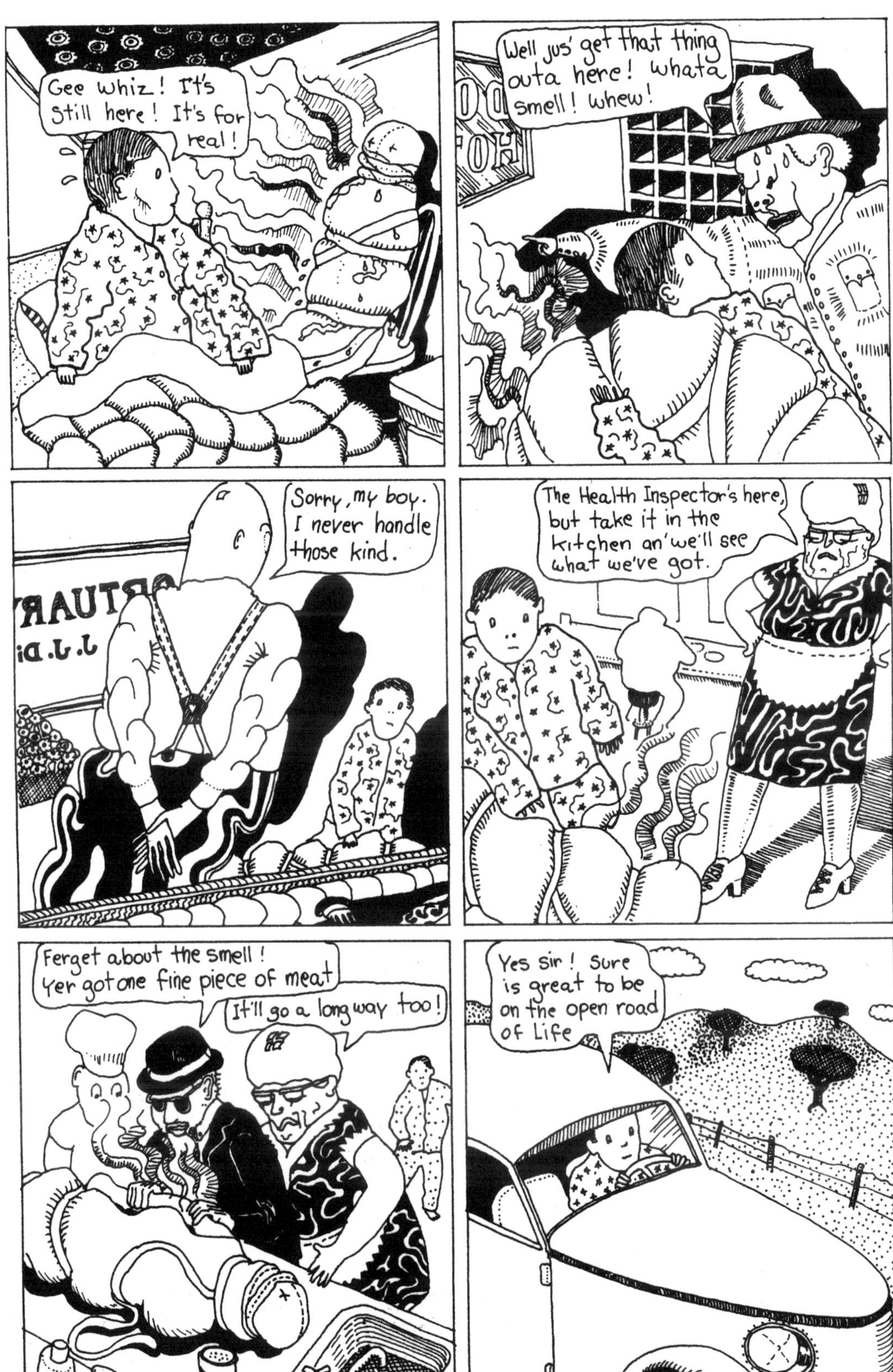
Gee whiz! It's still here! It's for real!
Well jus' get that thing outa here! whata smell! whew!
Sorry, my boy. I never handle those kind.
The Health Inspector's here, but take it in the kitchen an' we'll see what we've got.
Ferget about the smell! Yer got one fine piece of meat
It'll go a long way too!
Yes sir! Sure is great to be on the open road of Life

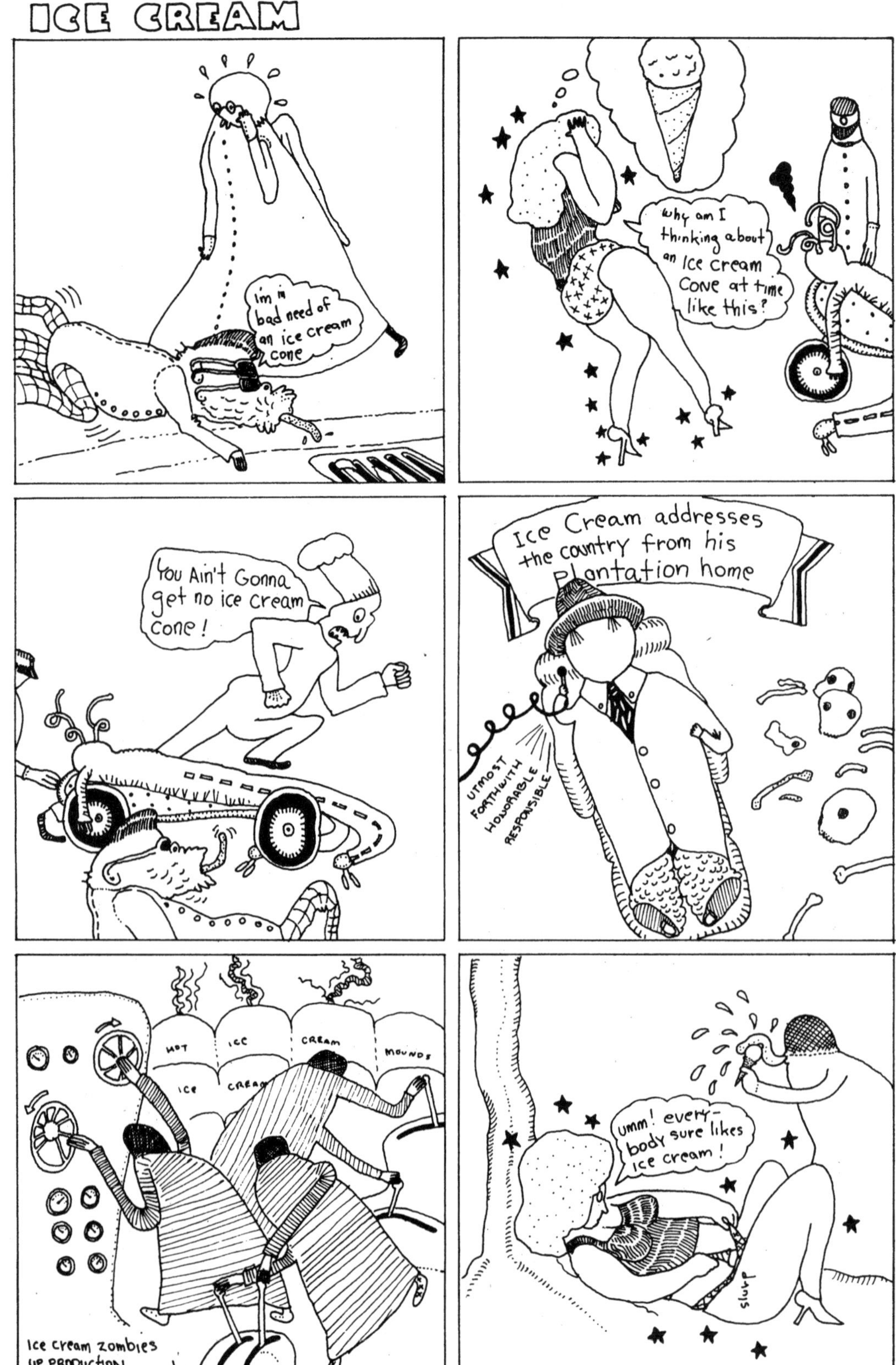
ICE CREAM
im in bad need of an ice cream cone
why am I thinking about an Ice cream cone at time like this?
You Ain't Gonna get no ice cream cone!
Ice Cream addresses the country from his plantation home
UTMOST
FORTHWITH
HONORABLE
RESPONSIBLE
HOT ICE CREAM MOUNDS
ICE CREAM
Ice cream zombies up PRODUCTION eight hundred percent
umm! every-body sure likes ice cream!
slurp
m. Mcmillan

Summertime along the POTOMAC

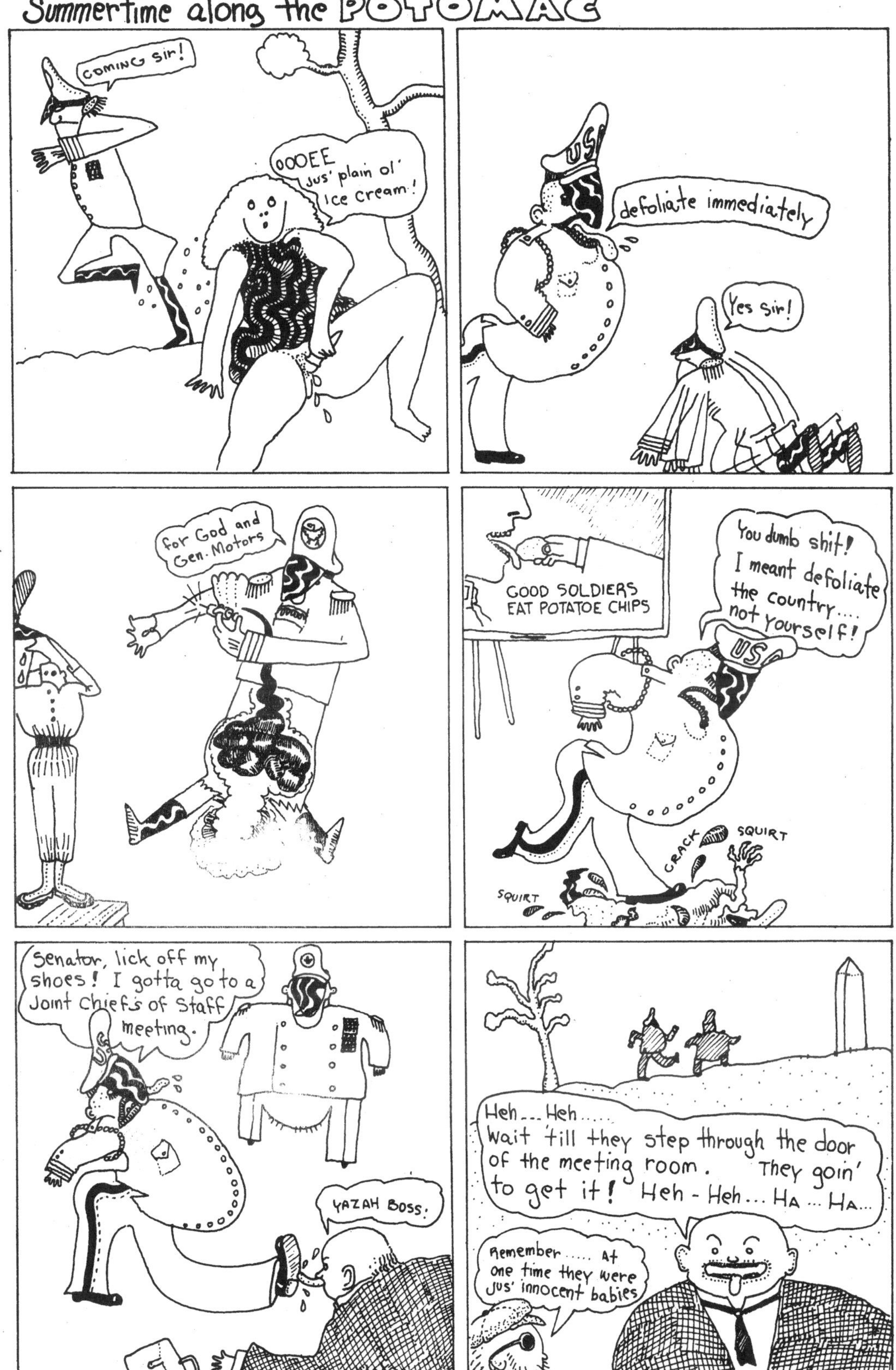

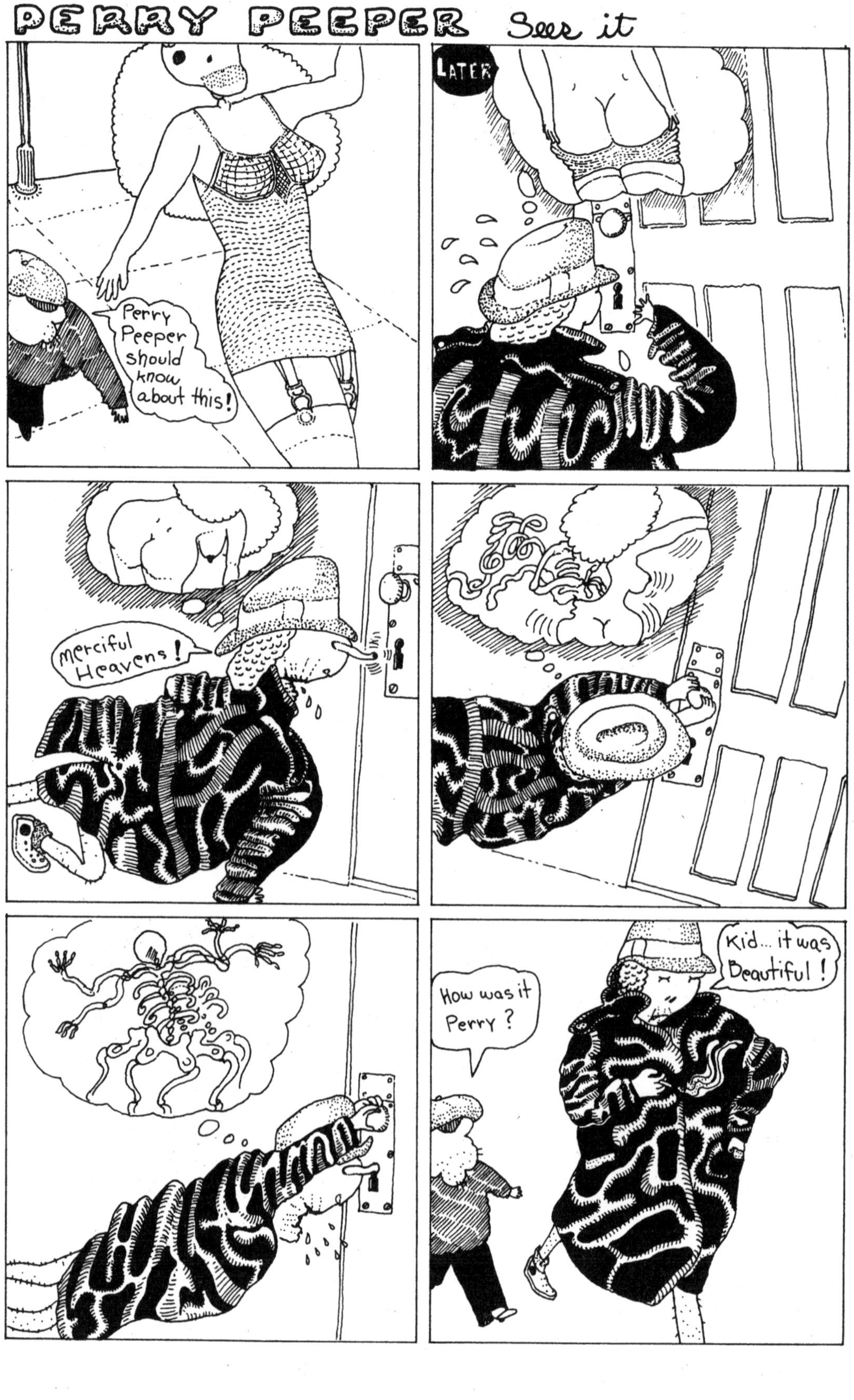

PERRY PEEPER Sees it

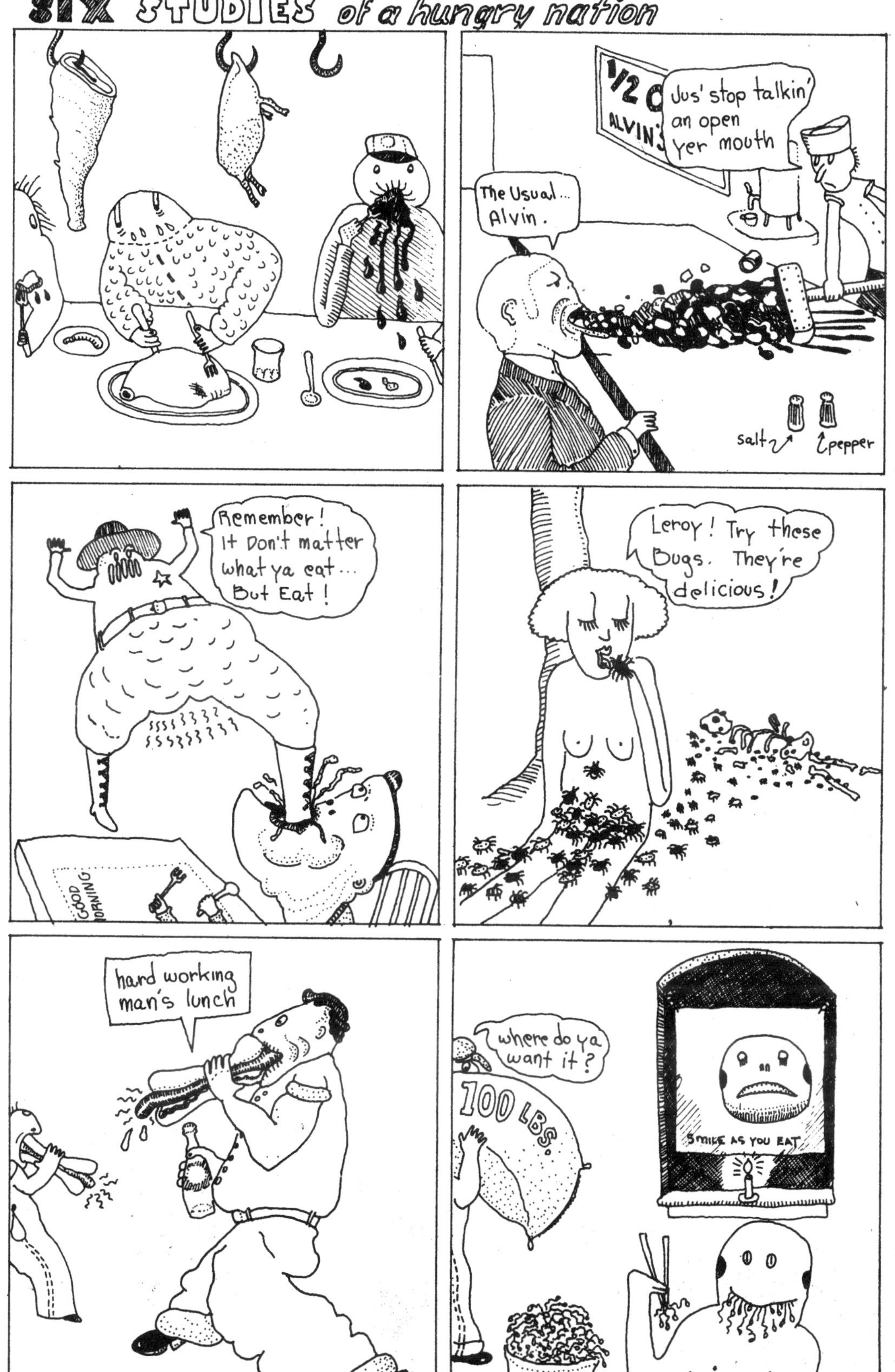
SIX STUDIES of a hungry nation
1/2 C
ALVIN'S
Jus' stop talkin' an open yer mouth
The Usual... Alvin.
salt
pepper
Remember! It Don't matter what ya eat... But Eat!
GOOD
ORNING
Leroy! Try these Bugs. They're delicious!
hard working man's lunch
where do ya want it?
100 LBS.
SMILE AS YOU EAT

Prologue to "THE UNDEAD FIENDS"

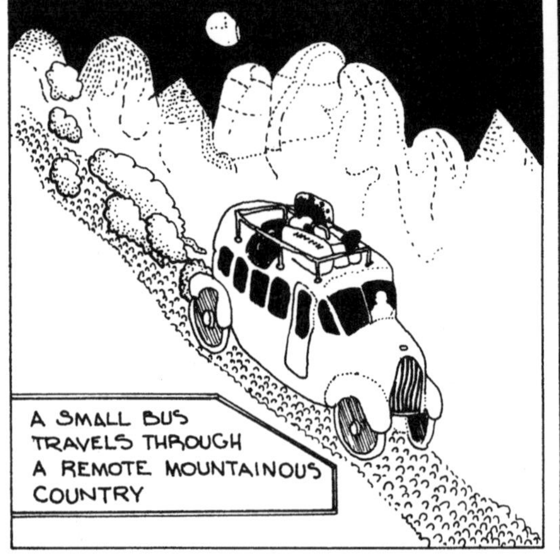

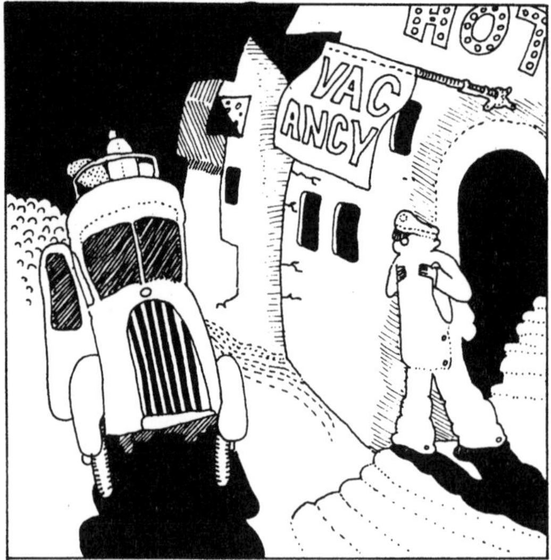

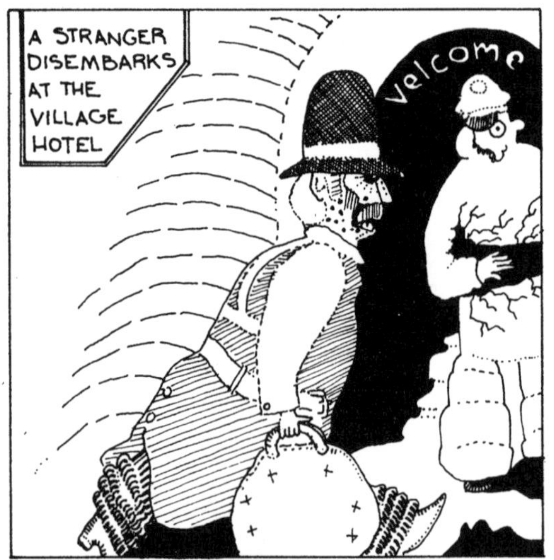

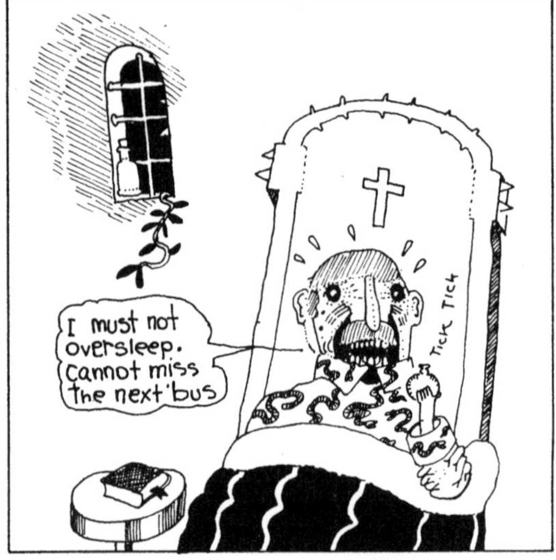

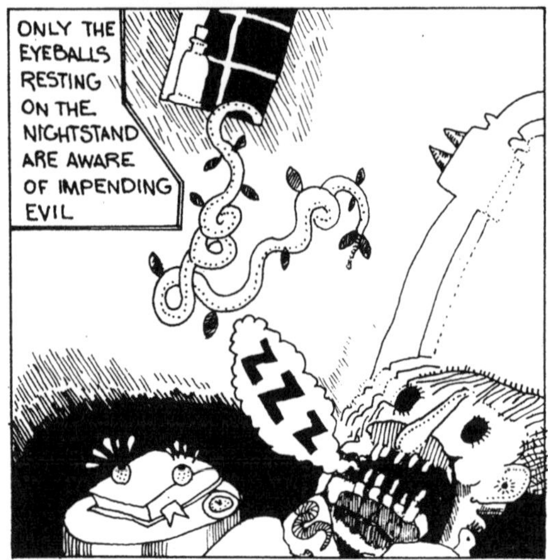

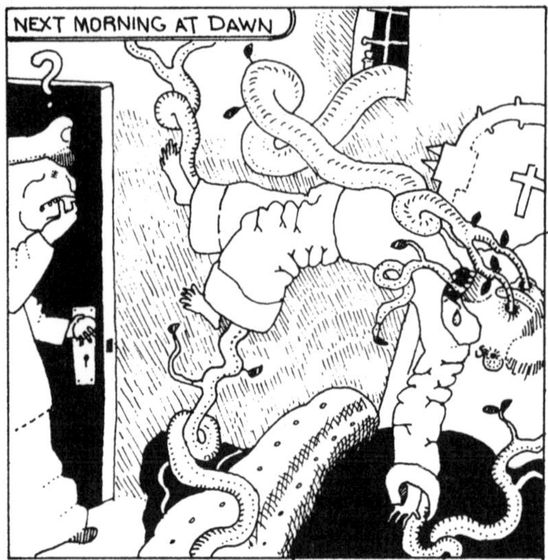

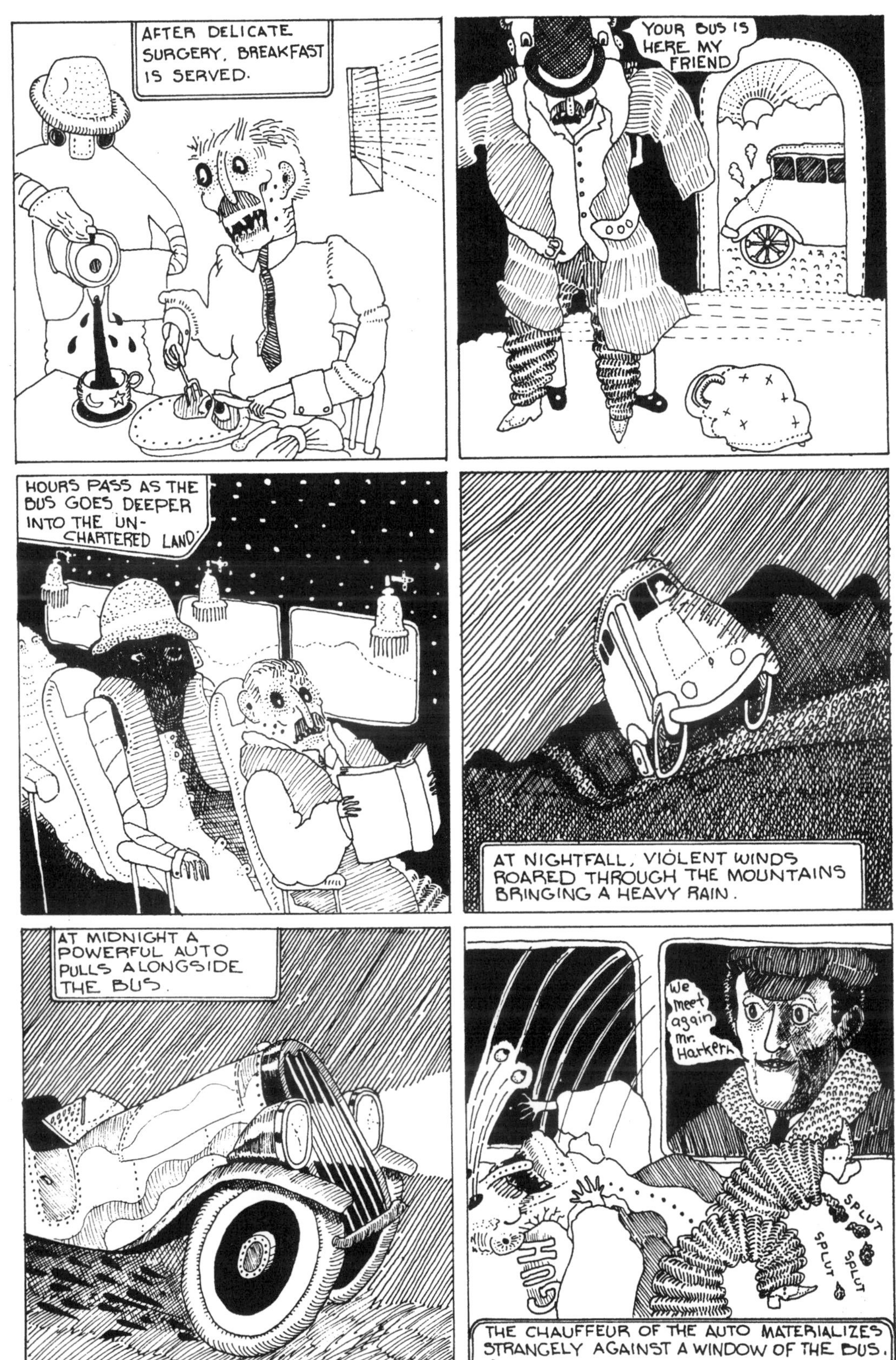
AFTER DELICATE SURGERY, BREAKFAST IS SERVED.
YOUR BUS IS HERE MY FRIEND
HOURS PASS AS THE BUS GOES DEEPER INTO THE UN-CHARTERED LAND.
AT NIGHTFALL, VIOLENT WINDS ROARED THROUGH THE MOUNTAINS BRINGING A HEAVY RAIN.
AT MIDNIGHT A POWERFUL AUTO PULLS ALONGSIDE THE BUS.
We meet again mr. Harker.
HOG
SPLUT
SPLUT
SPLUT
THE CHAUFFEUR OF THE AUTO MATERIALIZES STRANGELY AGAINST A WINDOW OF THE BUS.

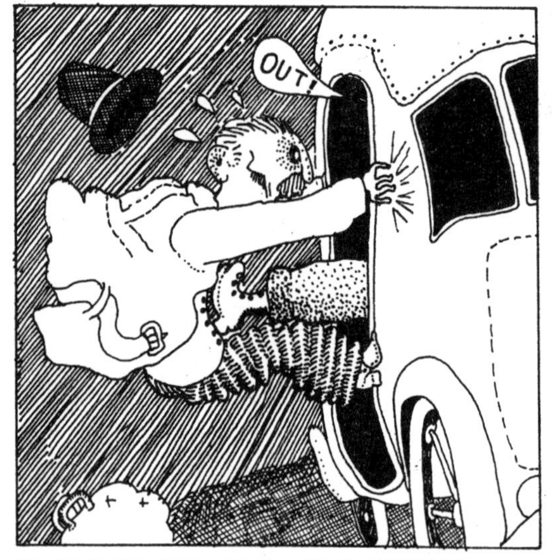
OUT!
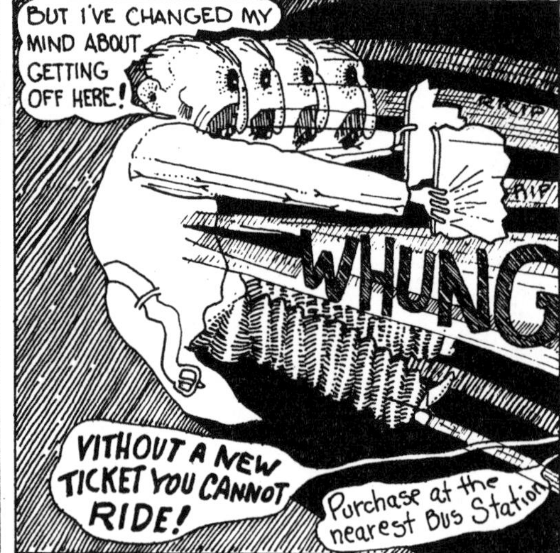
BUT I'VE CHANGED MY MIND ABOUT GETTING OFF HERE!
WHUNG
VITHOUT A NEW TICKET YOU CANNOT RIDE!
Purchase at the nearest Bus Station
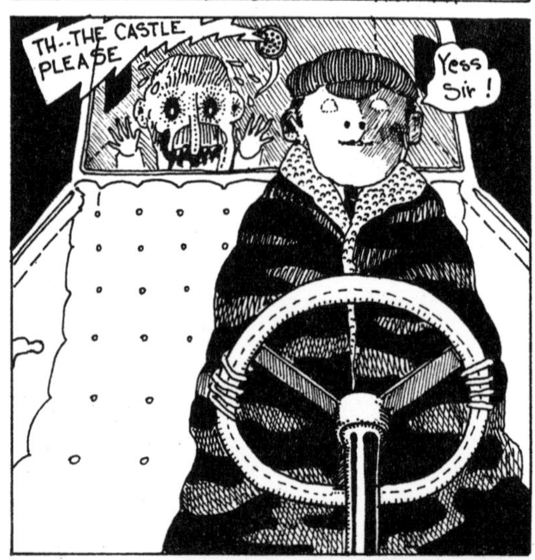
TH--THE CASTLE PLEASE
Yess Sir!
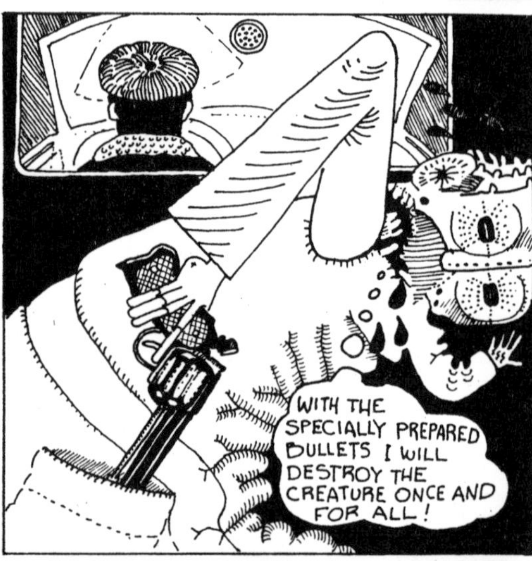
WITH THE SPECIALLY PREPARED BULLETS I WILL DESTROY THE CREATURE ONCE AND FOR ALL!
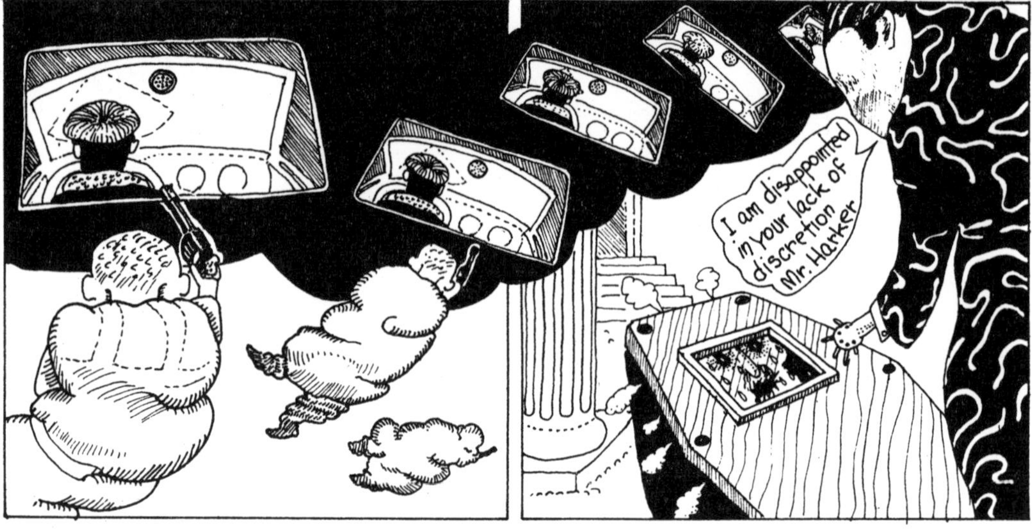
I am disappointed in your lack of discretion Mr. Harker

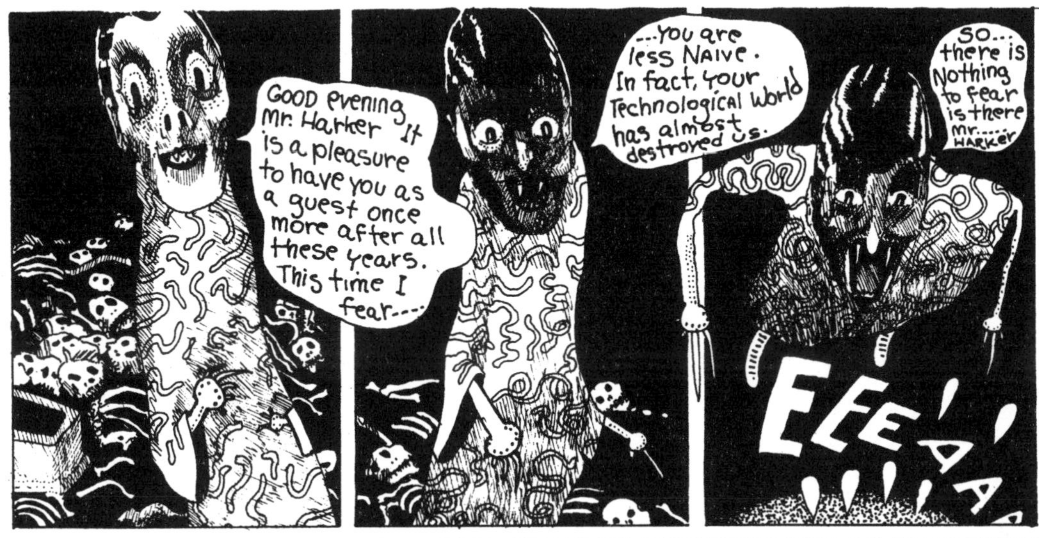
GOOD evening, Mr. Harker. It is a pleasure to have you as a guest once more after all these years. This time I fear---
---you are less NAIVE. In fact, your Technological World has almost destroyed us.
SO... there is Nothing to fear is there Mr..... HARKER
EEE AA

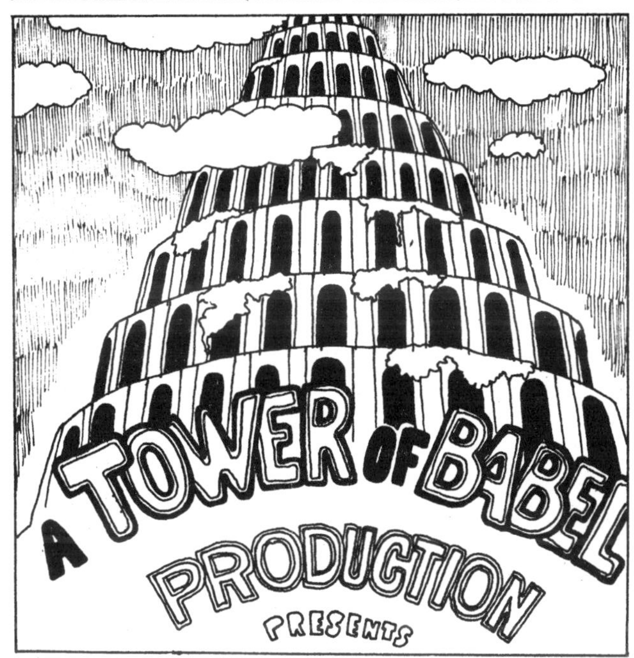
A TOWER OF BABEL PRODUCTION PRESENTS

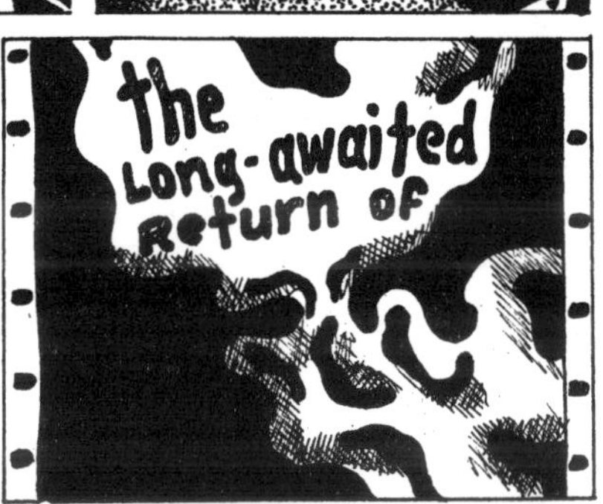
the Long-awaited Return of

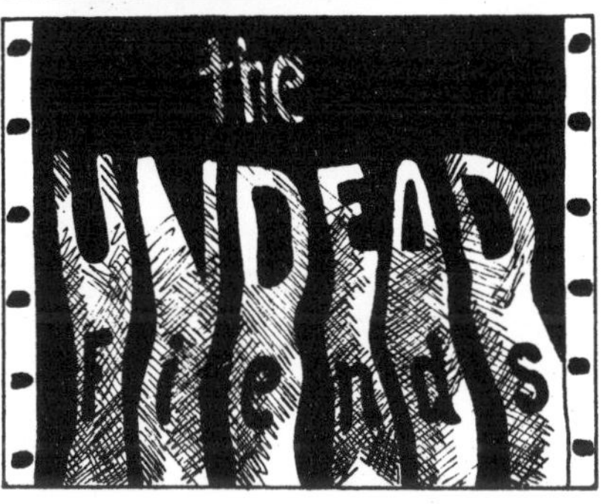
the UNDEAD fiends

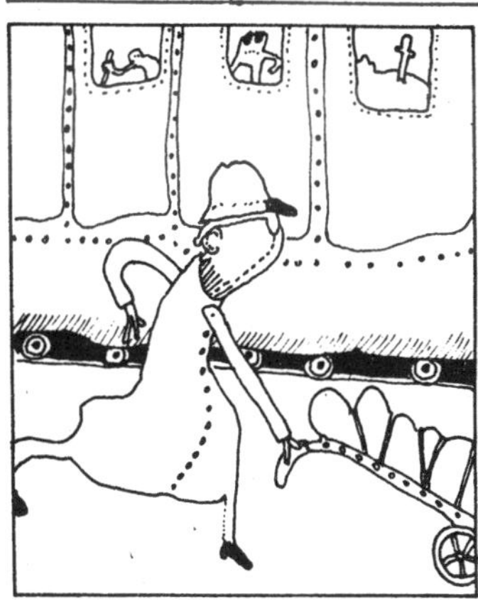

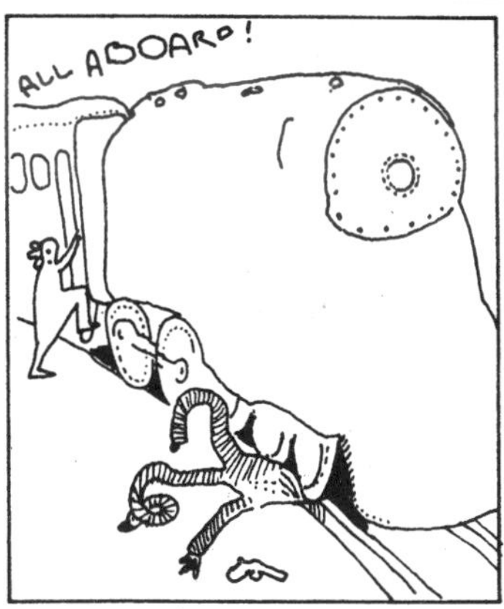
ALL ABOARD!

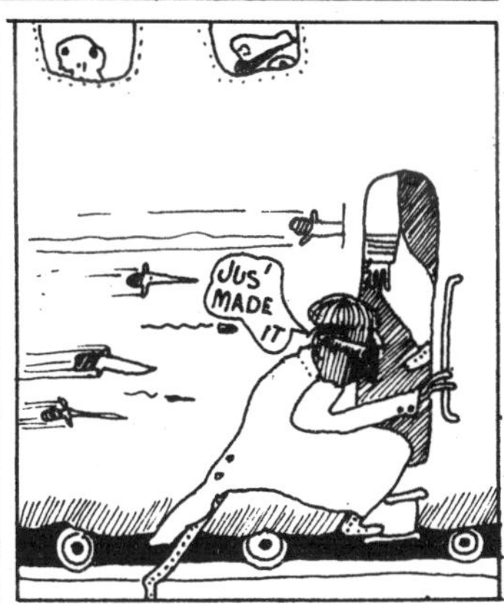
JUS' MADE IT

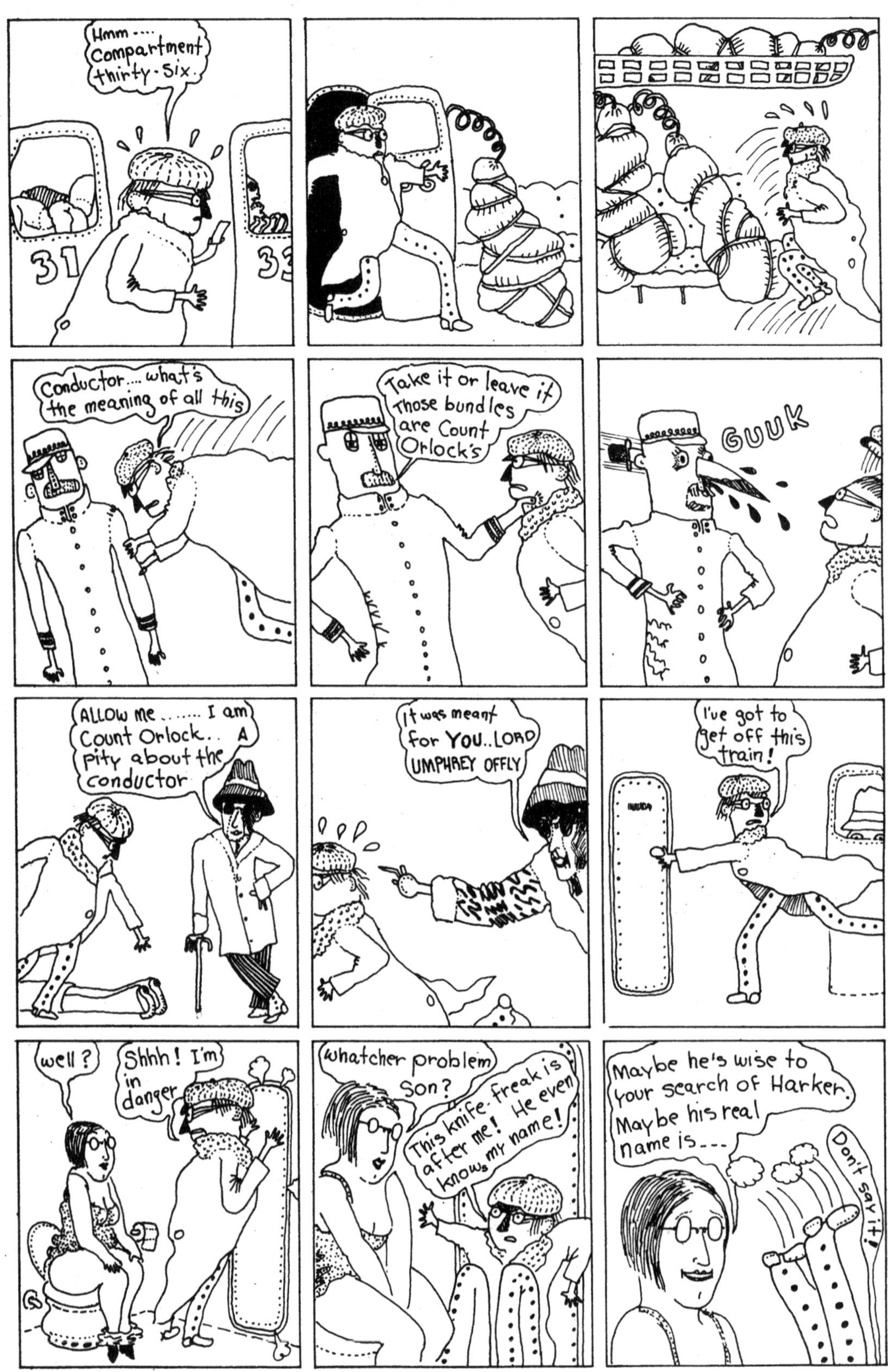
Hmm.... Compartment thirty-six.
Conductor.... what's the meaning of all this
Take it or leave it Those bundles are Count Orlock's
GUUK
ALLOW me...... I am Count Orlock.. A pity about the conductor
It was meant for YOU..LORD UMPHREY OFFLY
I've got to get off this train!
well?
Shhh! I'm in danger
whatcher problem Son?
This knife-freak is after me! He even knows my name!
Maybe he's wise to your search of Harker. Maybe his real name is...
Don't say it!

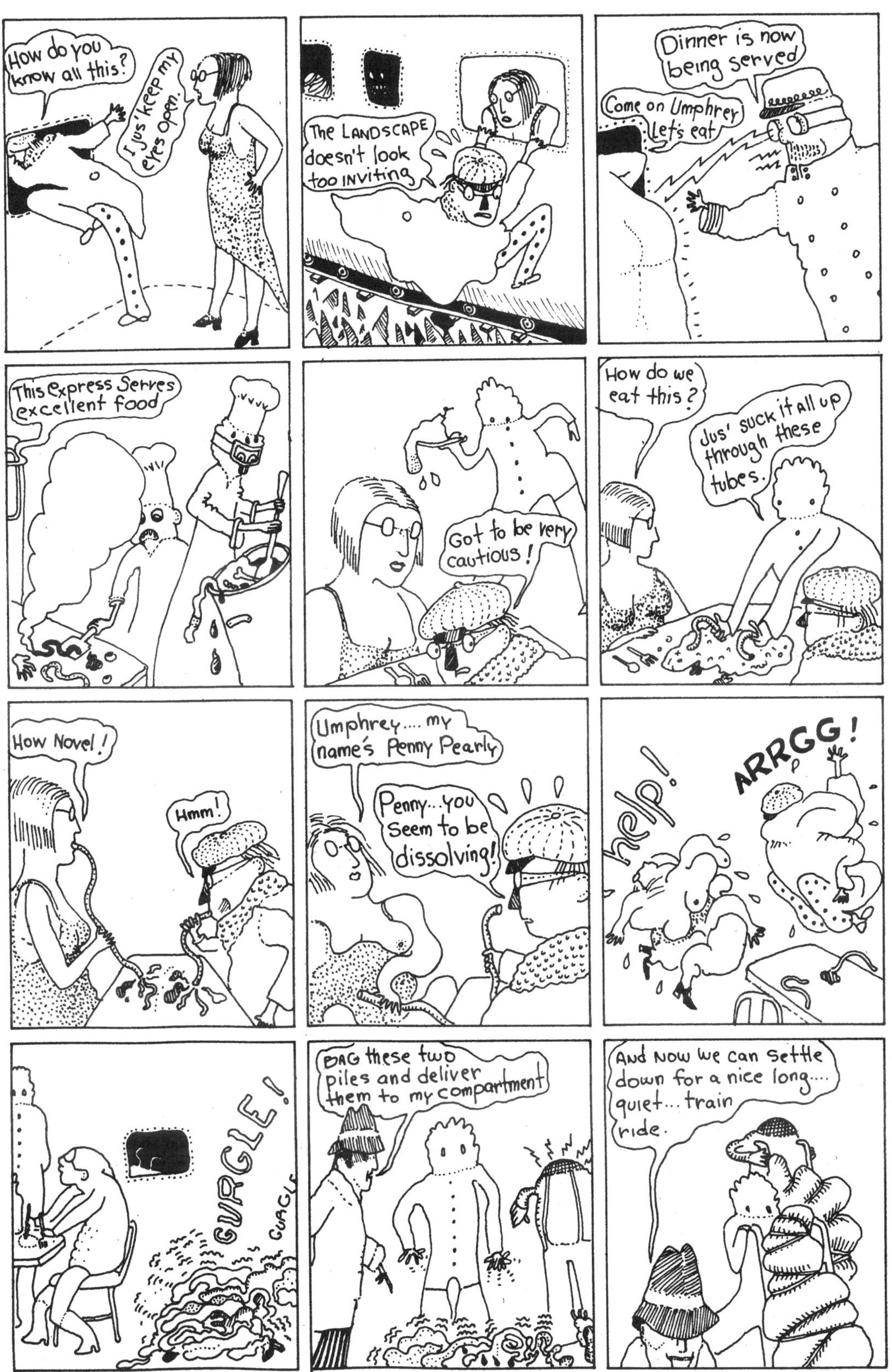
How do you know all this?
I jus' keep my eyes open.
The LANDSCAPE doesn't look too INVITING
Dinner is now being served
Come on Umphrey Let's eat
This express serves excellent food
Got to be very cautious!
How do we eat this?
Jus' suck it all up through these tubes.
How Novel!
Hmm!
Umphrey.... my name's Penny Pearly
Penny...you seem to be dissolving!
help!
ARRGG!
GURGLE!
GURGLE
BAG these two piles and deliver them to my compartment
And now we can settle down for a nice long.... quiet... train ride.

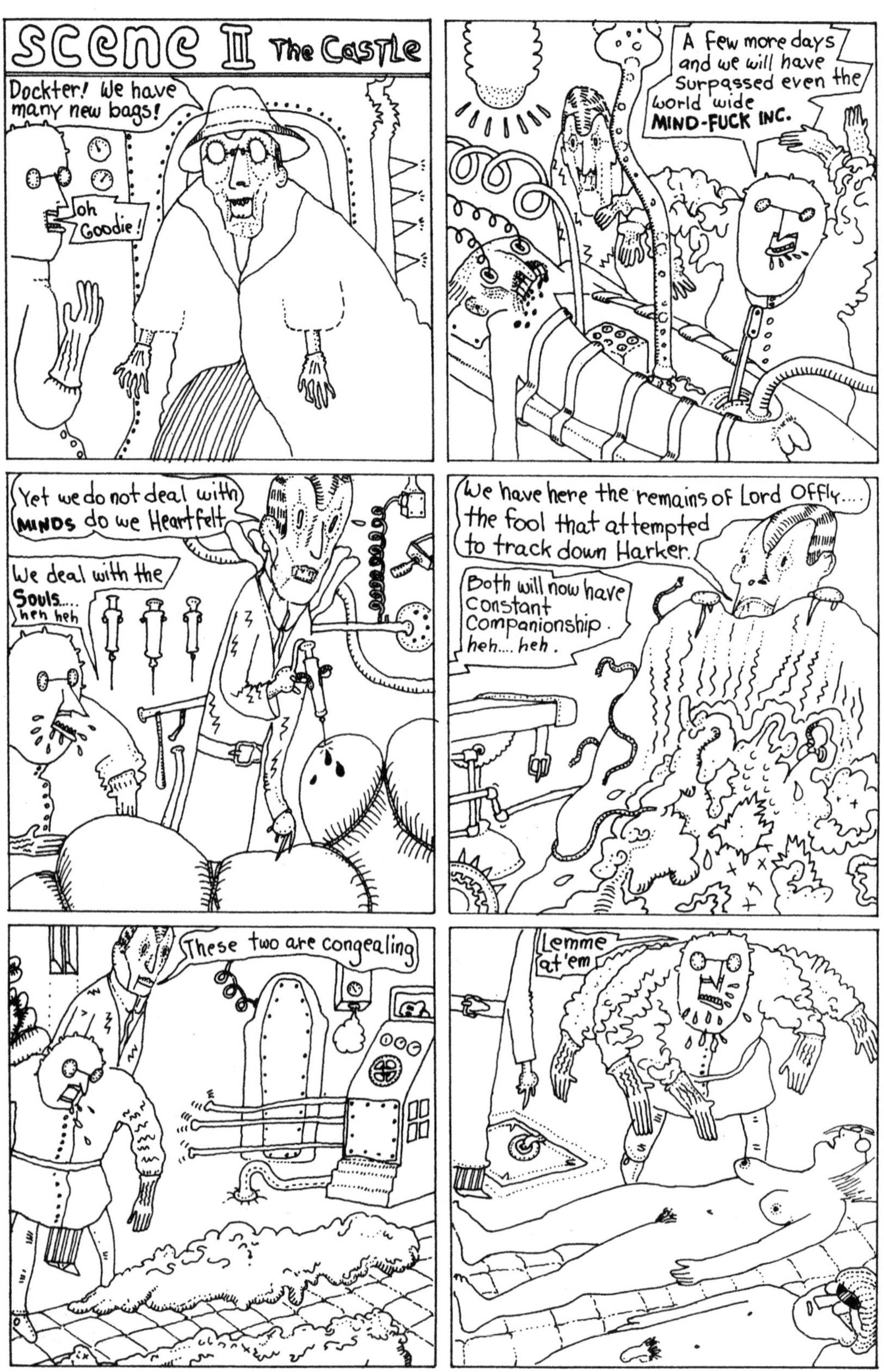
SCENE II The Castle
Dockter! We have many new bags!
oh Goodie!
A few more days and we will have surpassed even the world wide MIND-FUCK INC.
Yet we do not deal with MINDS do we Heartfelt
We deal with the SOULS.... heh heh
We have here the remains of Lord Offly.... the fool that attempted to track down Harker.
Both will now have constant companionship. heh.... heh.
These two are congealing
Lemme at'em

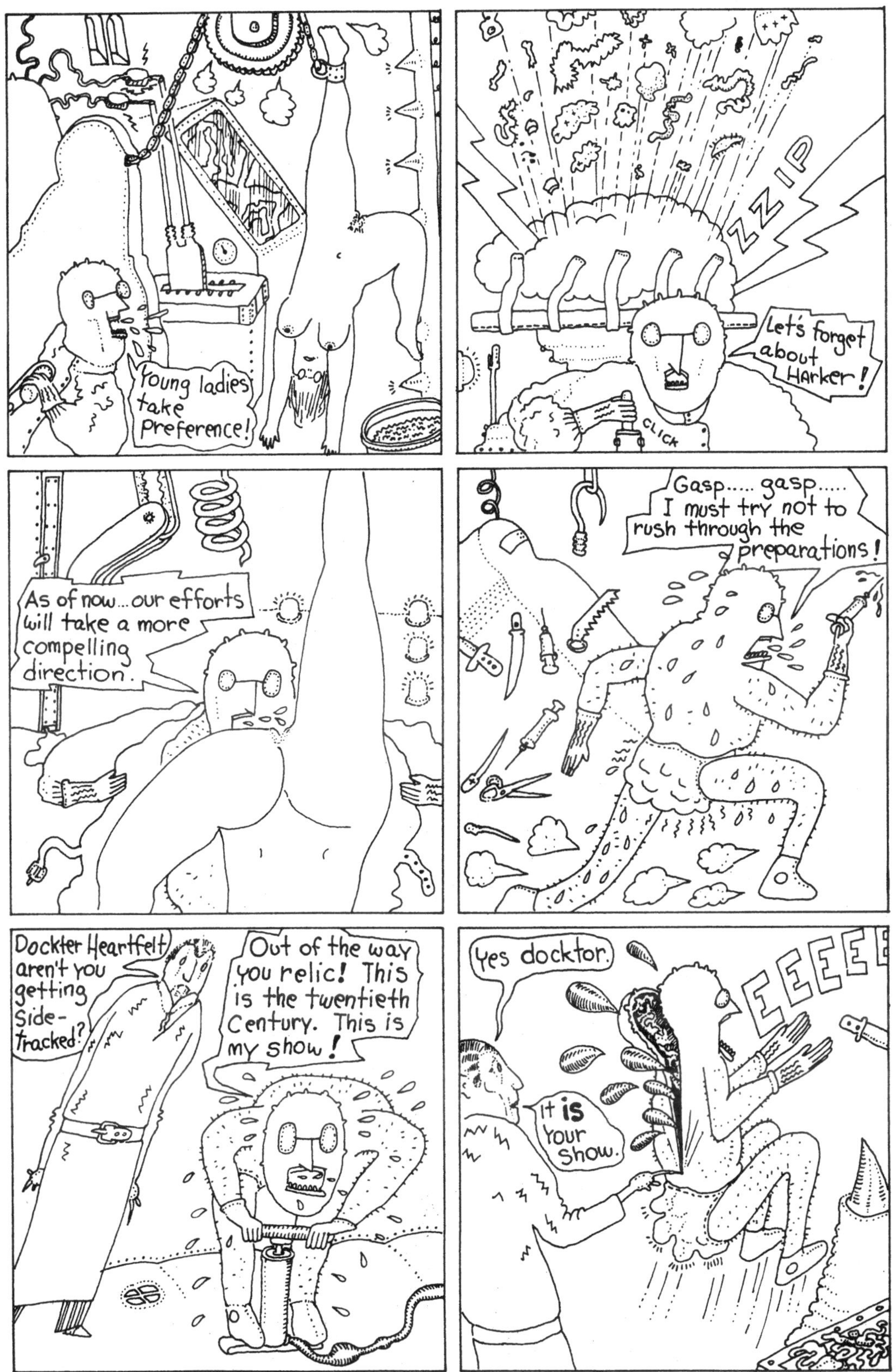
Young ladies take preference!
Let's forget about Harker!
CLICK
ZZIP
As of now...our efforts will take a more compelling direction.
Gasp..... gasp..... I must try not to rush through the preparations!
Dockter Heartfelt aren't you getting side-tracked?
Out of the way you relic! This is the twentieth Century. This is my show!
Yes docktor.
It is your show.
EEEEE

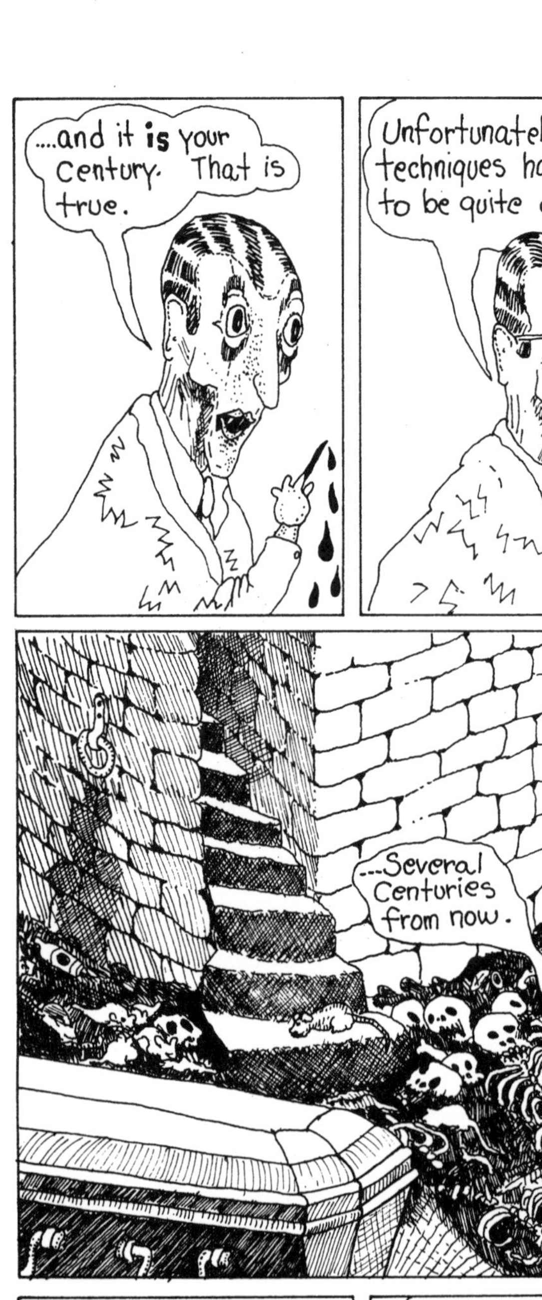

....and it **is** your Century. That is true.
Unfortunately our techniques have proven to be quite dissimilar.

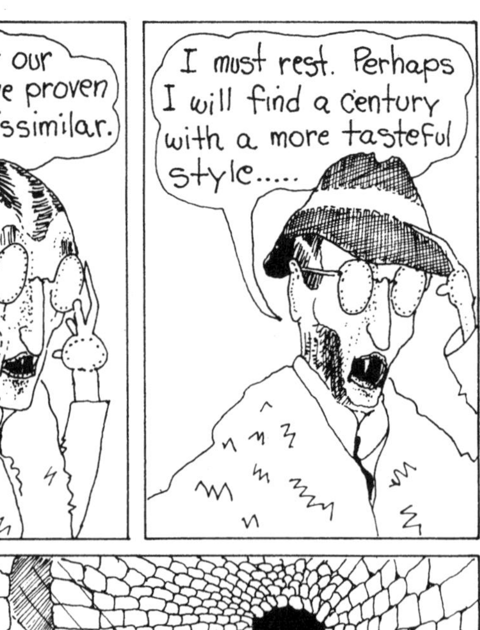

I must rest. Perhaps I will find a century with a more tasteful style.....

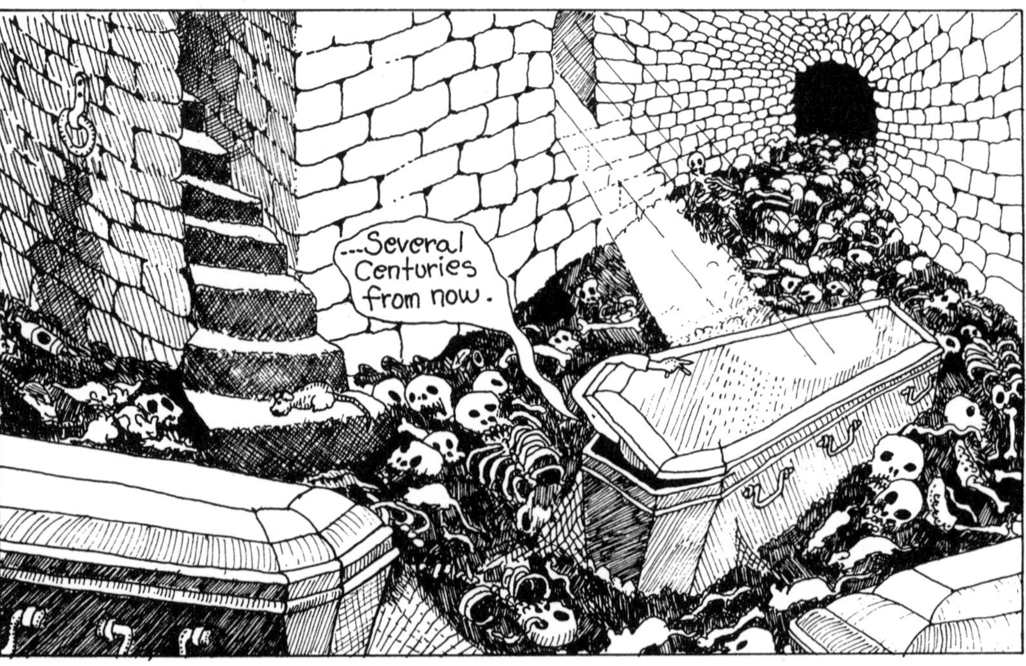

...Several Centuries from now.

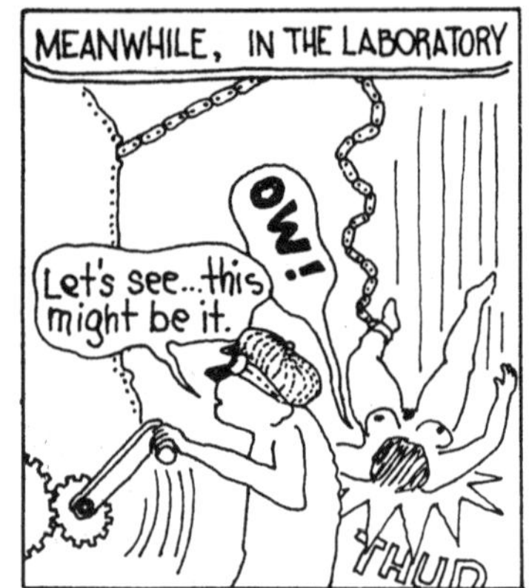

MEANWHILE, IN THE LABORATORY
Let's see...this might be it.
OW!
THUD

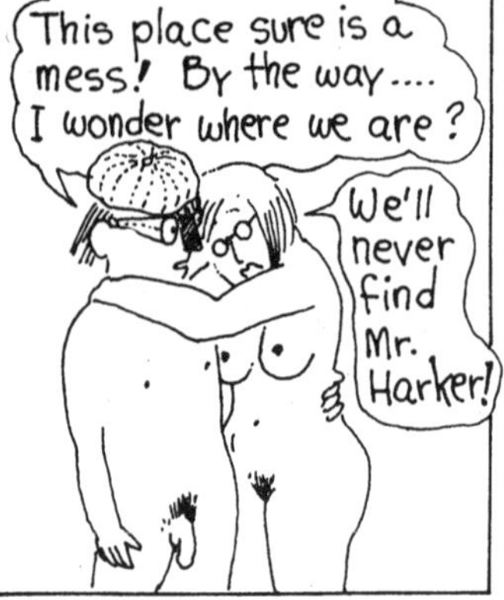

This place sure is a mess! By the way.... I wonder where we are?
We'll never find Mr. Harker!

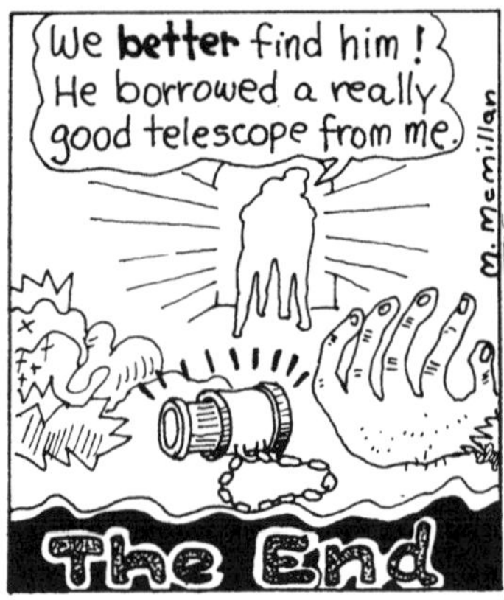

We **better** find him! He borrowed a really good telescope from me.
M. McMillan
The End

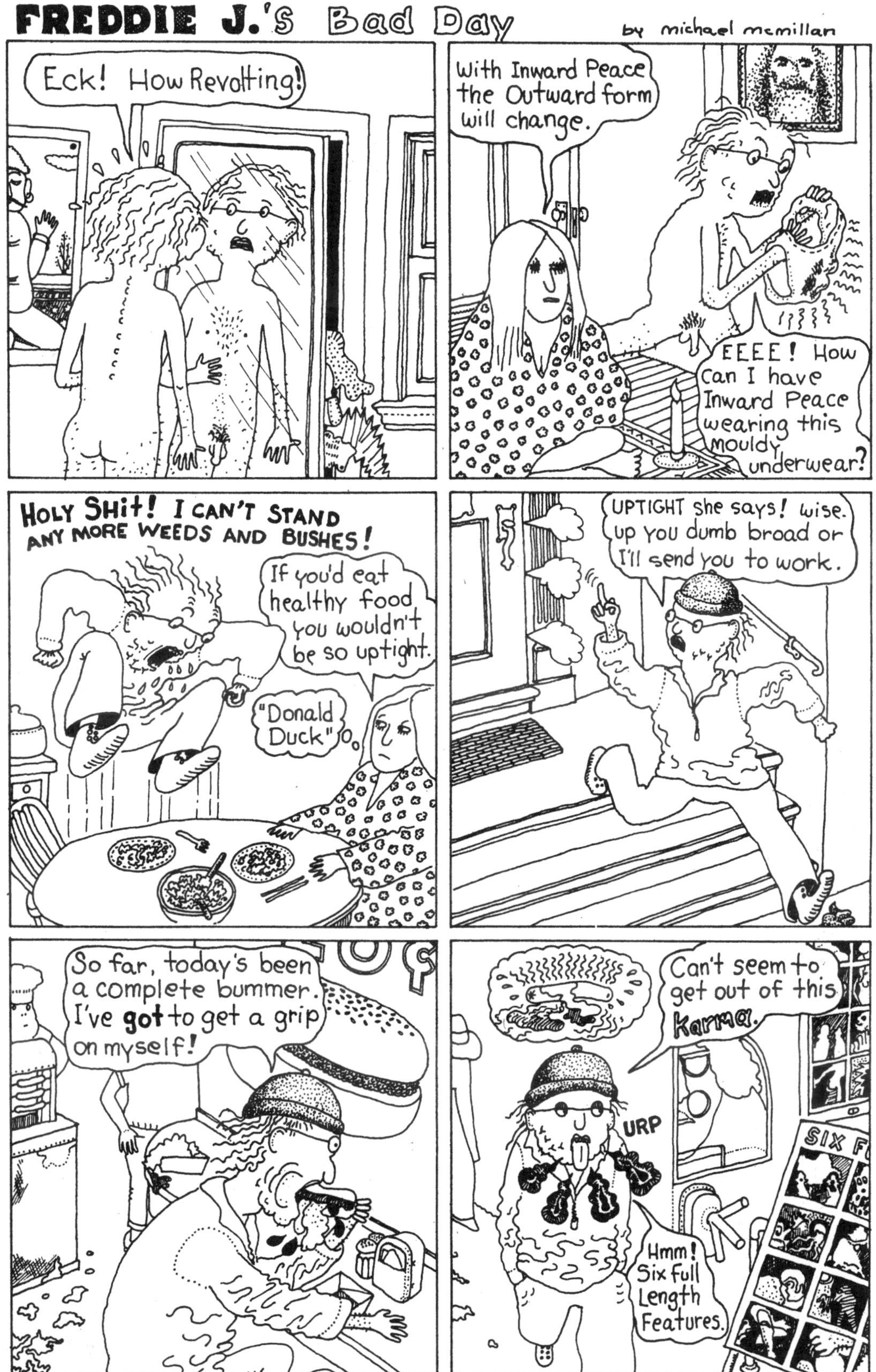
FREDDIE J.'S Bad Day
by michael mcmillan
Eck! How Revolting!
With Inward Peace the Outward form will change.
EEEE! How can I have Inward Peace wearing this mouldy underwear?
HOLY SHIT! I CAN'T STAND ANY MORE WEEDS AND BUSHES!
If you'd eat healthy food you wouldn't be so uptight.
"Donald Duck"
UPTIGHT she says! wise. up you dumb broad or I'll send you to work.
So far, today's been a complete bummer. I've got to get a grip on myself!
Can't seem to get out of this Karma.
URP
Hmm! Six Full Length Features.
SIX F

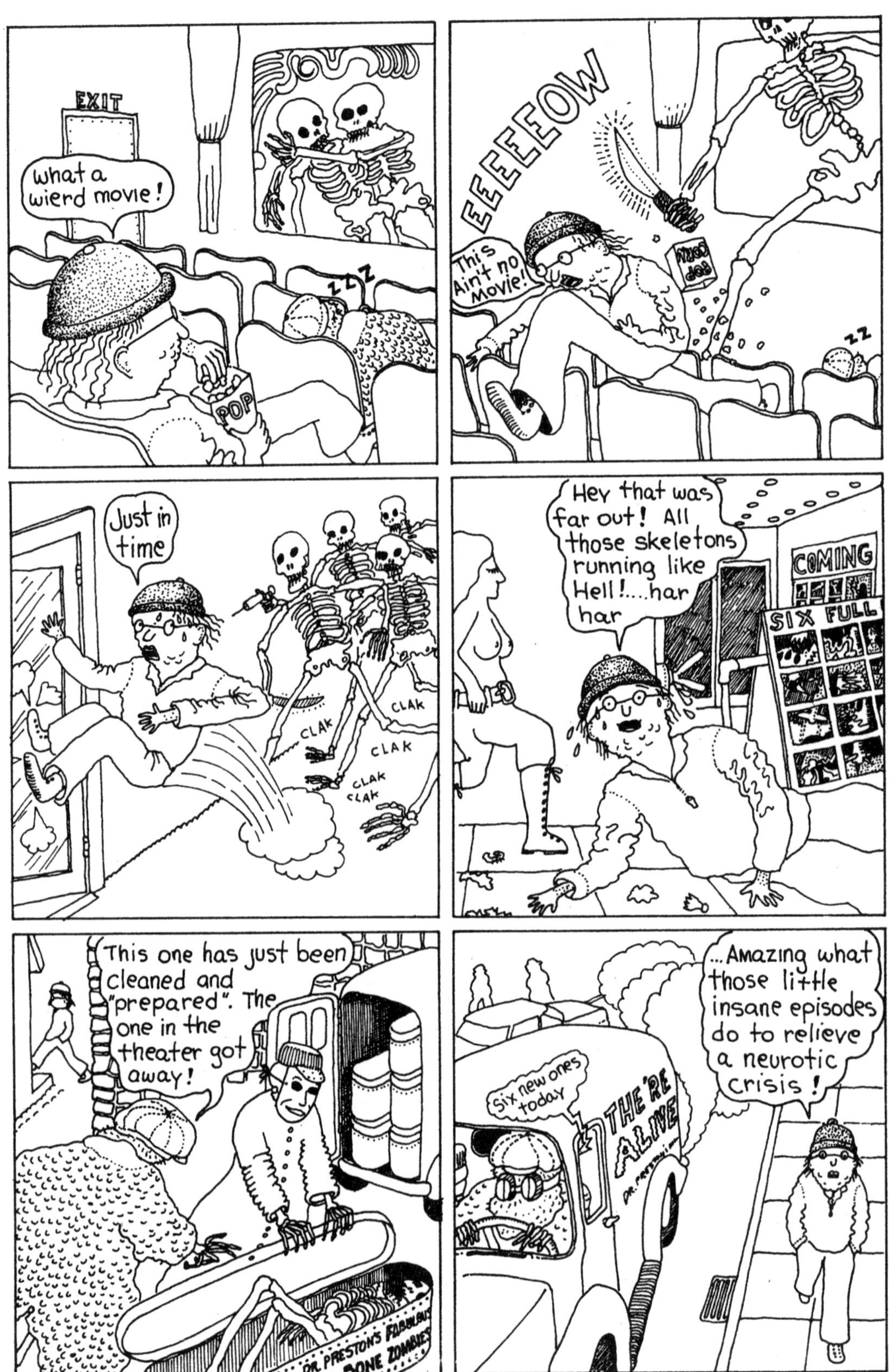

EXIT
what a wierd movie!
Z Z Z
POP
EEEEEOW
This Ain't no Movie!
Z Z
Just in time
CLAK
CLAK
CLAK
CLAK
CLAK
Hey that was far out! All those skeletons running like Hell!....har har
COMING
SIX FULL
This one has just been cleaned and "prepared". The one in the theater got away!
DR. PRESTON'S FABULOUS BONE ZOMBIES
...Amazing what those little insane episodes do to relieve a neurotic crisis!
Six new ones today
THE'RE ALIVE

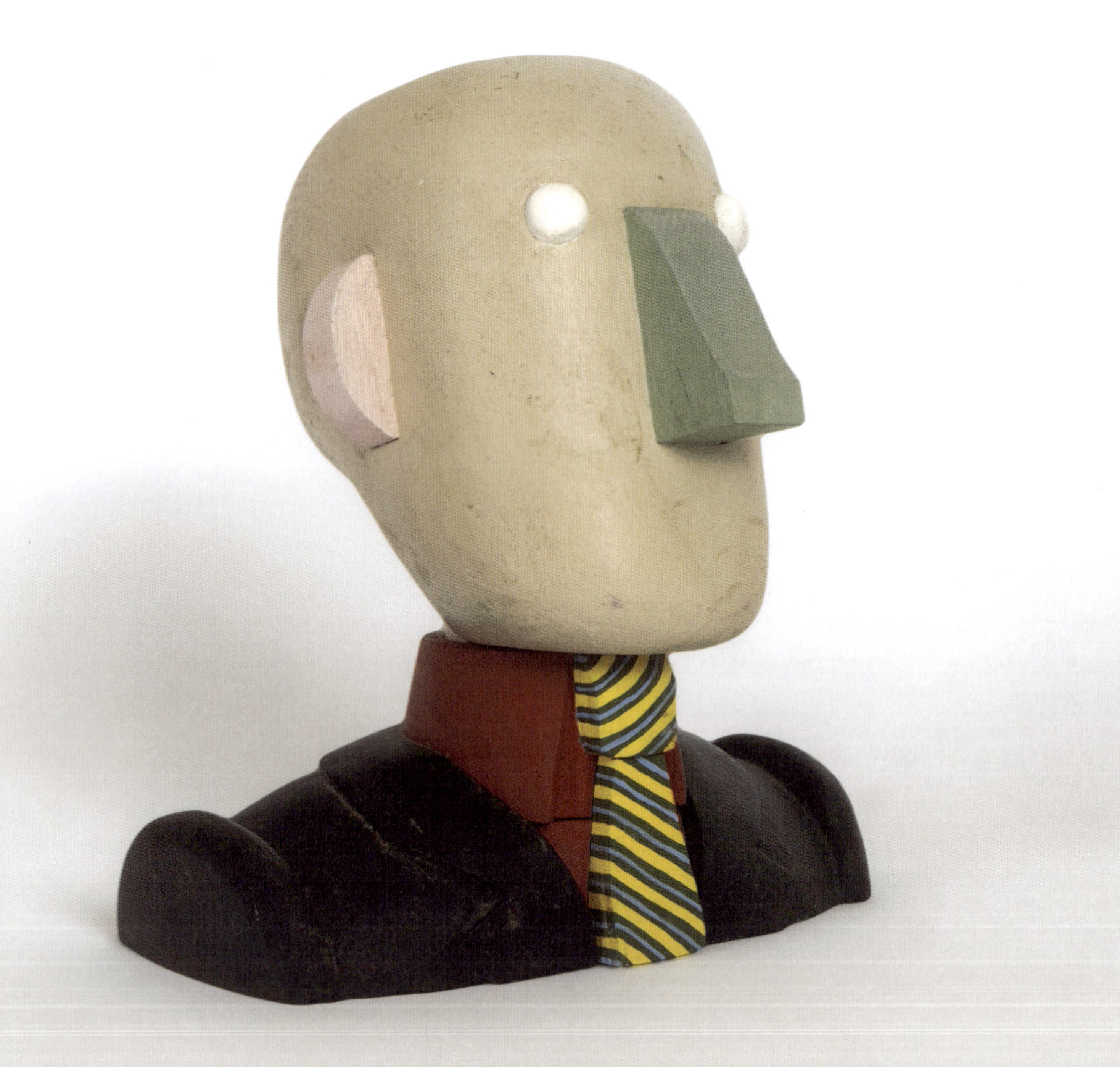

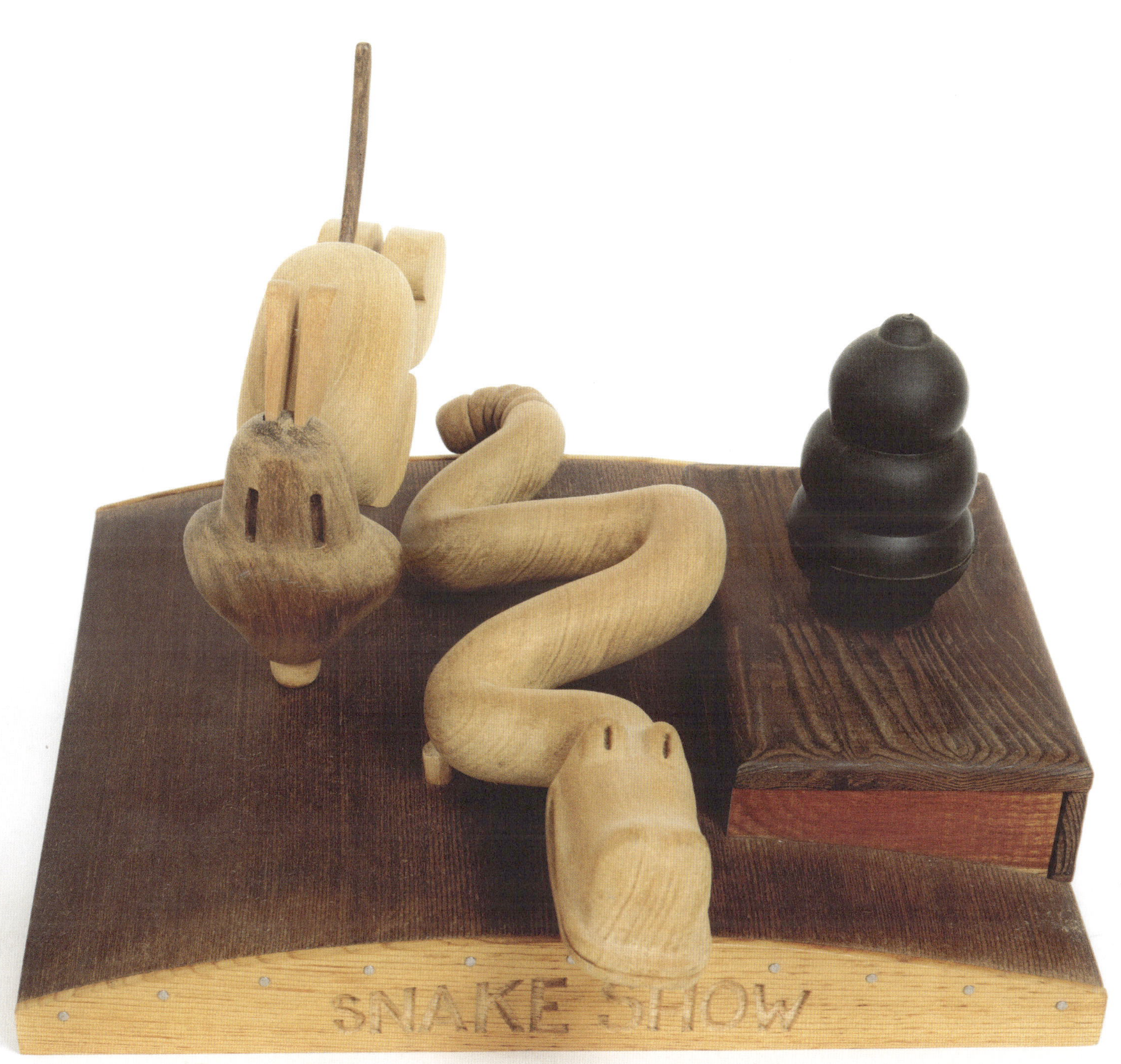
SNAKE SHOW

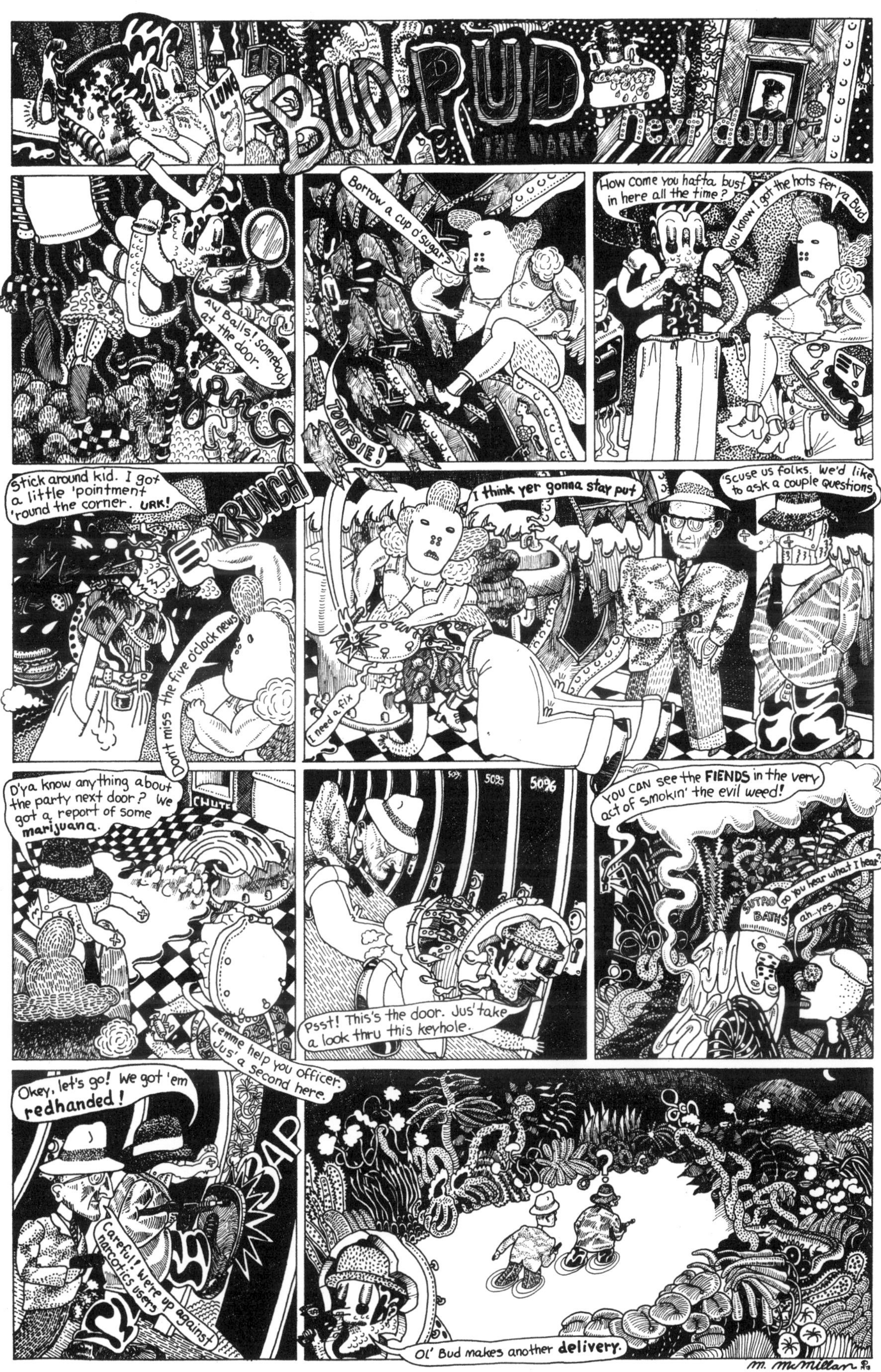
BUD PUD
THE NARK
next door
LONG
aw Balls! Somebody at the door.
Borrow a cup o'sugar,
TOOTSIE!
How come you hafta bust in here all the time?
You know I got the hots fer ya Bud.
Stick around kid. I got a little 'pointment 'round the corner. URK!
KRUNCH
Don't miss the five o'clock news
I think yer gonna stay put
I need a fix
'Scuse us folks. We'd like to ask a couple questions
D'ya know anything about the party next door? We got a report of some marijuana.
CHUTE
Lemme help you officer. Jus' a second here.
Psst! This's the door. Jus' take a look thru this keyhole.
You can see the FIENDS in the very act of smokin' the evil weed!
SUTRO BATHS
Do you hear what I hear?
ah-yes.
Okey, let's go! We got 'em redhanded!
BAP
Careful! We're up against narcotics users
Ol' Bud makes another delivery.
M. McMillan

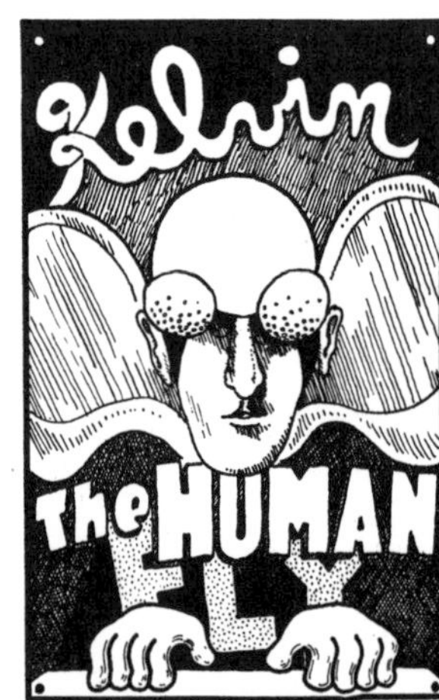
Kelvin
The HUMAN FLY

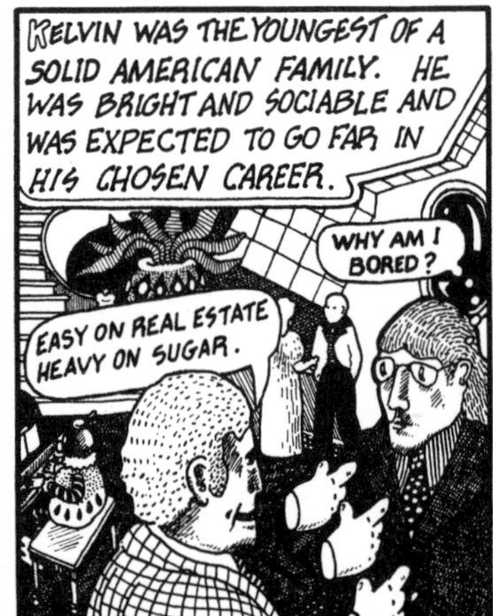
KELVIN WAS THE YOUNGEST OF A SOLID AMERICAN FAMILY. HE WAS BRIGHT AND SOCIABLE AND WAS EXPECTED TO GO FAR IN HIS CHOSEN CAREER.
WHY AM I BORED?
EASY ON REAL ESTATE HEAVY ON SUGAR.

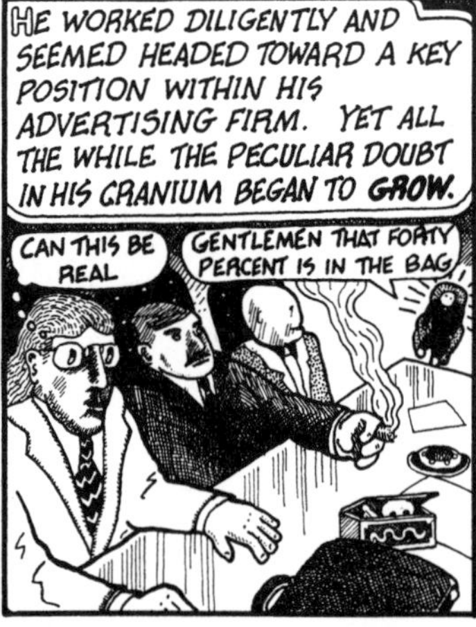
HE WORKED DILIGENTLY AND SEEMED HEADED TOWARD A KEY POSITION WITHIN HIS ADVERTISING FIRM. YET ALL THE WHILE THE PECULIAR DOUBT IN HIS CRANIUM BEGAN TO GROW.
CAN THIS BE REAL
GENTLEMEN THAT FORTY PERCENT IS IN THE BAG

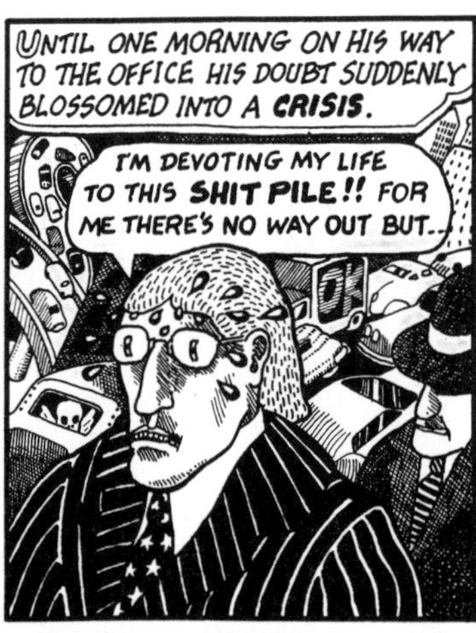
UNTIL ONE MORNING ON HIS WAY TO THE OFFICE HIS DOUBT SUDDENLY BLOSSOMED INTO A CRISIS.
I'M DEVOTING MY LIFE TO THIS SHIT PILE!! FOR ME THERE'S NO WAY OUT BUT..

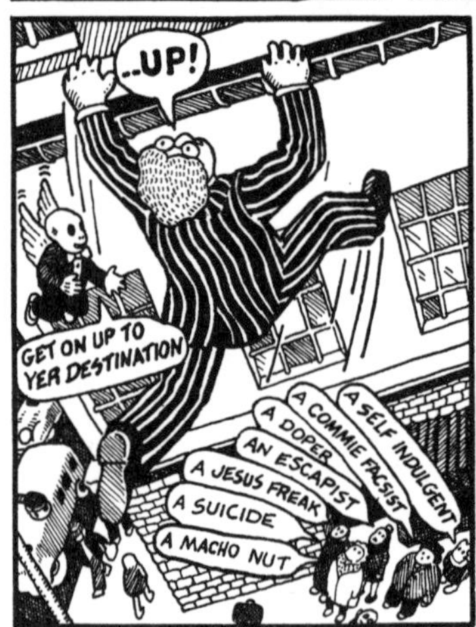
..UP!
GET ON UP TO YER DESTINATION
A SELF INDULGENT
A COMMIE FACSIST
A DOPER
AN ESCAPIST
A JESUS FREAK
A SUICIDE
A MACHO NUT

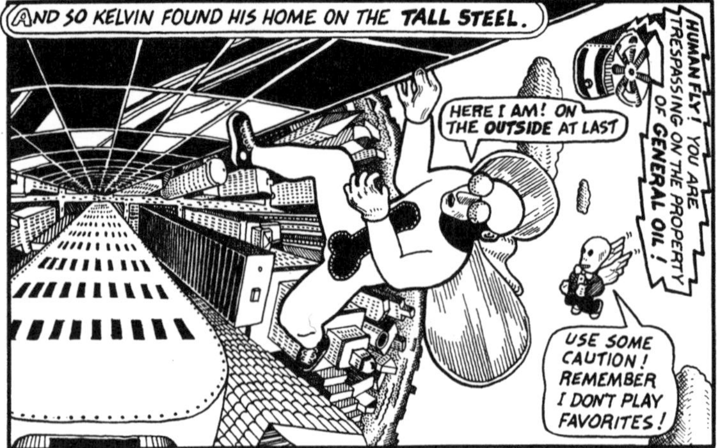
AND SO KELVIN FOUND HIS HOME ON THE TALL STEEL.
HERE I AM! ON THE OUTSIDE AT LAST
HUMAN FLY! YOU ARE TRESPASSING ON THE PROPERTY OF GENERAL OIL!
USE SOME CAUTION! REMEMBER I DON'T PLAY FAVORITES!

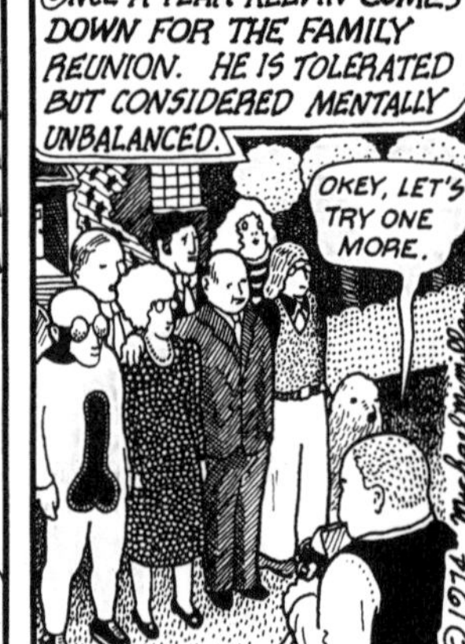
ONCE A YEAR KELVIN COMES DOWN FOR THE FAMILY REUNION. HE IS TOLERATED BUT CONSIDERED MENTALLY UNBALANCED.
OKEY, LET'S TRY ONE MORE.
© 1974 michael mcmillan

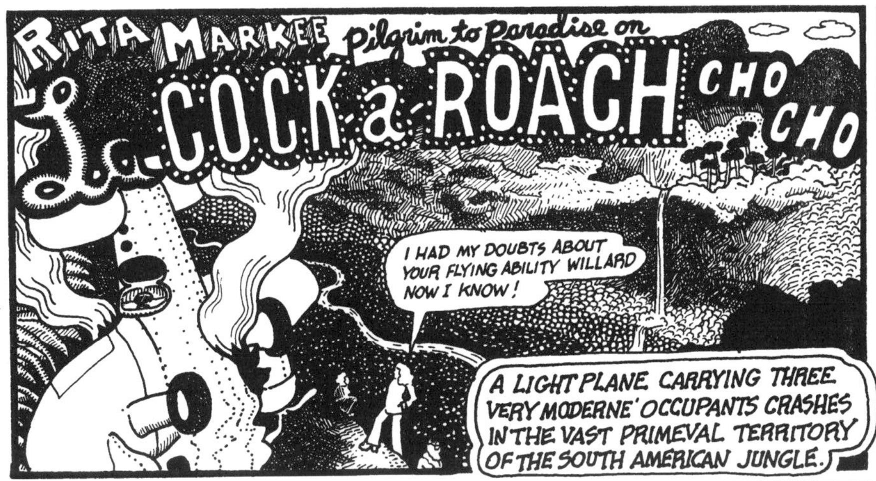
RITA MARKEE Pilgrim to Paradise on
La COCK a ROACH CHO CHO
I HAD MY DOUBTS ABOUT YOUR FLYING ABILITY WILLARD NOW I KNOW!
A LIGHT PLANE CARRYING THREE VERY MODERNE' OCCUPANTS CRASHES IN THE VAST PRIMEVAL TERRITORY OF THE SOUTH AMERICAN JUNGLE.

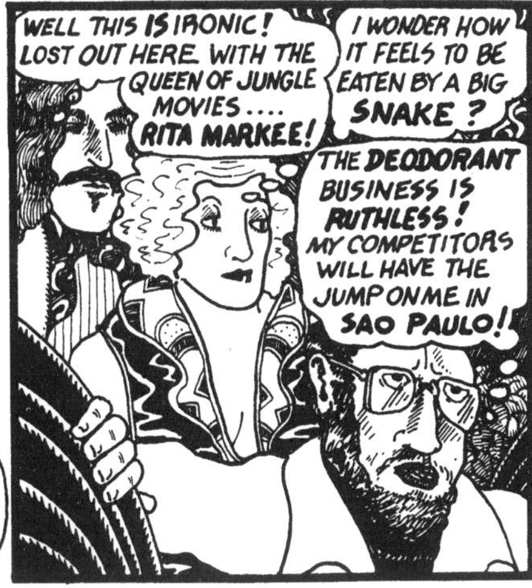
WELL THIS IS IRONIC! LOST OUT HERE WITH THE QUEEN OF JUNGLE MOVIES.... RITA MARKEE!
I WONDER HOW IT FEELS TO BE EATEN BY A BIG SNAKE?
THE DEODORANT BUSINESS IS RUTHLESS! MY COMPETITORS WILL HAVE THE JUMP ON ME IN SAO PAULO!

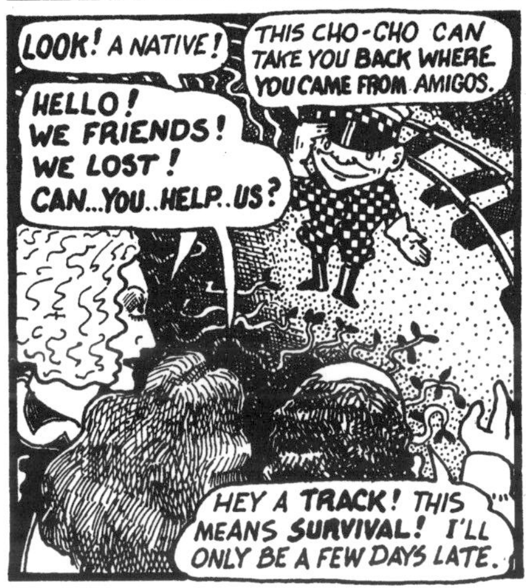
LOOK! A NATIVE!
THIS CHO-CHO CAN TAKE YOU BACK WHERE YOU CAME FROM AMIGOS.
HELLO! WE FRIENDS! WE LOST! CAN...YOU..HELP..US?
HEY A TRACK! THIS MEANS SURVIVAL! I'LL ONLY BE A FEW DAYS LATE.

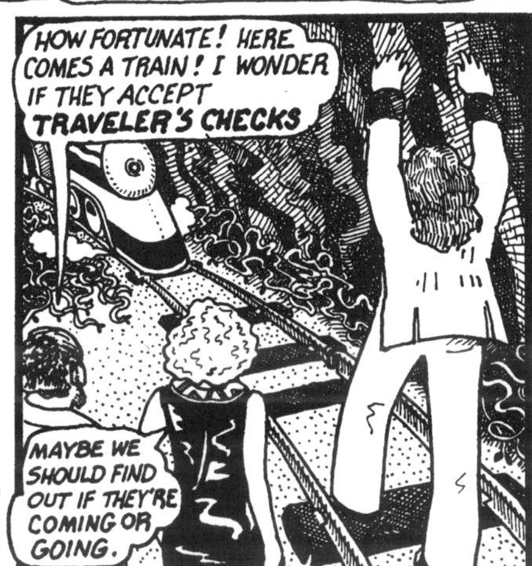
HOW FORTUNATE! HERE COMES A TRAIN! I WONDER IF THEY ACCEPT TRAVELER'S CHECKS
MAYBE WE SHOULD FIND OUT IF THEY'RE COMING OR GOING.

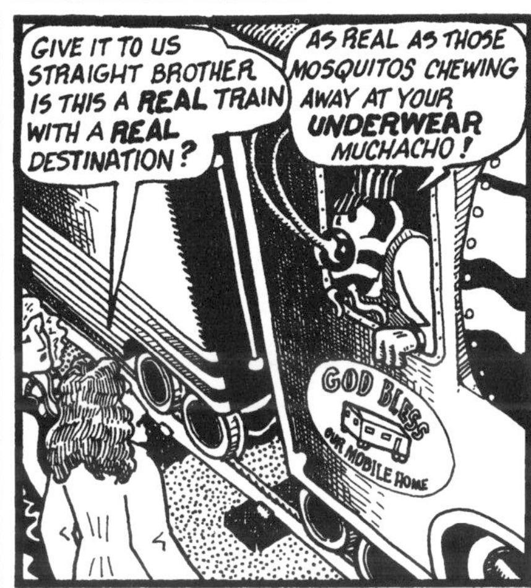
GIVE IT TO US STRAIGHT BROTHER IS THIS A REAL TRAIN WITH A REAL DESTINATION?
AS REAL AS THOSE MOSQUITOS CHEWING AWAY AT YOUR UNDERWEAR MUCHACHO!
GOD BLESS OUR MOBILE HOME

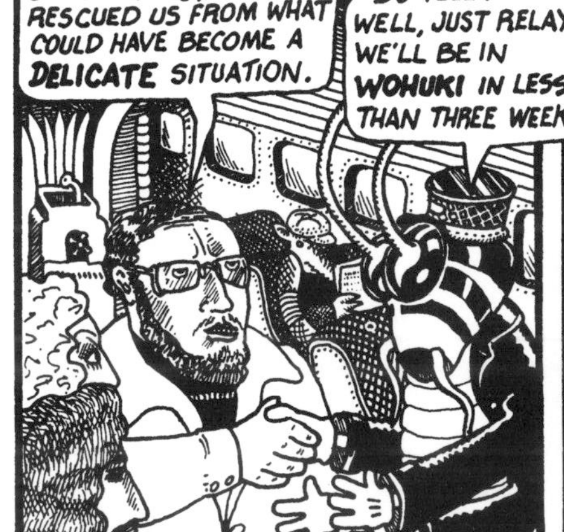
CONDUCTOR, YOU'VE RESCUED US FROM WHAT COULD HAVE BECOME A DELICATE SITUATION.
DO TELL! WELL, JUST RELAX. WE'LL BE IN WOHUKI IN LESS THAN THREE WEEKS.

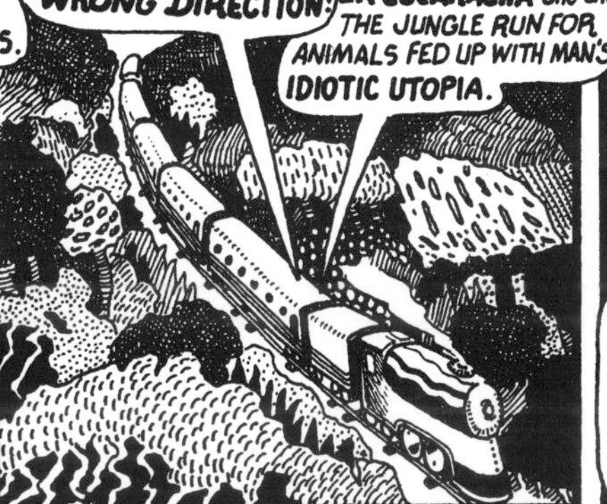
WOHUKI! THAT'S PART OF THE DEEPEST BUSH! YOU'RE GOING IN THE WRONG DIRECTION!
MAYBE THE WRONG DIRECTION FOR YOU SENIOR. THIS IS LA CUCARACHA CHO-CHO. THE JUNGLE RUN FOR ANIMALS FED UP WITH MAN'S IDIOTIC UTOPIA.

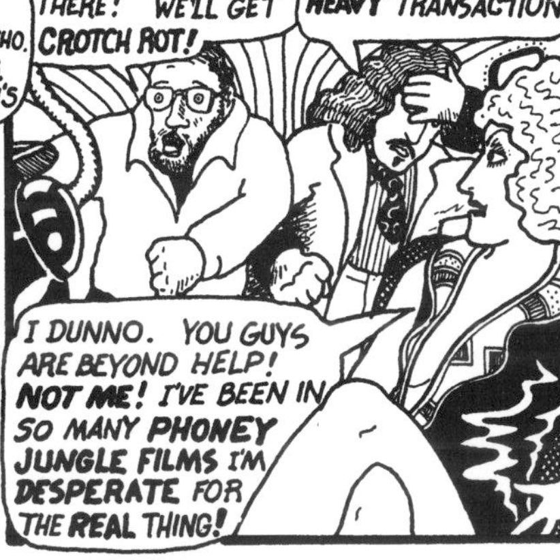
YOU CAN'T DO THIS! NO MAN CAN LIVE OUT THERE! WE'LL GET CROTCH ROT!
THIS IS INSANE! I'M BOOKED FOR A HEAVY TRANSACTION!
I DUNNO. YOU GUYS ARE BEYOND HELP! NOT ME! I'VE BEEN IN SO MANY PHONEY JUNGLE FILMS I'M DESPERATE FOR THE REAL THING!

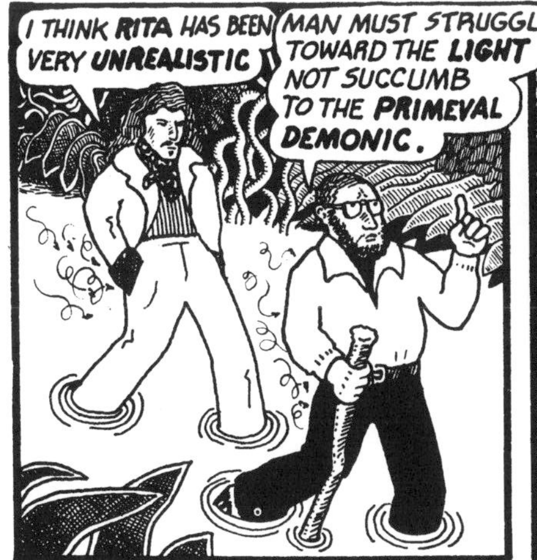
I THINK RITA HAS BEEN VERY UNREALISTIC
MAN MUST STRUGGLE TOWARD THE LIGHT NOT SUCCUMB TO THE PRIMEVAL DEMONIC.

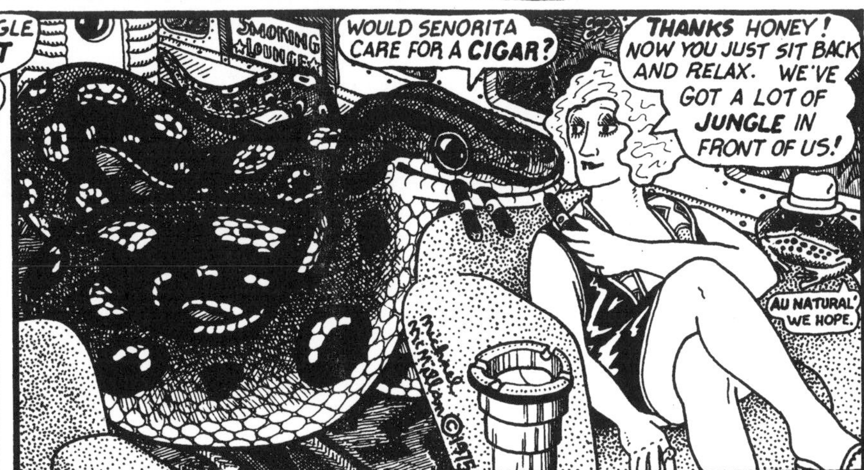
SMOKING LOUNGE
WOULD SENORITA CARE FOR A CIGAR?
THANKS HONEY! NOW YOU JUST SIT BACK AND RELAX. WE'VE GOT A LOT OF JUNGLE IN FRONT OF US!
AU NATURAL WE HOPE.

CAPTAIN
FLASHLIGHT
by michael mcmillan
GGUK
meets the Short Order
GHOUL

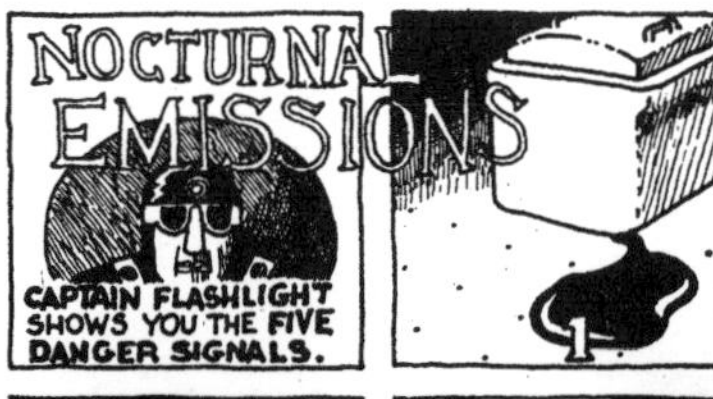
NOCTURNAL
EMISSIONS
CAPTAIN FLASHLIGHT SHOWS YOU THE FIVE DANGER SIGNALS.
1

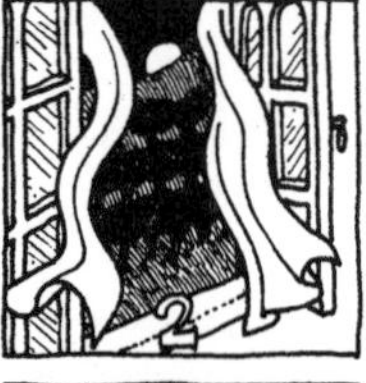
2

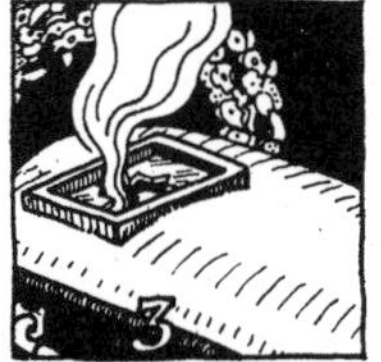
3

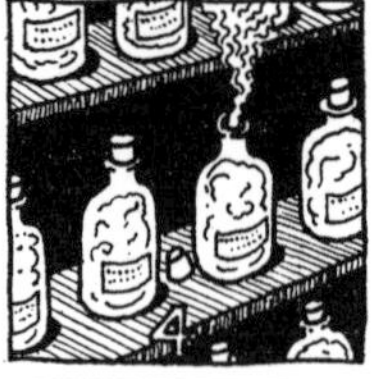
4

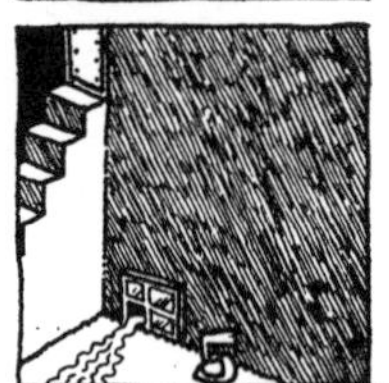
5

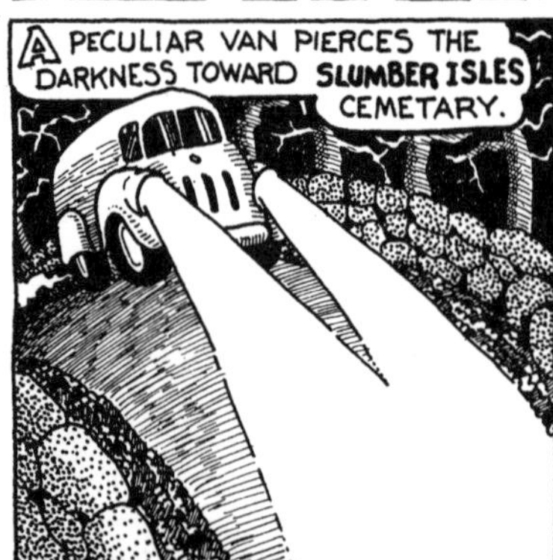
A PECULIAR VAN PIERCES THE DARKNESS TOWARD SLUMBER ISLES CEMETARY.

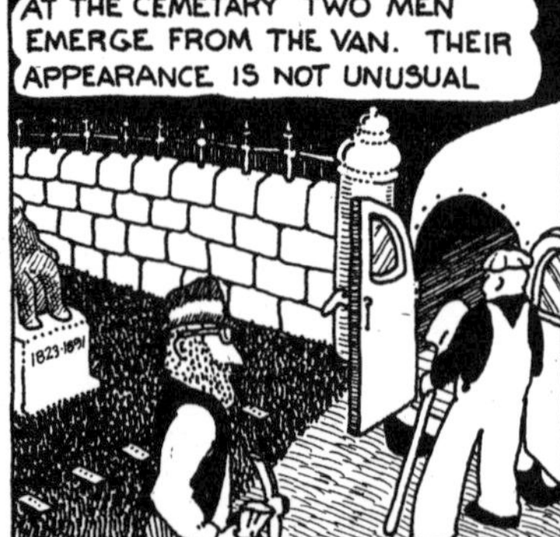
AT THE CEMETARY TWO MEN EMERGE FROM THE VAN. THEIR APPEARANCE IS NOT UNUSUAL
1823-1891

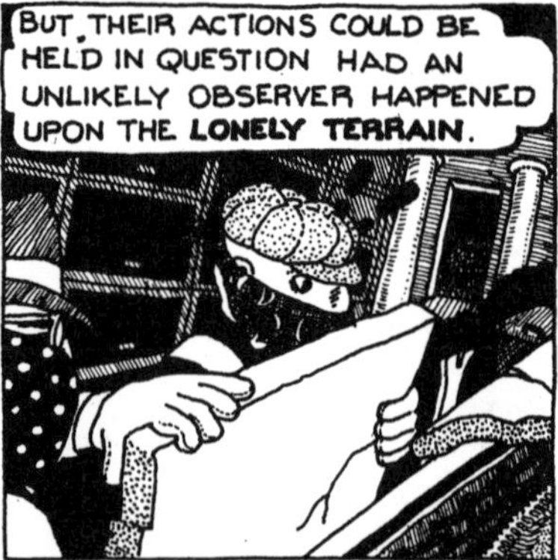
BUT THEIR ACTIONS COULD BE HELD IN QUESTION HAD AN UNLIKELY OBSERVER HAPPENED UPON THE LONELY TERRAIN.

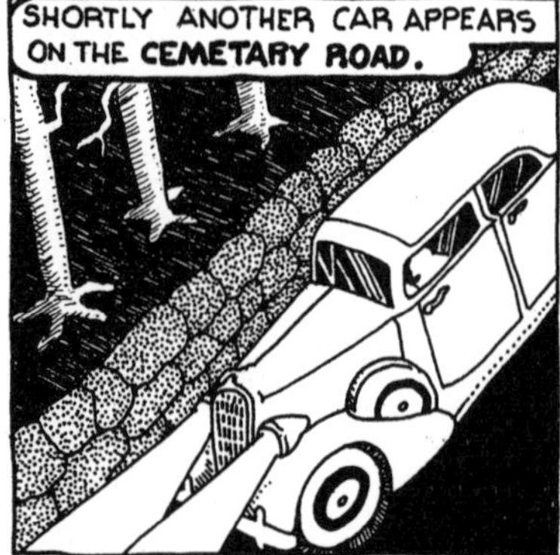
SHORTLY ANOTHER CAR APPEARS ON THE CEMETARY ROAD.

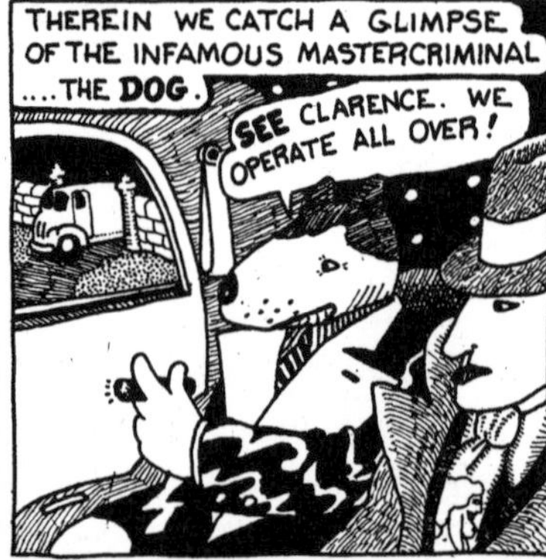
THEREIN WE CATCH A GLIMPSE OF THE INFAMOUS MASTERCRIMINAL ....THE DOG.
SEE CLARENCE. WE OPERATE ALL OVER!

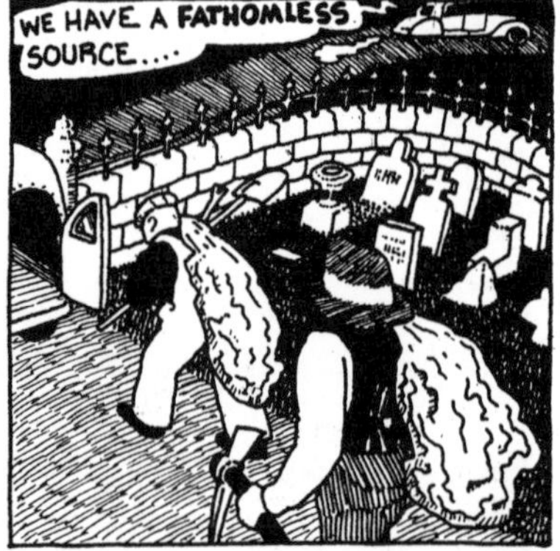
WE HAVE A FATHOMLESS SOURCE....

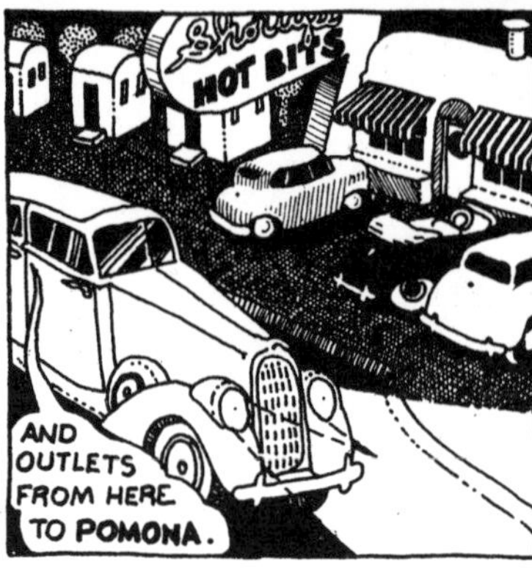
HOT BITS
AND OUTLETS FROM HERE TO POMONA.

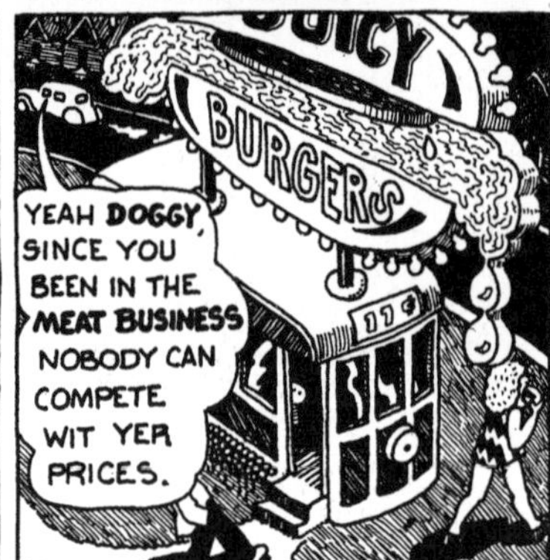
JUICY
BURGERS
YEAH DOGGY, SINCE YOU BEEN IN THE MEAT BUSINESS NOBODY CAN COMPETE WIT YER PRICES.

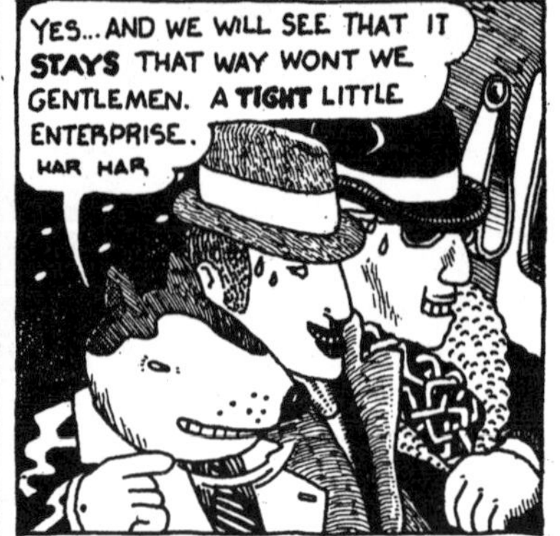
YES...AND WE WILL SEE THAT IT STAYS THAT WAY WONT WE GENTLEMEN. A TIGHT LITTLE ENTERPRISE.
HAR HAR

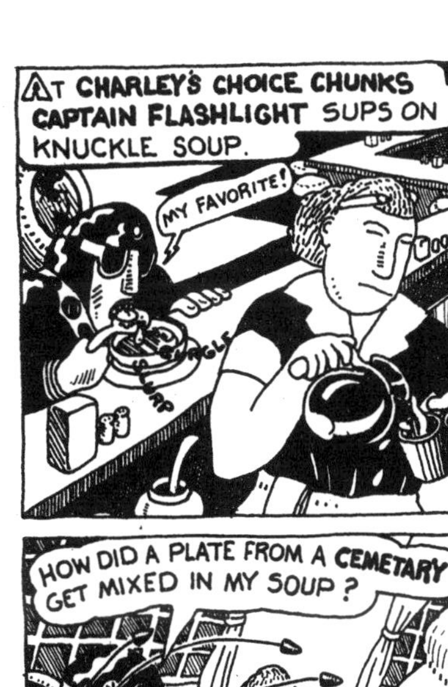
AT CHARLEY'S CHOICE CHUNKS CAPTAIN FLASHLIGHT SUPS ON KNUCKLE SOUP.
MY FAVORITE!

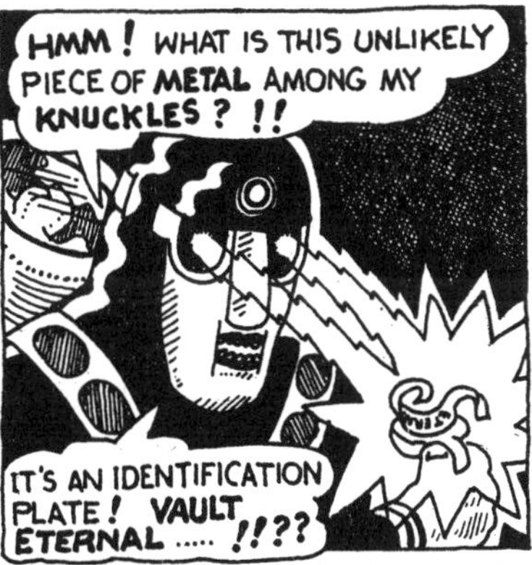
HMM! WHAT IS THIS UNLIKELY PIECE OF METAL AMONG MY KNUCKLES? !!
IT'S AN IDENTIFICATION PLATE! VAULT ETERNAL ..... !!??

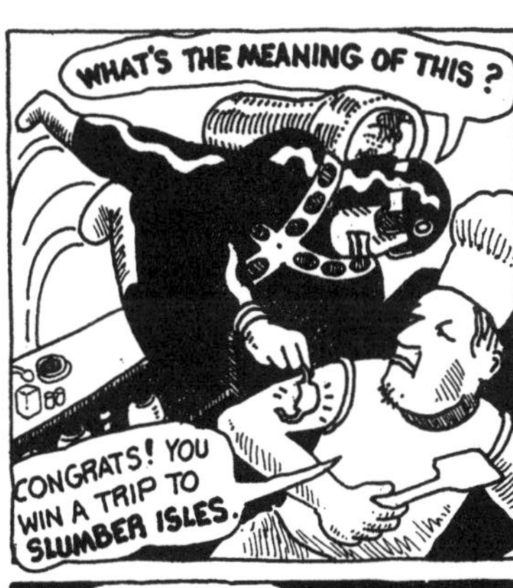
WHAT'S THE MEANING OF THIS?
CONGRATS! YOU WIN A TRIP TO SLUMBER ISLES.

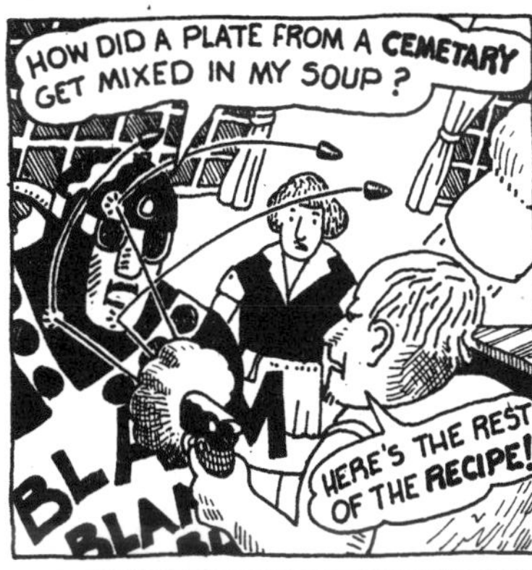
HOW DID A PLATE FROM A CEMETARY GET MIXED IN MY SOUP?
HERE'S THE REST OF THE RECIPE!

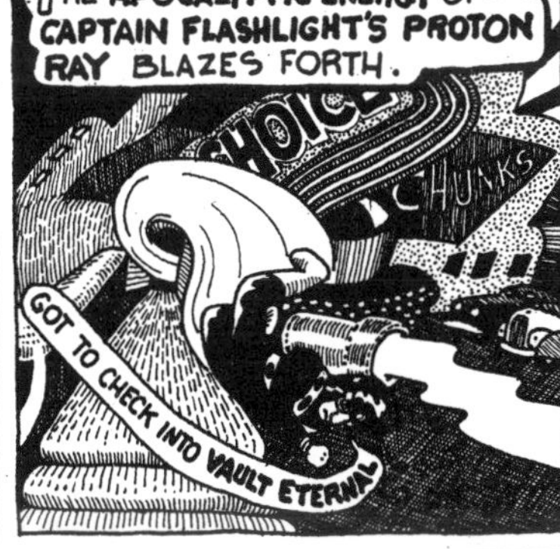
THE APOCALYPTIC ENERGY OF CAPTAIN FLASHLIGHT'S PROTON RAY BLAZES FORTH.
CHOICE
CHUNKS
GOT TO CHECK INTO VAULT ETERNAL

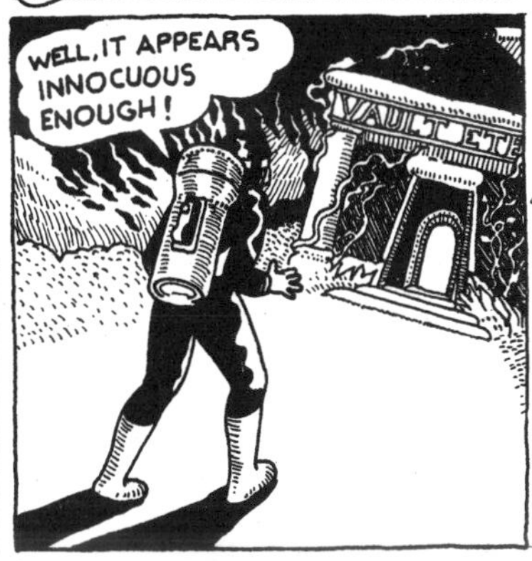
WELL, IT APPEARS INNOCUOUS ENOUGH!

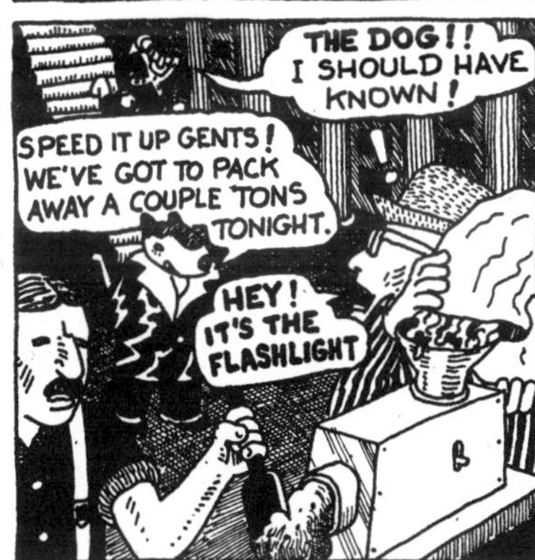
THE DOG!! I SHOULD HAVE KNOWN!
SPEED IT UP GENTS! WE'VE GOT TO PACK AWAY A COUPLE TONS TONIGHT.
HEY! IT'S THE FLASHLIGHT

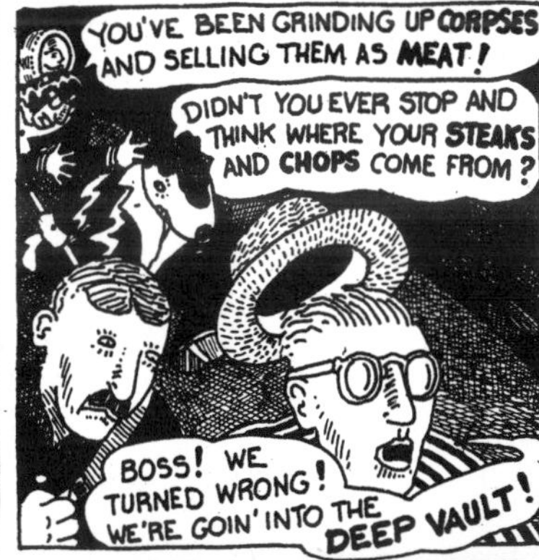
YOU'VE BEEN GRINDING UP CORPSES AND SELLING THEM AS MEAT!
DIDN'T YOU EVER STOP AND THINK WHERE YOUR STEAKS AND CHOPS COME FROM?
BOSS! WE TURNED WRONG! WE'RE GOIN' INTO THE DEEP VAULT!

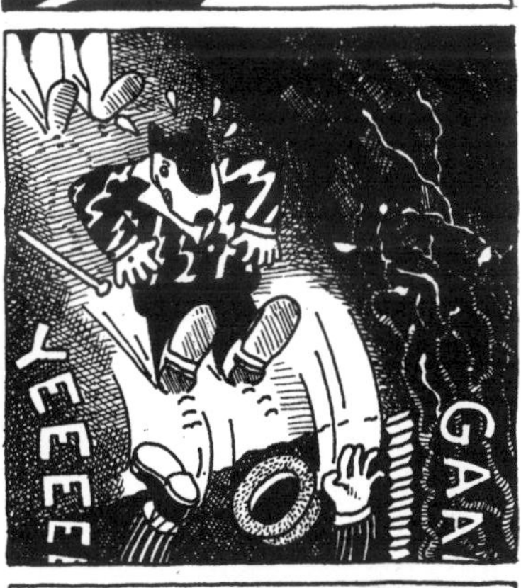
YEEEE
GAA

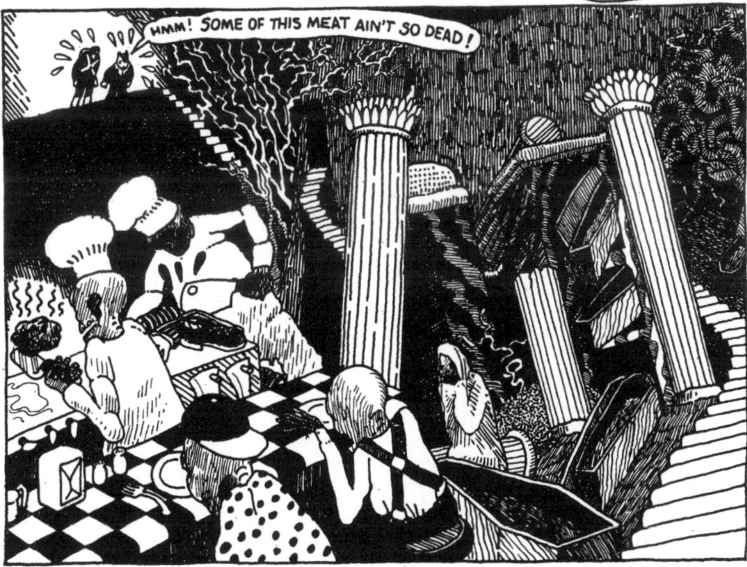
HMM! SOME OF THIS MEAT AIN'T SO DEAD!

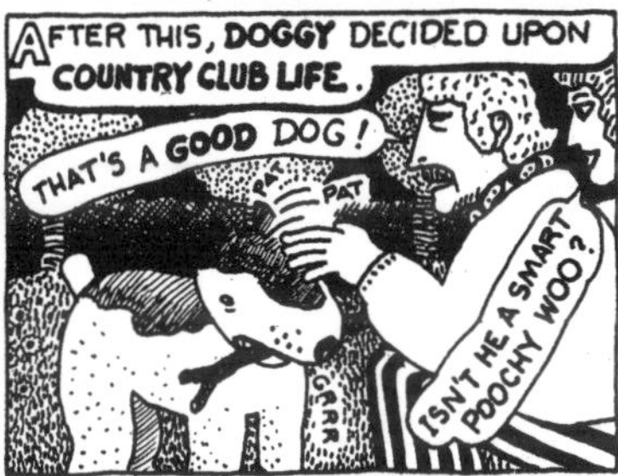
AFTER THIS, DOGGY DECIDED UPON COUNTRY CLUB LIFE.
THAT'S A GOOD DOG!
PAT
ISN'T HE A SMART POOCHY WOO?
GRRR

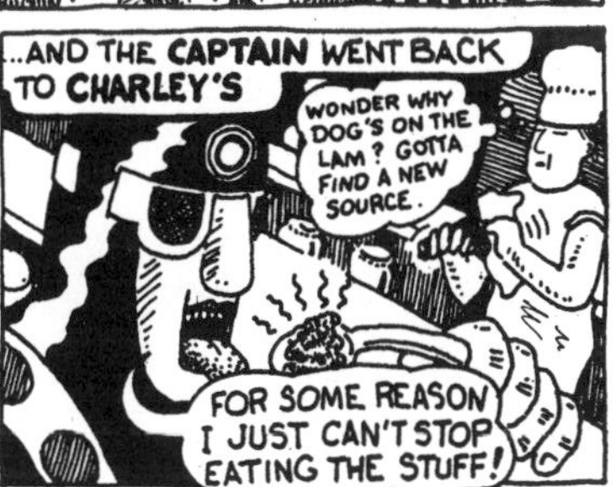
...AND THE CAPTAIN WENT BACK TO CHARLEY'S
WONDER WHY DOG'S ON THE LAM? GOTTA FIND A NEW SOURCE.
FOR SOME REASON I JUST CAN'T STOP EATING THE STUFF!

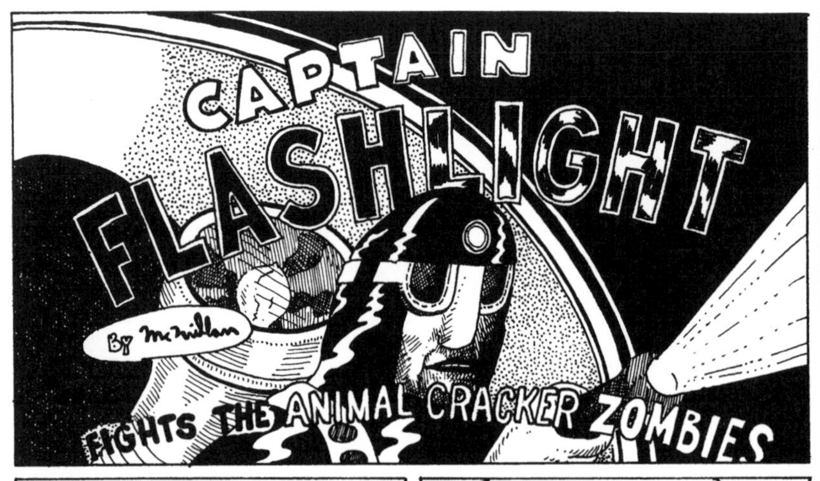
CAPTAIN
FLASHLIGHT
By McMillan
FIGHTS THE ANIMAL CRACKER ZOMBIES

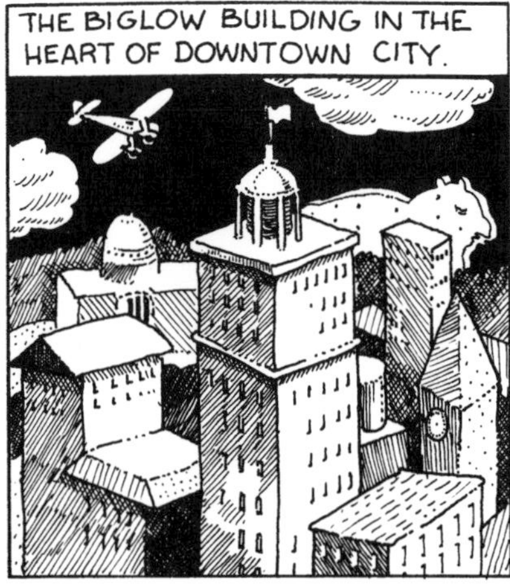
THE BIGLOW BUILDING IN THE HEART OF DOWNTOWN CITY.

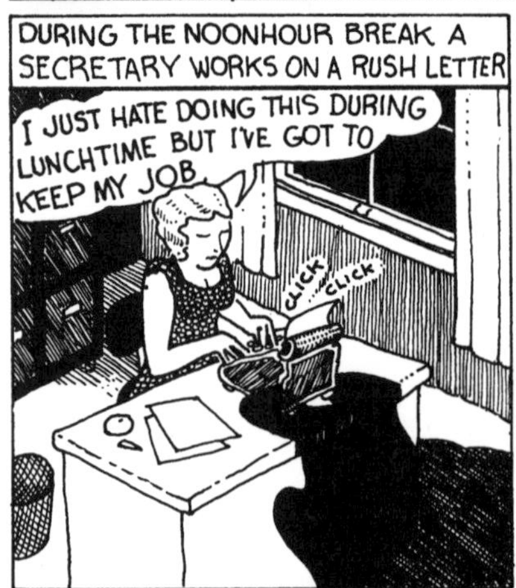
DURING THE NOONHOUR BREAK A SECRETARY WORKS ON A RUSH LETTER
I JUST HATE DOING THIS DURING LUNCHTIME BUT I'VE GOT TO KEEP MY JOB.
CLICK CLICK

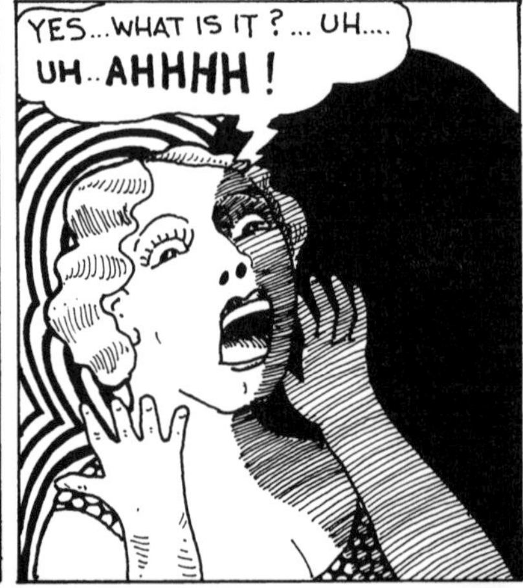
YES... WHAT IS IT ?... UH.... UH.. AHHHH !

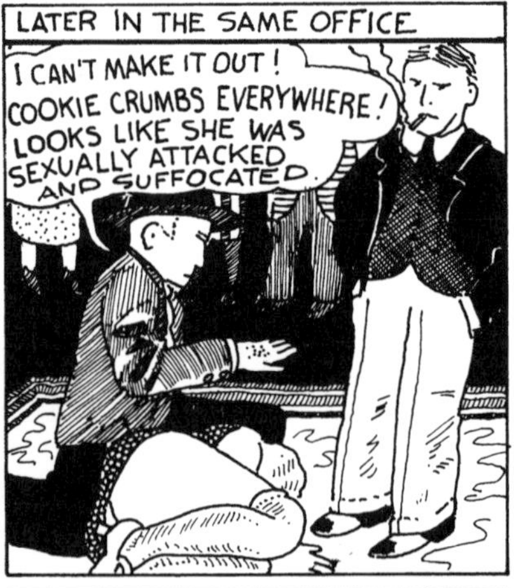
LATER IN THE SAME OFFICE
I CAN'T MAKE IT OUT ! COOKIE CRUMBS EVERYWHERE ! LOOKS LIKE SHE WAS SEXUALLY ATTACKED AND SUFFOCATED.

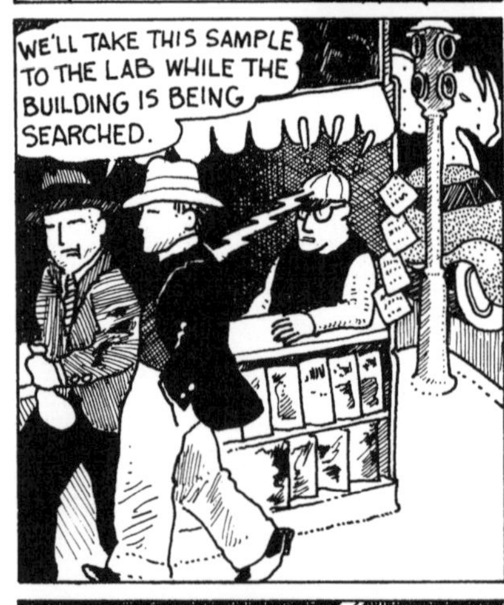
WE'LL TAKE THIS SAMPLE TO THE LAB WHILE THE BUILDING IS BEING SEARCHED.

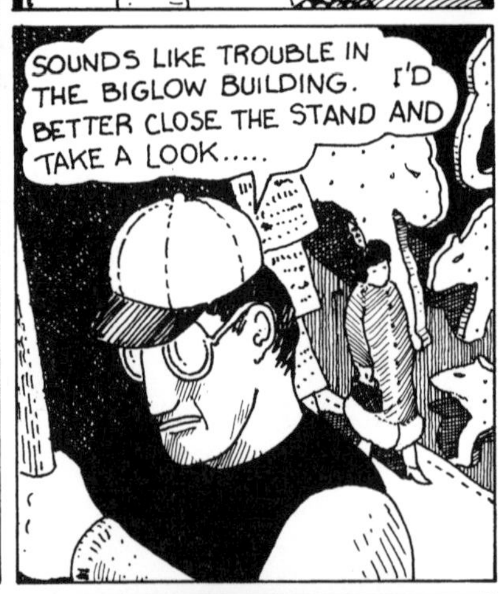
SOUNDS LIKE TROUBLE IN THE BIGLOW BUILDING. I'D BETTER CLOSE THE STAND AND TAKE A LOOK.....

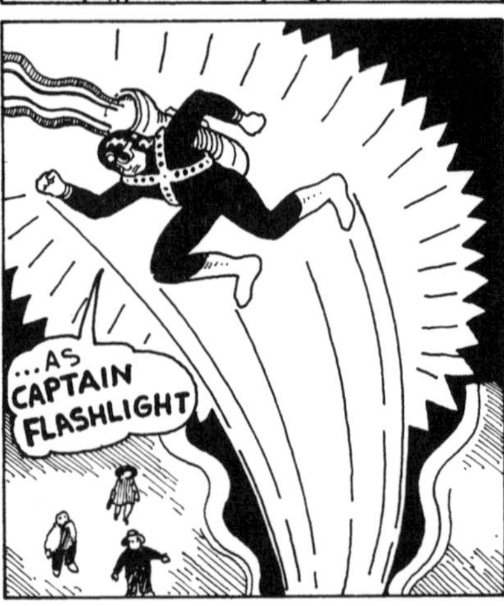
...AS CAPTAIN FLASHLIGHT

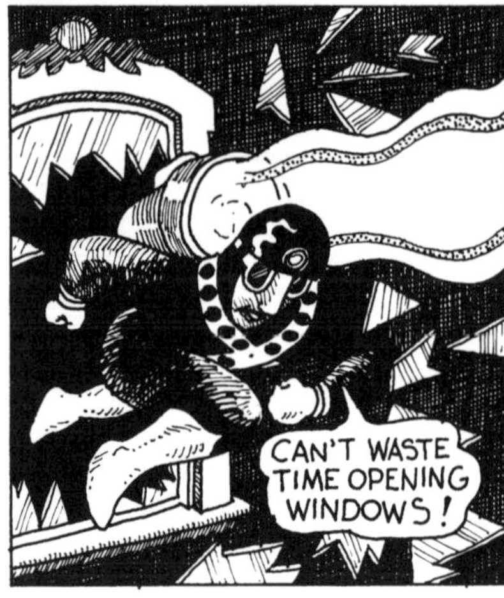
CAN'T WASTE TIME OPENING WINDOWS !

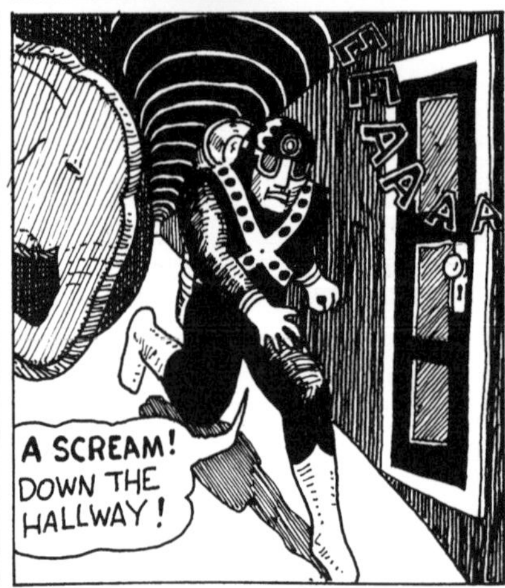
EEEAAAA
A SCREAM! DOWN THE HALLWAY !

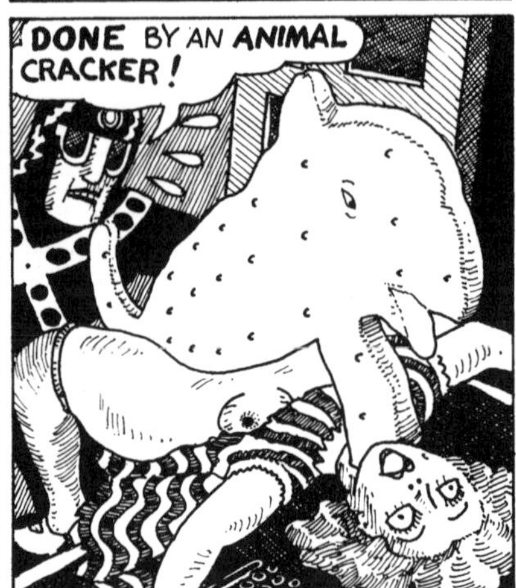
DONE BY AN ANIMAL CRACKER !

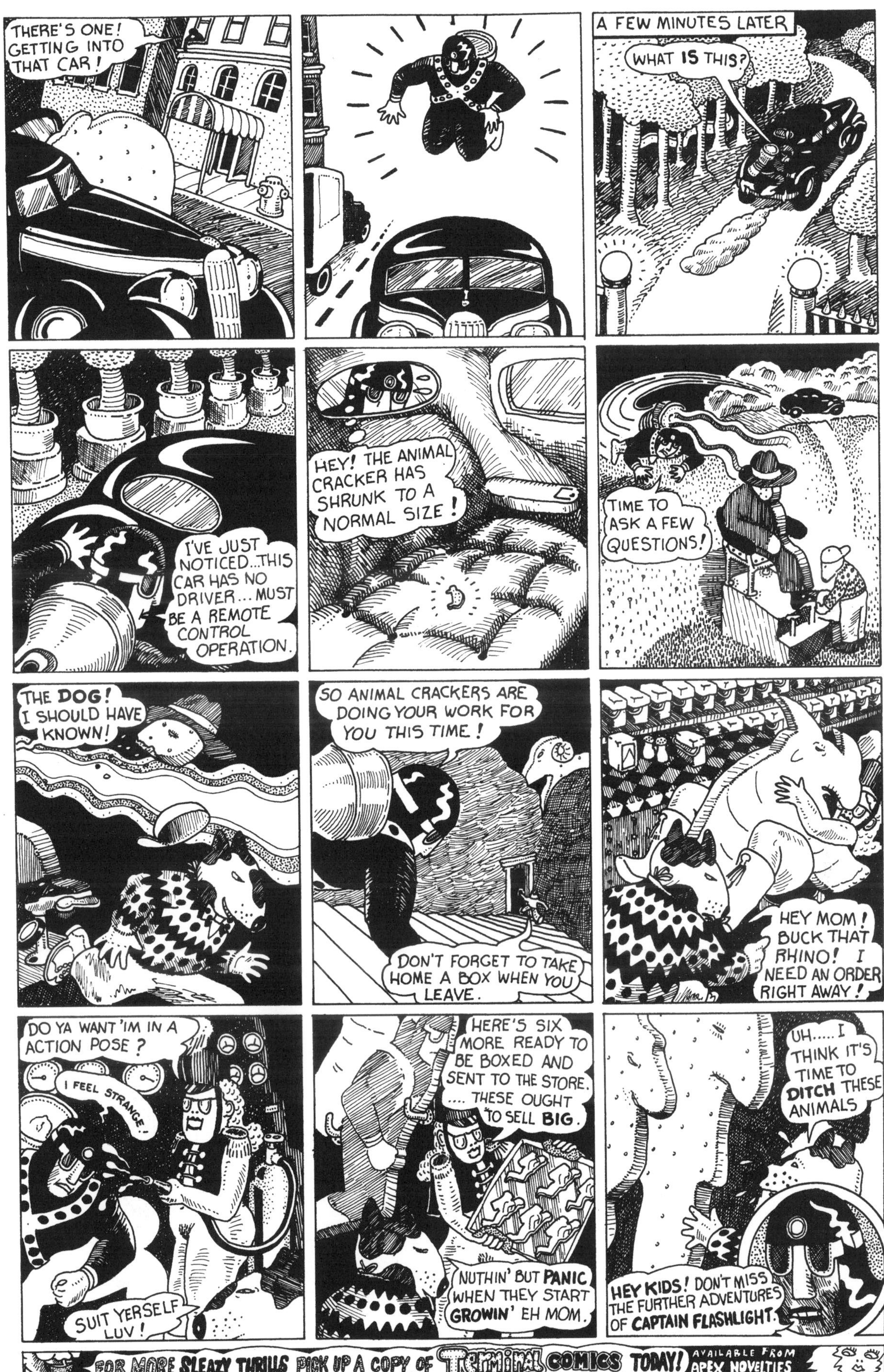
THERE'S ONE! GETTING INTO THAT CAR!
A FEW MINUTES LATER
WHAT IS THIS?
I'VE JUST NOTICED...THIS CAR HAS NO DRIVER... MUST BE A REMOTE CONTROL OPERATION.
HEY! THE ANIMAL CRACKER HAS SHRUNK TO A NORMAL SIZE!
TIME TO ASK A FEW QUESTIONS!
THE DOG! I SHOULD HAVE KNOWN!
SO ANIMAL CRACKERS ARE DOING YOUR WORK FOR YOU THIS TIME!
DON'T FORGET TO TAKE HOME A BOX WHEN YOU LEAVE.
HEY MOM! BUCK THAT RHINO! I NEED AN ORDER RIGHT AWAY!
DO YA WANT 'IM IN A ACTION POSE?
I FEEL STRANGE.
SUIT YERSELF LUV!
HERE'S SIX MORE READY TO BE BOXED AND SENT TO THE STORE. .... THESE OUGHT TO SELL BIG.
NUTHIN' BUT PANIC WHEN THEY START GROWIN' EH MOM.
UH.... I THINK IT'S TIME TO DITCH THESE ANIMALS
HEY KIDS! DON'T MISS THE FURTHER ADVENTURES OF CAPTAIN FLASHLIGHT.
FOR MORE SLEAZY THRILLS PICK UP A COPY OF TERMINAL COMICS TODAY! AVAILABLE FROM APEX NOVELTIES

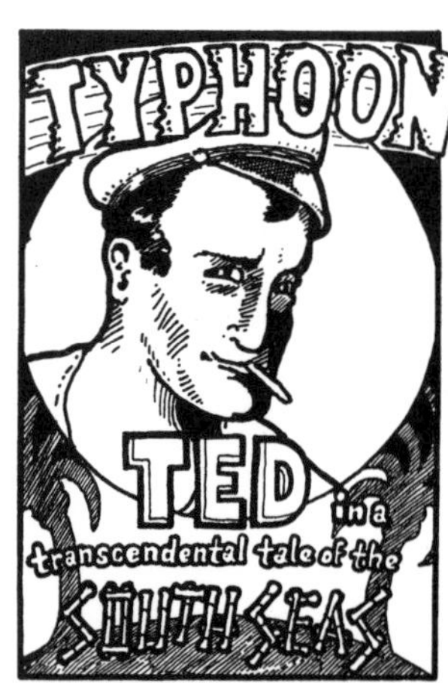
TYPHOON
TED in a
transcendental tale of the
SOUTH SEAS

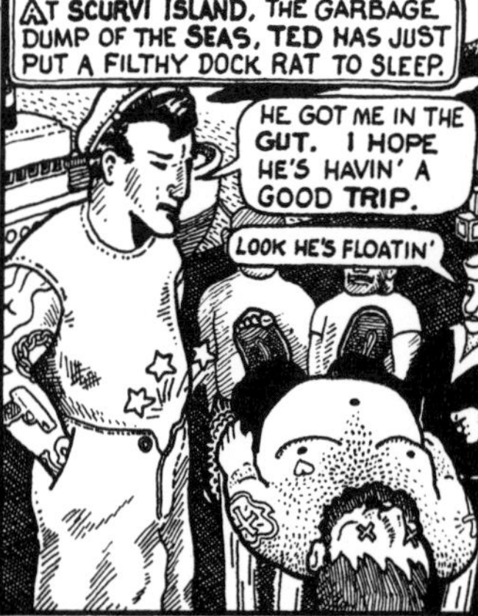
AT SCURVI ISLAND, THE GARBAGE DUMP OF THE SEAS, TED HAS JUST PUT A FILTHY DOCK RAT TO SLEEP.
HE GOT ME IN THE GUT. I HOPE HE'S HAVIN' A GOOD TRIP.
LOOK HE'S FLOATIN'

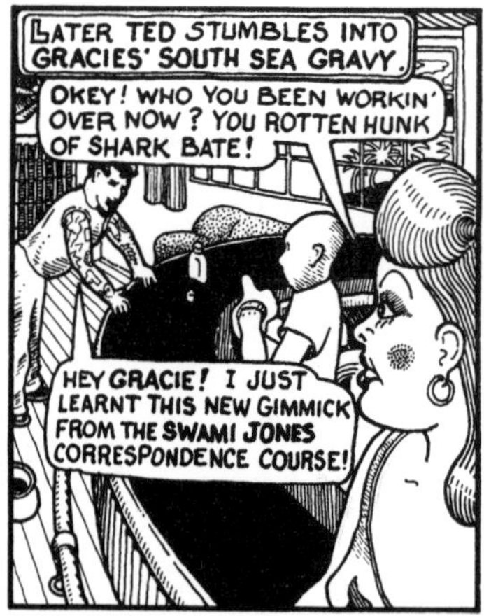
LATER TED STUMBLES INTO GRACIES' SOUTH SEA GRAVY.
OKEY! WHO YOU BEEN WORKIN' OVER NOW? YOU ROTTEN HUNK OF SHARK BATE!
HEY GRACIE! I JUST LEARNT THIS NEW GIMMICK FROM THE SWAMI JONES CORRESPONDENCE COURSE!

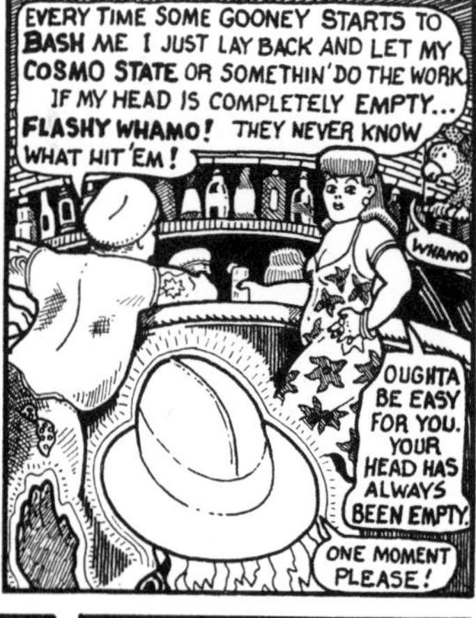
EVERY TIME SOME GOONEY STARTS TO BASH ME I JUST LAY BACK AND LET MY COSMO STATE OR SOMETHIN' DO THE WORK. IF MY HEAD IS COMPLETELY EMPTY... FLASHY WHAMO! THEY NEVER KNOW WHAT HIT 'EM!
WHAMO
OUGHTA BE EASY FOR YOU. YOUR HEAD HAS ALWAYS BEEN EMPTY.
ONE MOMENT PLEASE!

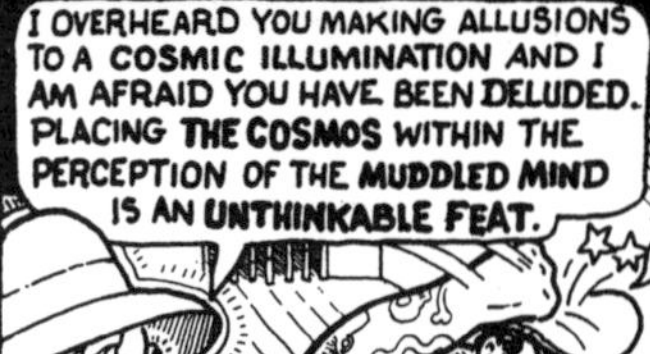
I OVERHEARD YOU MAKING ALLUSIONS TO A COSMIC ILLUMINATION AND I AM AFRAID YOU HAVE BEEN DELUDED. PLACING THE COSMOS WITHIN THE PERCEPTION OF THE MUDDLED MIND IS AN UNTHINKABLE FEAT.

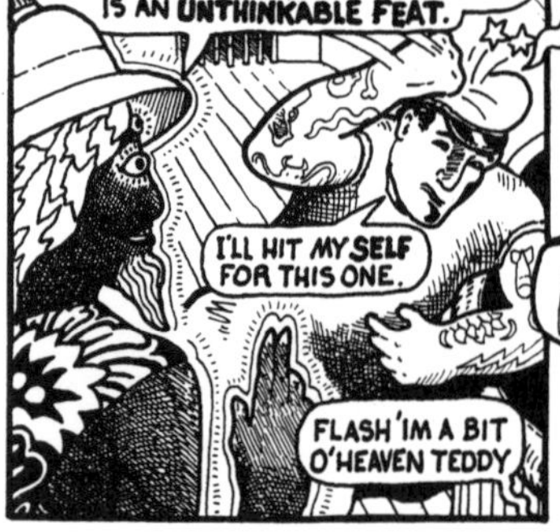
I'LL HIT MY SELF FOR THIS ONE.
FLASH 'IM A BIT O'HEAVEN TEDDY

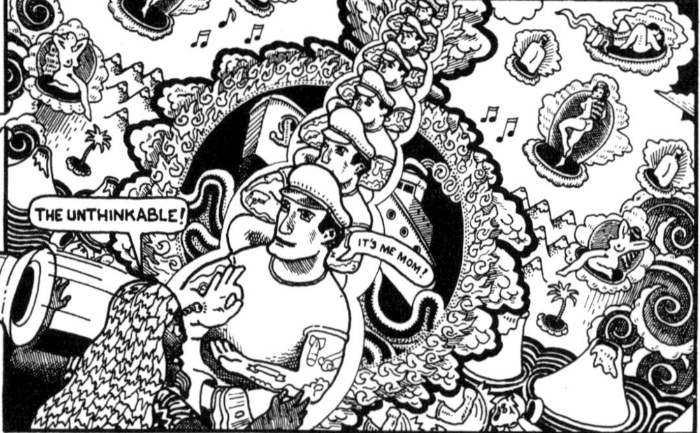
THE UNTHINKABLE!
IT'S ME MOM!

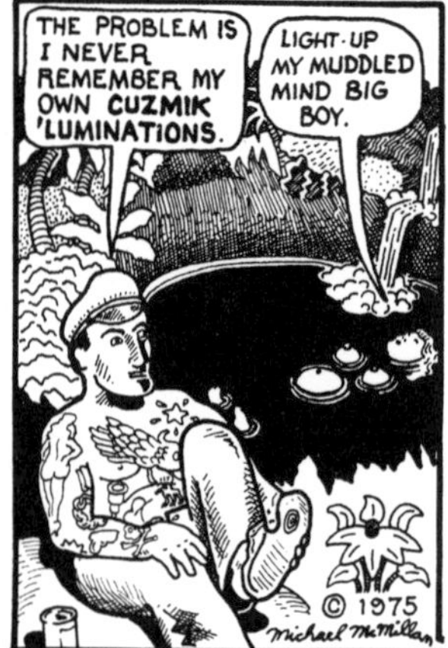
THE PROBLEM IS I NEVER REMEMBER MY OWN CUZMIK 'LUMINATIONS.
LIGHT-UP MY MUDDLED MIND BIG BOY.
© 1975
Michael McMillan

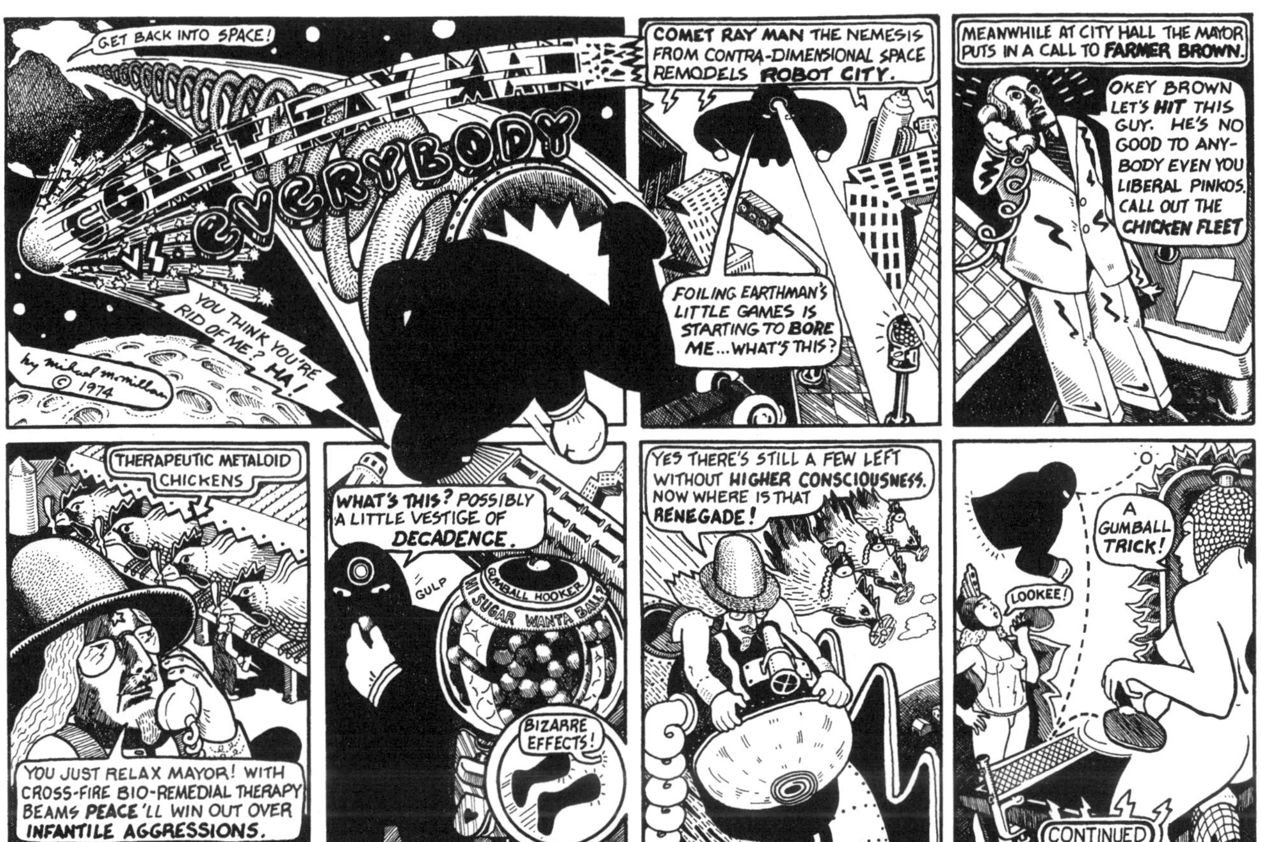
GET BACK INTO SPACE!
COMET RAY MAN VS. EVERYBODY
YOU THINK YOU'RE RID OF ME? HA!
by michael mcmillan © 1974
COMET RAY MAN THE NEMESIS FROM CONTRA-DIMENSIONAL SPACE REMODELS ROBOT CITY.
FOILING EARTHMAN'S LITTLE GAMES IS STARTING TO BORE ME...WHAT'S THIS?
MEANWHILE AT CITY HALL THE MAYOR PUTS IN A CALL TO FARMER BROWN.
OKEY BROWN LET'S HIT THIS GUY. HE'S NO GOOD TO ANYBODY EVEN YOU LIBERAL PINKOS. CALL OUT THE CHICKEN FLEET
THERAPEUTIC METALOID CHICKENS
YOU JUST RELAX MAYOR! WITH CROSS-FIRE BIO-REMEDIAL THERAPY BEAMS PEACE'LL WIN OUT OVER INFANTILE AGGRESSIONS.
WHAT'S THIS? POSSIBLY A LITTLE VESTIGE OF DECADENCE.
GULP
GUMBALL HOOKER
HI SUGAR WANTA BALL?
BIZARRE EFFECTS!
YES THERE'S STILL A FEW LEFT WITHOUT HIGHER CONSCIOUSNESS. NOW WHERE IS THAT RENEGADE!
LOOKEE!
A GUMBALL TRICK!
CONTINUED

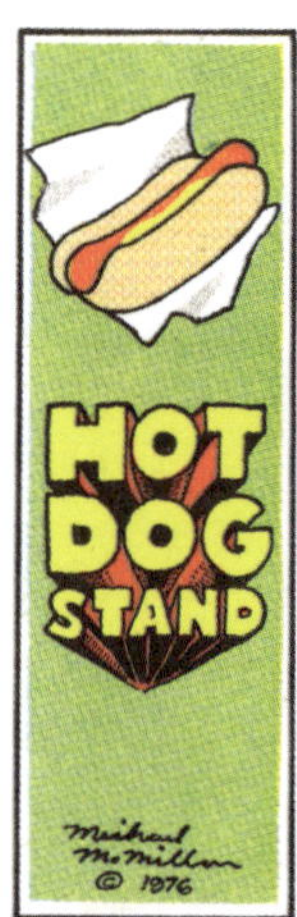
HOT DOG STAND
michael McMillan
© 1976

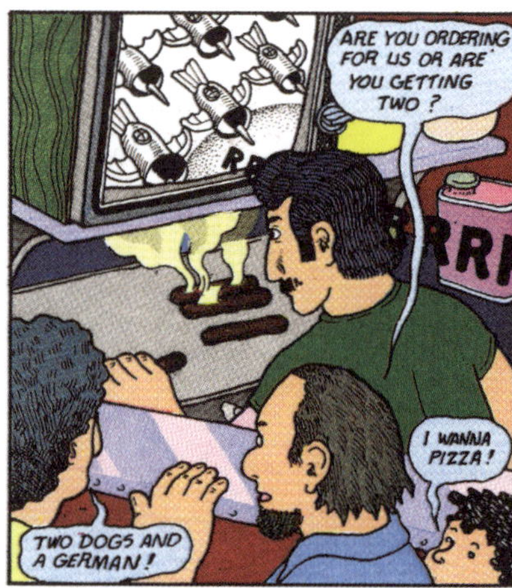
ARE YOU ORDERING FOR US OR ARE YOU GETTING TWO ?
I WANNA PIZZA!
TWO DOGS AND A GERMAN!

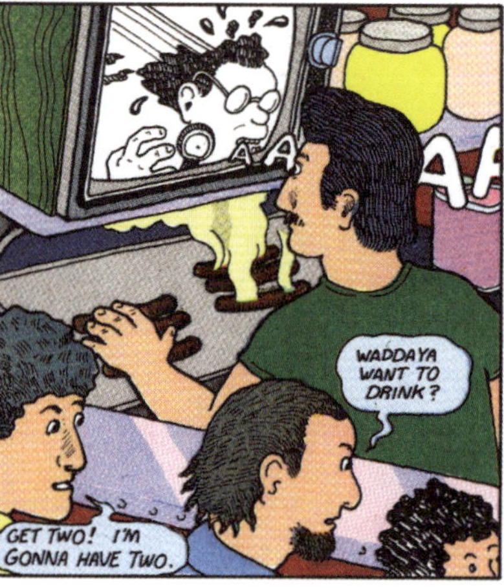
WADDAYA WANT TO DRINK?
GET TWO! I'M GONNA HAVE TWO.

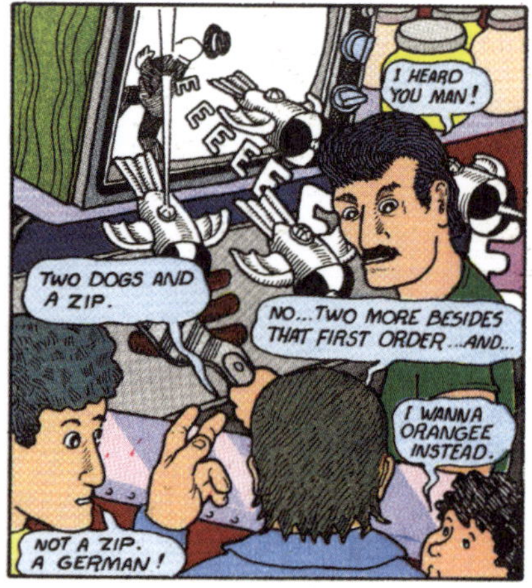
I HEARD YOU MAN!
TWO DOGS AND A ZIP.
NO...TWO MORE BESIDES THAT FIRST ORDER...AND...
I WANNA ORANGEE INSTEAD.
NOT A ZIP. A GERMAN!

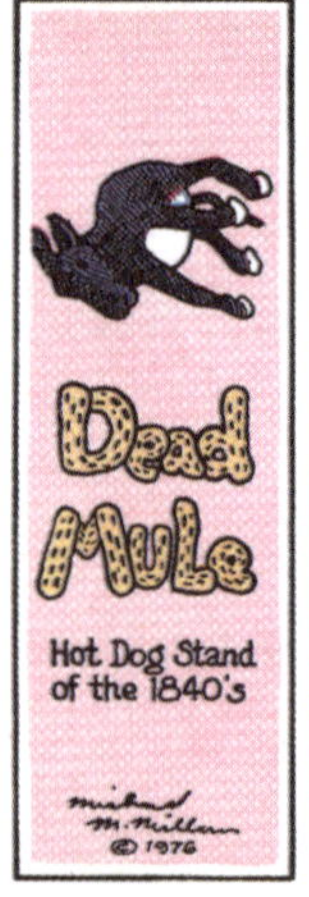
Dead Mule
Hot Dog Stand of the 1840's
michael McMillan
© 1976

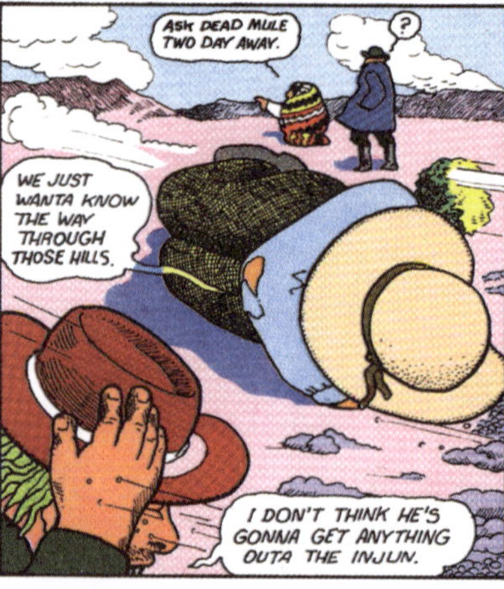
ASK DEAD MULE TWO DAY AWAY.
?
WE JUST WANTA KNOW THE WAY THROUGH THOSE HILLS.
I DON'T THINK HE'S GONNA GET ANYTHING OUTA THE INJUN.

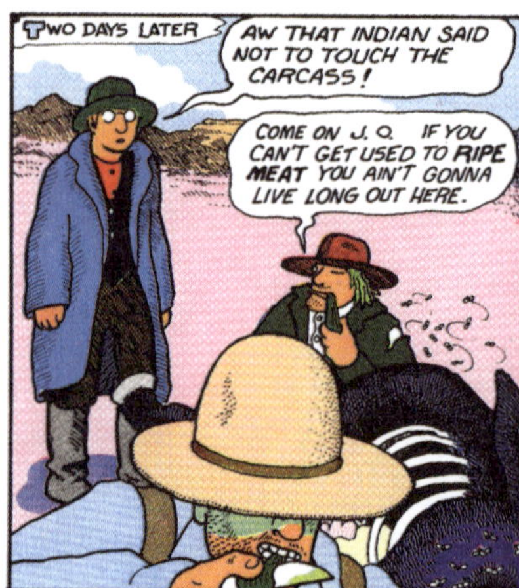
TWO DAYS LATER
AW THAT INDIAN SAID NOT TO TOUCH THE CARCASS!
COME ON J. Q. IF YOU CAN'T GET USED TO RIPE MEAT YOU AIN'T GONNA LIVE LONG OUT HERE.

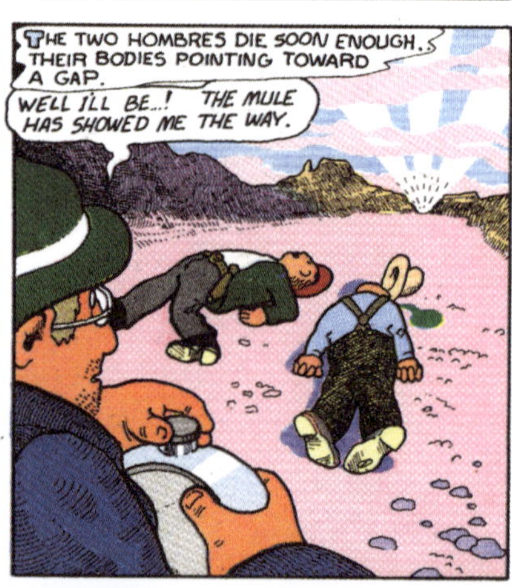
THE TWO HOMBRES DIE SOON ENOUGH. THEIR BODIES POINTING TOWARD A GAP.
WELL I'LL BE...! THE MULE HAS SHOWED ME THE WAY.

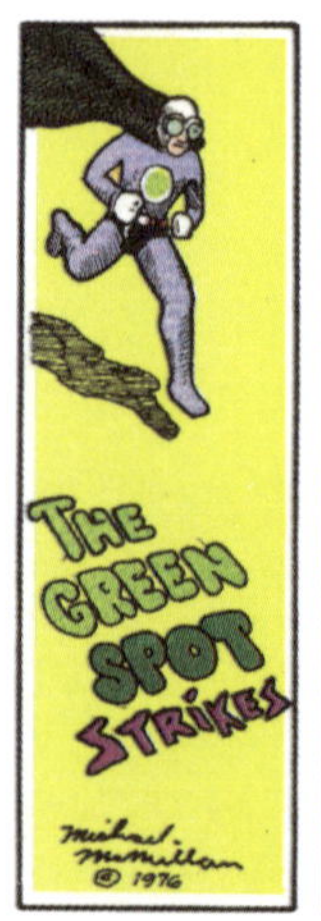
THE GREEN SPOT STRIKES
michael McMillan
© 1976

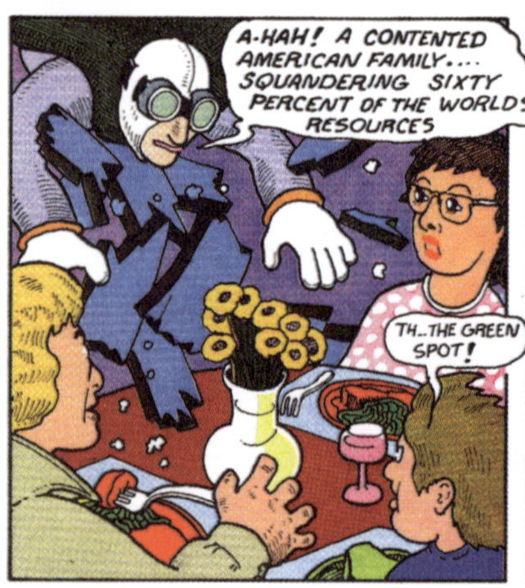
A-HAH! A CONTENTED AMERICAN FAMILY.... SQUANDERING SIXTY PERCENT OF THE WORLDS RESOURCES
TH...THE GREEN SPOT!

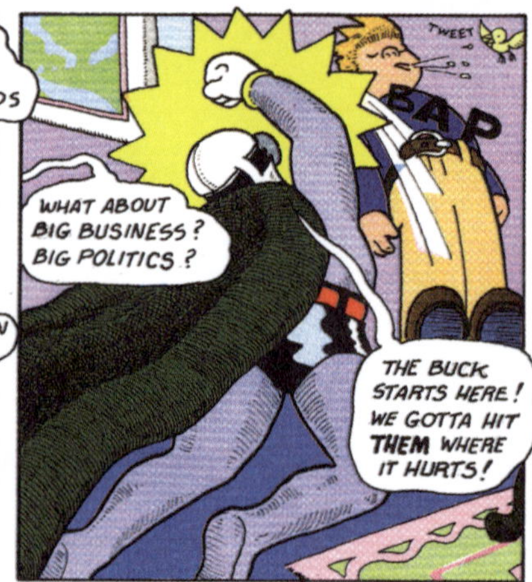
TWEET
BAP
WHAT ABOUT BIG BUSINESS? BIG POLITICS?
THE BUCK STARTS HERE! WE GOTTA HIT THEM WHERE IT HURTS!

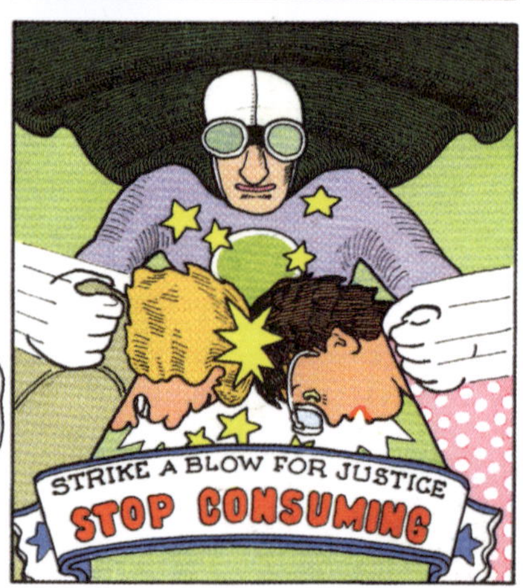
STRIKE A BLOW FOR JUSTICE
STOP CONSUMING

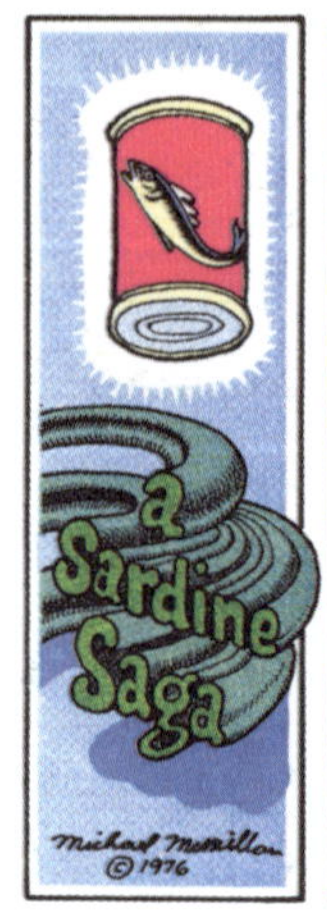
a Sardine Saga
michael McMillan
© 1976

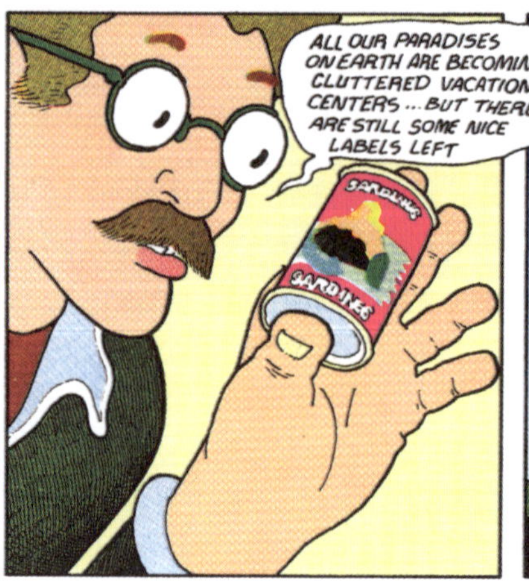
ALL OUR PARADISES ON EARTH ARE BECOMING CLUTTERED VACATION CENTERS... BUT THERE ARE STILL SOME NICE LABELS LEFT
SARDINES

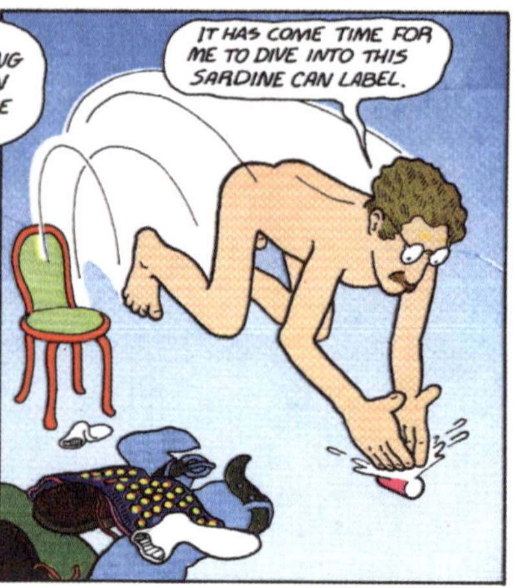
IT HAS COME TIME FOR ME TO DIVE INTO THIS SARDINE CAN LABEL.

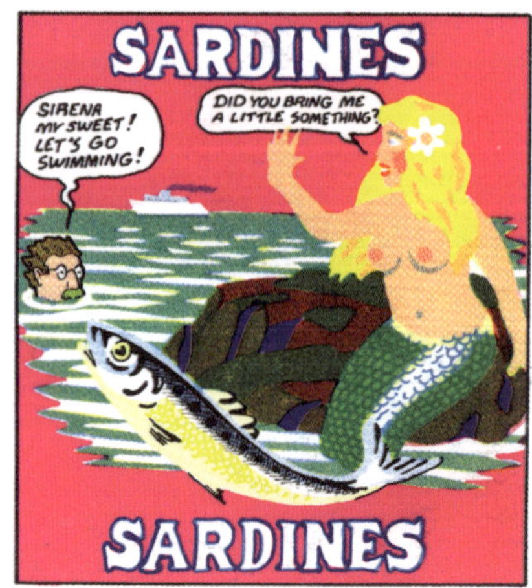
SARDINES
SIRENA MY SWEET! LET'S GO SWIMMING!
DID YOU BRING ME A LITTLE SOMETHING?
SARDINES

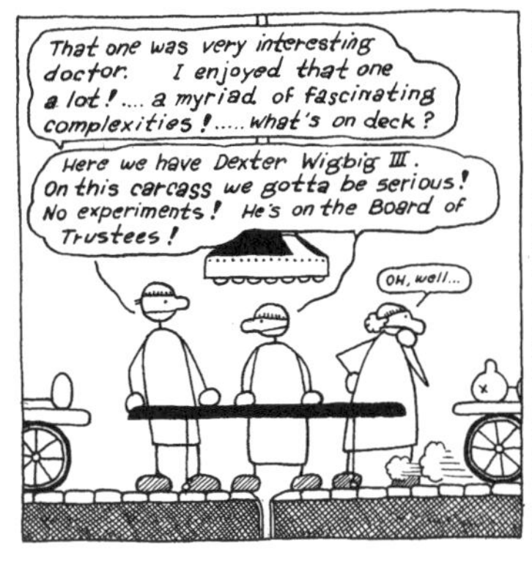
That one was very interesting doctor. I enjoyed that one a lot! .... a myriad of fascinating complexities! ..... what's on deck?
Here we have Dexter Wigbig III. On this carcass we gotta be serious! No experiments! He's on the Board of Trustees!
OH, well...

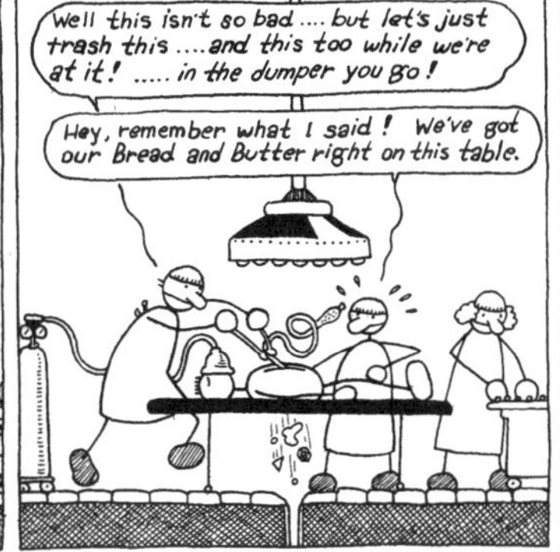
Well this isn't so bad .... but let's just trash this .... and this too while we're at it! ..... in the dumper you go!
Hey, remember what I said! We've got our Bread and Butter right on this table.

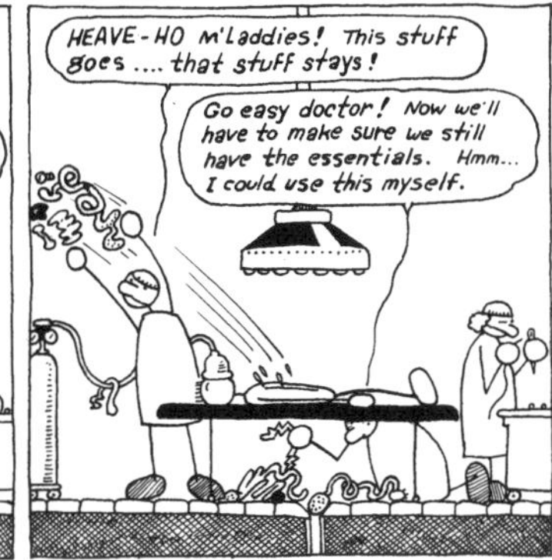
HEAVE-HO M'Laddies! This stuff goes .... that stuff stays!
Go easy doctor! Now we'll have to make sure we still have the essentials. Hmm... I could use this myself.

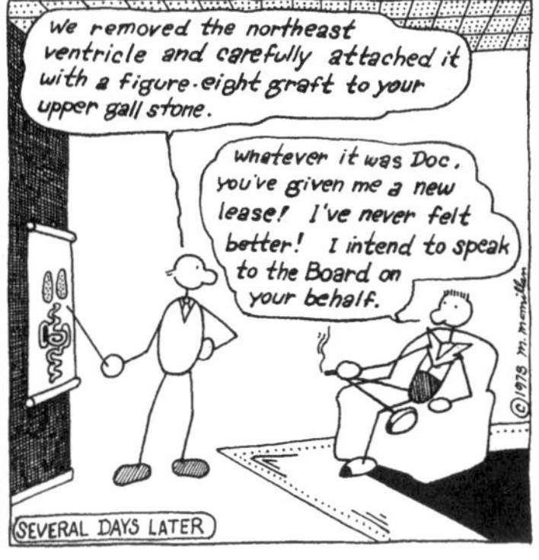
We removed the northeast ventricle and carefully attached it with a figure-eight graft to your upper gall stone.
whatever it was Doc, you've given me a new lease! I've never felt better! I intend to speak to the Board on your behalf.
SEVERAL DAYS LATER

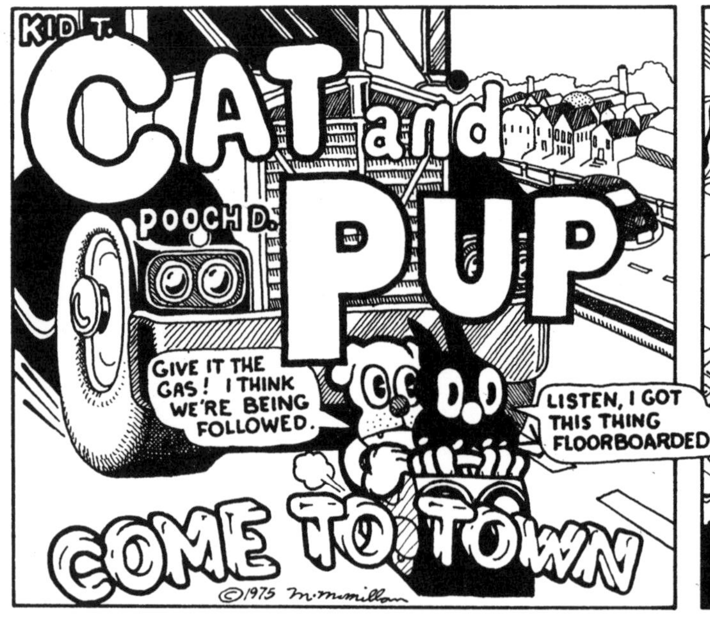
KID T.
CAT and
POOCH D.
PUP
GIVE IT THE GAS! I THINK WE'RE BEING FOLLOWED.
LISTEN, I GOT THIS THING FLOORBOARDED!
COME TO TOWN
©1975 M. McMillan

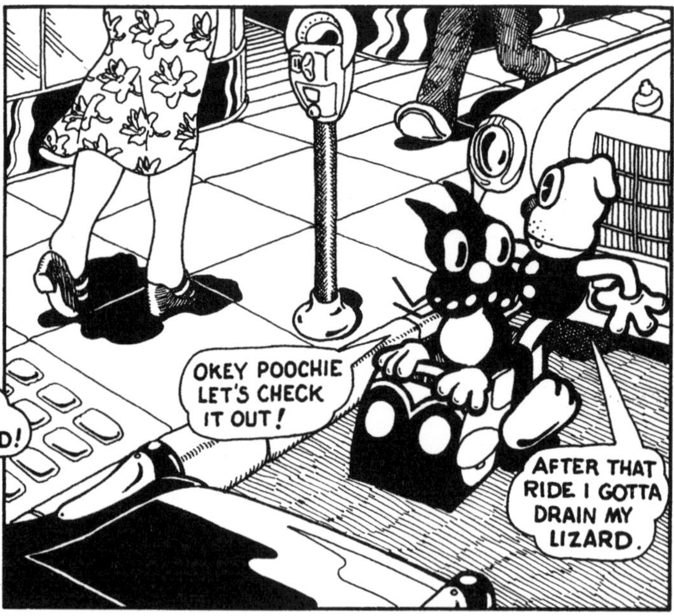
OKEY POOCHIE LET'S CHECK IT OUT!
AFTER THAT RIDE I GOTTA DRAIN MY LIZARD.

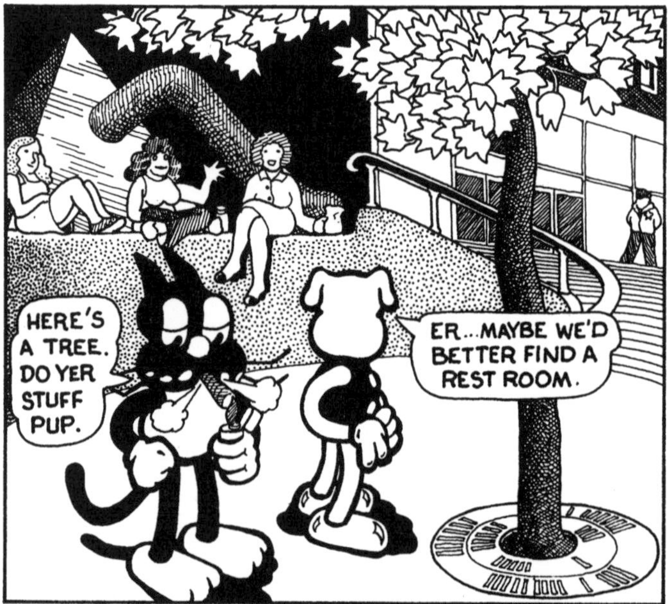
HERE'S A TREE. DO YER STUFF PUP.
ER... MAYBE WE'D BETTER FIND A REST ROOM.

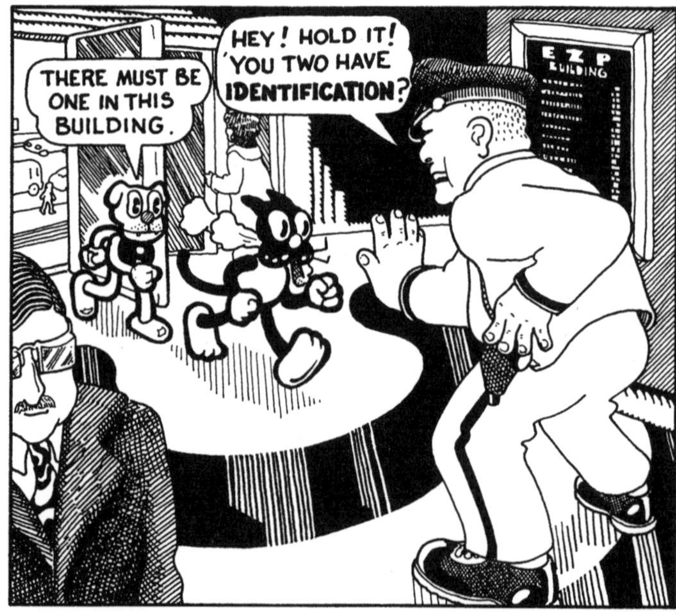
THERE MUST BE ONE IN THIS BUILDING.
HEY! HOLD IT! YOU TWO HAVE IDENTIFICATION?
E Z P BUILDING

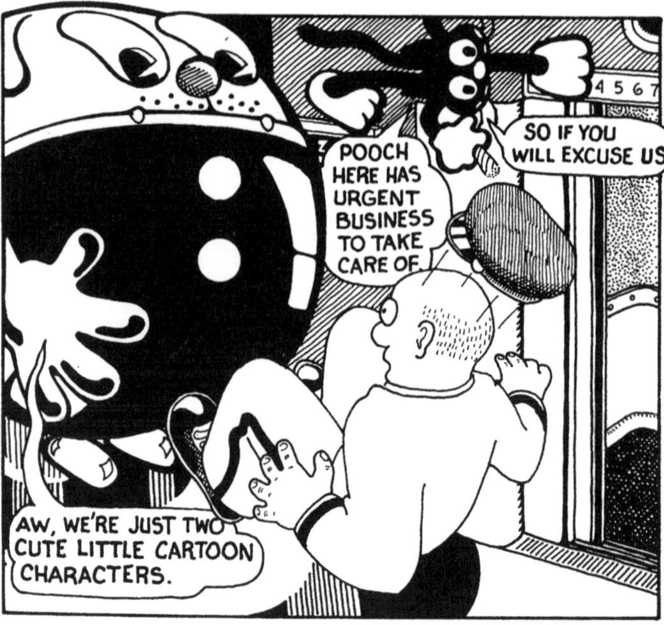
4 5 6 7
POOCH HERE HAS URGENT BUSINESS TO TAKE CARE OF.
SO IF YOU WILL EXCUSE US
AW, WE'RE JUST TWO CUTE LITTLE CARTOON CHARACTERS.

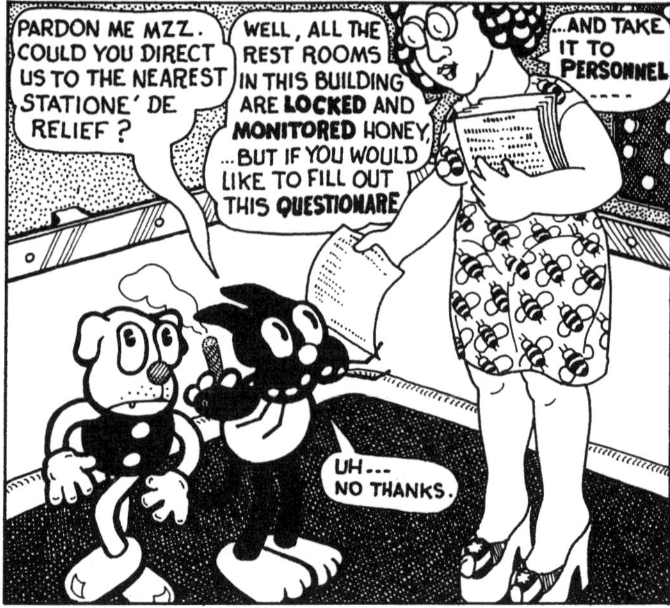
PARDON ME MZZ. COULD YOU DIRECT US TO THE NEAREST STATIONE' DE RELIEF?
WELL, ALL THE REST ROOMS IN THIS BUILDING ARE LOCKED AND MONITORED HONEY ...BUT IF YOU WOULD LIKE TO FILL OUT THIS QUESTIONARE
...AND TAKE IT TO PERSONNEL ---
UH... NO THANKS.

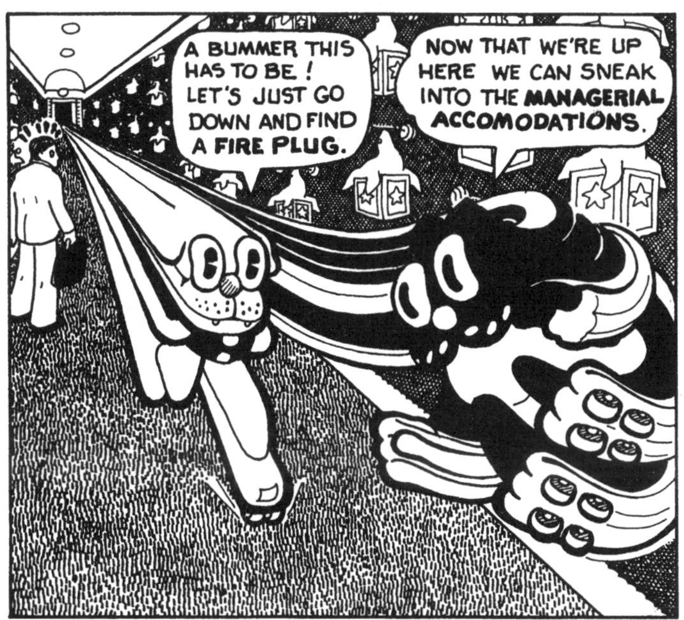
A BUMMER THIS HAS TO BE! LET'S JUST GO DOWN AND FIND A FIRE PLUG.
NOW THAT WE'RE UP HERE WE CAN SNEAK INTO THE MANAGERIAL ACCOMODATIONS.

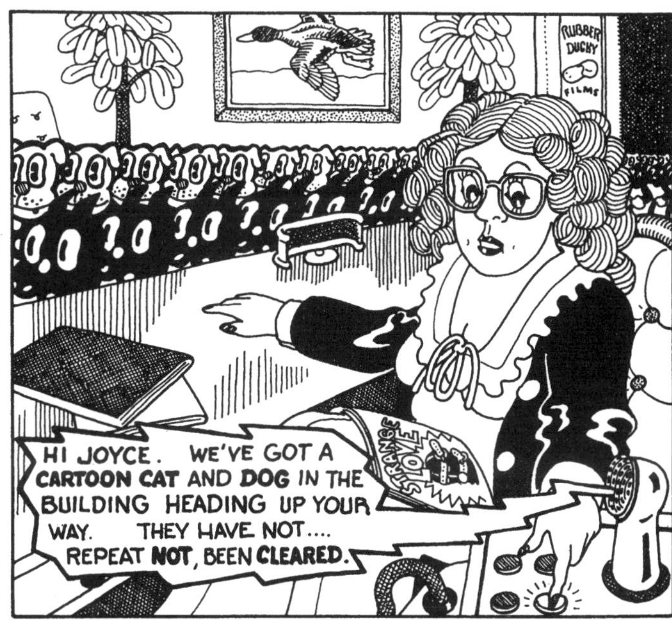
RUBBER DUCKY FILMS
HI JOYCE. WE'VE GOT A CARTOON CAT AND DOG IN THE BUILDING HEADING UP YOUR WAY. THEY HAVE NOT.... REPEAT NOT, BEEN CLEARED.

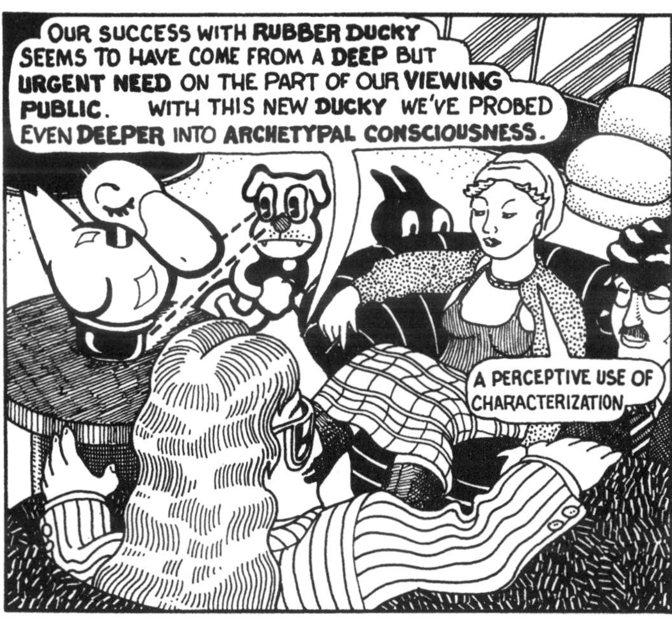
OUR SUCCESS WITH RUBBER DUCKY SEEMS TO HAVE COME FROM A DEEP BUT URGENT NEED ON THE PART OF OUR VIEWING PUBLIC. WITH THIS NEW DUCKY WE'VE PROBED EVEN DEEPER INTO ARCHETYPAL CONSCIOUSNESS.
A PERCEPTIVE USE OF CHARACTERIZATION.

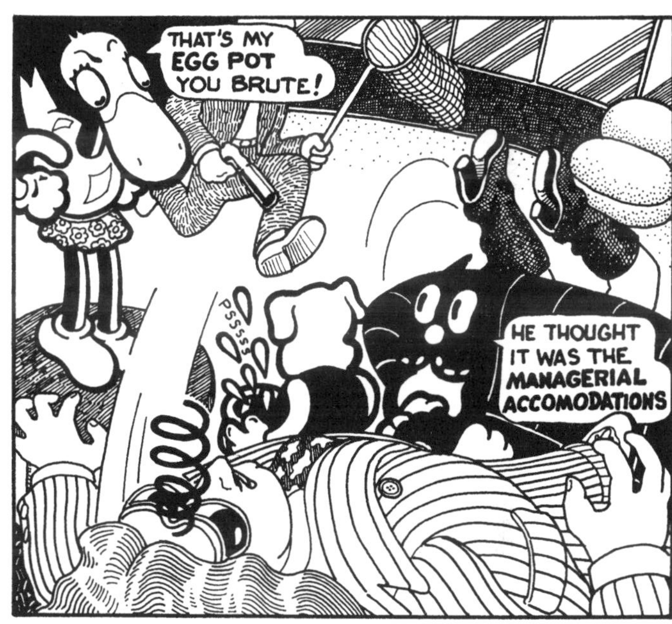
THAT'S MY EGG POT YOU BRUTE!
PSSSSS
HE THOUGHT IT WAS THE MANAGERIAL ACCOMODATIONS

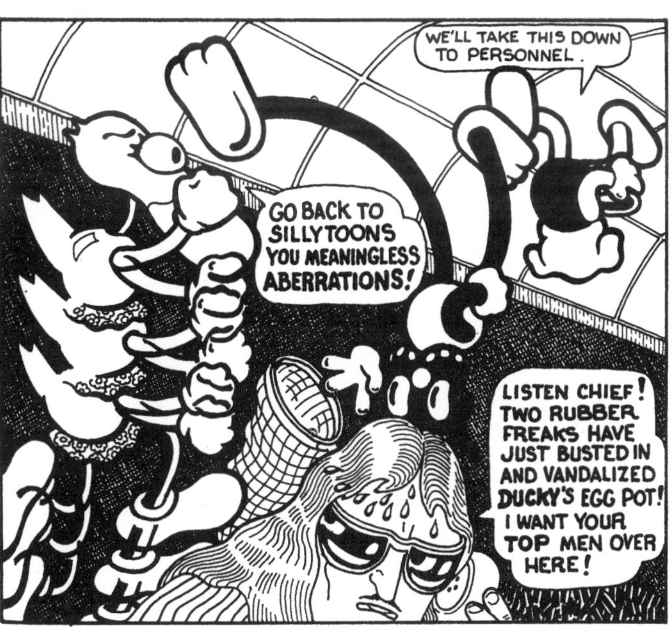
WE'LL TAKE THIS DOWN TO PERSONNEL.
GO BACK TO SILLYTOONS YOU MEANINGLESS ABERRATIONS!
LISTEN CHIEF! TWO RUBBER FREAKS HAVE JUST BUSTED IN AND VANDALIZED DUCKY'S EGG POT! I WANT YOUR TOP MEN OVER HERE!

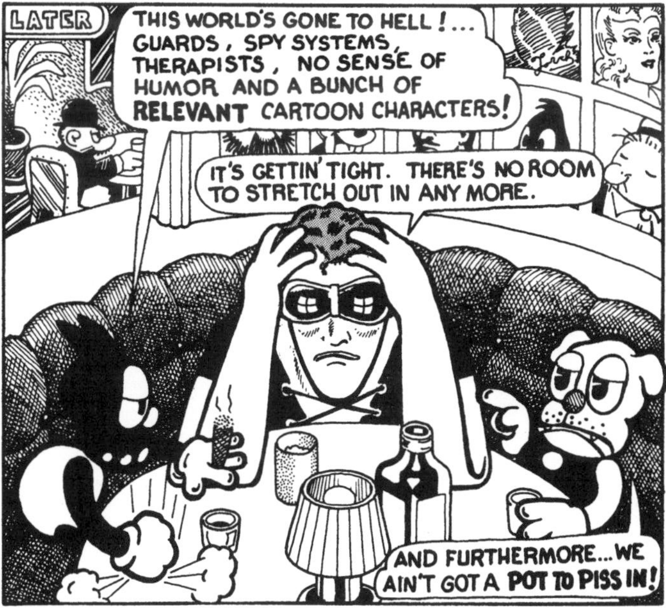
LATER
THIS WORLD'S GONE TO HELL!... GUARDS, SPY SYSTEMS, THERAPISTS, NO SENSE OF HUMOR AND A BUNCH OF RELEVANT CARTOON CHARACTERS!
IT'S GETTIN' TIGHT. THERE'S NO ROOM TO STRETCH OUT IN ANY MORE.
AND FURTHERMORE... WE AIN'T GOT A POT TO PISS IN!

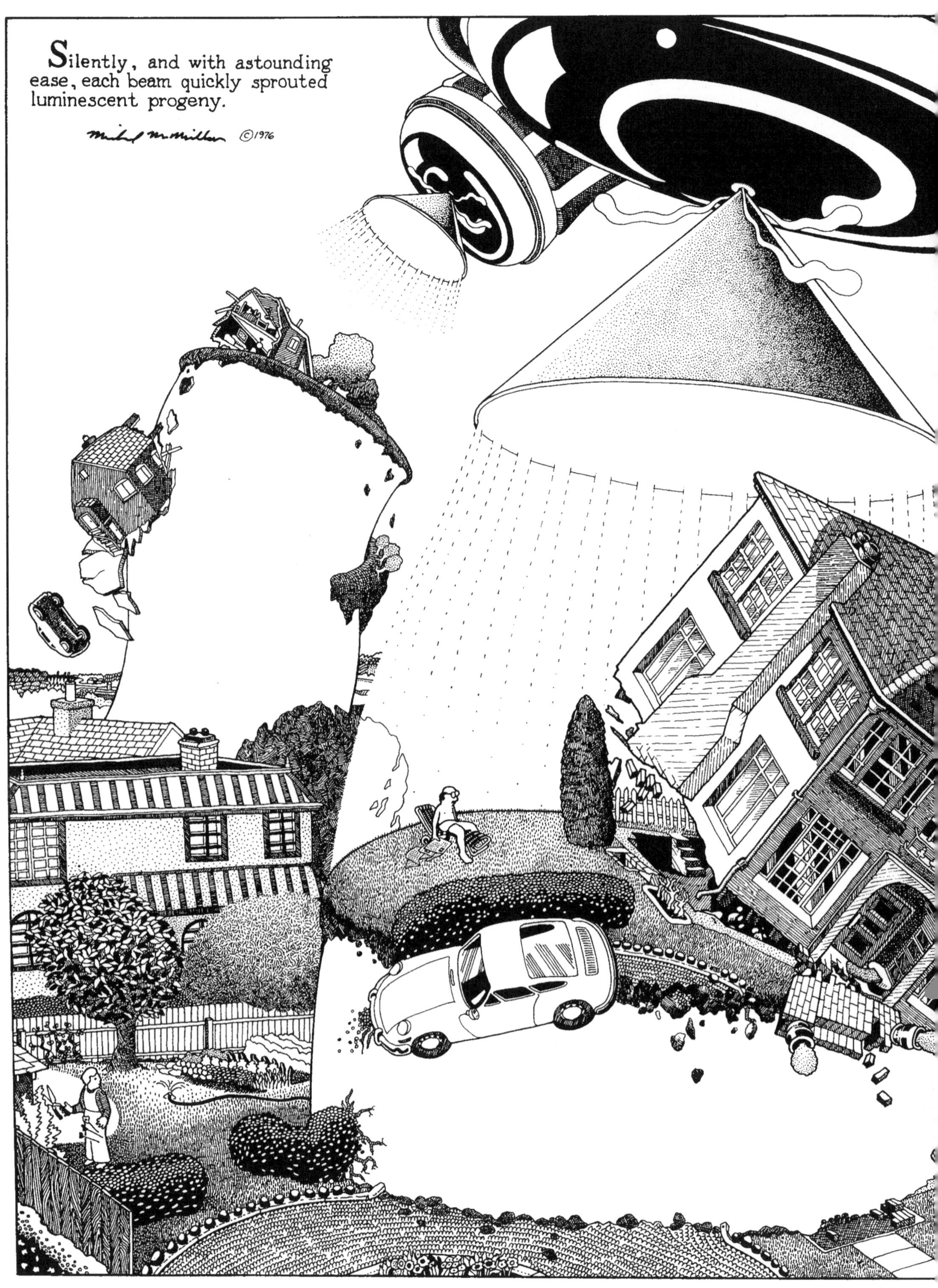
Silently, and with astounding ease, each beam quickly sprouted luminescent progeny.
©1976

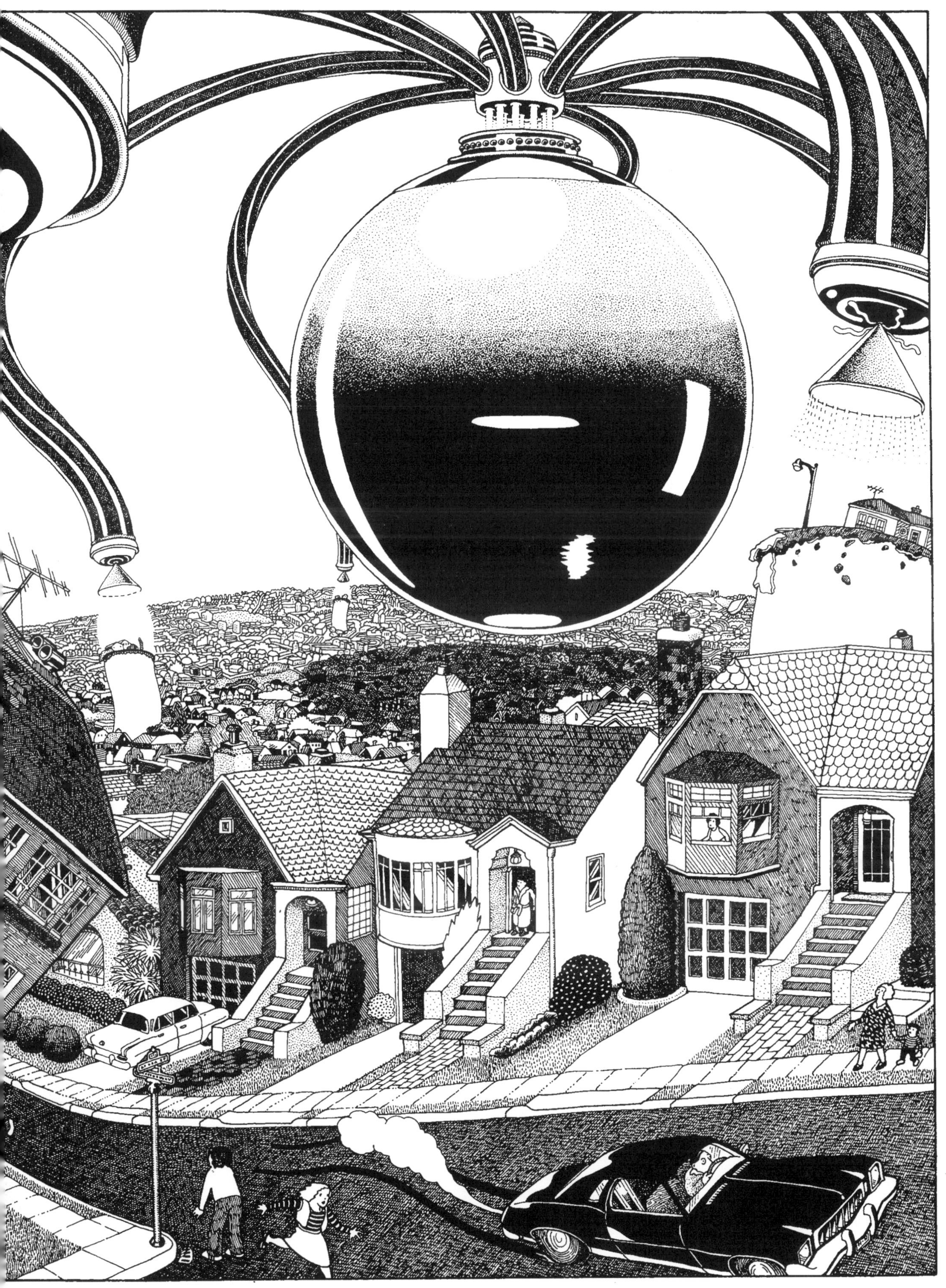

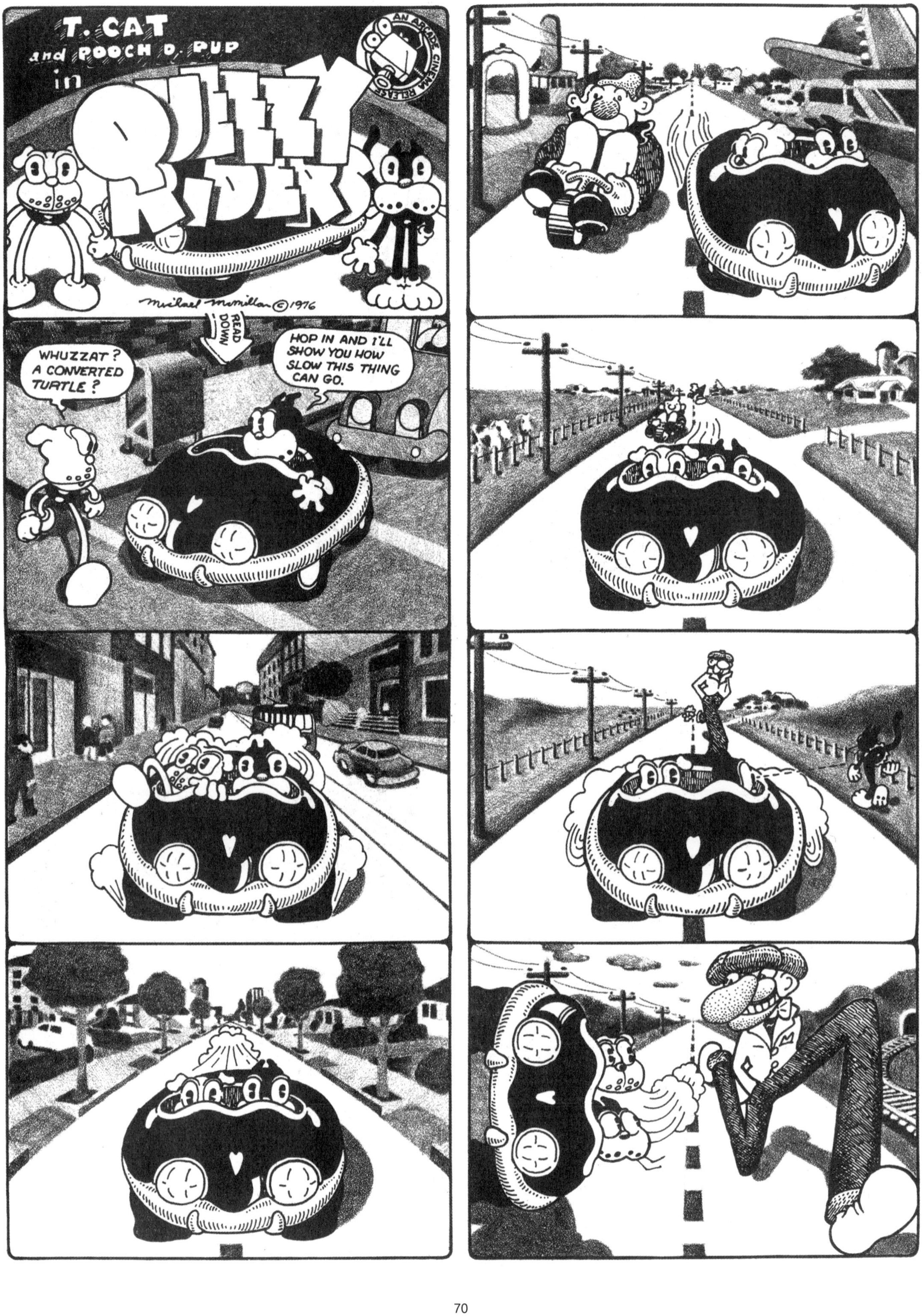

T. CAT
and POOCH D. PUP
in
QUEEZY RIDERS

AN ARCADE CINEMA RELEASE

Michael McMillan ©1976

READ DOWN

WHUZZAT? A CONVERTED TURTLE?

HOP IN AND I'LL SHOW YOU HOW SLOW THIS THING CAN GO.

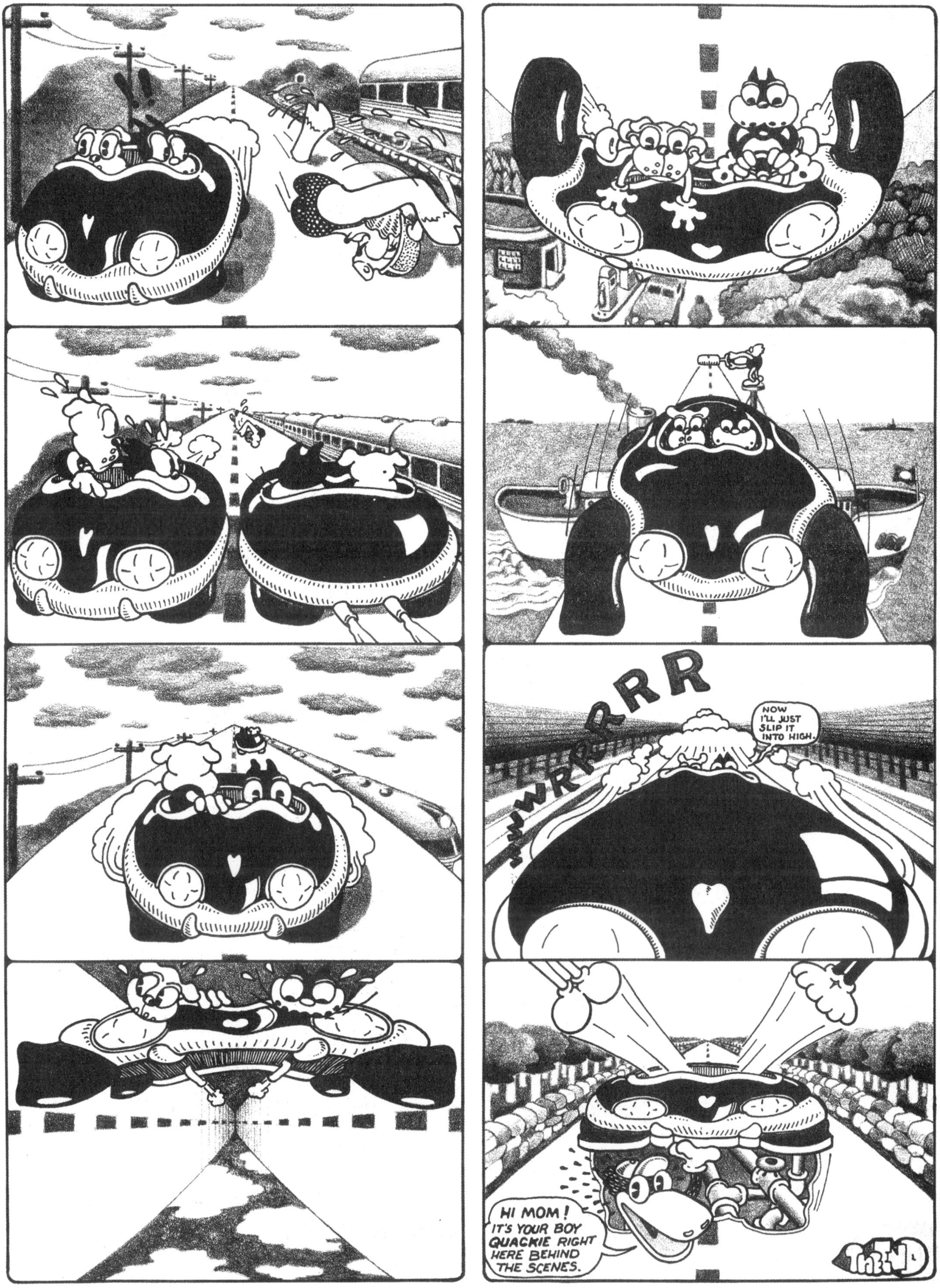

!!

WWWWRRRRRRR

NOW I'LL JUST SLIP IT INTO HIGH.

HI MOM! IT'S YOUR BOY QUACKIE RIGHT HERE BEHIND THE SCENES.

THE END

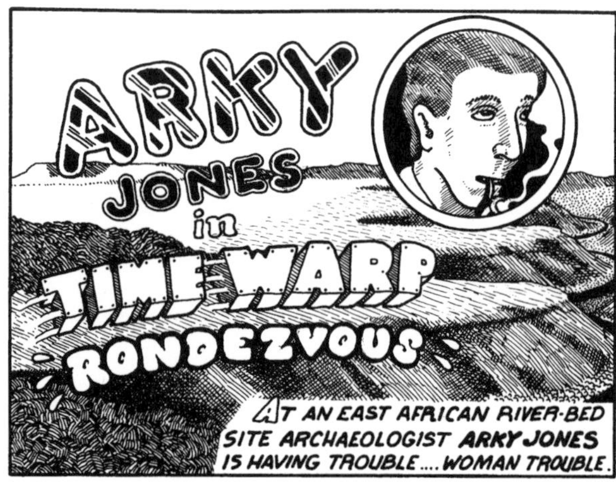
ARKY
JONES
in
TIME WARP
RONDEZVOUS
AT AN EAST AFRICAN RIVER-BED SITE ARCHAEOLOGIST ARKY JONES IS HAVING TROUBLE.... WOMAN TROUBLE.

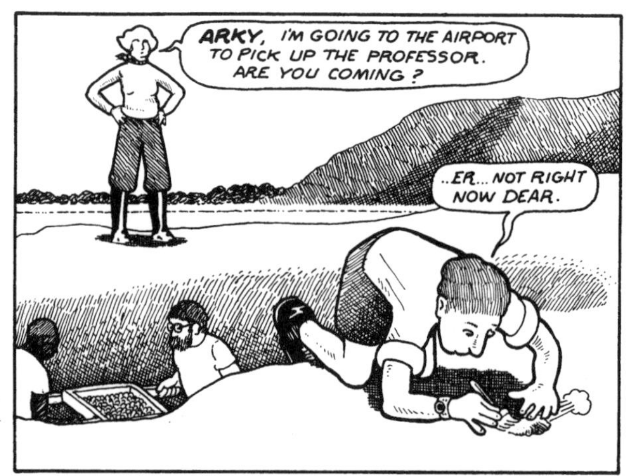
ARKY, I'M GOING TO THE AIRPORT TO PICK UP THE PROFESSOR. ARE YOU COMING?
..ER... NOT RIGHT NOW DEAR.

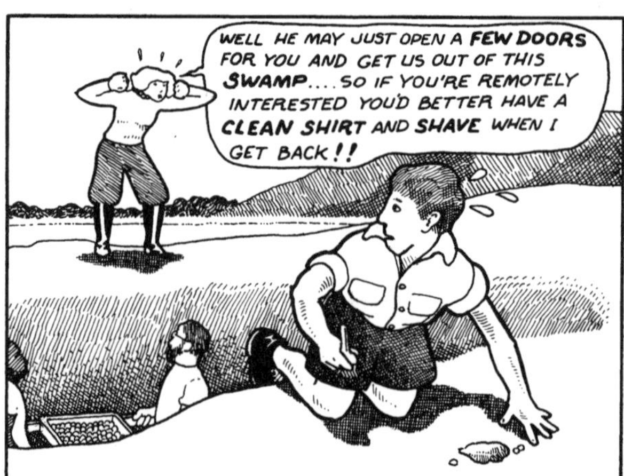
WELL HE MAY JUST OPEN A FEW DOORS FOR YOU AND GET US OUT OF THIS SWAMP.... SO IF YOU'RE REMOTELY INTERESTED YOU'D BETTER HAVE A CLEAN SHIRT AND SHAVE WHEN I GET BACK!!

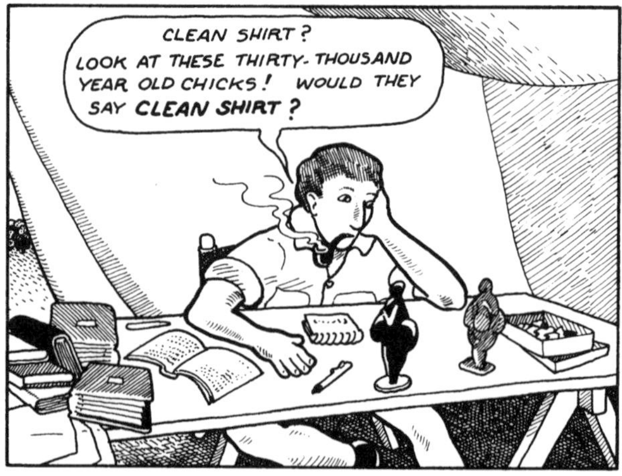
CLEAN SHIRT? LOOK AT THESE THIRTY-THOUSAND YEAR OLD CHICKS! WOULD THEY SAY CLEAN SHIRT?

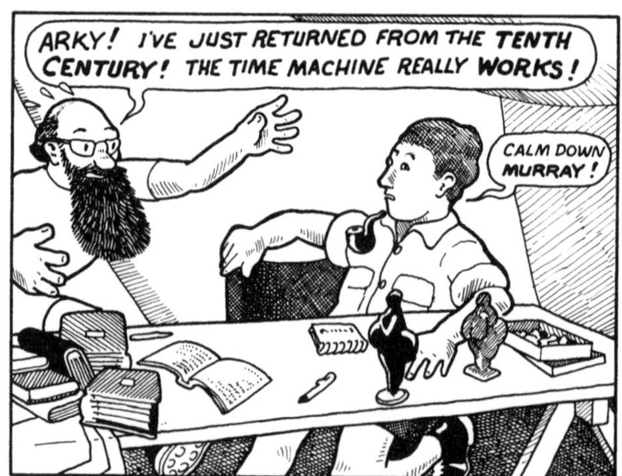
ARKY! I'VE JUST RETURNED FROM THE TENTH CENTURY! THE TIME MACHINE REALLY WORKS!
CALM DOWN MURRAY!

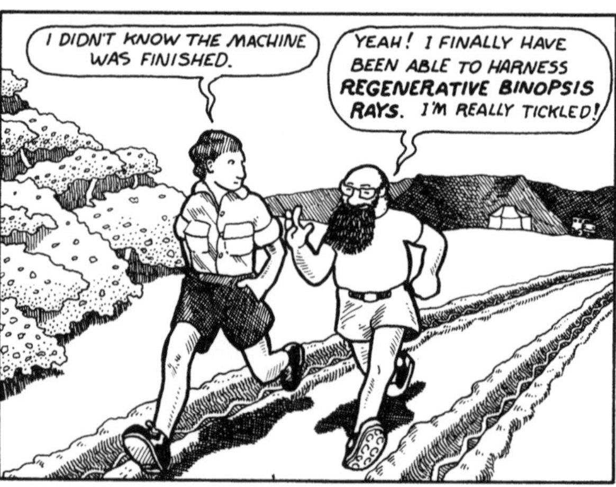
I DIDN'T KNOW THE MACHINE WAS FINISHED.
YEAH! I FINALLY HAVE BEEN ABLE TO HARNESS REGENERATIVE BINOPSIS RAYS. I'M REALLY TICKLED!

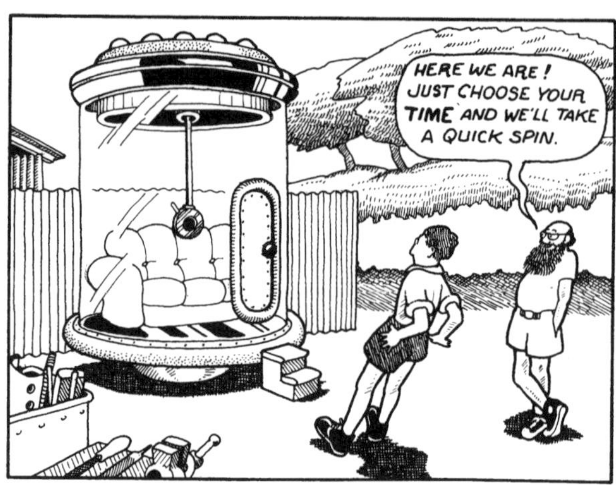
HERE WE ARE! JUST CHOOSE YOUR TIME AND WE'LL TAKE A QUICK SPIN.

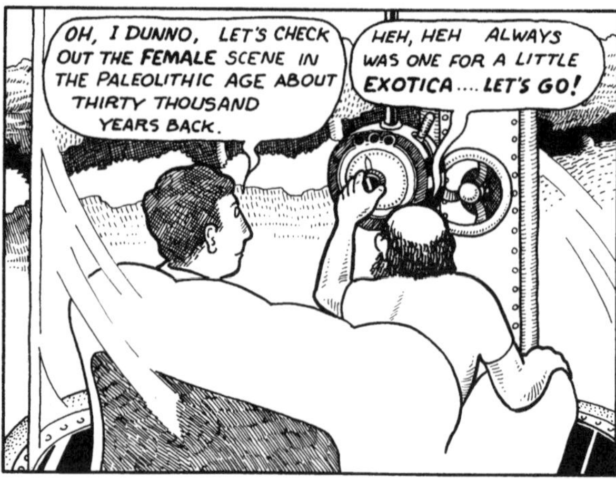
OH, I DUNNO, LET'S CHECK OUT THE FEMALE SCENE IN THE PALEOLITHIC AGE ABOUT THIRTY THOUSAND YEARS BACK.
HEH, HEH ALWAYS WAS ONE FOR A LITTLE EXOTICA.... LET'S GO!

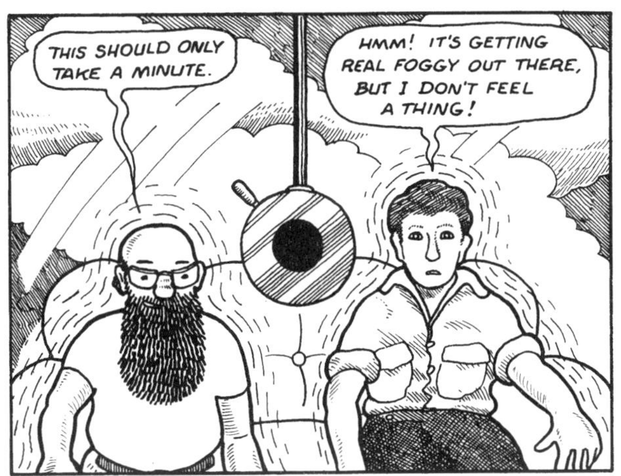
THIS SHOULD ONLY TAKE A MINUTE.
HMM! IT'S GETTING REAL FOGGY OUT THERE, BUT I DON'T FEEL A THING!

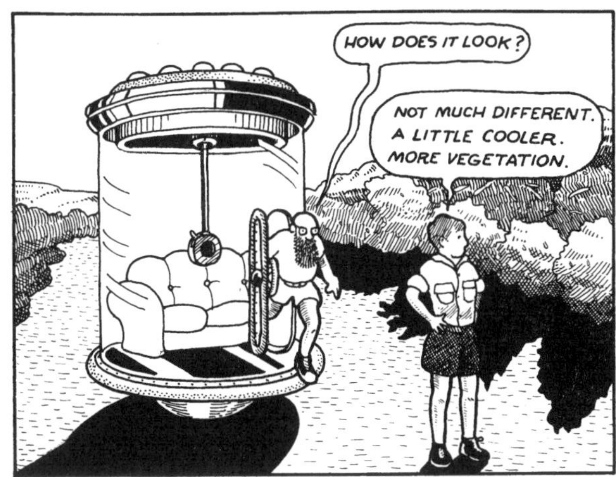
HOW DOES IT LOOK?
NOT MUCH DIFFERENT. A LITTLE COOLER. MORE VEGETATION.

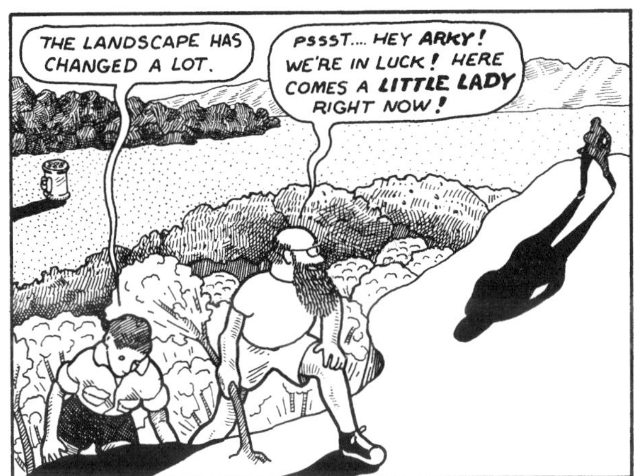
THE LANDSCAPE HAS CHANGED A LOT.
PSSST.... HEY ARKY! WE'RE IN LUCK! HERE COMES A LITTLE LADY RIGHT NOW!

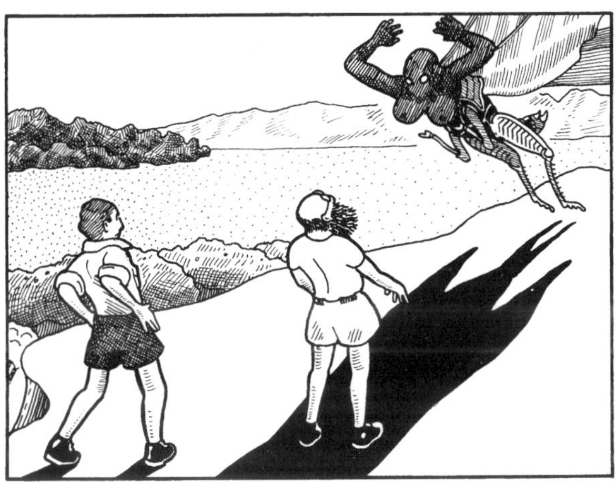

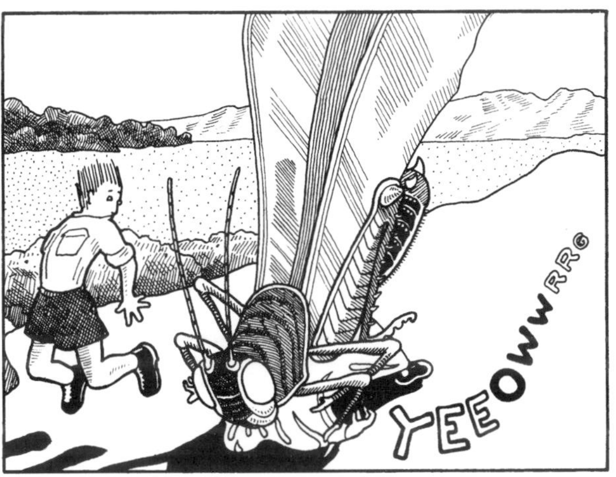
YEEOWWRRG

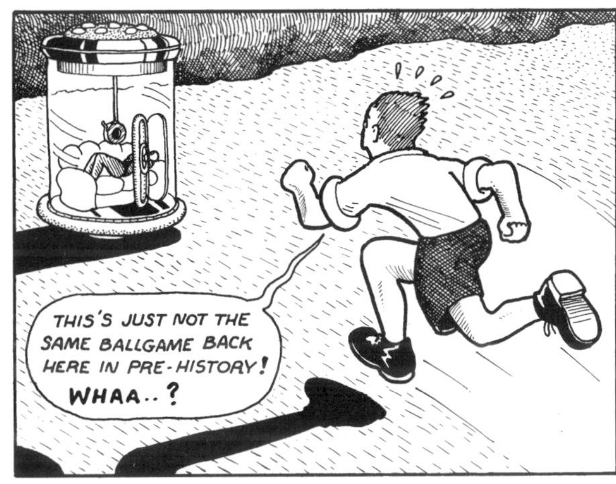
THIS'S JUST NOT THE SAME BALLGAME BACK HERE IN PRE-HISTORY! WHAA..?

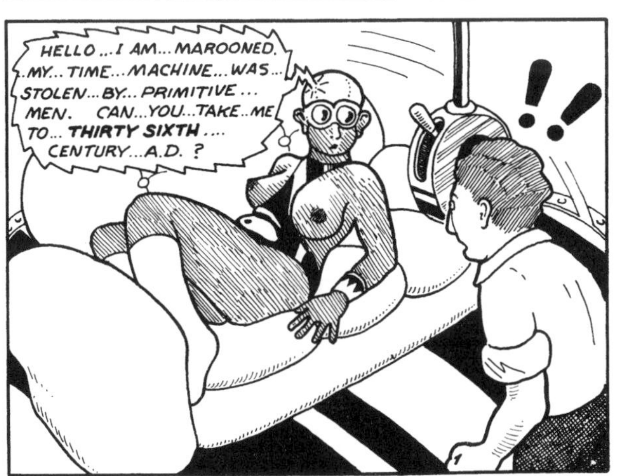
HELLO...I AM...MAROONED. MY...TIME...MACHINE...WAS... STOLEN...BY...PRIMITIVE... MEN. CAN...YOU...TAKE...ME TO... THIRTY SIXTH.... CENTURY...A.D.?
!!

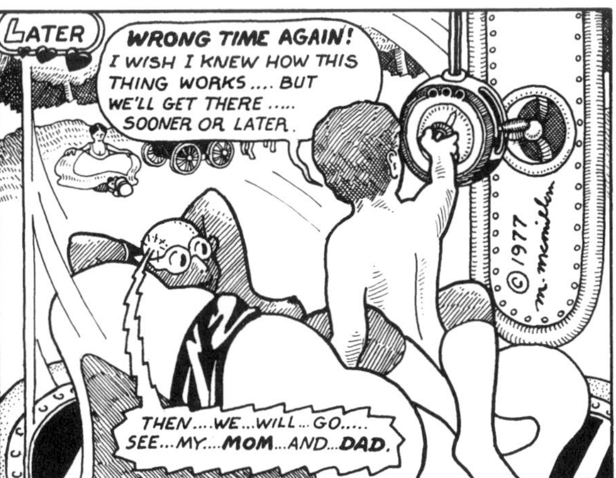
LATER
WRONG TIME AGAIN! I WISH I KNEW HOW THIS THING WORKS.... BUT WE'LL GET THERE..... SOONER OR LATER.
THEN....WE...WILL...GO.... SEE...MY....MOM...AND...DAD.
© 1977 m. mcmillan

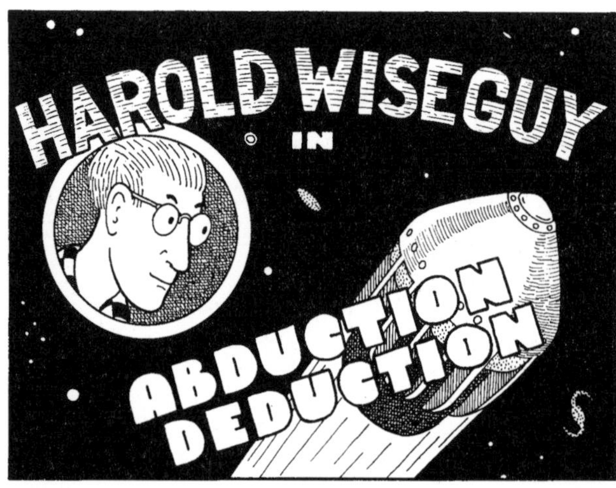
HAROLD WISEGUY
IN
ABDUCTION DEDUCTION

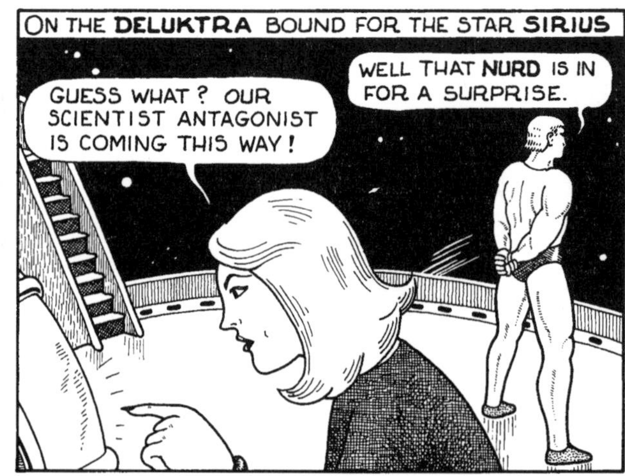
ON THE DELUKTRA BOUND FOR THE STAR SIRIUS
GUESS WHAT? OUR SCIENTIST ANTAGONIST IS COMING THIS WAY!
WELL THAT NURD IS IN FOR A SURPRISE.

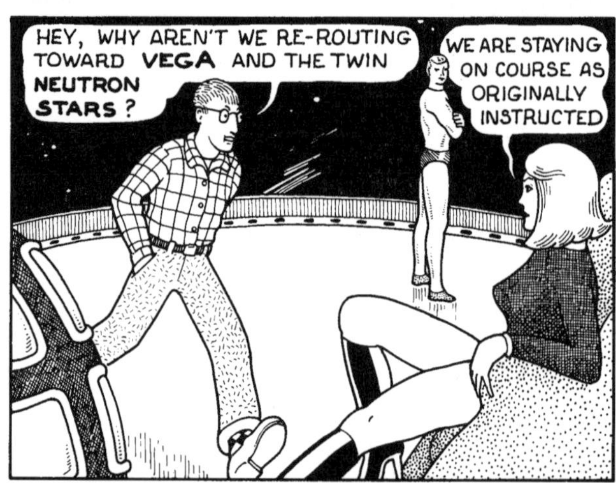
HEY, WHY AREN'T WE RE-ROUTING TOWARD VEGA AND THE TWIN NEUTRON STARS?
WE ARE STAYING ON COURSE AS ORIGINALLY INSTRUCTED

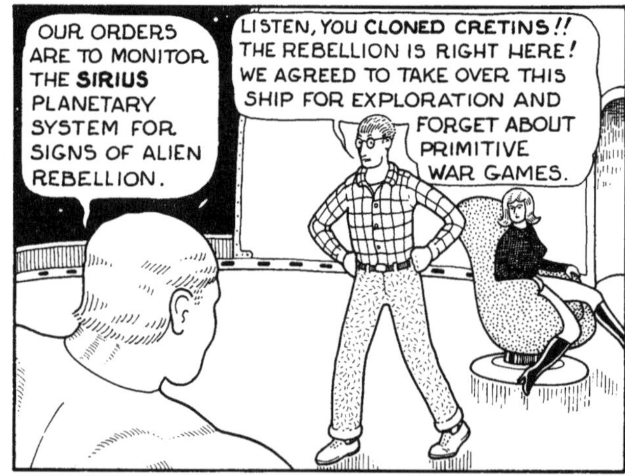
OUR ORDERS ARE TO MONITOR THE SIRIUS PLANETARY SYSTEM FOR SIGNS OF ALIEN REBELLION.
LISTEN, YOU CLONED CRETINS!! THE REBELLION IS RIGHT HERE! WE AGREED TO TAKE OVER THIS SHIP FOR EXPLORATION AND FORGET ABOUT PRIMITIVE WAR GAMES.

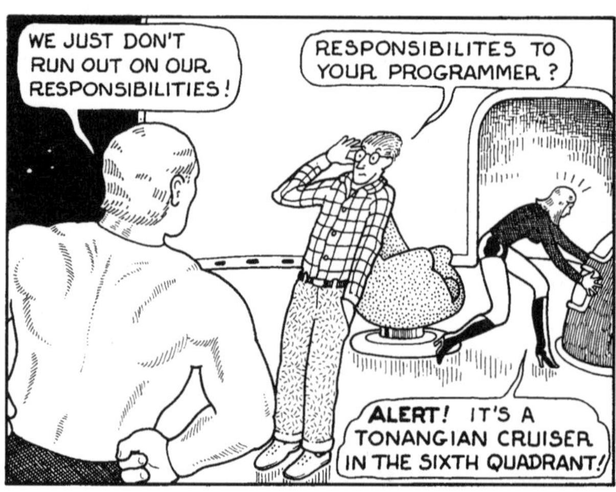
WE JUST DON'T RUN OUT ON OUR RESPONSIBILITIES!
RESPONSIBILITES TO YOUR PROGRAMMER?
ALERT! IT'S A TONANGIAN CRUISER IN THE SIXTH QUADRANT!

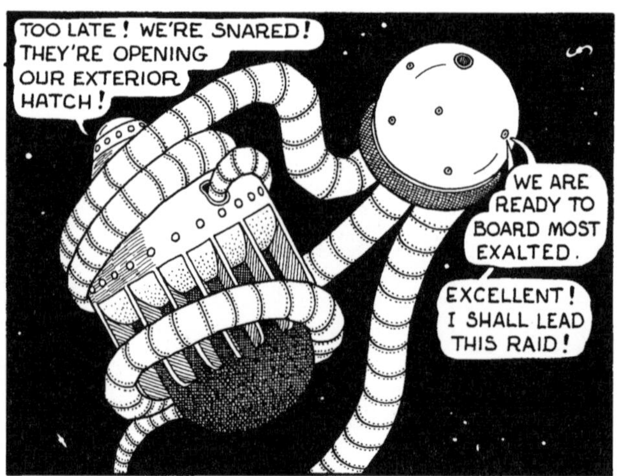
TOO LATE! WE'RE SNARED! THEY'RE OPENING OUR EXTERIOR HATCH!
WE ARE READY TO BOARD MOST EXALTED.
EXCELLENT! I SHALL LEAD THIS RAID!

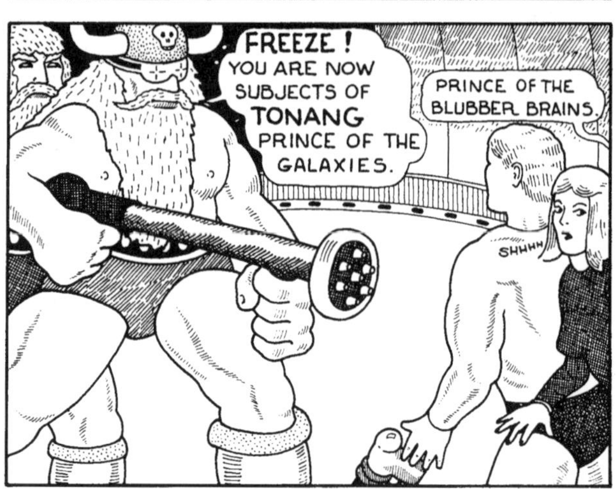
FREEZE! YOU ARE NOW SUBJECTS OF TONANG PRINCE OF THE GALAXIES.
PRINCE OF THE BLUBBER BRAINS.
SHHHH

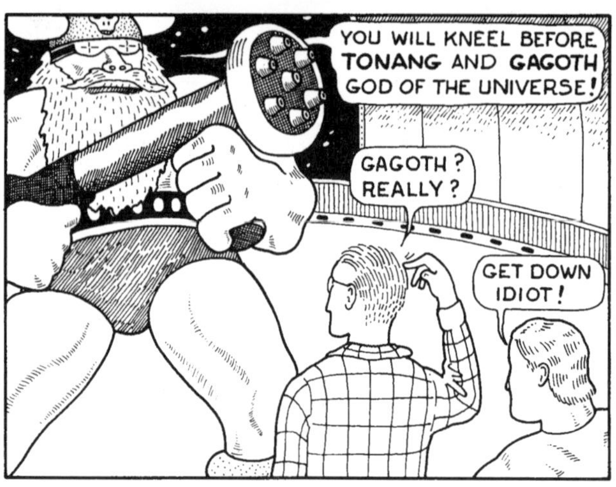
YOU WILL KNEEL BEFORE TONANG AND GAGOTH GOD OF THE UNIVERSE!
GAGOTH? REALLY?
GET DOWN IDIOT!

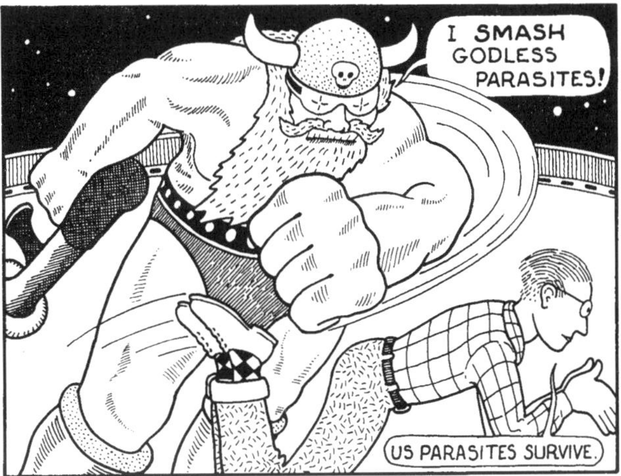
I SMASH GODLESS PARASITES!
US PARASITES SURVIVE.

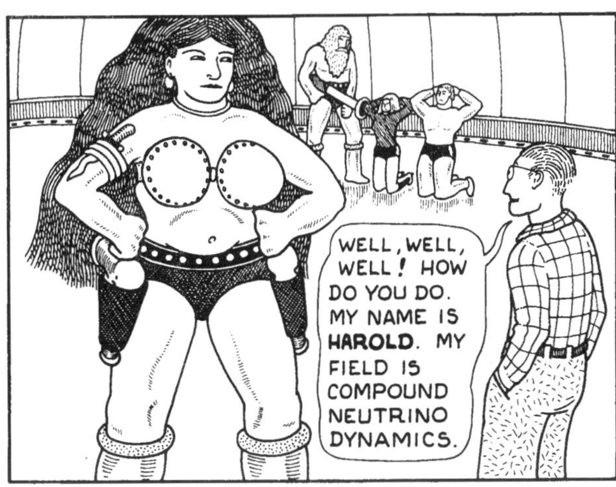
WELL, WELL, WELL! HOW DO YOU DO. MY NAME IS HAROLD. MY FIELD IS COMPOUND NEUTRINO DYNAMICS.

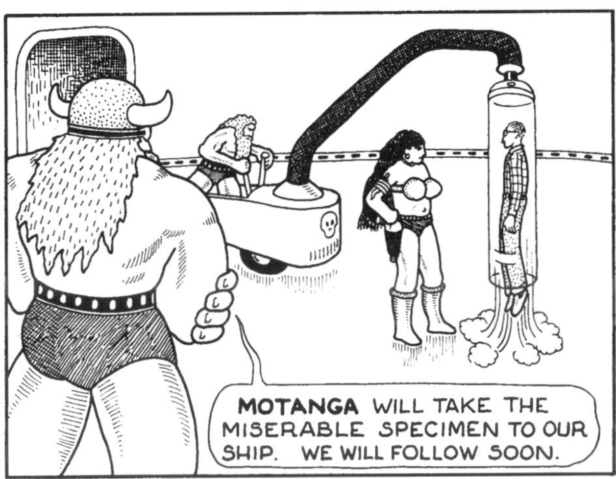
MOTANGA WILL TAKE THE MISERABLE SPECIMEN TO OUR SHIP. WE WILL FOLLOW SOON.

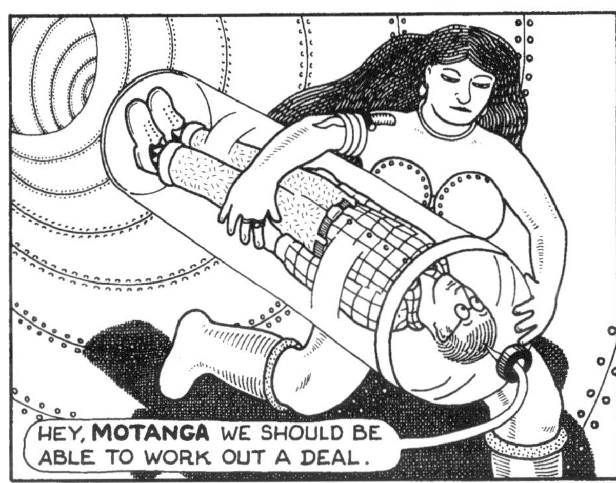
HEY, MOTANGA WE SHOULD BE ABLE TO WORK OUT A DEAL.

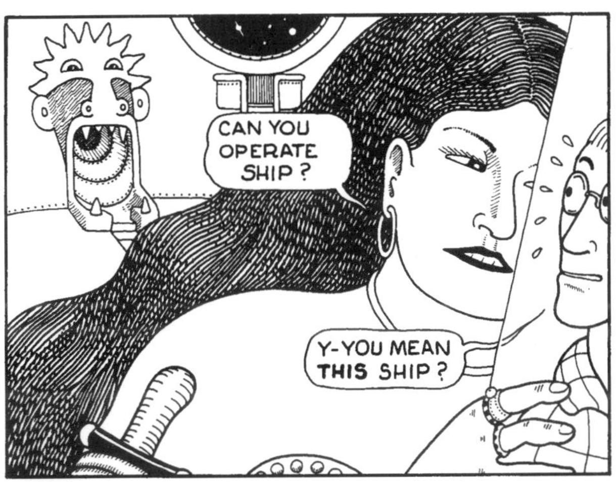
CAN YOU OPERATE SHIP?
Y-YOU MEAN THIS SHIP?

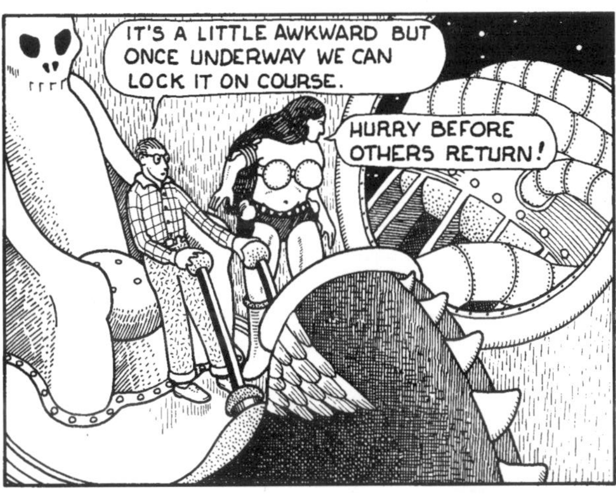
IT'S A LITTLE AWKWARD BUT ONCE UNDERWAY WE CAN LOCK IT ON COURSE.
HURRY BEFORE OTHERS RETURN!

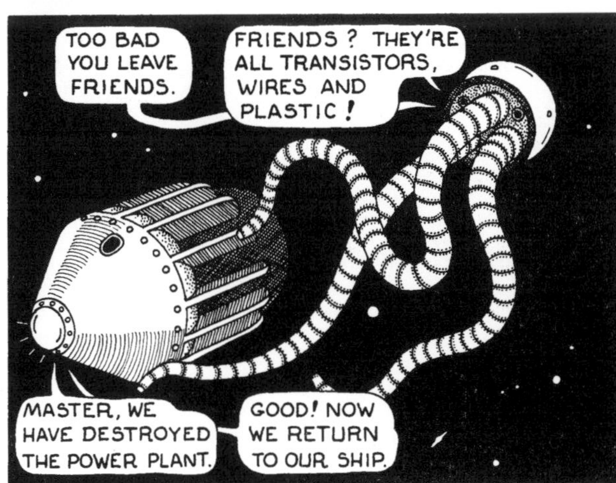
TOO BAD YOU LEAVE FRIENDS.
FRIENDS? THEY'RE ALL TRANSISTORS, WIRES AND PLASTIC!
MASTER, WE HAVE DESTROYED THE POWER PLANT.
GOOD! NOW WE RETURN TO OUR SHIP.

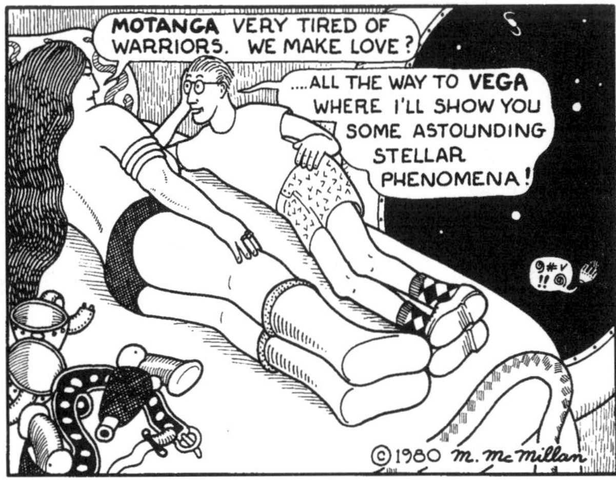
MOTANGA VERY TIRED OF WARRIORS. WE MAKE LOVE?
....ALL THE WAY TO VEGA WHERE I'LL SHOW YOU SOME ASTOUNDING STELLAR PHENOMENA!
©1980 m. McMillan

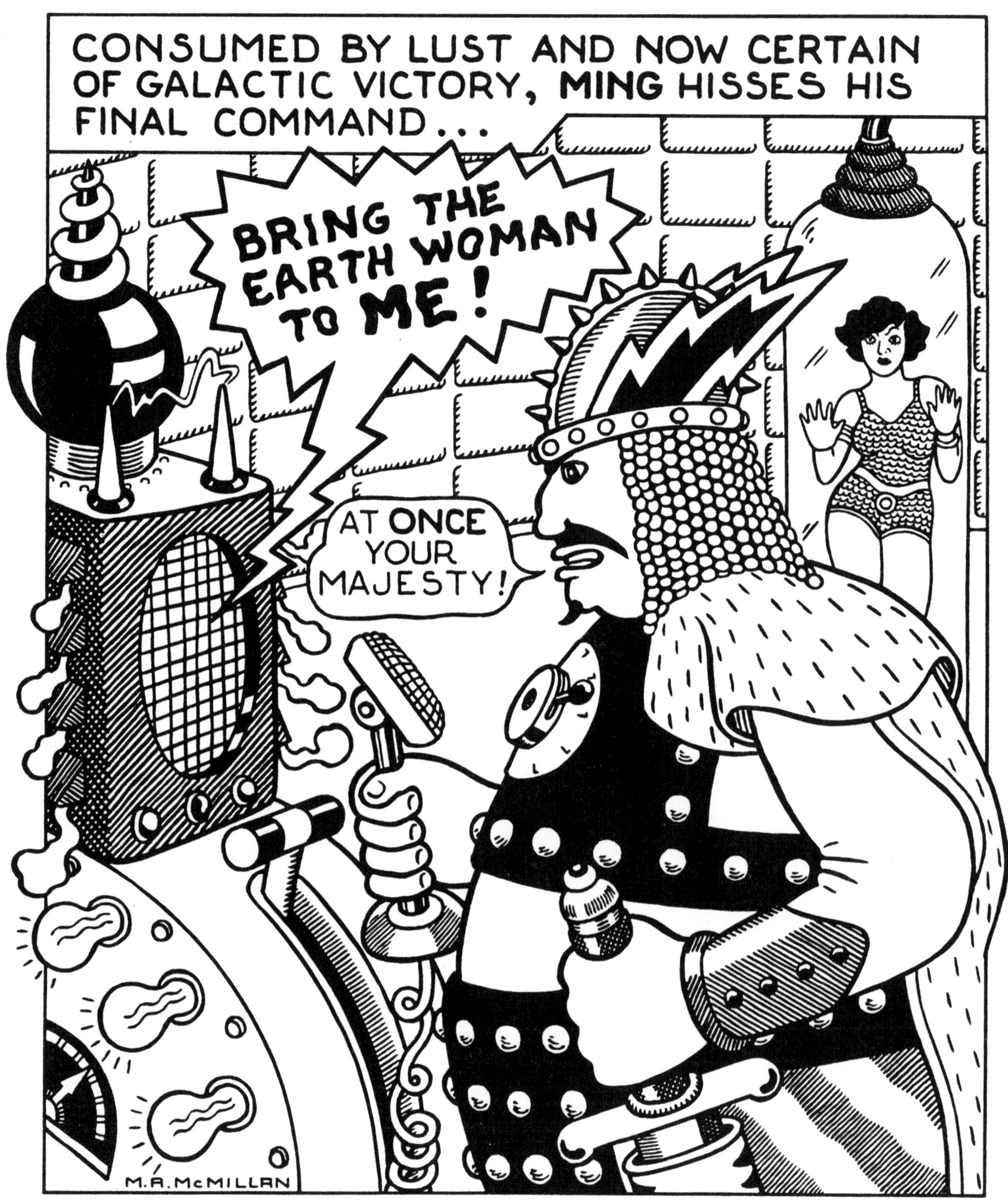
CONSUMED BY LUST AND NOW CERTAIN OF GALACTIC VICTORY, MING HISSES HIS FINAL COMMAND...
BRING THE EARTH WOMAN TO ME!
AT ONCE YOUR MAJESTY!
M.A. McMILLAN

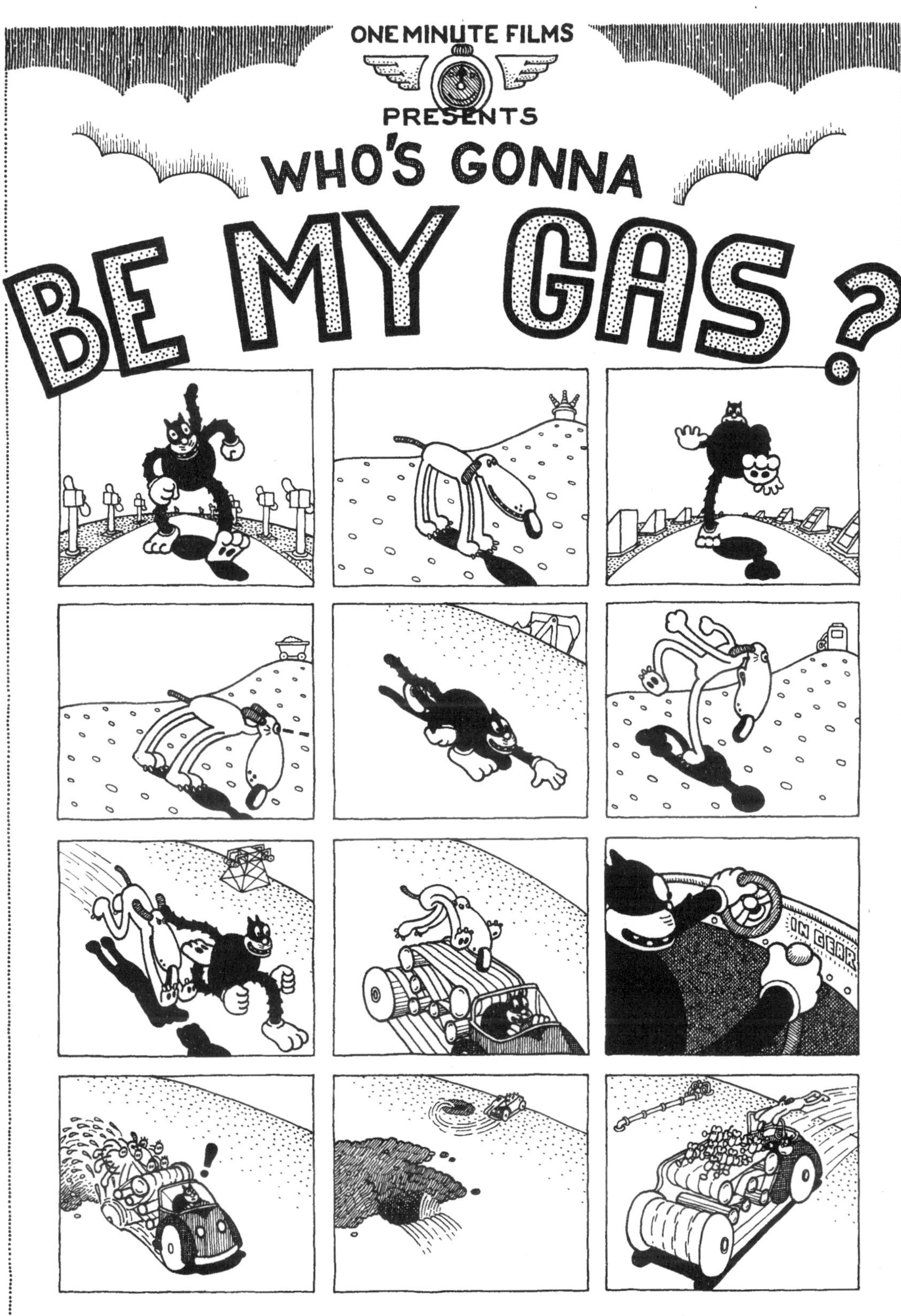

K.O. KITTY attempts to beat the gas crunch by exploiting the basic instincts of R. MUTT JR. The over-zealous MUTT causes the "Doggie-Wagon" to submerge where those aggressive little rodents THE BROTHERS RATTUS become "gas" uncontrollable.

AND SO IT GOES!

DESIGN AND ANIMATION BY Michael McMillan and Diane Balter
MUSIC BY Bob Armstrong and Al Dodge

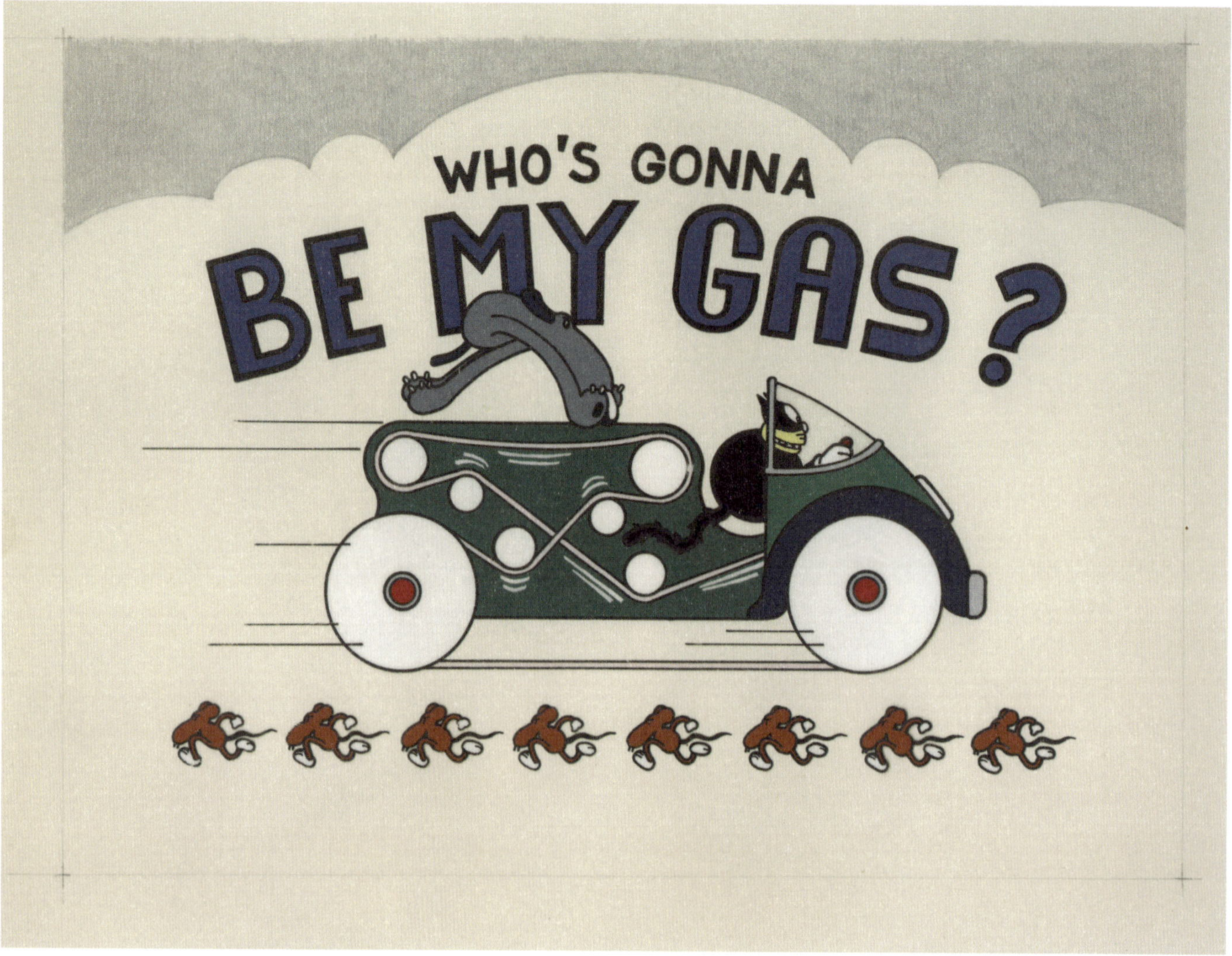

WHO'S GONNA

BE MY GAS?

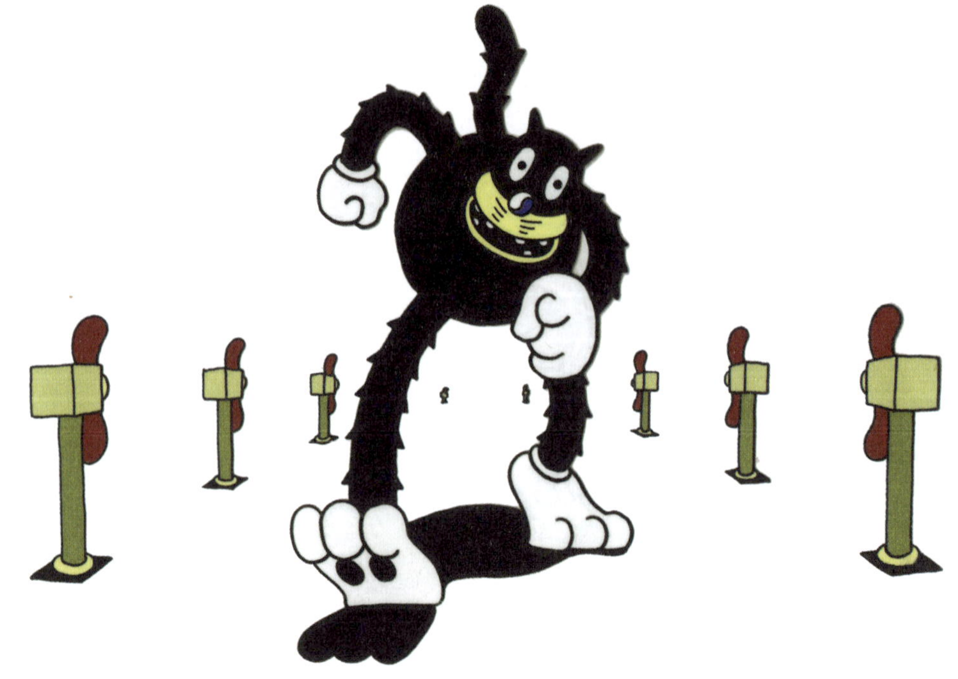

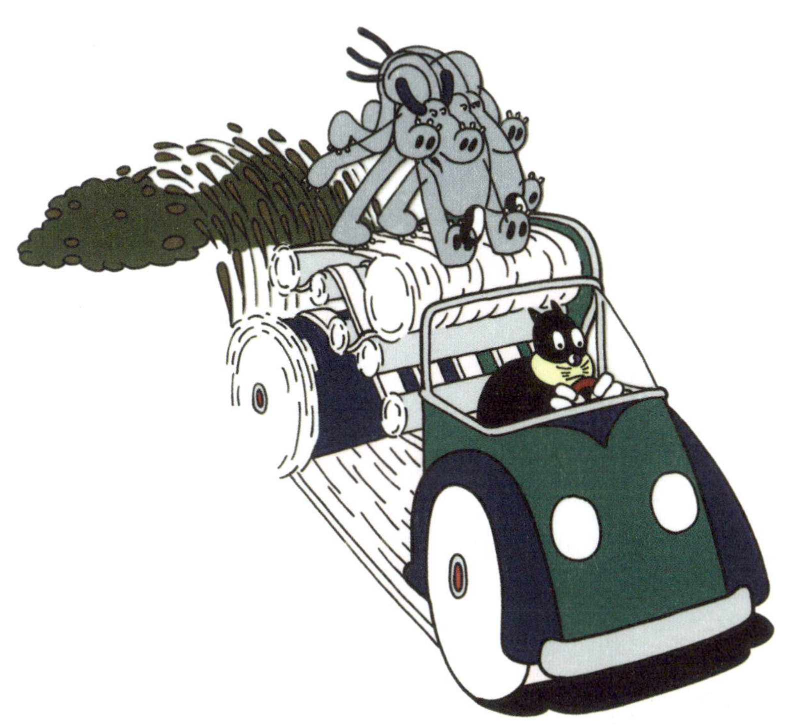

Be My Gas *was a self-produced animated film inspired by the simplistic early Disney and Fleischer productions. It received some attention at the 1980 Ottawa International Animation Festival which resulted in wider distribution.*

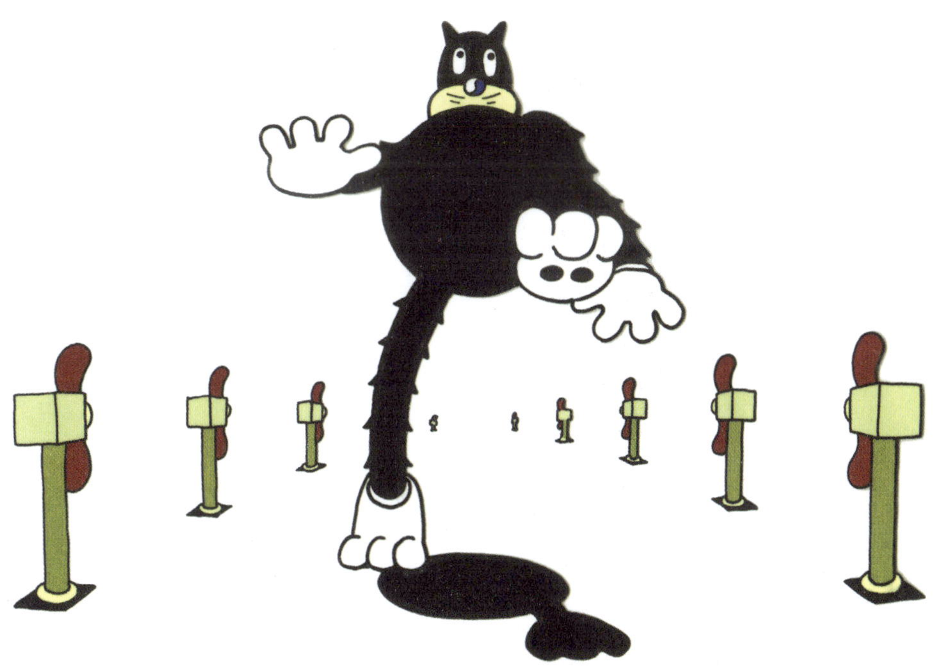

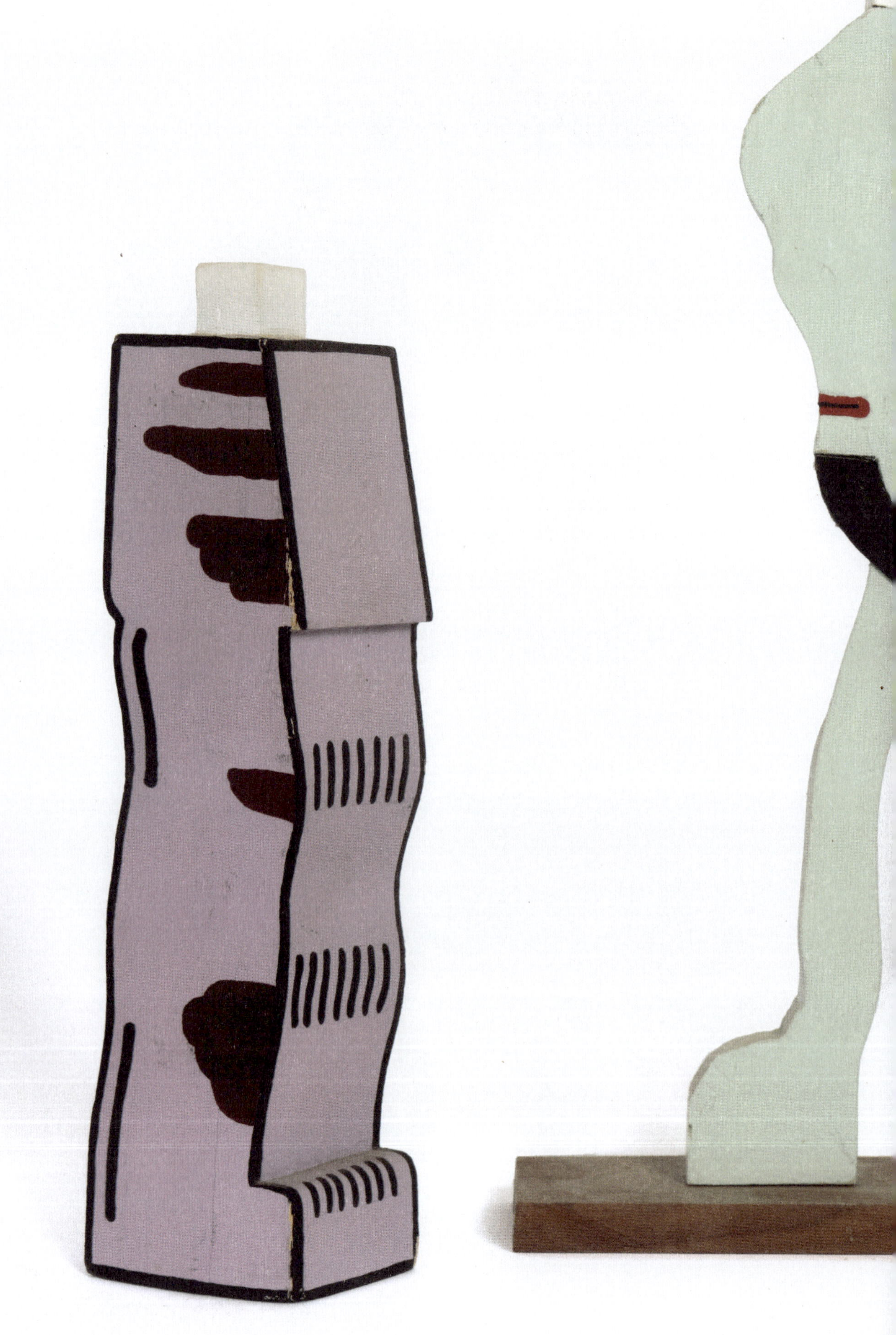

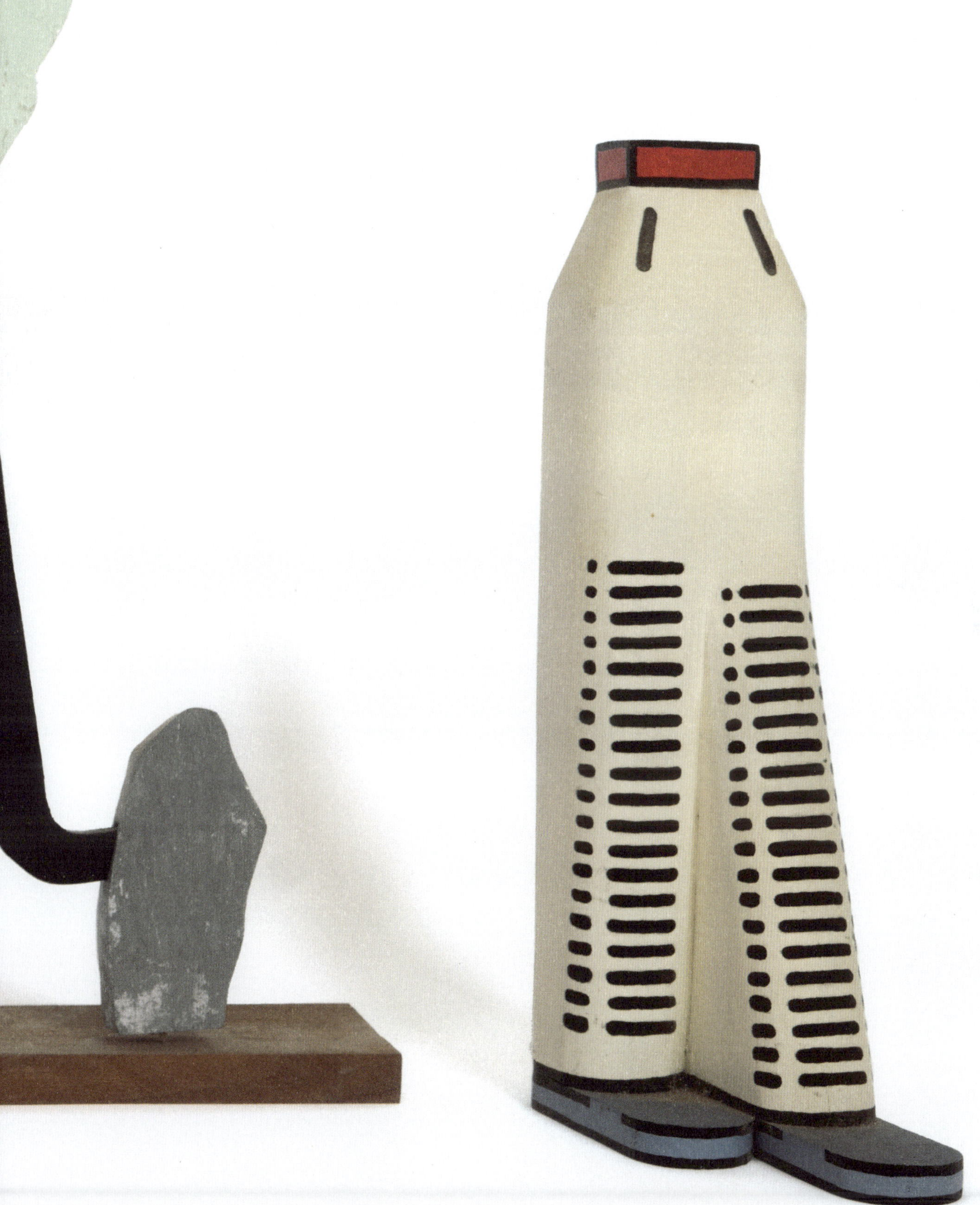

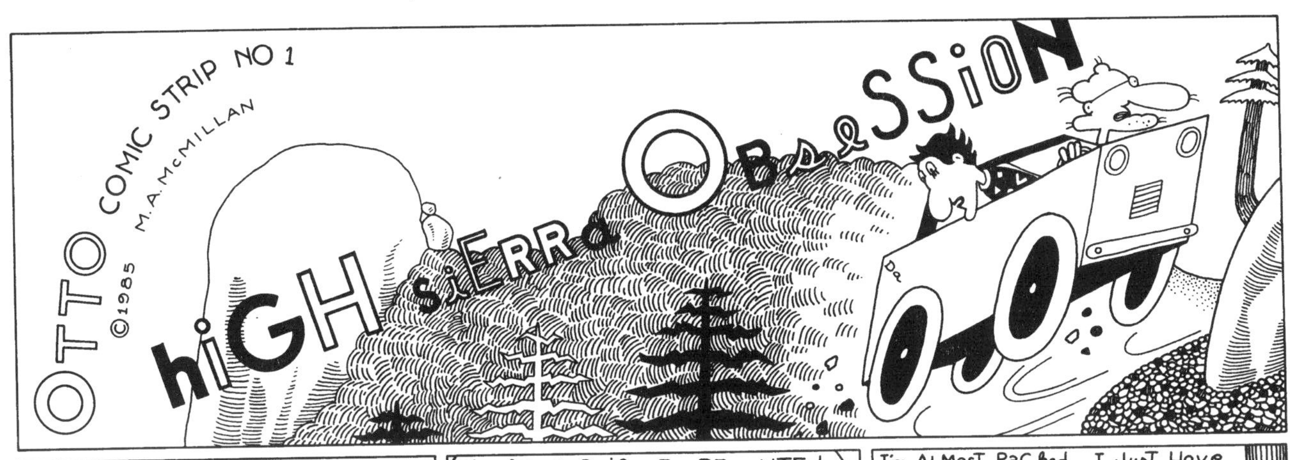
OTTO COMIC STRIP NO 1
©1985 M.A.McMILLAN
hiGH siERRa OBsessioN

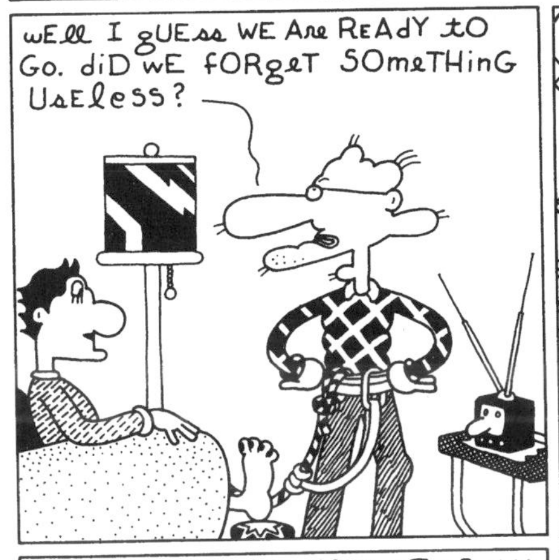
wELL I gUEss WE ARe READY to Go. diD wE fORget SOmeTHinG UsELess?

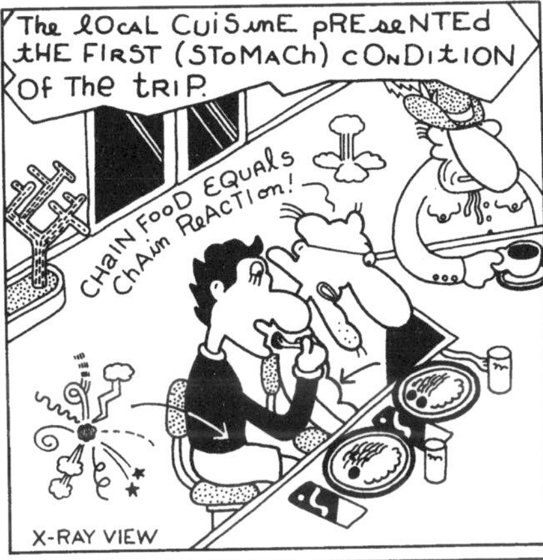
The LOcaL CUiSine PRESENTED THE FIRST (STOMACH) CONDITION OF The tRIP.
CHAIN FOOD EQUALS CHAIN REACTION!
X-RAY VIEW

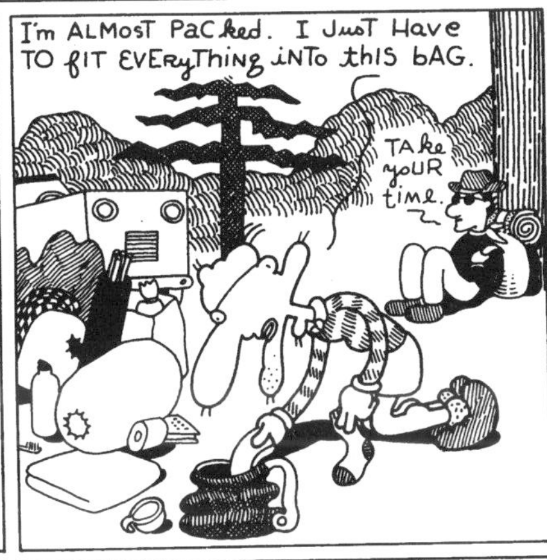
I'm ALMOST PacKed. I JUST Have TO fit EVERyThing iNTo this bAG.
Take YOUR time.

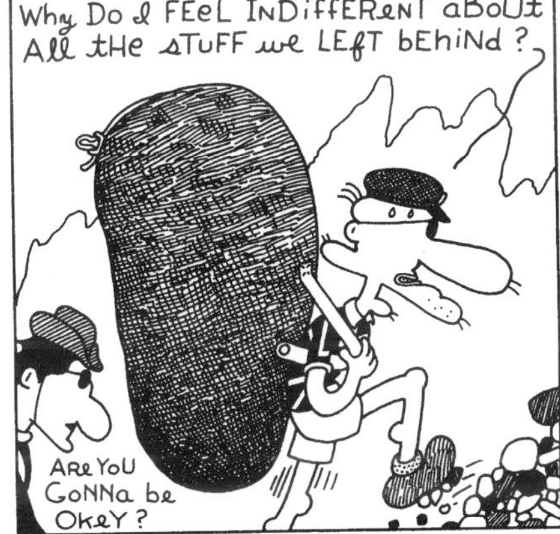
Why Do I FEEL INDIFFERENT aBOUT ALL tHe stUFF we LEFT bEhiND?
ARe YOU GONNa be OKeY?

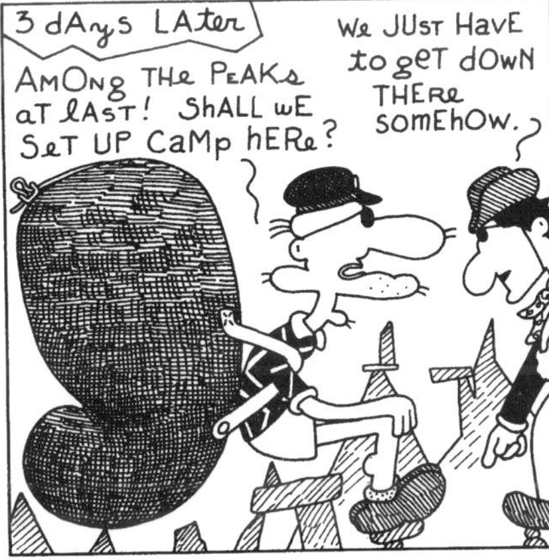
3 dAys LAter
AMONG THe PEAKs aT LAST! SHALL wE SET UP CaMp hERe?
We JUST HAVE to get dOWN THERe SOMEhOW.

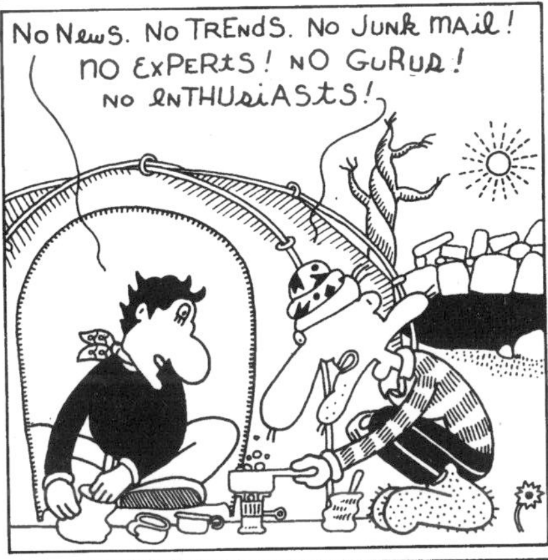
No News. No TRENDS. No JUNK MAIL!
NO EXPERTS! NO GURUS!
NO ENTHUSIASTS!

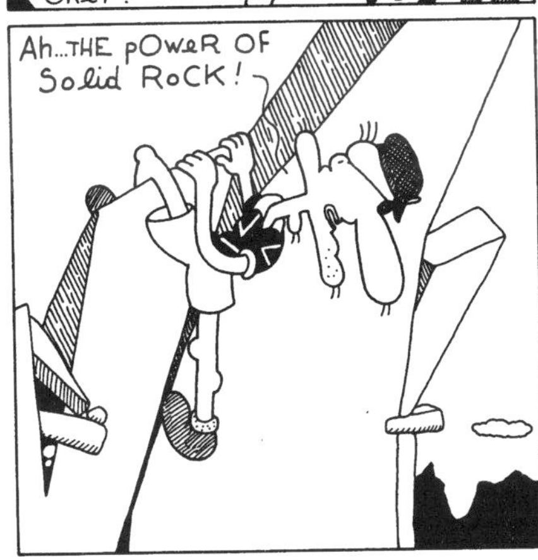
Ah...THE pOWeR OF Solid RoCK!

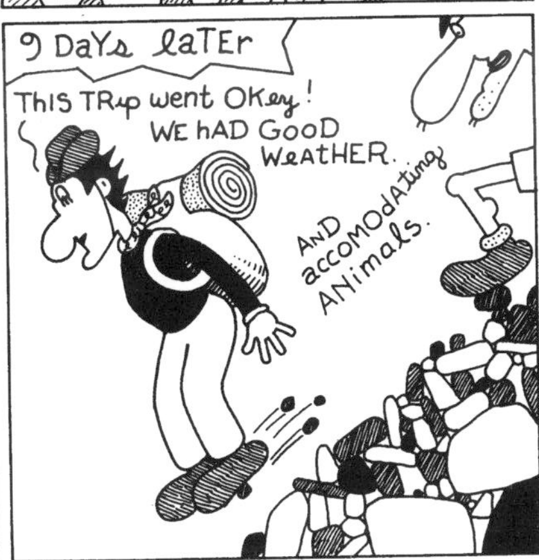
9 DAYs LaTer
THIS TRip went OKey! WE hAD GOOD WeatHER.
AND accomODating ANimals.

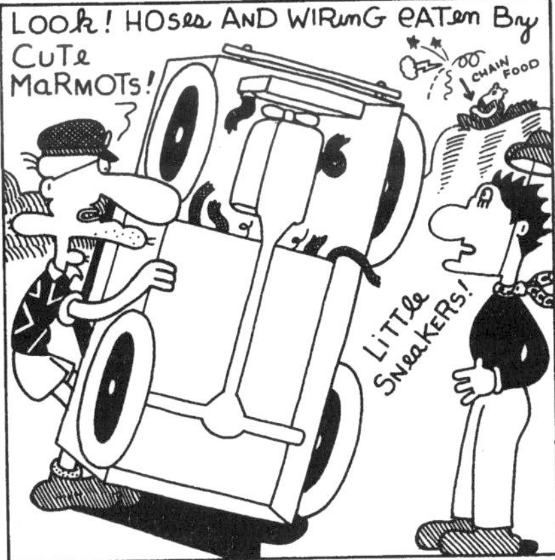
LOOK! HOSes AND WIRinG EATen By CUTe MaRMOTS!
CHAIN FOOD
LITTLe SNeaKERS!

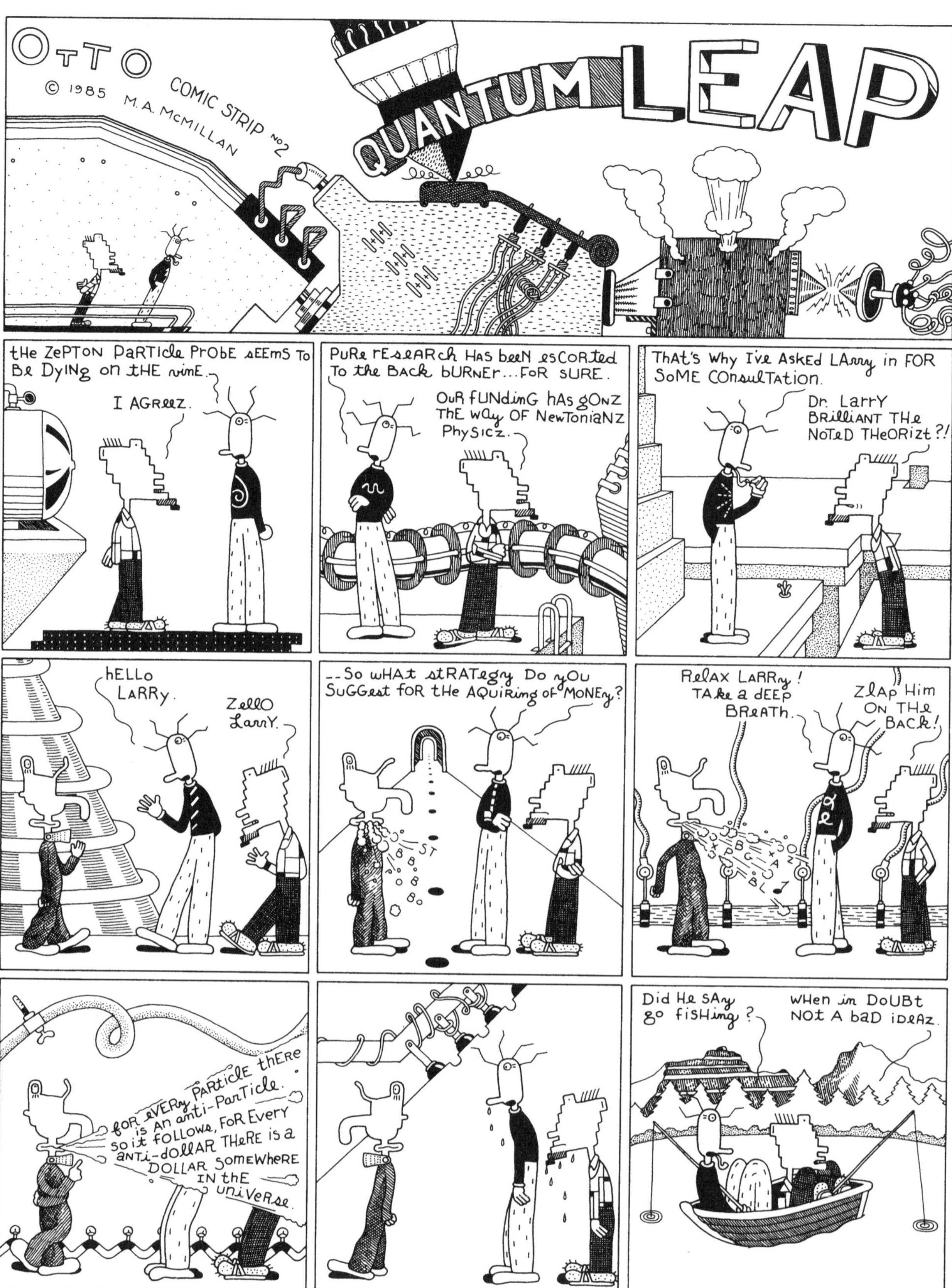
OTTO
COMIC STRIP No 2
© 1985 M.A. McMILLAN
QUANTUM LEAP
THE ZEPTON PARTICLE PROBE SEEMS TO BE DYING ON THE VINE.
I AGREEZ.
PURE RESEARCH HAS BEEN ESCORTED TO THE BACK BURNER... FOR SURE.
OUR FUNDING HAS GONZ THE WAY OF NEWTONIANZ PHYSICZ.
THAT'S WHY I'VE ASKED LARRY IN FOR SOME CONSULTATION.
DR. LARRY BRILLIANT THE NOTED THEORIZT?!
HELLO LARRY.
ZELLO LARRY.
--SO WHAT STRATEGY DO YOU SUGGEST FOR THE AQUIRING OF MONEY?
RELAX LARRY! TAKE A DEEP BREATH.
ZLAP HIM ON THE BACK!
FOR EVERY PARTICLE THERE IS AN ANTI-PARTICLE. SO IT FOLLOWS, FOR EVERY ANTI-DOLLAR THERE IS A DOLLAR SOMEWHERE IN THE UNIVERSE.
DID HE SAY GO FISHING?
WHEN IN DOUBT NOT A BAD IDEAZ.

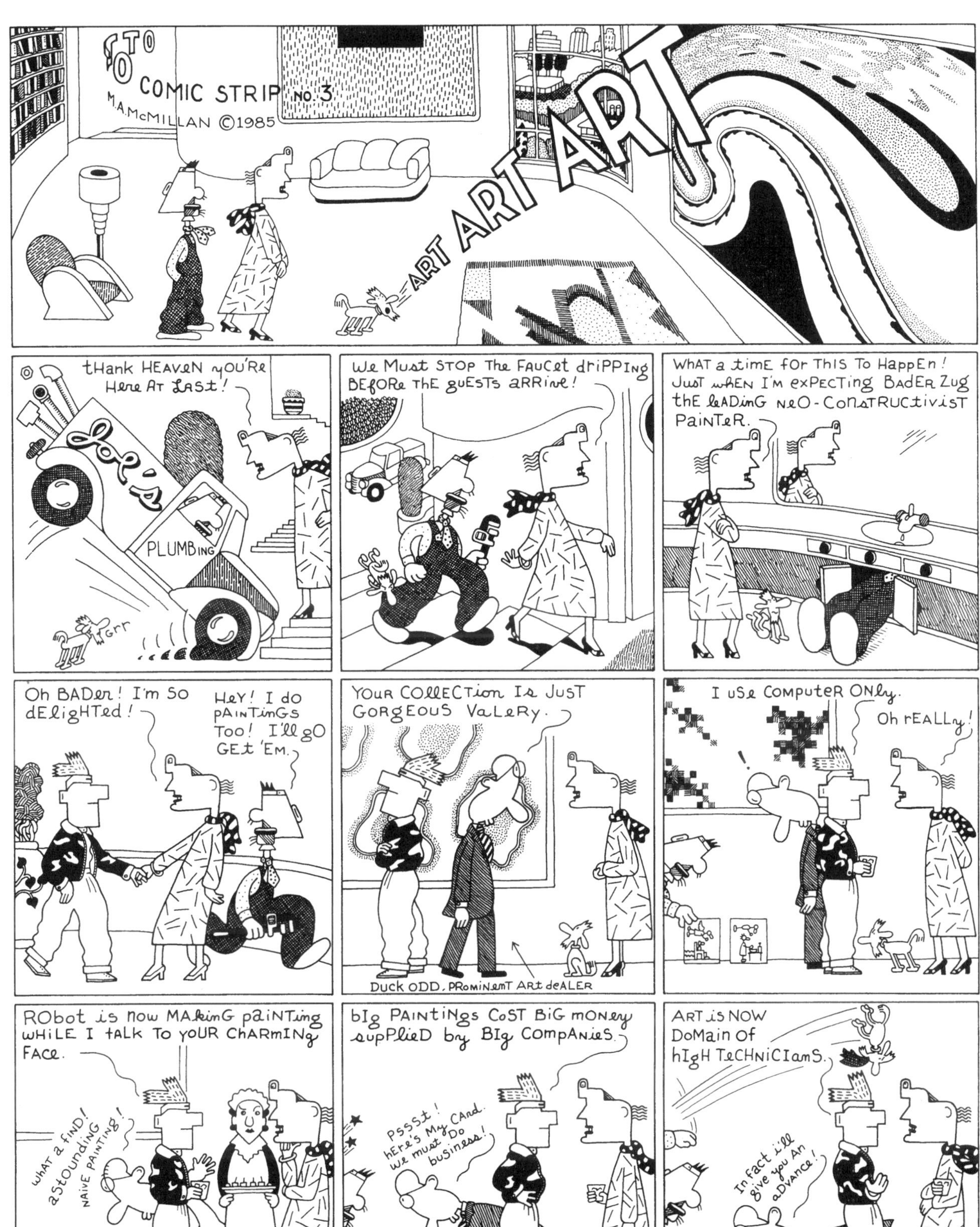

SOTO COMIC STRIP NO.3
M.A.McMILLAN ©1985
ART ART ART ART
tHank HEAVEN yOU'RE Here AT Last!
PLUMBing
Grr
We Must STOP The FAUCet dripping BEfORe THE guests arrive!
WHAT a time fOr THIS TO HappEn! Just when I'M expecting BadEr Zug the leading neO-ConstRUCtivist PainTeR.
Oh BADer! I'm SO dElighted!
HeY! I do paintings Too! I'll gO GEt 'EM.
YOUR COLLECTion Is JUST GORGEOUS VaLeRy.
DUCK ODD, PROminent ARt deALER
I use COMPUTER ONly.
Oh rEALLy!
ROBot is now MAking painting wHILE I tALK TO YOUR ChARMING FACE.
WHAT a FIND! astounding NAIVE PAINTING!
bIg PAINTINGs CoST BIG money supplieD by BIg COMPANIES.
Pssst! hEre's My CArd. We must Do business!
ART is NOW DoMain Of hIgH TeCHNICIamS.
In fact i'll give you An aDVance!

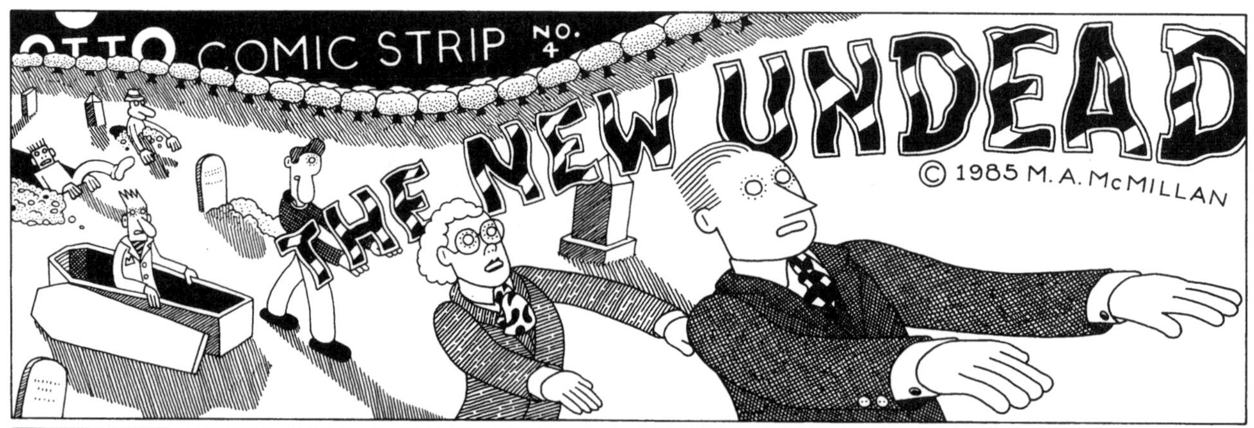
OTTO COMIC STRIP NO. 4
THE NEW UNDEAD
© 1985 M. A. McMILLAN

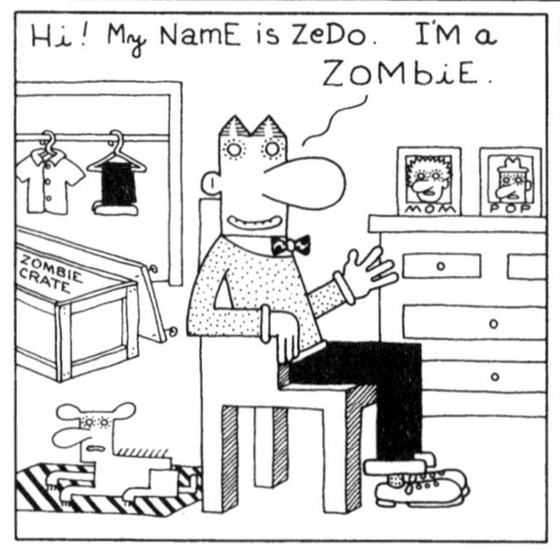
Hi! My NamE is ZeDo. I'M a ZOMbiE.
ZOMBIE CRATE
MOM
POP

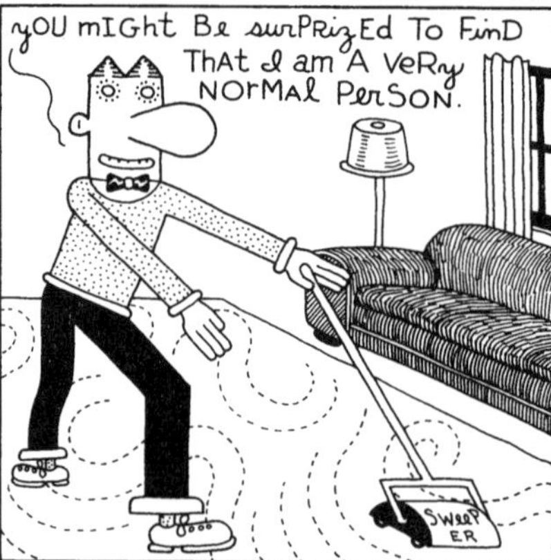
YOU mIGht Be surPRizEd TO FinD ThAt I am A VeRy NORMAl PerSON.
SWEEPER

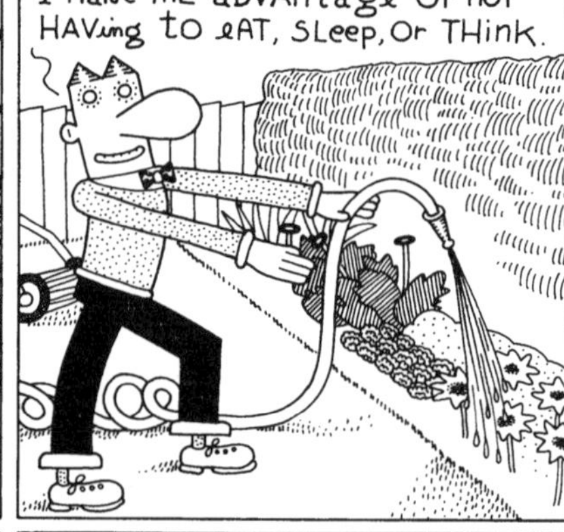
I Have ThE aDvAntage Of noT HAVing to eAT, SLeep, Or THink.

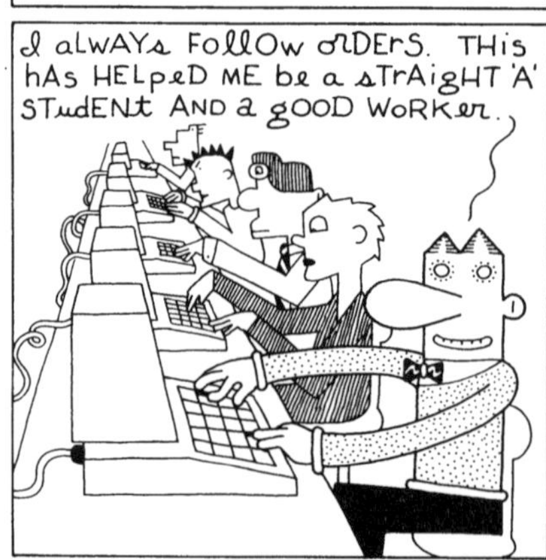
I alWAYs FOllOw oRDErS. THis hAs HELPeD ME be a sTrAighT 'A' STudENt AND a gOOD WorKer.

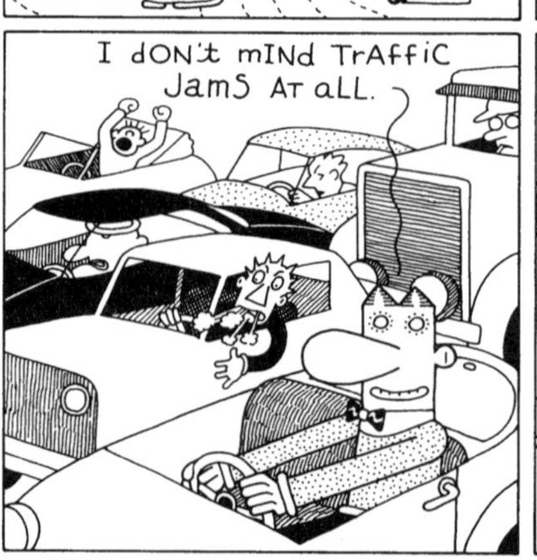
I dON't mINd TrAffiC Jams At aLL.

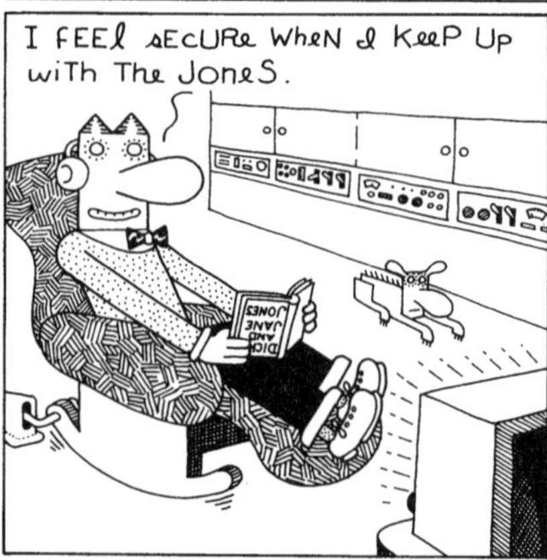
I FEEl sECURe WheN I KeeP Up with The JoneS.
DICK JANE JONES

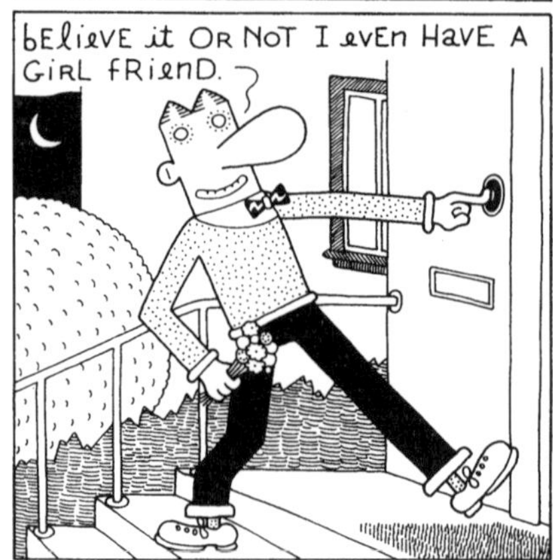
bElieVE it OR NoT I even HAVE A GIRL fRienD.

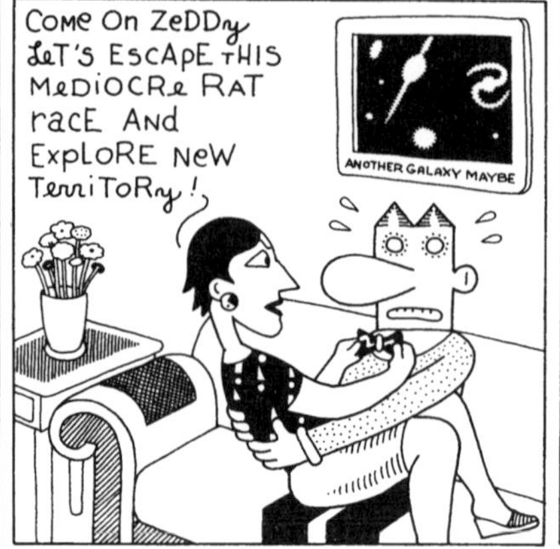
Come On ZeDDy LeT'S ESCAPE THIS MeDIOCRe RAT racE AND ExploRE New TerriToRy!
ANOTHER GALAXY MAYBE

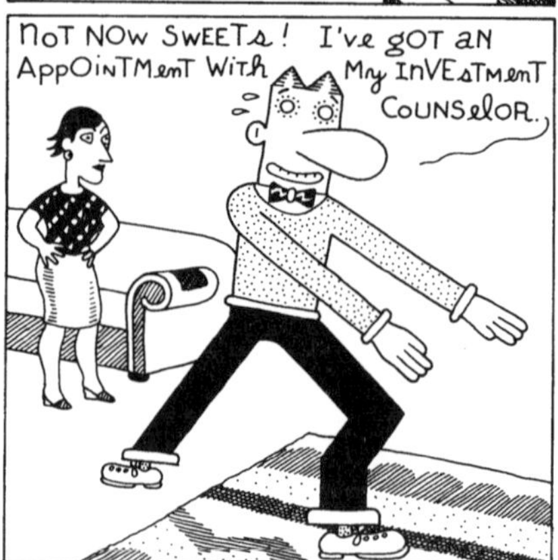
NoT NOW SWEETs! I've gOT aN AppOinTMenT With My InVEsTMenT COUNSelOR.

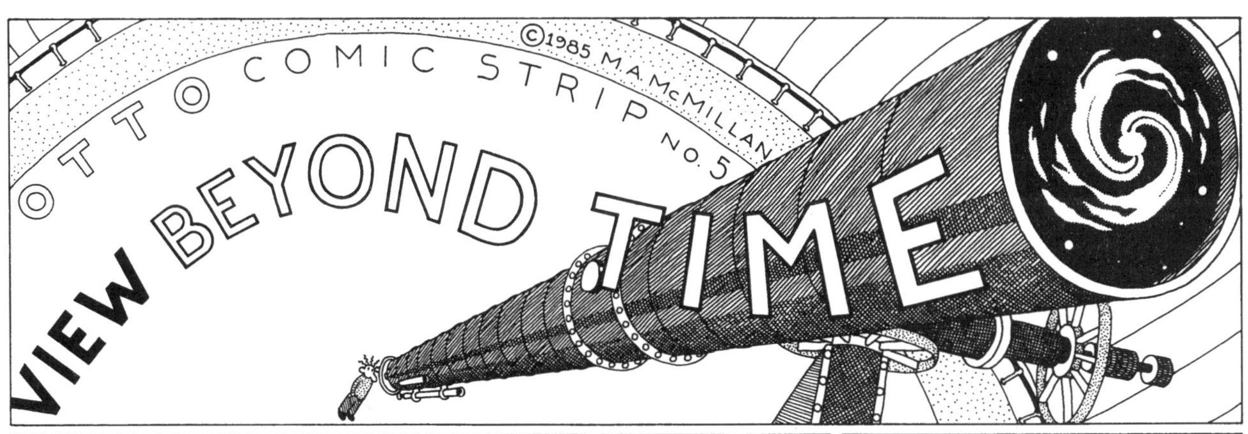
©1985 M.A. McMILLAN
OTTO COMIC STRIP No. 5
VIEW BEYOND TIME

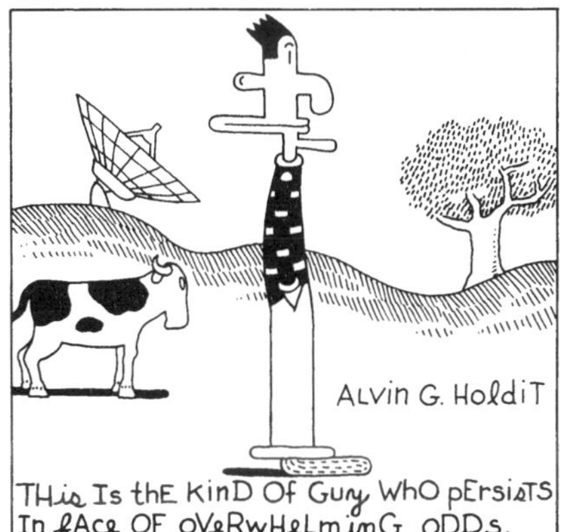
ALVIN G. HOLDIT
THIS IS THE KIND OF GUY WHO PERSISTS IN FACE OF OVERWHELMING ODDS.

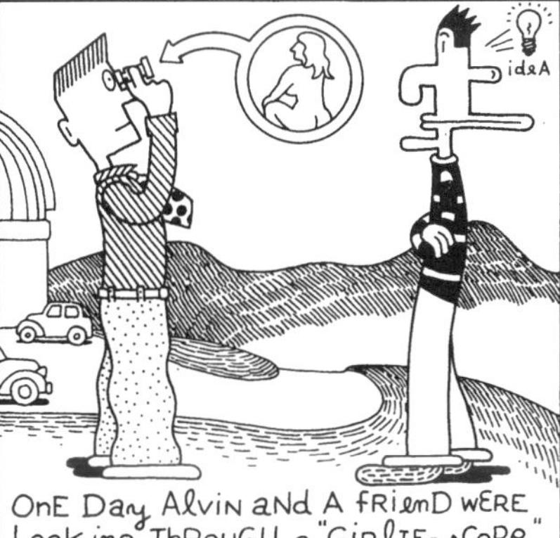
IDEA
ONE DAY ALVIN AND A FRIEND WERE LOOKING THROUGH A "GIRLIE-SCOPE."

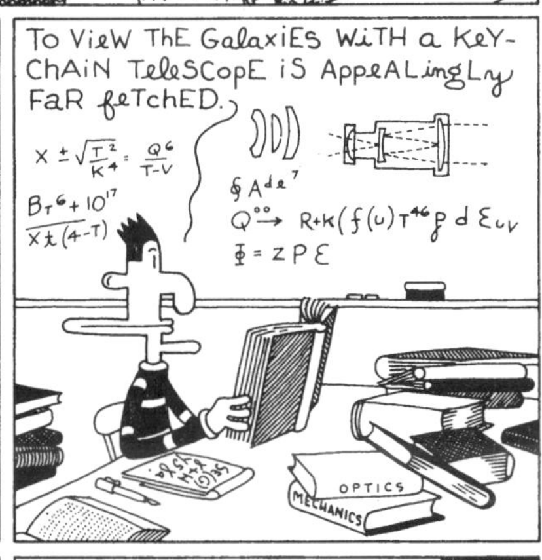
TO VIEW THE GALAXIES WITH A KEY-CHAIN TELESCOPE IS APPEALINGLY FAR FETCHED.
OPTICS
MECHANICS

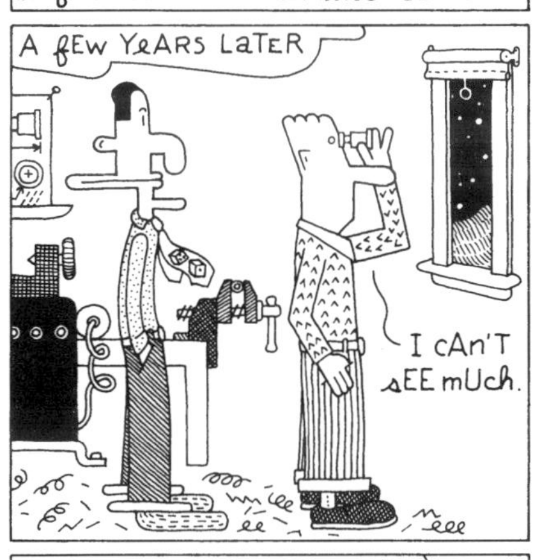
A FEW YEARS LATER
I CAN'T SEE MUCH.

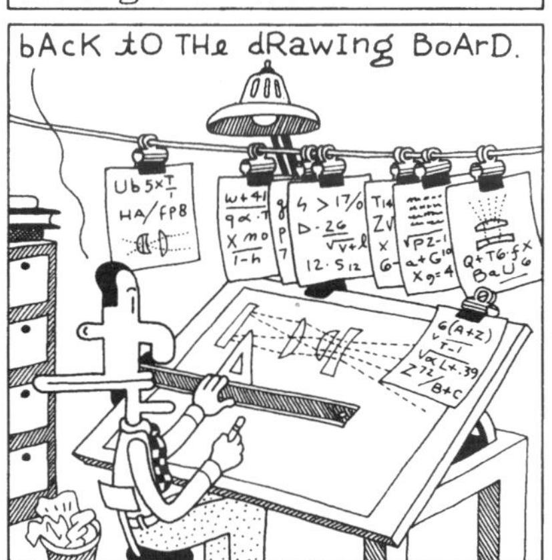
BACK TO THE DRAWING BOARD.

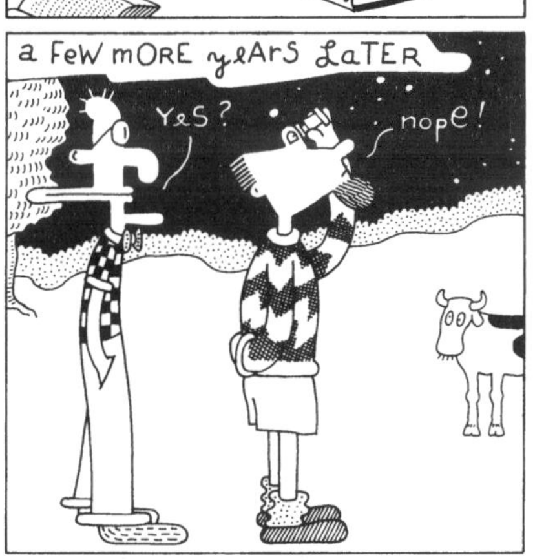
A FEW MORE YEARS LATER
YES?
NOPE!

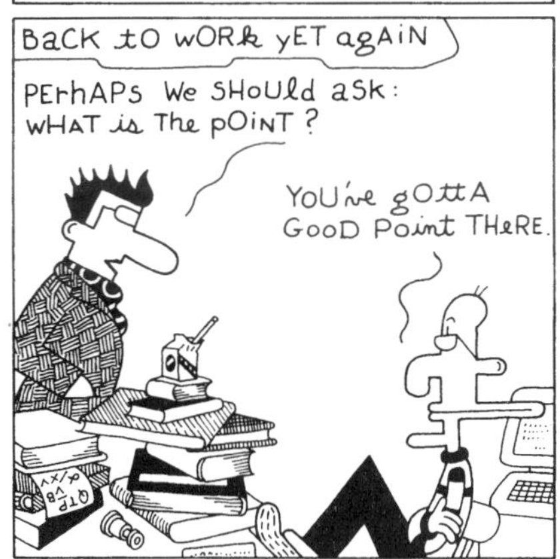
BACK TO WORK YET AGAIN
PERHAPS WE SHOULD ASK: WHAT IS THE POINT?
YOU'VE GOTTA GOOD POINT THERE.

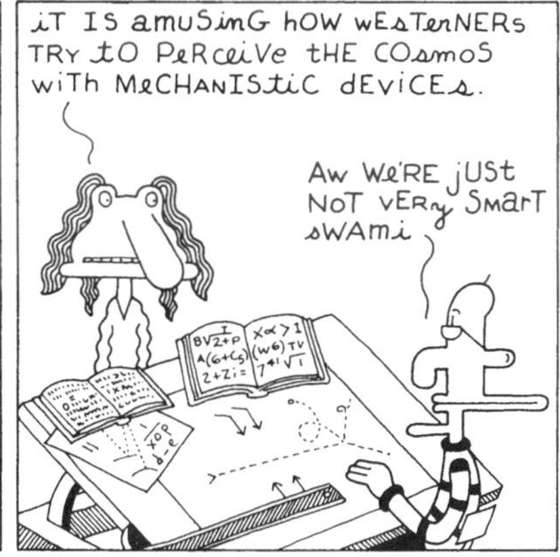
IT IS AMUSING HOW WESTERNERS TRY TO PERCEIVE THE COSMOS WITH MECHANISTIC DEVICES.
AW WE'RE JUST NOT VERY SMART SWAMI

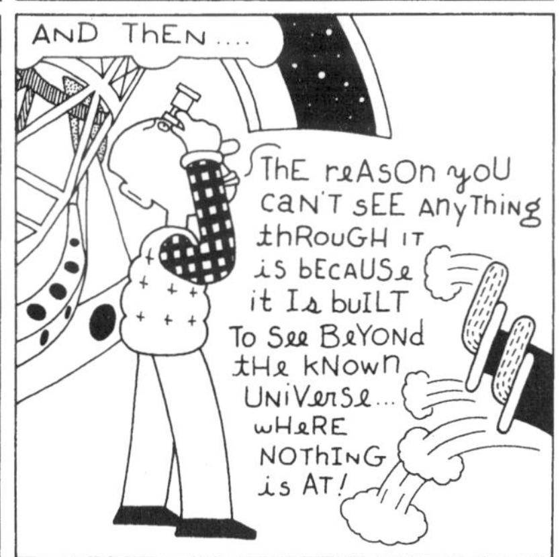
AND THEN....
THE REASON YOU CAN'T SEE ANYTHING THROUGH IT IS BECAUSE IT IS BUILT TO SEE BEYOND THE KNOWN UNIVERSE... WHERE NOTHING IS AT!

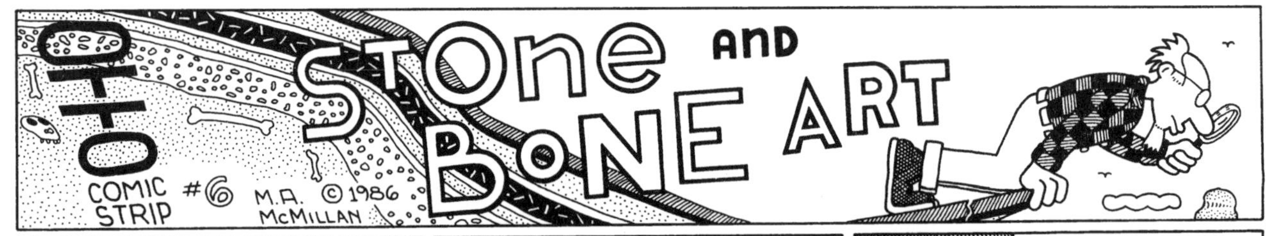
OTTO
STONE AND BONE ART
COMIC STRIP #6
M.A. McMILLAN
©1986

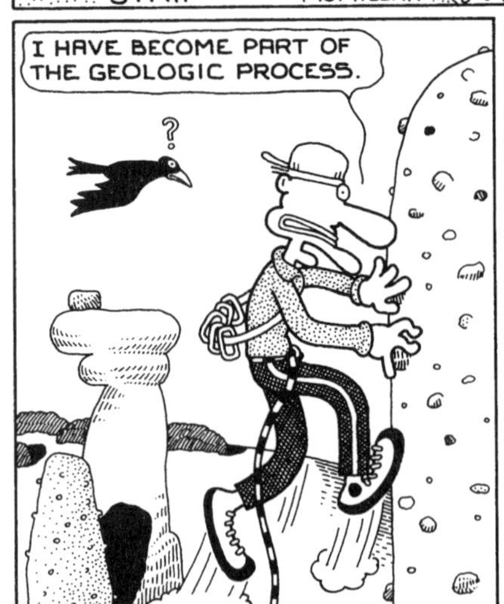
I HAVE BECOME PART OF THE GEOLOGIC PROCESS.
?

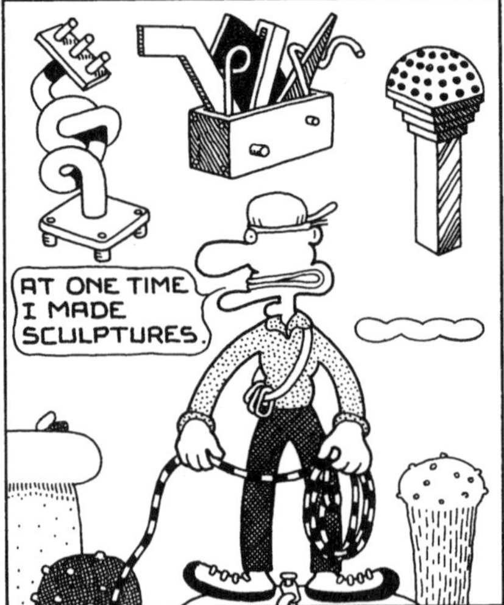
AT ONE TIME I MADE SCULPTURES.

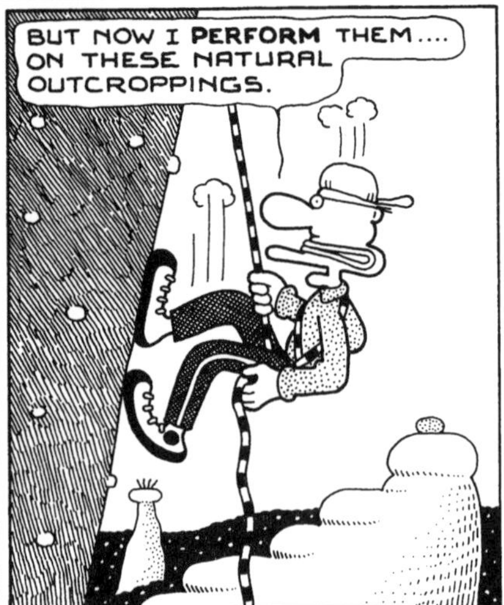
BUT NOW I **PERFORM** THEM.... ON THESE NATURAL OUTCROPPINGS.

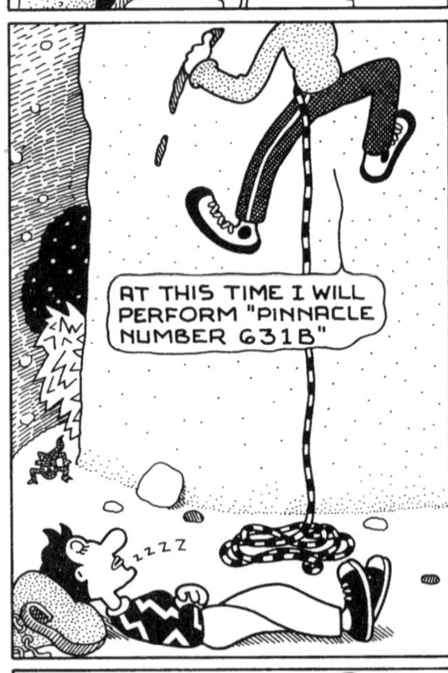
AT THIS TIME I WILL PERFORM "PINNACLE NUMBER 631B"
ZZZZ

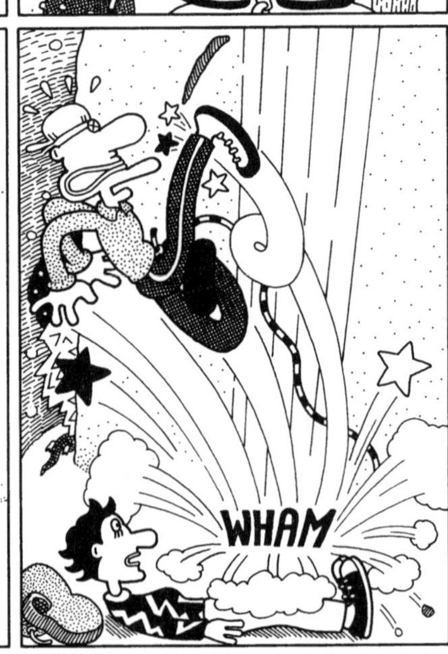
WHAM

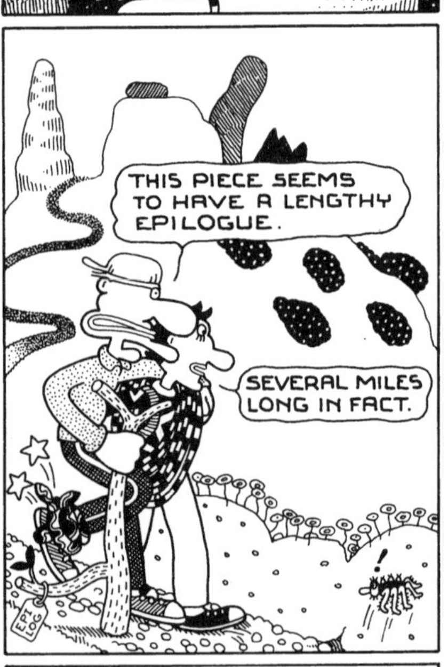
THIS PIECE SEEMS TO HAVE A LENGTHY EPILOGUE.
SEVERAL MILES LONG IN FACT.
!

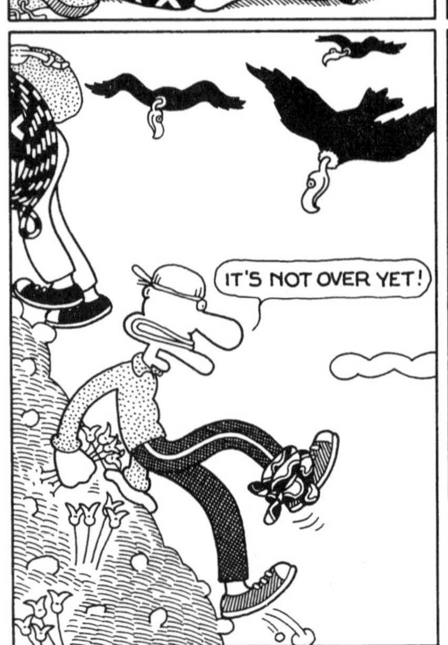
IT'S NOT OVER YET!

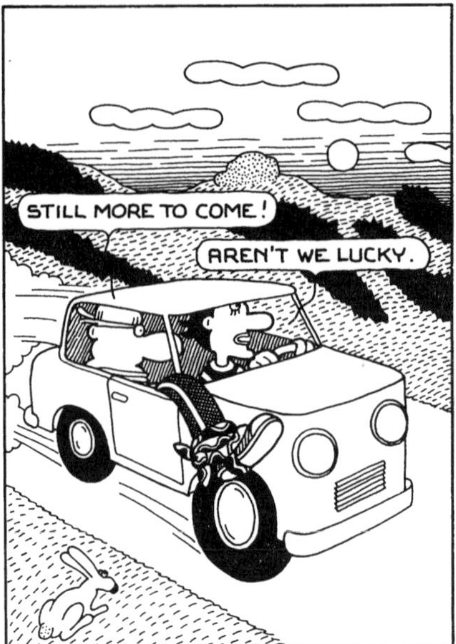
STILL MORE TO COME!
AREN'T WE LUCKY.

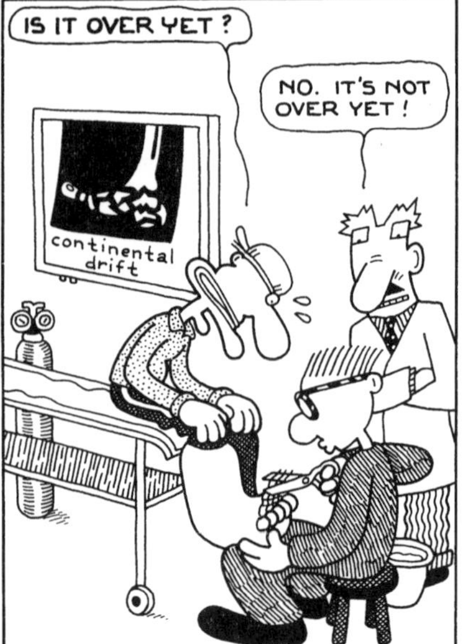
IS IT OVER YET?
NO. IT'S NOT OVER YET!
continental drift

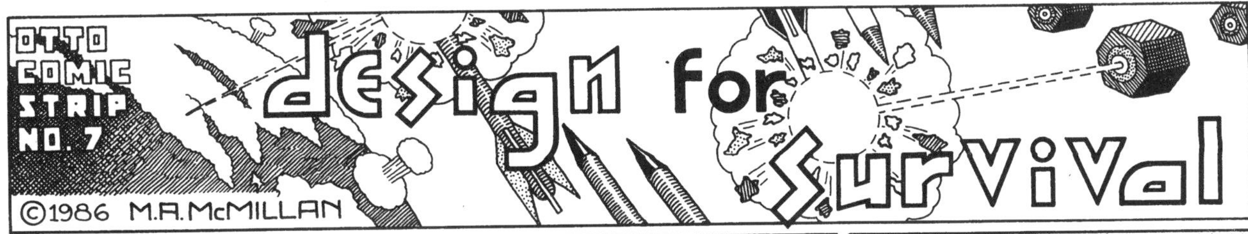
OTTO COMIC STRIP NO. 7
design for Survival
©1986 M.A. McMILLAN

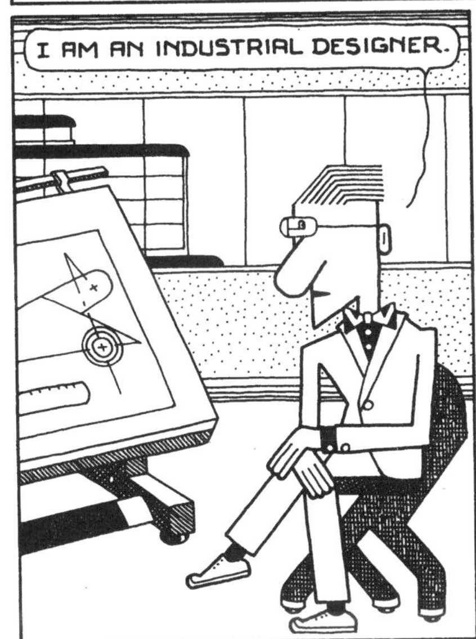
I AM AN INDUSTRIAL DESIGNER.

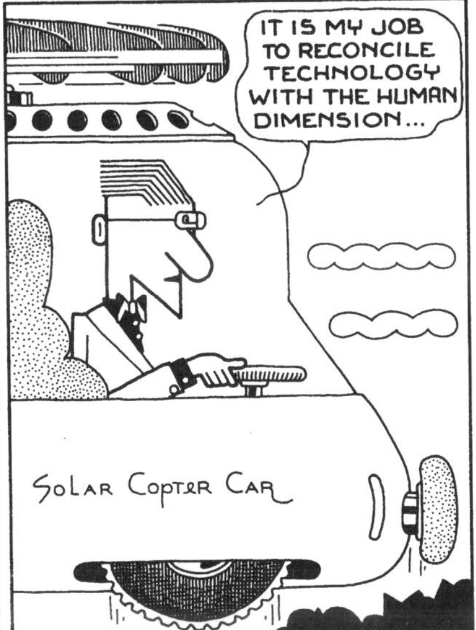
IT IS MY JOB TO RECONCILE TECHNOLOGY WITH THE HUMAN DIMENSION...
SoLAR Copter CaR

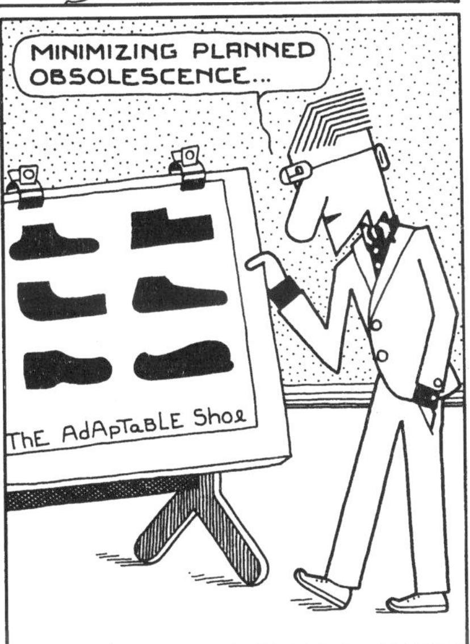
MINIMIZING PLANNED OBSOLESCENCE...
THE AdApTaBLE Shoe

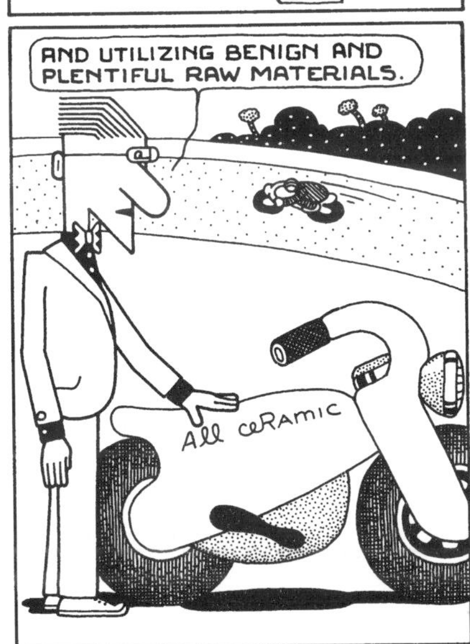
AND UTILIZING BENIGN AND PLENTIFUL RAW MATERIALS.
All ceRamic

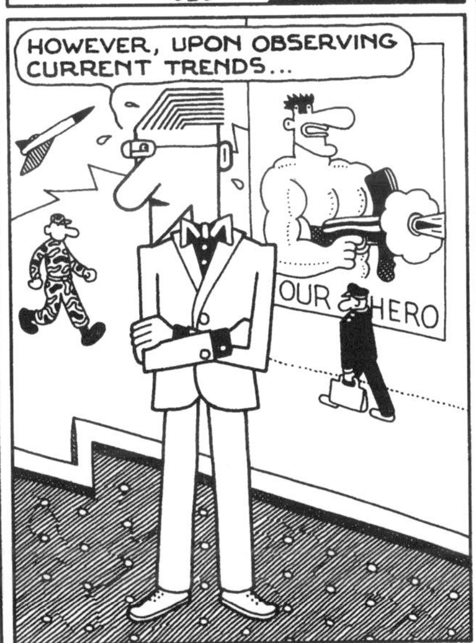
HOWEVER, UPON OBSERVING CURRENT TRENDS...
OUR HERO

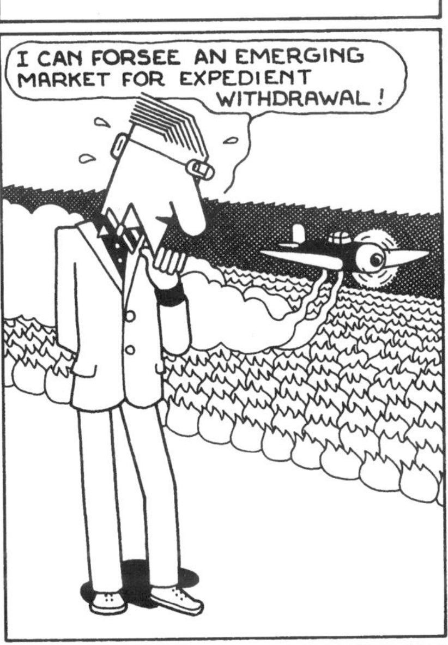
I CAN FORSEE AN EMERGING MARKET FOR EXPEDIENT WITHDRAWAL!

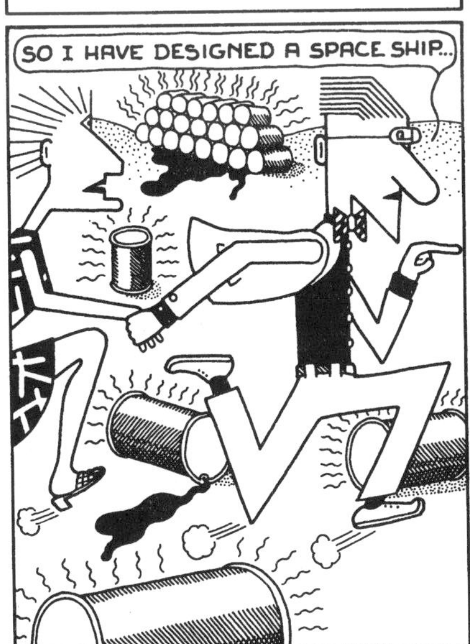
SO I HAVE DESIGNED A SPACE SHIP...

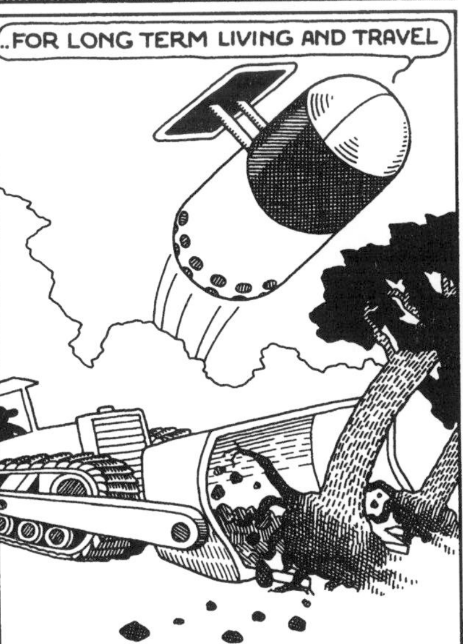
..FOR LONG TERM LIVING AND TRAVEL

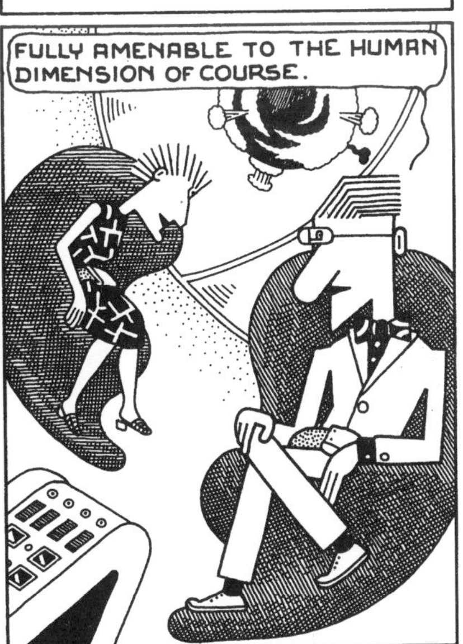
FULLY AMENABLE TO THE HUMAN DIMENSION OF COURSE.

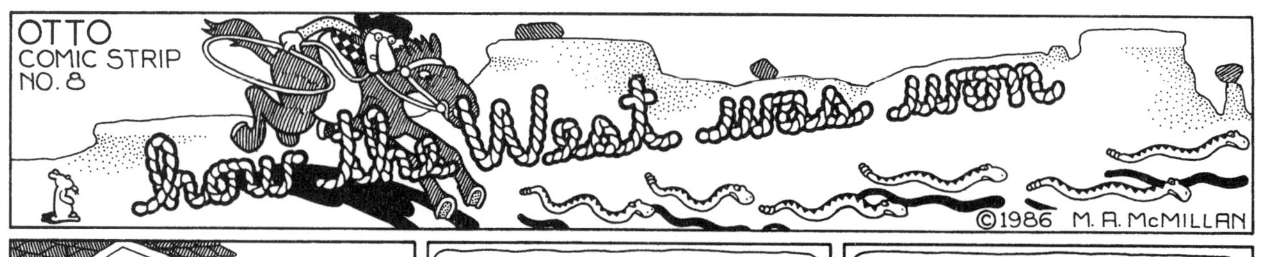
OTTO
COMIC STRIP
NO. 8
how the West was won
©1986 M. A. McMILLAN

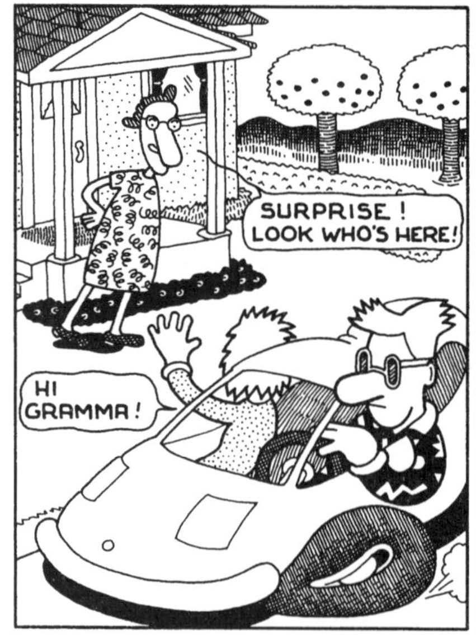
SURPRISE! LOOK WHO'S HERE!
HI GRAMMA!

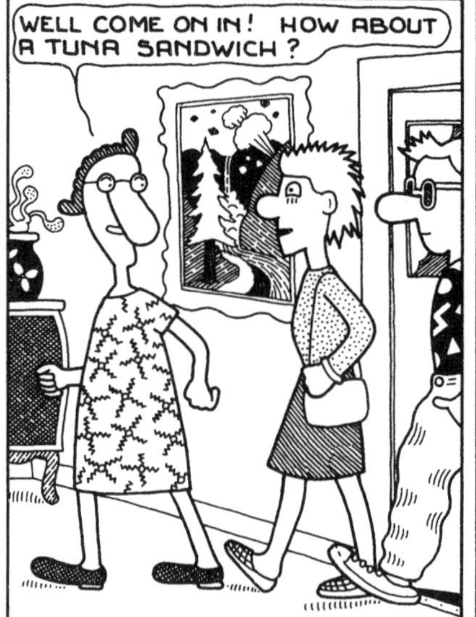
WELL COME ON IN! HOW ABOUT A TUNA SANDWICH?

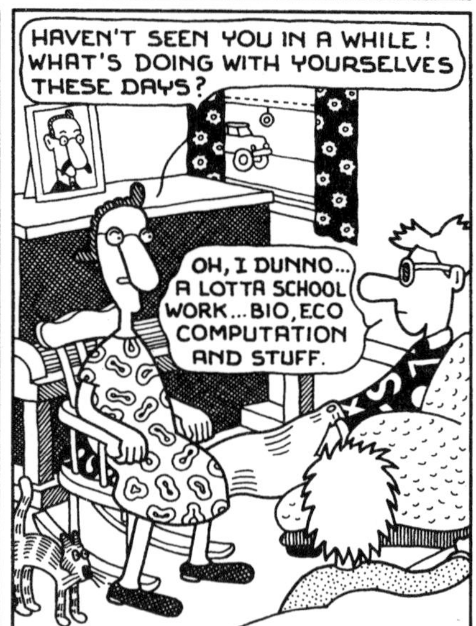
HAVEN'T SEEN YOU IN A WHILE! WHAT'S DOING WITH YOURSELVES THESE DAYS?
OH, I DUNNO... A LOTTA SCHOOL WORK... BIO, ECO COMPUTATION AND STUFF.

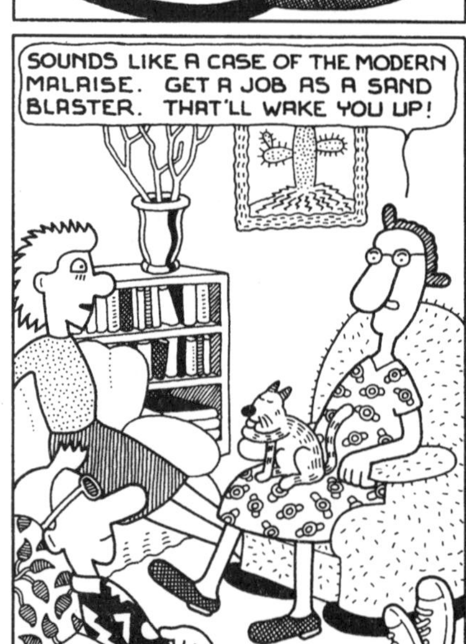
SOUNDS LIKE A CASE OF THE MODERN MALAISE. GET A JOB AS A SAND BLASTER. THAT'LL WAKE YOU UP!

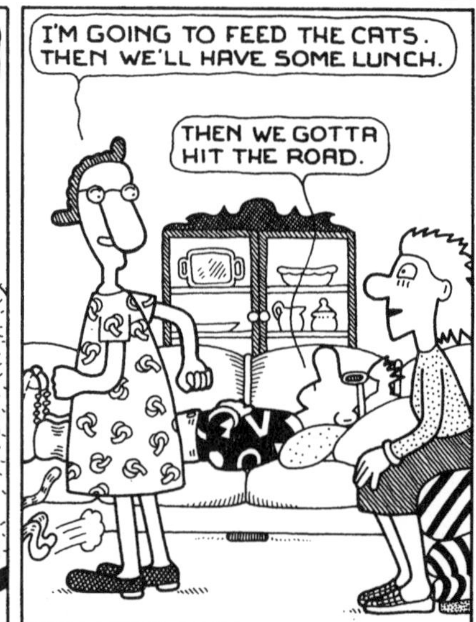
I'M GOING TO FEED THE CATS. THEN WE'LL HAVE SOME LUNCH.
THEN WE GOTTA HIT THE ROAD.

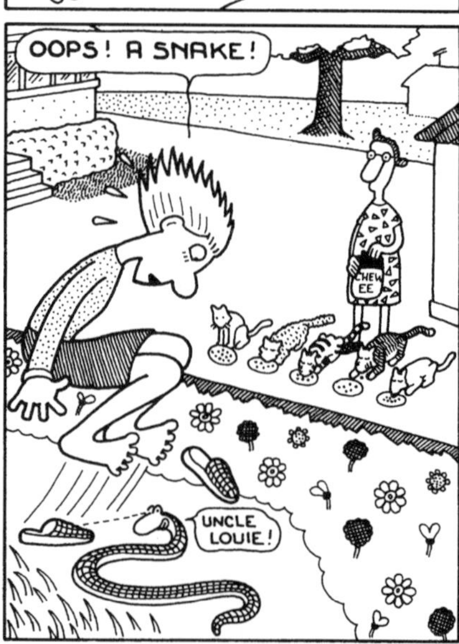
OOPS! A SNAKE!
CHEW EE
UNCLE LOUIE!

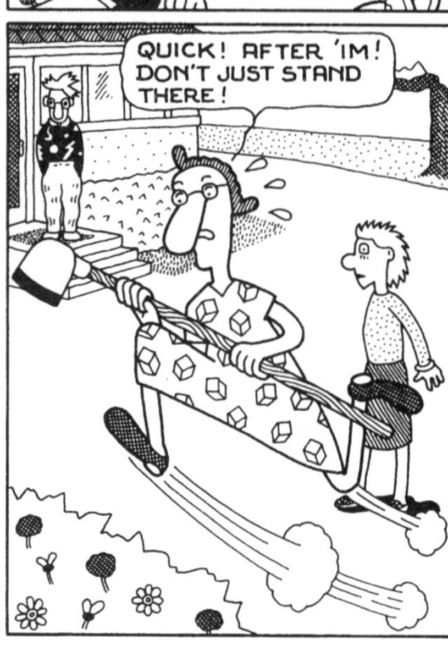
QUICK! AFTER 'IM! DON'T JUST STAND THERE!

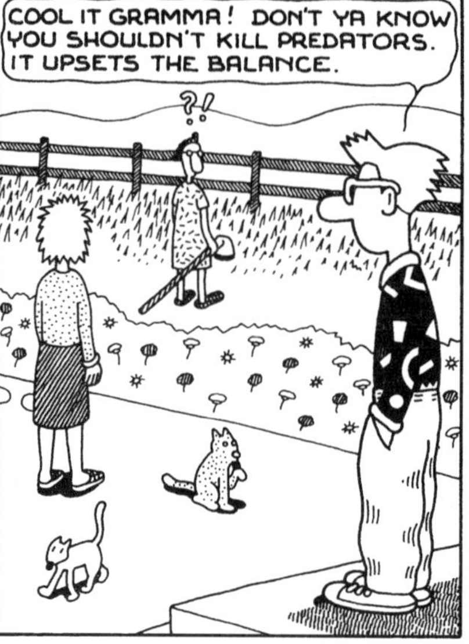
COOL IT GRAMMA! DON'T YA KNOW YOU SHOULDN'T KILL PREDATORS. IT UPSETS THE BALANCE.
?!

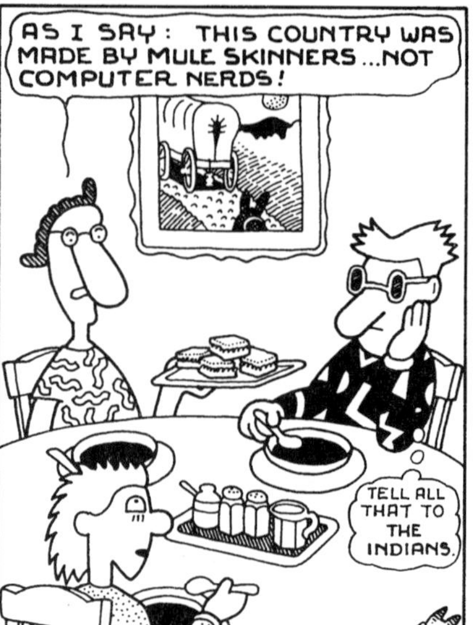
AS I SAY: THIS COUNTRY WAS MADE BY MULE SKINNERS... NOT COMPUTER NERDS!
TELL ALL THAT TO THE INDIANS.

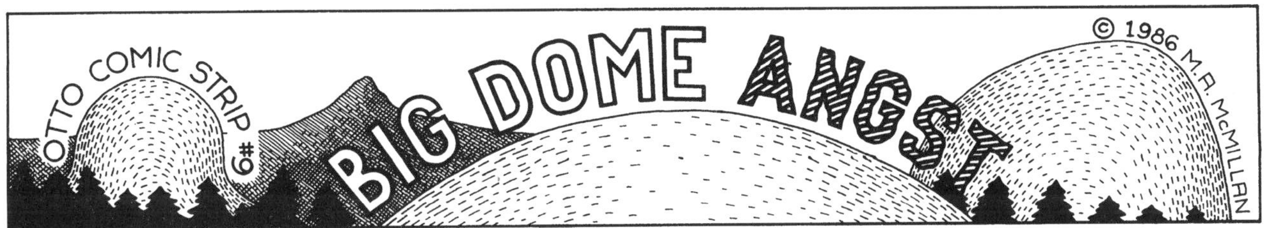
OTTO COMIC STRIP #9
BIG DOME ANGST
© 1986 M.A. McMILLAN

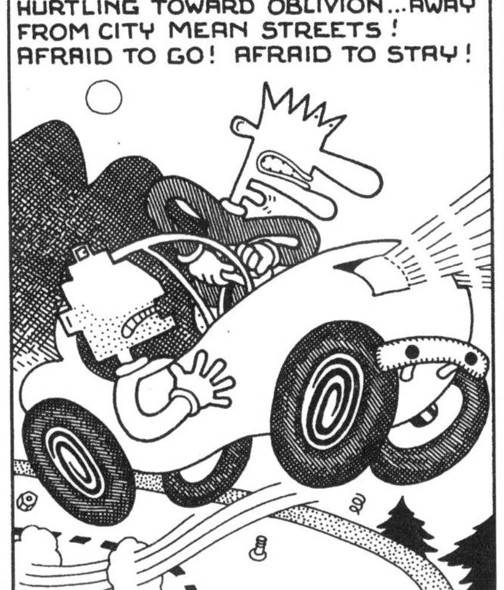
HURTLING TOWARD OBLIVION...AWAY FROM CITY MEAN STREETS! AFRAID TO GO! AFRAID TO STAY!

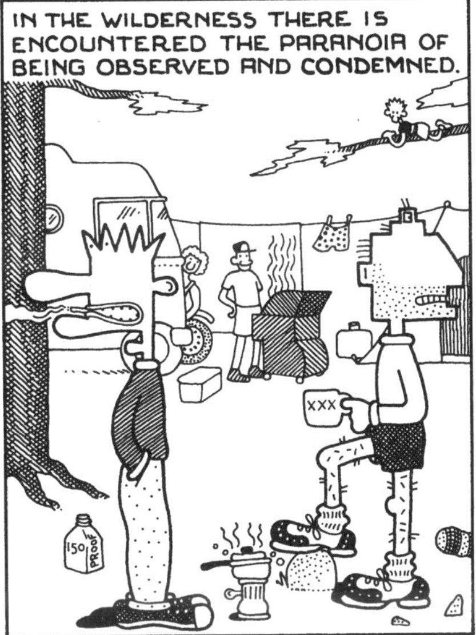
IN THE WILDERNESS THERE IS ENCOUNTERED THE PARANOIA OF BEING OBSERVED AND CONDEMNED.
XXX
150 PROOF

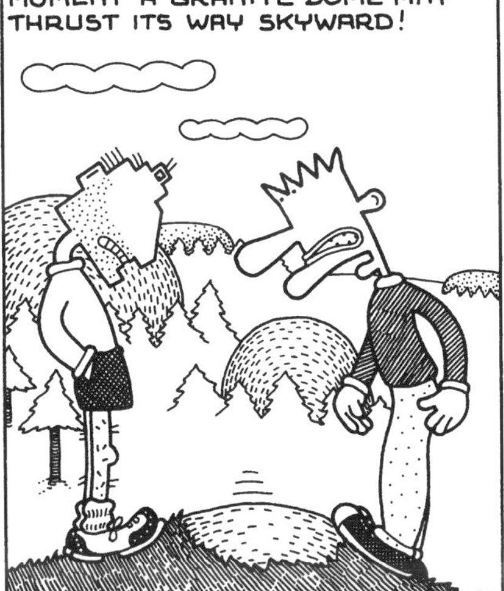
EXAMINATION OF THE TERRAIN PROVOKES UNEASE. AT ANY MOMENT A GRANITE DOME MAY THRUST ITS WAY SKYWARD!

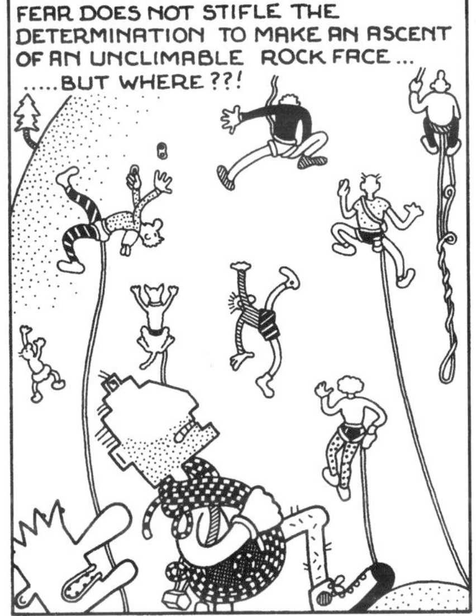
FEAR DOES NOT STIFLE THE DETERMINATION TO MAKE AN ASCENT OF AN UNCLIMABLE ROCK FACE... .....BUT WHERE??!

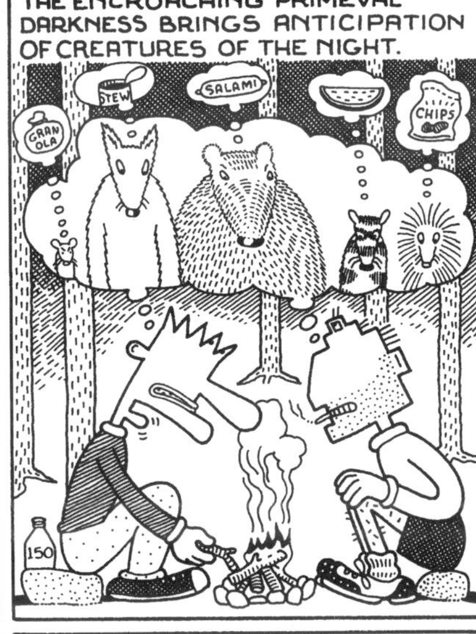
THE ENCROACHING PRIMEVAL DARKNESS BRINGS ANTICIPATION OF CREATURES OF THE NIGHT.
STEW
SALAMI
CHIPS
GRAN OLA
150

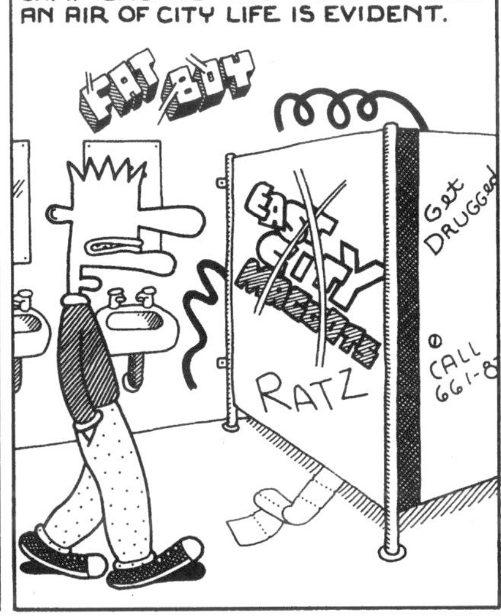
SOME RESPITE IS FOUND IN THE CAMP GROUND REST ROOM WHERE AN AIR OF CITY LIFE IS EVIDENT.
FAT BOY
Get DRUGGED
RATZ
CALL 661-8

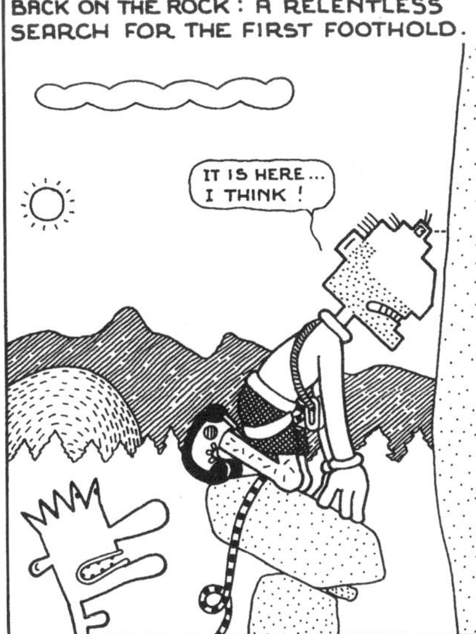
BACK ON THE ROCK: A RELENTLESS SEARCH FOR THE FIRST FOOTHOLD.
IT IS HERE... I THINK!

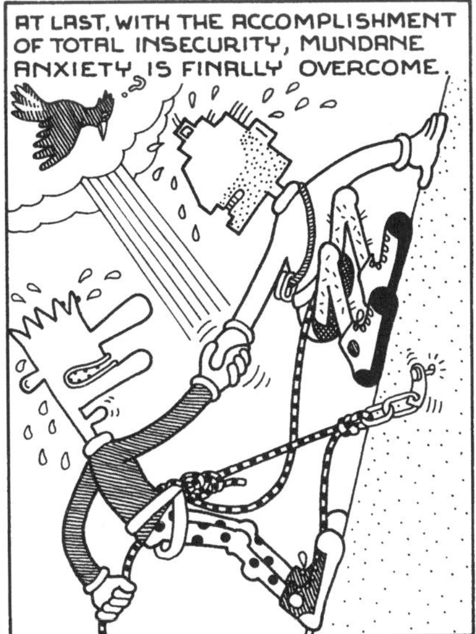
AT LAST, WITH THE ACCOMPLISHMENT OF TOTAL INSECURITY, MUNDANE ANXIETY IS FINALLY OVERCOME.

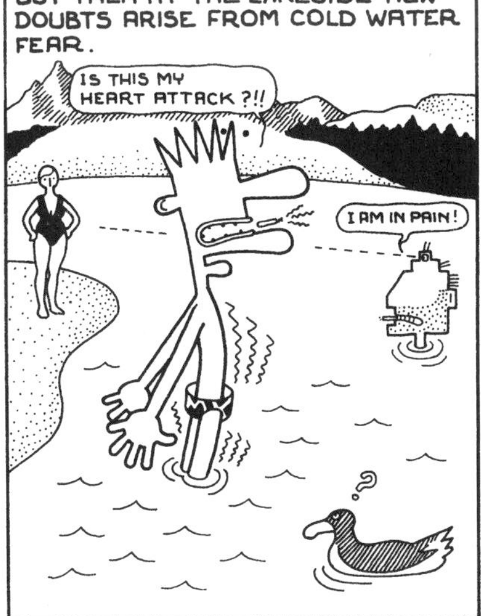
BUT THEN AT THE LAKESIDE NEW DOUBTS ARISE FROM COLD WATER FEAR.
IS THIS MY HEART ATTACK?!!
I AM IN PAIN!

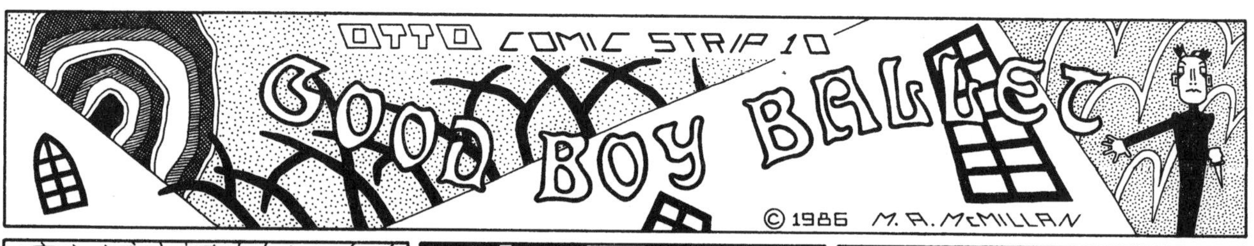
OTTO COMIC STRIP 10
GOOD BOY BALLET
©1986 M.A. McMILLAN

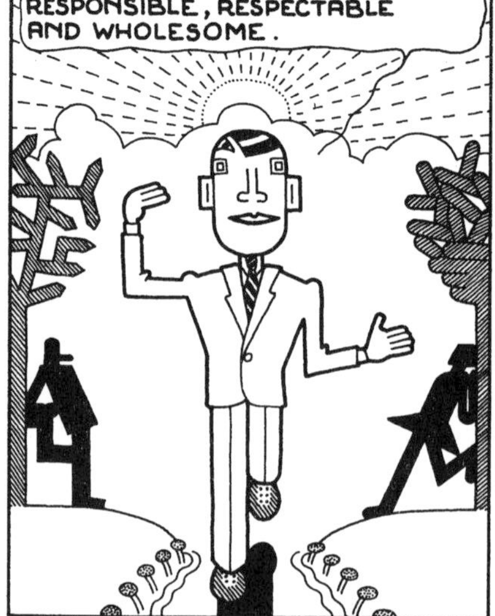
I AM SUCH A GOOD BOY... RELIABLE RESPONSIBLE, RESPECTABLE AND WHOLESOME.

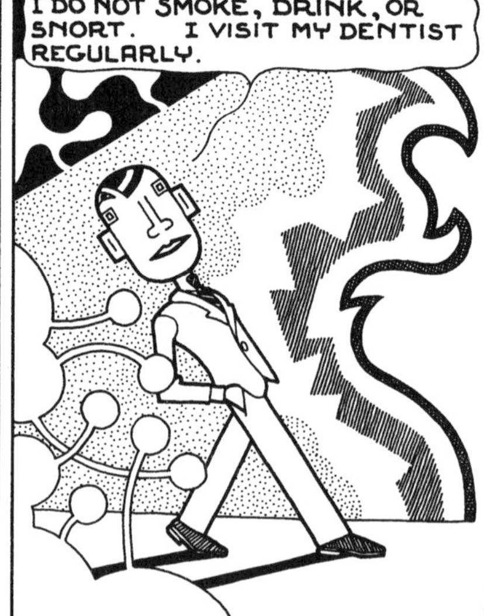
I DO NOT SMOKE, DRINK, OR SNORT. I VISIT MY DENTIST REGULARLY.

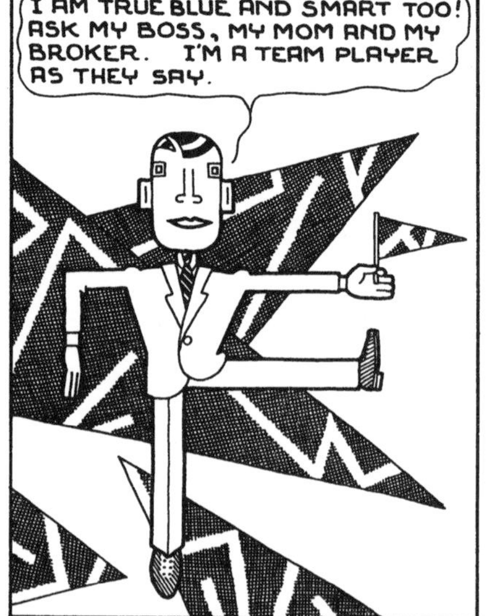
I AM TRUE BLUE AND SMART TOO! ASK MY BOSS, MY MOM AND MY BROKER. I'M A TEAM PLAYER AS THEY SAY.

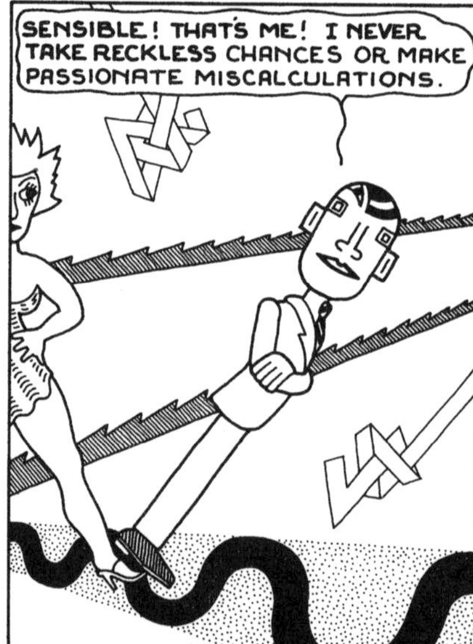
SENSIBLE! THAT'S ME! I NEVER TAKE RECKLESS CHANCES OR MAKE PASSIONATE MISCALCULATIONS.

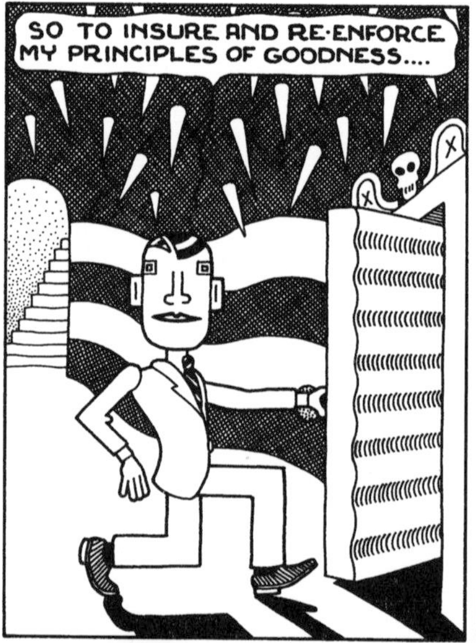
SO TO INSURE AND RE-ENFORCE MY PRINCIPLES OF GOODNESS....

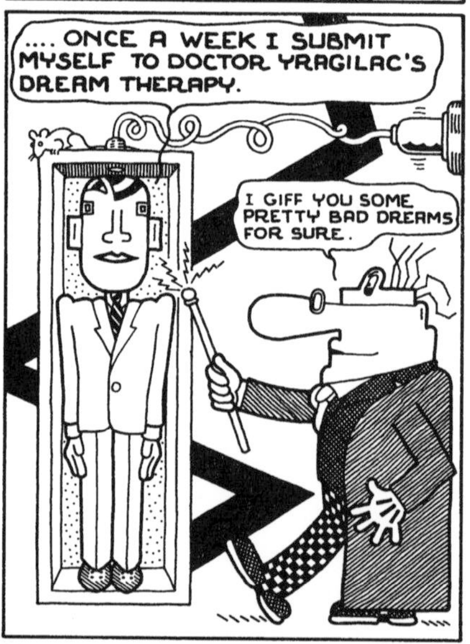
.... ONCE A WEEK I SUBMIT MYSELF TO DOCTOR YRAGILAC'S DREAM THERAPY.
I GIFF YOU SOME PRETTY BAD DREAMS FOR SURE.

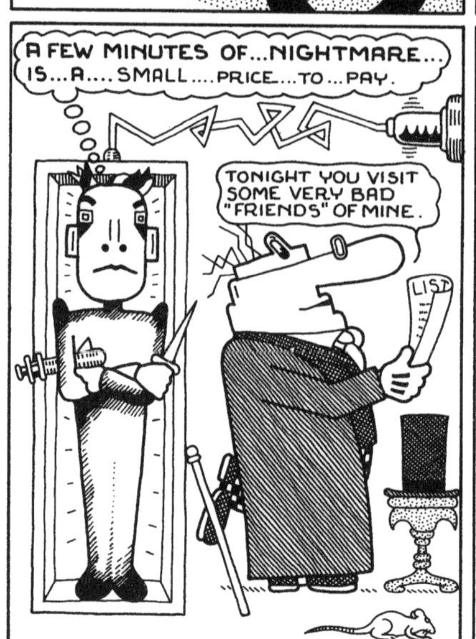
A FEW MINUTES OF... NIGHTMARE... IS... A.... SMALL.... PRICE.... TO... PAY.
TONIGHT YOU VISIT SOME VERY BAD "FRIENDS" OF MINE.
LIST

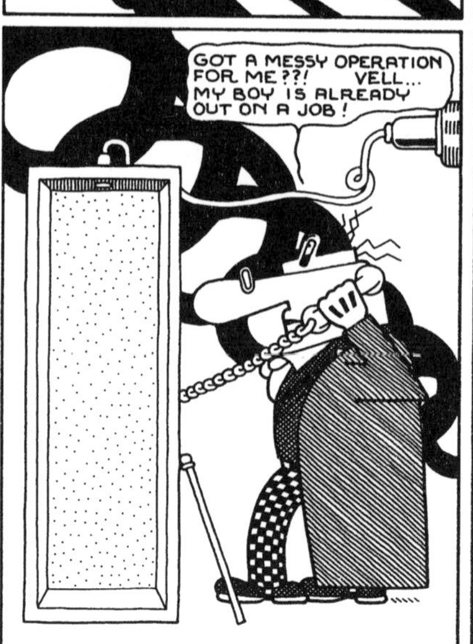
GOT A MESSY OPERATION FOR ME??! VELL... MY BOY IS ALREADY OUT ON A JOB!

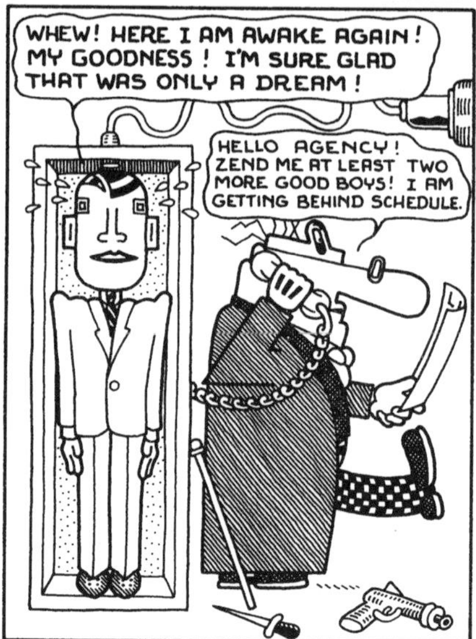
WHEW! HERE I AM AWAKE AGAIN! MY GOODNESS! I'M SURE GLAD THAT WAS ONLY A DREAM!
HELLO AGENCY! ZEND ME AT LEAST TWO MORE GOOD BOYS! I AM GETTING BEHIND SCHEDULE.

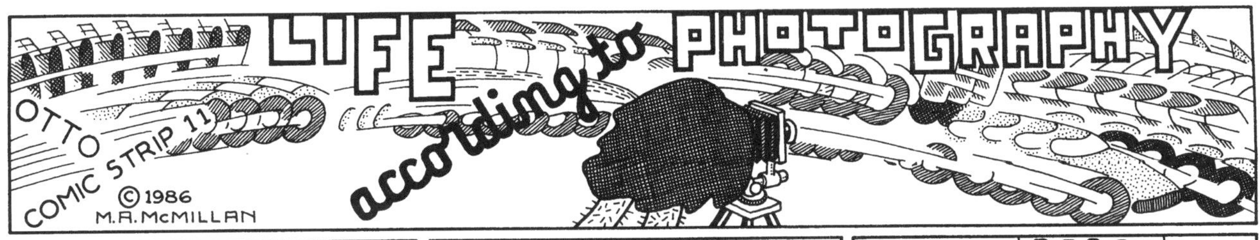
LIFE according to PHOTOGRAPHY
OTTO
COMIC STRIP 11
© 1986
M.A. McMILLAN

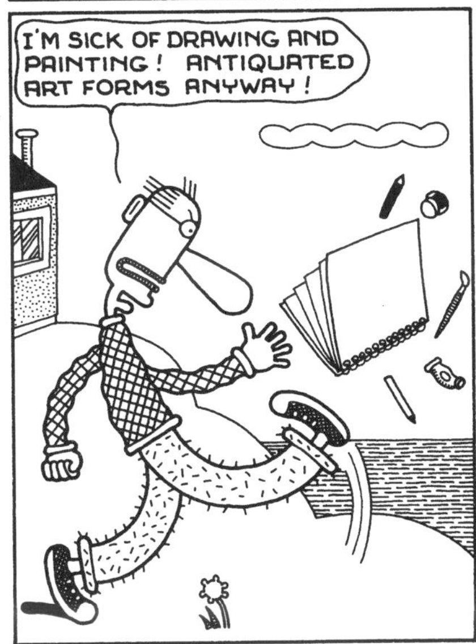
I'M SICK OF DRAWING AND PAINTING! ANTIQUATED ART FORMS ANYWAY!

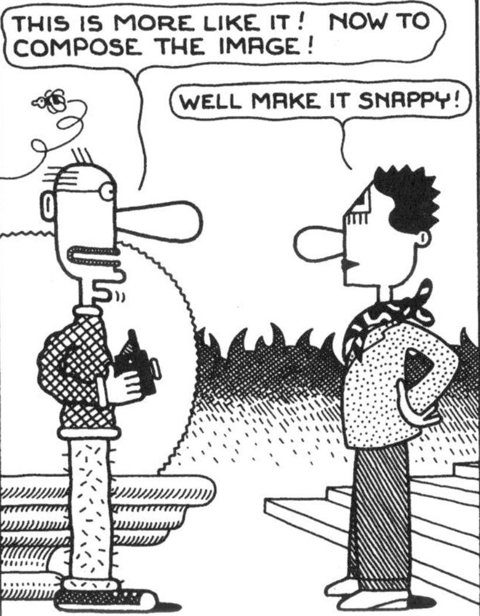
THIS IS MORE LIKE IT! NOW TO COMPOSE THE IMAGE!
WELL MAKE IT SNAPPY!

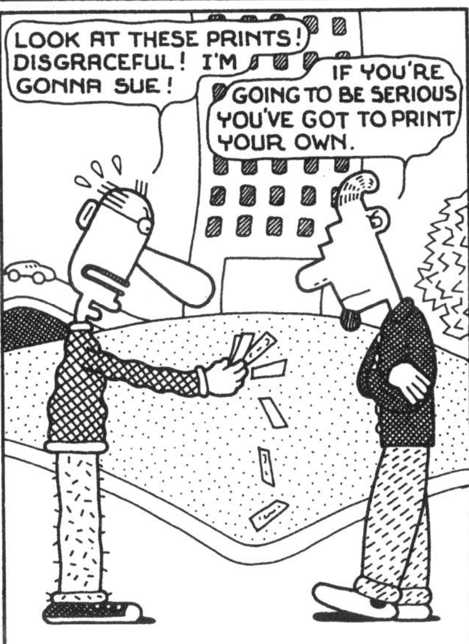
LOOK AT THESE PRINTS! DISGRACEFUL! I'M GONNA SUE!
IF YOU'RE GOING TO BE SERIOUS YOU'VE GOT TO PRINT YOUR OWN.

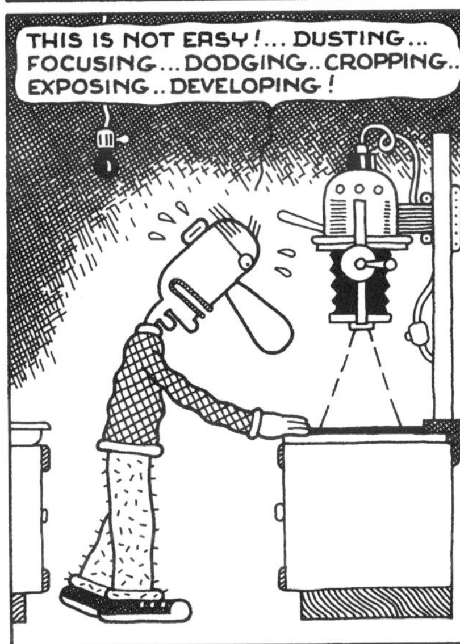
THIS IS NOT EASY!... DUSTING... FOCUSING...DODGING..CROPPING.. EXPOSING..DEVELOPING!

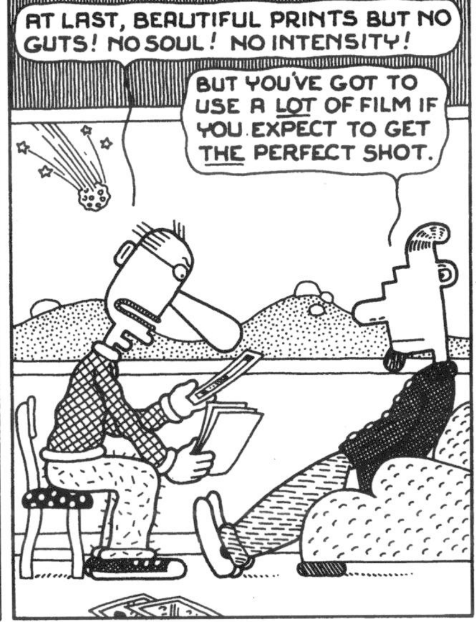
AT LAST, BEAUTIFUL PRINTS BUT NO GUTS! NO SOUL! NO INTENSITY!
BUT YOU'VE GOT TO USE A LOT OF FILM IF YOU EXPECT TO GET THE PERFECT SHOT.

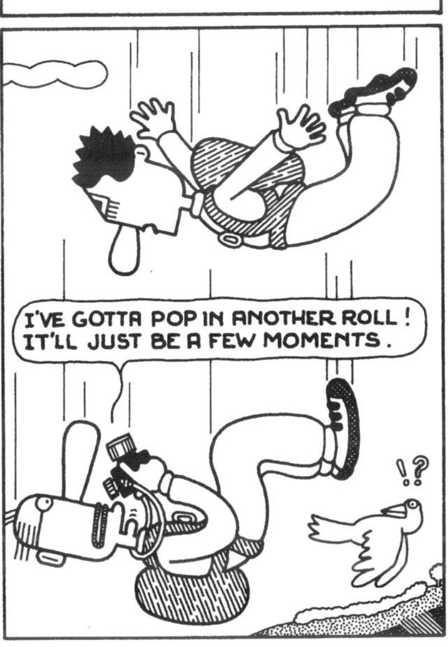
I'VE GOTTA POP IN ANOTHER ROLL! IT'LL JUST BE A FEW MOMENTS.
!?

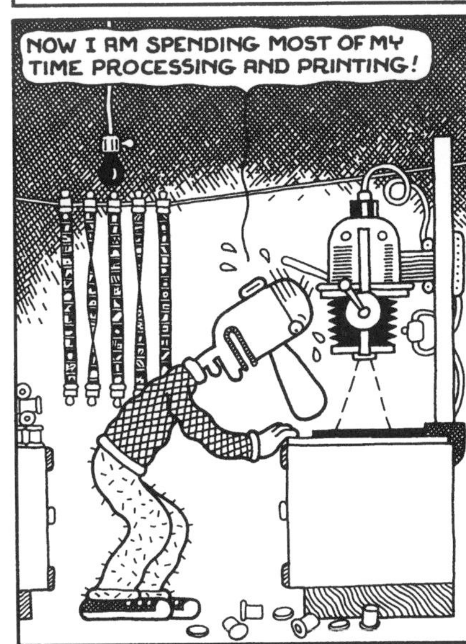
NOW I AM SPENDING MOST OF MY TIME PROCESSING AND PRINTING!

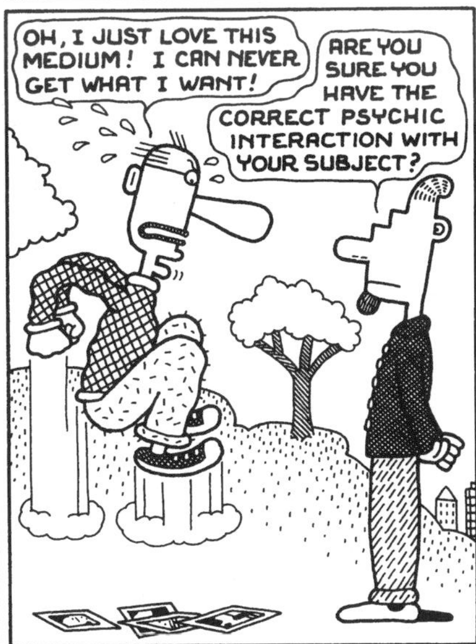
OH, I JUST LOVE THIS MEDIUM! I CAN NEVER GET WHAT I WANT!
ARE YOU SURE YOU HAVE THE CORRECT PSYCHIC INTERACTION WITH YOUR SUBJECT?

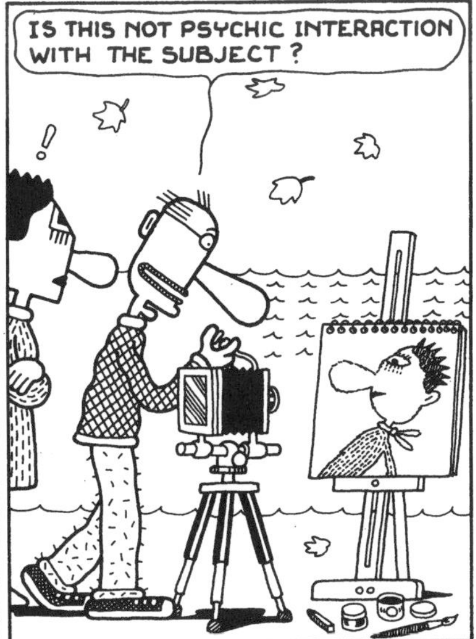
IS THIS NOT PSYCHIC INTERACTION WITH THE SUBJECT?
!

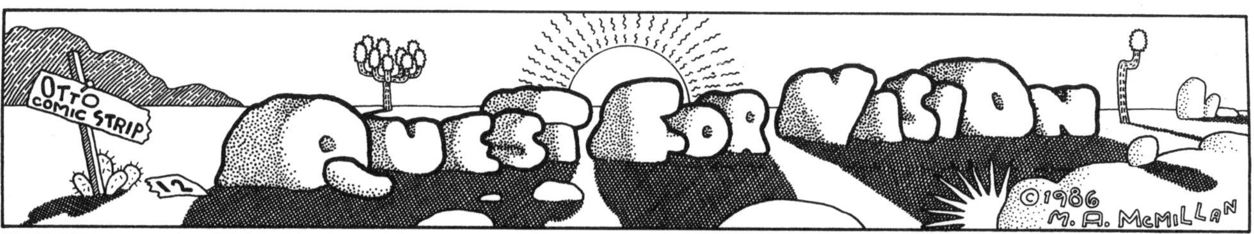
OTTO COMIC STRIP
QUEST FOR VISION
12
©1986 M. A. McMILLAN

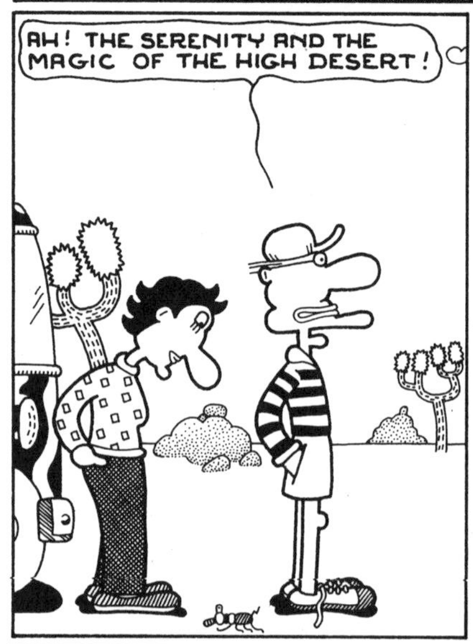
AH! THE SERENITY AND THE MAGIC OF THE HIGH DESERT!

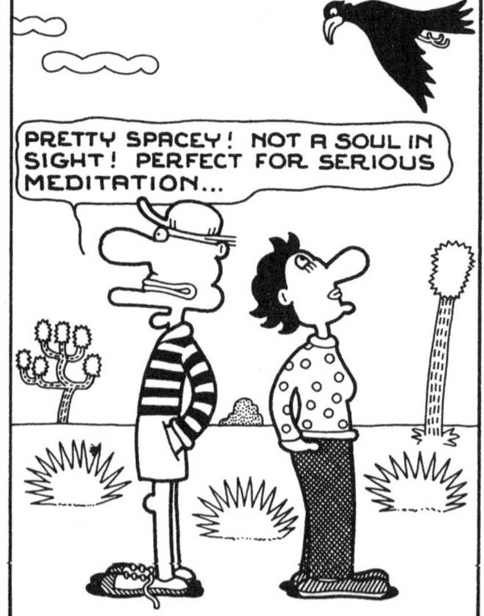
PRETTY SPACEY! NOT A SOUL IN SIGHT! PERFECT FOR SERIOUS MEDITATION...

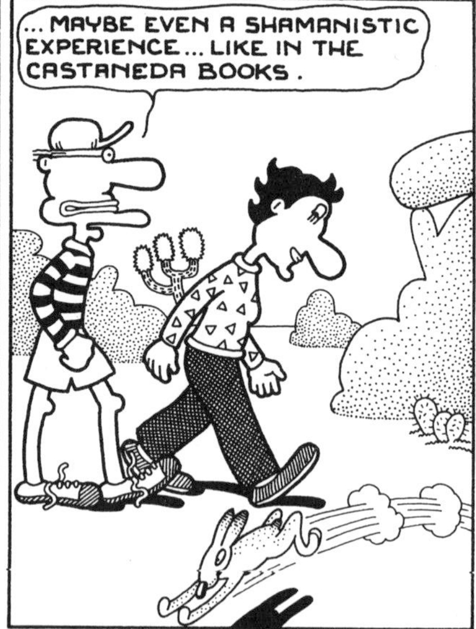
... MAYBE EVEN A SHAMANISTIC EXPERIENCE... LIKE IN THE CASTANEDA BOOKS.

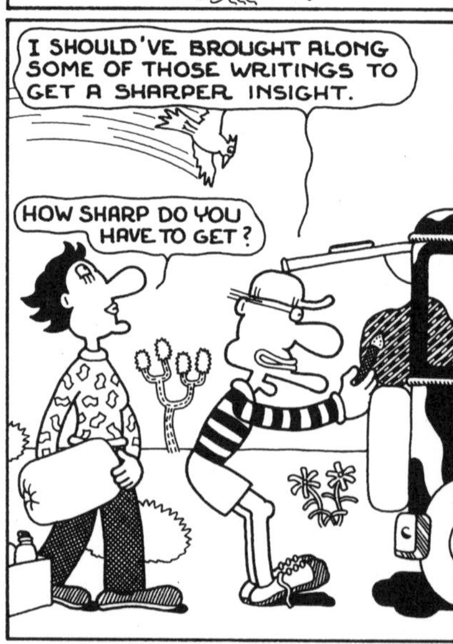
I SHOULD'VE BROUGHT ALONG SOME OF THOSE WRITINGS TO GET A SHARPER INSIGHT.
HOW SHARP DO YOU HAVE TO GET?

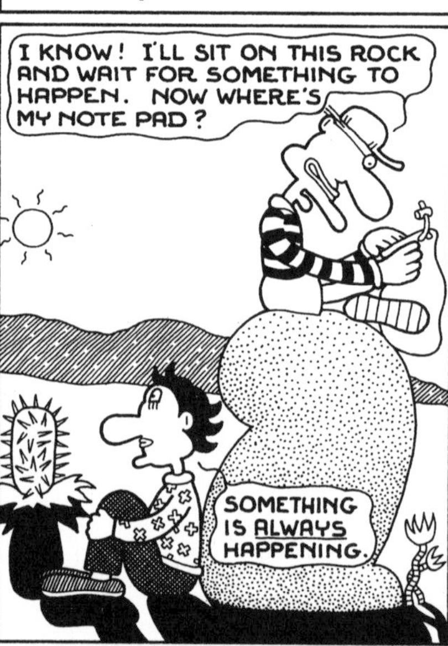
I KNOW! I'LL SIT ON THIS ROCK AND WAIT FOR SOMETHING TO HAPPEN. NOW WHERE'S MY NOTE PAD?
SOMETHING IS ALWAYS HAPPENING.

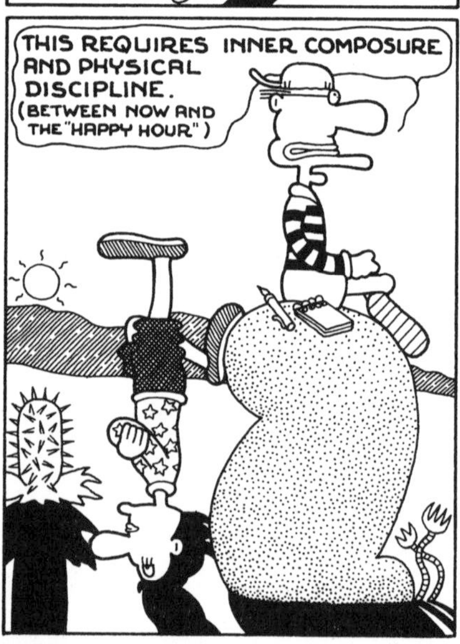
THIS REQUIRES INNER COMPOSURE AND PHYSICAL DISCIPLINE. (BETWEEN NOW AND THE "HAPPY HOUR")

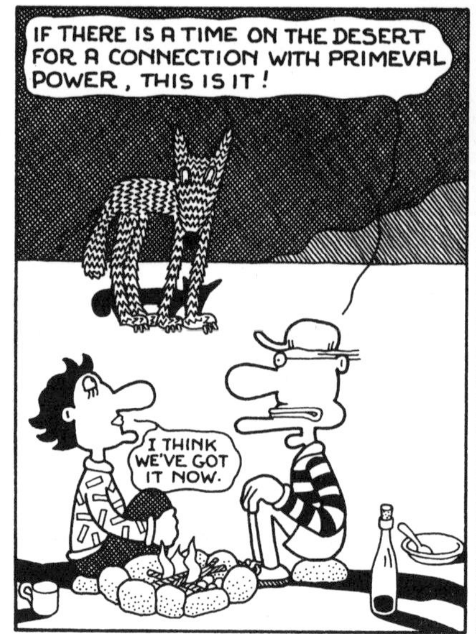
IF THERE IS A TIME ON THE DESERT FOR A CONNECTION WITH PRIMEVAL POWER, THIS IS IT!
I THINK WE'VE GOT IT NOW.

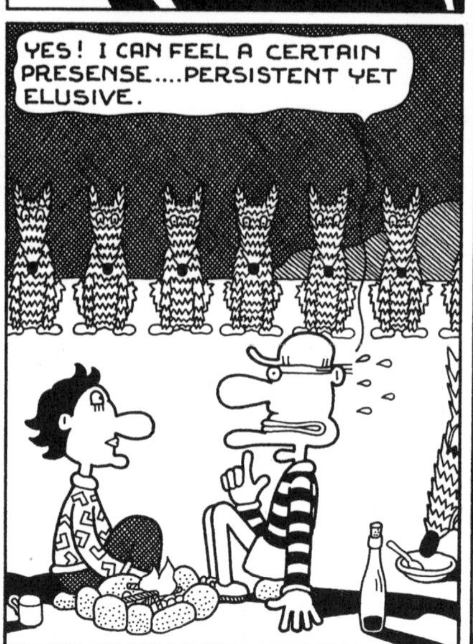
YES! I CAN FEEL A CERTAIN PRESENSE....PERSISTENT YET ELUSIVE.

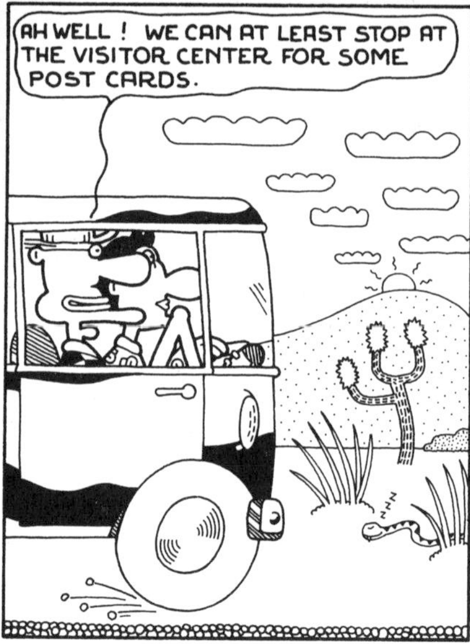
AH WELL! WE CAN AT LEAST STOP AT THE VISITOR CENTER FOR SOME POST CARDS.

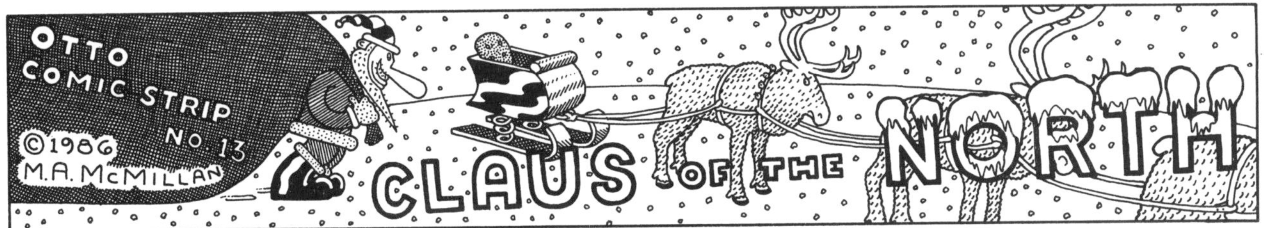
OTTO COMIC STRIP NO. 13
©1986 M.A. McMILLAN
CLAUS OF THE NORTH

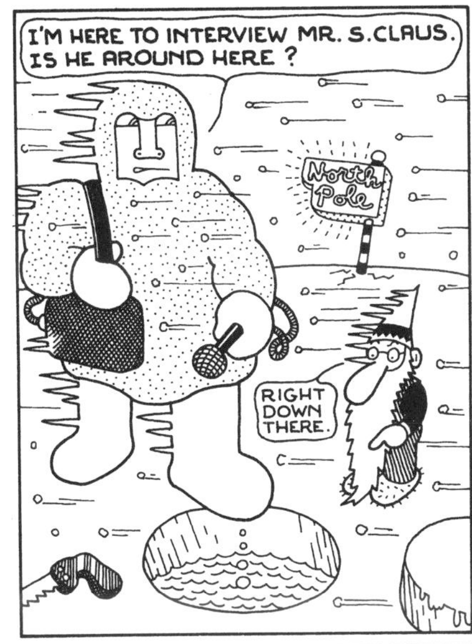
I'M HERE TO INTERVIEW MR. S.CLAUS. IS HE AROUND HERE ?
North Pole
RIGHT DOWN THERE.

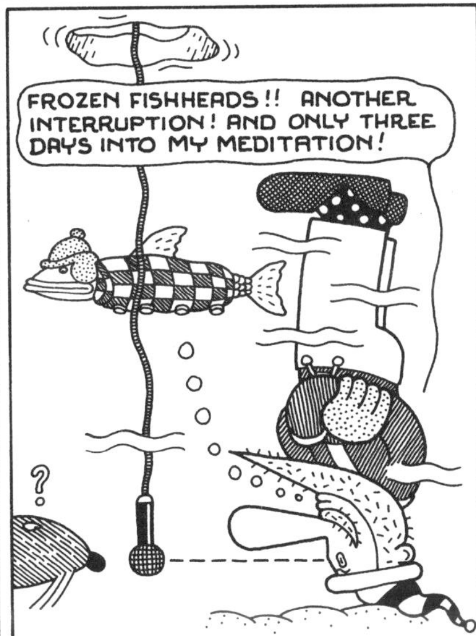
FROZEN FISHHEADS!! ANOTHER INTERRUPTION! AND ONLY THREE DAYS INTO MY MEDITATION!
?

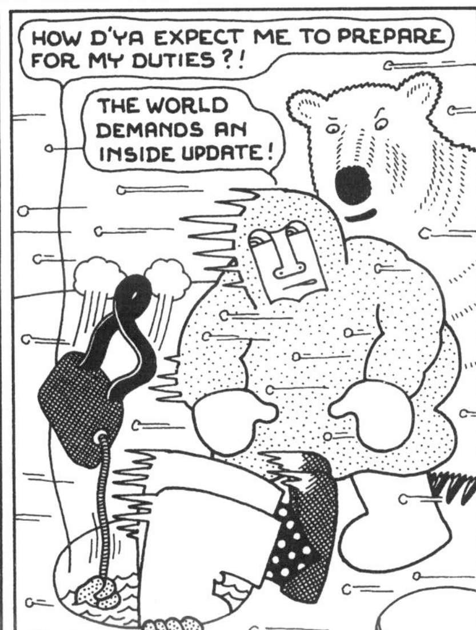
HOW D'YA EXPECT ME TO PREPARE FOR MY DUTIES ?!
THE WORLD DEMANDS AN INSIDE UPDATE!

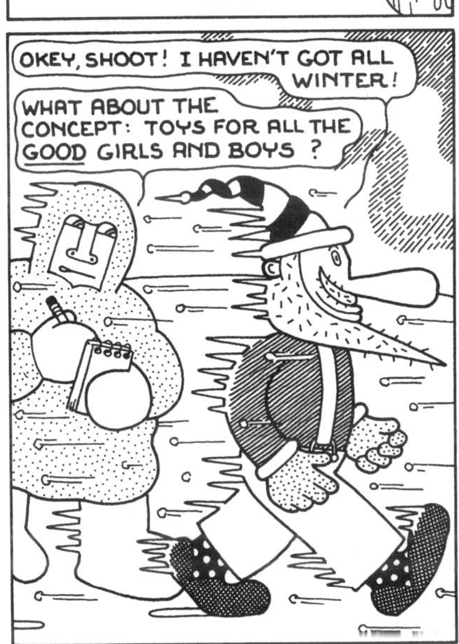
OKEY, SHOOT! I HAVEN'T GOT ALL WINTER!
WHAT ABOUT THE CONCEPT: TOYS FOR ALL THE GOOD GIRLS AND BOYS ?

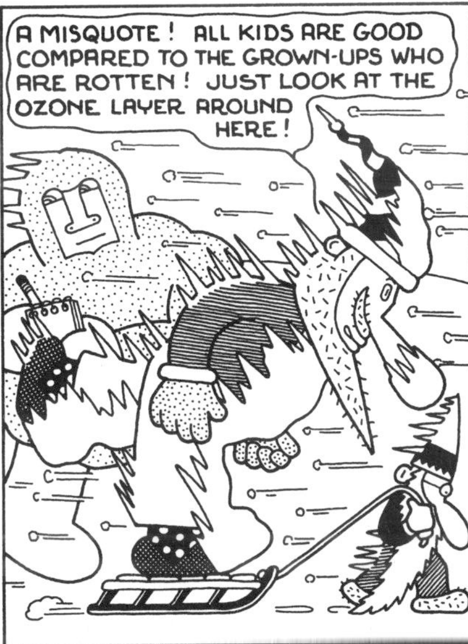
A MISQUOTE! ALL KIDS ARE GOOD COMPARED TO THE GROWN-UPS WHO ARE ROTTEN! JUST LOOK AT THE OZONE LAYER AROUND HERE!

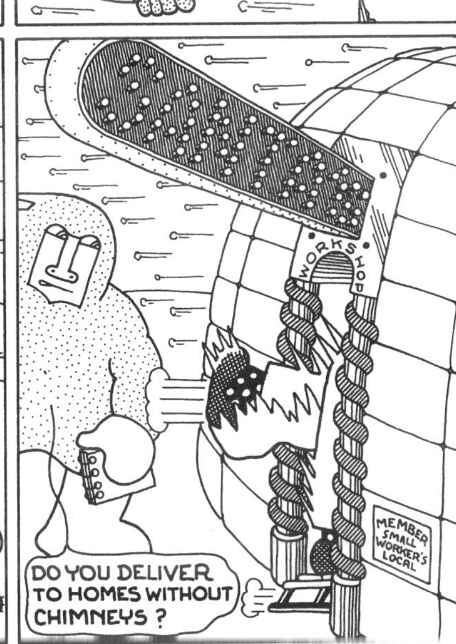
WORKSHOP
MEMBER SMALL WORKER'S LOCAL
DO YOU DELIVER TO HOMES WITHOUT CHIMNEYS ?

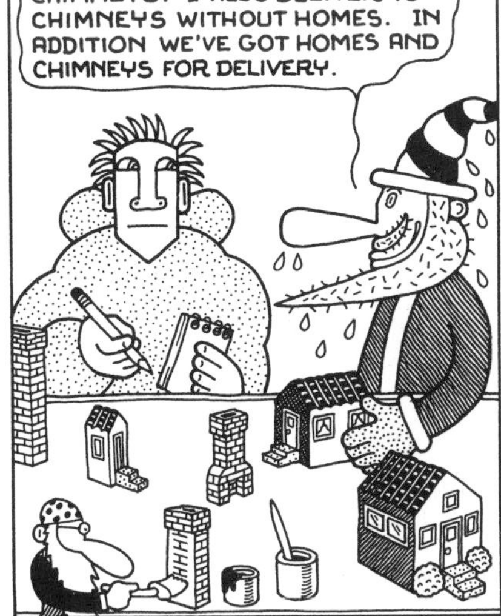
I DELIVER TO HOMES WITHOUT CHIMNEYS. I ALSO DELIVER TO CHIMNEYS WITHOUT HOMES. IN ADDITION WE'VE GOT HOMES AND CHIMNEYS FOR DELIVERY.

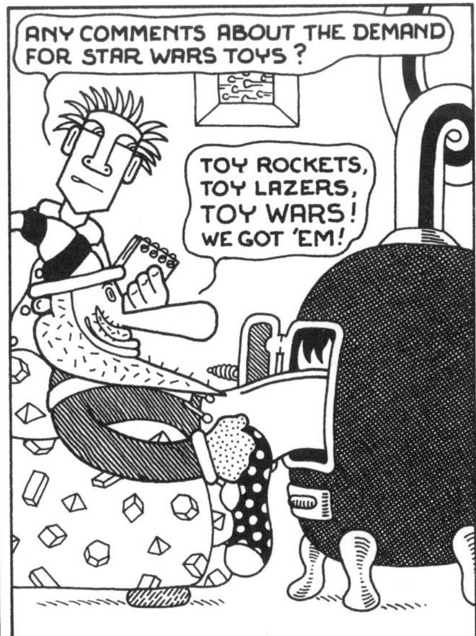
ANY COMMENTS ABOUT THE DEMAND FOR STAR WARS TOYS ?
TOY ROCKETS, TOY LAZERS, TOY WARS! WE GOT 'EM!

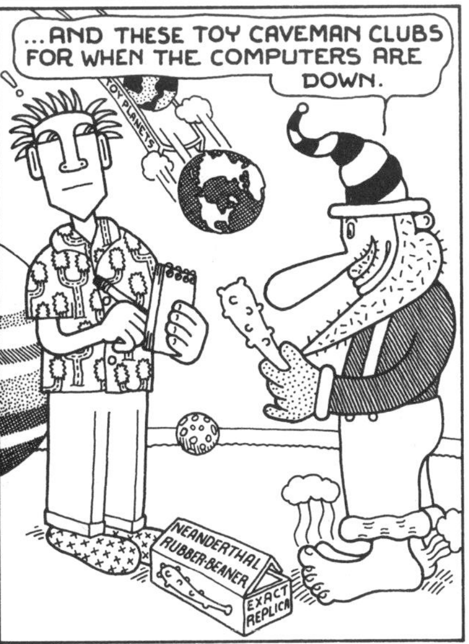
...AND THESE TOY CAVEMAN CLUBS FOR WHEN THE COMPUTERS ARE DOWN.
!
NEANDERTHAL RUBBER-BEANER
EXACT REPLICA

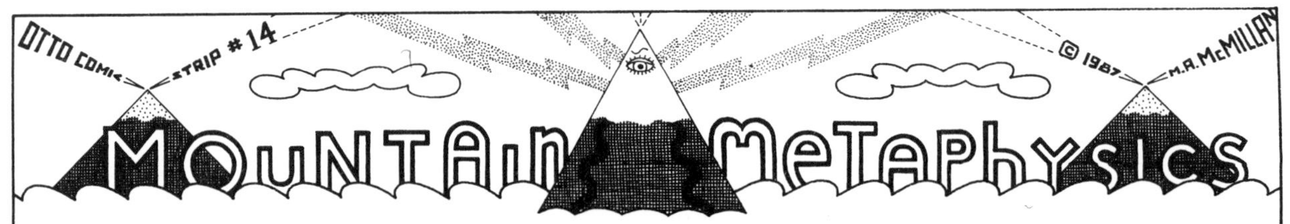
OTTO COMIC STRIP #14
© 1987
M.A. McMILLAN
MOUNTAIN METAPHYSICS

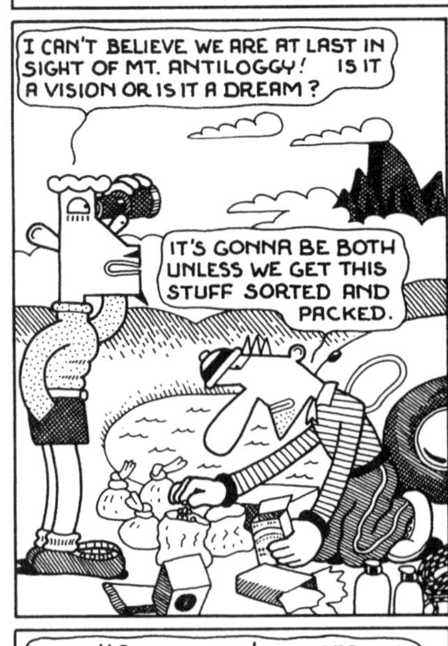
I CAN'T BELIEVE WE ARE AT LAST IN SIGHT OF MT. ANTILOGGY! IS IT A VISION OR IS IT A DREAM?
IT'S GONNA BE BOTH UNLESS WE GET THIS STUFF SORTED AND PACKED.

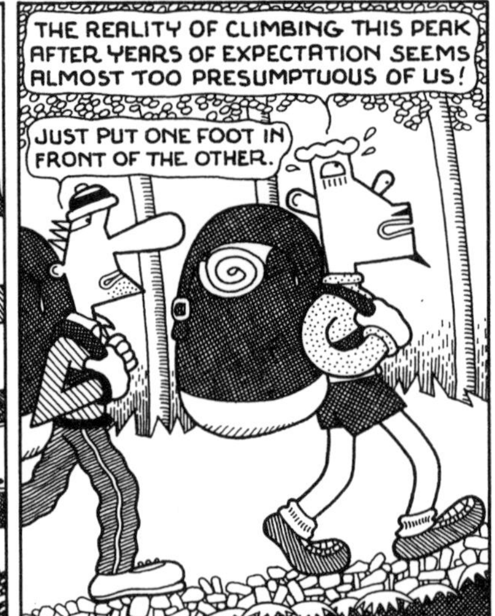
THE REALITY OF CLIMBING THIS PEAK AFTER YEARS OF EXPECTATION SEEMS ALMOST TOO PRESUMPTUOUS OF US!
JUST PUT ONE FOOT IN FRONT OF THE OTHER.

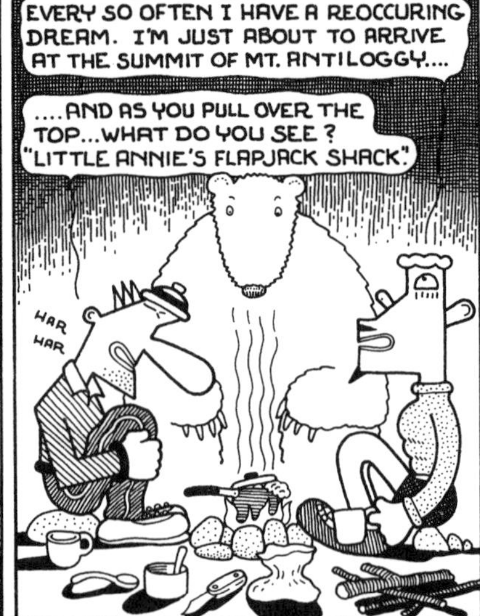
EVERY SO OFTEN I HAVE A REOCCURING DREAM. I'M JUST ABOUT TO ARRIVE AT THE SUMMIT OF MT. ANTILOGGY....
....AND AS YOU PULL OVER THE TOP...WHAT DO YOU SEE? "LITTLE ANNIE'S FLAPJACK SHACK".
HAR HAR

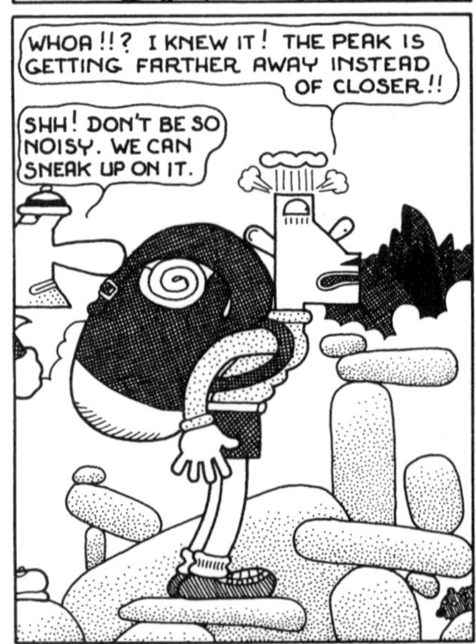
WHOA!!? I KNEW IT! THE PEAK IS GETTING FARTHER AWAY INSTEAD OF CLOSER!!
SHH! DON'T BE SO NOISY. WE CAN SNEAK UP ON IT.

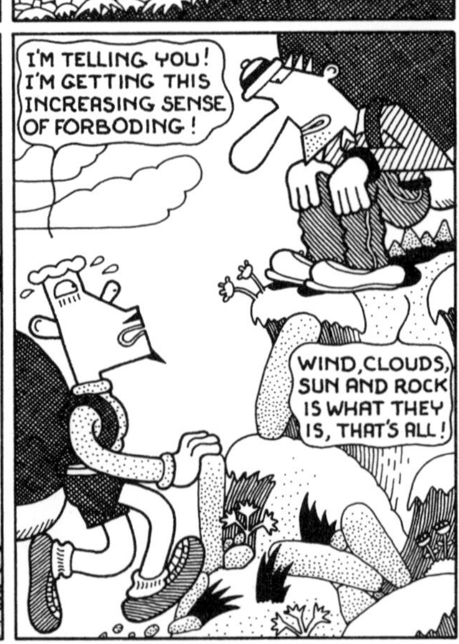
I'M TELLING YOU! I'M GETTING THIS INCREASING SENSE OF FORBODING!
WIND, CLOUDS, SUN AND ROCK IS WHAT THEY IS, THAT'S ALL!

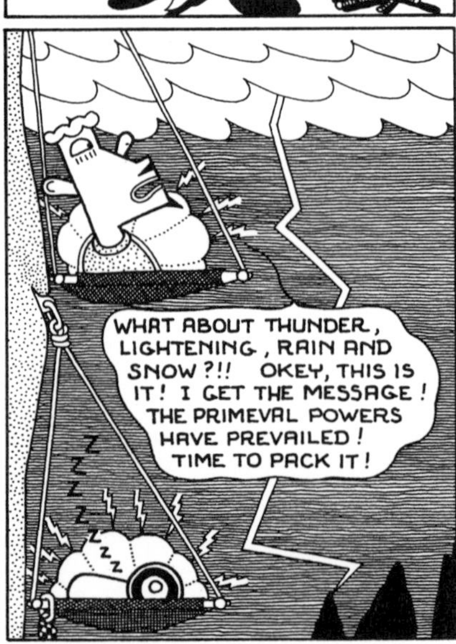
WHAT ABOUT THUNDER, LIGHTENING, RAIN AND SNOW?!! OKEY, THIS IS IT! I GET THE MESSAGE! THE PRIMEVAL POWERS HAVE PREVAILED! TIME TO PACK IT!
ZZZZ

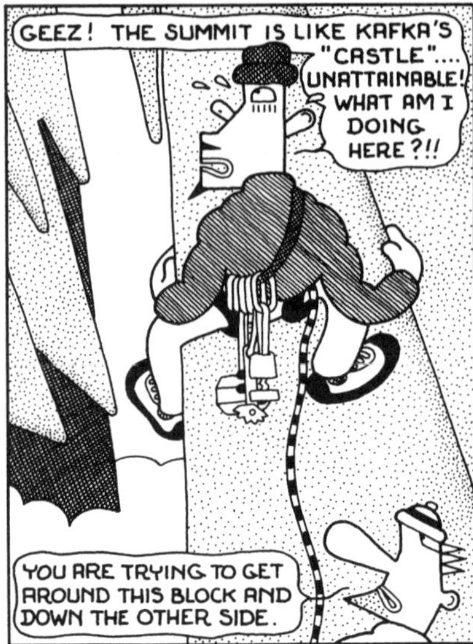
GEEZ! THE SUMMIT IS LIKE KAFKA'S "CASTLE"... UNATTAINABLE! WHAT AM I DOING HERE?!!
YOU ARE TRYING TO GET AROUND THIS BLOCK AND DOWN THE OTHER SIDE.

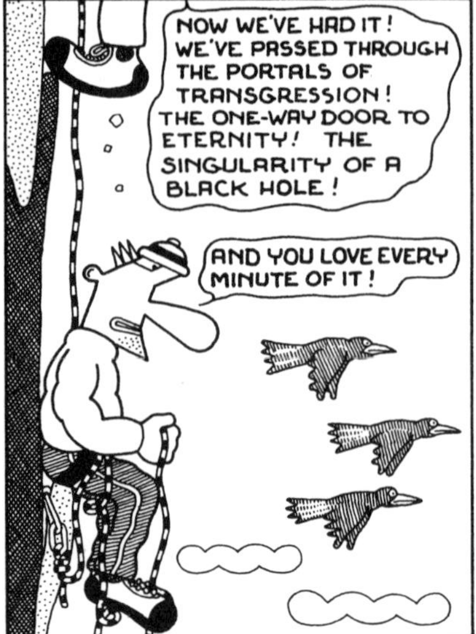
NOW WE'VE HAD IT! WE'VE PASSED THROUGH THE PORTALS OF TRANSGRESSION! THE ONE-WAY DOOR TO ETERNITY! THE SINGULARITY OF A BLACK HOLE!
AND YOU LOVE EVERY MINUTE OF IT!

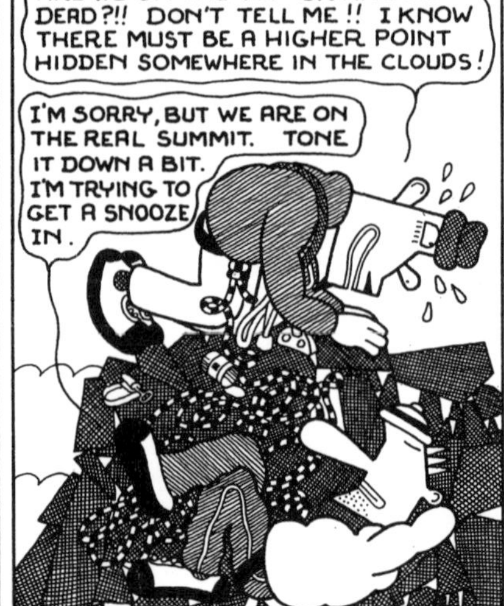
ARE WE ON THE TOP OR ARE WE DEAD?!! DON'T TELL ME!! I KNOW THERE MUST BE A HIGHER POINT HIDDEN SOMEWHERE IN THE CLOUDS!
I'M SORRY, BUT WE ARE ON THE REAL SUMMIT. TONE IT DOWN A BIT. I'M TRYING TO GET A SNOOZE IN.

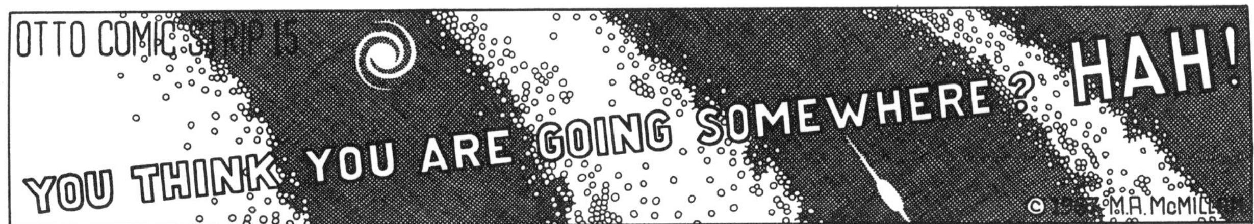
OTTO COMIC STRIP 15
YOU THINK YOU ARE GOING SOMEWHERE? HAH!
© M.A. McMILLAN

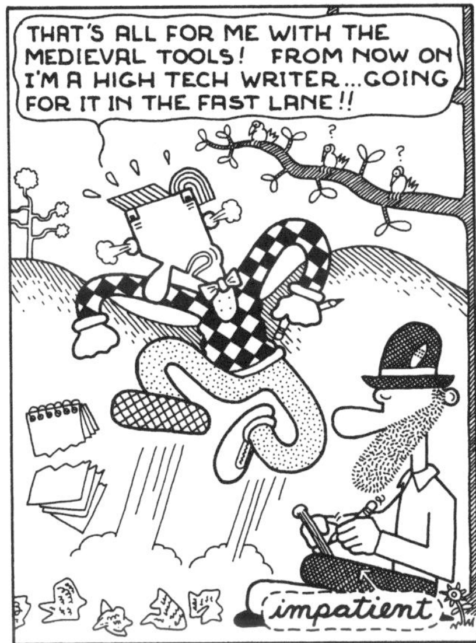
THAT'S ALL FOR ME WITH THE MEDIEVAL TOOLS! FROM NOW ON I'M A HIGH TECH WRITER...GOING FOR IT IN THE FAST LANE!!
impatient

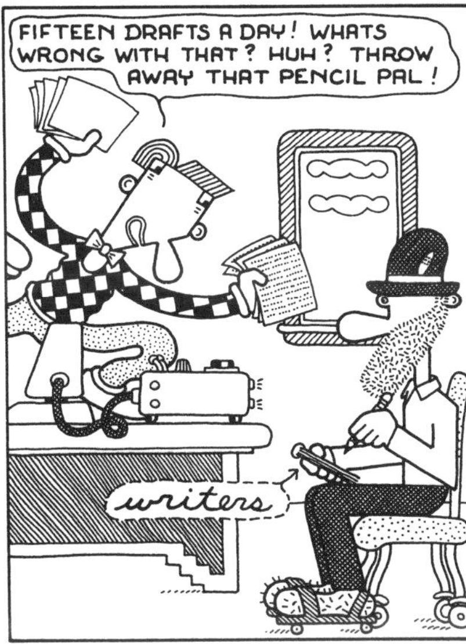
FIFTEEN DRAFTS A DAY! WHATS WRONG WITH THAT? HUH? THROW AWAY THAT PENCIL PAL!
writers

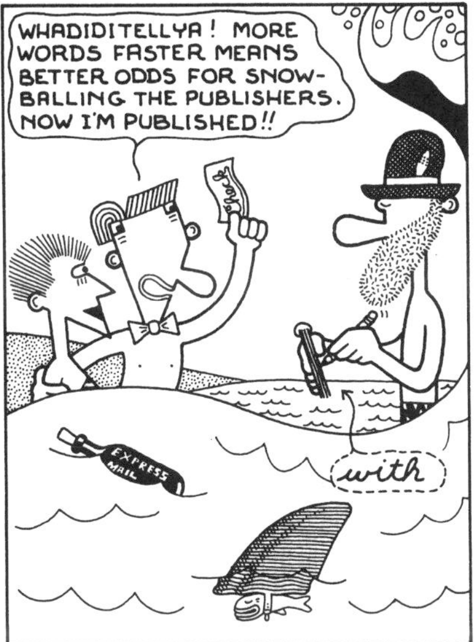
WHADIDITELLYA! MORE WORDS FASTER MEANS BETTER ODDS FOR SNOW-BALLING THE PUBLISHERS. NOW I'M PUBLISHED!!
EXPRESS MAIL
with

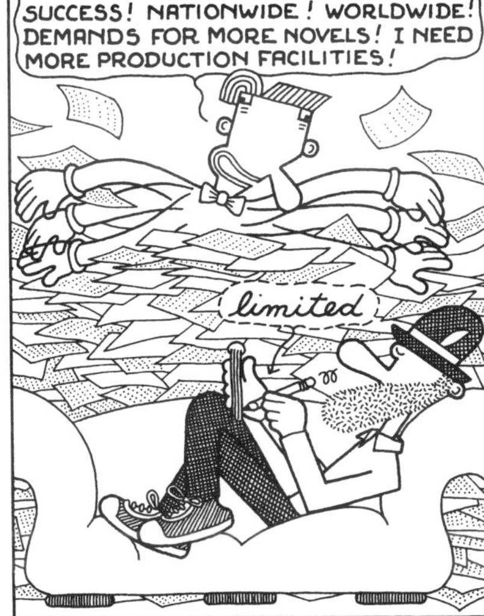
IT'S FANTASTIC! AN AVALANCE OF SUCCESS! NATIONWIDE! WORLDWIDE! DEMANDS FOR MORE NOVELS! I NEED MORE PRODUCTION FACILITIES!
limited

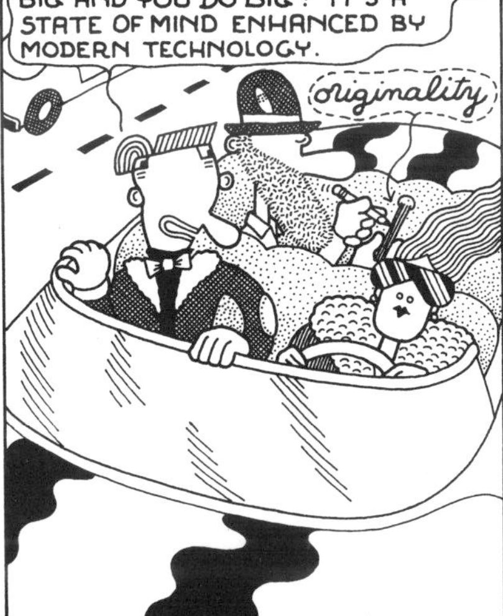
YOU SEE, MY BOY, IT'S LIKE THIS: THINK BIG AND YOU DO BIG! IT'S A STATE OF MIND ENHANCED BY MODERN TECHNOLOGY.
originality

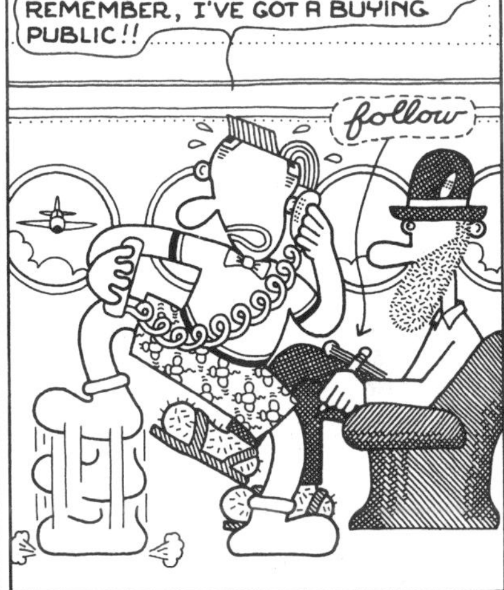
LOOK! I DON'T CARE WHAT THOSE STUFFED SHIRTS SAY! I'M GOING AHEAD WITH MY LIFE STORY! JUST REMEMBER, I'VE GOT A BUYING PUBLIC!!
follow

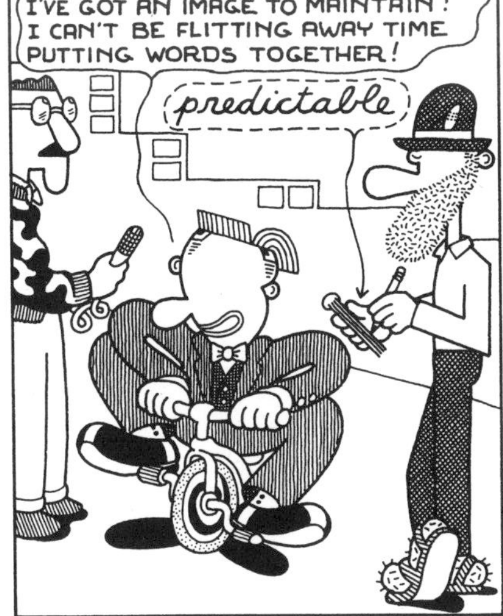
SURE I'M USING A TEAM OF WRITERS. I'VE GOT AN IMAGE TO MAINTAIN! I CAN'T BE FLITTING AWAY TIME PUTTING WORDS TOGETHER!
predictable

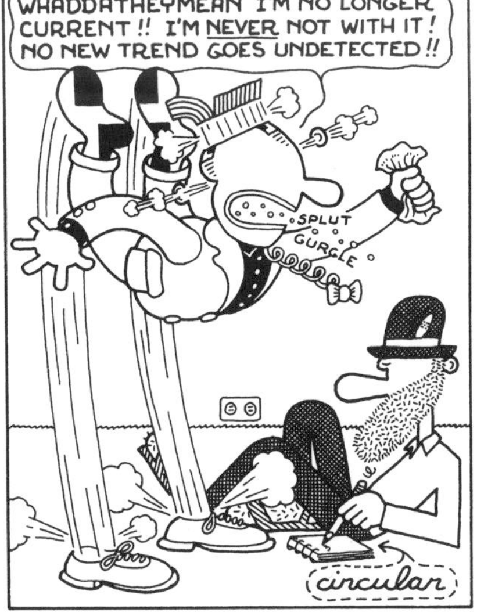
WHADDATHEYMEAN I'M NO LONGER CURRENT!! I'M NEVER NOT WITH IT! NO NEW TREND GOES UNDETECTED!!
SPLUT
GURGLE
circular

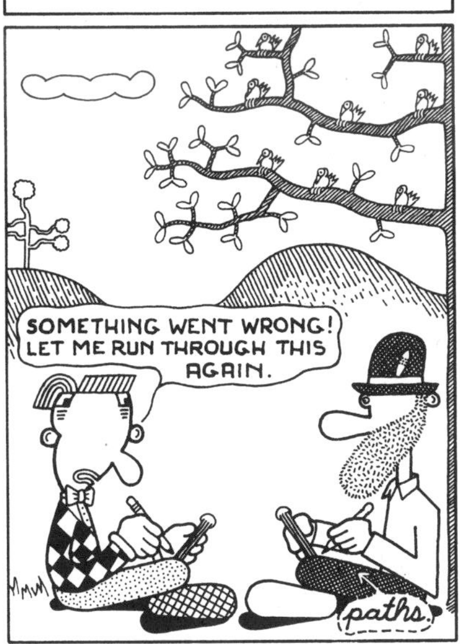
SOMETHING WENT WRONG! LET ME RUN THROUGH THIS AGAIN.
paths.

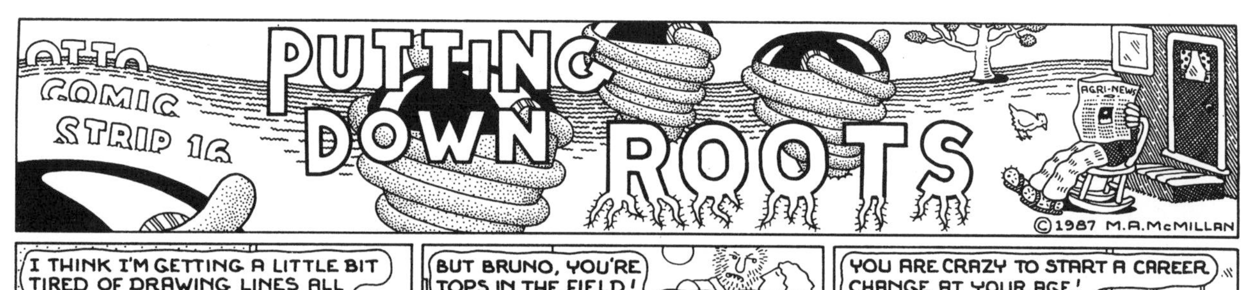
OTTO
COMIC
STRIP 16
PUTTING DOWN ROOTS
AGRI-NEWS
©1987 M.A.McMILLAN

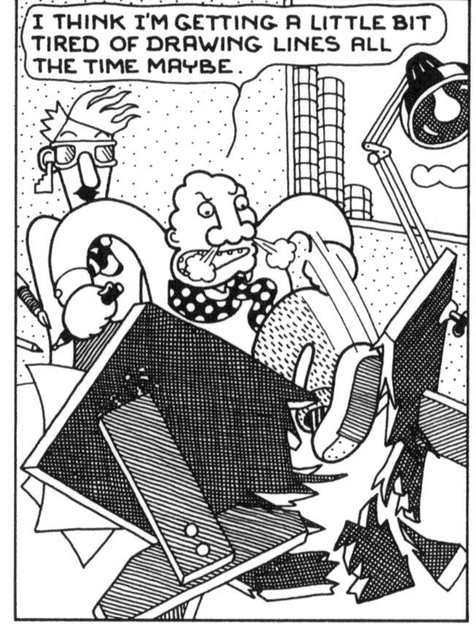
I THINK I'M GETTING A LITTLE BIT TIRED OF DRAWING LINES ALL THE TIME MAYBE.

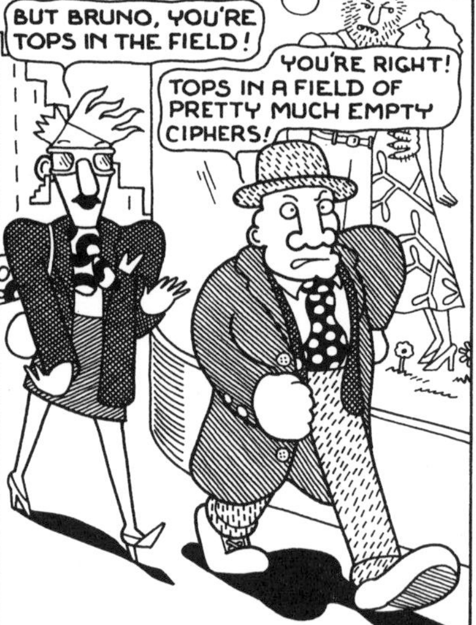
BUT BRUNO, YOU'RE TOPS IN THE FIELD!
YOU'RE RIGHT! TOPS IN A FIELD OF PRETTY MUCH EMPTY CIPHERS!

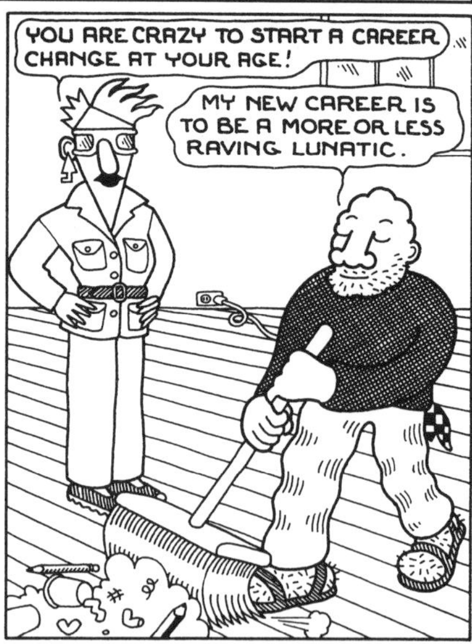
YOU ARE CRAZY TO START A CAREER CHANGE AT YOUR AGE!
MY NEW CAREER IS TO BE A MORE OR LESS RAVING LUNATIC.

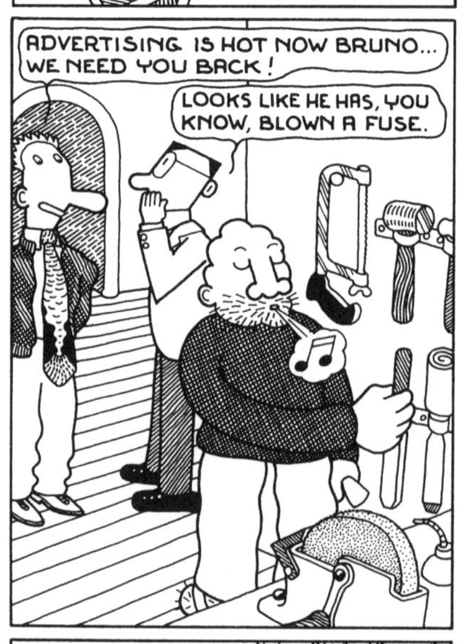
ADVERTISING IS HOT NOW BRUNO... WE NEED YOU BACK!
LOOKS LIKE HE HAS, YOU KNOW, BLOWN A FUSE.

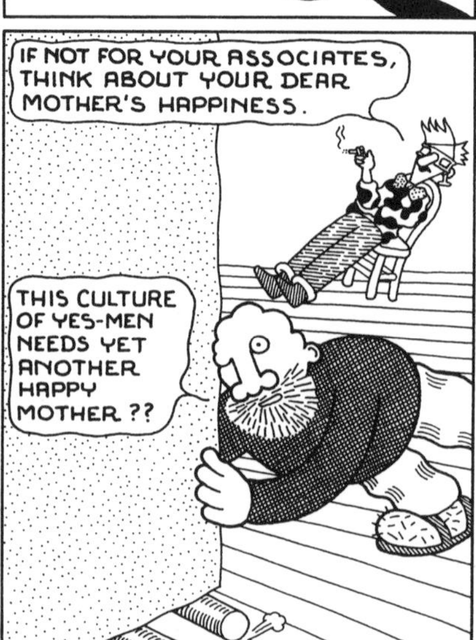
IF NOT FOR YOUR ASSOCIATES, THINK ABOUT YOUR DEAR MOTHER'S HAPPINESS.
THIS CULTURE OF YES-MEN NEEDS YET ANOTHER HAPPY MOTHER ??

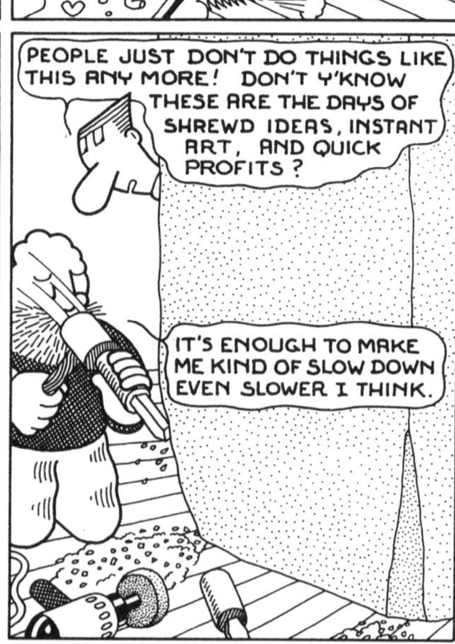
PEOPLE JUST DON'T DO THINGS LIKE THIS ANY MORE! DON'T Y'KNOW THESE ARE THE DAYS OF SHREWD IDEAS, INSTANT ART, AND QUICK PROFITS ?
IT'S ENOUGH TO MAKE ME KIND OF SLOW DOWN EVEN SLOWER I THINK.

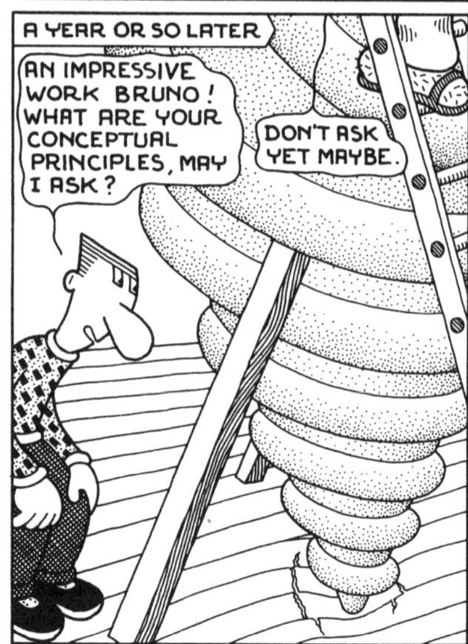
A YEAR OR SO LATER
AN IMPRESSIVE WORK BRUNO! WHAT ARE YOUR CONCEPTUAL PRINCIPLES, MAY I ASK?
DON'T ASK YET MAYBE.

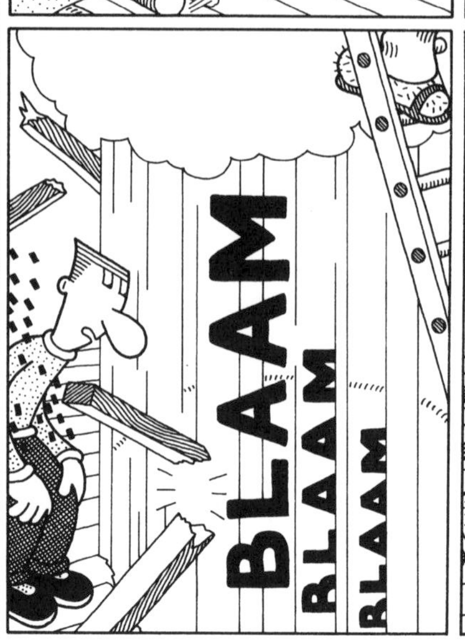
BLAAM
BLAAM
BLAAM

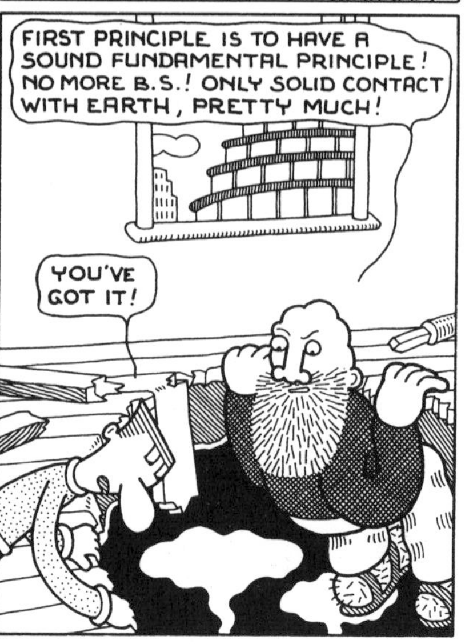
FIRST PRINCIPLE IS TO HAVE A SOUND FUNDAMENTAL PRINCIPLE! NO MORE B.S.! ONLY SOLID CONTACT WITH EARTH, PRETTY MUCH!
YOU'VE GOT IT!

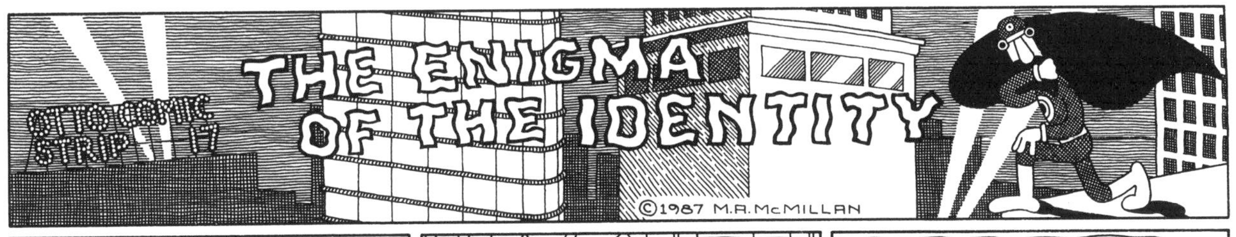
OTTO COMIC STRIP #17
THE ENIGMA OF THE IDENTITY
©1987 M.A.McMILLAN

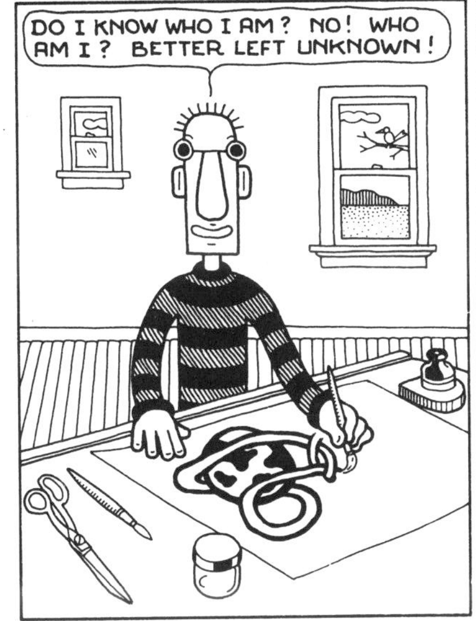
DO I KNOW WHO I AM? NO! WHO AM I? BETTER LEFT UNKNOWN!

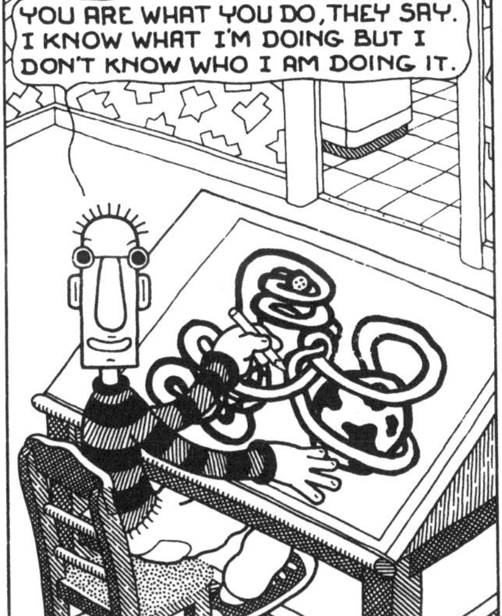
YOU ARE WHAT YOU DO, THEY SAY. I KNOW WHAT I'M DOING BUT I DON'T KNOW WHO I AM DOING IT.

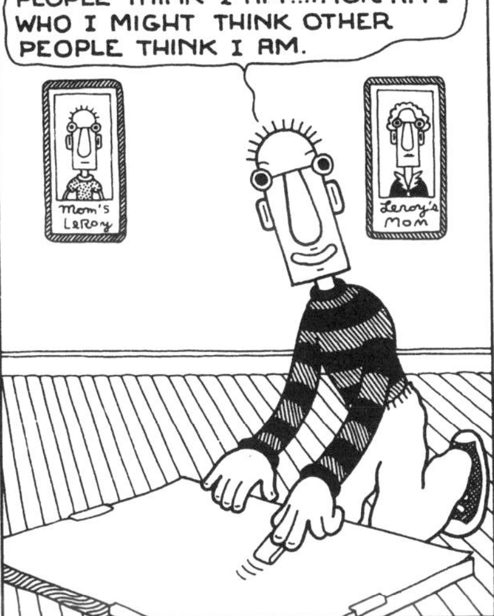
I KNOW I AM NOT WHO OTHER PEOPLE THINK I AM.... NOR AM I WHO I MIGHT THINK OTHER PEOPLE THINK I AM.
Mom's LeRoy
Leroy's Mom

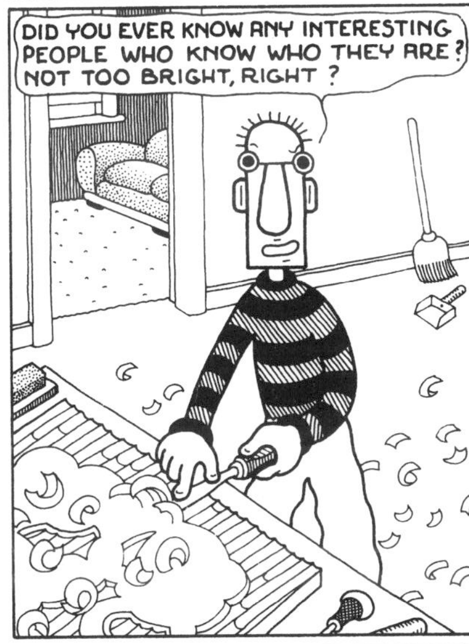
DID YOU EVER KNOW ANY INTERESTING PEOPLE WHO KNOW WHO THEY ARE? NOT TOO BRIGHT, RIGHT?

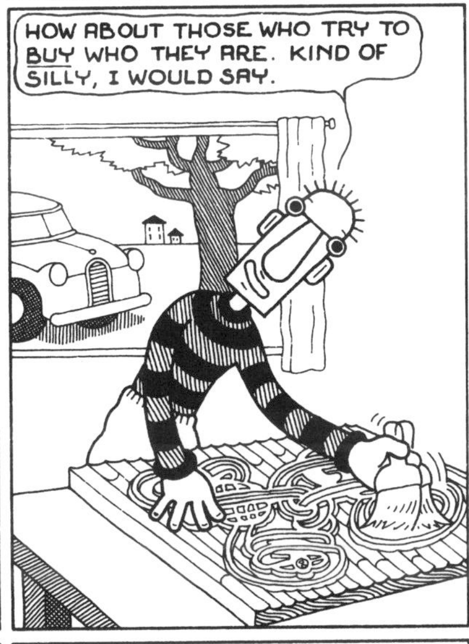
HOW ABOUT THOSE WHO TRY TO BUY WHO THEY ARE. KIND OF SILLY, I WOULD SAY.

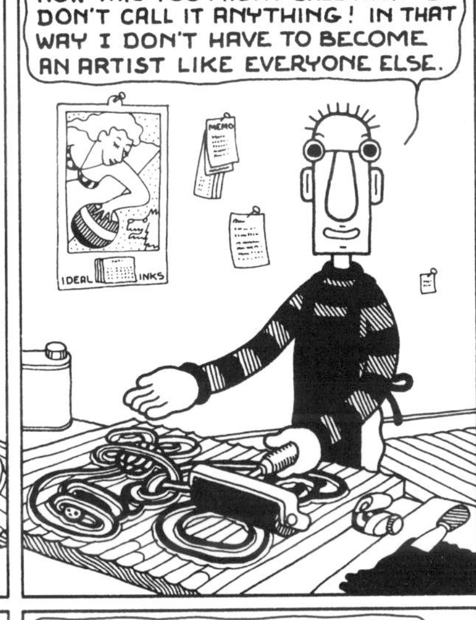
NOW THIS YOU MIGHT CALL ART. I DON'T CALL IT ANYTHING! IN THAT WAY I DON'T HAVE TO BECOME AN ARTIST LIKE EVERYONE ELSE.
IDEAL INKS

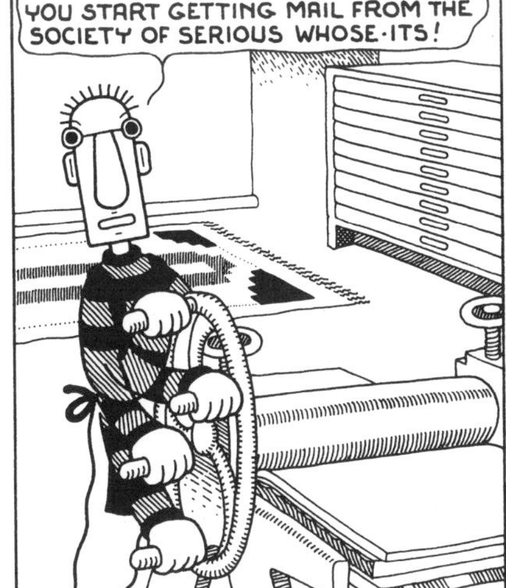
ONCE YOU CALL YOURSELF SOMETHING ...THERE YOU GO! INTO THE DUMPER! YOU START GETTING MAIL FROM THE SOCIETY OF SERIOUS WHOSE-ITS!

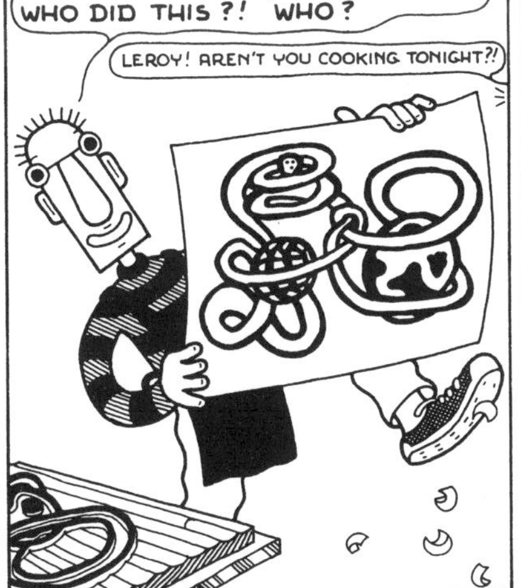
IF YOU ARE REALLY SERIOUS YOU'VE GOTTA SNEAK UP ON YOURSELF. THEN PRESTO! .... HEY, NOT BAD!...... WHO DID THIS?! WHO?
LEROY! AREN'T YOU COOKING TONIGHT?!

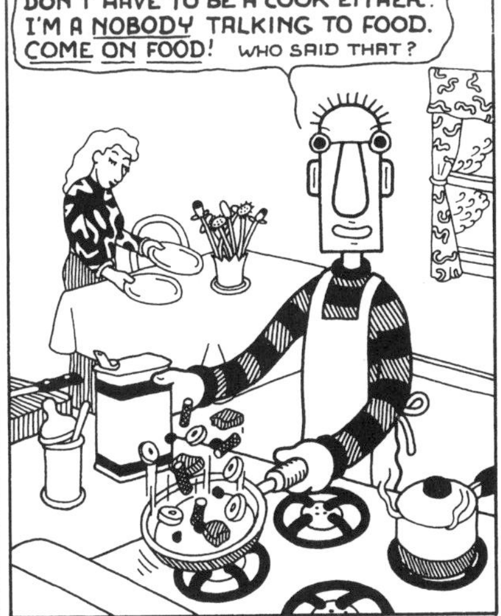
AS LONG AS I'M NOT AN ARTIST, I DON'T HAVE TO BE A COOK EITHER. I'M A NOBODY TALKING TO FOOD. COME ON FOOD! WHO SAID THAT?

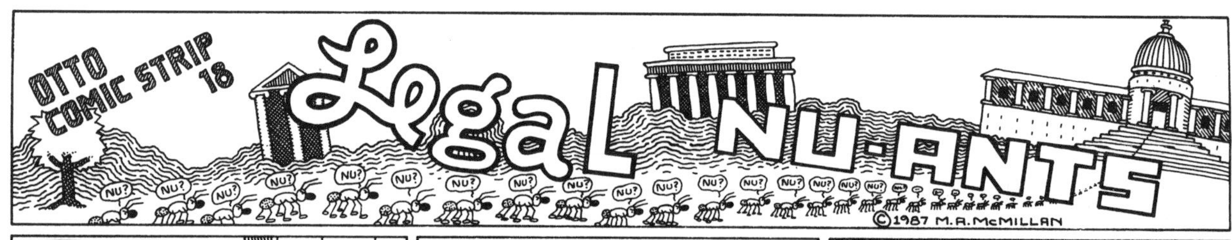
OTTO COMIC STRIP 18
Legal NU-ANTS
©1987 M.A. McMILLAN

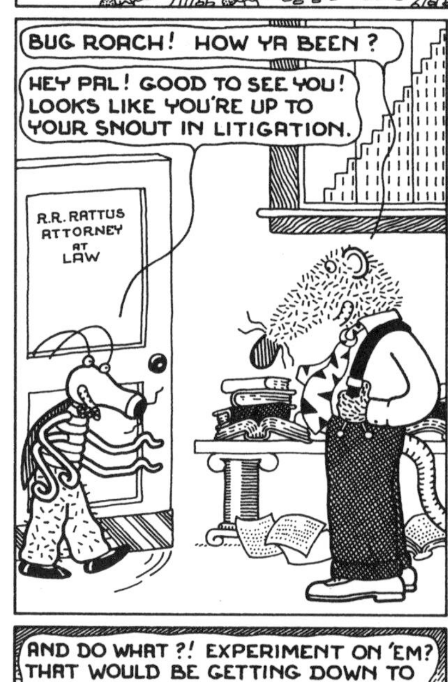
BUG ROACH! HOW YA BEEN?
HEY PAL! GOOD TO SEE YOU! LOOKS LIKE YOU'RE UP TO YOUR SNOUT IN LITIGATION.
R.R. RATTUS ATTORNEY AT LAW

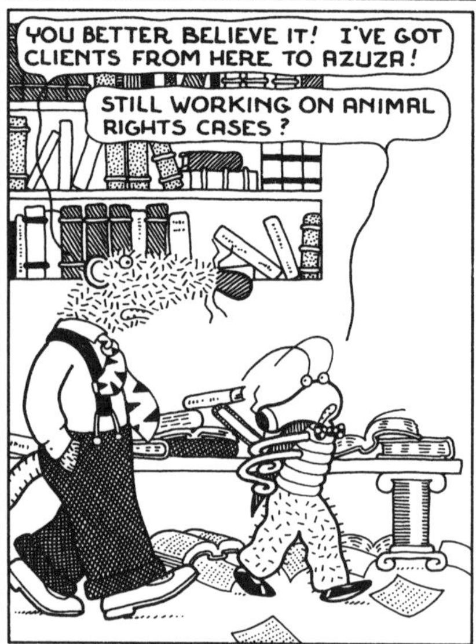
YOU BETTER BELIEVE IT! I'VE GOT CLIENTS FROM HERE TO AZUZA!
STILL WORKING ON ANIMAL RIGHTS CASES?

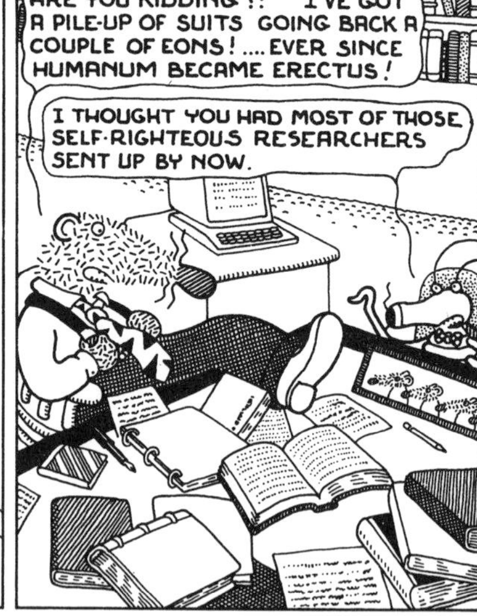
ARE YOU KIDDING?! I'VE GOT A PILE-UP OF SUITS GOING BACK A COUPLE OF EONS! .... EVER SINCE HUMANUM BECAME ERECTUS!
I THOUGHT YOU HAD MOST OF THOSE SELF-RIGHTEOUS RESEARCHERS SENT UP BY NOW.

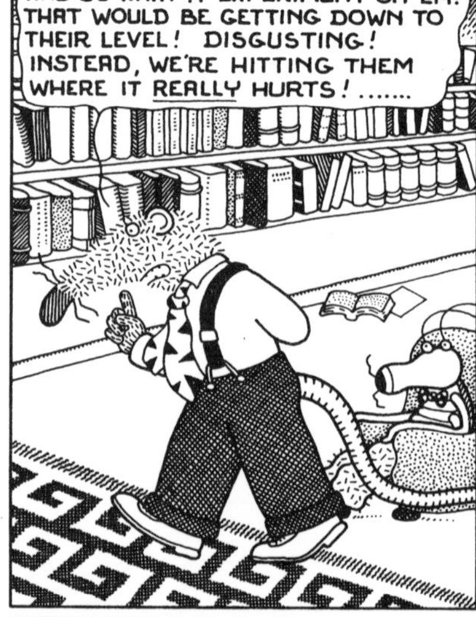
AND DO WHAT?! EXPERIMENT ON 'EM? THAT WOULD BE GETTING DOWN TO THEIR LEVEL! DISGUSTING! INSTEAD, WE'RE HITTING THEM WHERE IT REALLY HURTS! ....

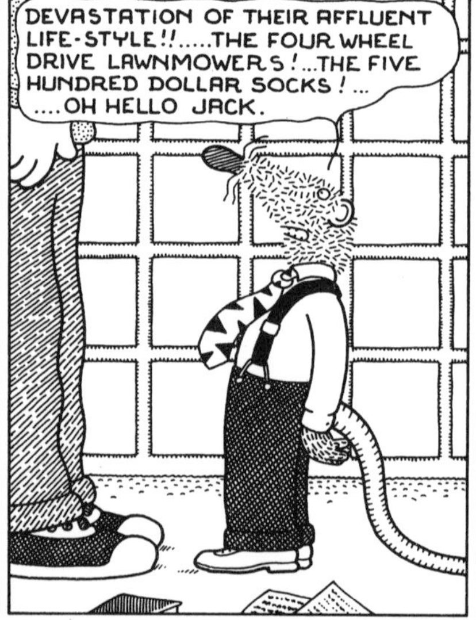
DEVASTATION OF THEIR AFFLUENT LIFE-STYLE!! ..... THE FOUR WHEEL DRIVE LAWNMOWERS! ... THE FIVE HUNDRED DOLLAR SOCKS! ... . OH HELLO JACK.

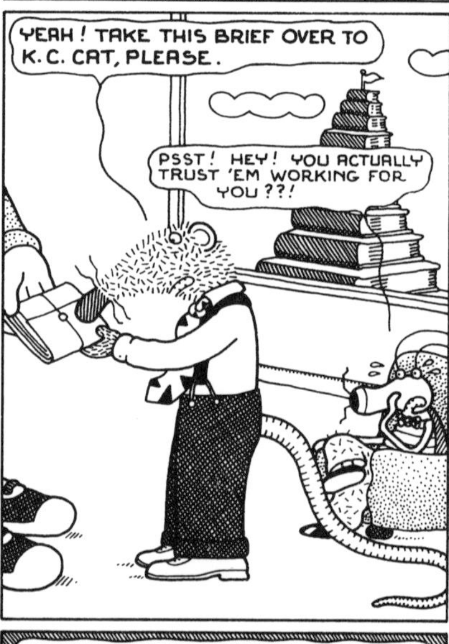
YEAH! TAKE THIS BRIEF OVER TO K. C. CAT, PLEASE.
PSST! HEY! YOU ACTUALLY TRUST 'EM WORKING FOR YOU ??!

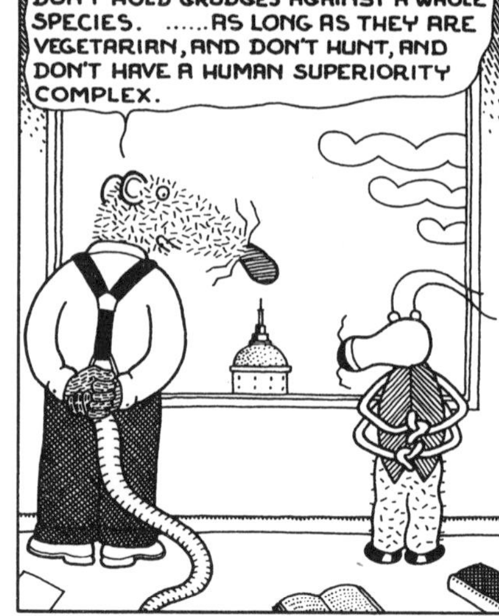
LOOK! I'M AN OPEN MINDED GUY! I DON'T HOLD GRUDGES AGAINST A WHOLE SPECIES. ...... AS LONG AS THEY ARE VEGETARIAN, AND DON'T HUNT, AND DON'T HAVE A HUMAN SUPERIORITY COMPLEX.

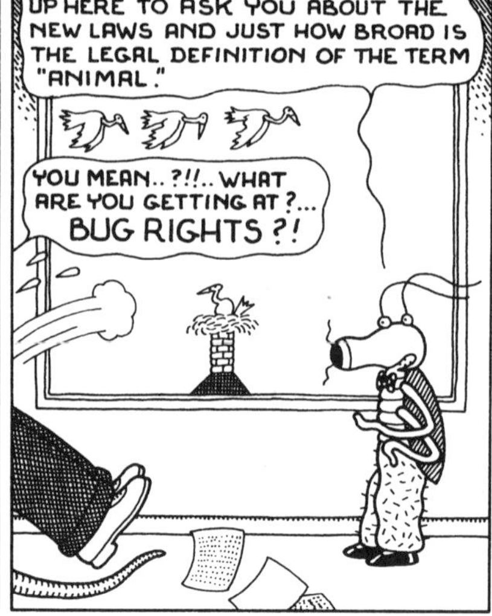
SPEAKING OF SPECIES, I SCURRIED UP HERE TO ASK YOU ABOUT THE NEW LAWS AND JUST HOW BROAD IS THE LEGAL DEFINITION OF THE TERM "ANIMAL."
YOU MEAN..?!!.. WHAT ARE YOU GETTING AT?... BUG RIGHTS?!

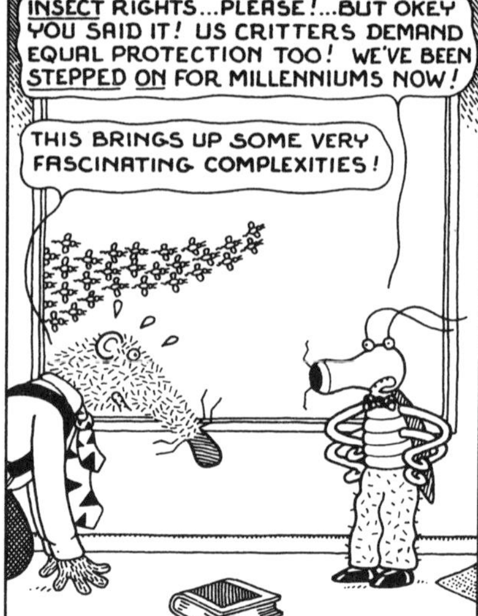
INSECT RIGHTS... PLEASE! ... BUT OKEY YOU SAID IT! US CRITTERS DEMAND EQUAL PROTECTION TOO! WE'VE BEEN STEPPED ON FOR MILLENNIUMS NOW!
THIS BRINGS UP SOME VERY FASCINATING COMPLEXITIES!

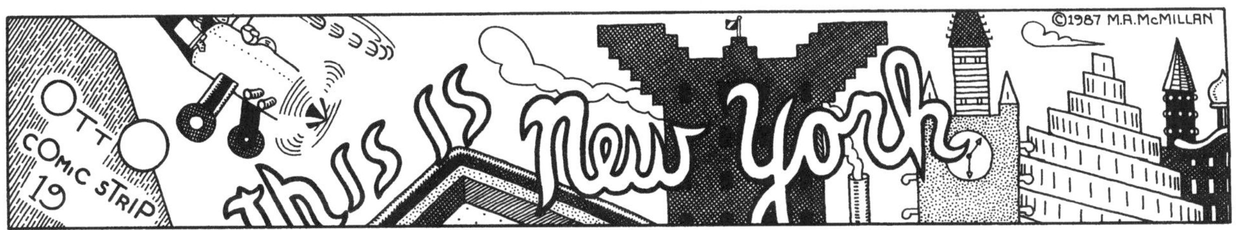

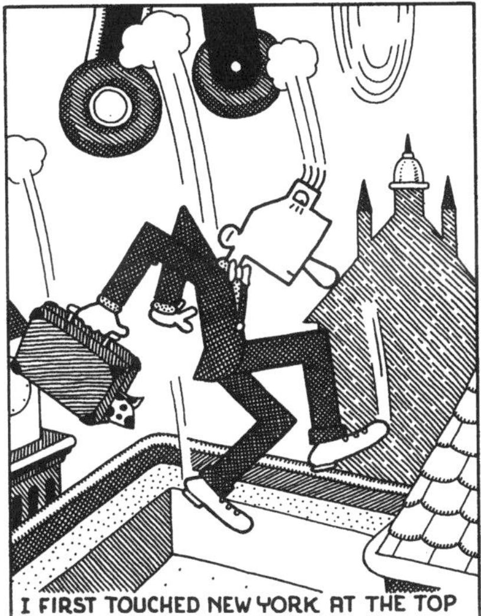

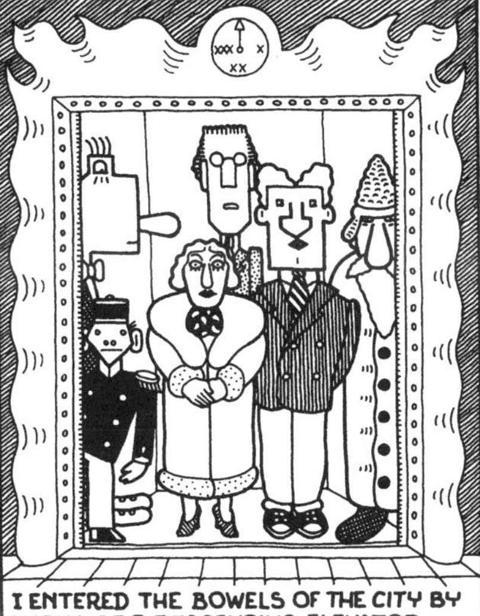

ALMOST IMMEDIATELY, AT THE NEAREST STREET CORNER, I BECAME AWARE OF THE PHENOMENON KNOWN AS "GRIDLOCK."

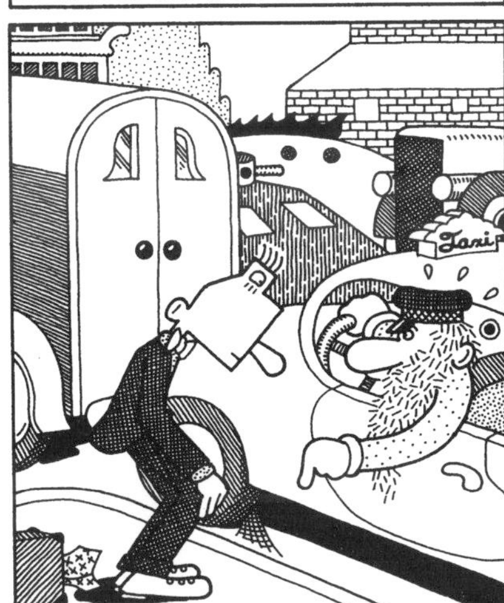

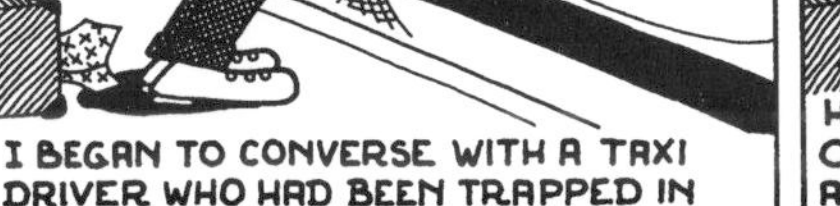

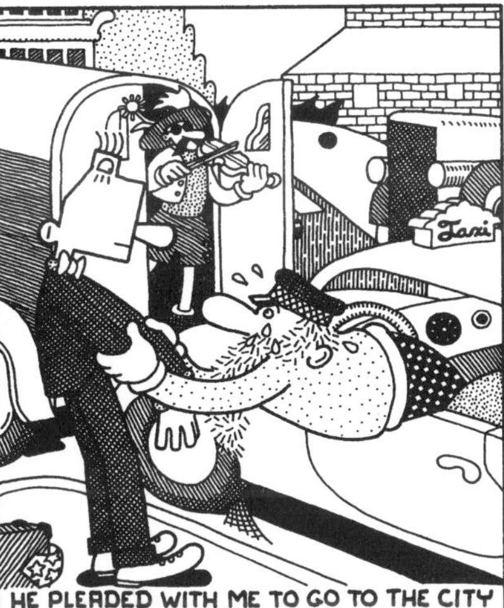

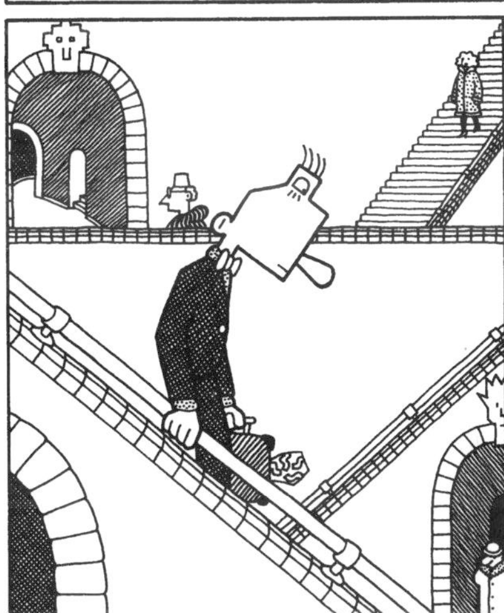

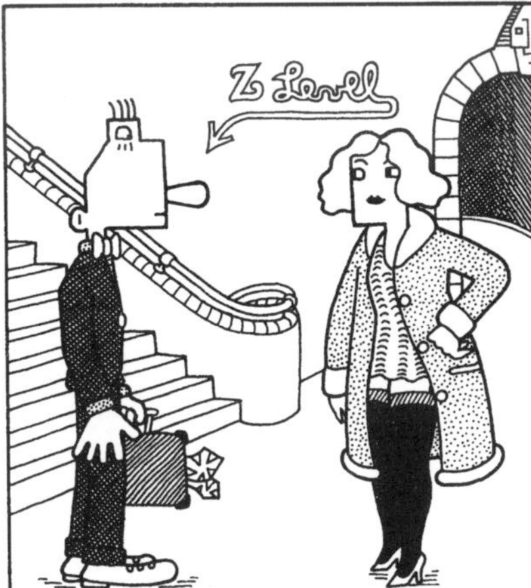

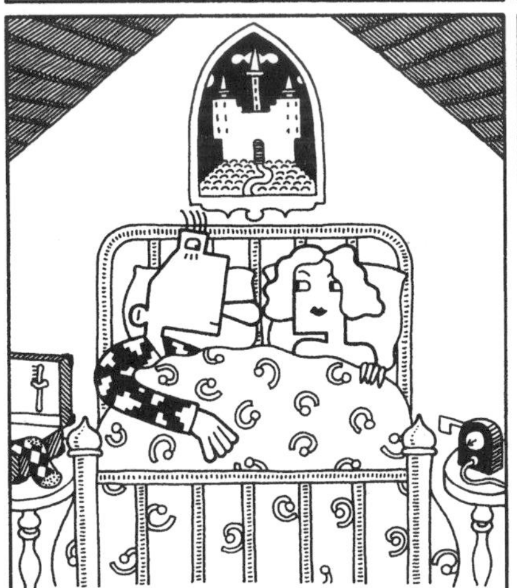

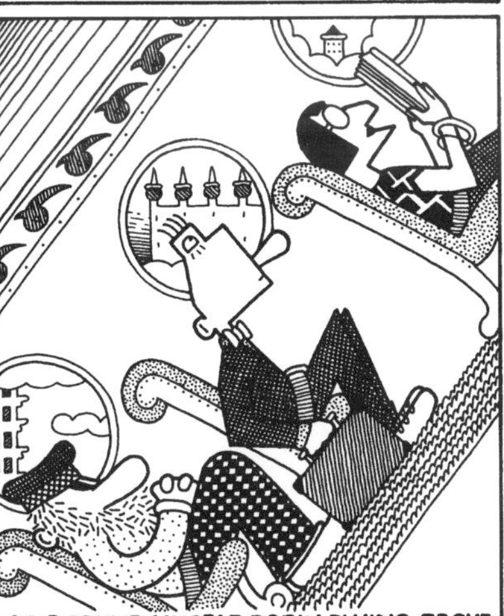

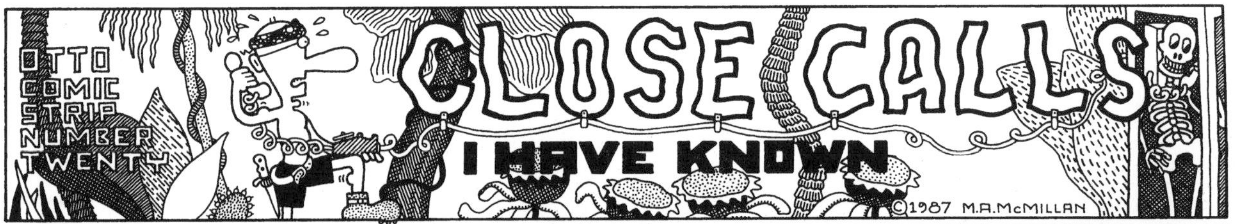
OTTO COMIC STRIP NUMBER TWENTY
CLOSE CALLS
I HAVE KNOWN
©1987 M.A.McMILLAN

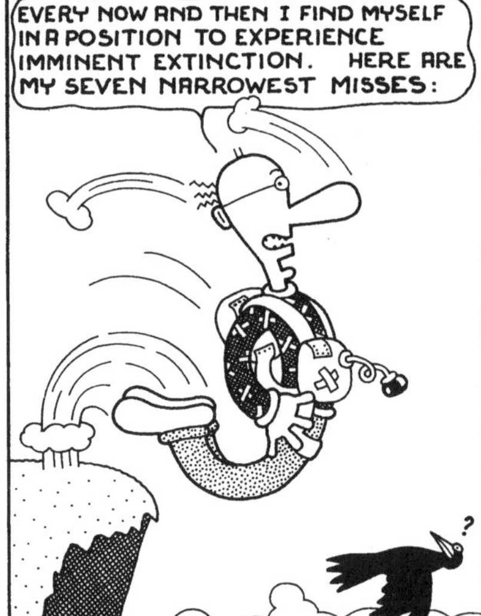
EVERY NOW AND THEN I FIND MYSELF IN A POSITION TO EXPERIENCE IMMINENT EXTINCTION. HERE ARE MY SEVEN NARROWEST MISSES:

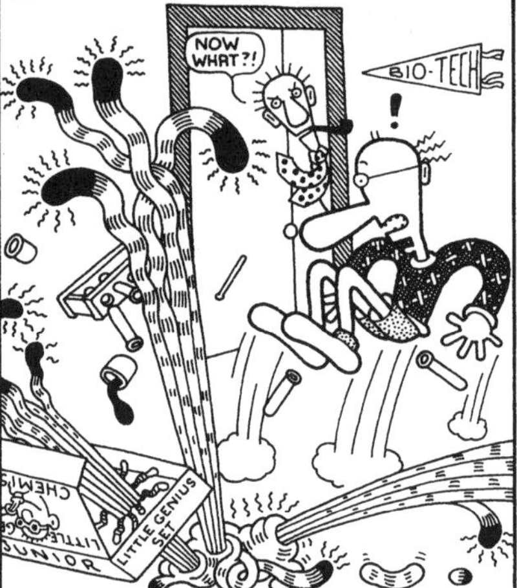
NOW WHAT?!
BIO-TECH
LITTLE GENIUS SET
ONE: AFTER MONTHS OF FUTILE EXPERIMENTS WITH MY "JUNIOR" CHEMISTRY SET, I HAD AT LAST ATTAINED THE INEVITABLE SOLUTION: DEVASTATION!

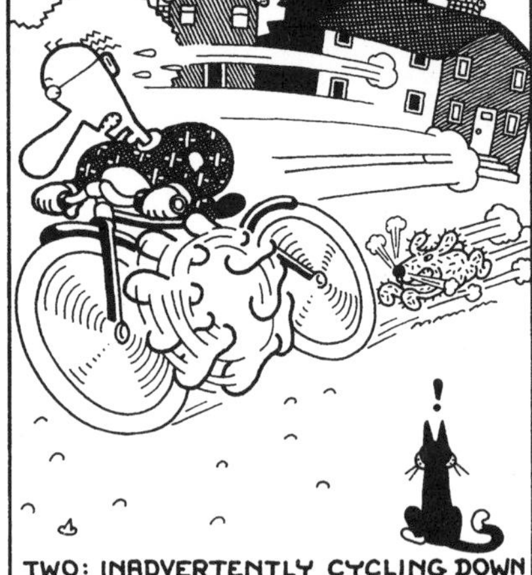
TWO: INADVERTENTLY CYCLING DOWN AN UNFAMILIAR STREET, I COULD BARELY PEDAL FAST ENOUGH TO ESCAPE THE JAWS OF A SNORTING CARPATHIAN TERRIER!

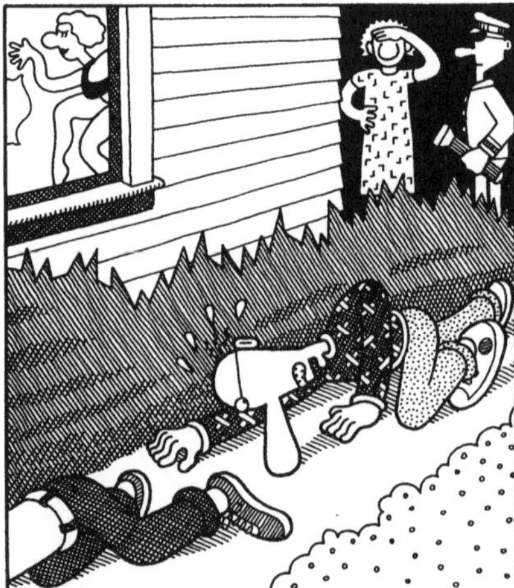

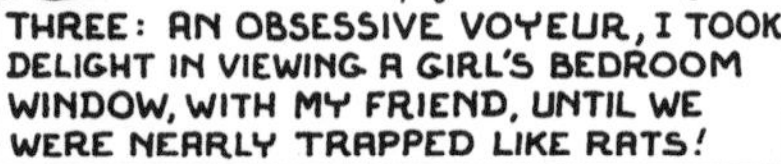
THREE: AN OBSESSIVE VOYEUR, I TOOK DELIGHT IN VIEWING A GIRL'S BEDROOM WINDOW, WITH MY FRIEND, UNTIL WE WERE NEARLY TRAPPED LIKE RATS!

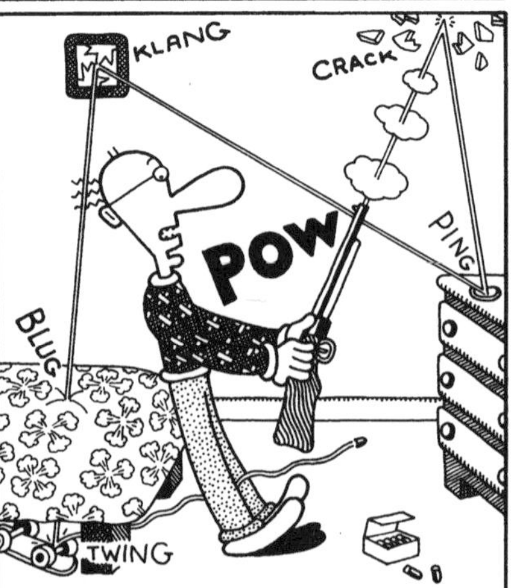
KLANG
CRACK
POW
PING
BLUG
TWING
FOUR: MY FIRST AND ONLY GUN WAS SENT TO ME BY MY FATHER WHO WAS CONCERNED THAT I SHOULD LEARN THE TRICKS OF THE COUNTRY'S MAJOR PASTIME.

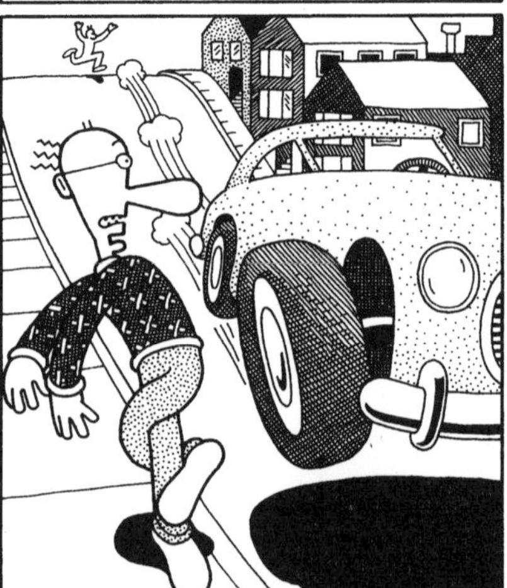
FIVE: IN A HILLY CITY.... AS I NONCHALANTLY STROLLED DOWN A STREET, I WAS CLOSELY MISSED BY AN AUTO WITH NO ONE IN IT!

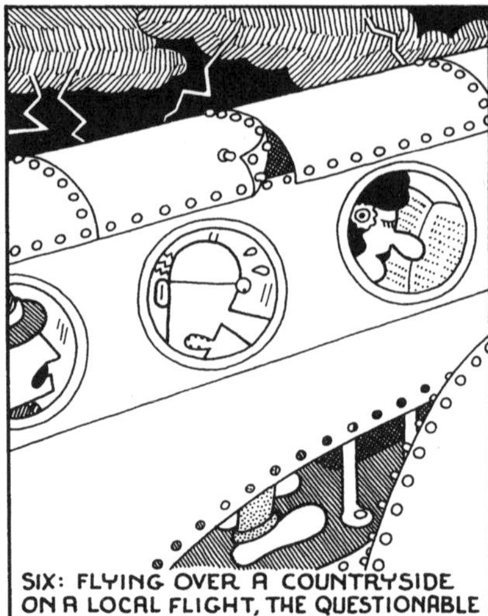
SIX: FLYING OVER A COUNTRYSIDE ON A LOCAL FLIGHT, THE QUESTIONABLE SOUNDNESS OF THE PLANE BECAME QUITE EVIDENT DURING TURBULENT WEATHER.

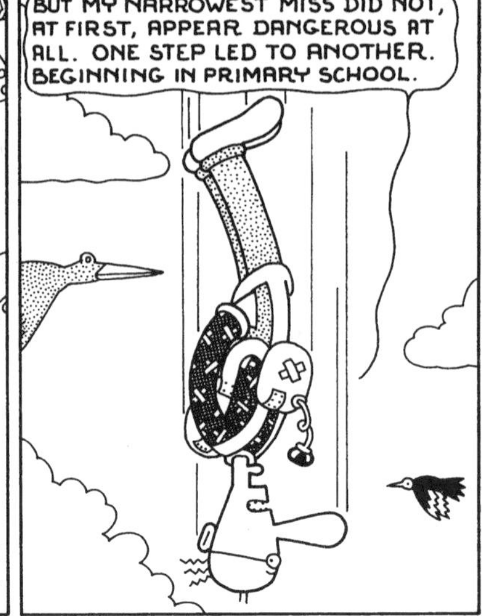
BUT MY NARROWEST MISS DID NOT, AT FIRST, APPEAR DANGEROUS AT ALL. ONE STEP LED TO ANOTHER. BEGINNING IN PRIMARY SCHOOL.

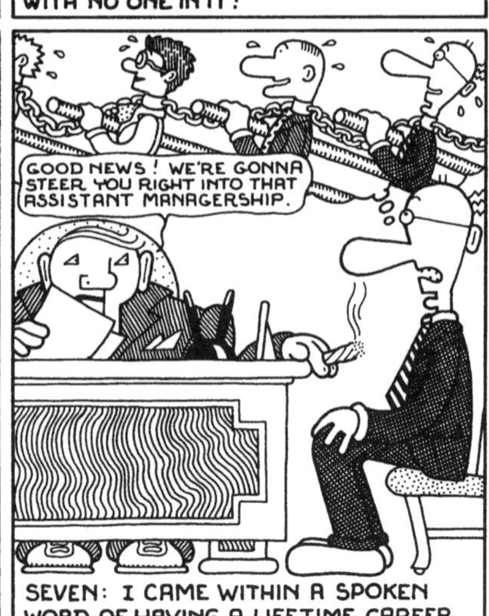
GOOD NEWS! WE'RE GONNA STEER YOU RIGHT INTO THAT ASSISTANT MANAGERSHIP.
SEVEN: I CAME WITHIN A SPOKEN WORD OF HAVING A LIFETIME CAREER IN THE OFFICES OF "SECURE SECURITIES SECURITY, INC." !!

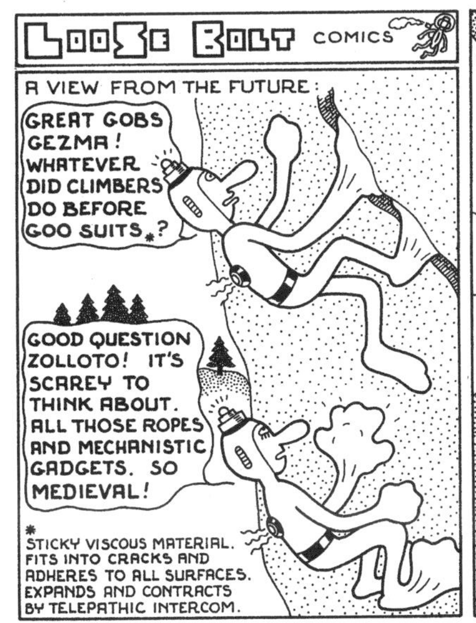
LOOSE BOLT COMICS
A VIEW FROM THE FUTURE:
GREAT GOBS GEZMA! WHATEVER DID CLIMBERS DO BEFORE GOO SUITS*?
GOOD QUESTION ZOLLOTO! IT'S SCAREY TO THINK ABOUT. ALL THOSE ROPES AND MECHANISTIC GADGETS. SO MEDIEVAL!
* STICKY VISCOUS MATERIAL. FITS INTO CRACKS AND ADHERES TO ALL SURFACES. EXPANDS AND CONTRACTS BY TELEPATHIC INTERCOM.
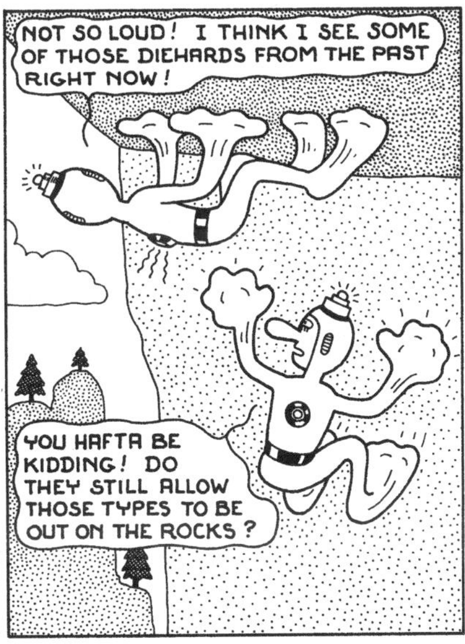
NOT SO LOUD! I THINK I SEE SOME OF THOSE DIEHARDS FROM THE PAST RIGHT NOW!
YOU HAFTA BE KIDDING! DO THEY STILL ALLOW THOSE TYPES TO BE OUT ON THE ROCKS?
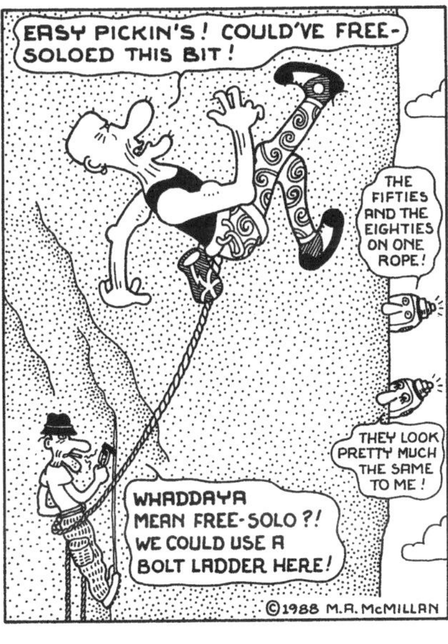
EASY PICKIN'S! COULD'VE FREE-SOLOED THIS BIT!
THE FIFTIES AND THE EIGHTIES ON ONE ROPE!
THEY LOOK PRETTY MUCH THE SAME TO ME!
WHADDAYA MEAN FREE-SOLO?! WE COULD USE A BOLT LADDER HERE!
©1988 M.A. McMILLAN
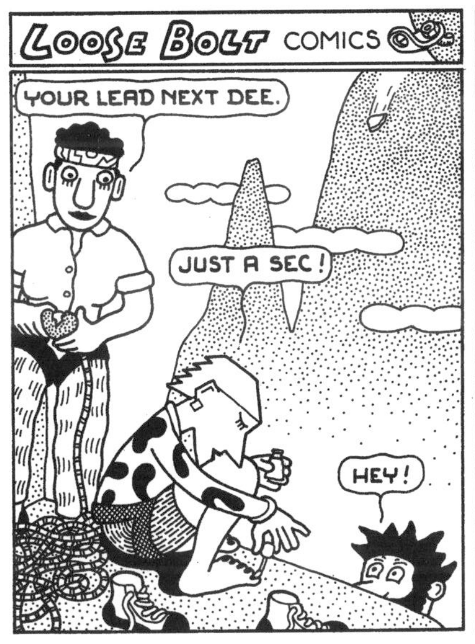
LOOSE BOLT COMICS
YOUR LEAD NEXT DEE.
JUST A SEC!
HEY!
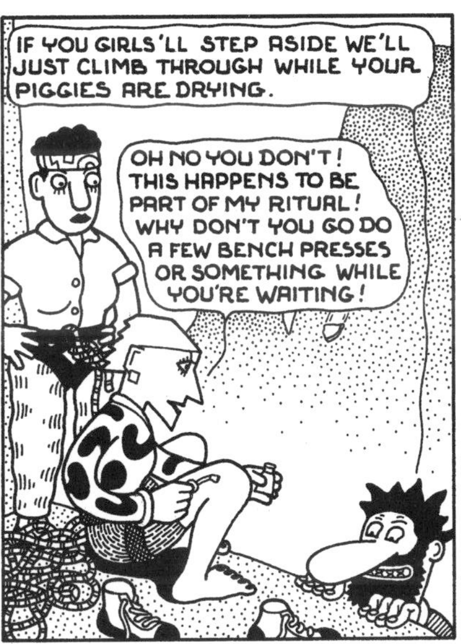
IF YOU GIRLS'LL STEP ASIDE WE'LL JUST CLIMB THROUGH WHILE YOUR PIGGIES ARE DRYING.
OH NO YOU DON'T! THIS HAPPENS TO BE PART OF MY RITUAL! WHY DON'T YOU GO DO A FEW BENCH PRESSES OR SOMETHING WHILE YOU'RE WAITING!
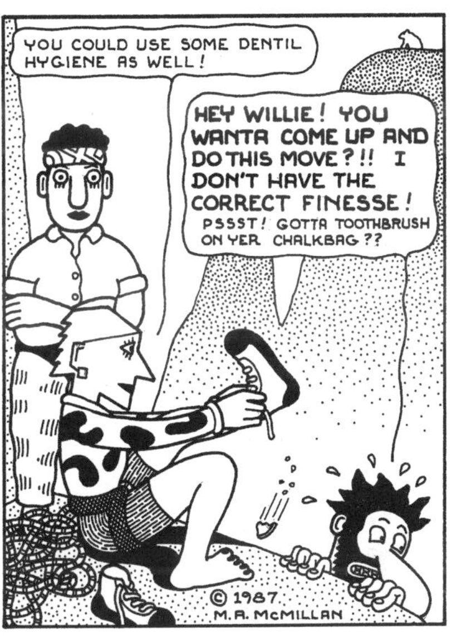
YOU COULD USE SOME DENTIL HYGIENE AS WELL!
HEY WILLIE! YOU WANTA COME UP AND DO THIS MOVE?!! I DON'T HAVE THE CORRECT FINESSE!
PSSST! GOTTA TOOTHBRUSH ON YER CHALKBAG??
© 1987. M.A. McMILLAN
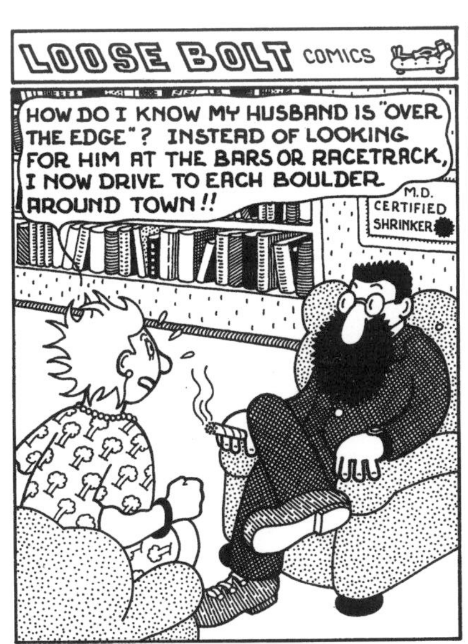
LOOSE BOLT COMICS
HOW DO I KNOW MY HUSBAND IS "OVER THE EDGE"? INSTEAD OF LOOKING FOR HIM AT THE BARS OR RACETRACK, I NOW DRIVE TO EACH BOULDER AROUND TOWN!!
M.D. CERTIFIED SHRINKER
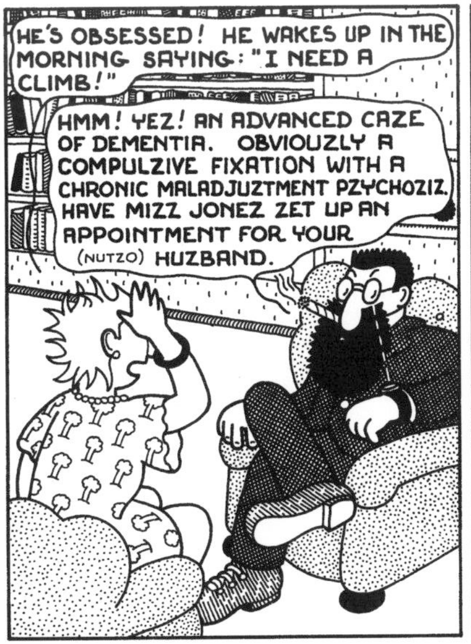
HE'S OBSESSED! HE WAKES UP IN THE MORNING SAYING: "I NEED A CLIMB!"
HMM! YEZ! AN ADVANCED CAZE OF DEMENTIA. OBVIOUZLY A COMPULZIVE FIXATION WITH A CHRONIC MALADJUZTMENT PZYCHOZIZ. HAVE MIZZ JONEZ ZET UP AN APPOINTMENT FOR YOUR (NUTZO) HUZBAND.
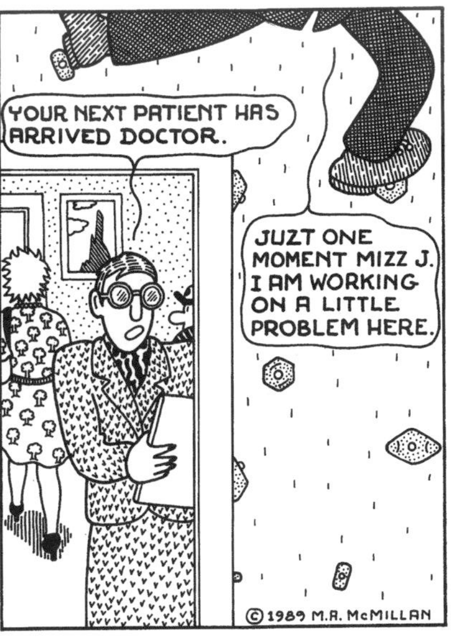
YOUR NEXT PATIENT HAS ARRIVED DOCTOR.
JUZT ONE MOMENT MIZZ J. I AM WORKING ON A LITTLE PROBLEM HERE.
©1989 M.A. McMILLAN

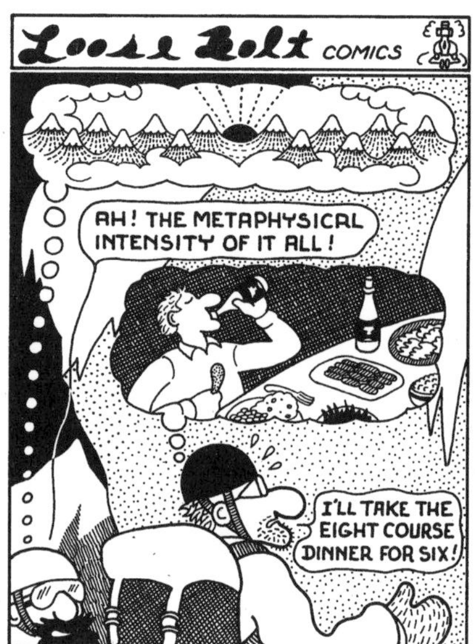
Loose Bolt COMICS
AH! THE METAPHYSICAL INTENSITY OF IT ALL!
I'LL TAKE THE EIGHT COURSE DINNER FOR SIX!

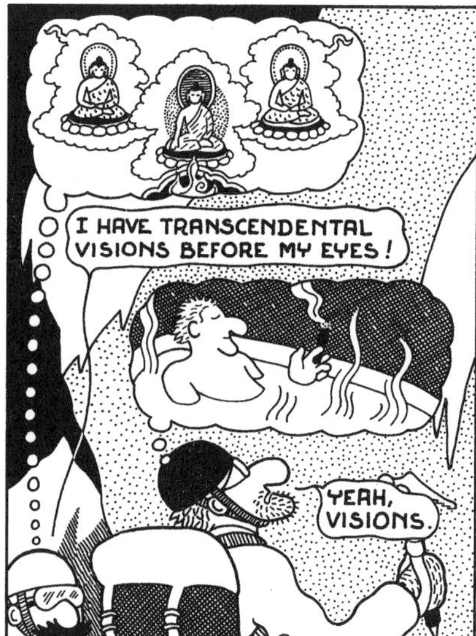
I HAVE TRANSCENDENTAL VISIONS BEFORE MY EYES!
YEAH, VISIONS.
©1989 M.A. McMILLAN

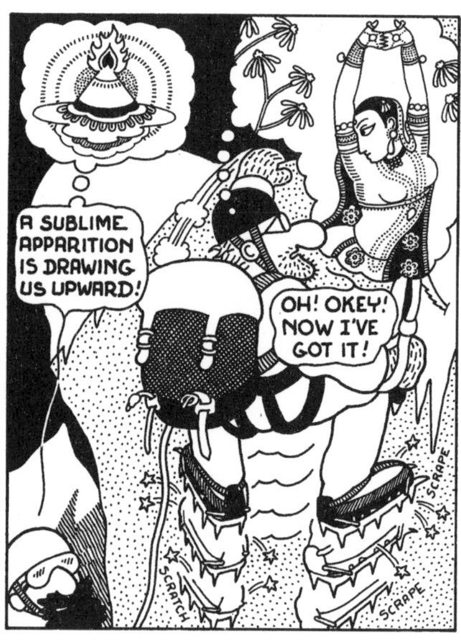
A SUBLIME APPARITION IS DRAWING US UPWARD!
OH! OKEY! NOW I'VE GOT IT!
SCRATCH
SCRAPE
SCRAPE

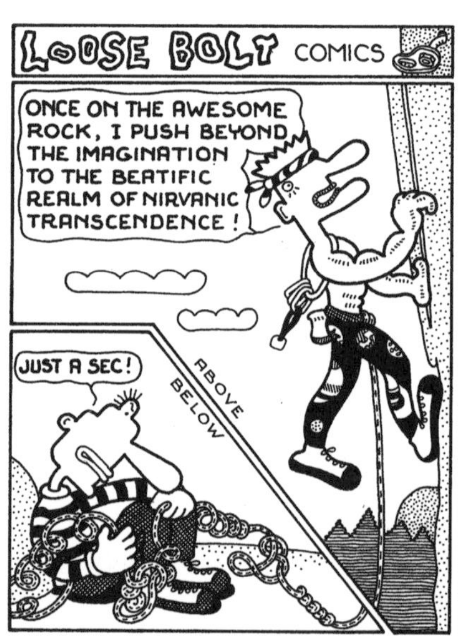
LOOSE BOLT COMICS
ONCE ON THE AWESOME ROCK, I PUSH BEYOND THE IMAGINATION TO THE BEATIFIC REALM OF NIRVANIC TRANSCENDENCE!
JUST A SEC!
ABOVE
BELOW

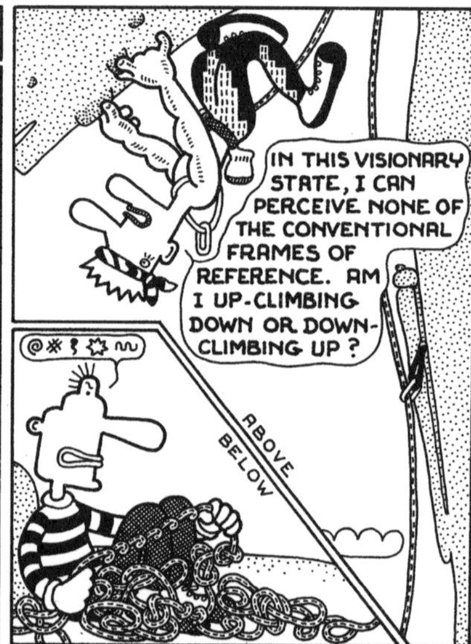
IN THIS VISIONARY STATE, I CAN PERCEIVE NONE OF THE CONVENTIONAL FRAMES OF REFERENCE. AM I UP-CLIMBING DOWN OR DOWN-CLIMBING UP?
ABOVE
BELOW

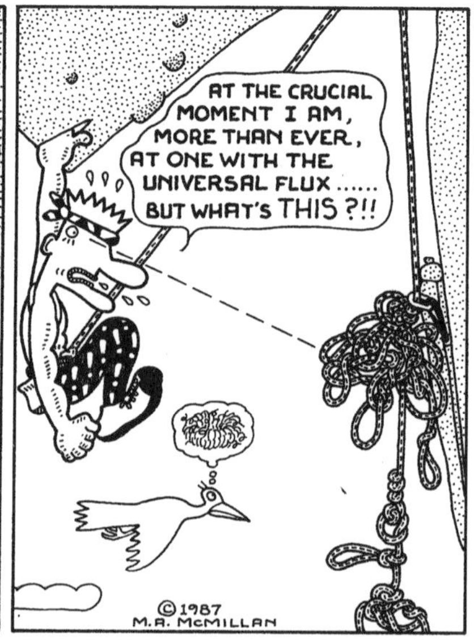
AT THE CRUCIAL MOMENT I AM, MORE THAN EVER, AT ONE WITH THE UNIVERSAL FLUX...... BUT WHAT'S THIS?!!
©1987 M.A. McMILLAN

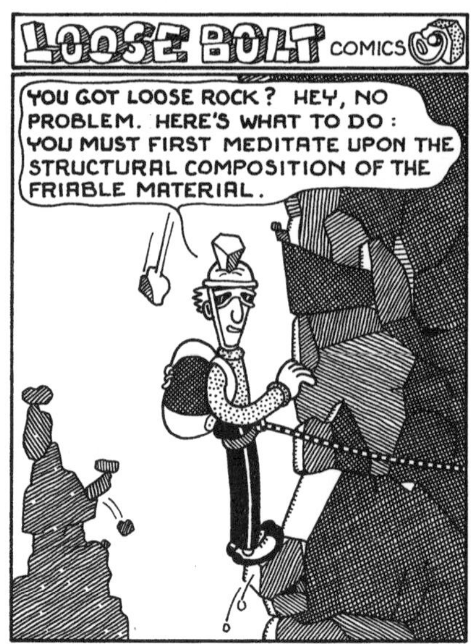
LOOSE BOLT COMICS
YOU GOT LOOSE ROCK? HEY, NO PROBLEM. HERE'S WHAT TO DO: YOU MUST FIRST MEDITATE UPON THE STRUCTURAL COMPOSITION OF THE FRIABLE MATERIAL.

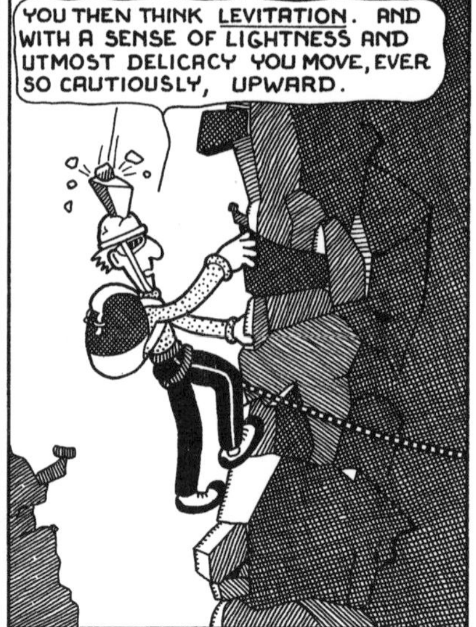
YOU THEN THINK LEVITATION. AND WITH A SENSE OF LIGHTNESS AND UTMOST DELICACY YOU MOVE, EVER SO CAUTIOUSLY, UPWARD.

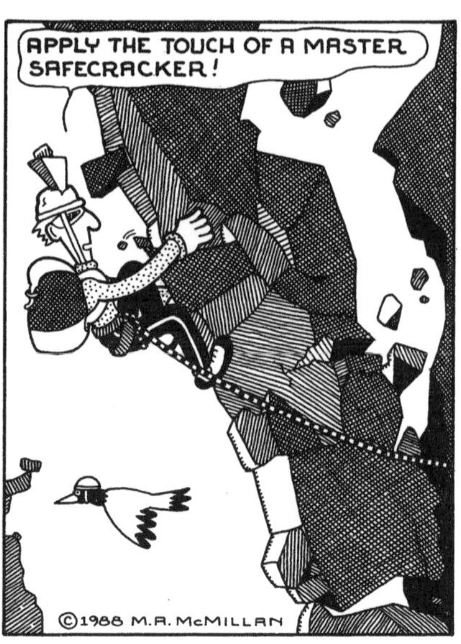
APPLY THE TOUCH OF A MASTER SAFECRACKER!
©1988 M.A. McMILLAN

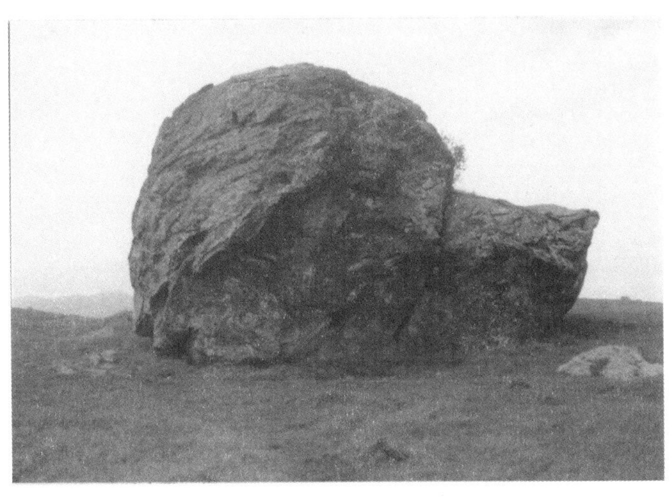

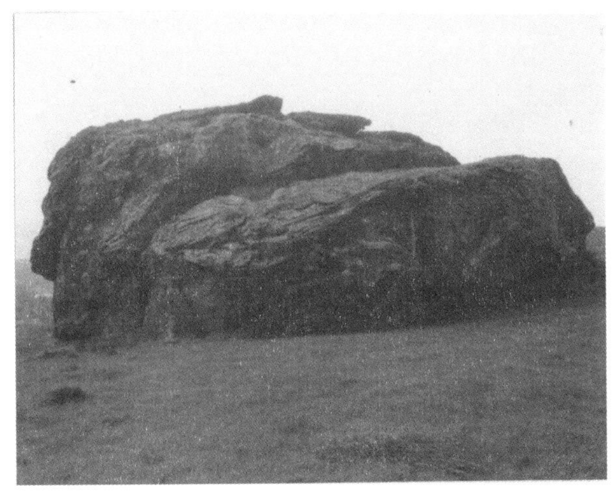

turtle rock   east side

north side

BOULDER AT RING MOUNTAIN
Marin COUNTY

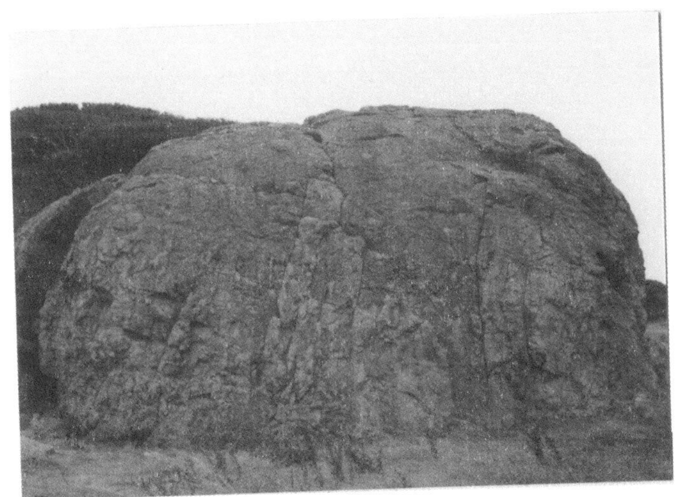

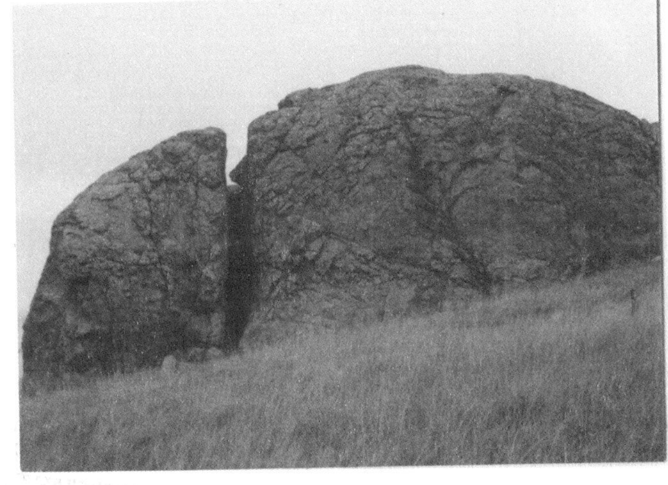

split rock   west face

south face

BOULDER AT RING MOUNTAIN
Marin COUNTY

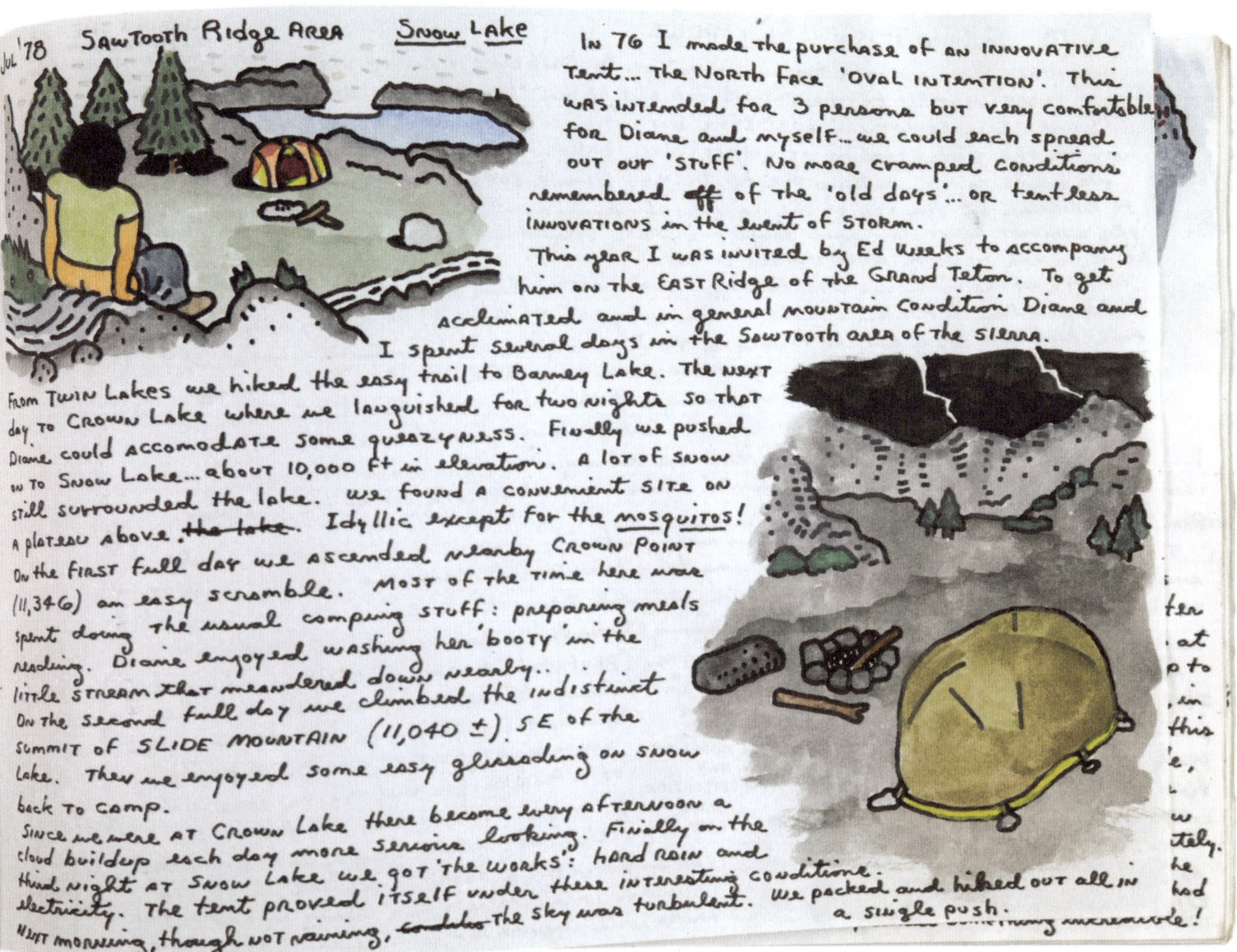

Jul '78 SawTooth Ridge Area Snow Lake

In 76 I made the purchase of an innovative tent... The North Face 'Oval Intention'. This was intended for 3 persons but very comfortable for Diane and myself... we could each spread out our 'stuff'. No more cramped conditions remembered ~~off~~ of the 'old days'... or tentless innovations in the event of storm.

This year I was invited by Ed Weeks to accompany him on the East Ridge of the Grand Teton. To get acclimated and in general mountain condition Diane and I spent several days in the Sawtooth area of the Sierra.

From Twin Lakes we hiked the easy trail to Barney Lake. The next day to Crown Lake where we languished for two nights so that Diane could accomodate some queazyness. Finally we pushed on to Snow Lake... about 10,000 ft in elevation. A lot of snow still surrounded the lake. We found a convenient site on a plateau above ~~the lake~~. Idyllic except for the mosquitos!

On the first full day we ascended nearby Crown Point (11,346) an easy scramble. Most of the time here was spent doing the usual camping stuff: preparing meals reading. Diane enjoyed washing her 'booty' in the little stream that meandered down nearby..

On the second full day we climbed the indistinct summit of Slide Mountain (11,040 ±) SE of the lake. Then we enjoyed some easy glissading on snow back to camp.

Since we were at Crown Lake there become every afternoon a cloud buildup each day more serious looking. Finally on the third night at Snow Lake we got 'the works': hard rain and electricity. The tent proved itself under these interesting conditions. Next morning, though not raining, ~~conditions~~ the sky was turbulent. We packed and hiked out all in a single push.

I was a climber of mountains, crags, and boulders from 1951 to 2004. There is a climb route at Pinnacles National Monument called "Adrenaline Junkies,`" which adequately described my climbing fix. The elation after getting away with a risky commitment. By 1988 I'd recorded each outing in journals, with illustrations. There are four volumes.

May '58 Mt. Shasta Attempt with Snow Storm

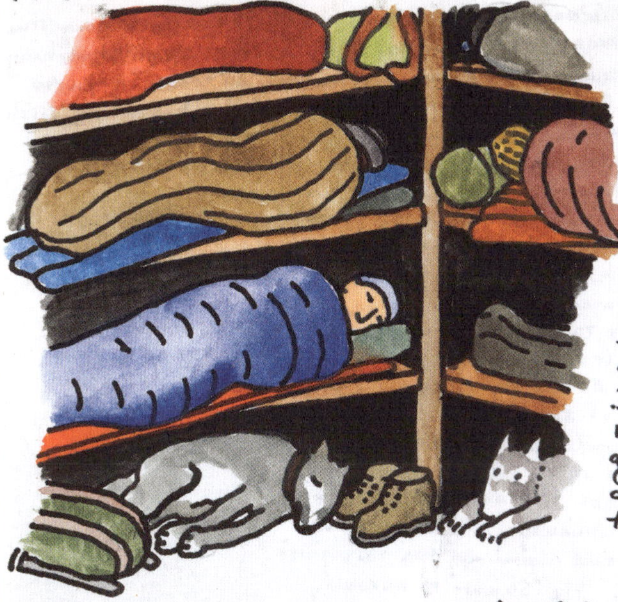

On memorial Day weekend the Sierra Club had a double outing in Northern California: Castle Crags and or Mt. Shasta. I choose Mt. Shasta. The problem was it was stormy for most of the weekend. I drove my VW as far as possible on a severely rutted road then hiked on snow a couple of miles to the small stone hut on the south side of the mountain.

As evening came more and more aspirants showed up… including people from L.A. and a group from Portland with two large dogs! As a storm intensified we found ourselves packed together… though a spirited and amenible crowd.

At six A.M. next morning the sky was still overcast, wind still blowing… but two others (can't remember names) and myself …and a couple other teams decided to go for it.

We pressed on in near white out for hours …up! At the steep section (Red Banks?) I was going full steam then paused to adjust something … taking off a glove.

It blew down the slope giving my friends the chance to rationalize turning around.

This has been my high point on Shasta: the trade route but certainly extreme conditions.

The L.A. skiers made the summit.

I think the dogs remained hut bound.

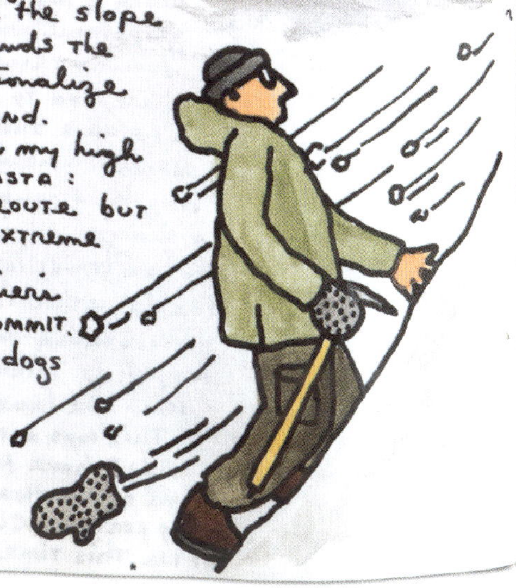

17 Apr Fri 1998 Mortar & Indian Rock Bench Wall 3rd Ascent

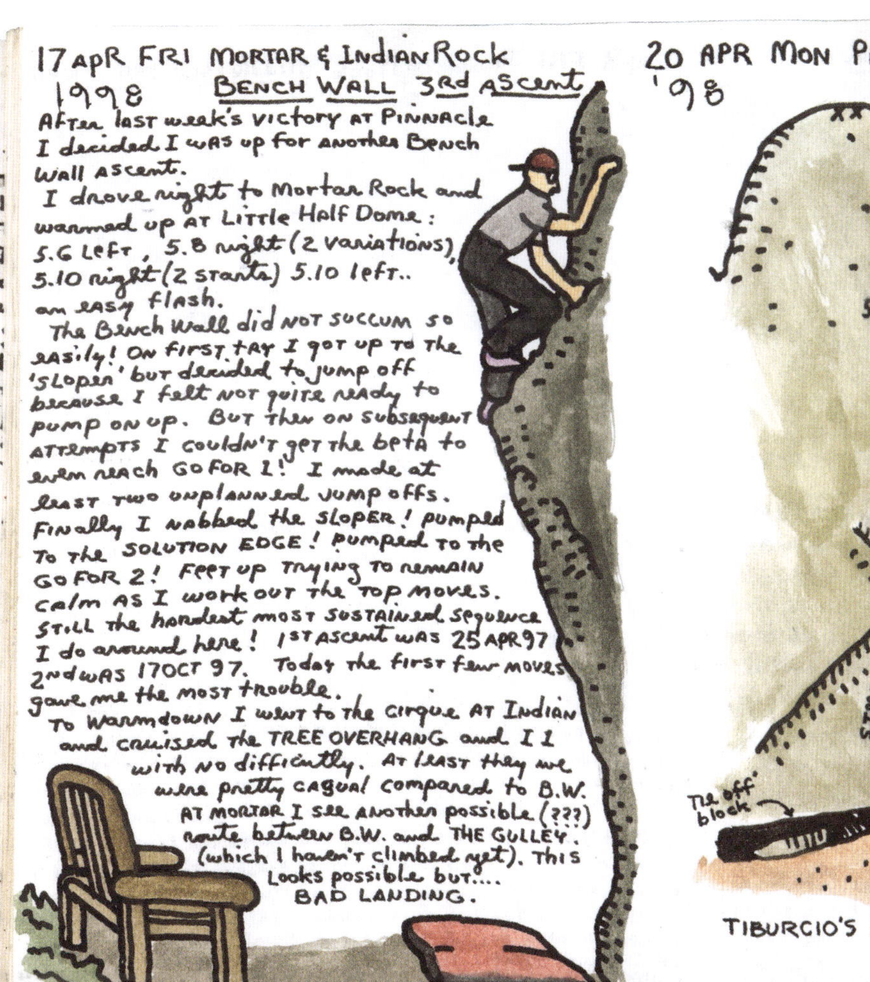

After last week's victory at Pinnacle I decided I was up for another Bench Wall ascent.

I drove right to Mortar Rock and warmed up at Little Half Dome: 5.6 left, 5.8 right (2 variations), 5.10 right (2 starts) 5.10 left.. an easy flash.

The Bench Wall did not succum so easily! On first try I got up to the 'sloper' but decided to jump off because I felt not quite ready to pump on up. But then on subsequent attempts I couldn't get the beta to even reach go for 1! I made at least two unplanned jump offs. Finally I nabbed the sloper! pumped to the solution edge! pumped to the go for 2! Feet up trying to remain calm as I work out the top moves. Still the hardest most sustained sequence I do around here! 1st ascent was 25 APR 97 2nd was 17 OCT 97. Today the first few moves gave me the most trouble.

To warmdown I went to the cirque at Indian and cruised the tree overhang and I 1 with no difficulty. At least they we were pretty casual compared to B.W. At Mortar I see another possible (???) route between B.W. and the Gulley (which I haven't climbed yet). This looks possible but…. BAD LANDING.

20 Apr Mon '98 Pinnacles Coyote Ugly on Tiburcio's X ★ my opinion ★★★

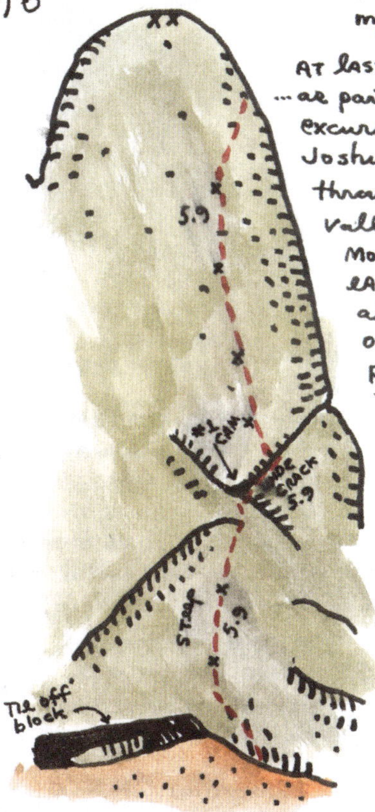

At last a trip to Pinnacles …as part of a driving excursion to include Joshua Tree and back through the central valley.

Mon at Pinnacles east side was almost all to ourselves. My plan was to climb Tiburcio's X (Coyote Ugly)…an intriguing name as well as a spectacular locale for a route… but I wanted to have a look before commiting.

At the site I had several second thoughts. One was there did not seem to be any convenient anchor. Two was Diane wanted to take a nap so I would have to self belay. Three was: this is a steep and long route!

5.9
#1 CAM
Wide crack 5.9
Step
5.9
The off block

TIBURCIO'S X SOUTH SIDE

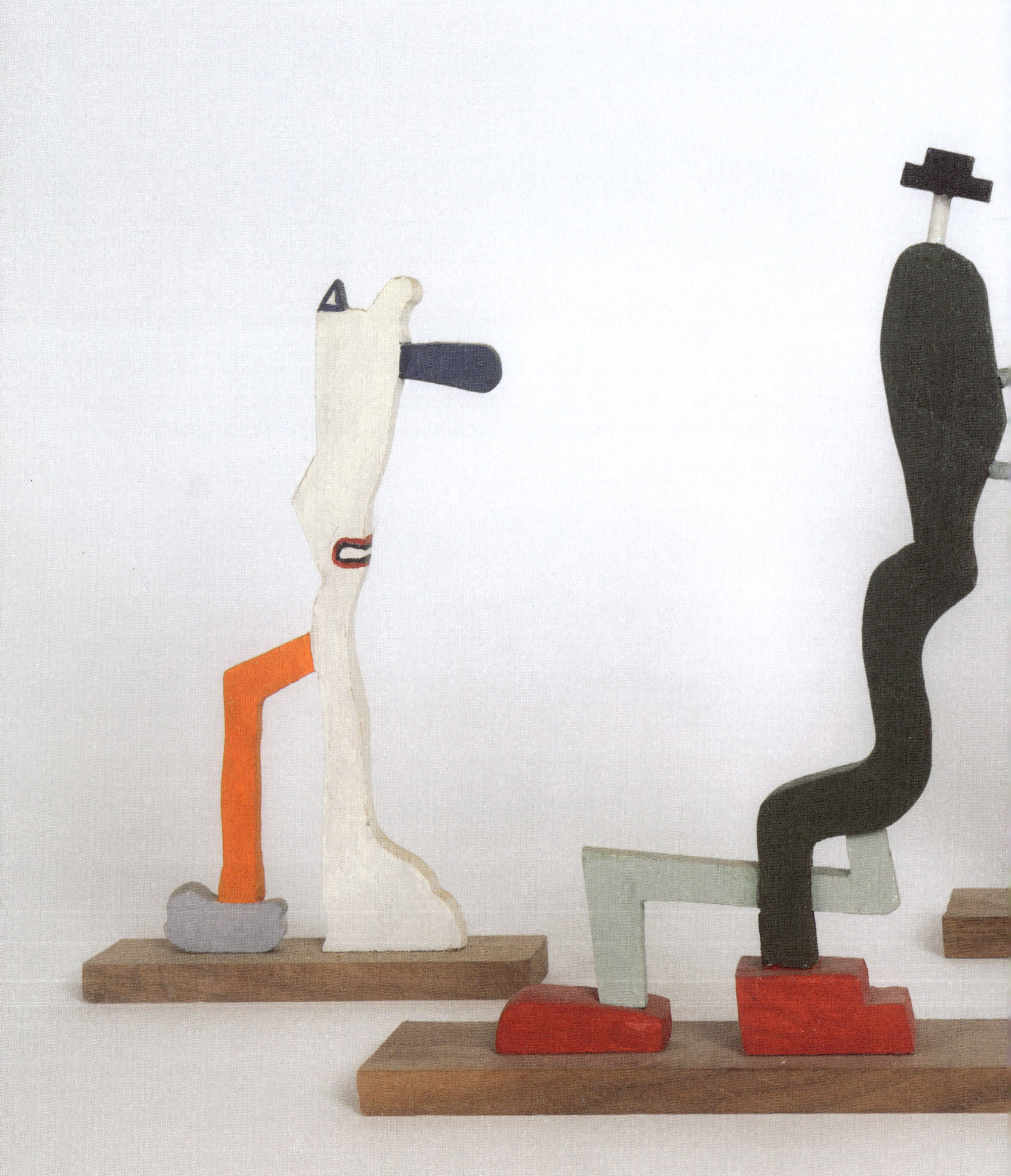

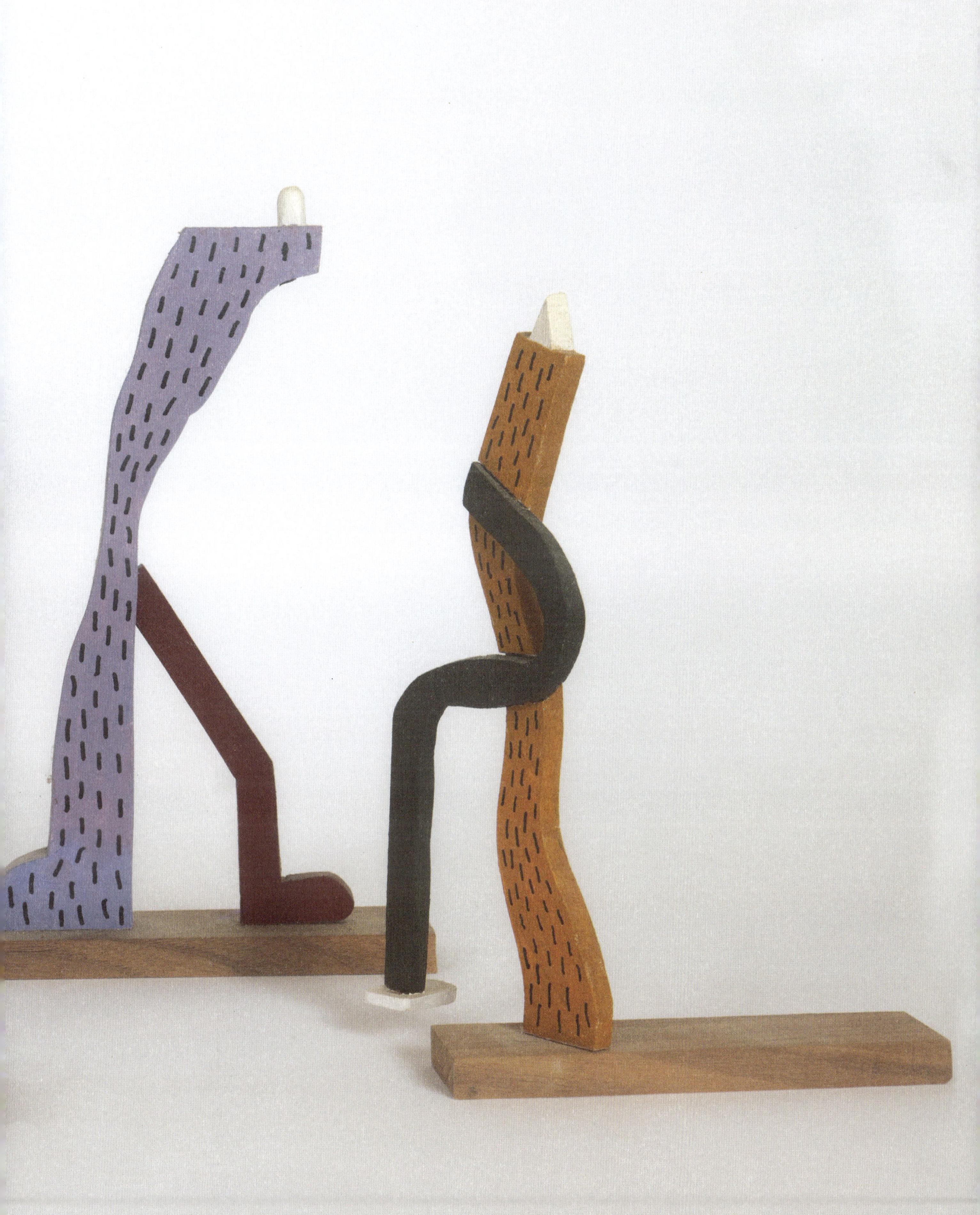

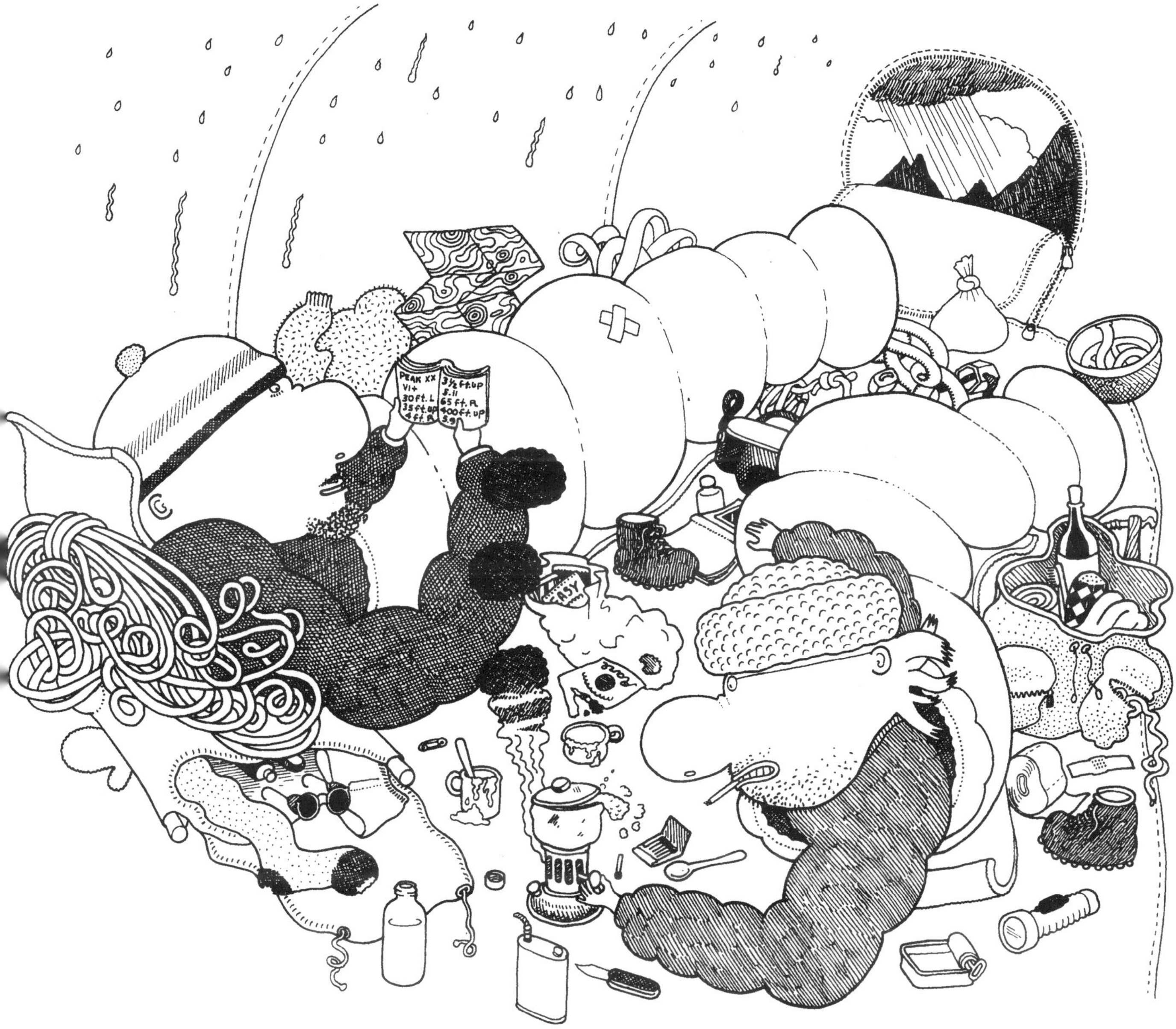

Home Sweet Home

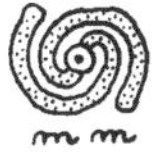

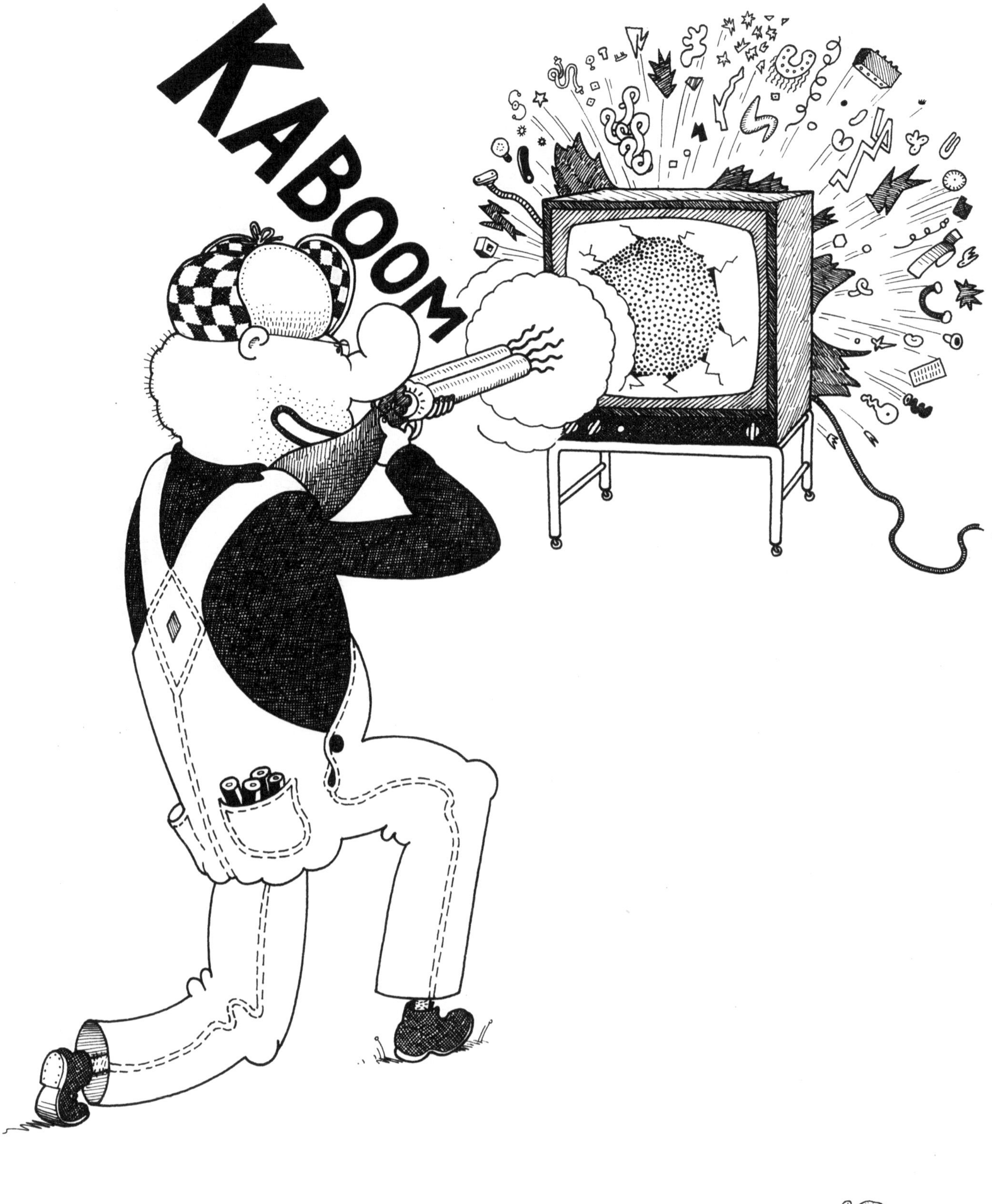

KABOOM

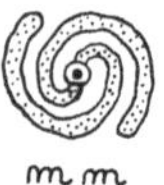

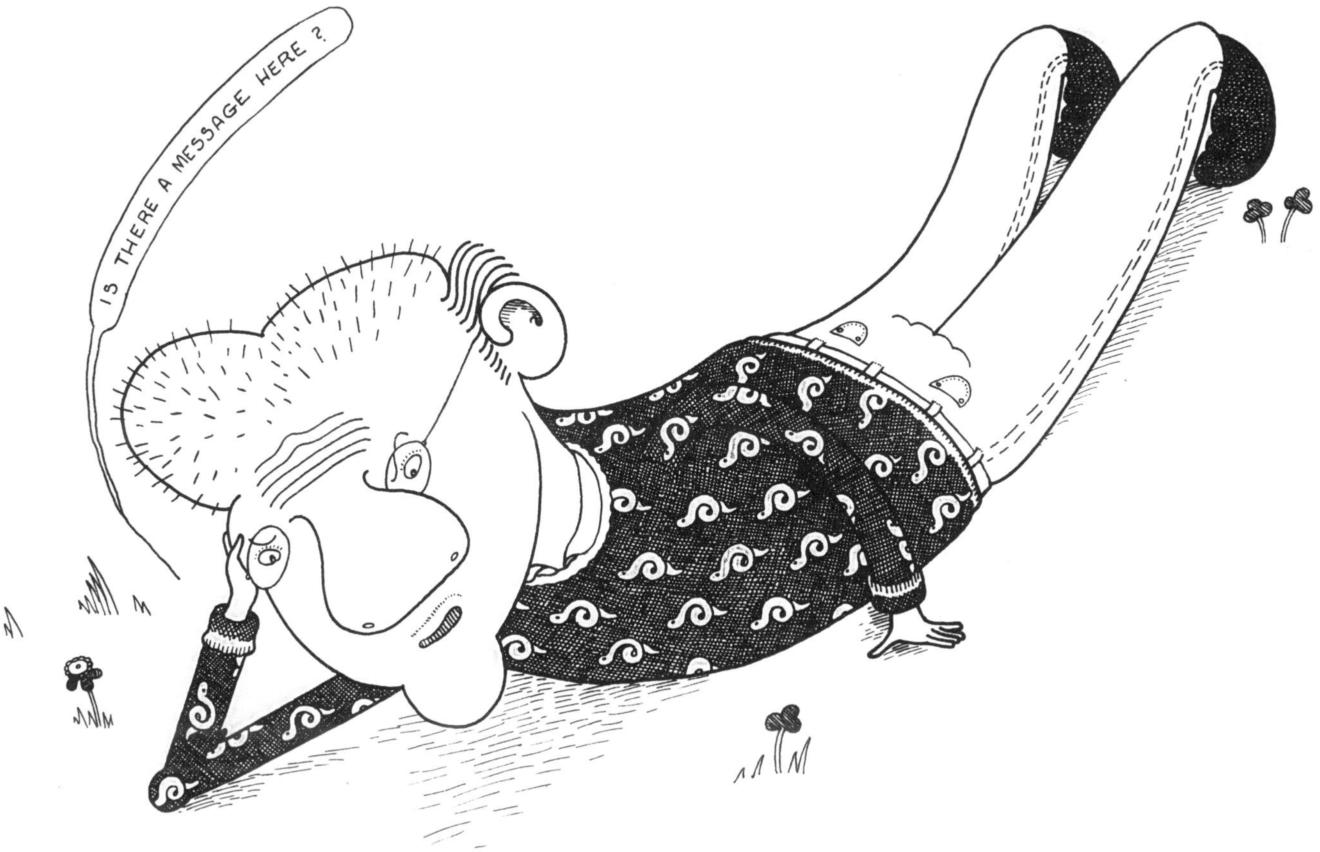

IS THERE A MESSAGE HERE ?

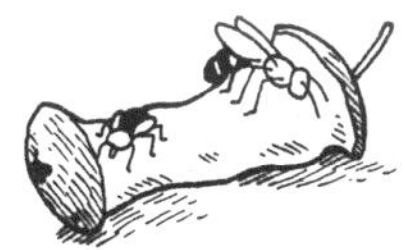

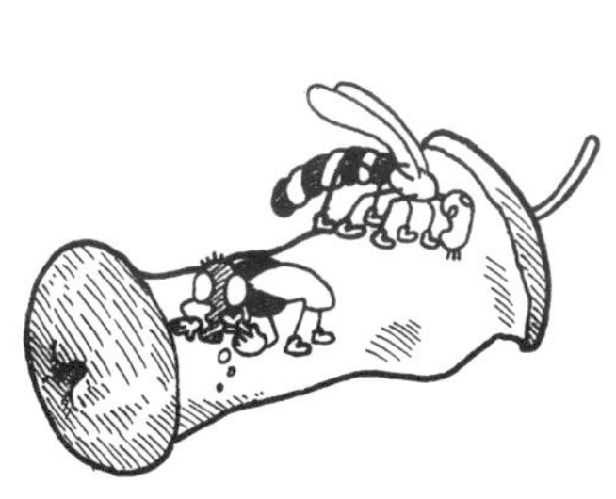

In the Park I happened to observe the following incident: A WASP and a FLY were compatibly taking lunch at the same "table."

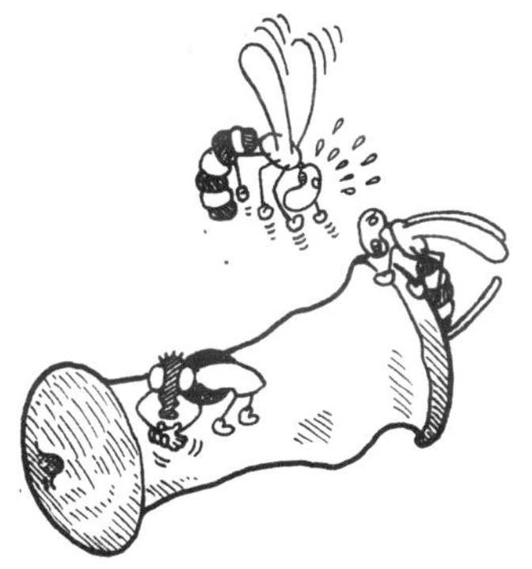

Enter WASP "B" causing WASP "A" to fly into a state of acute nervous agitation. This made it impossible for the two WASPS to "sit down" together.

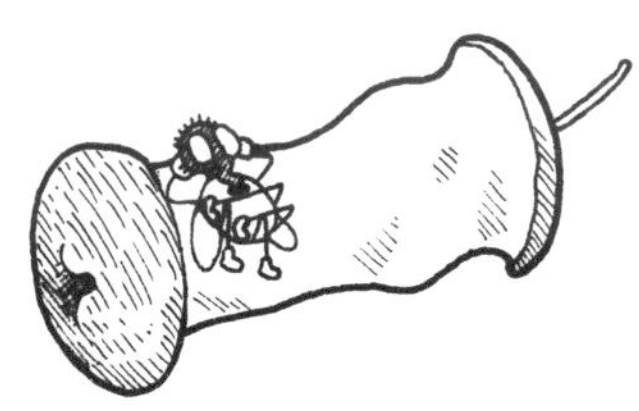

Meanwhile the FLY, wholly indifferent to the excited WASPS, continued to round out his meal in peaceful seclusion.

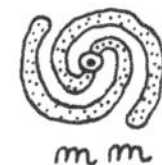

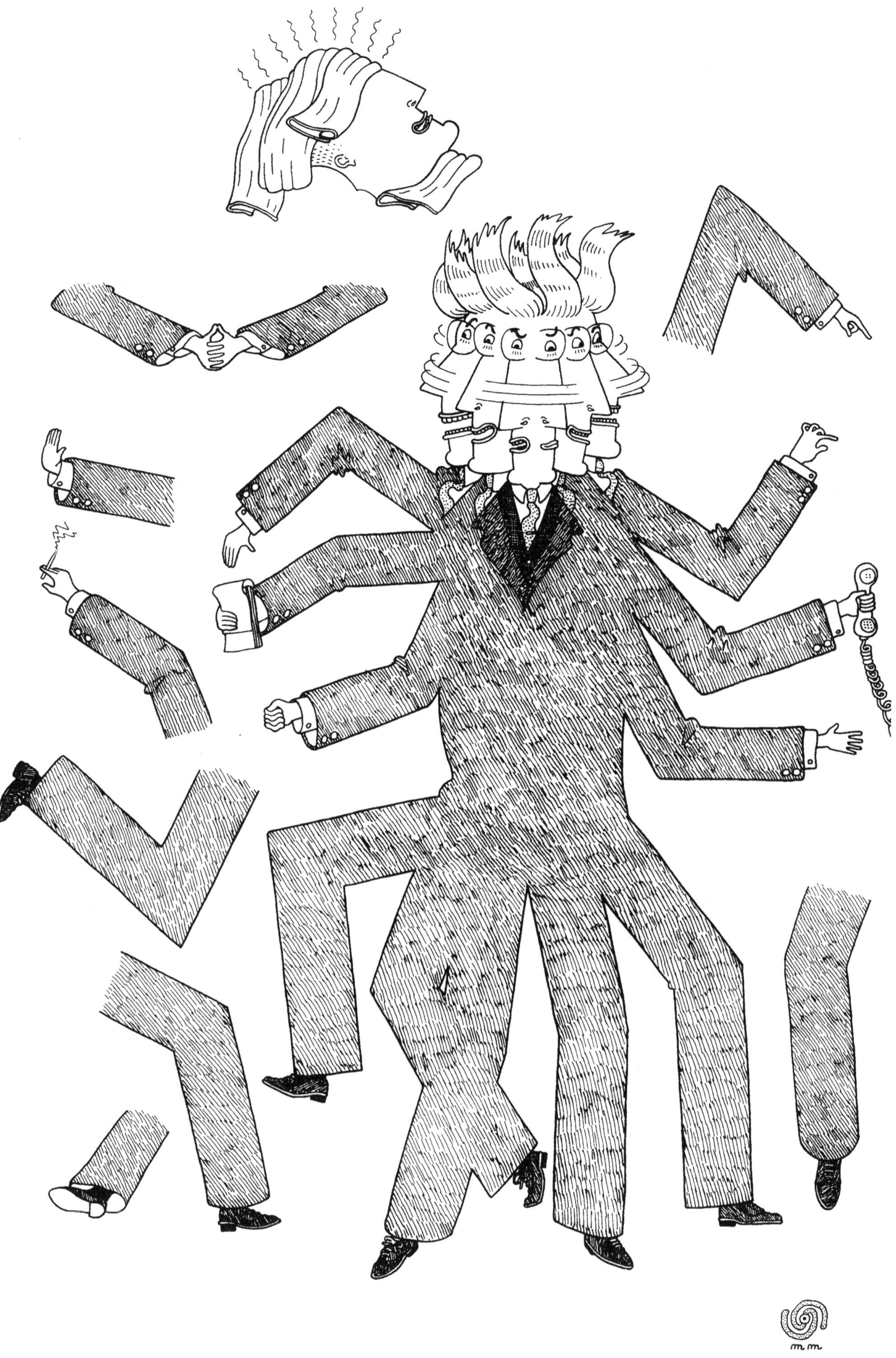

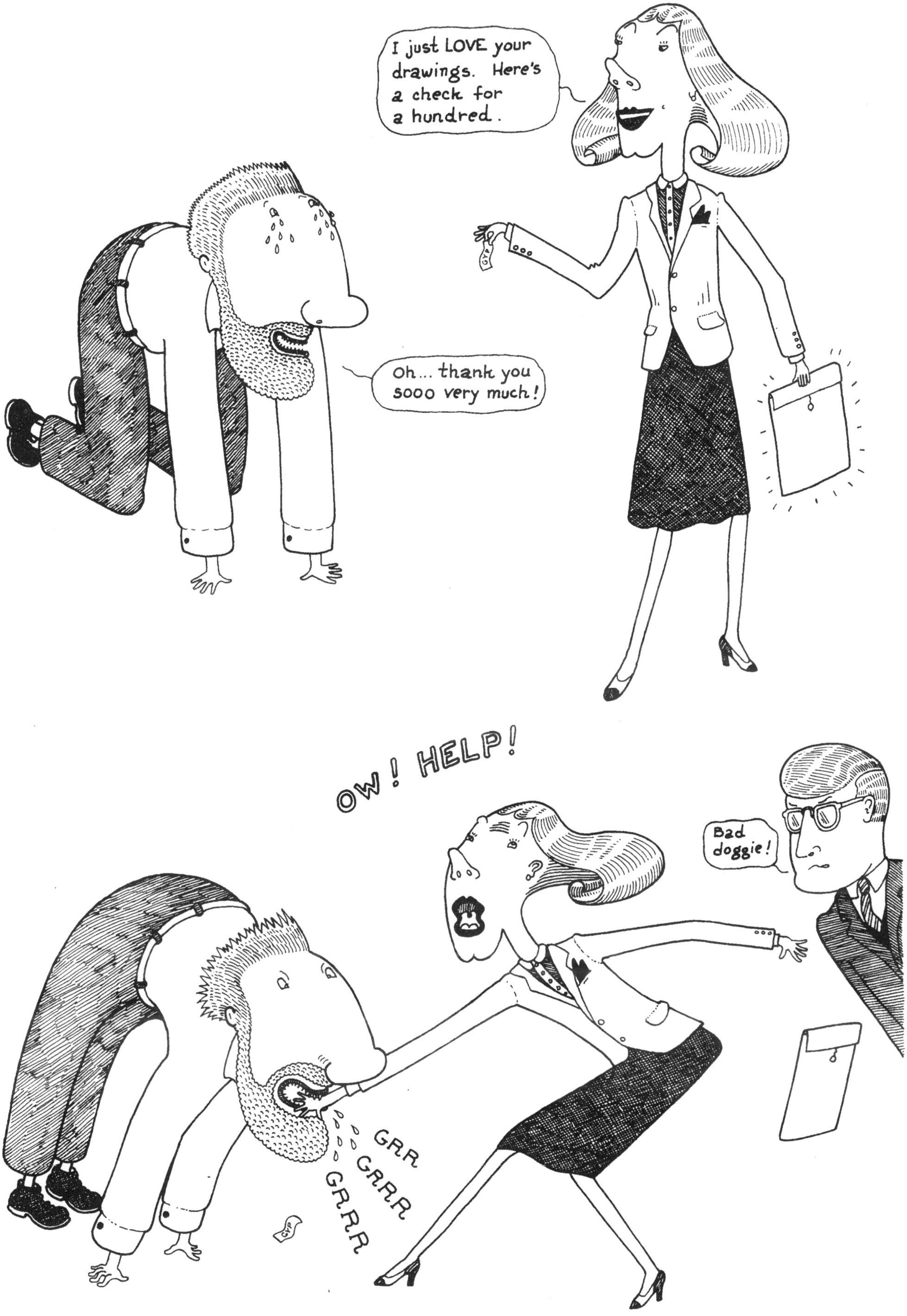

I just LOVE your drawings. Here's a check for a hundred.

Oh... thank you sooo very much!

OW! HELP!

Bad doggie!

GRR

GRRR

GRRR

Biting The Hand That Feeds

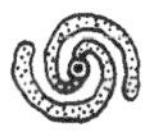

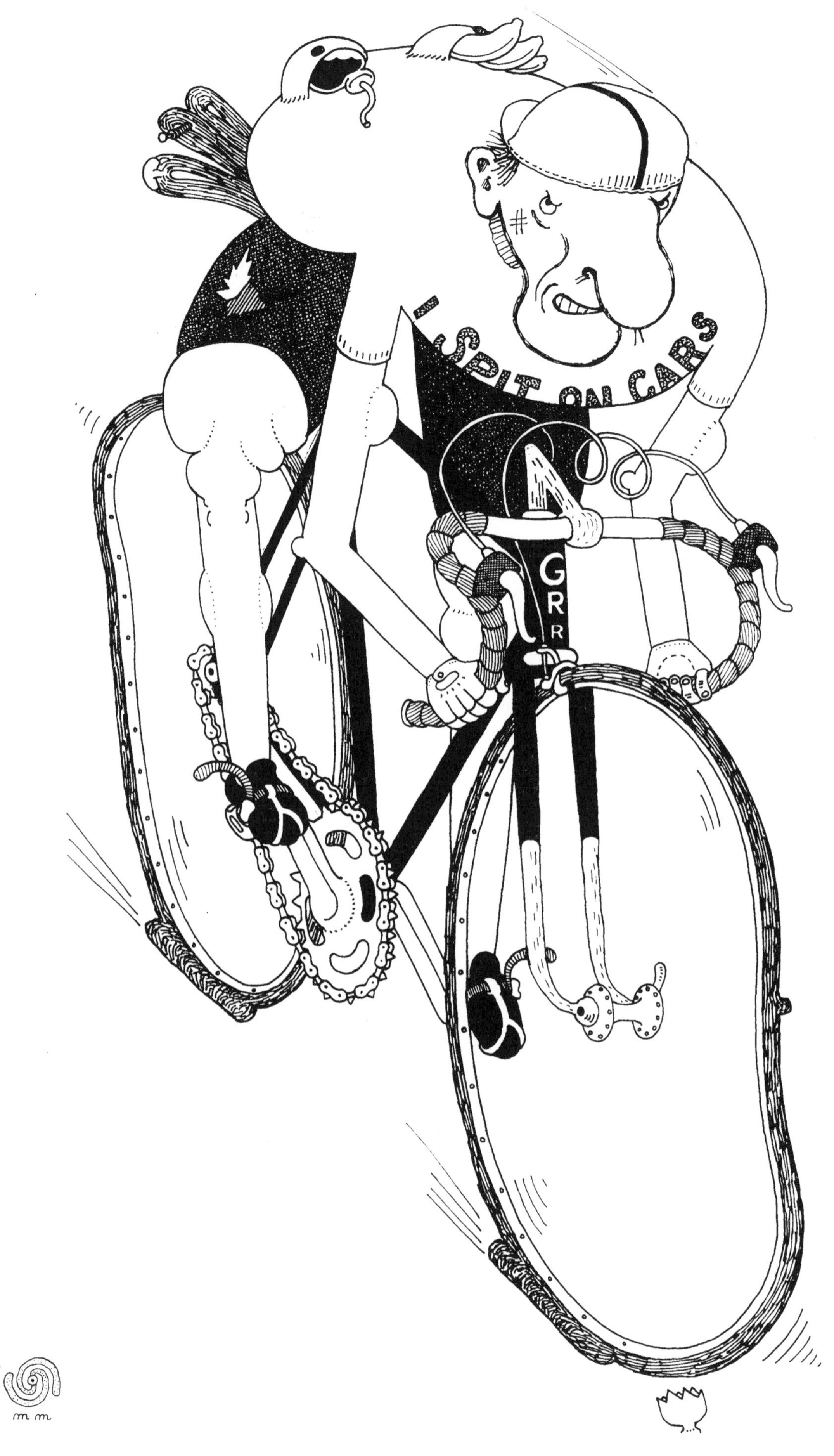
I SPIT ON CARS
GRR

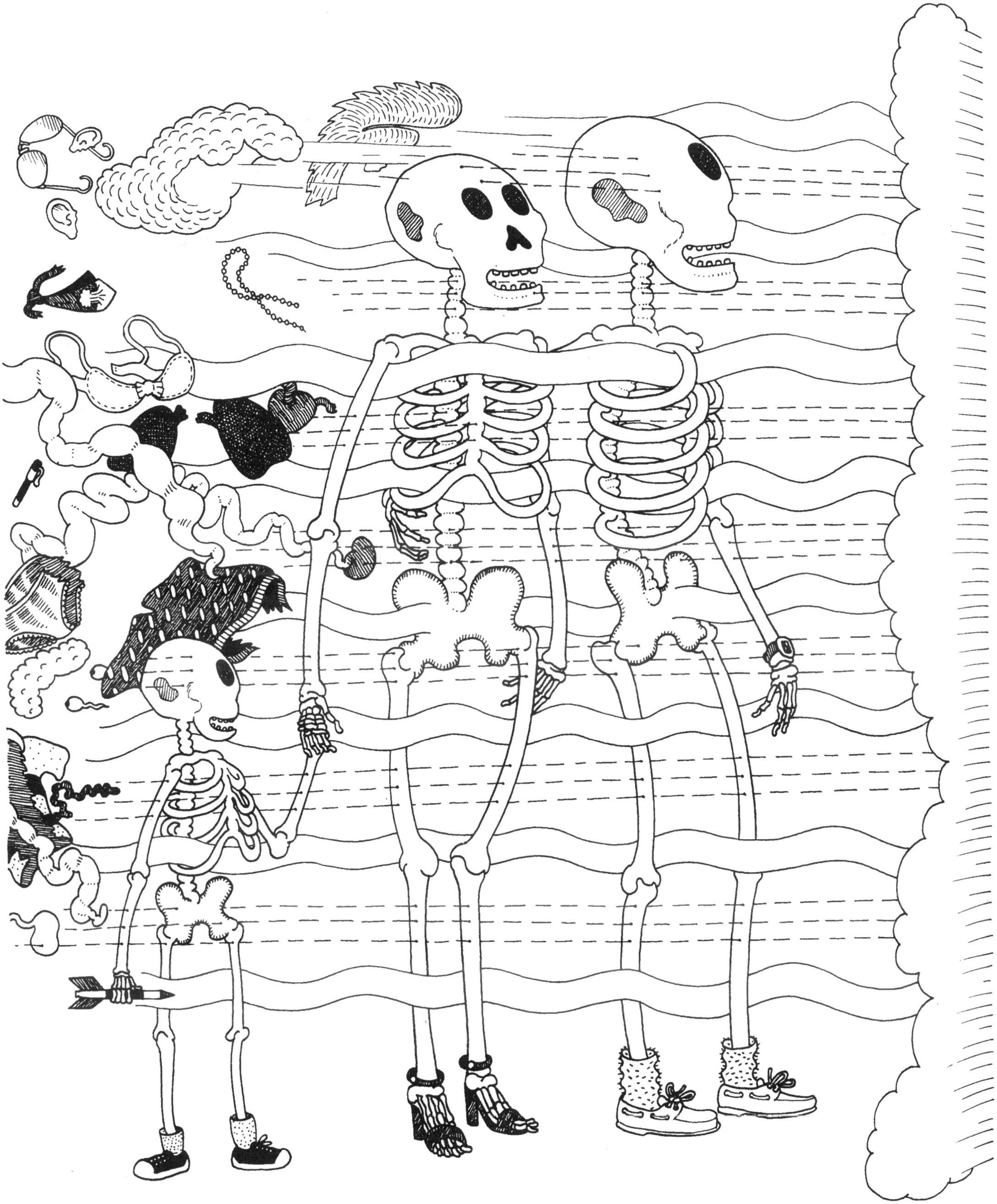

The Nuclear Family

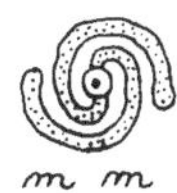

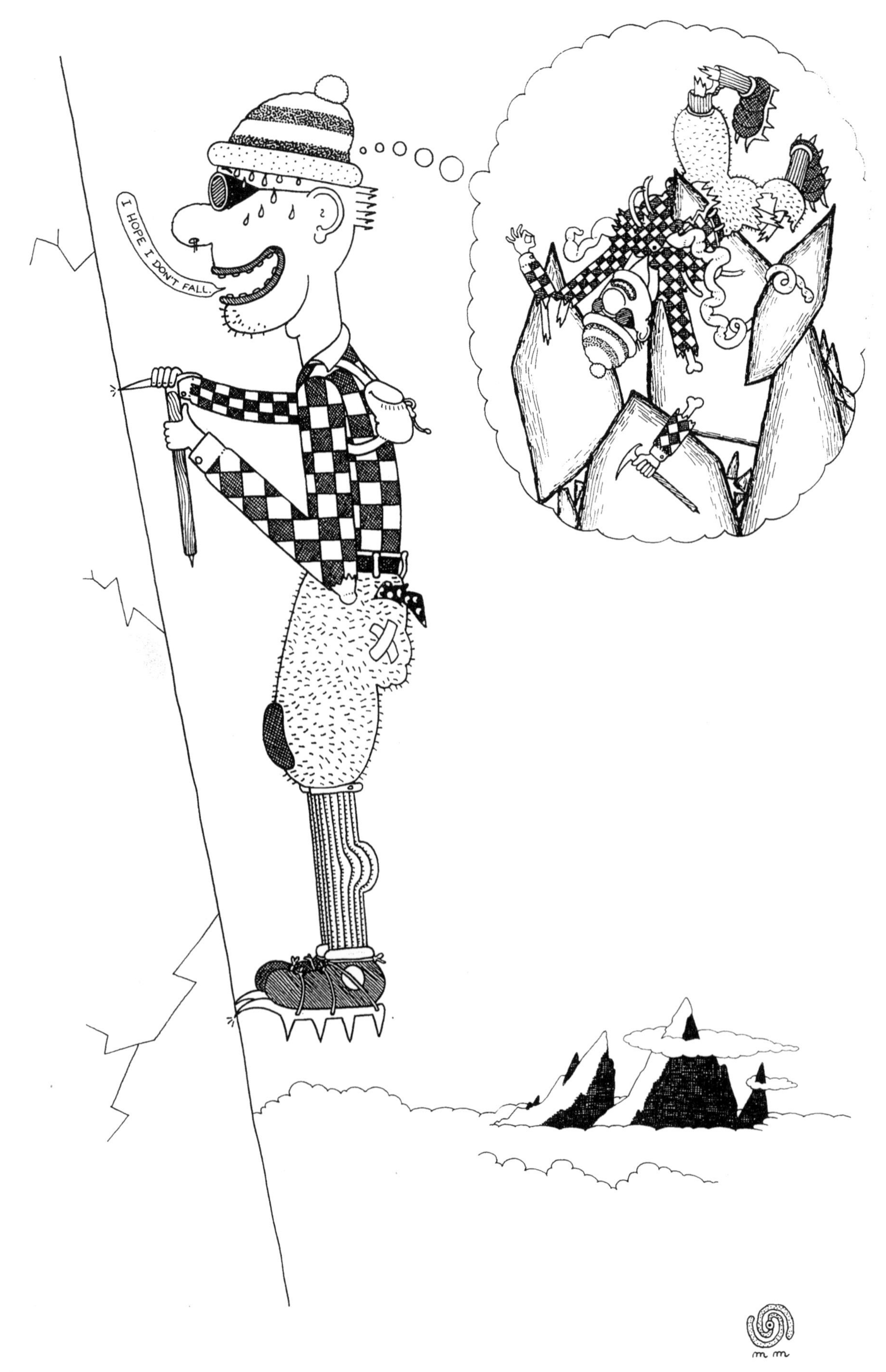
I HOPE I DON'T FALL.

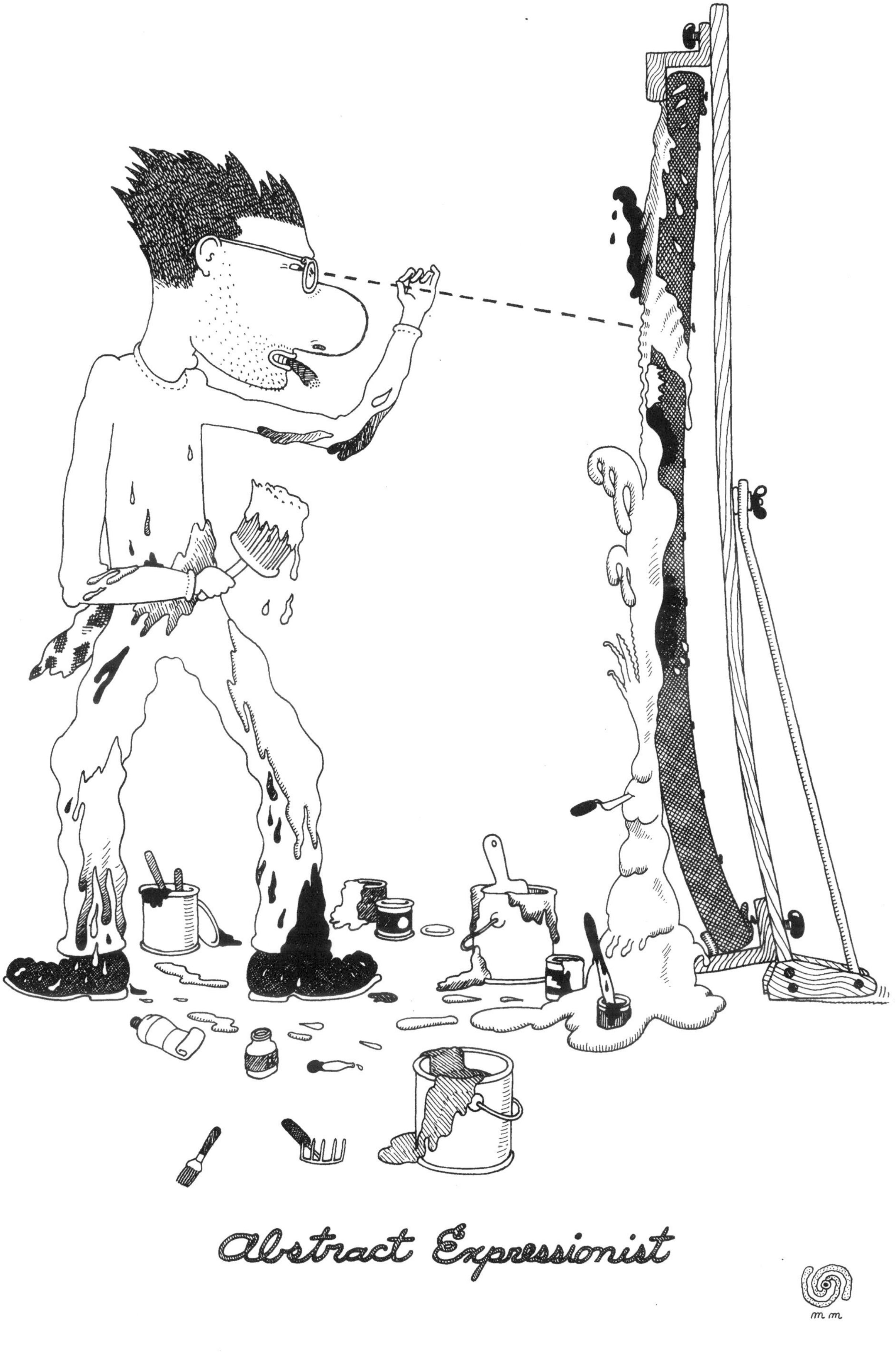

Abstract Expressionist

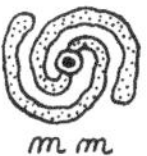

Happy Holidays!

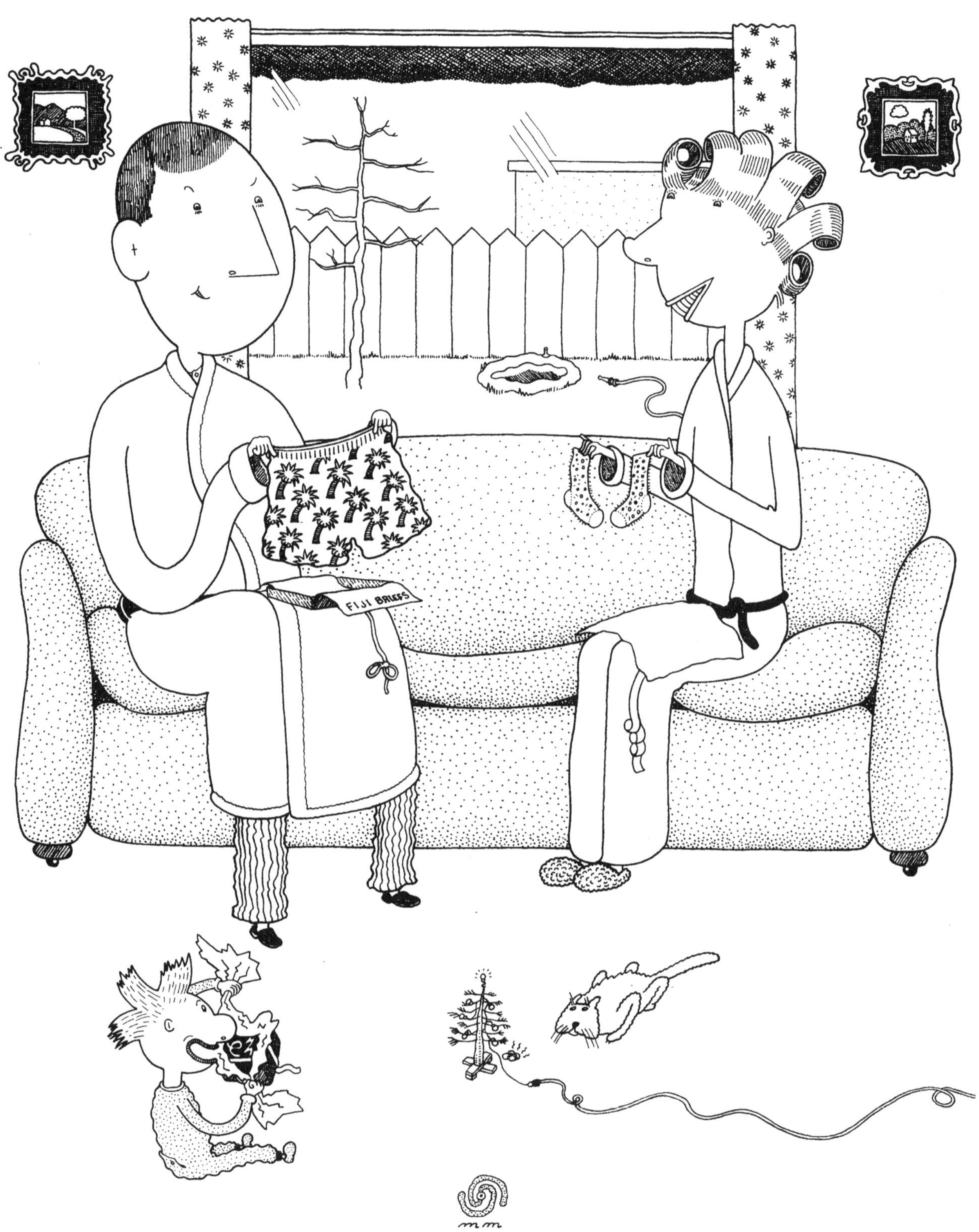

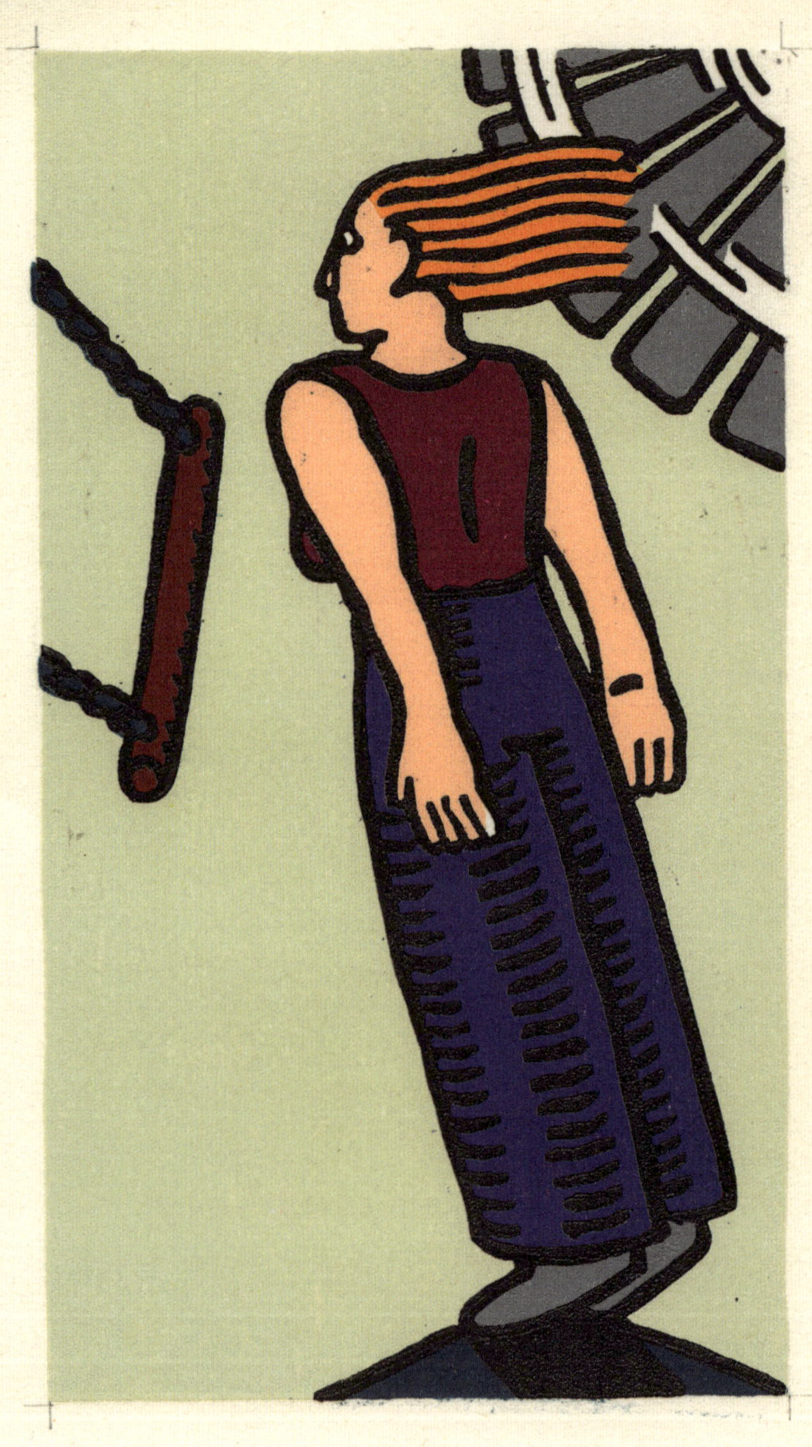

10/10 M.A.M. 90

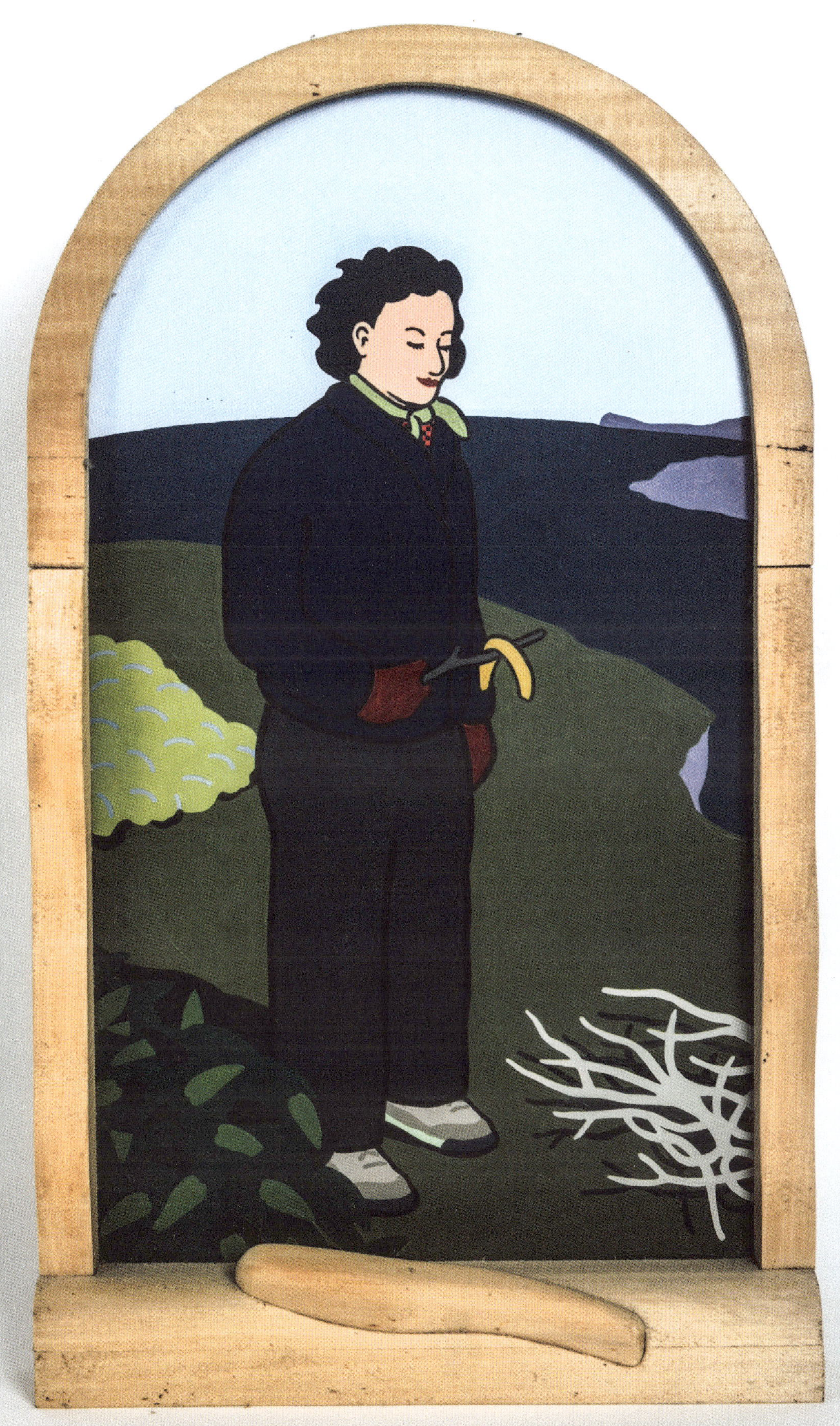

Saw this on a walk in the city park. "Oh, look—a terrestrial gastropod!" "Don't step on it." (It is rare to see one of those in the city.) Diane found a stick to move the banana slug into the bushes at the side of the walkway.

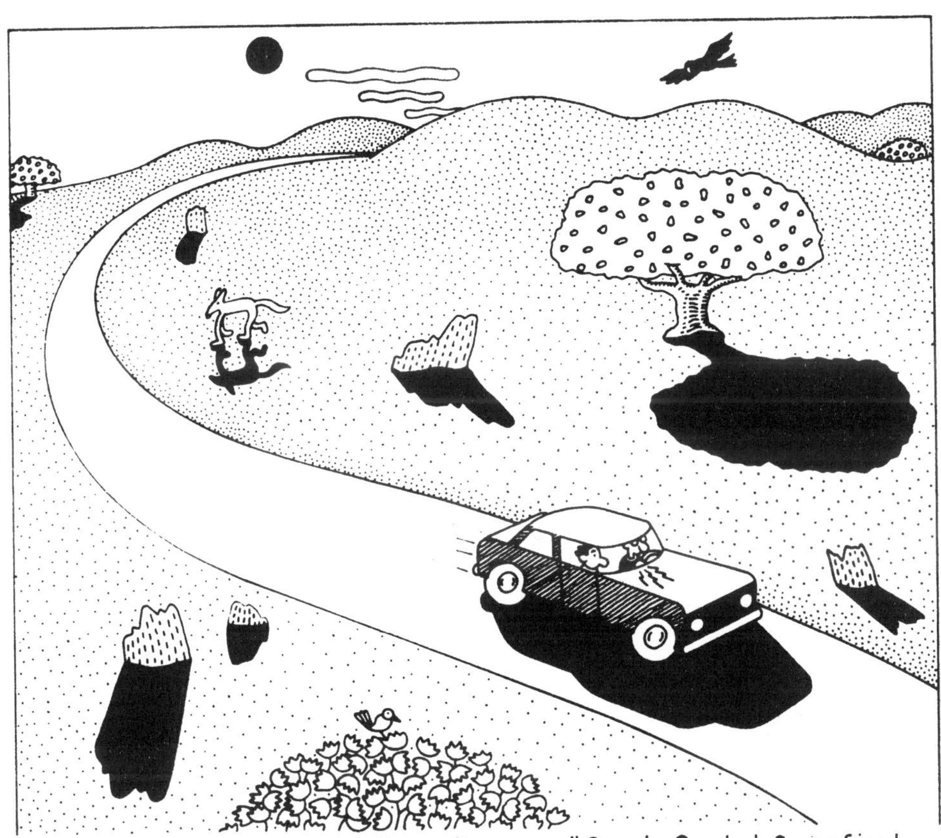

Motoring in the country with the radio on: "Crack Cartel Crossfire! Paramilitary Bible Camp! Nice Guy Runs Amuck! Playworld Sniper Makes Demands! Hospital Chickenblood Scandal! Shoe Fetish Cult Holds Hostages! High Tech Gang Wars! Kamikaze Bomber Rams Skyscraper! Poison Gas Leaks Into Exclusive Suburb! Threeway Plane Crash Destroys Fastfood Warehouse! These stories and more coming up!"

© 1988 M.A.M.

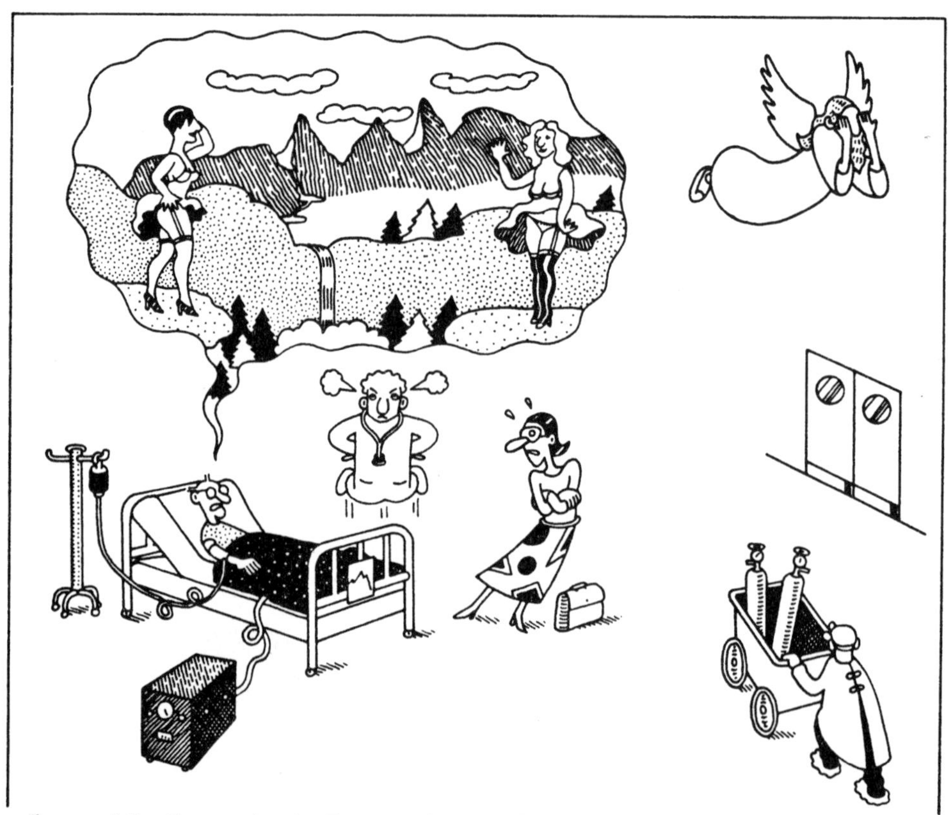

For a while I was dead. I was out of my body looking down on myself...and my doctor and my therapist. I felt perfectly calm. Next, there was a blinding light. "Oh-oh, here comes the Man", I thought. Instead, a grand panorama opened before me: The majestic high mountains that have inspired my life! Two scantily dressed curvaceous women were to be my guides. But it was not to be. Modern technology brought me back. I told of my wonderous experience. The professionals were not amused.

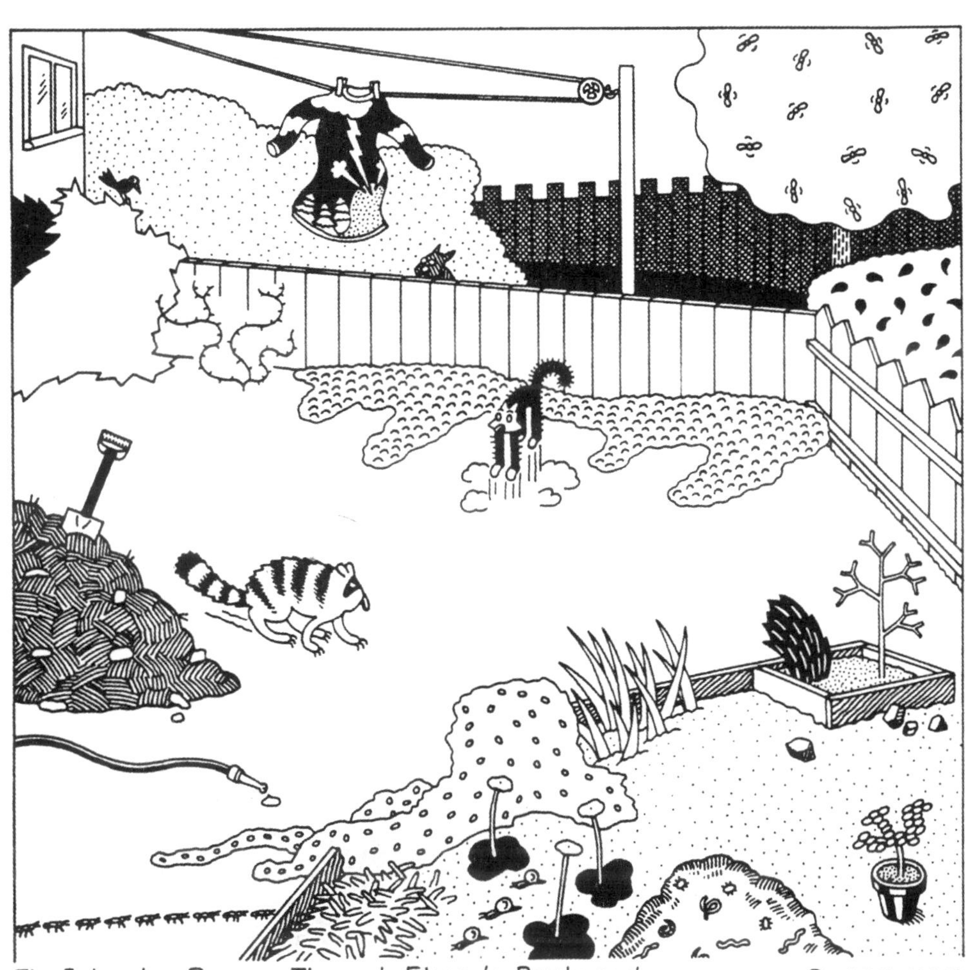

The Intruder Passes Through Elmer's Backyard

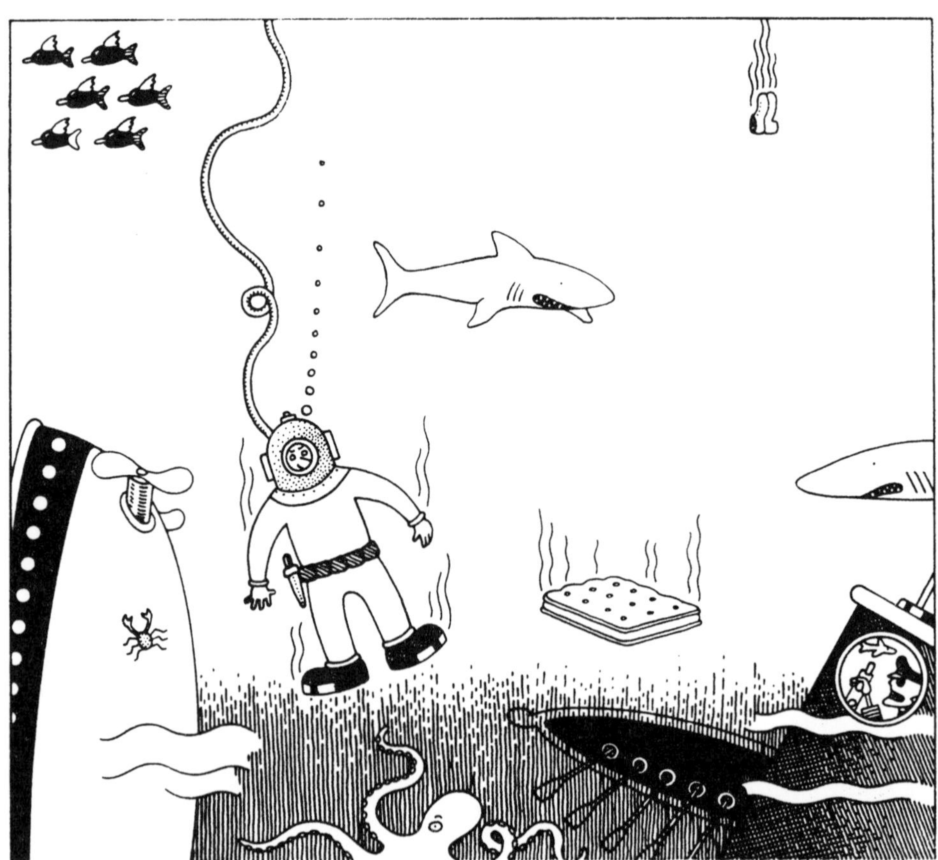

When I become fed up with the rat race and all its scumballs, I get into my old diving suit and head for the Bottom. There is nothing like walking around Davey Jone's Locker for peace of mind and calm reflection.

© 1988 M.A.M.

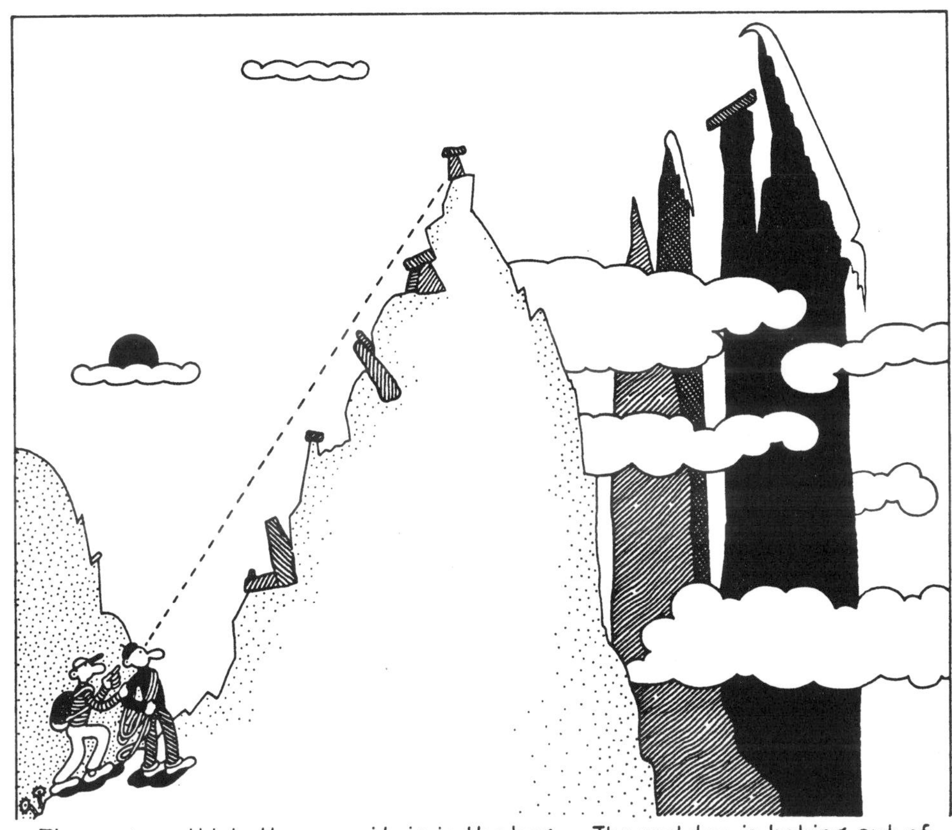

These guys think the summit is in the bag. The real top is lurking out of sight as an exquisitely unapproachable possibility.

So as they rest in full view of the true situation deciding whether to admit defeat and turn around or claim success and turn around, they can at least say that here the real nature of things has been revealed. This is better than most of the time in a society where the real nature of things is usually obscured by fog.

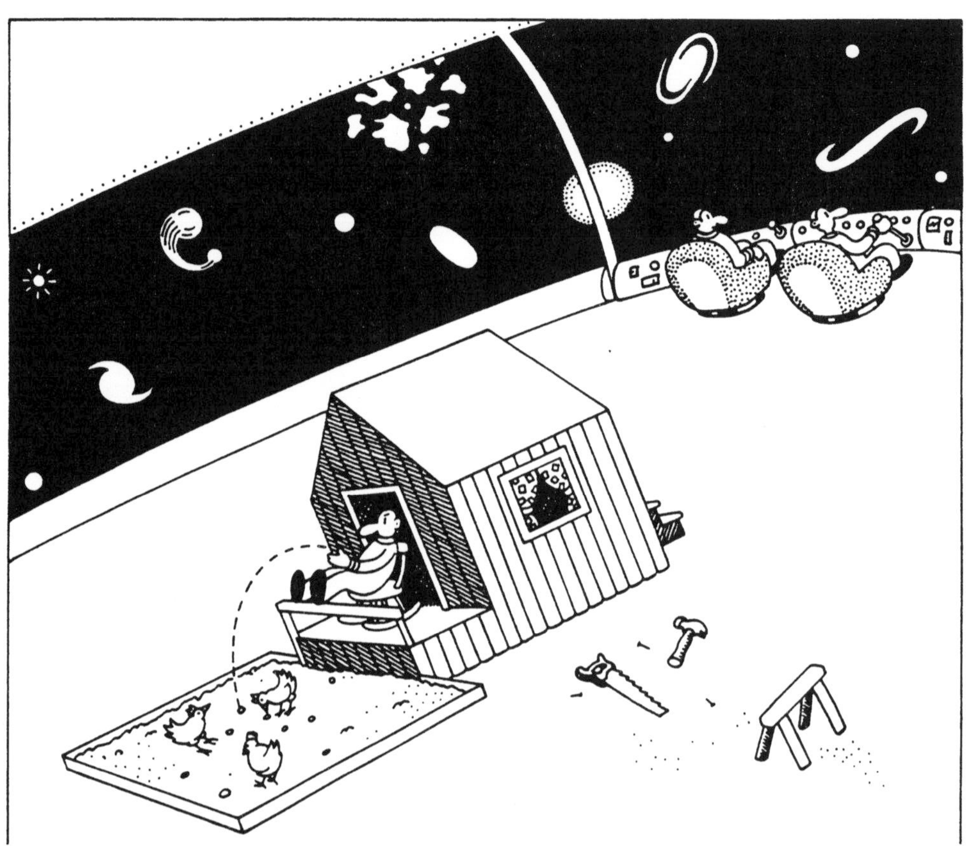

Ever spend time aboard a space ship amidst the marvels of technologic sterility and the interminable presence of super novas, colliding galaxies and black holes? After a decade or so the effect of such astounding phenomena wears thin. You surprise yourself that you are fondly recalling scenes of urban squalor or the rustic shack in the piney woods.

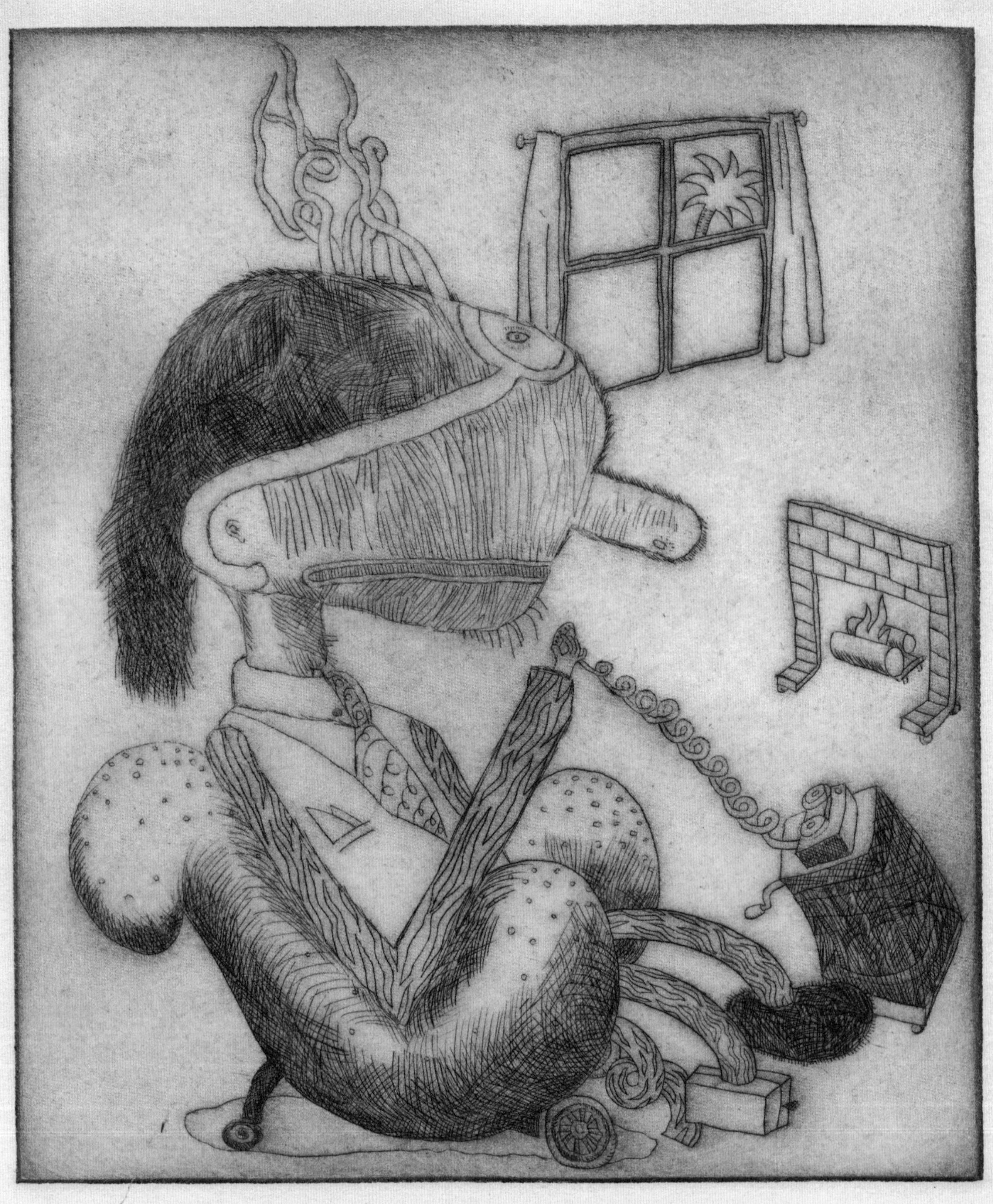
Fireside Chat
M.M.

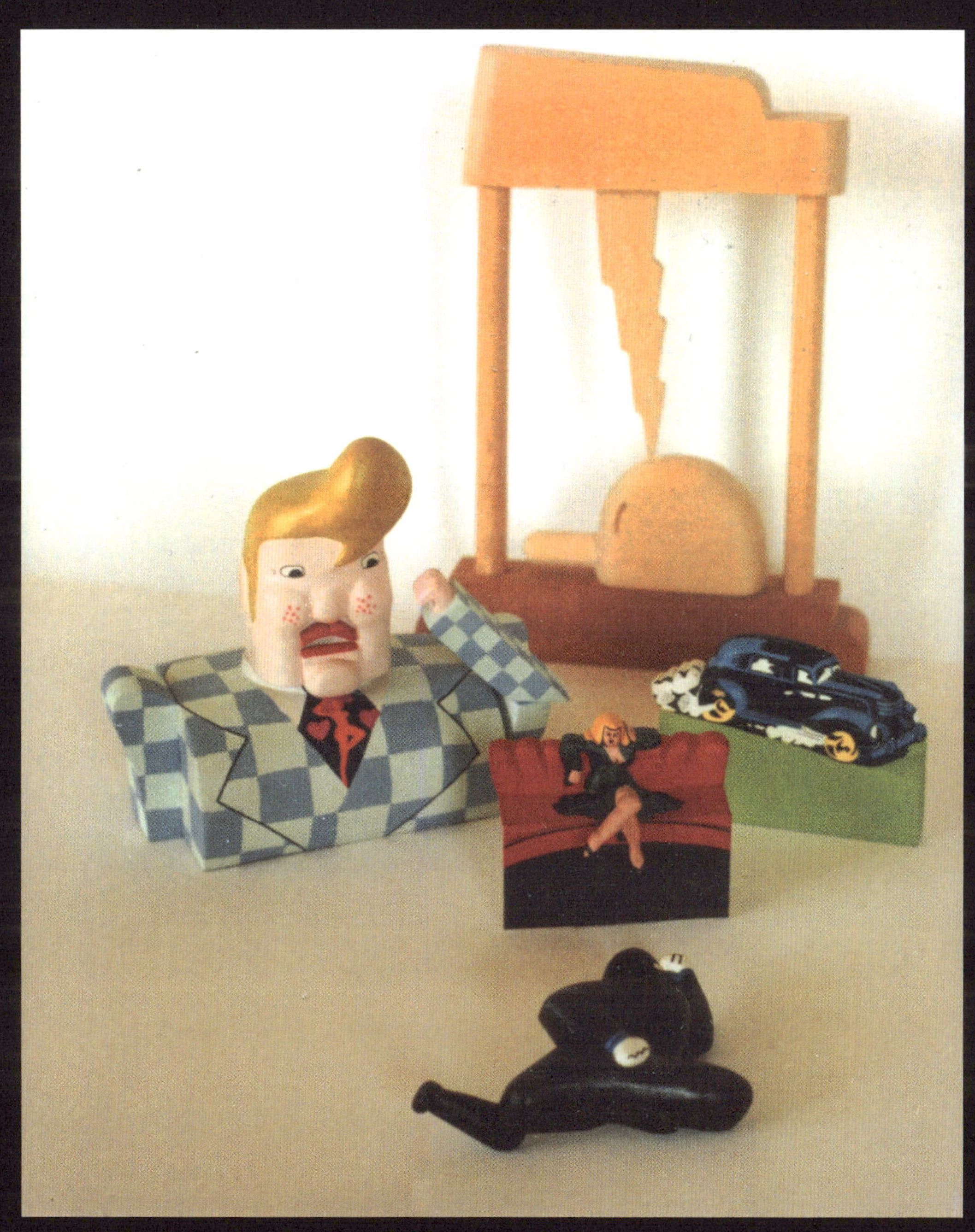

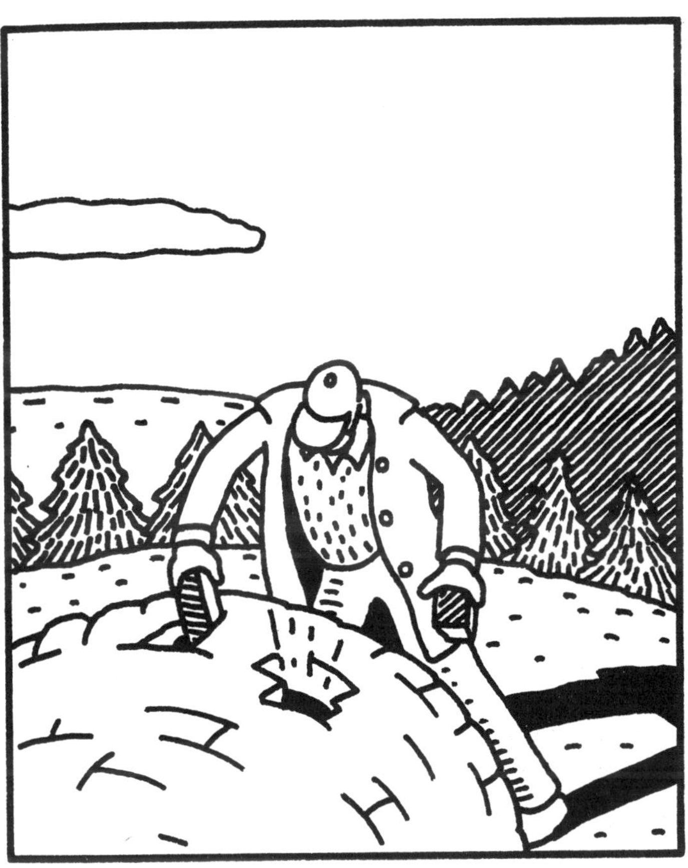

I approached cautiously
The small brick dome
There were some openings
I removed loose bricks
Looked down inside

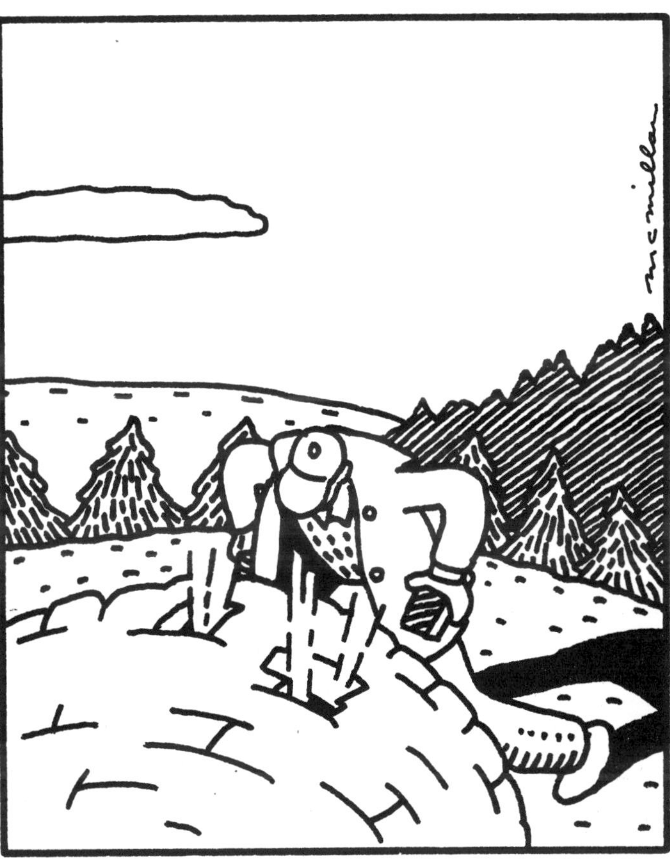

To see
A still glowing meteor
What to make of this imposition
A pain in the butt
I replaced the bricks

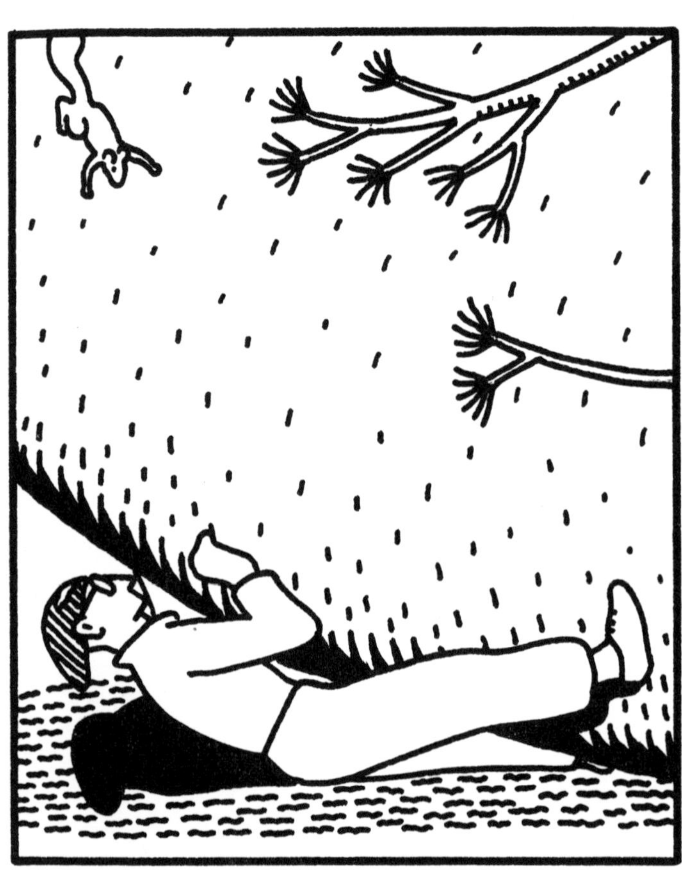

My butt is on the ground
I am relaxed
But I am fully focused
I am ready to climb
I am going nowhere but up

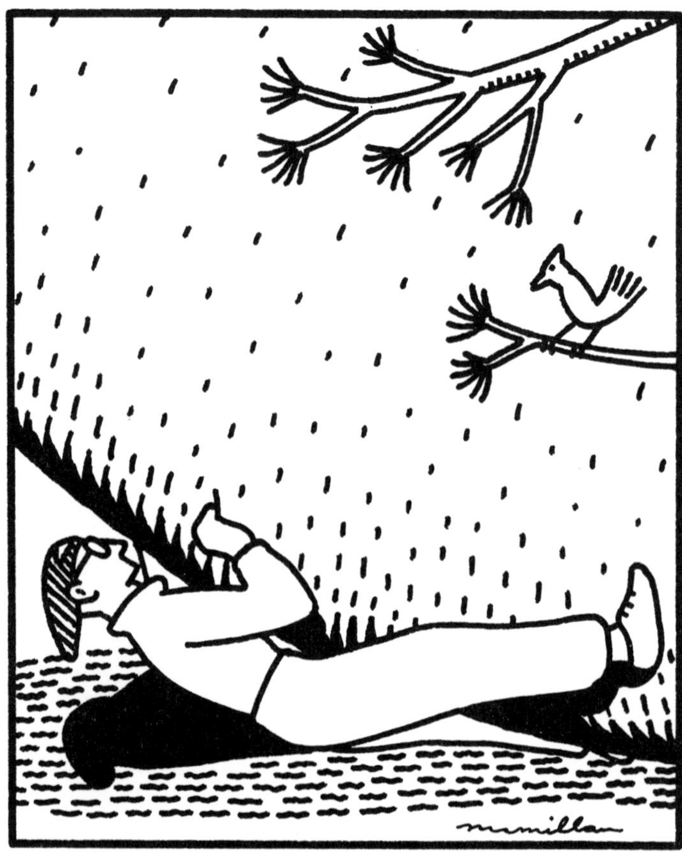

Now I am not relaxed
Now I am applying maximum power
All stops out
Total facilitation
Waiting for movement

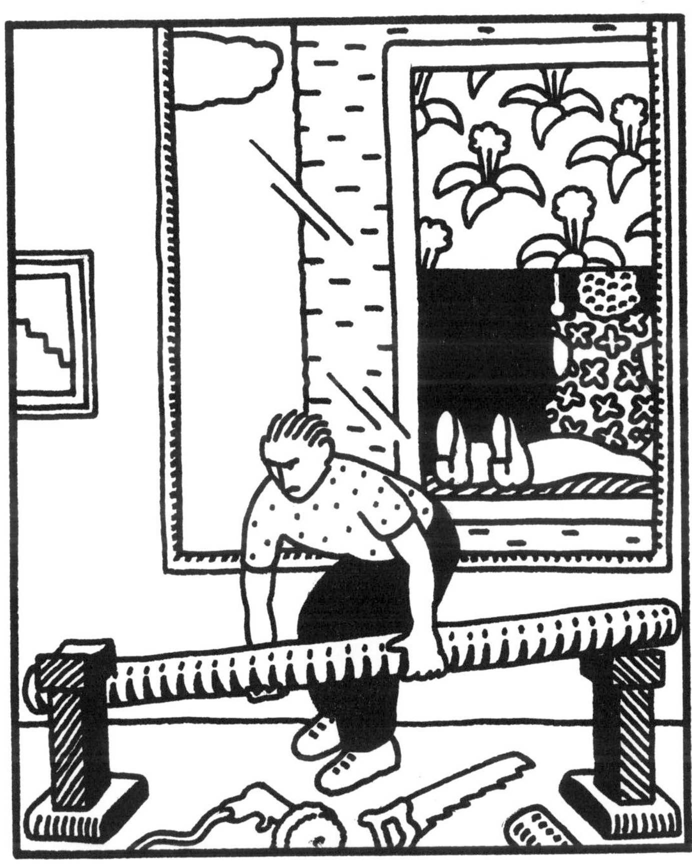

And now this completes
My latest construction
Incorporating the principles
Of geometric symmetry and balance
Abstract and transcendent

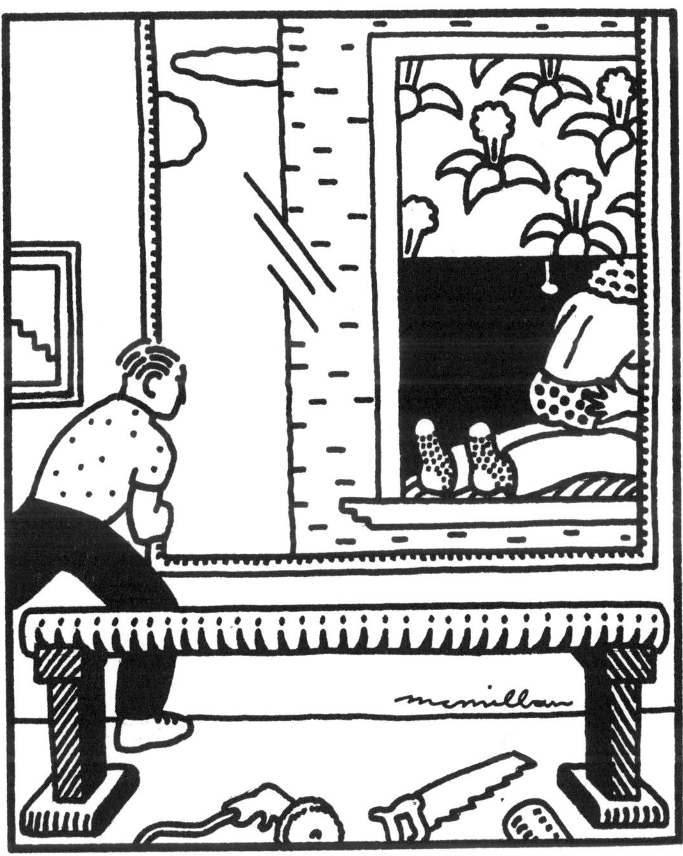

Yet how can I presume to challenge
The power of pulsating organisms
And the slurpy interactions
Occuring in every nook and cranny
Of the biological universe

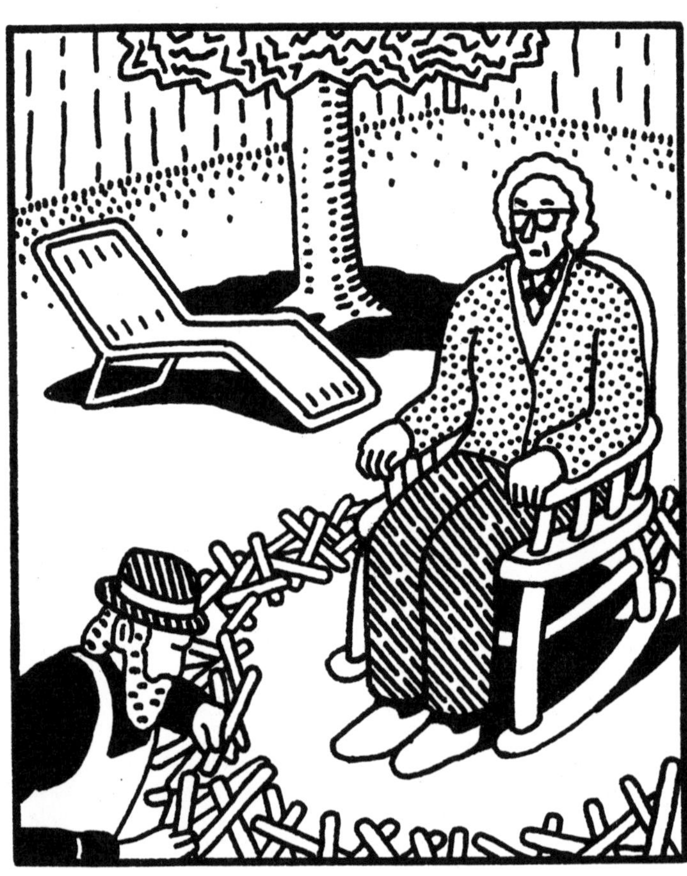

I realize that Mother
Has never understood my work
So I have designed a sculpture-event
With her as the central component
Here Mom

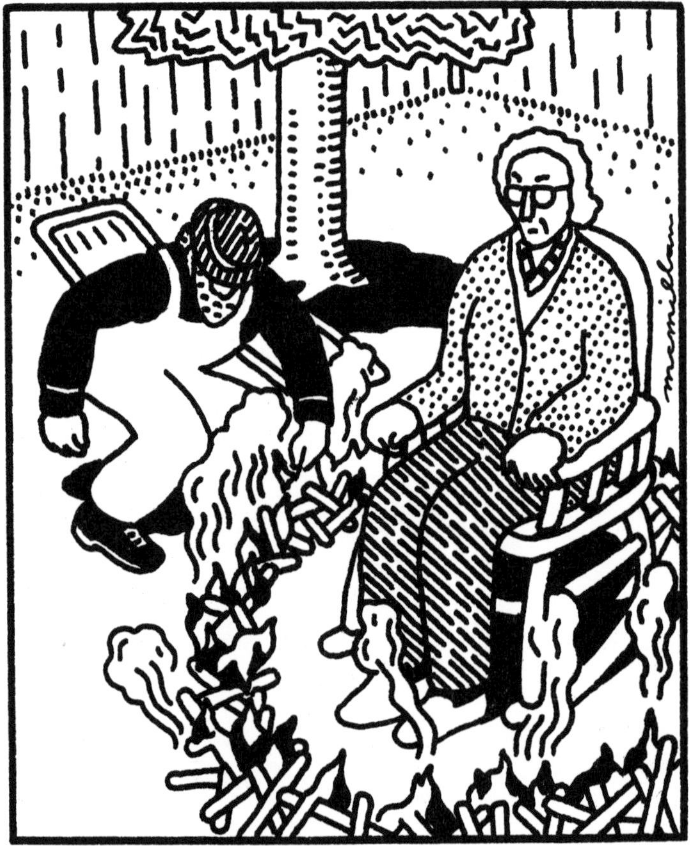

I hope this will do the job
Make the connection
And at the same time
Illuminate my most primary
Motivational guidelines

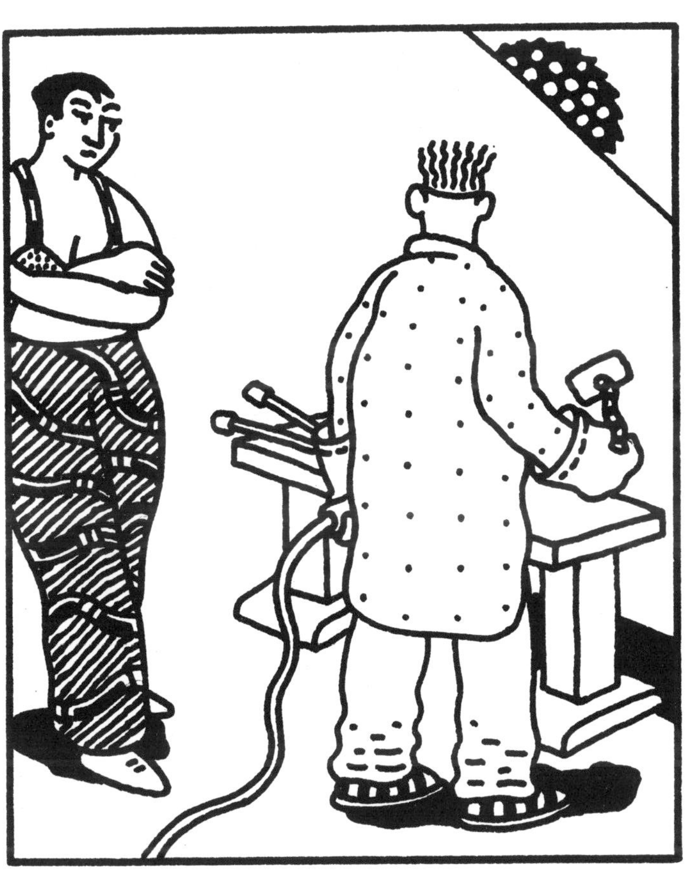

Excuse me
But I'm waiting for a confirmation
Are you coasting into shore
Or shall I put everything
Back in the refrigerator

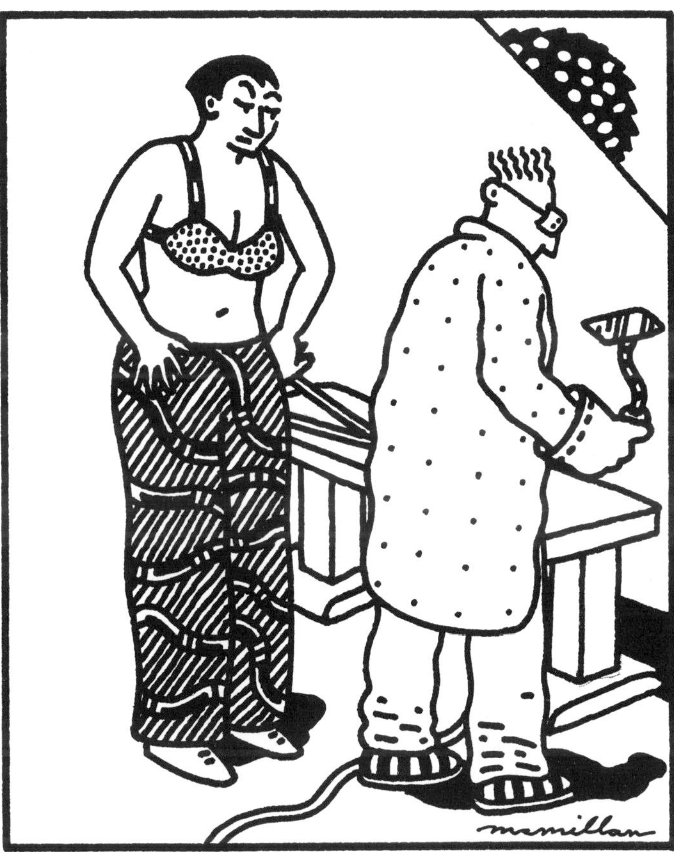

Absolutely not
Despite tottering on the edge here
Approaching the decisive formulation
With the probability of total failure
I'll take pastrami on rye..tomato on the side

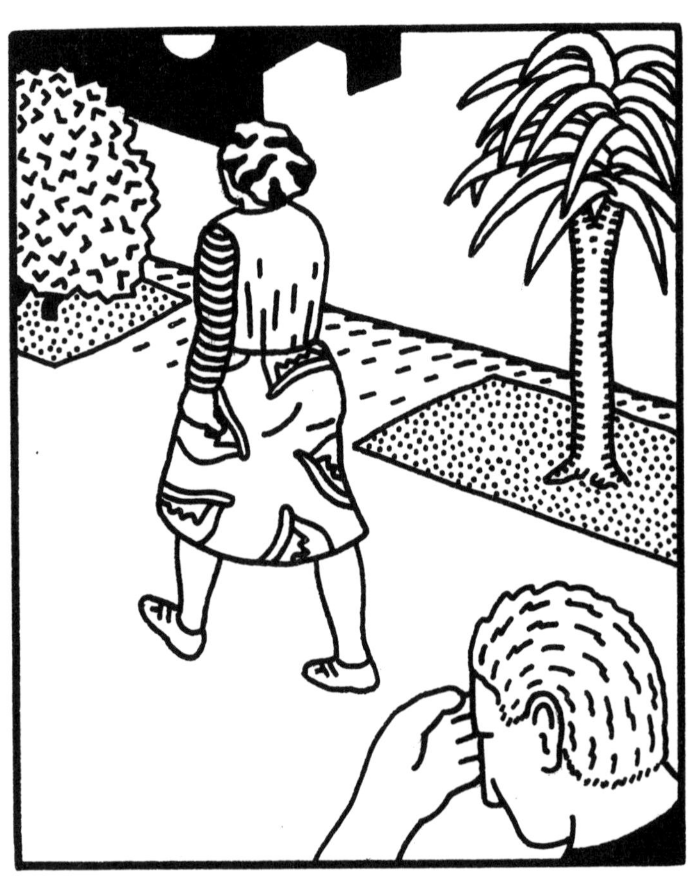

I try so hard to ignore
But once I see those swaying hips
I am driven
A victim of compulsion
Immune to psychotherapy

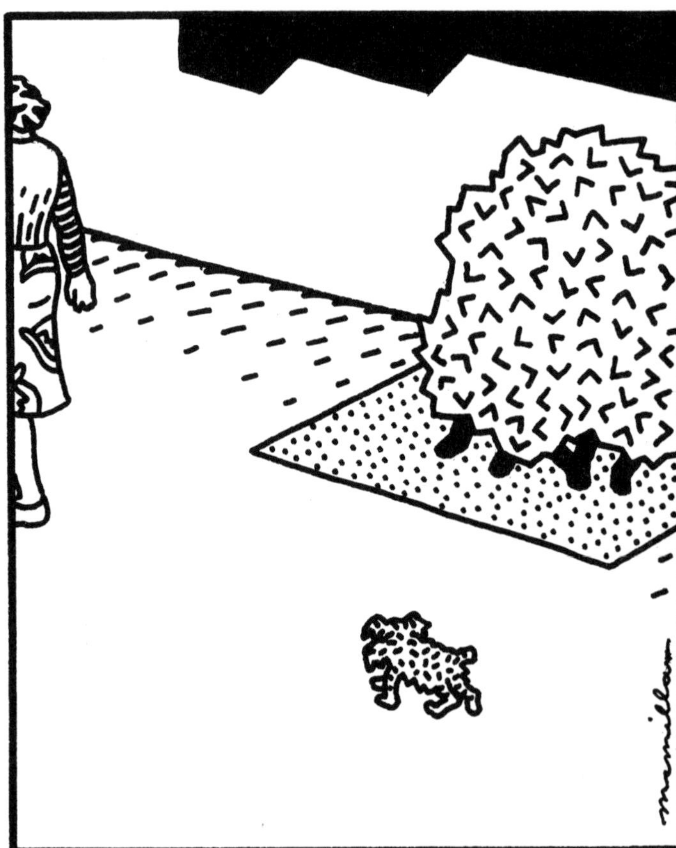

Because once the moon is full
The transformation begins
From man to beast
I become a wereterrier
I want to be her pookums

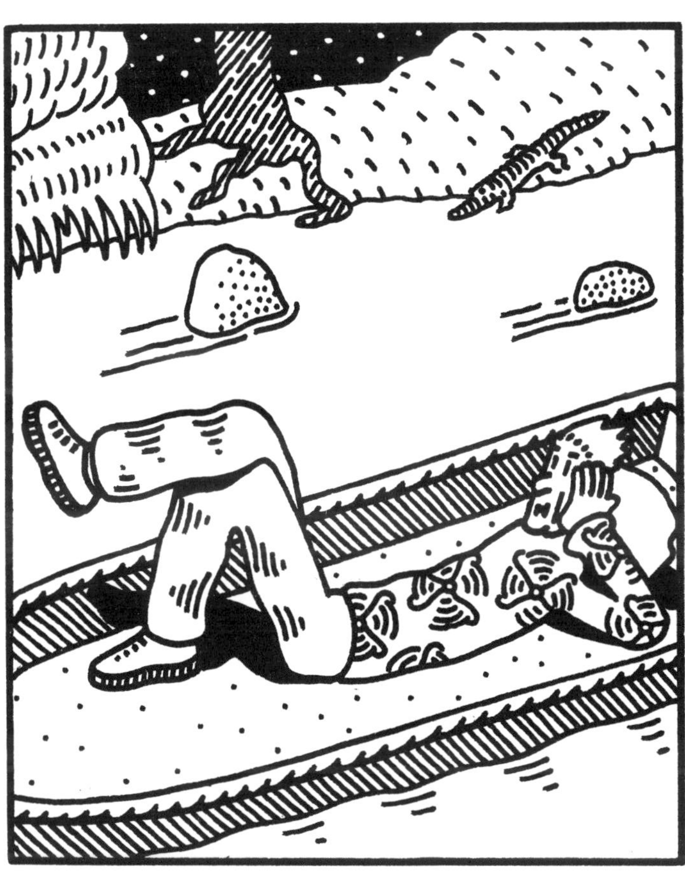

Floating adrift
Down the proverbial river
The situation is this
I can acquiesce
Or I can struggle

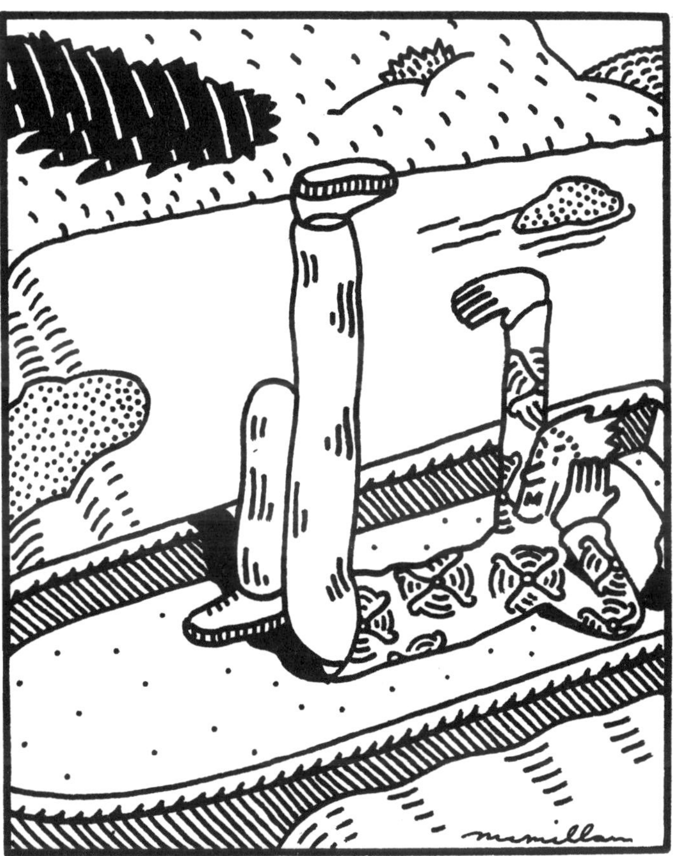

Let's take struggle
Here's something then
As good or better than passivity
So they say
Position one of self assertion

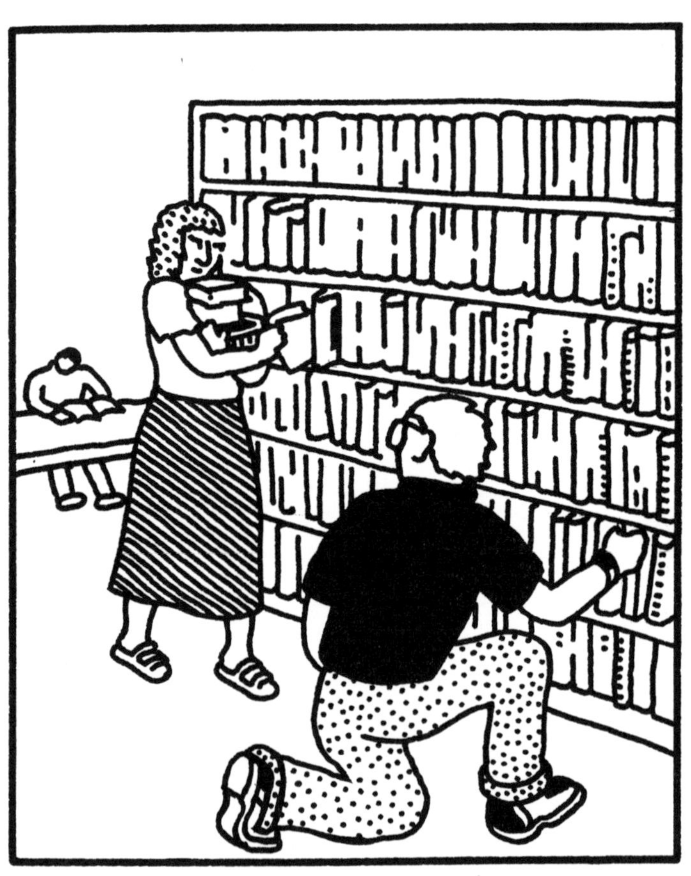

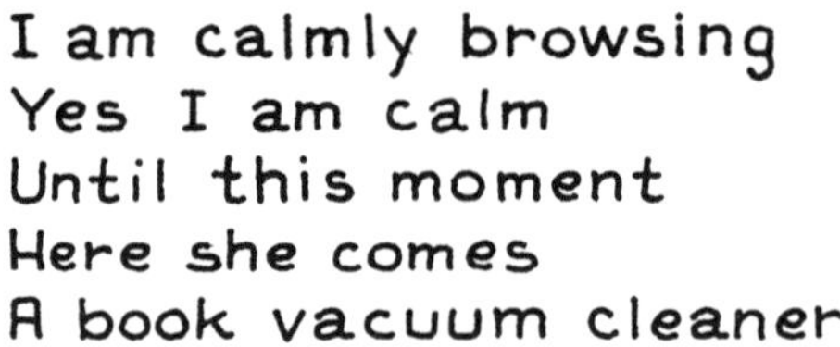

I am calmly browsing
Yes I am calm
Until this moment
Here she comes
A book vacuum cleaner

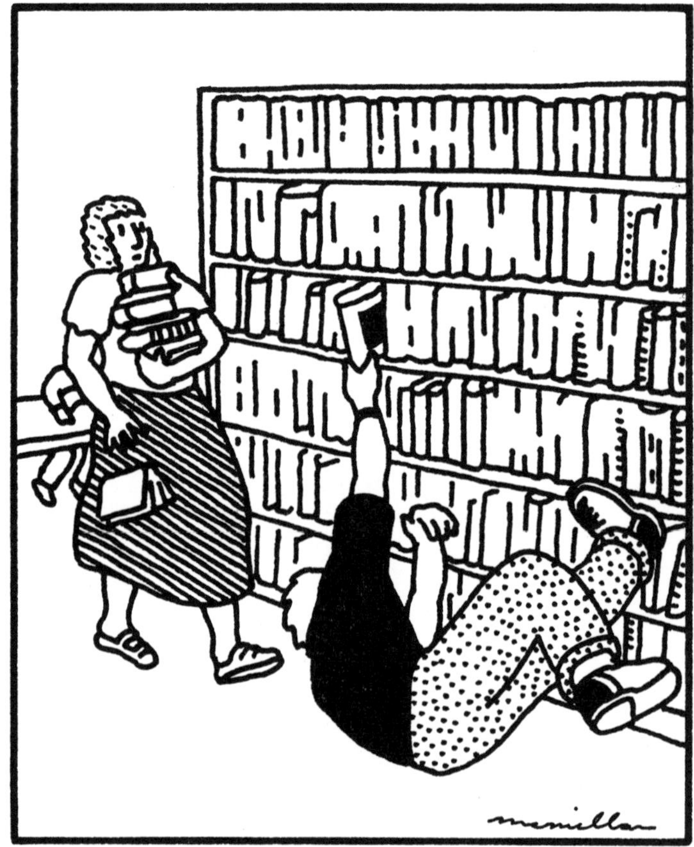

Now I am not calm
She is about to suck up
The book I passed on
The book that I now need
Requires a vigorous effort

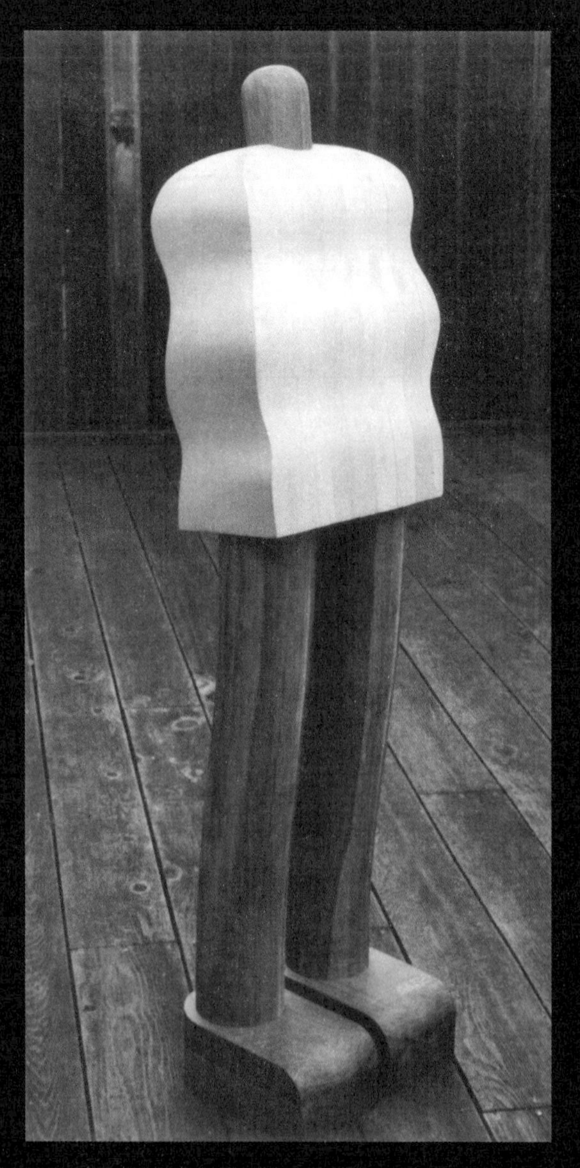

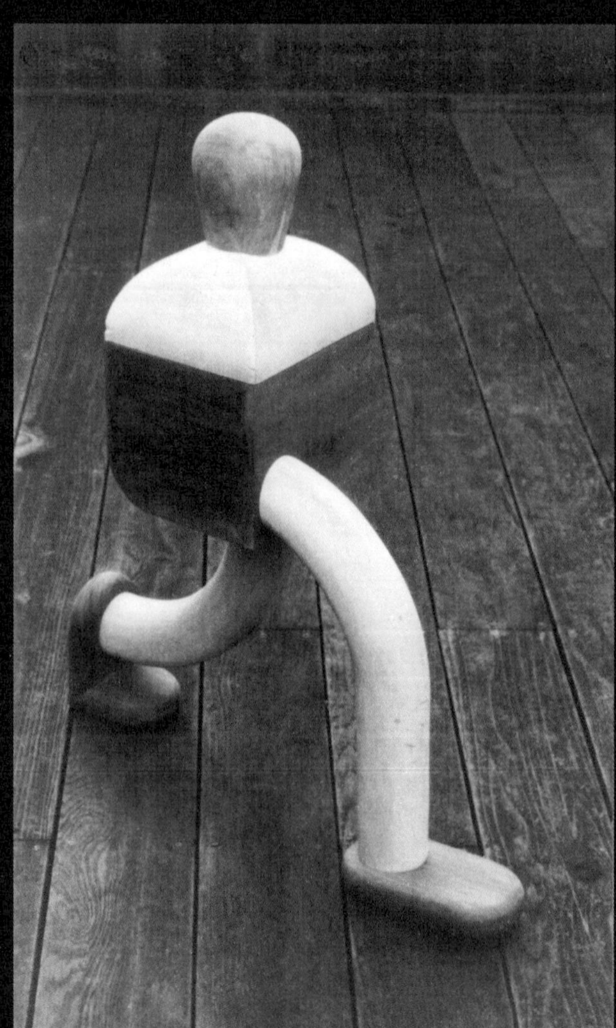

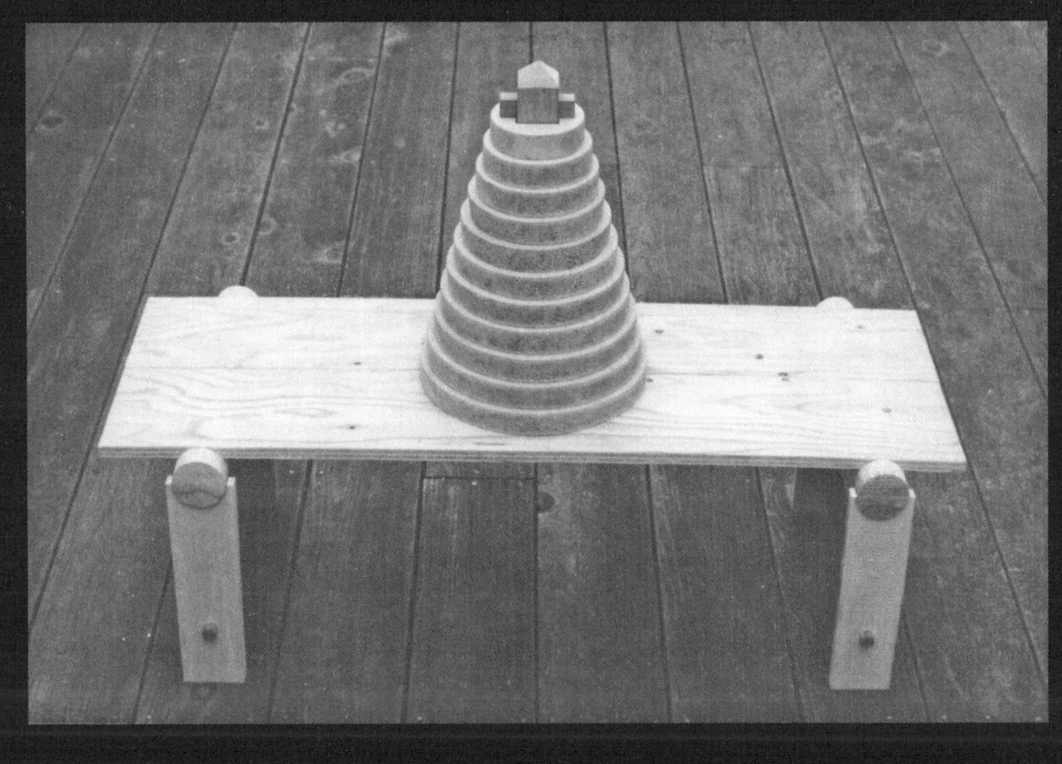

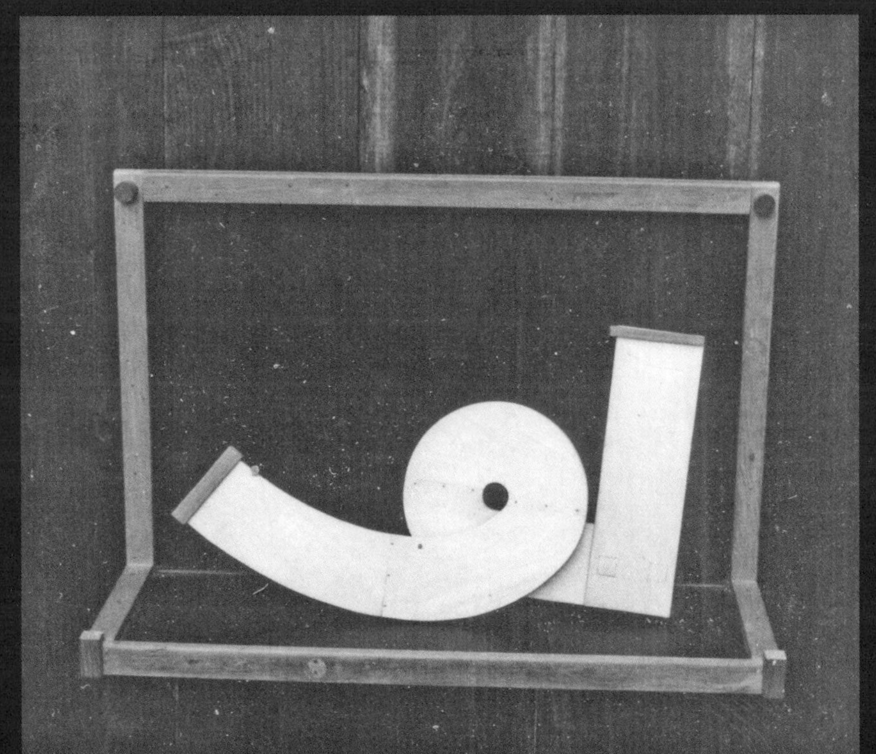

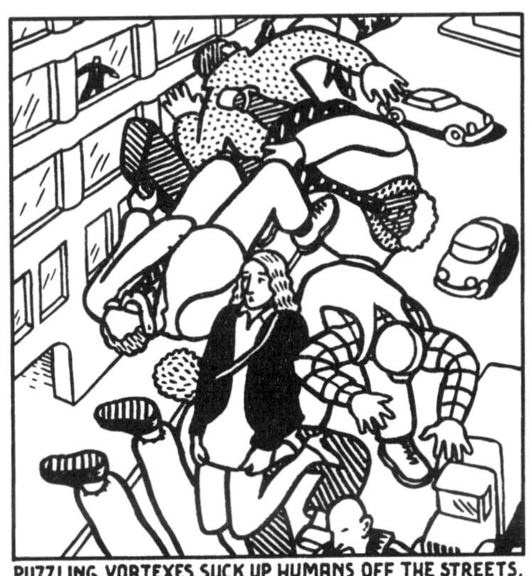
PUZZLING VORTEXES SUCK UP HUMANS OFF THE STREETS.

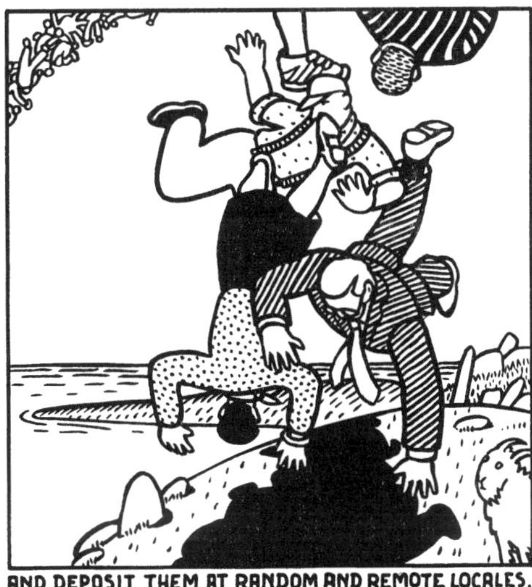
AND DEPOSIT THEM AT RANDOM AND REMOTE LOCALES.

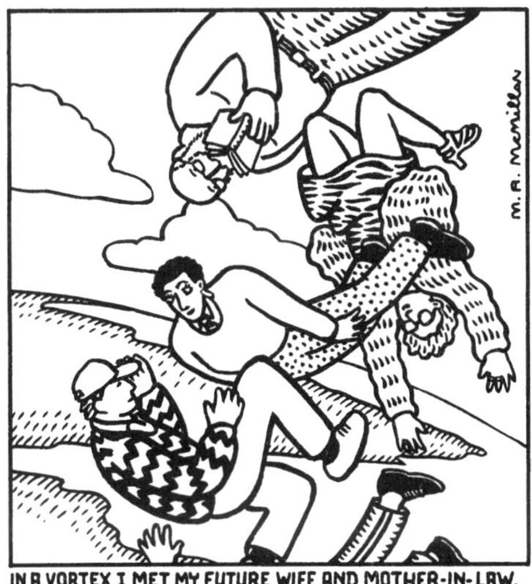

IN A VORTEX I MET MY FUTURE WIFE AND MOTHER-IN-LAW.

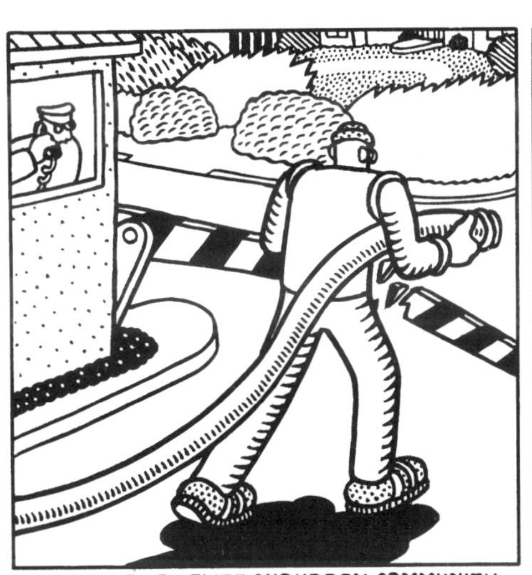
ZOMO ENTERS AN ELITE SUBURBAN COMMUNITY..

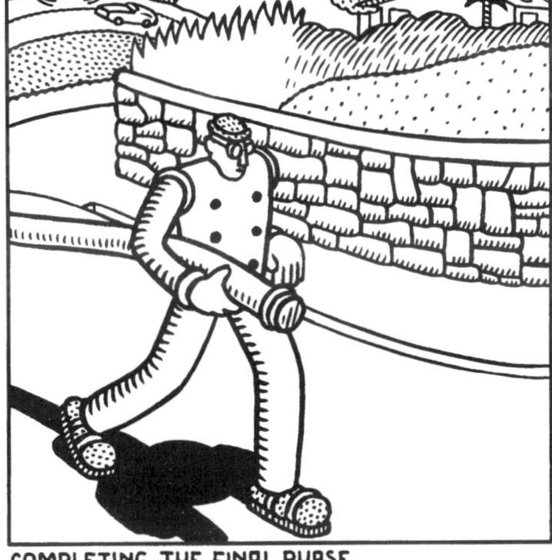
COMPLETING THE FINAL PHASE....

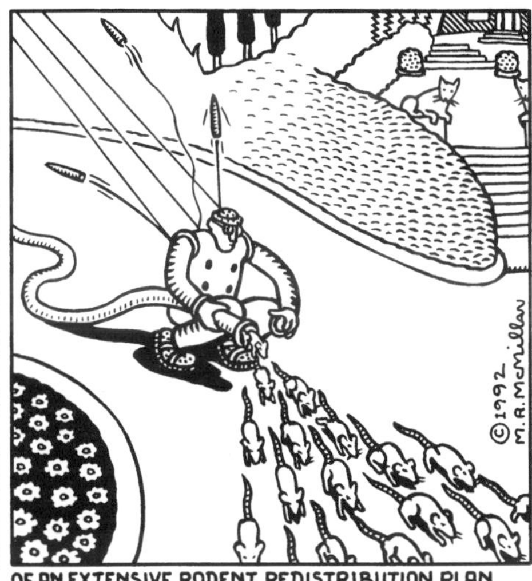

OF AN EXTENSIVE RODENT REDISTRIBUTION PLAN.

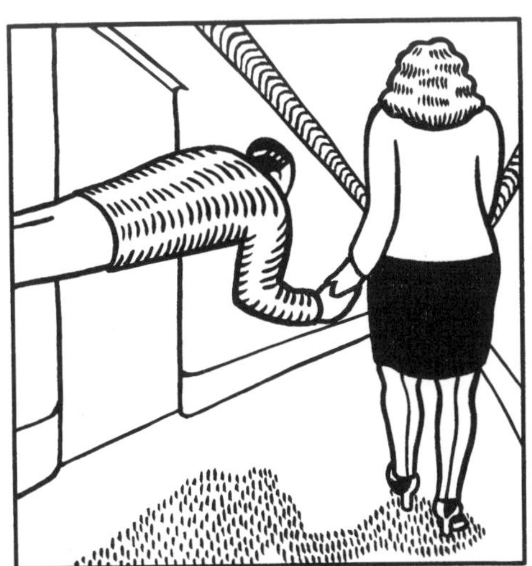
SHE LED ME THROUGH A MAZE OF CORRIDORS

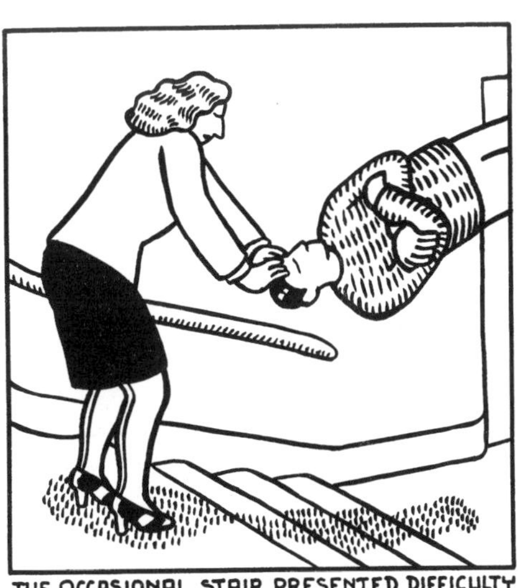
THE OCCASIONAL STAIR PRESENTED DIFFICULTY

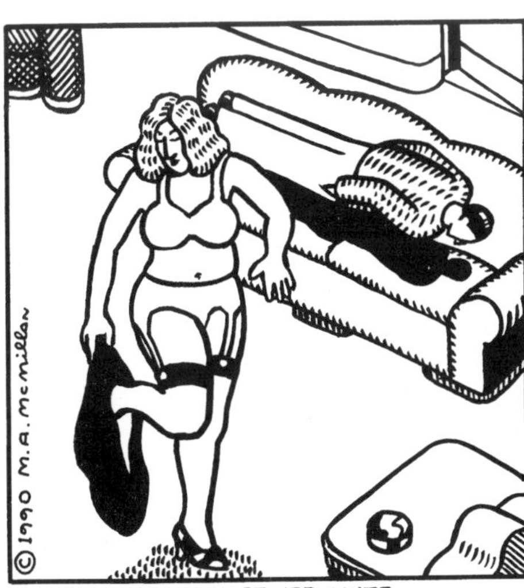

AT LAST WE ARRIVED AT HER SUITE

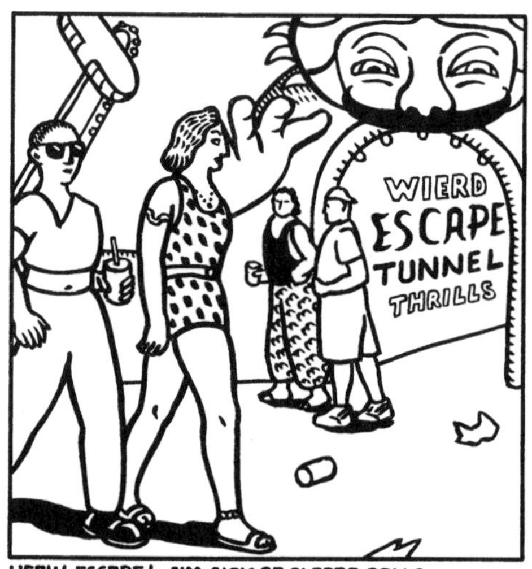

YEAH! ESCAPE! I'M SICK OF SLEAZE BALLS.

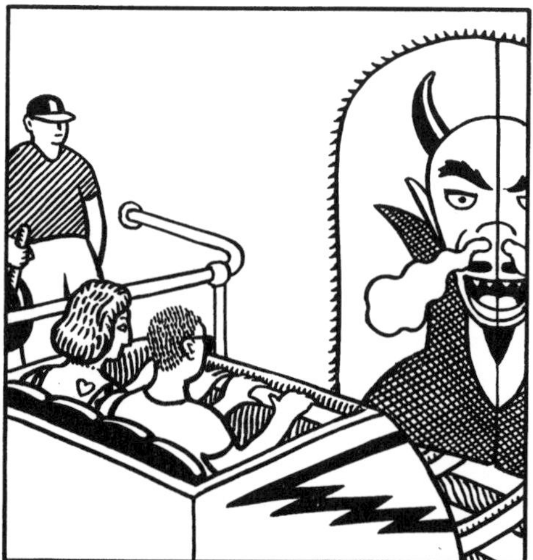
GOODBYE SOAP OPERA TRASH! NOW FOR SOMETHIN' DUMB.

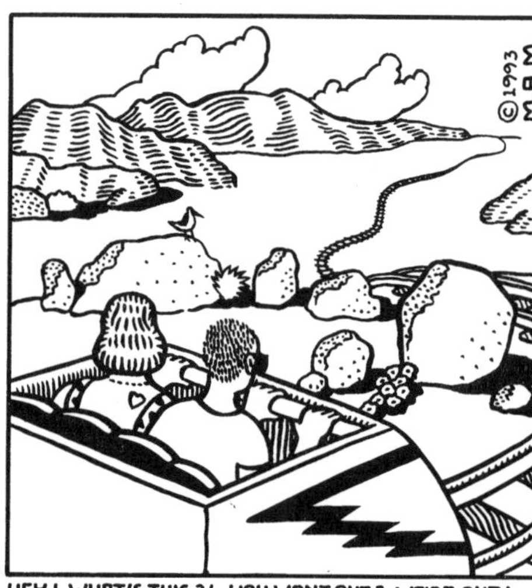

HEY! WHAT'S THIS?! YOU WANT OUT? WE'RE OUT!

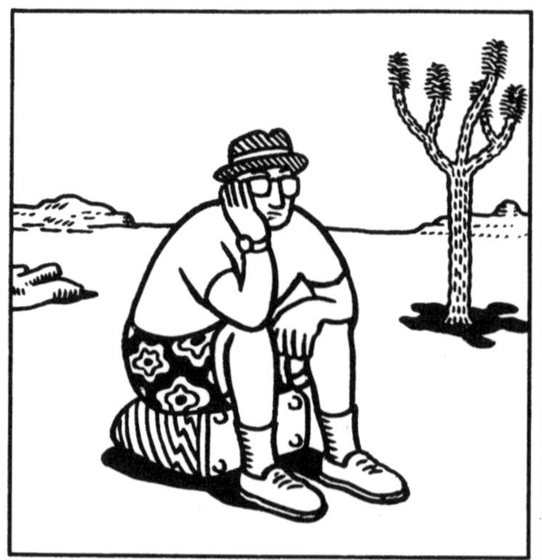
I AM HERE. ALMOST NOWHERE. WRITING FOR SOMETHING.

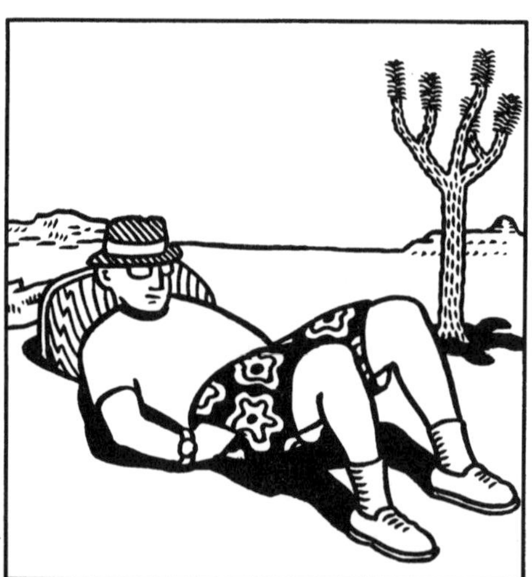
PREFERABLY NOT THEM..OF THE CRAWLING PERSUASION.

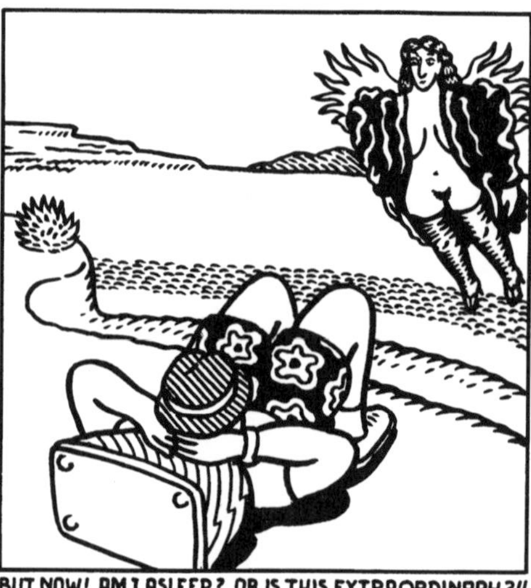
BUT NOW! AM I ASLEEP? OR IS THIS EXTRAORDINARY?!!

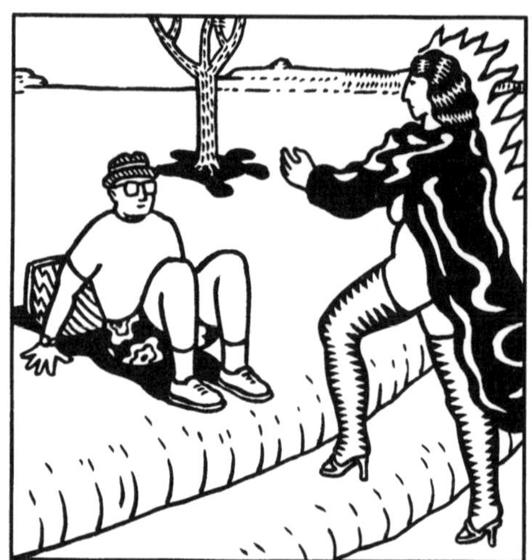
AN APPARITION MAKING A CURIOUS GESTURE.

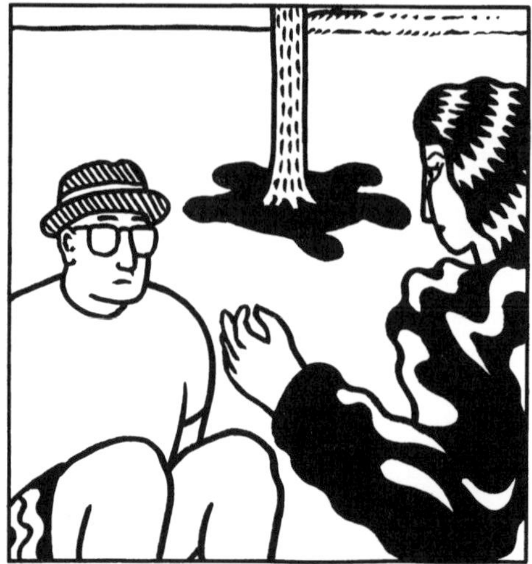
IS THIS GOING TO BE A RELIGIOUS EXPERIENCE?

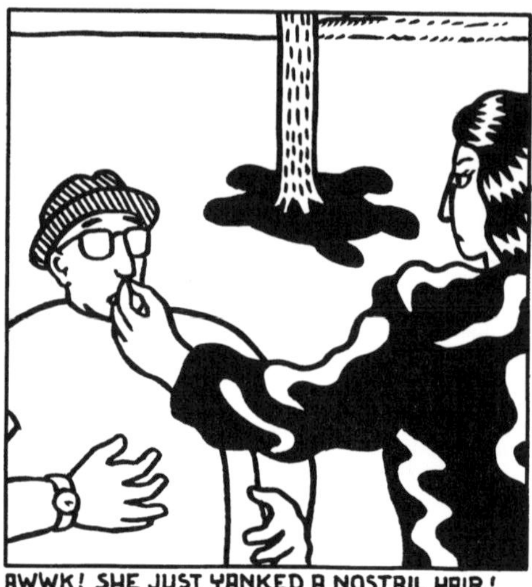
AWWK! SHE JUST YANKED A NOSTRIL HAIR!

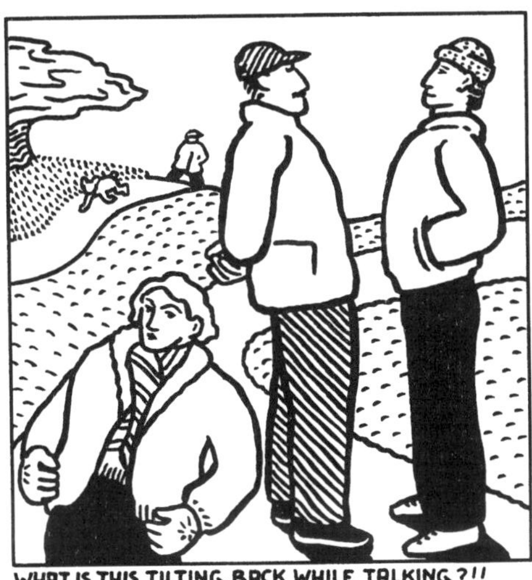

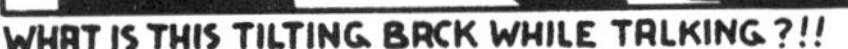

WHAT IS THIS TILTING BACK WHILE TALKING ?!!

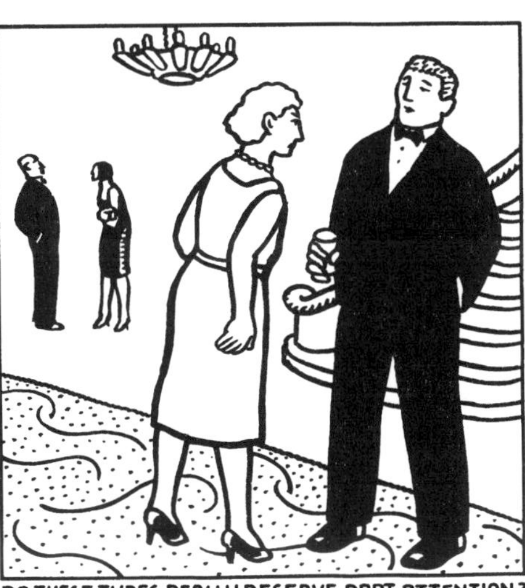

DO THESE TYPES REALLY DESERVE RAPT ATTENTION?

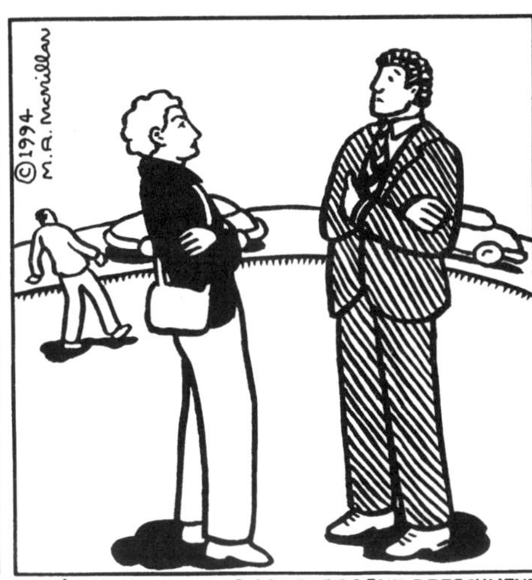

GIVE 'EM THEIR POSITION OF ARROGANT DETACHMENT.

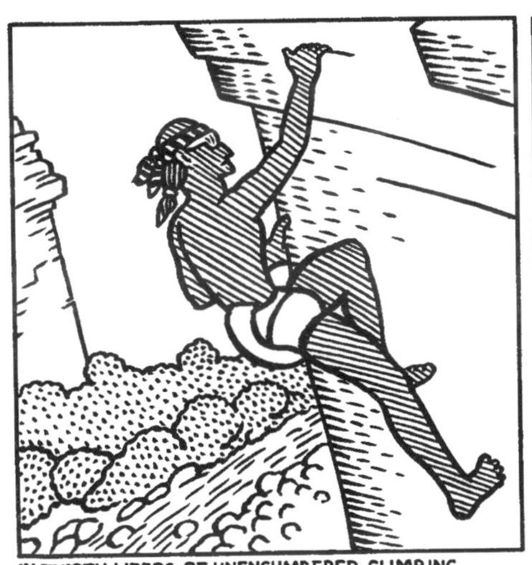

IN THIRTY YEARS OF UNENCUMBERED CLIMBING.......

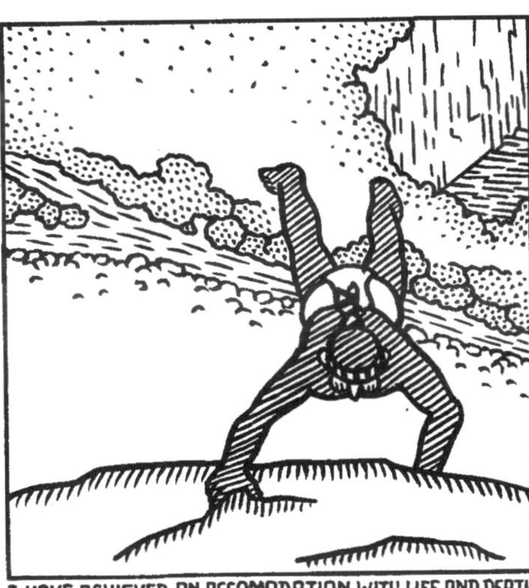

I HAVE ACHIEVED AN ACCOMODATION WITH LIFE AND DEATH.

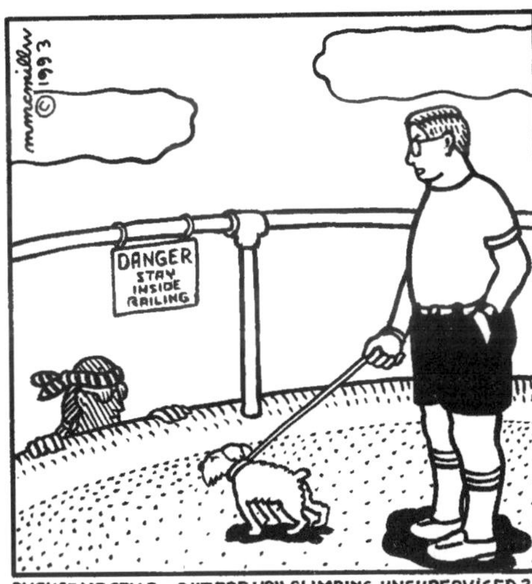

EXCUSE ME FELLA .. BUT ARE YOU CLIMBING UNSUPERVISED ?!

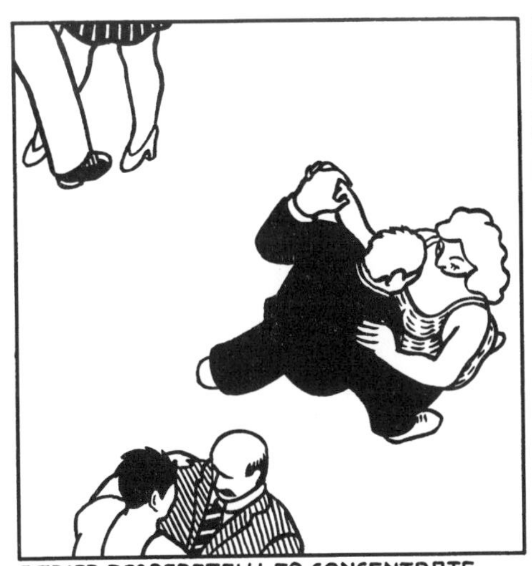

I TRIED DESPERATELY TO CONCENTRATE

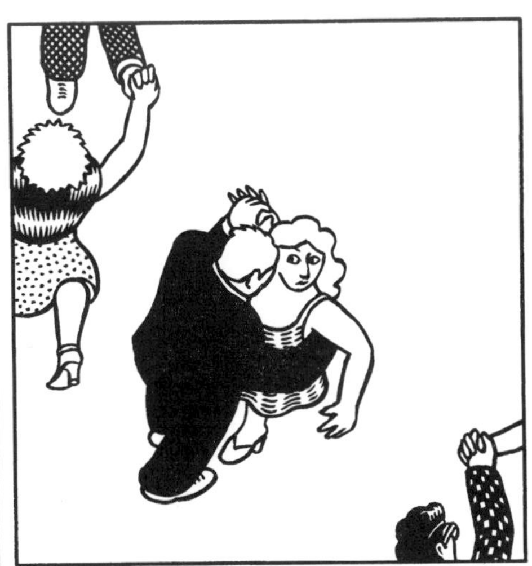

AS I FELT MYSELF GOING I HELD HER TIGHTLY

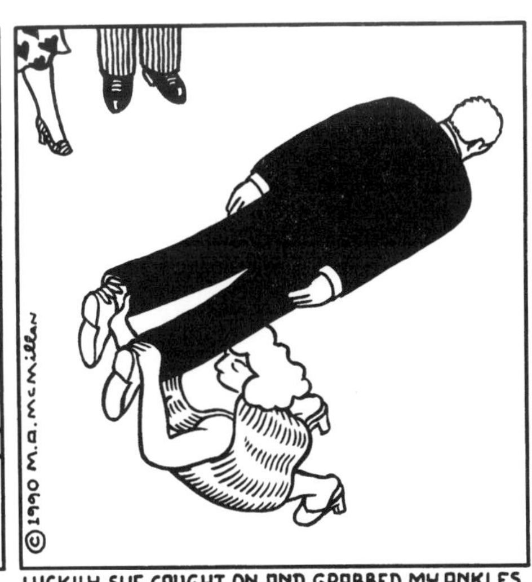

LUCKILY SHE CAUGHT ON AND GRABBED MY ANKLES

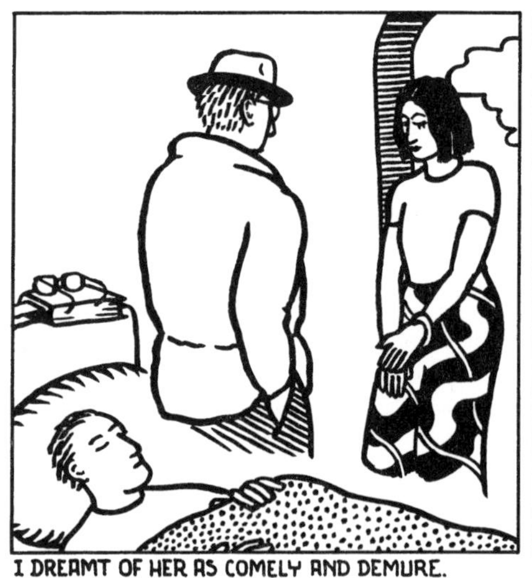

I DREAMT OF HER AS COMELY AND DEMURE.

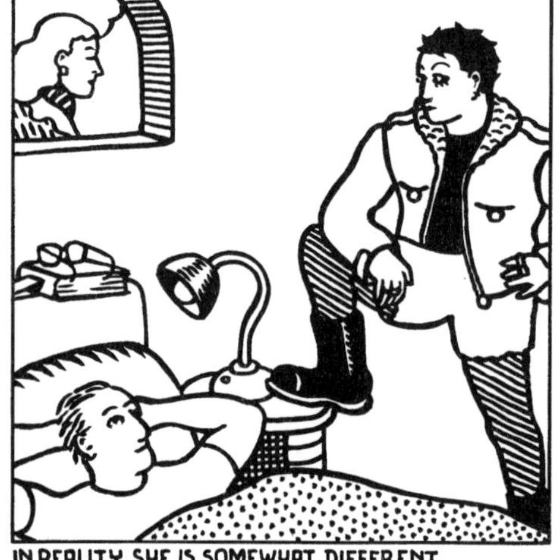

IN REALITY SHE IS SOMEWHAT DIFFERENT.

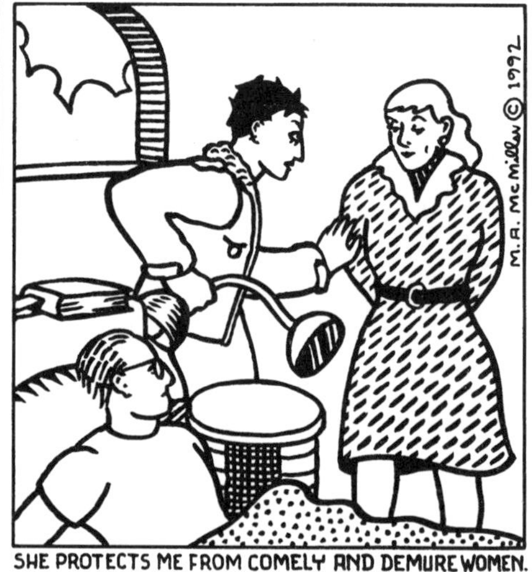

SHE PROTECTS ME FROM COMELY AND DEMURE WOMEN.

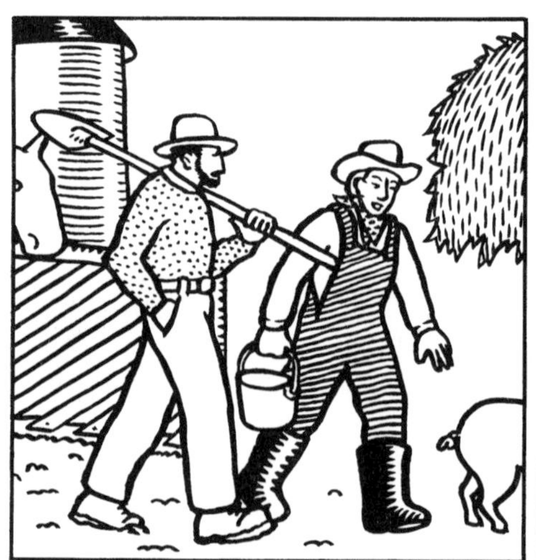

I'D RATHER BE BACK HERE WITH THE ANIMALS..THE MUD.

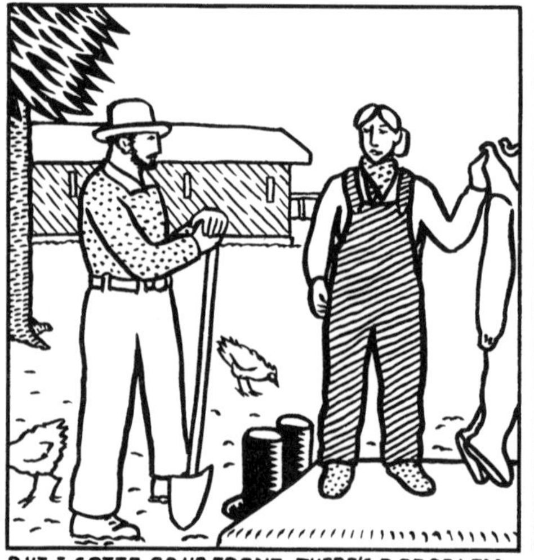

BUT I GOTTA GO UP FRONT. THERE'S A PROBLEM.

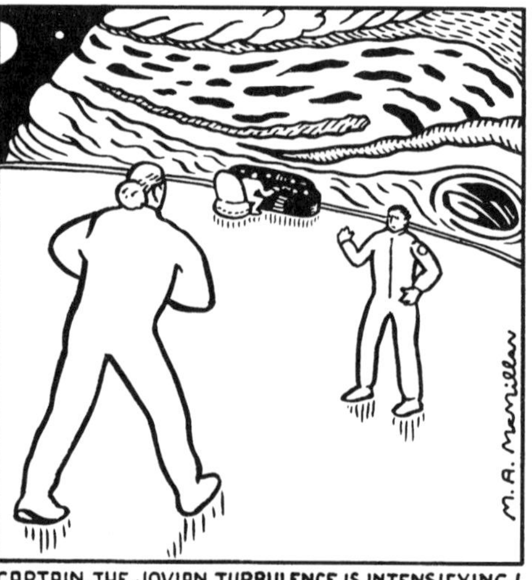

CAPTAIN, THE JOVIAN TURBULENCE IS INTENSIFYING!

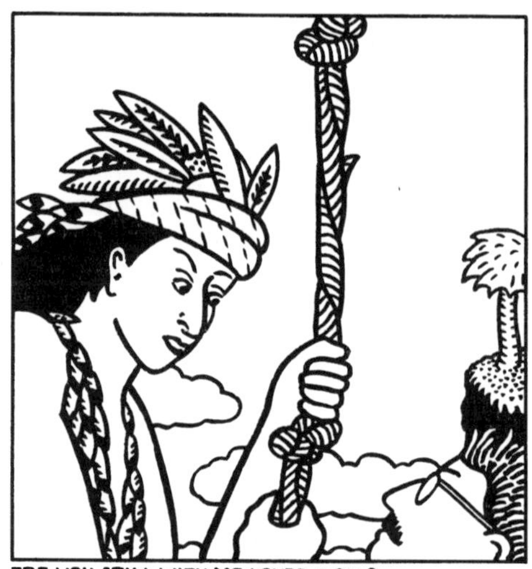

ARE YOU STILL WITH ME LOVER BOY ?

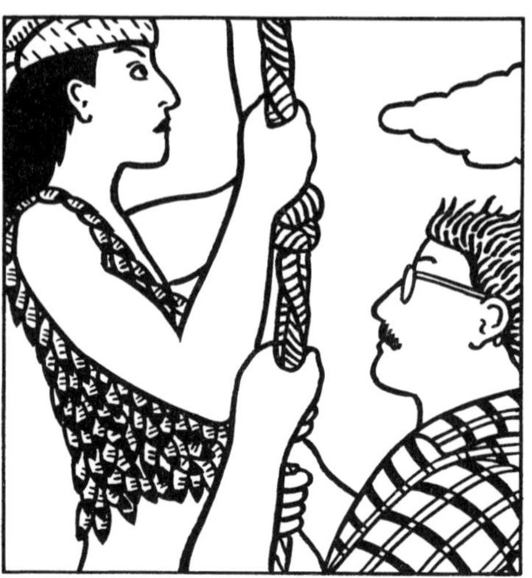

OKEY WE GO HIGHER. CAREFUL! THE ROPE IS ROTTEN!

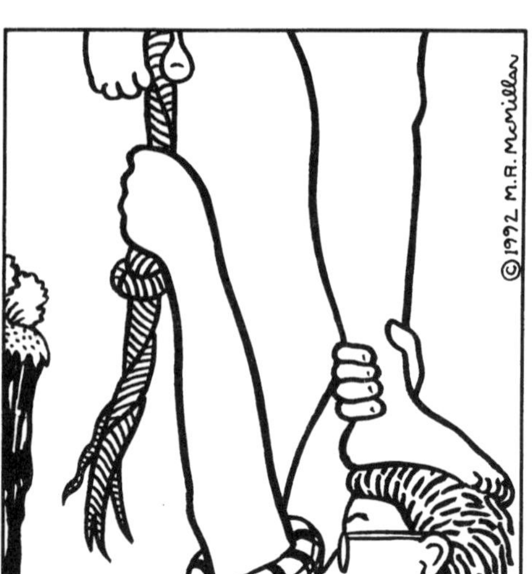

WE WORK AS A TEAM, YES ?

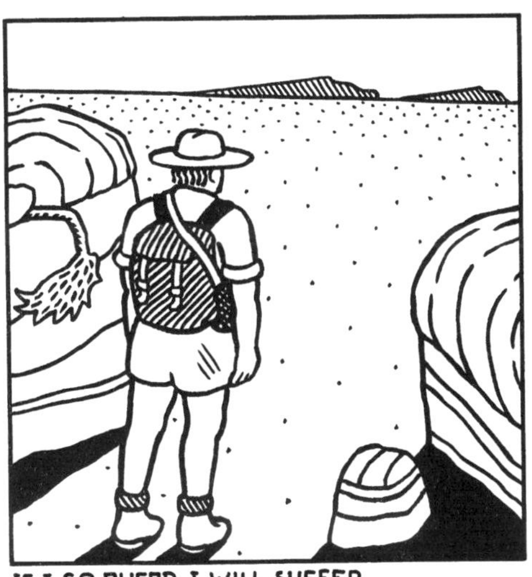

IF I GO AHEAD I WILL SUFFER

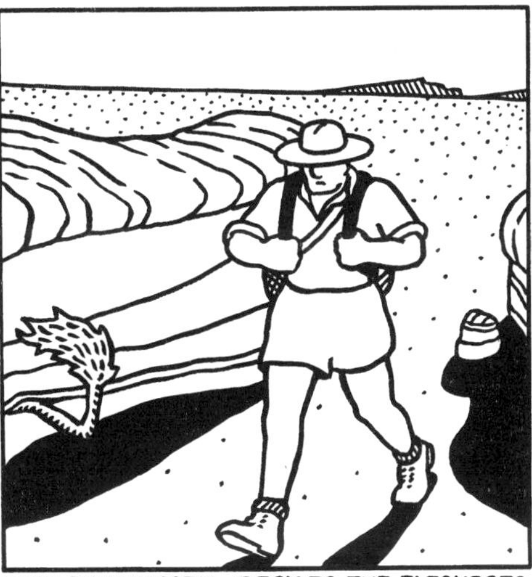

I AM ONLY HUMAN. BACK TO THE FLESHPOTS

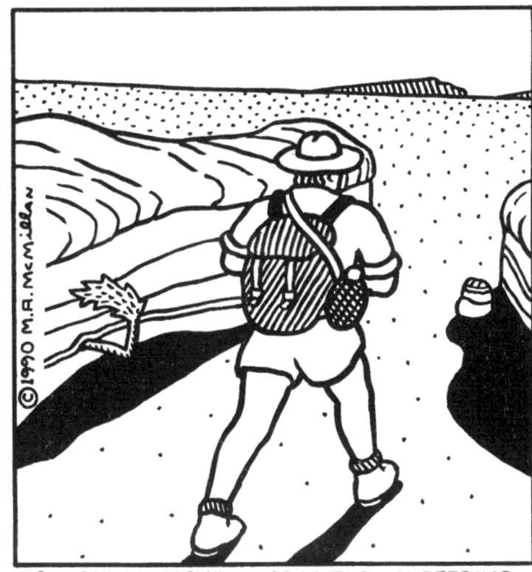

NO! "ONLY HUMAN" IS WORSE THAN SUFFERING

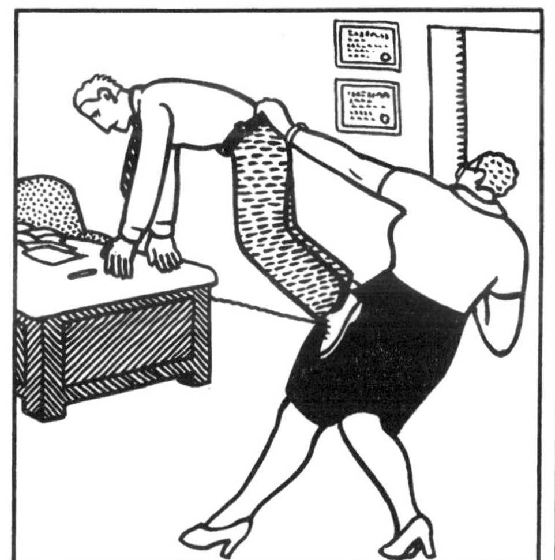

YOU MUST AVOID INTELLECTUAL BOOBY TRAPS.

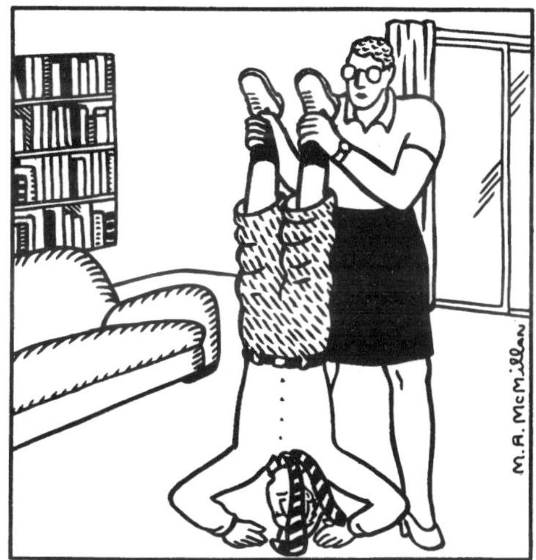

BE AWARE OF ALL YOUR DEVIOUS RATIONALIZATIONS.

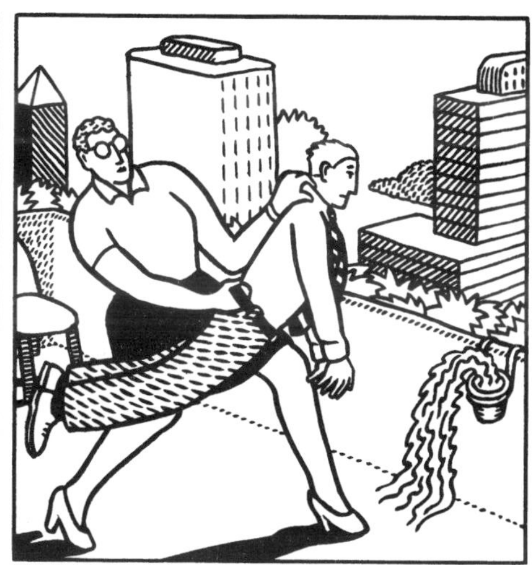

THEN WITH A STILL MIND LOOK TO THE SETTING SUN.

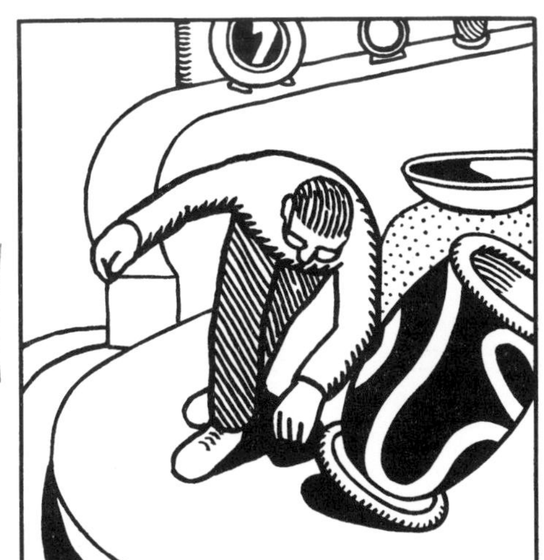

IT WAS ONLY A MINOR MISSTEP

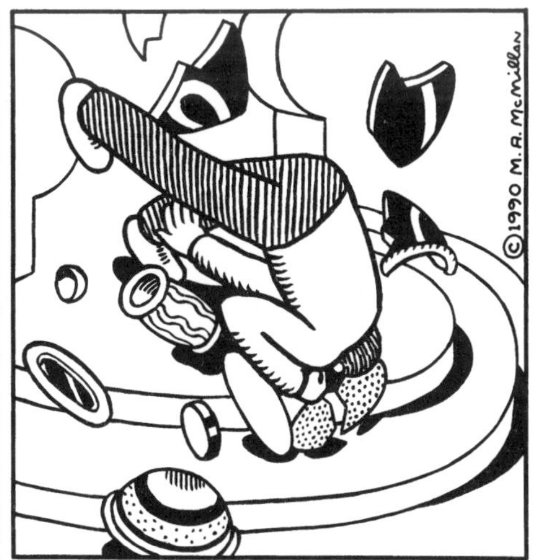

BUT ONE MISSTEP LED TO OTHERS

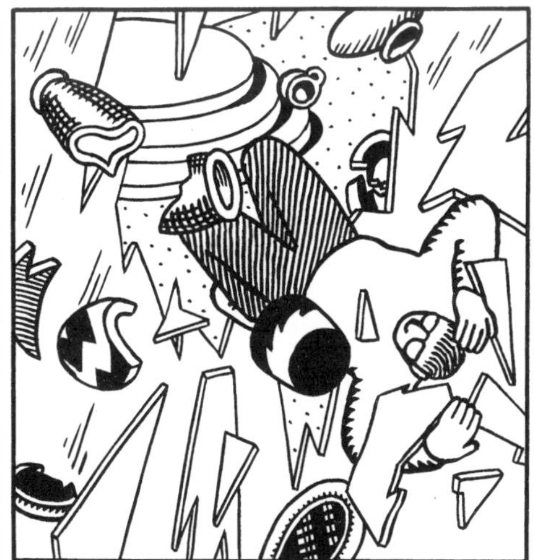

THE MOMENTUM ACCELERATED

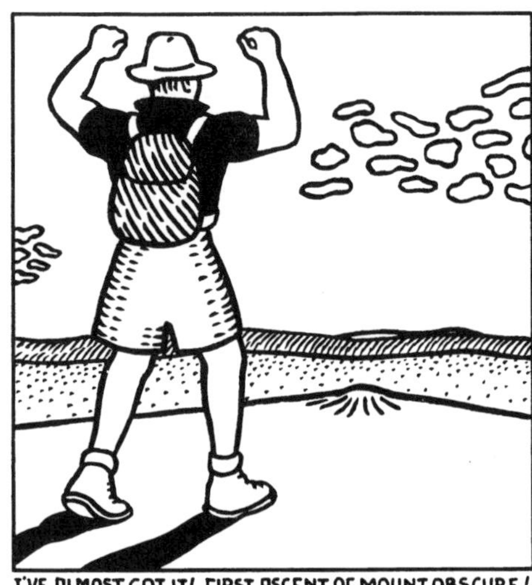
I'VE ALMOST GOT IT! FIRST ASCENT OF MOUNT OBSCURE!

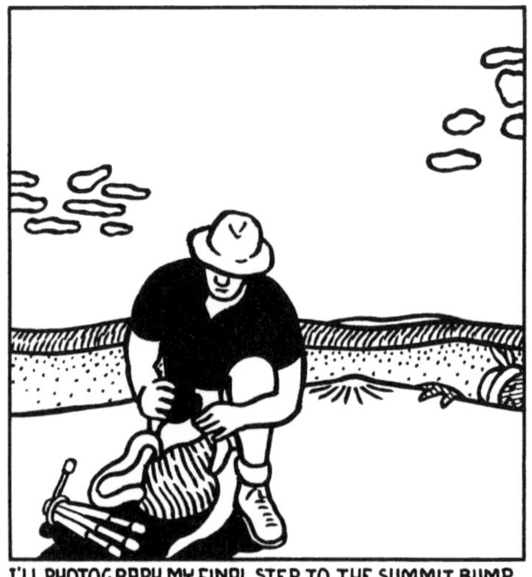
I'LL PHOTOGRAPH MY FINAL STEP TO THE SUMMIT BUMP.

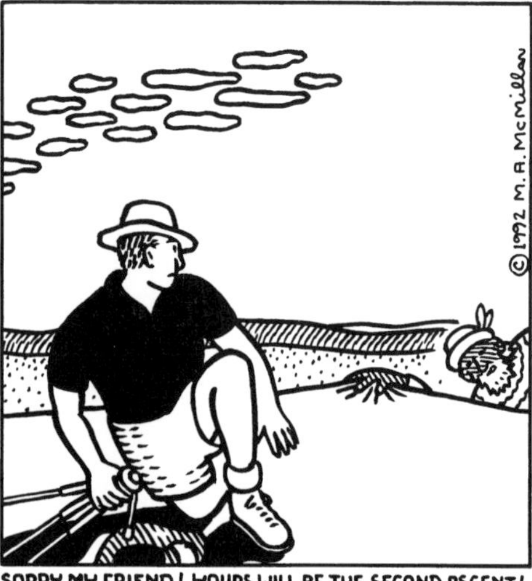

SORRY MY FRIEND! YOURS WILL BE THE SECOND ASCENT!

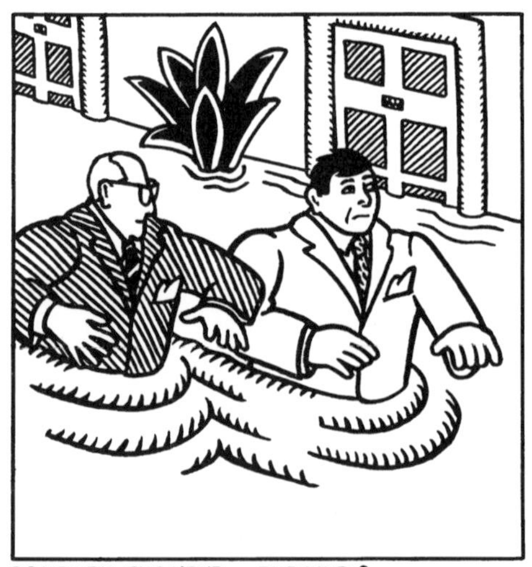
DO YOU ALWAYS HAVE .... THE MUD ?

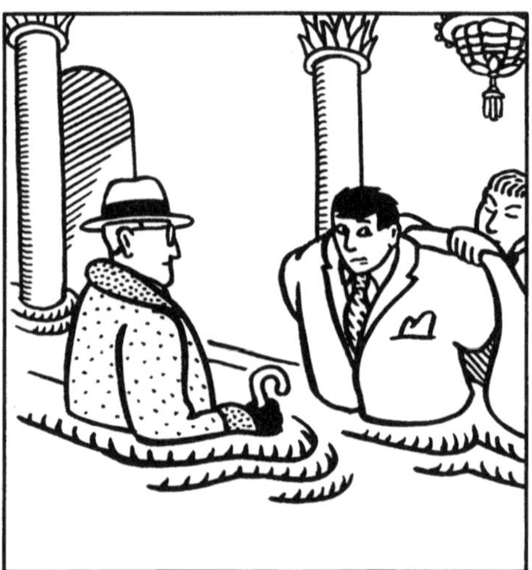
MUD WOULD BE A BLESSING. THIS IS WHAT WE CALL SLUDGE.

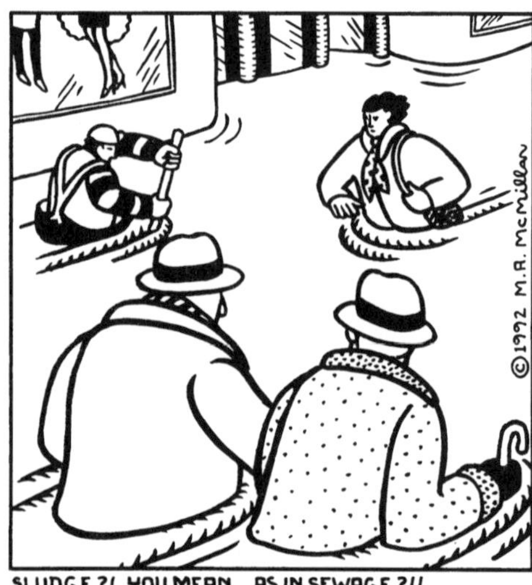

SLUDGE ?! YOU MEAN... AS IN SEWAGE ?!!

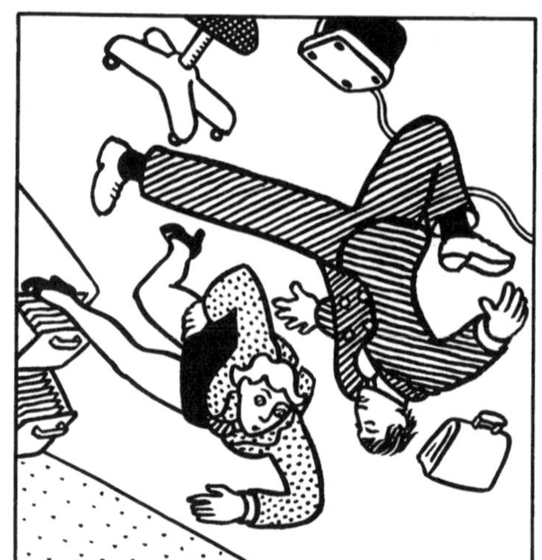
LIKE THE OZONE LAYER, GRAVITY IS LEAVING THE PLANET.

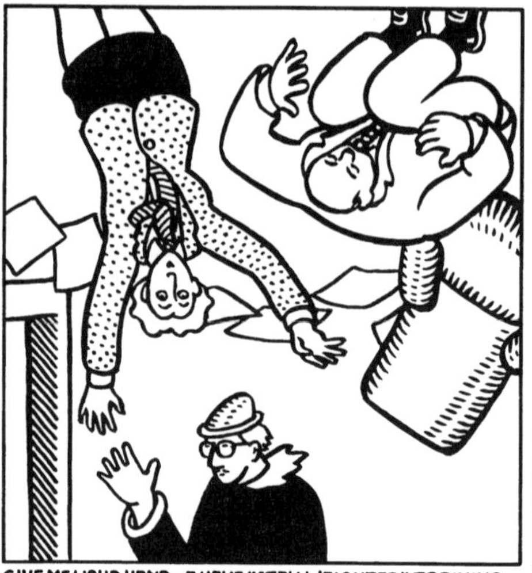
GIVE ME YOUR HAND. I HAVE "STAY WEIGHTED" TRAINING.

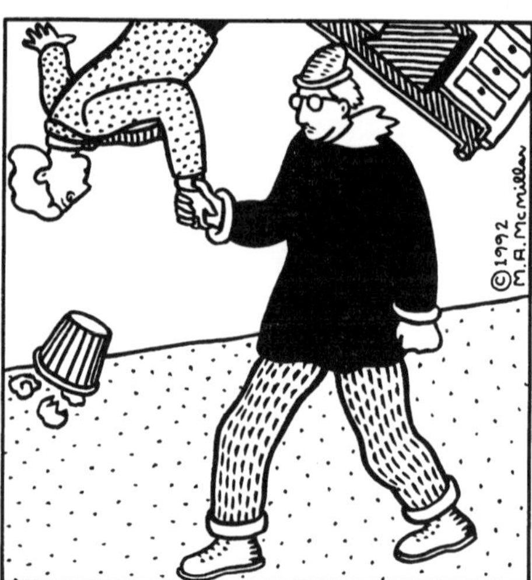

...TAKES CONCENTRATION THOUGH.

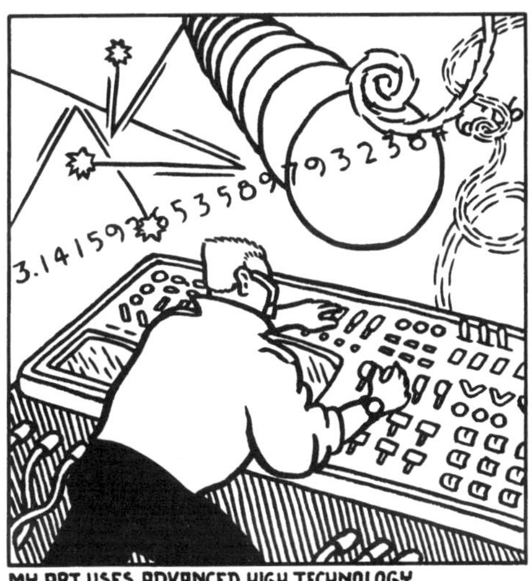
MY ART USES ADVANCED HIGH TECHNOLOGY.

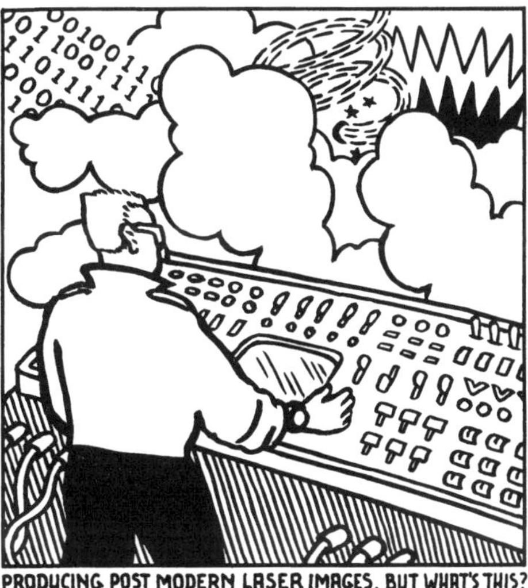
PRODUCING POST MODERN LASER IMAGES. BUT WHAT'S THIS?

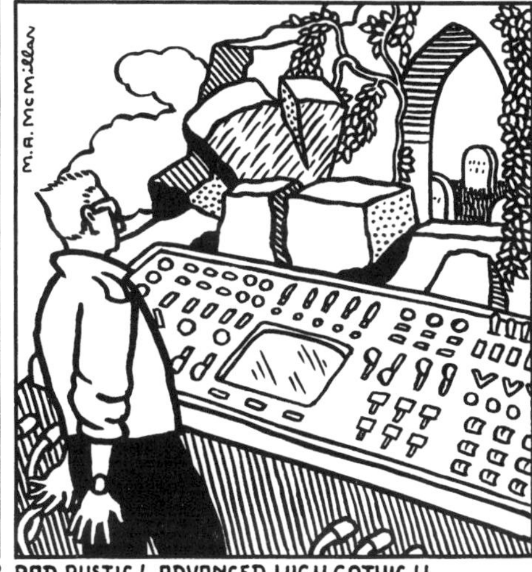
M.A. McMillan
RAD RUSTIC! ADVANCED HIGH GOTHIC!!

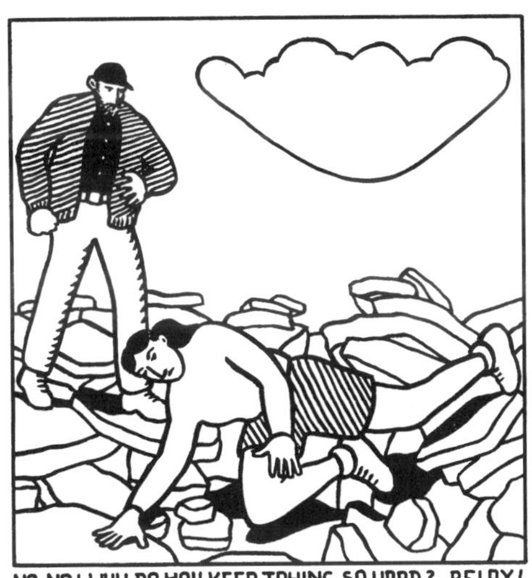
NO-NO! WHY DO YOU KEEP TRYING SO HARD? RELAX!

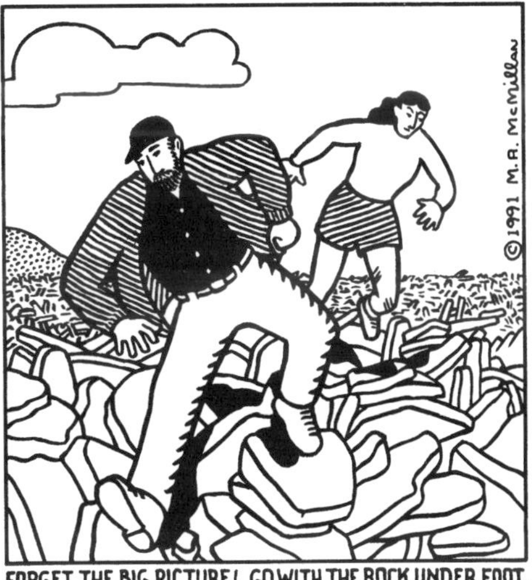
©1991 M.A. McMillan
FORGET THE BIG PICTURE! GO WITH THE ROCK UNDER FOOT.

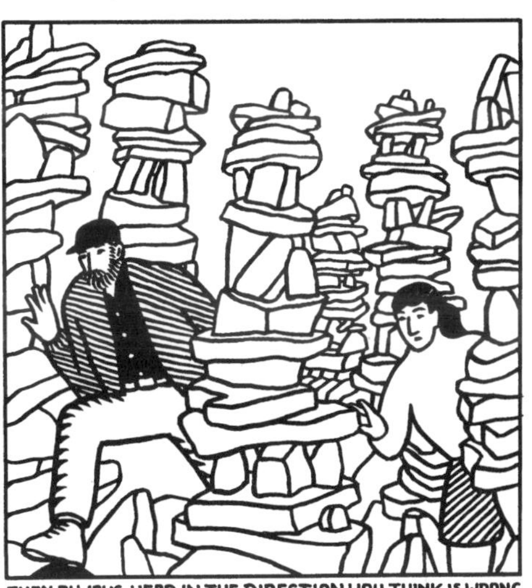
THEN ALWAYS HEAD IN THE DIRECTION YOU THINK IS WRONG.

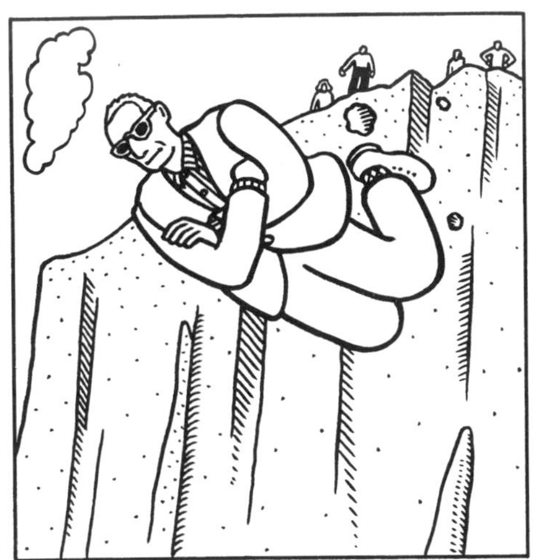

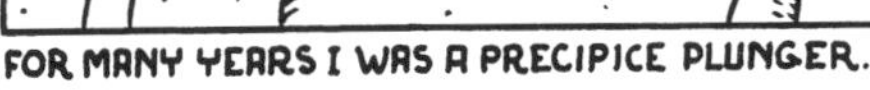
FOR MANY YEARS I WAS A PRECIPICE PLUNGER.

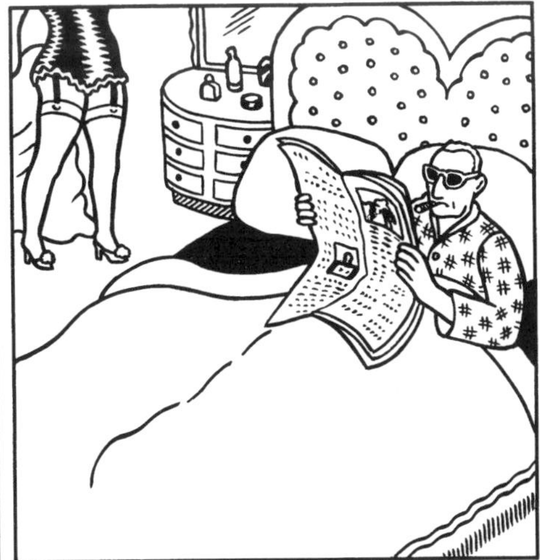
I RETIRED BUT GOT BORED WITH THE SOFT LIFE.

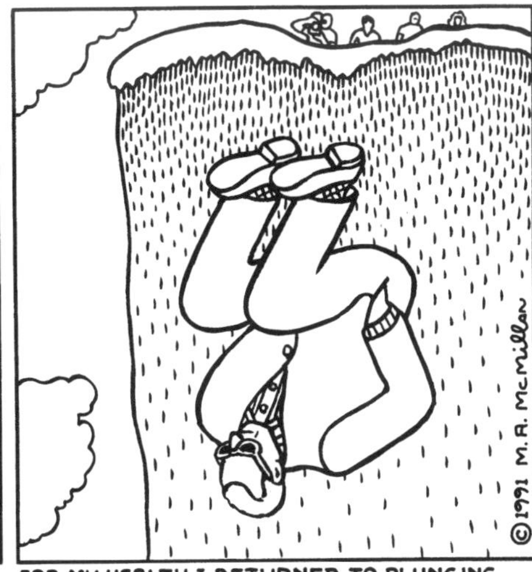
©1991 M.A. McMillan
FOR MY HEALTH I RETURNED TO PLUNGING.

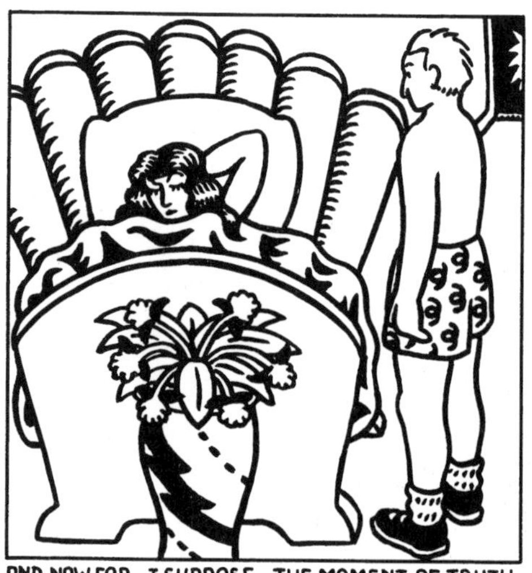

AND NOW FOR, I SUPPOSE, THE MOMENT OF TRUTH.

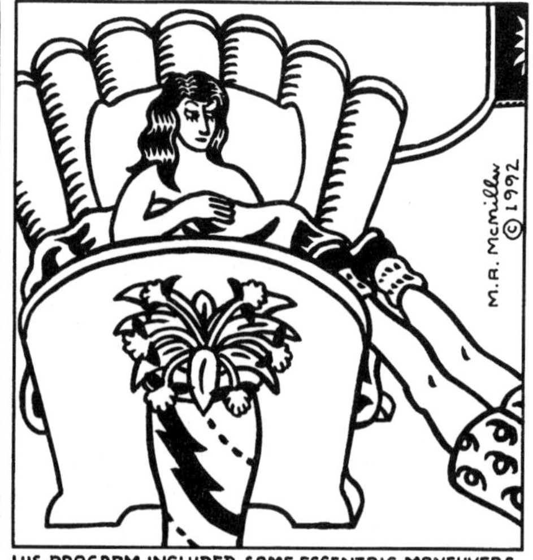

HIS PROGRAM INCLUDED SOME ECCENTRIC MANEUVERS.

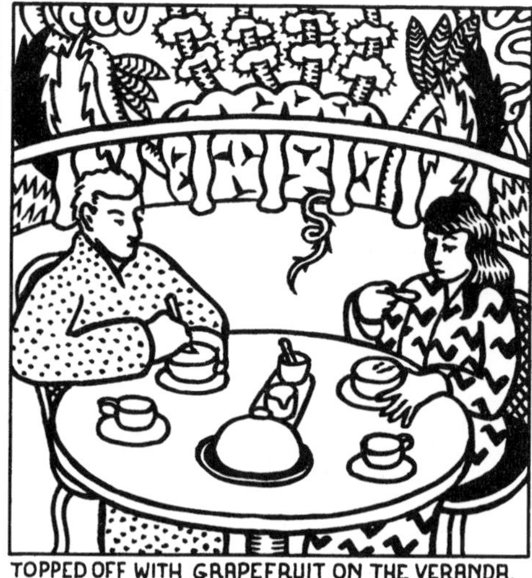

TOPPED OFF WITH GRAPEFRUIT ON THE VERANDA.

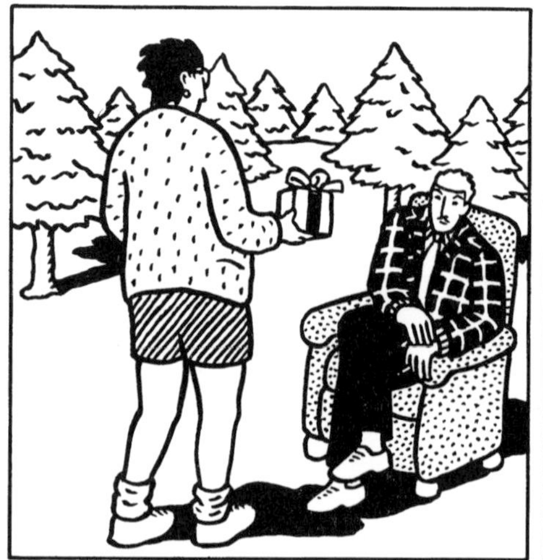

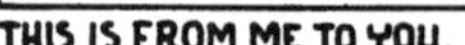
THIS IS FROM ME TO YOU.

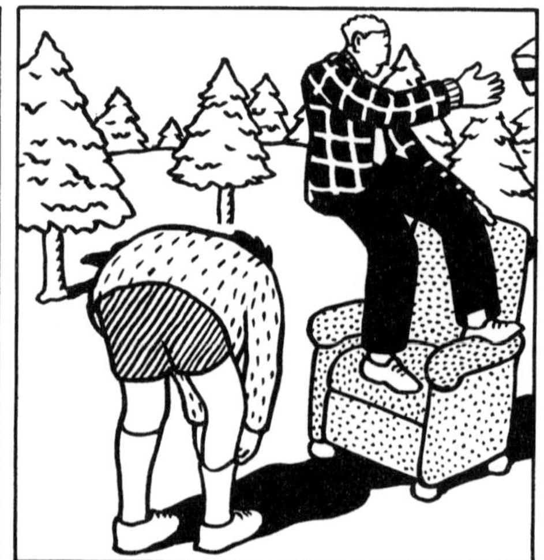

HOW THOUGHTFUL! JUST WHAT I'M NEEDING NO DOUBT.

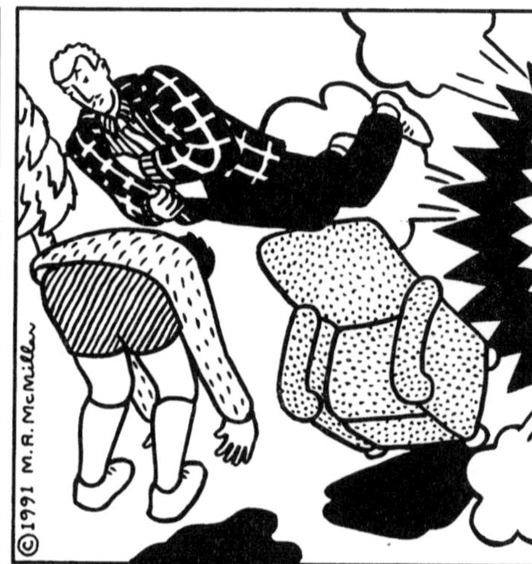

AND I DIDN'T FORGET YOUR LITTLE SOMETHING.

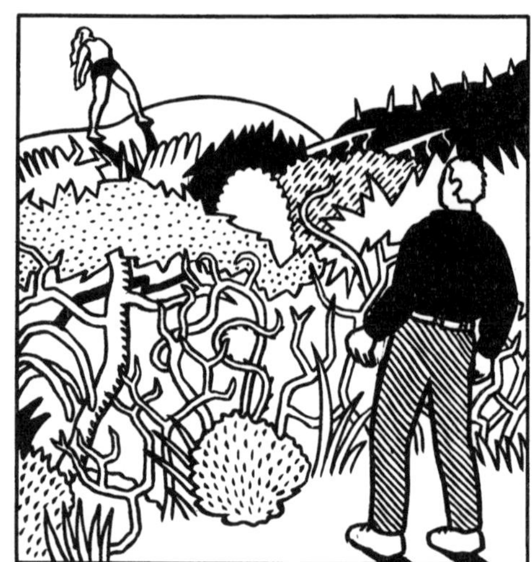

SHE WAS OBVIOUSLY PERSUADING ME TO APPROACH HER.

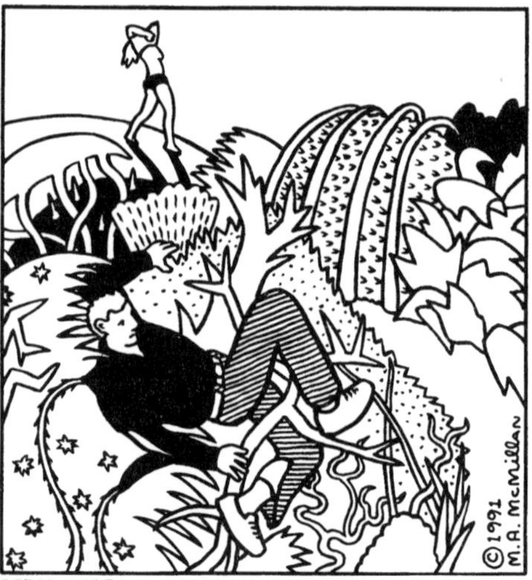

AFTER A FRANTIC EFFORT I FOUND A PATH. TOO SOON!

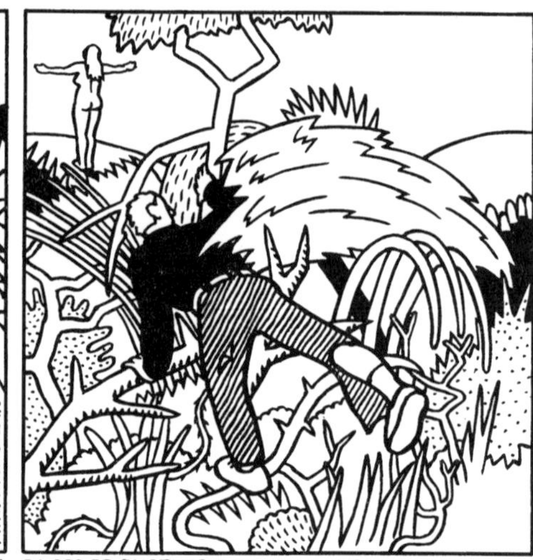

I NEEDED ANOTHER TEN MINUTES OF TORMENT.

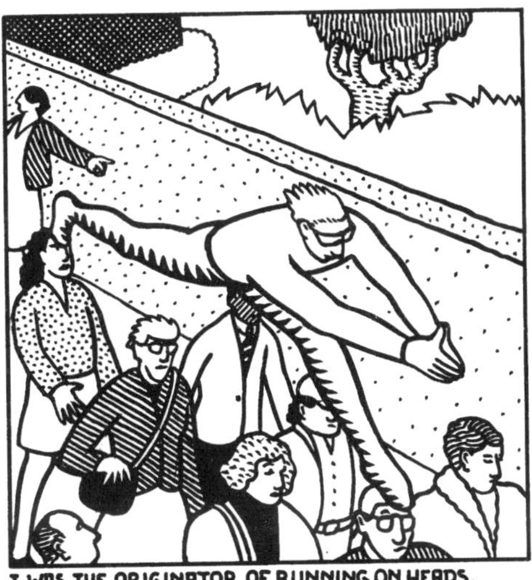
I WAS THE ORIGINATOR OF RUNNING ON HEADS.

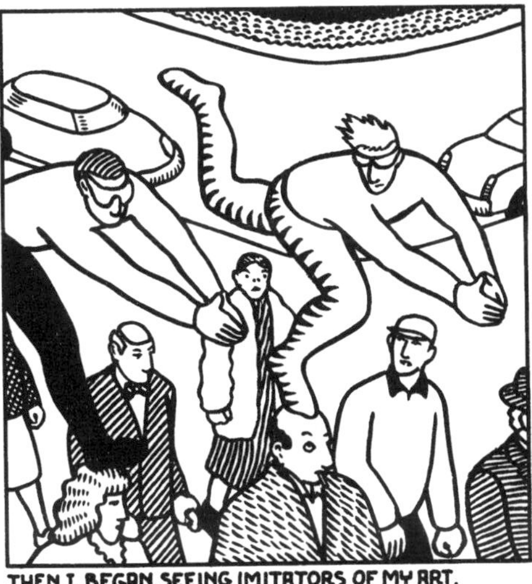
THEN I BEGAN SEEING IMITATORS OF MY ART.

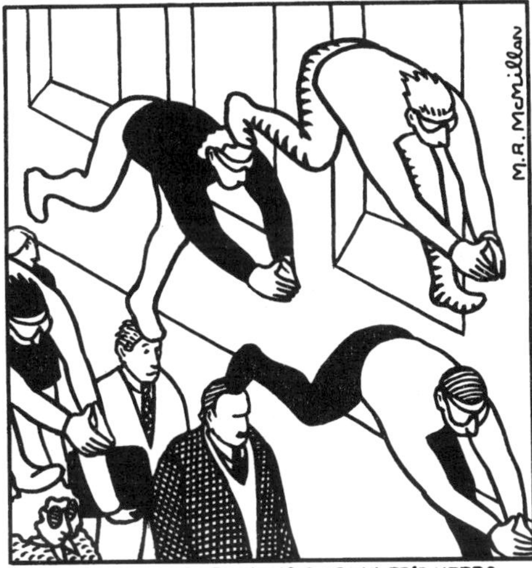

I UPPED THE ANTE BY RUNNING ON RUNNER'S HEADS.

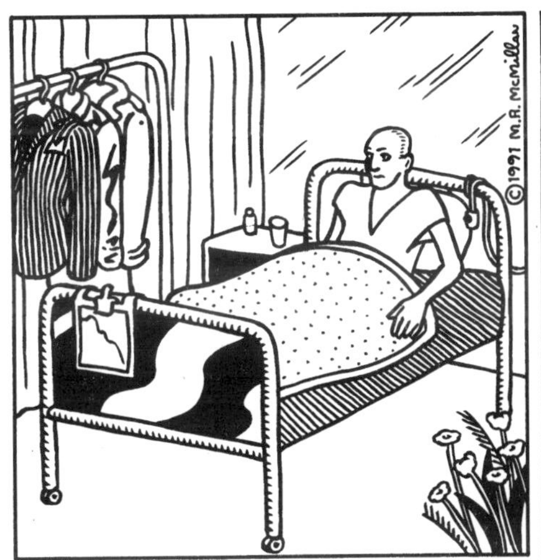

I JUST DIED! GOTTA SPLIT BEFORE IT BECOMES KNOWN.

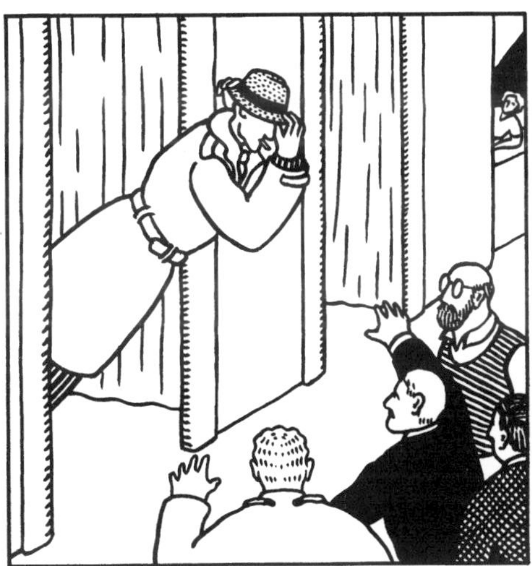
DOCTORS, LAWYERS, THERAPISTS, MORTICIANS!!

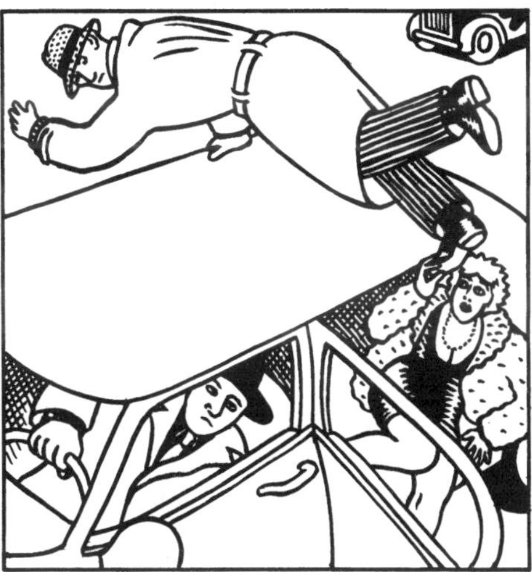
STEP ON IT TINY! I GOT THE RABBLE ON MY TAIL!

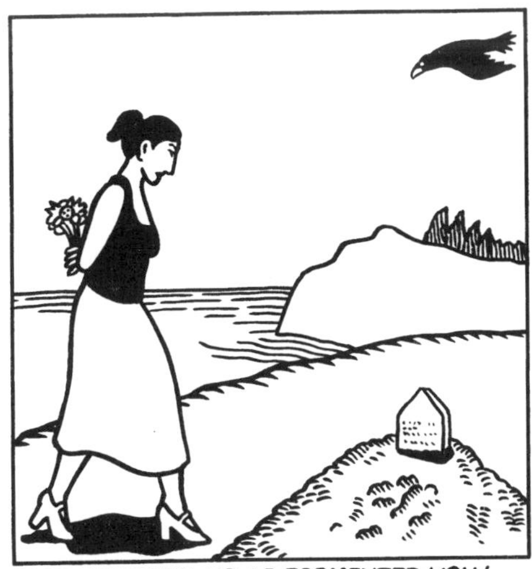
POOR REYNALDO, HOW I TORMENTED YOU!

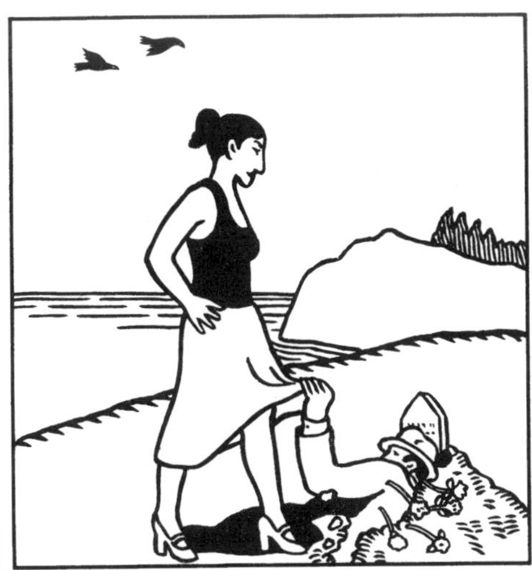
BUT YOU DESERVED IT, YOU BASTARD!

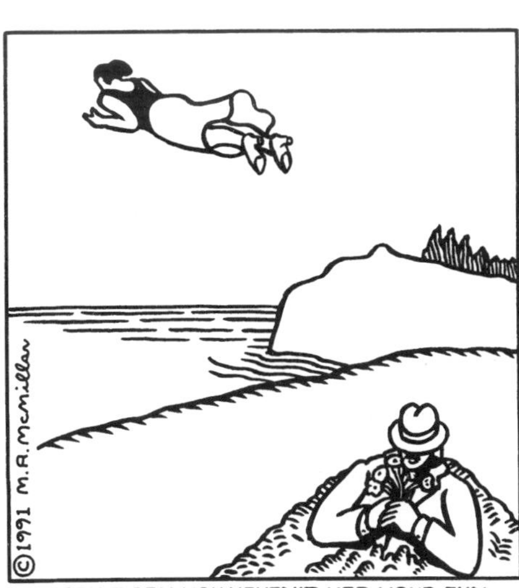

YOU CAN'T SAY YOU HAVEN'T HAD YOUR FUN.

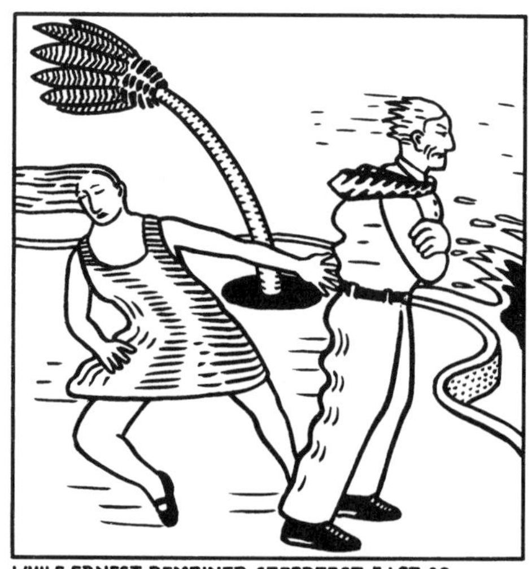

WHILE ERNEST REMAINED STEADFAST I LET GO.

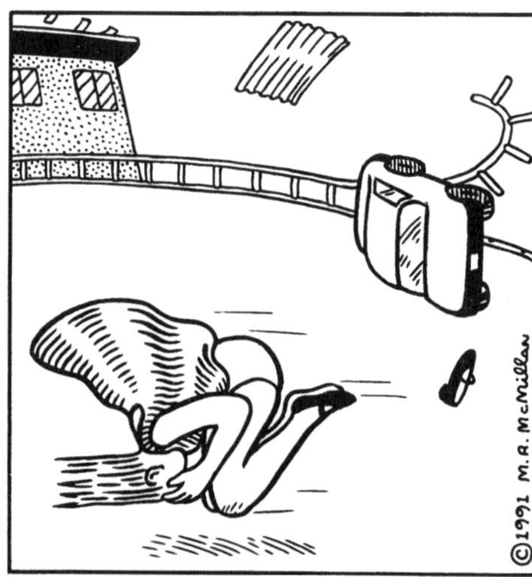

I WENT WITH THE WIND. IT ROLLED ME FOR MILES.

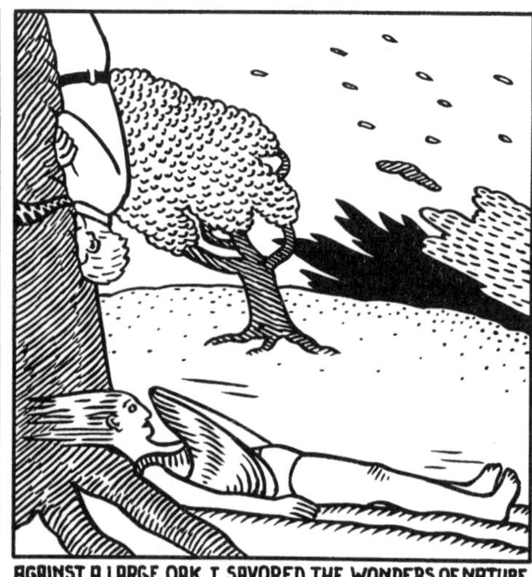

AGAINST A LARGE OAK I SAVORED THE WONDERS OF NATURE.

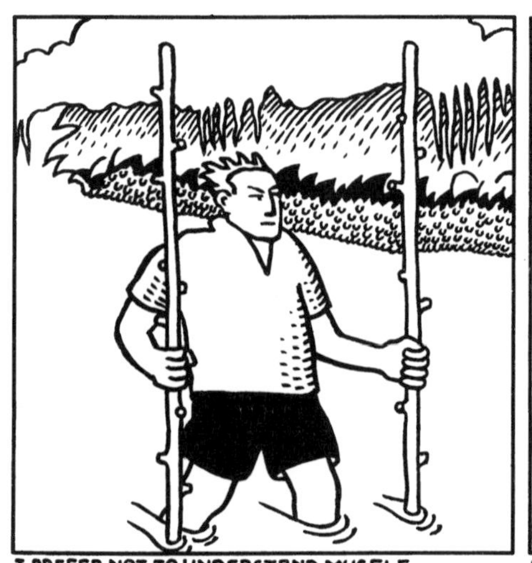

I PREFER NOT TO UNDERSTAND MYSELF

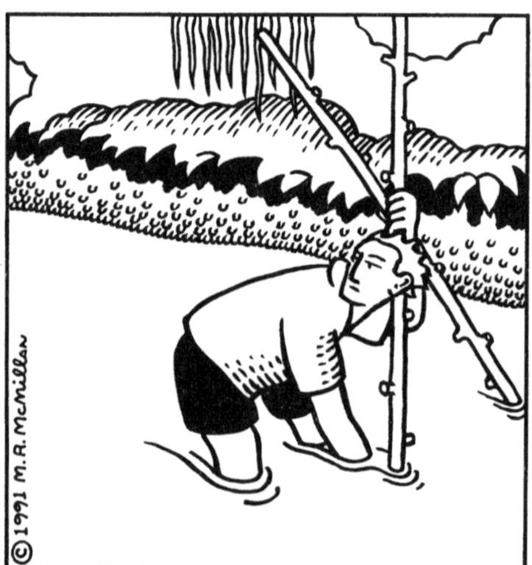

THEREBY OPENING THE DOOR TO SURPRISES....

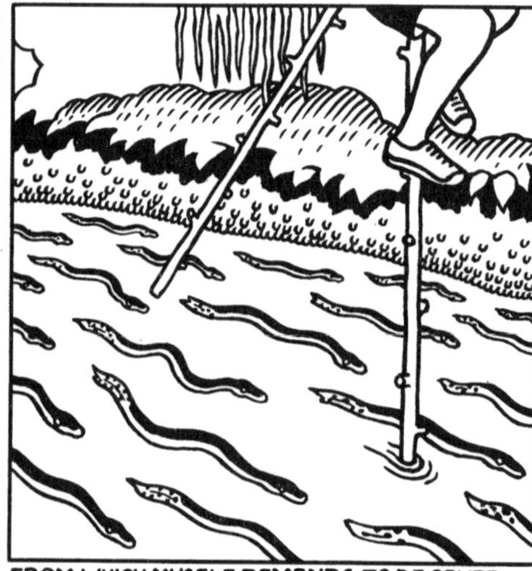

FROM WHICH MYSELF DEMANDS TO BE SAVED.

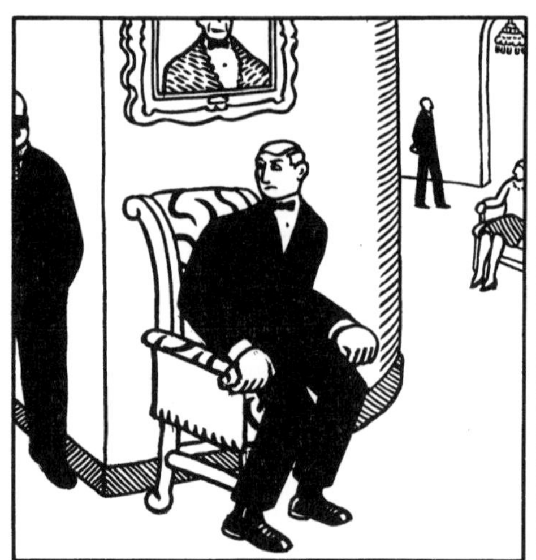

THIS IS THE FREE ENTERPRISE SYSTEM.

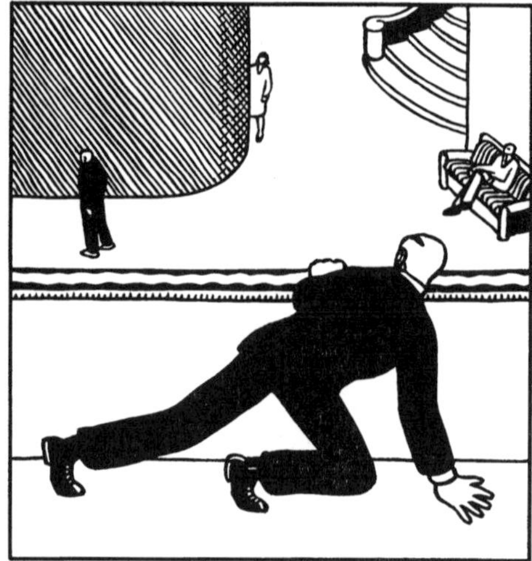

WHERE WE CAN UTILIZE OUR RESOURCEFULNESS.

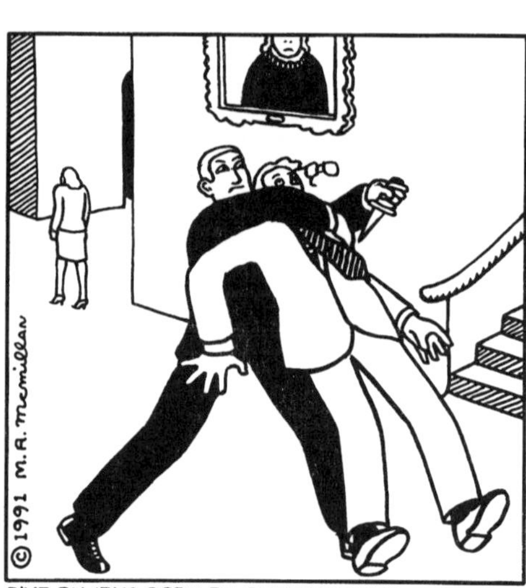

I'VE ALWAYS BEEN AN OVERACHIEVER

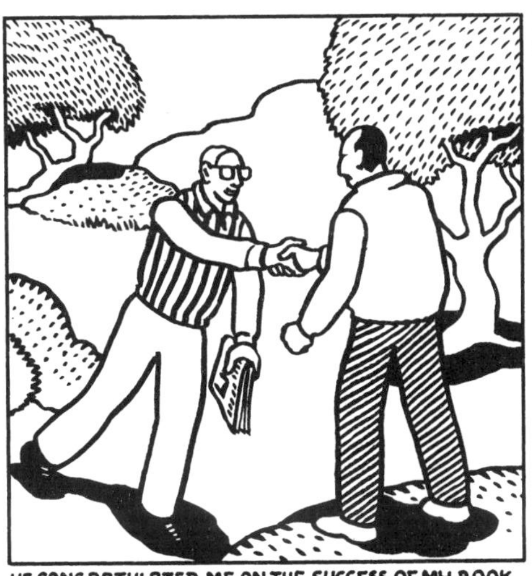

HE CONGRATULATED ME ON THE SUCCESS OF MY BOOK.

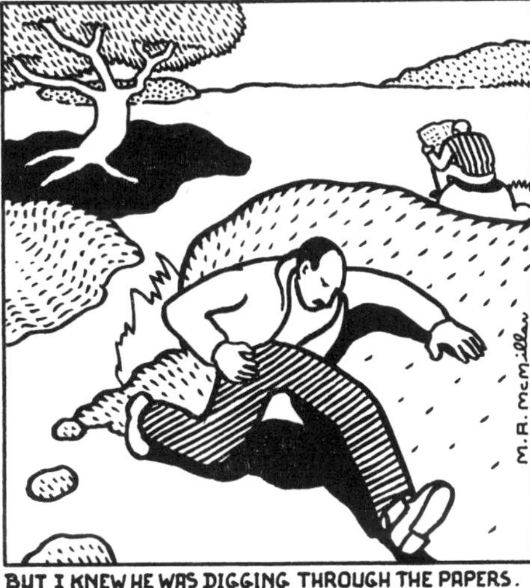

BUT I KNEW HE WAS DIGGING THROUGH THE PAPERS.

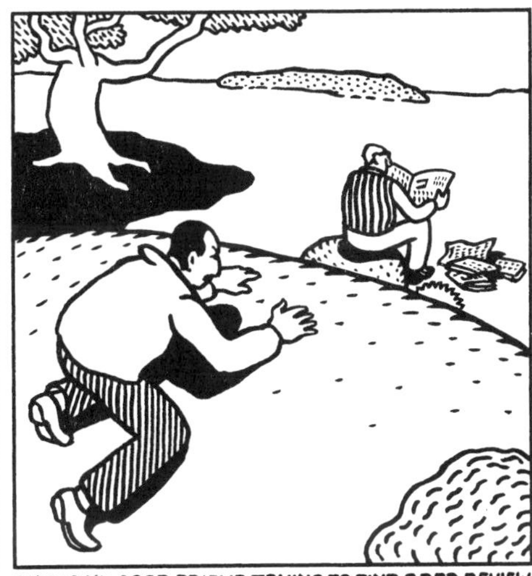

THIS IS MY GOOD FRIEND TRYING TO FIND A BAD REVIEW!

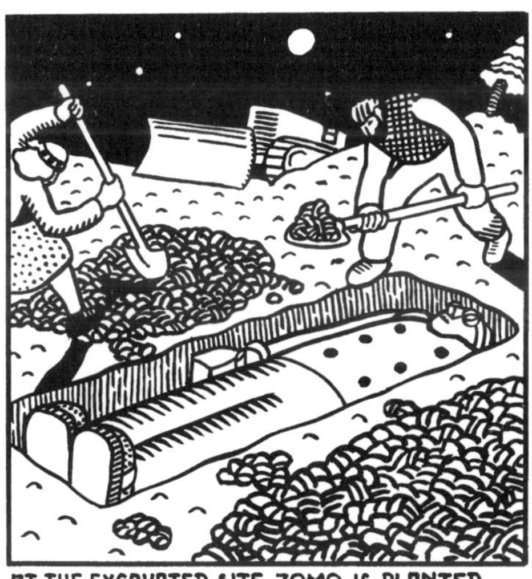

AT THE EXCAVATED SITE ZOMO IS PLANTED

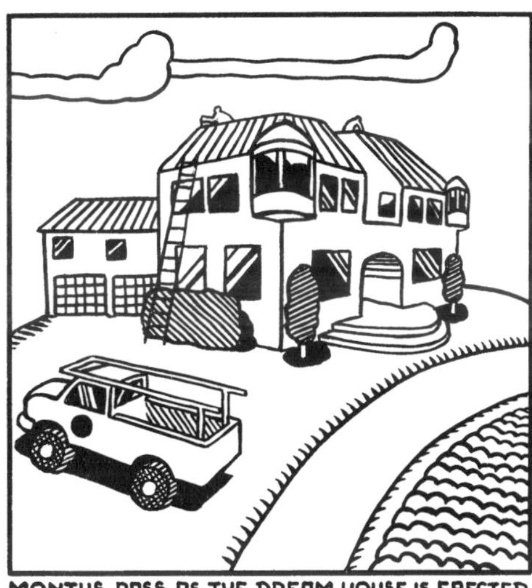

MONTHS PASS AS THE DREAM HOUSE IS ERECTED

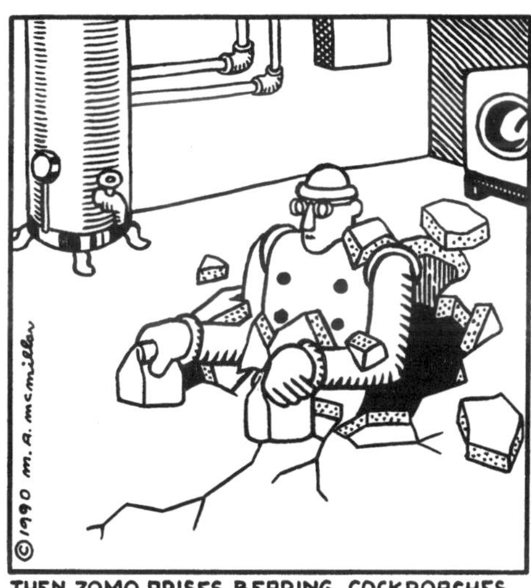

THEN ZOMO ARISES BEARING COCKROACHES

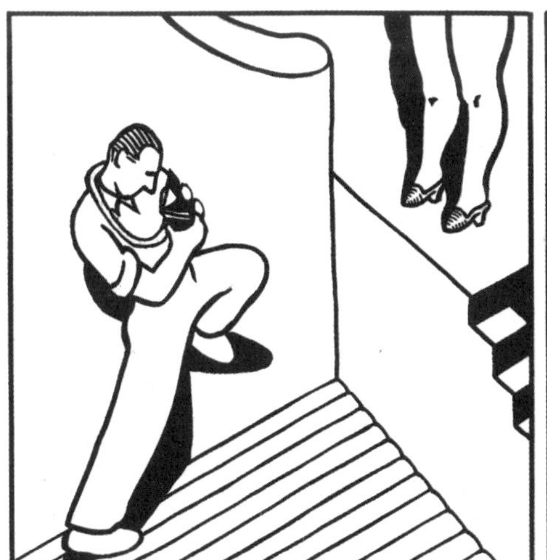

FIRST I SHOT THREE ROLLS OF HER

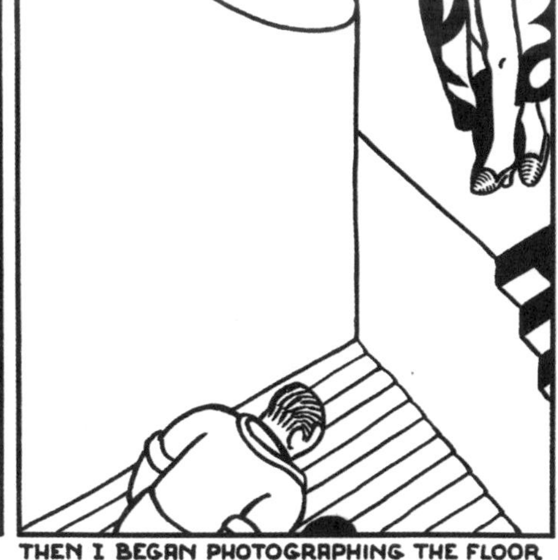

THEN I BEGAN PHOTOGRAPHING THE FLOOR

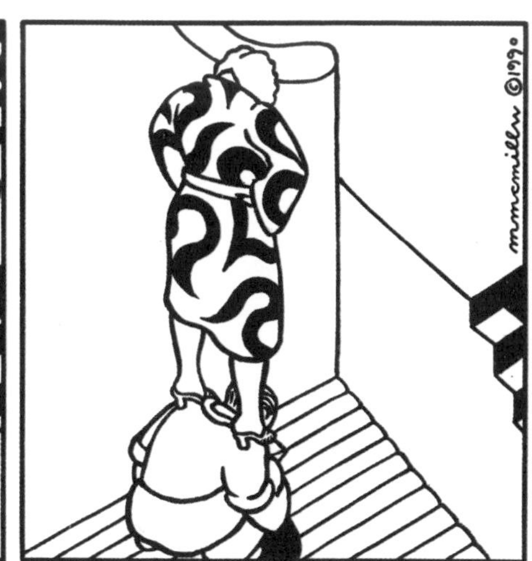

I BECAME OBSESSED DOWN THERE

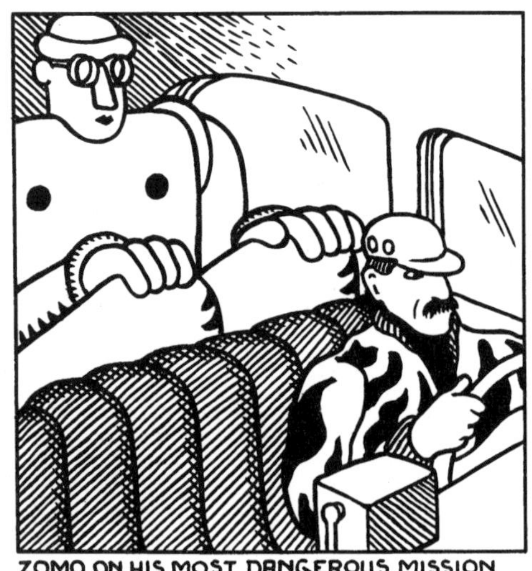
ZOMO ON HIS MOST DANGEROUS MISSION

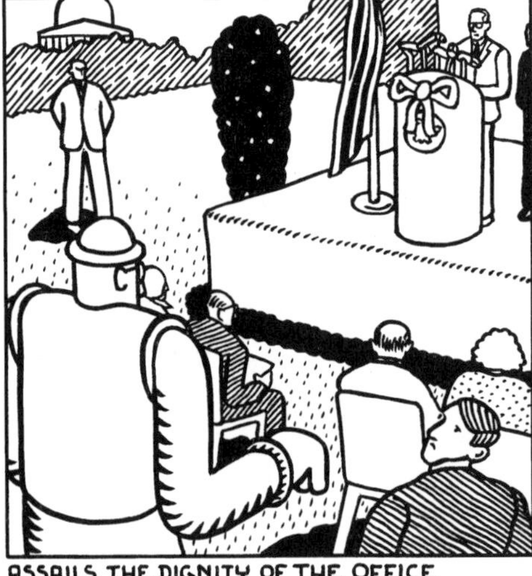
ASSAILS THE DIGNITY OF THE OFFICE

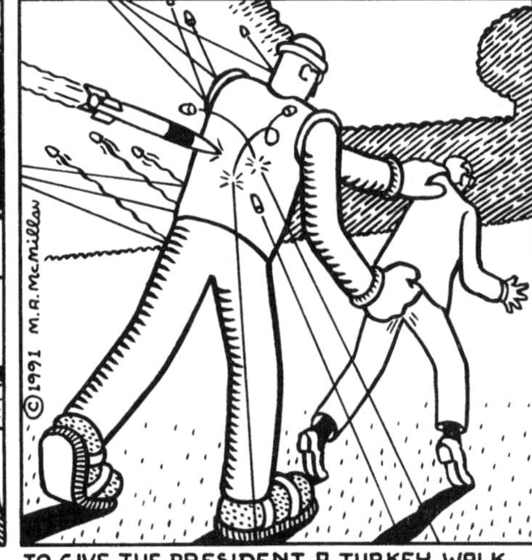

TO GIVE THE PRESIDENT A TURKEY WALK.

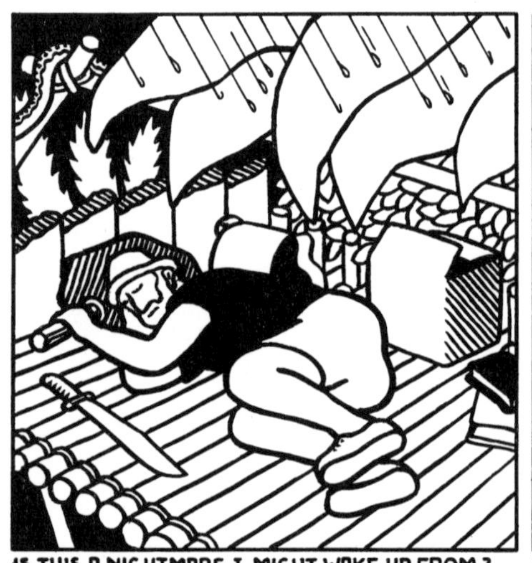
IS THIS A NIGHTMARE I MIGHT WAKE UP FROM?

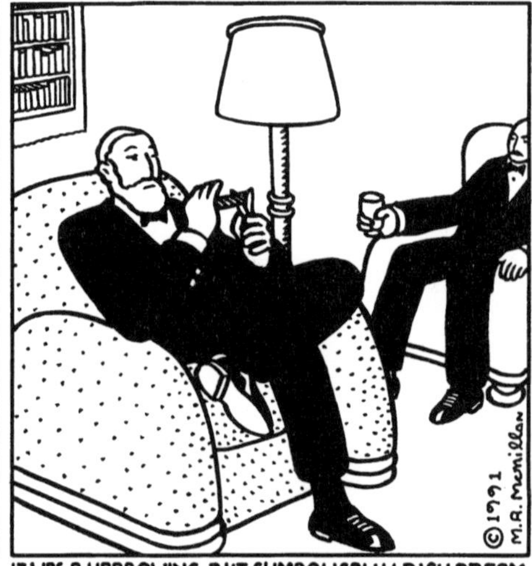

IT WAS A HARROWING BUT SYMBOLICALLY RICH DREAM.

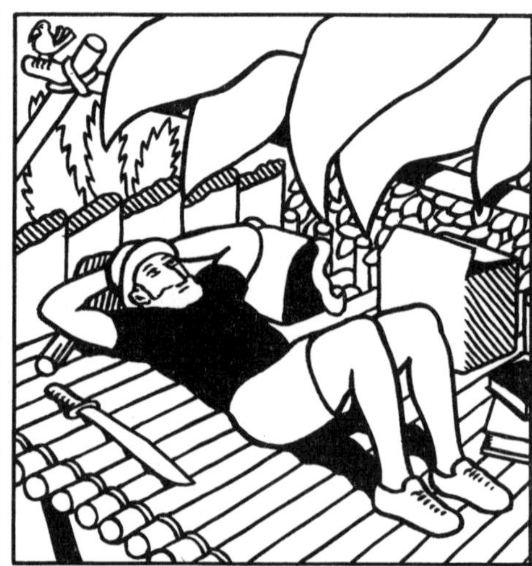
ANOTHER DRAWING ROOM SESSION! GIVE ME A BREAK!

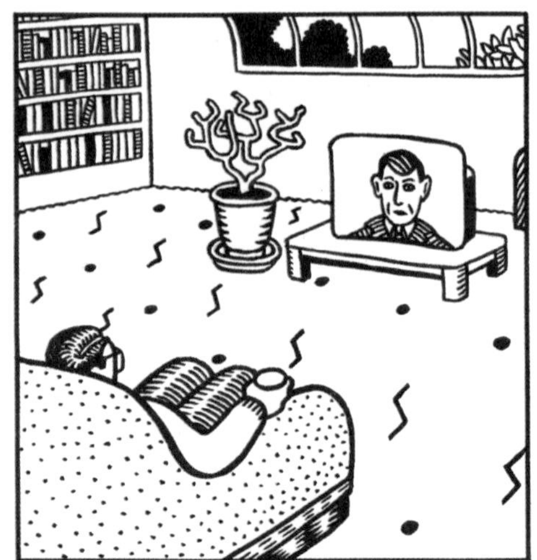
ONE MOMENT AT EASE IN THE PASTORAL SUBURBS

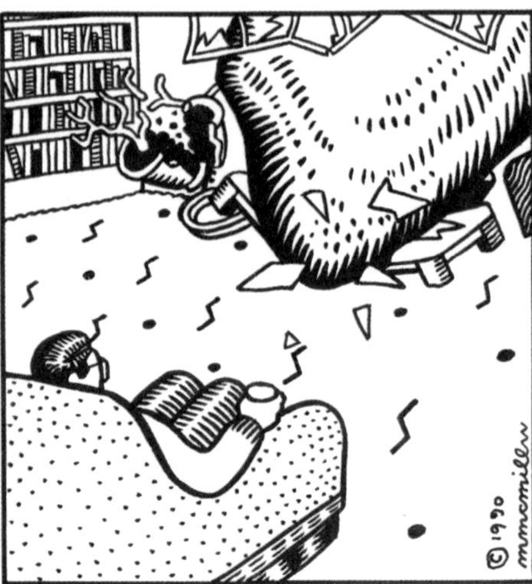

THE NEXT MOMENT...

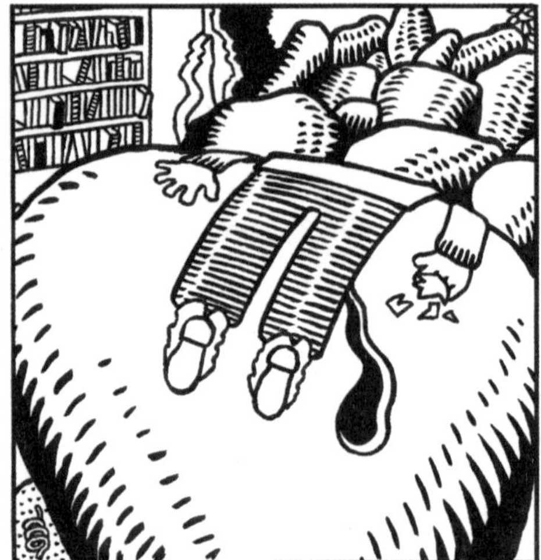
SQUASHED FLAT AS A BUG

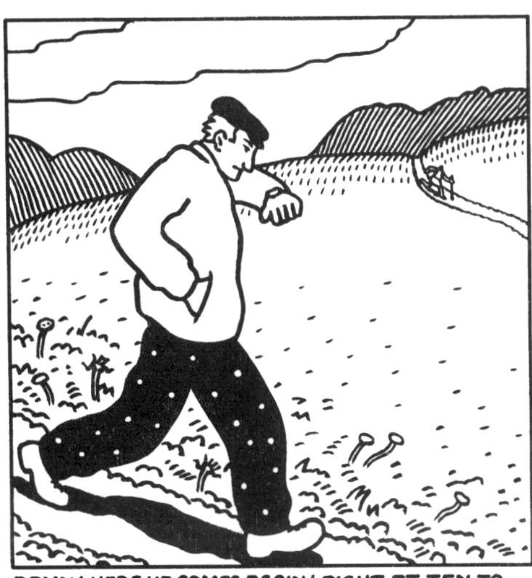
DAMN! HERE HE COMES AGAIN! RIGHT AT TEN TO.

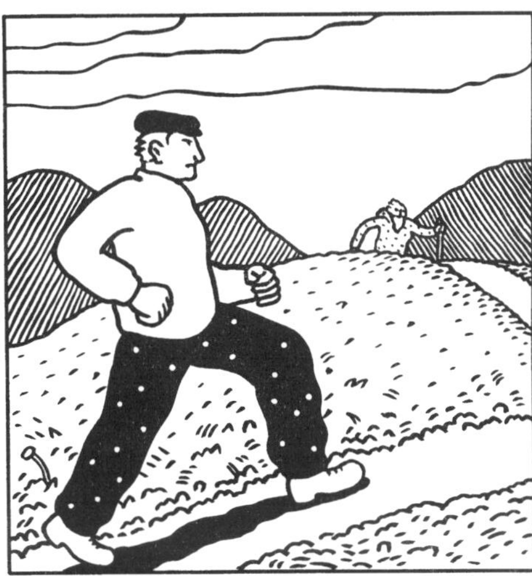
EVERY DAY I HAVE TO SPEED UP OR SLOW DOWN..

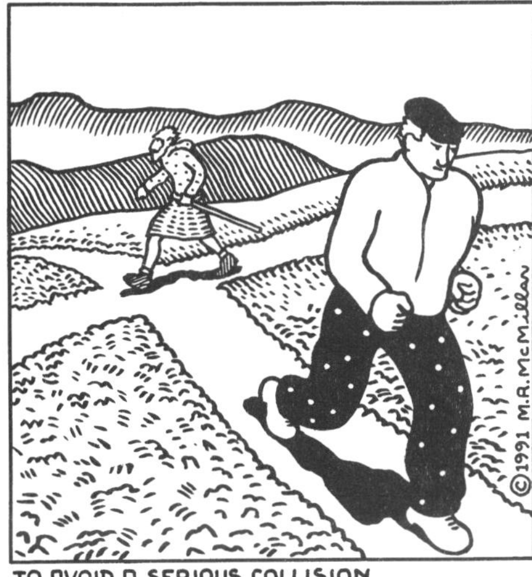

TO AVOID A SERIOUS COLLISION.

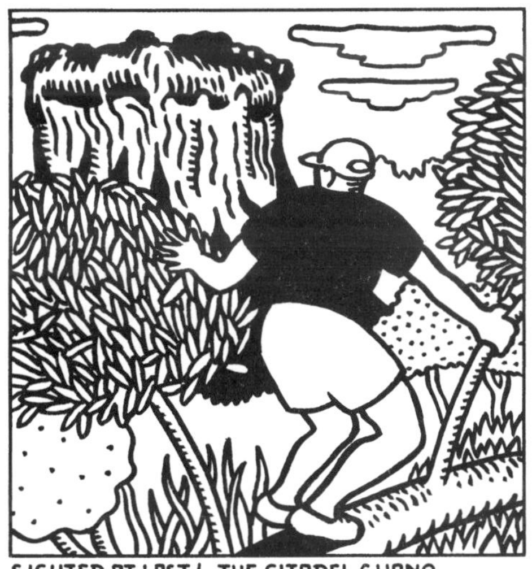
SIGHTED AT LAST! THE CITADEL GUANO.

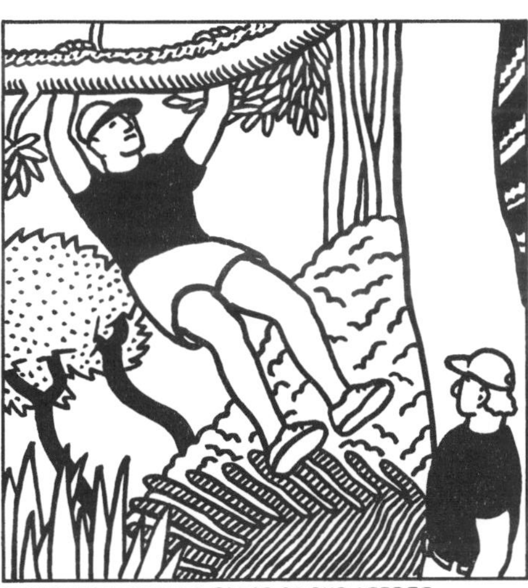
TO BE THE RESTING PLACE OF OUR LEADER.

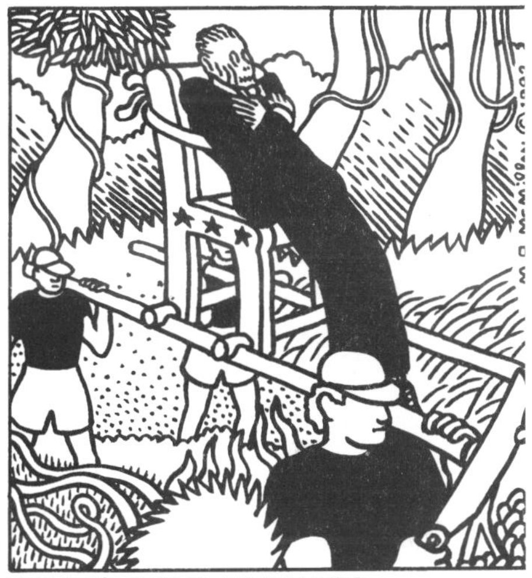
AMERICA'S LAST PRESIDENT KING.

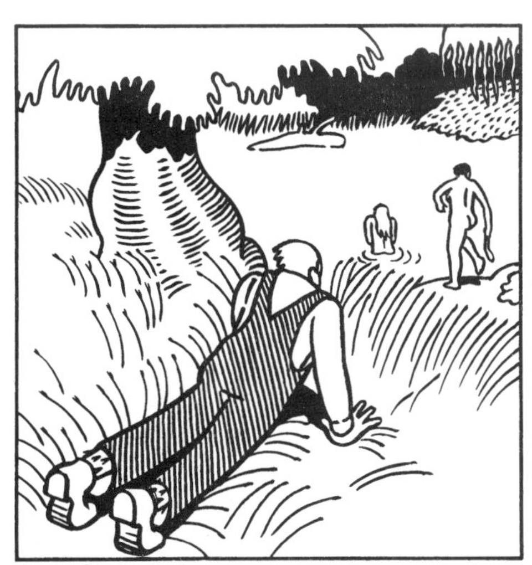
REDUCED TO SNEAKING IN THE GRASS.

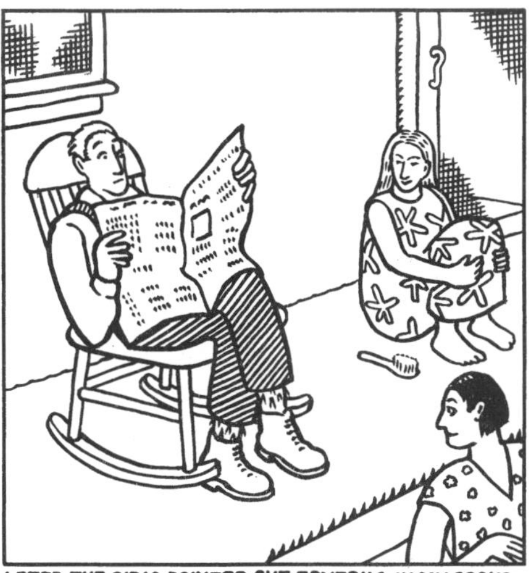
LATER THE GIRLS POINTED OUT FOXTAILS IN MY SOCKS.

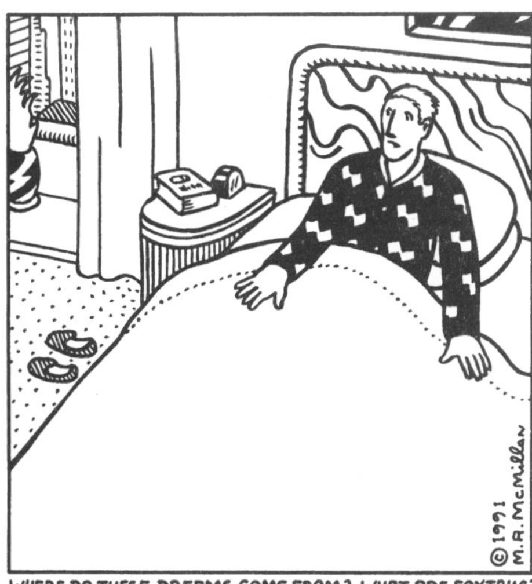

WHERE DO THESE DREAMS COME FROM? WHAT ARE FOXTAILS?

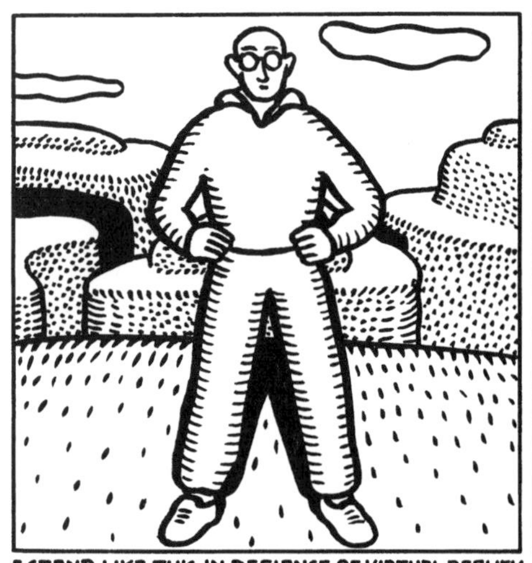
I STAND LIKE THIS IN DEFIANCE OF VIRTUAL REALITY.

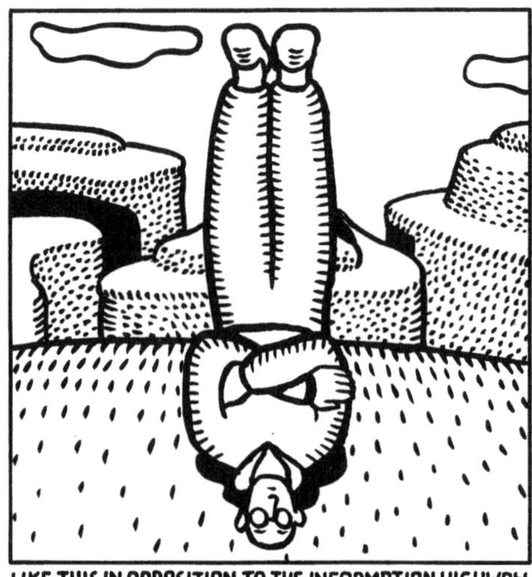
LIKE THIS IN OPPOSITION TO THE INFORMATION HIGHWAY.

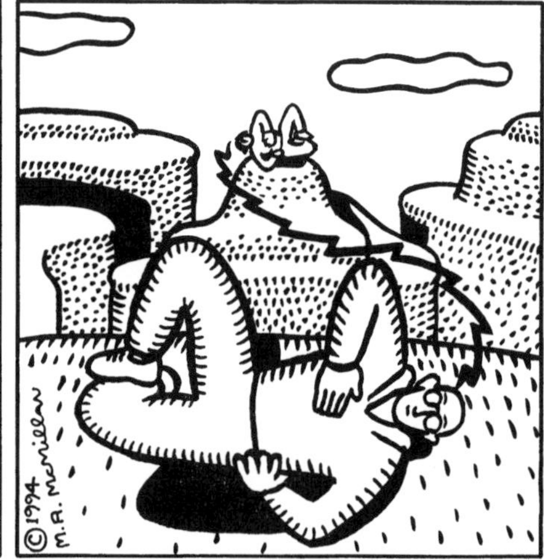

LIKE THIS FOR RECEIVING TELEPATHIC MESSAGES.

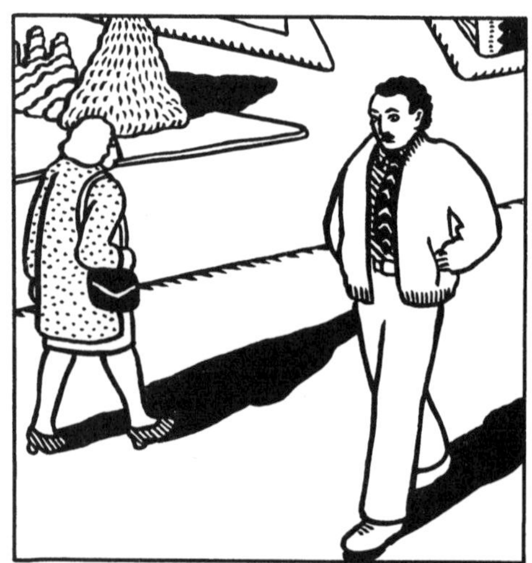
I WISH I COULD RELIVE THE PAST. WHERE IS SHE NOW?

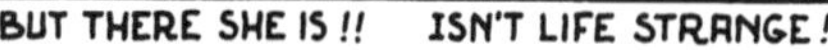
BUT THERE SHE IS!! ISN'T LIFE STRANGE!

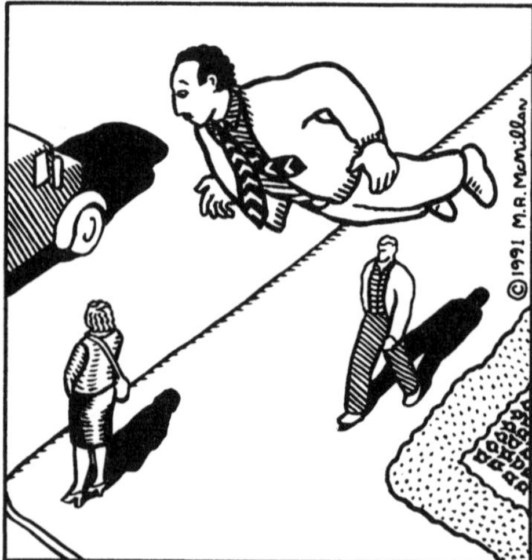

I WOULD SAY HELLO BUT I GOTTA GO.

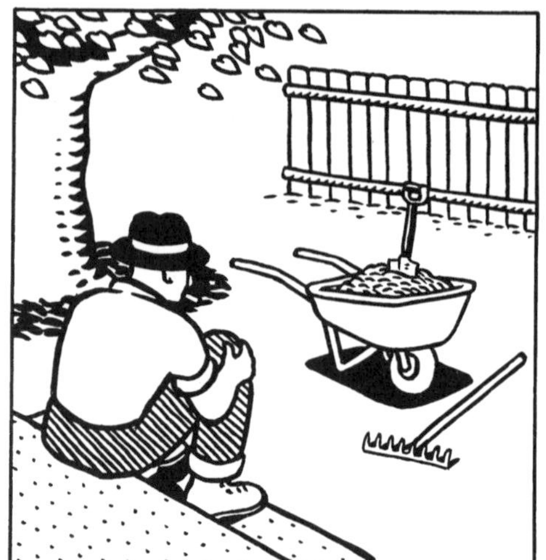
THIS WORK IS TAKING SHAPE.

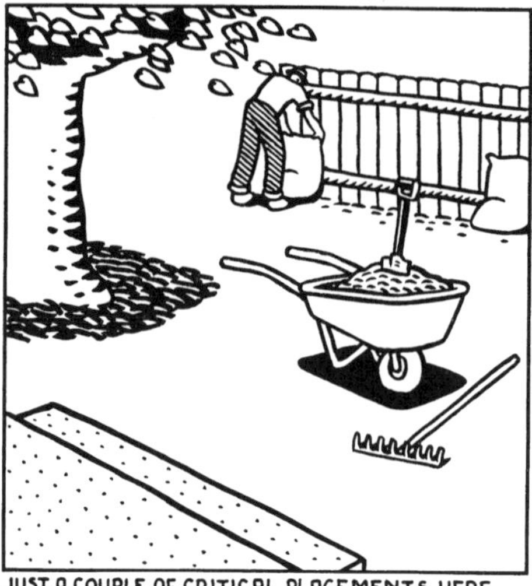
JUST A COUPLE OF CRITICAL PLACEMENTS HERE.

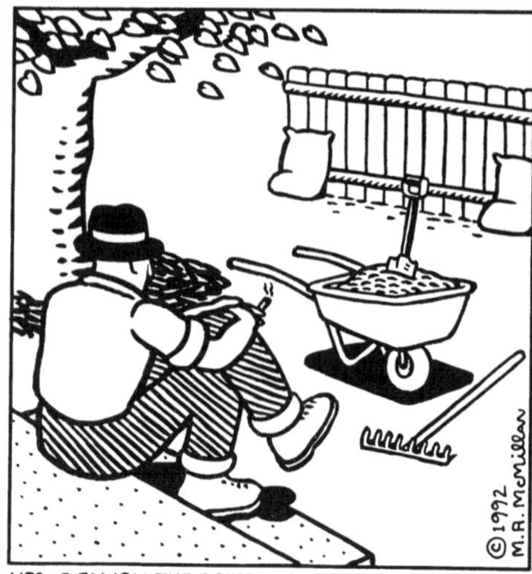

YES, I ENJOY THE SOMEWHAT CONTRIVED ASPECT.

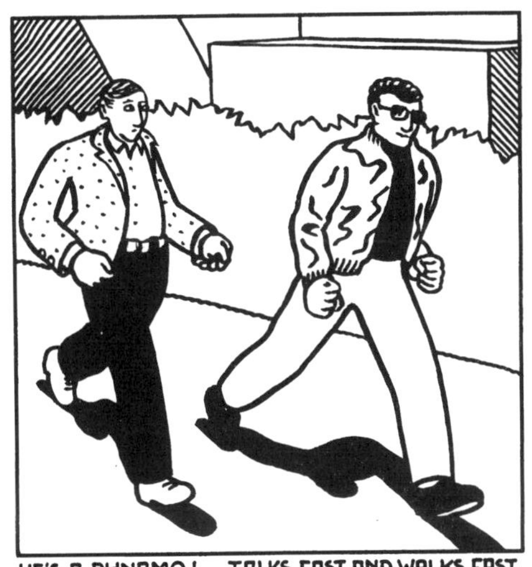

HE'S A DYNAMO! ... TALKS FAST AND WALKS FAST.

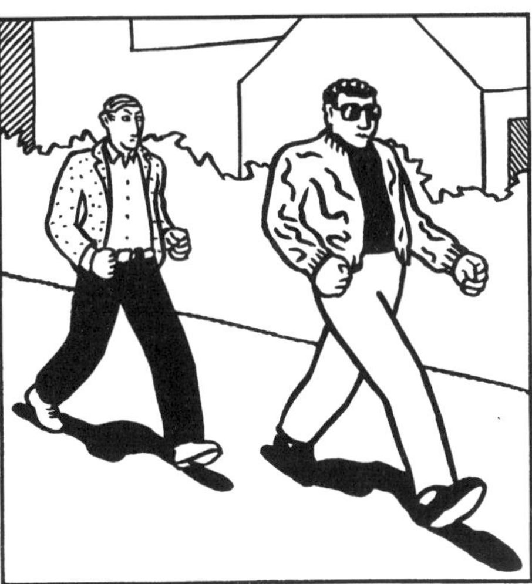

BUT TWO CAN PLAY THIS GAME!

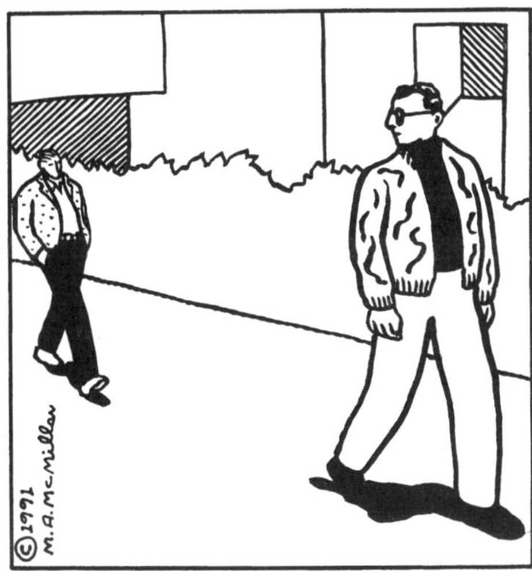

I WILL NOW APPLY THE SLOW TALK AND WALK REVOLT.

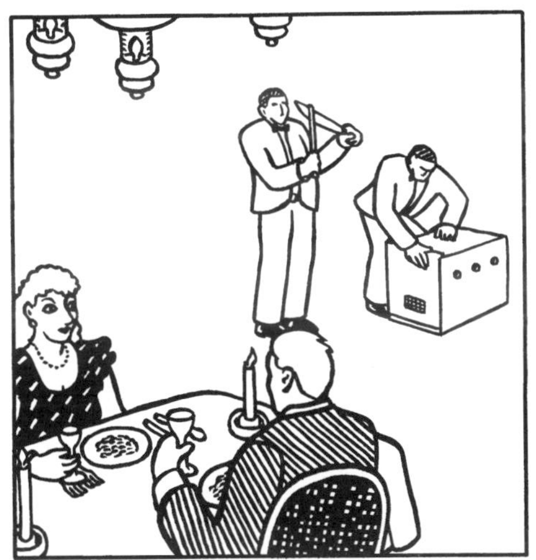

YOU'VE NEVER HAD WILD PIG OVER WILD RICE ?

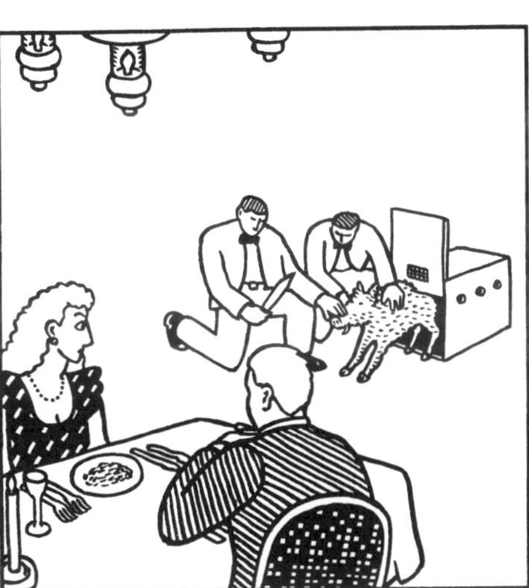

YOU ARE IN FOR A GREAT SHOW.

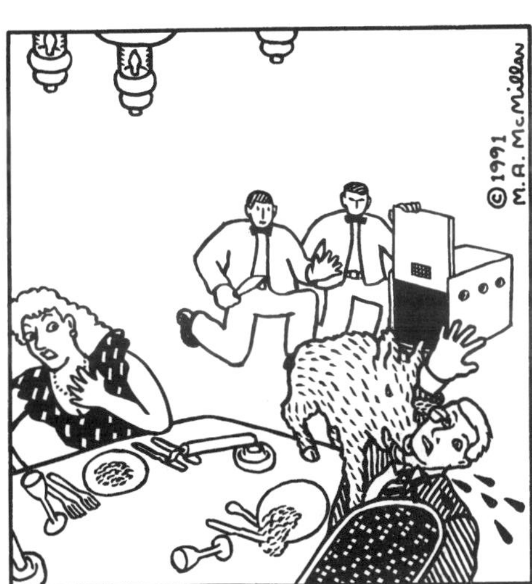

BE CAREFUL SIR HE'S HUNGRY!

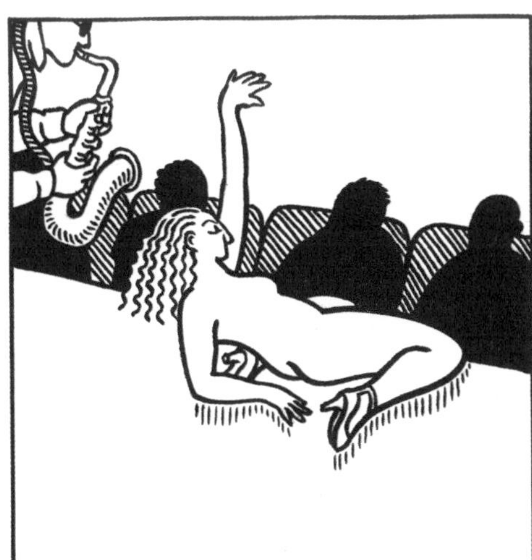

MY FANS RESPOND WHEN I GIVE MY ALL

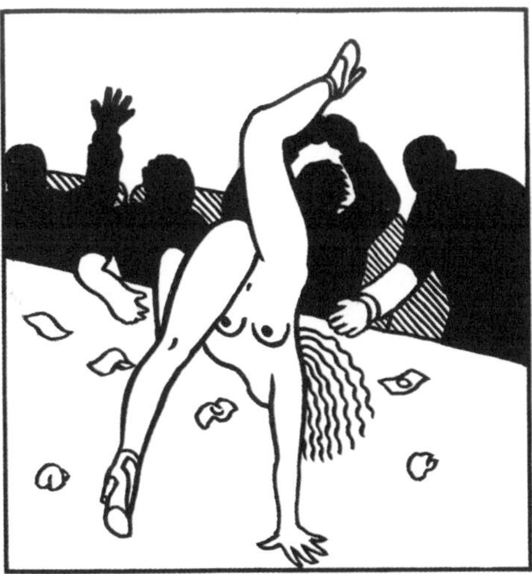

TO ACHIEVE THE MAGIC I MUST GO BEYOND DANCE

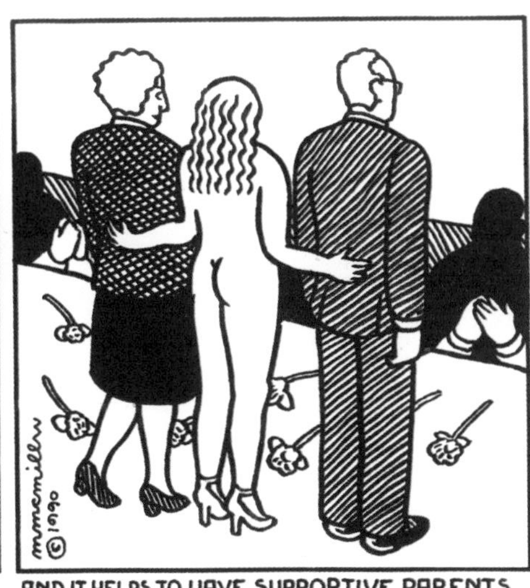

AND IT HELPS TO HAVE SUPPORTIVE PARENTS

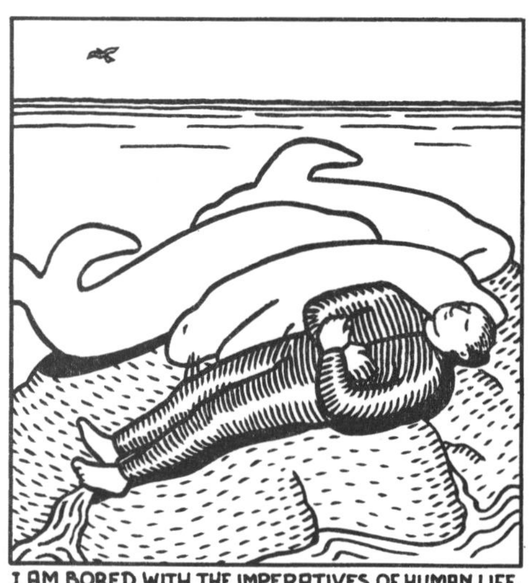

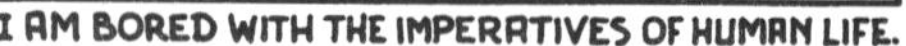

I AM BORED WITH THE IMPERATIVES OF HUMAN LIFE.

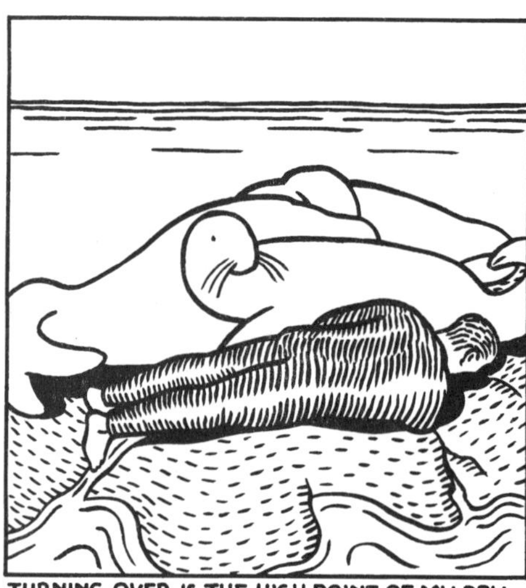

TURNING OVER IS THE HIGH POINT OF MY DAY.

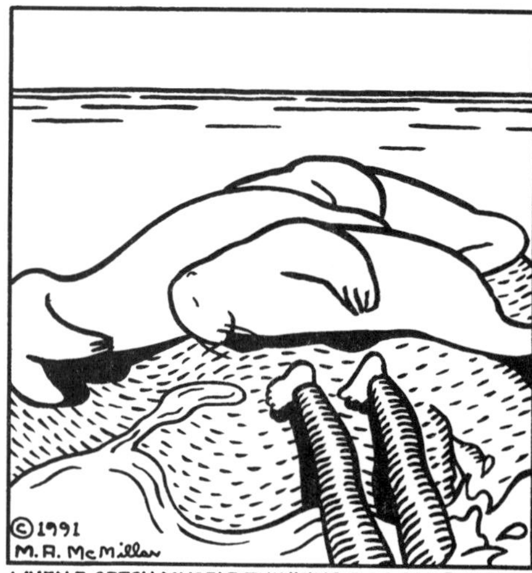

WHEN I CATCH MYSELF THINKING I GO FOR A SWIM.

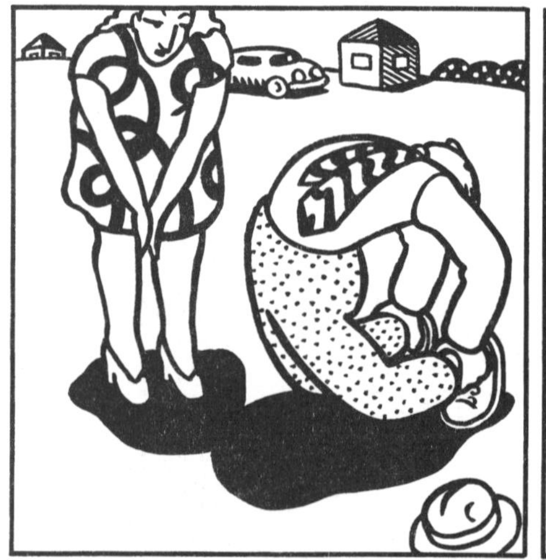

HE IS REJECTING HIS FORMALIST CHILDHOOD

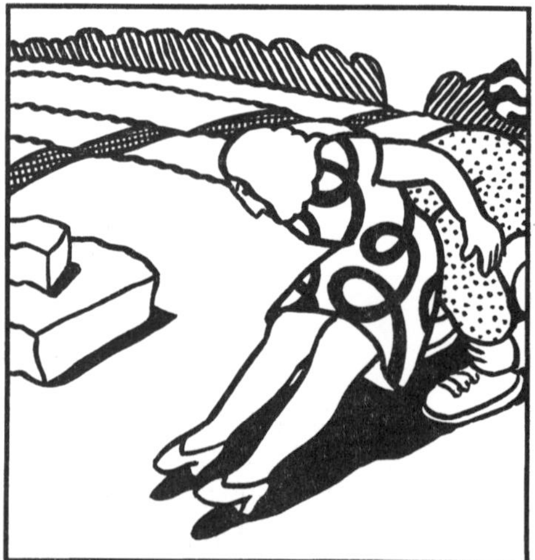

I DIDN'T REALLY WANT TO GET INVOLVED

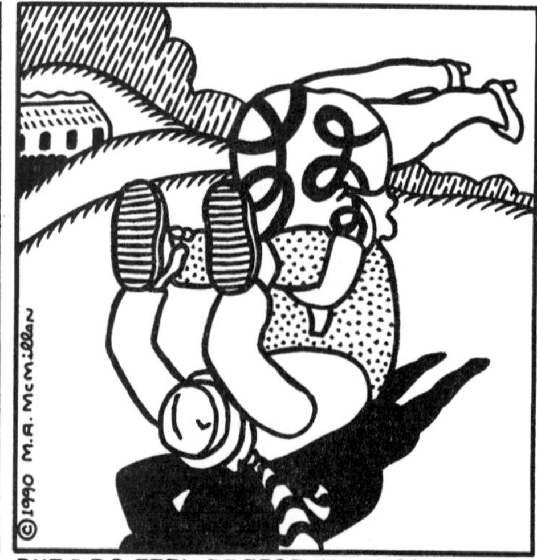

BUT I DO FEEL AT EASE IN HIS COMPANY

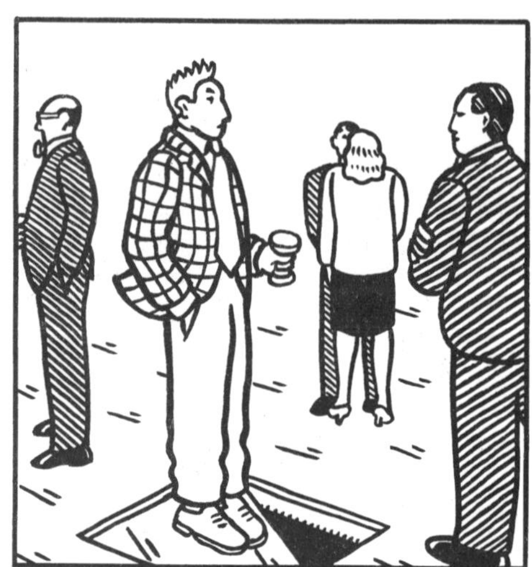

GREAT PARTY! NOW IF YOU WILL EXCUSE ME

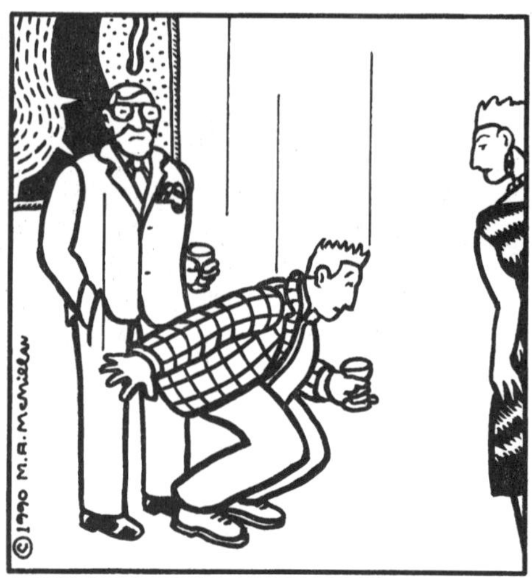

ART ENTHUSIASTS! WHAT NEXT?

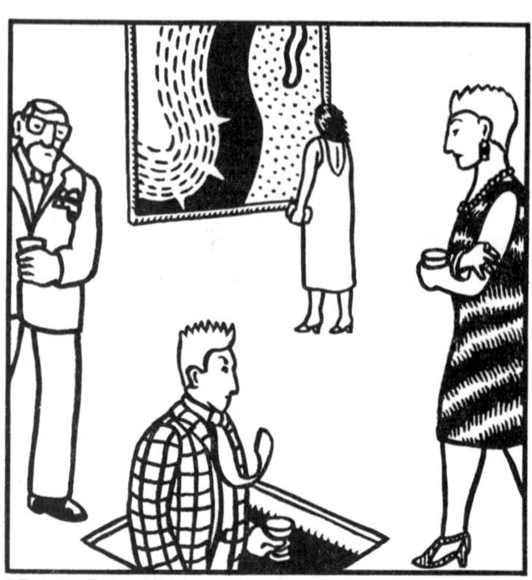

IT'S BEEN NICE! HEY... CUTE SHOES THERE

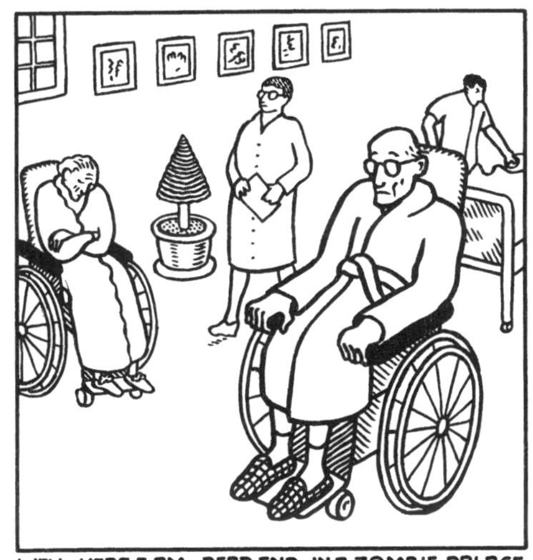

WELL, HERE I AM. DEAD END. IN A ZOMBIE PALACE.

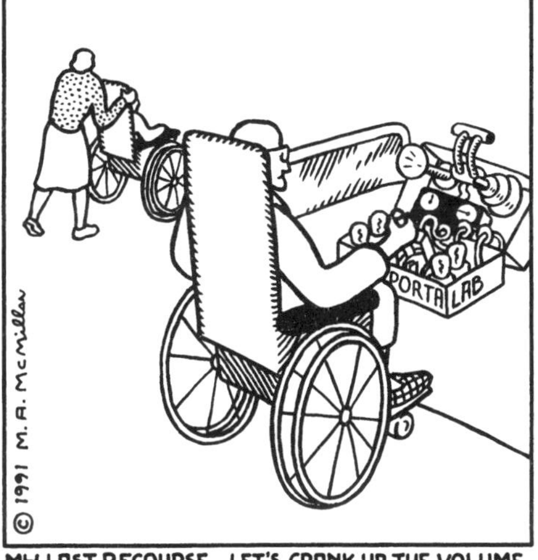

MY LAST RECOURSE. LET'S CRANK UP THE VOLUME.

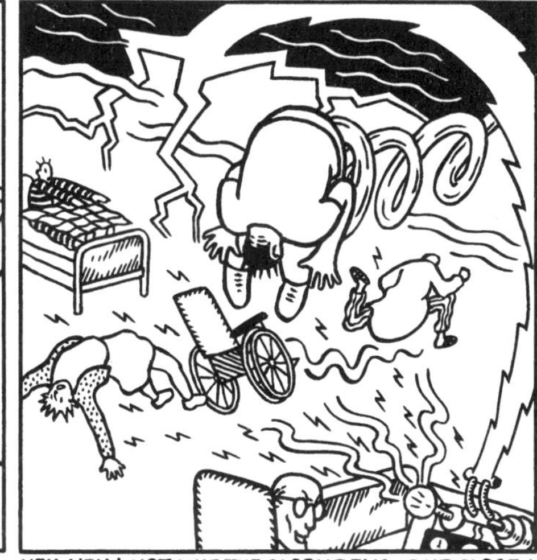

HEH HEH! NOT LIKE THE GLORY DAYS.. BUT CLOSE!

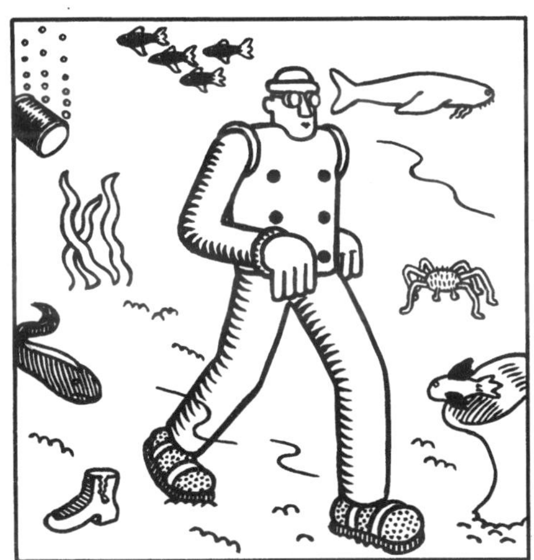

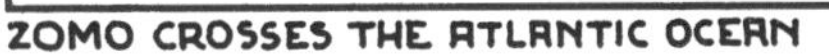
ZOMO CROSSES THE ATLANTIC OCEAN

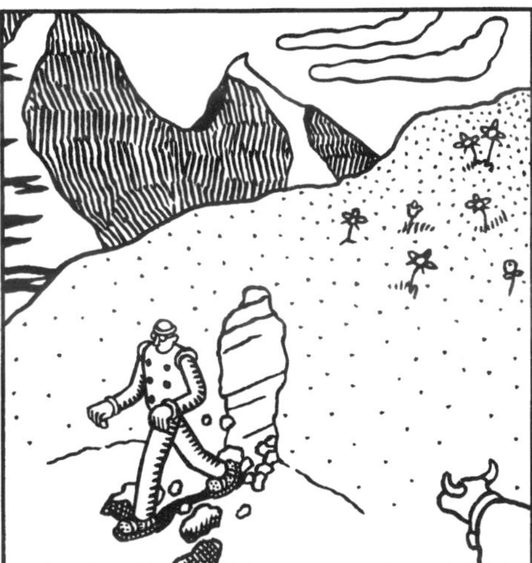

TAKES A DIRECT PATH TO HIS DESTINATION

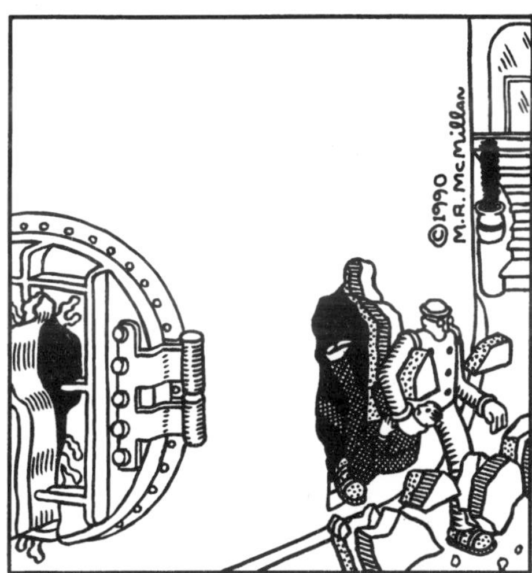

MAKES SWISS CHEESE OF SWISS BANKS

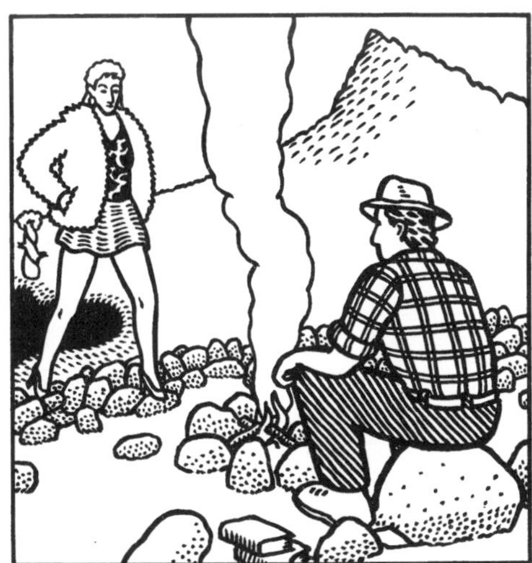

ONE EVENING SHE STUMBLED INTO MY CAMP

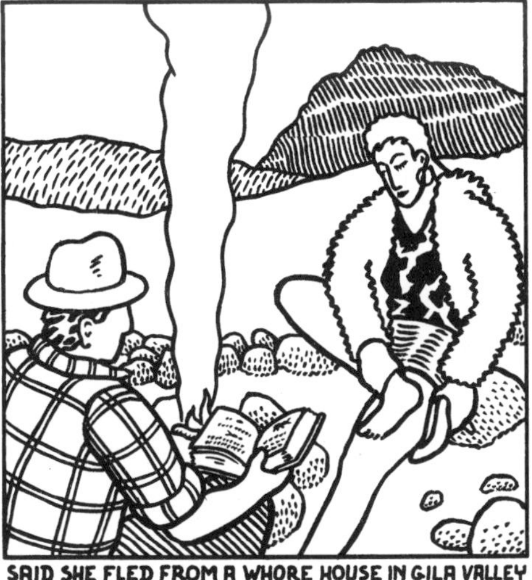

SAID SHE FLED FROM A WHORE HOUSE IN GILA VALLEY

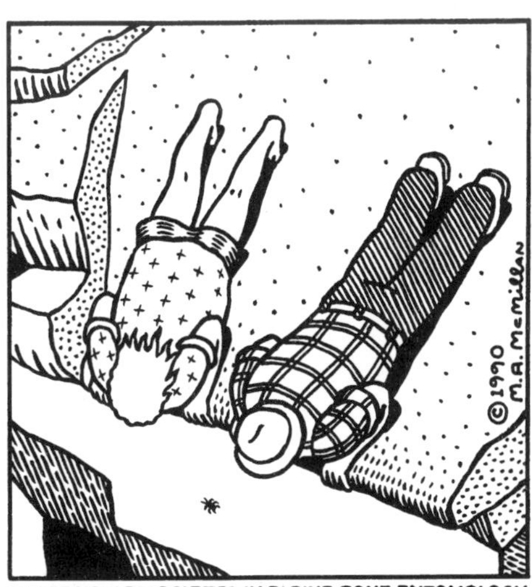

WE ARE NOW ASSOCIATES IN ALPINE ZONE ENTOMOLOGY

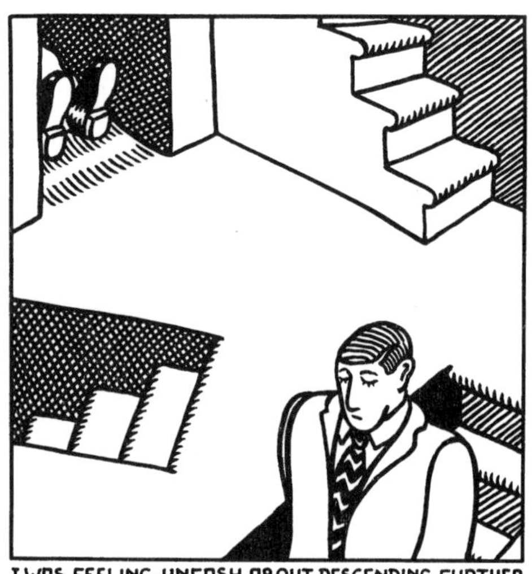
I WAS FEELING UNEASY ABOUT DESCENDING FURTHER

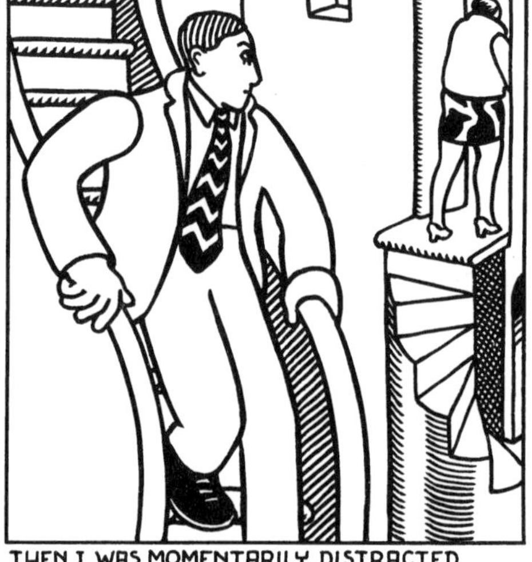
THEN I WAS MOMENTARILY DISTRACTED

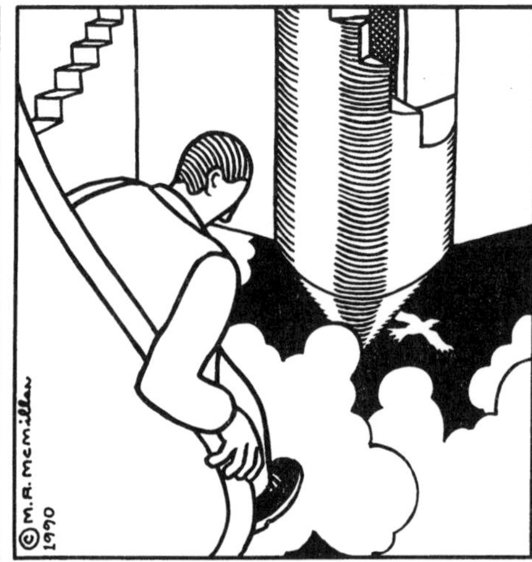

A FEW STEPS FROM OBLIVION

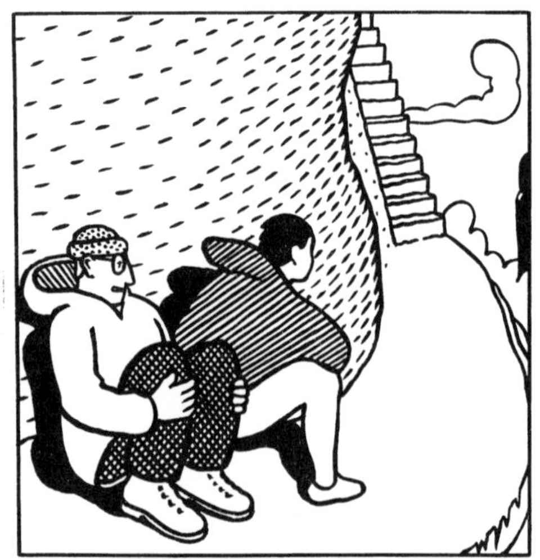
GUSTY WIND AND ICY ROCK! I'M NO LONGER CURIOUS!

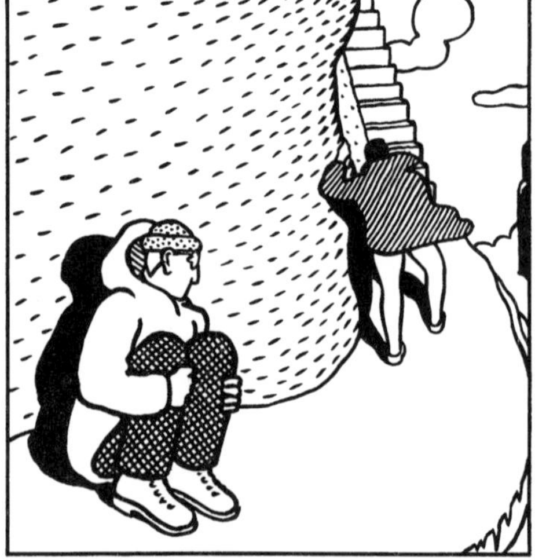
LET'S TRY SOMETHING. WALK VERY CAREFULLY.

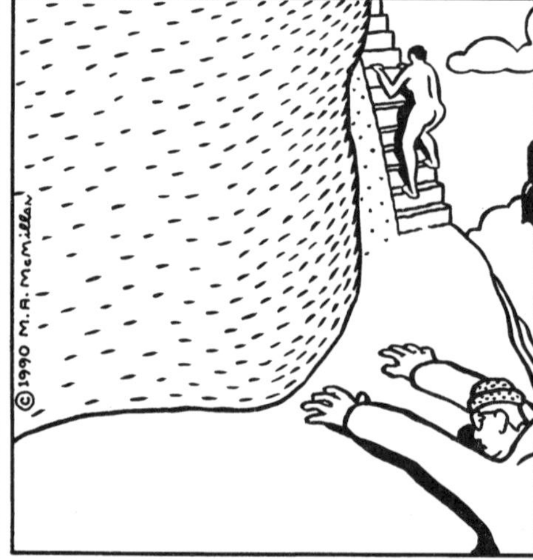

GET RID OF YOUR CLOTHES AND UP WE GO!

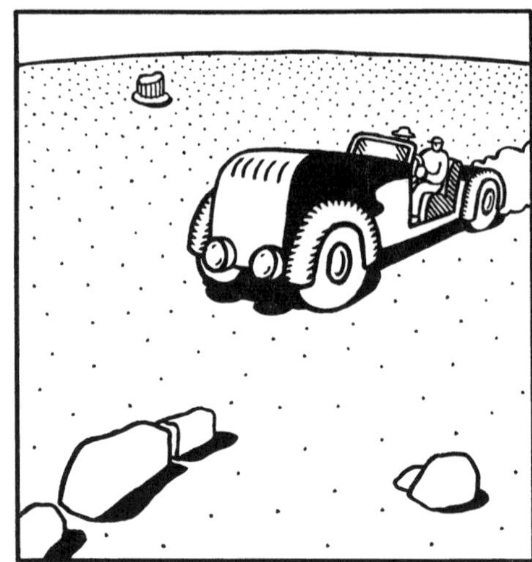
ONCE ACROSS THE GREAT DESERT

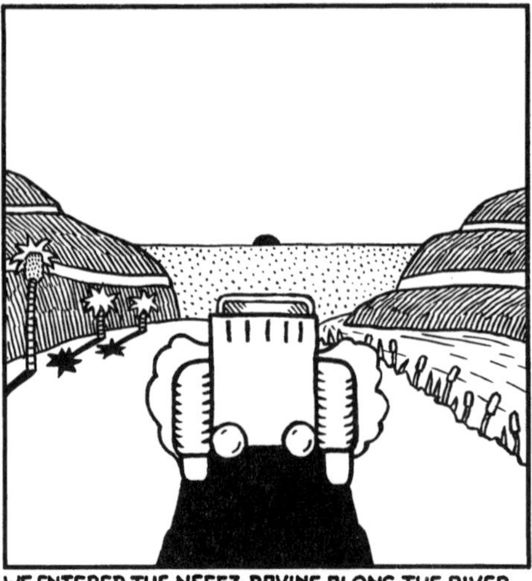
WE ENTERED THE NEFEZ RAVINE ALONG THE RIVER

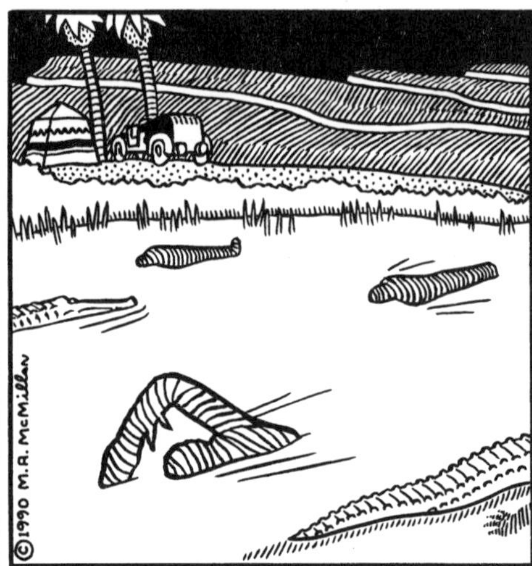

WHERE MUMMIES SWIM UPSTREAM AT NIGHT

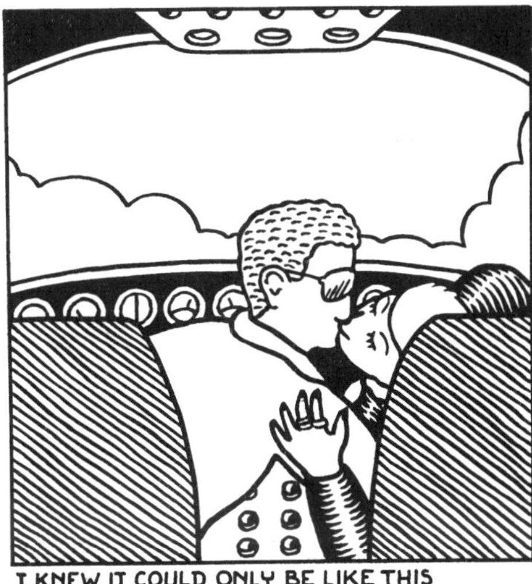
I KNEW IT COULD ONLY BE LIKE THIS

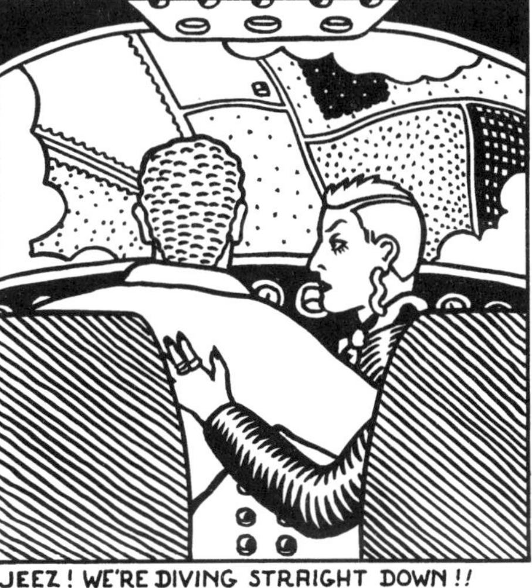
JEEZ! WE'RE DIVING STRAIGHT DOWN!!

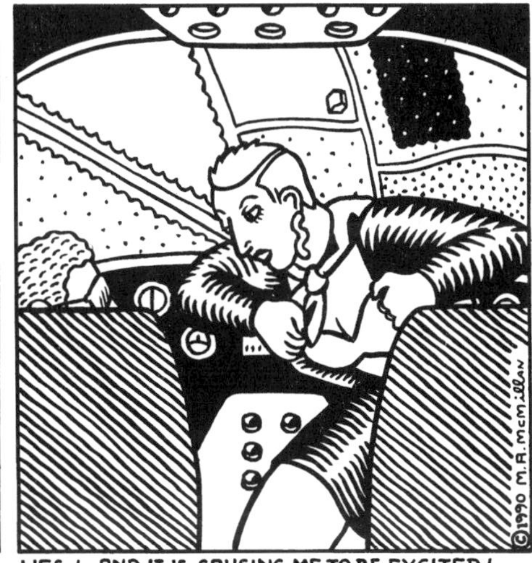

YES! AND IT IS CAUSING ME TO BE EXCITED!

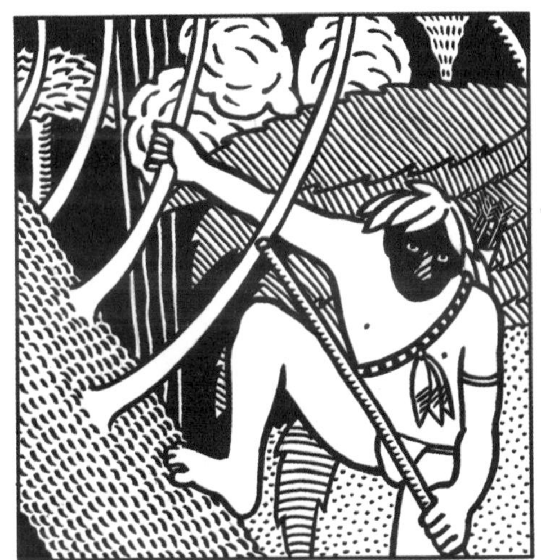
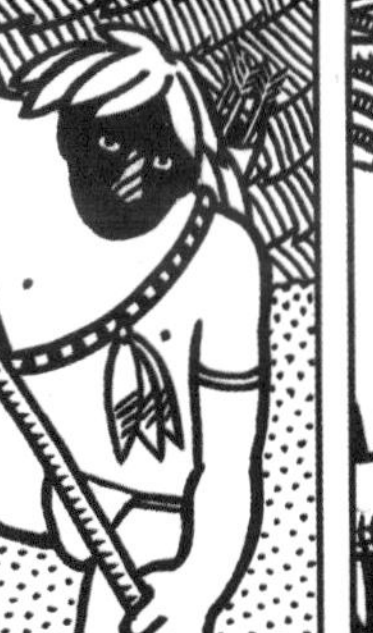
SOON I STOP MONKEY HUNTING. LEARN COMPUTER.

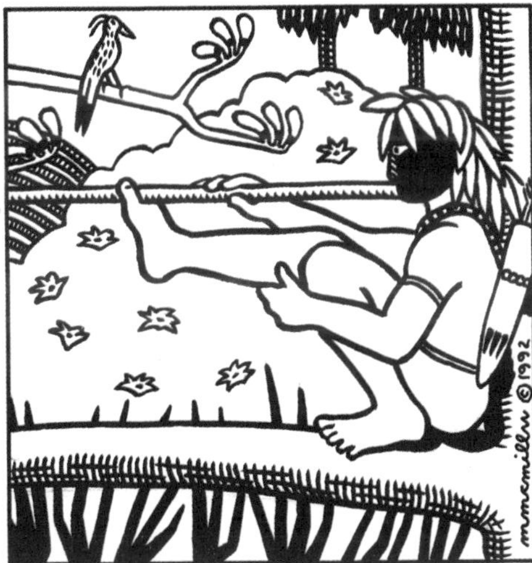

GET CELLULAR PHONE. LIVE IN SUBURBS WITH CREDIT CARD.

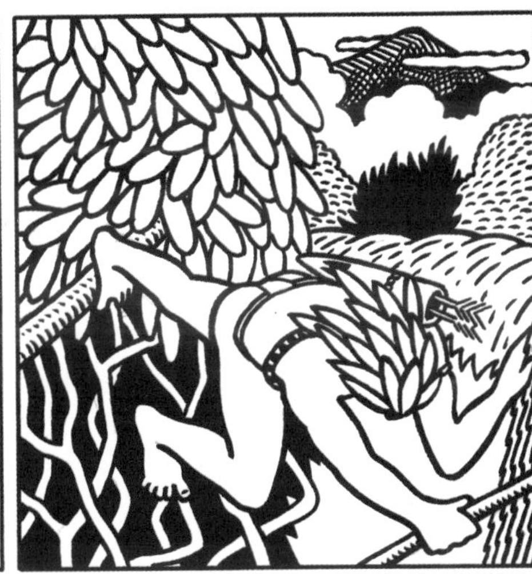
JOIN HEALTH CLUB. BEAT WIFE. GO ON SHOPPING MALL SHOOT UP.

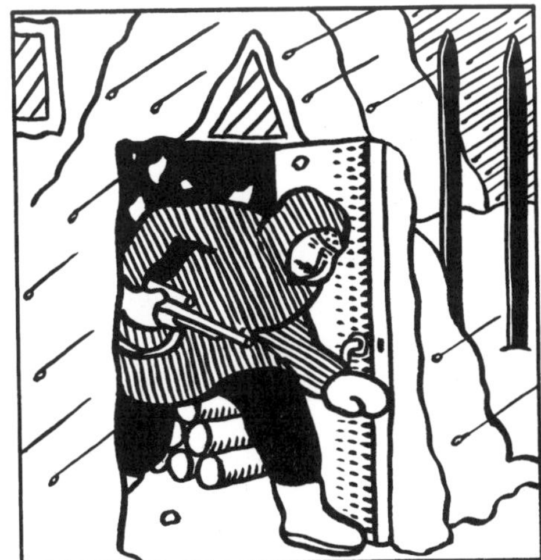
GOL DURN IT! WEDNESDAY AGAIN!

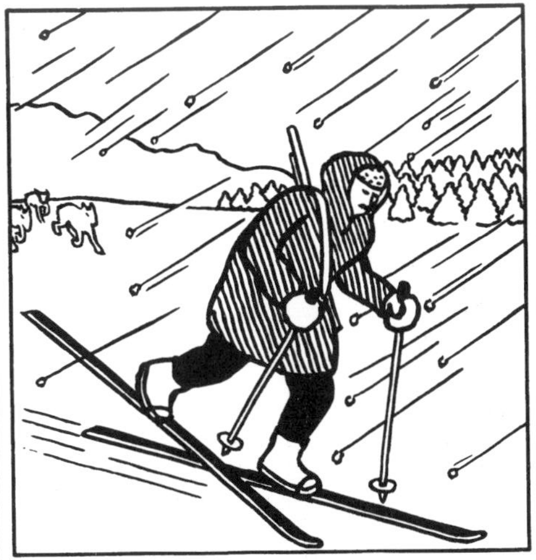
IF I CAN OUTRUN THE CRITTERS...

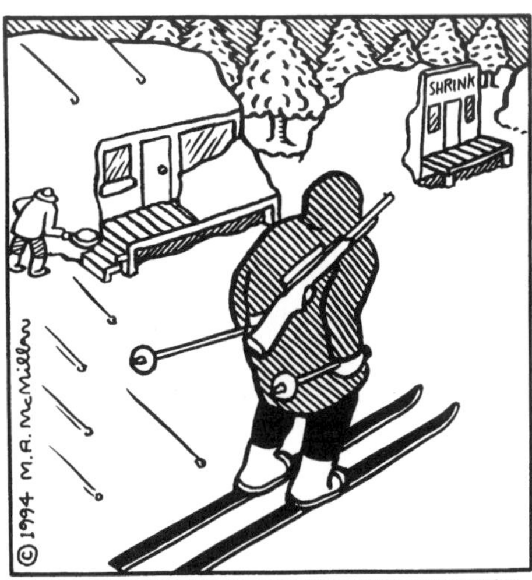

I CAN GET TO MY THERAPY APPOINTMENT ON TIME.

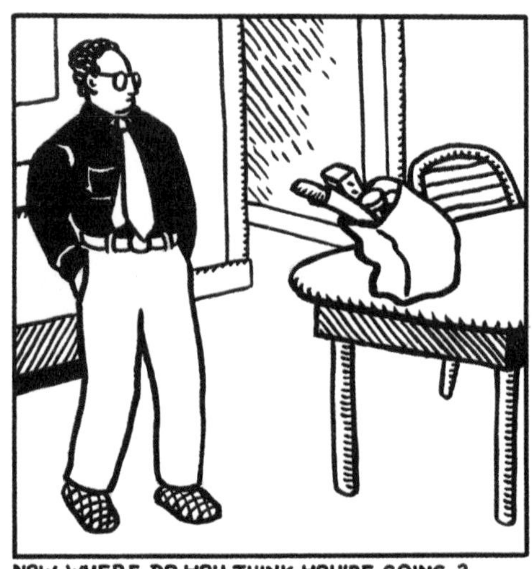
NOW WHERE DO YOU THINK YOU'RE GOING ?

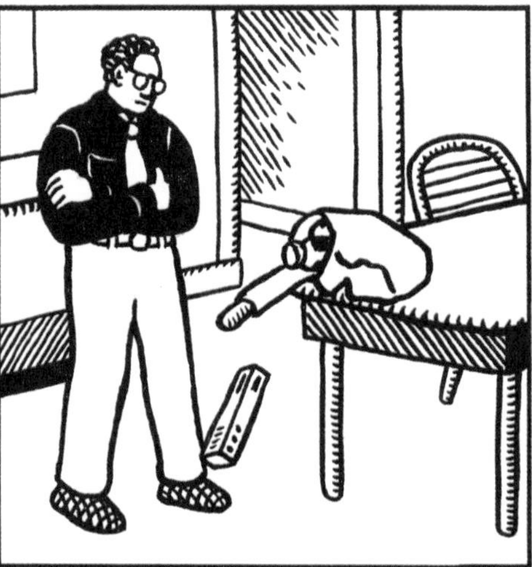
NEVER SATISFIED WITH YOUR APPOINTED POSITION ?

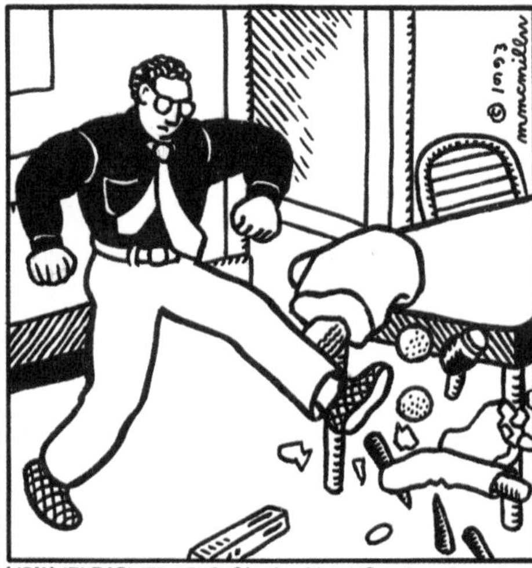

YOU WANT LOWER LEVEL ?! I'LL GIVE YOU LOWER LEVEL !

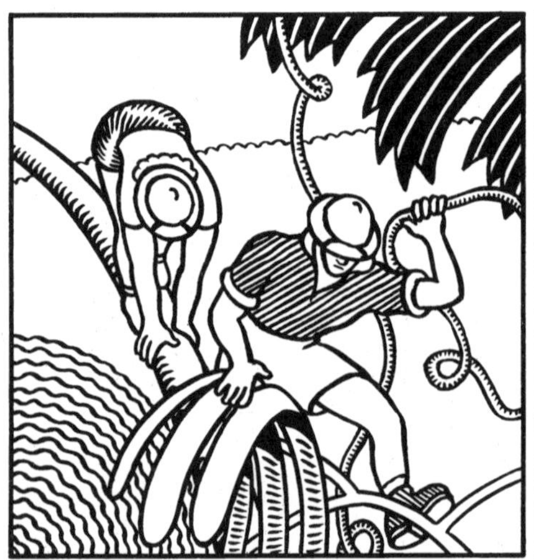
WE PUSHED HARD TO GET AWAY FROM CAMP

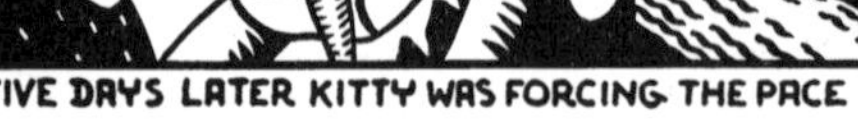
FIVE DAYS LATER KITTY WAS FORCING THE PACE

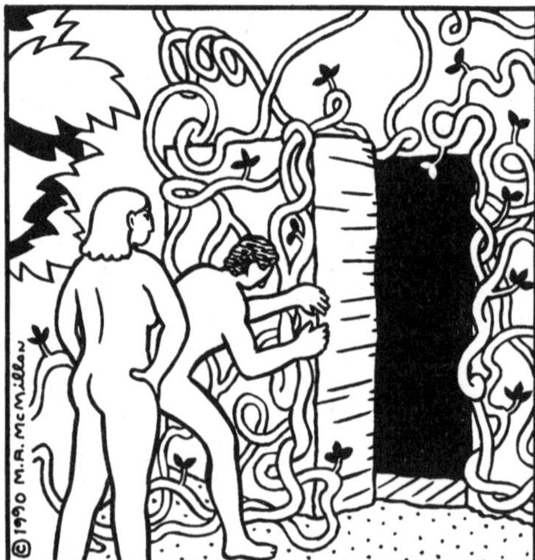

YET WE STILL FOUND REMANTS OF HUMAN MACHINATION

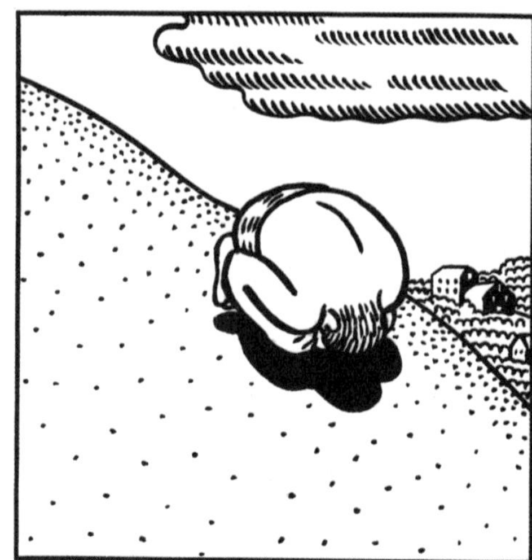
ONE DAY I WENT ROLLING ON THE LONG SLOPE

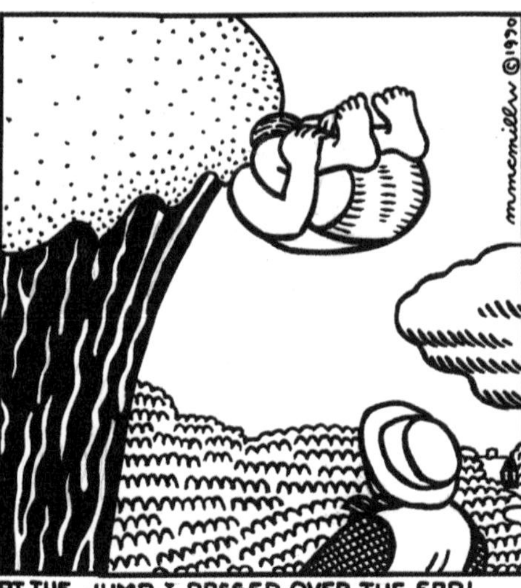

AT THE JUMP I PASSED OVER THE EARL

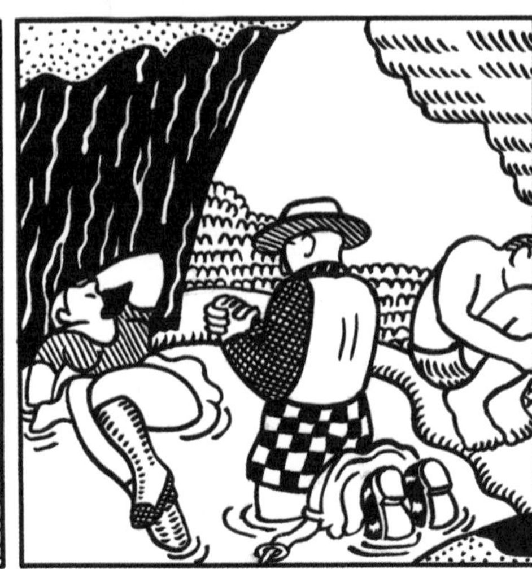
HE WAS ENTERTAINING LADY BOSWICK

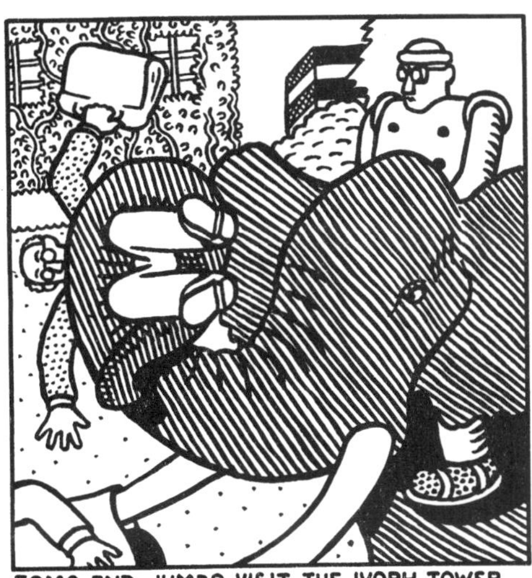
ZOMO AND JUMBO VISIT THE IVORY TOWER

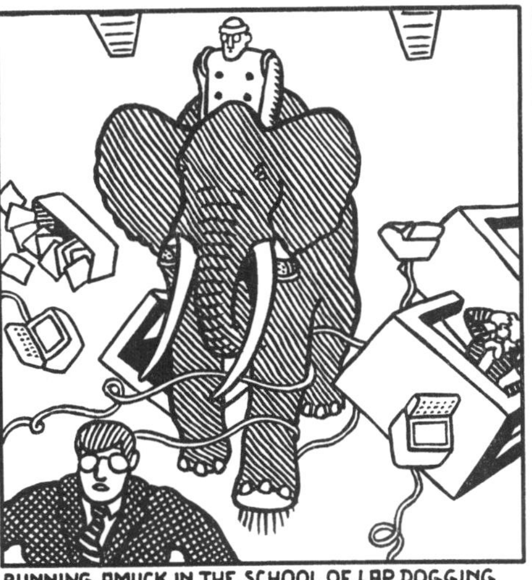
RUNNING AMUCK IN THE SCHOOL OF LAP DOGGING

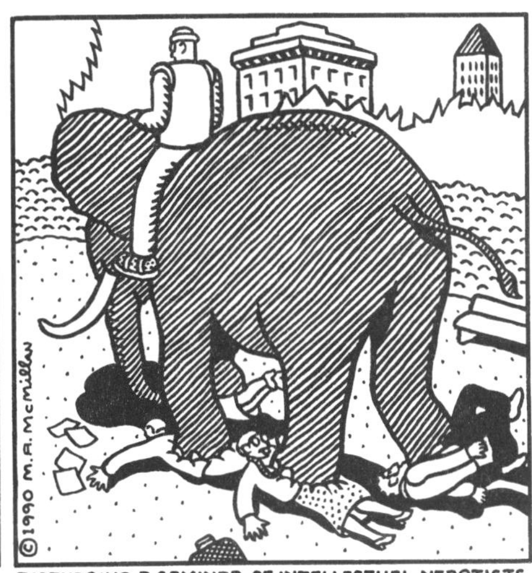

DISTURBING A SEMINAR OF INTELLECTUAL NEPOTISTS

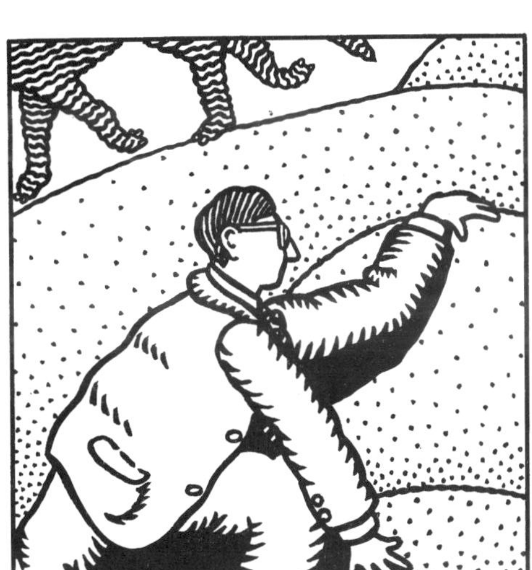
I AM ABOUT TO MEET THE SHAMAN OF THE NORTH

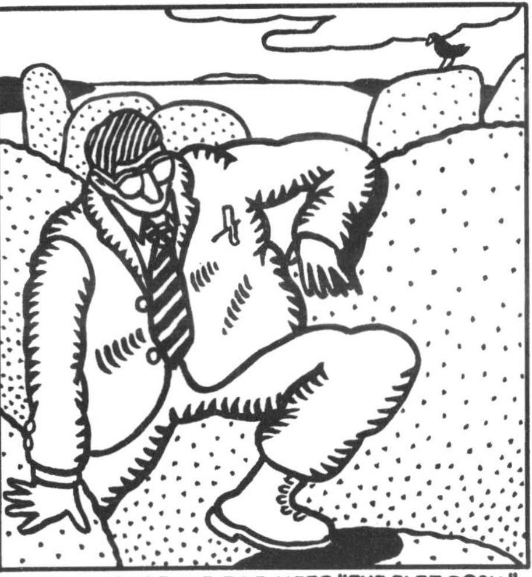
I FEEL A PRESENCE AS I NEAR "THE FLAT ROCK"

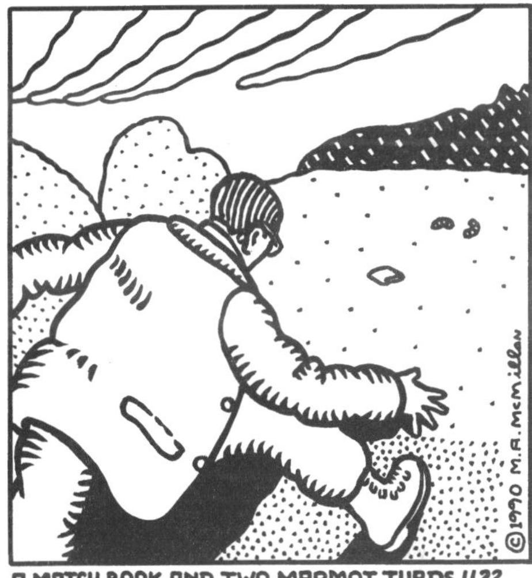

A MATCH BOOK AND TWO MARMOT TURDS !!??

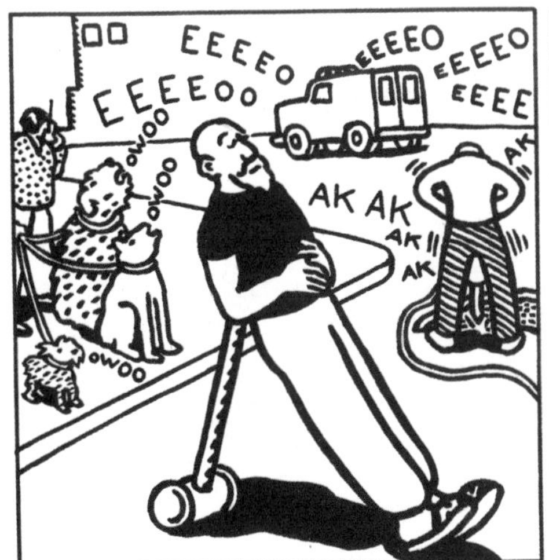

I AM CALM IN THE PRESENSE OF CITY NOISE

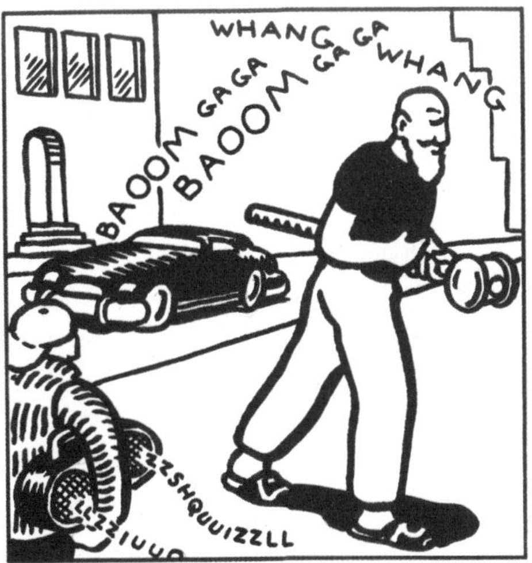

ONE MUST GO WITHIN ONESELF FOR COMPOSURE

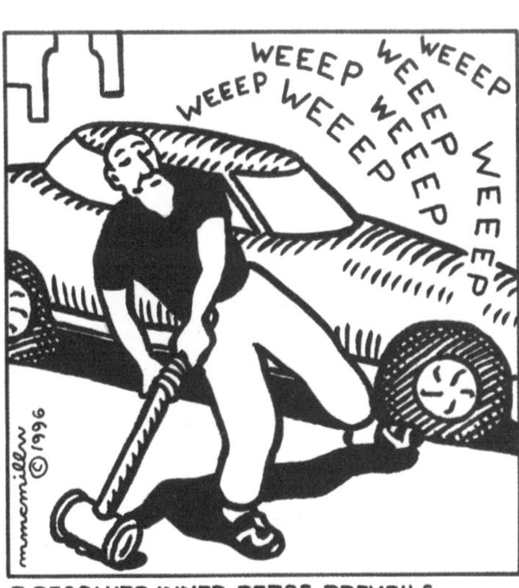

A RESOLUTE INNER PEACE PREVAILS

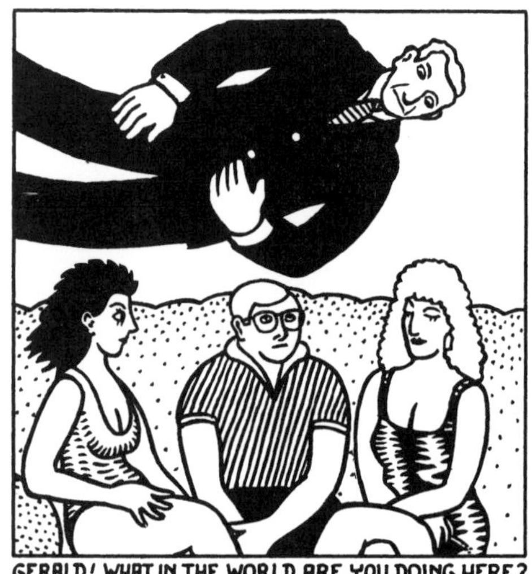
GERALD! WHAT IN THE WORLD ARE YOU DOING HERE?

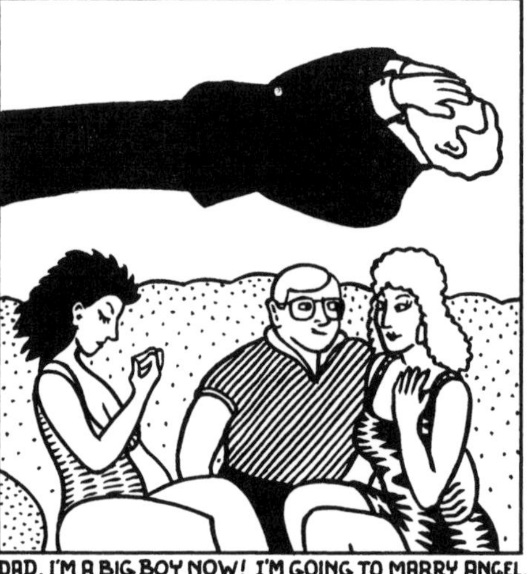
DAD, I'M A BIG BOY NOW! I'M GOING TO MARRY ANGEL.

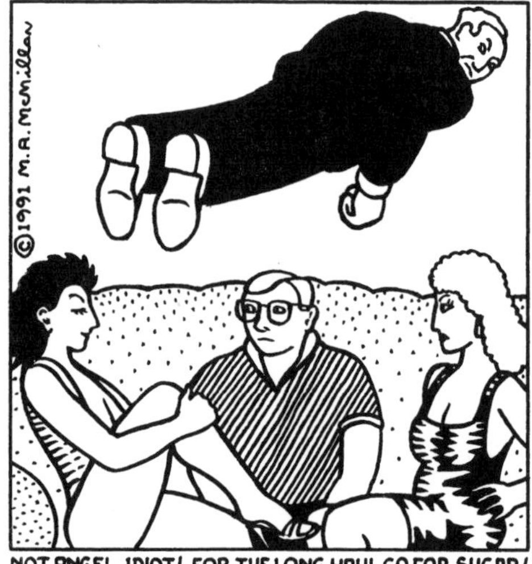

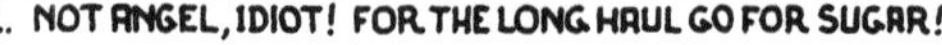
NOT ANGEL, IDIOT! FOR THE LONG HAUL GO FOR SUGAR!

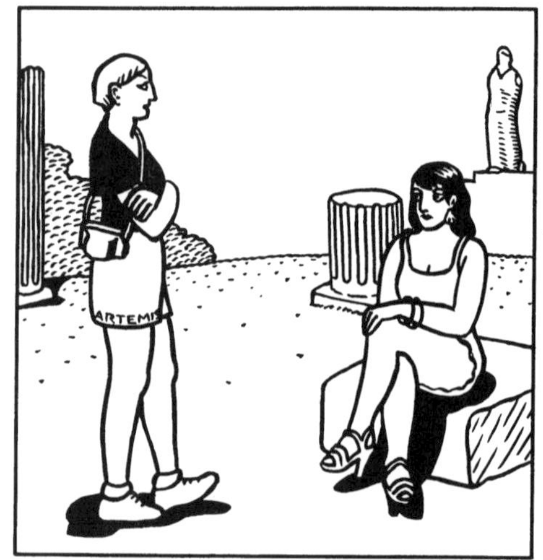

WELL, HERE WE ARE! WHERE'S THE BIG SHOT?

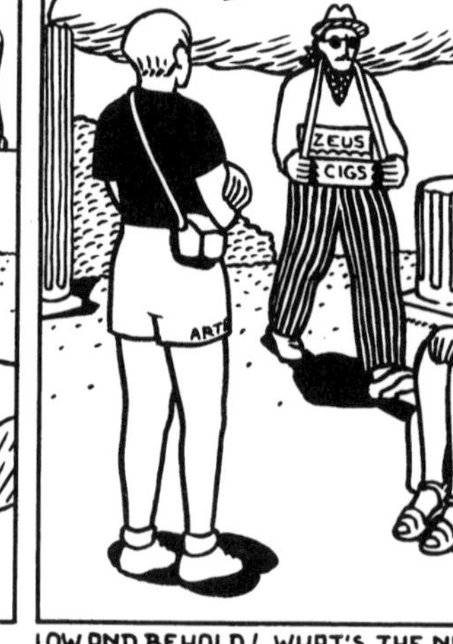

LOW AND BEHOLD! WHAT'S THE NEWS DAD?

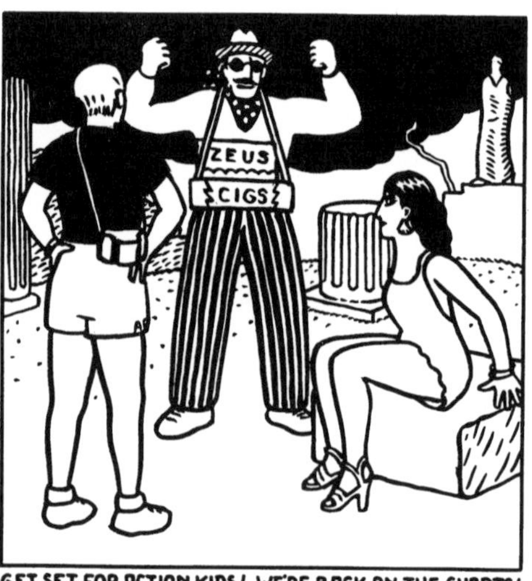

GET SET FOR ACTION KIDS! WE'RE BACK ON THE CHARTS!

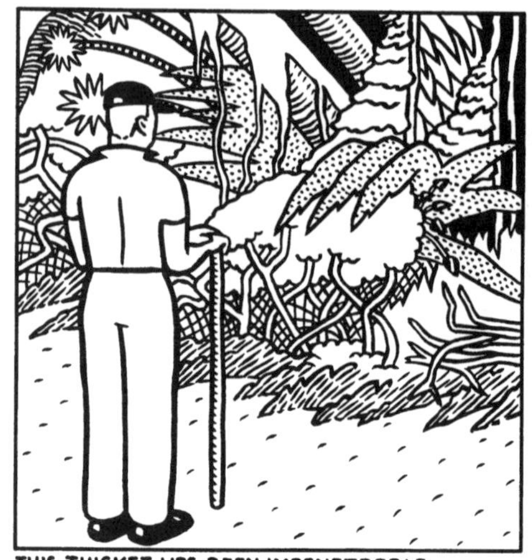
THIS THICKET HAS BEEN IMPENETRABLE.

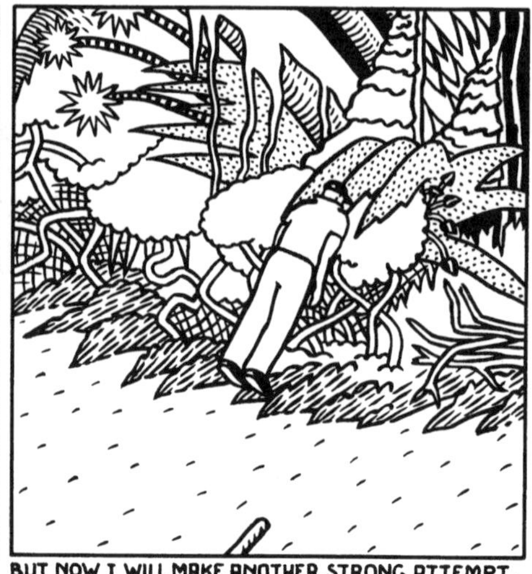
BUT NOW I WILL MAKE ANOTHER STRONG ATTEMPT.

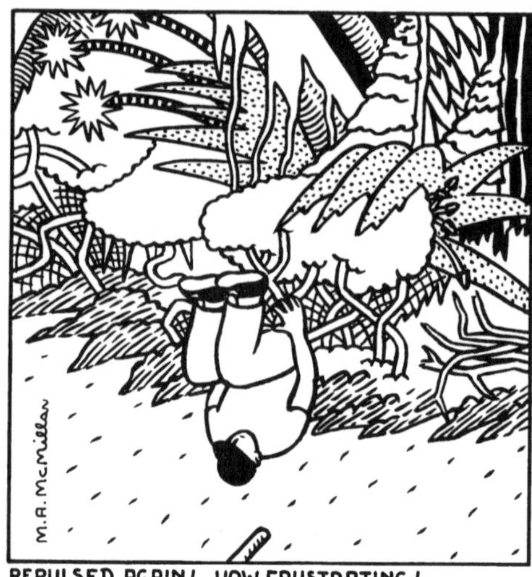

REPULSED AGAIN! HOW FRUSTRATING!

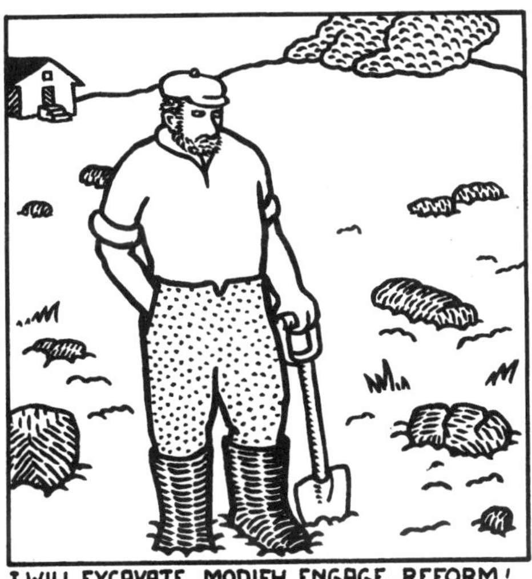
I WILL EXCAVATE, MODIFY, ENGAGE, REFORM!

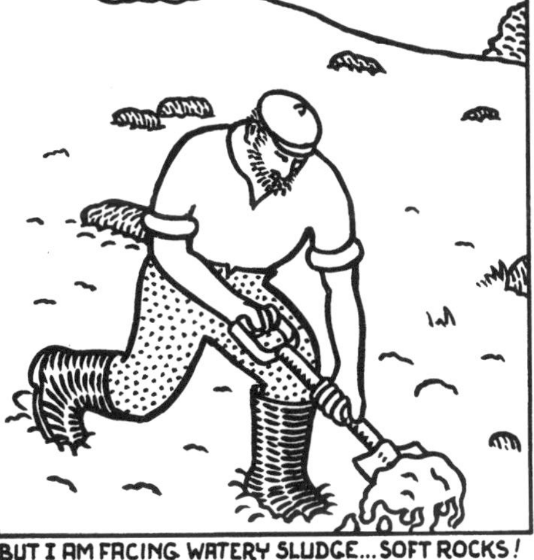
BUT I AM FACING WATERY SLUDGE... SOFT ROCKS!

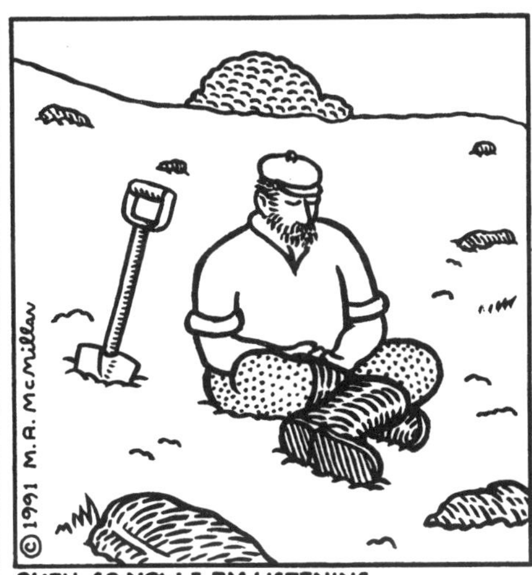

OKEY, SO NOW I AM LISTENING.

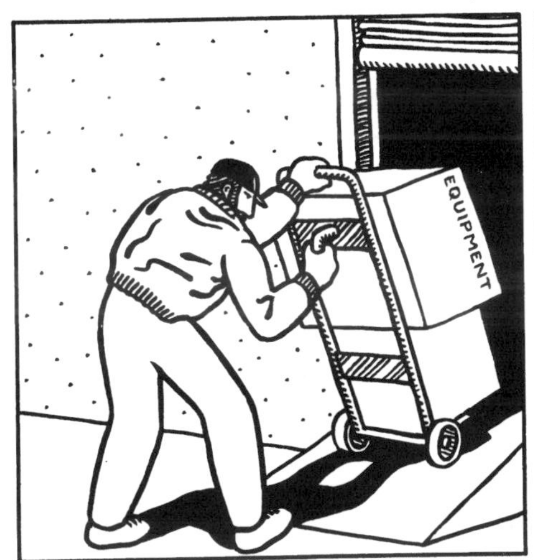

I HAVE EVERYTHING I NEED TO START MY PROJECT

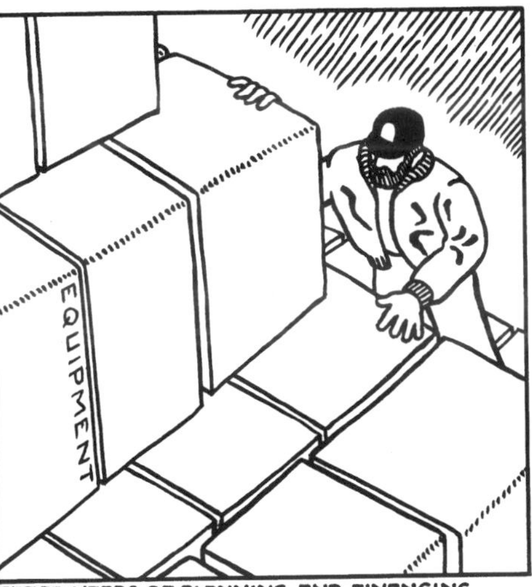

AFTER YEARS OF PLANNING AND FINANCING

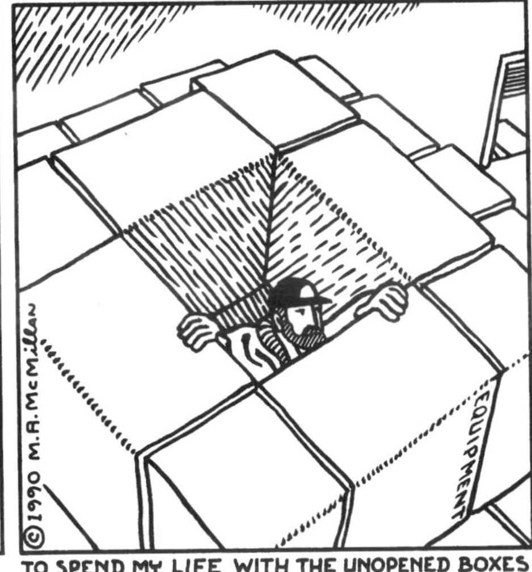

TO SPEND MY LIFE WITH THE UNOPENED BOXES

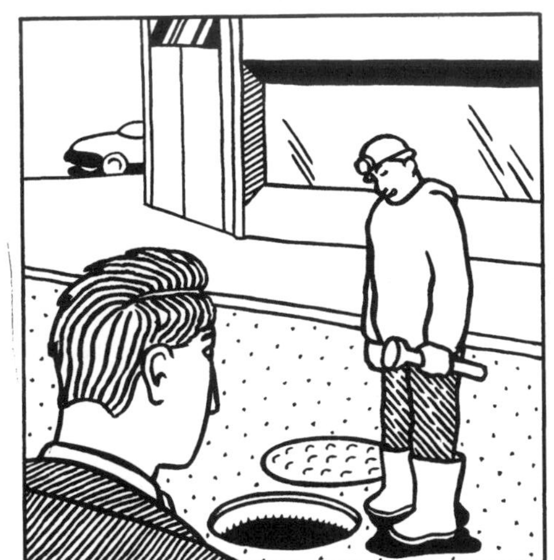
IT'S WAY OUT DOWN THERE

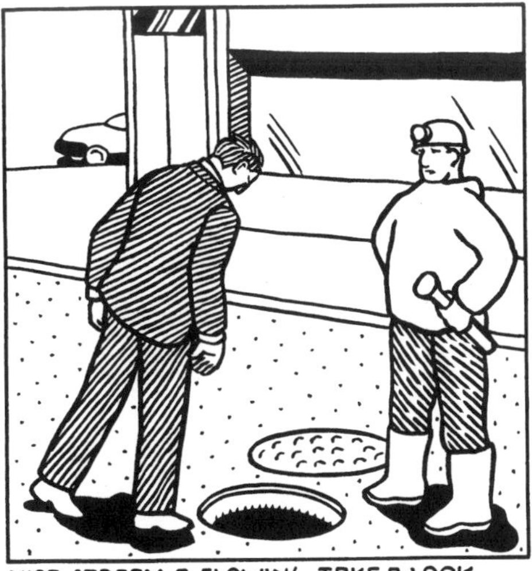
NICE STREAM A-FLOWIN'... TAKE A LOOK

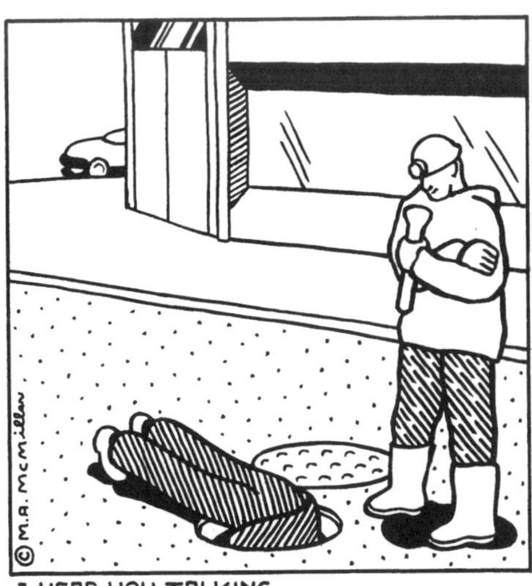

I HEAR YOU TALKING

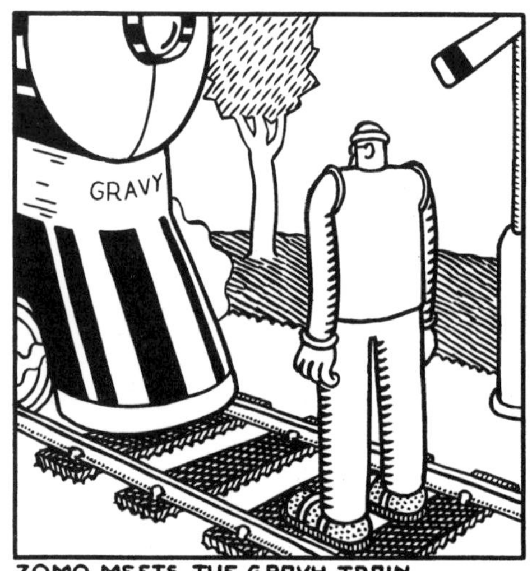

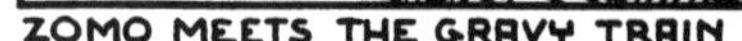
ZOMO MEETS THE GRAVY TRAIN

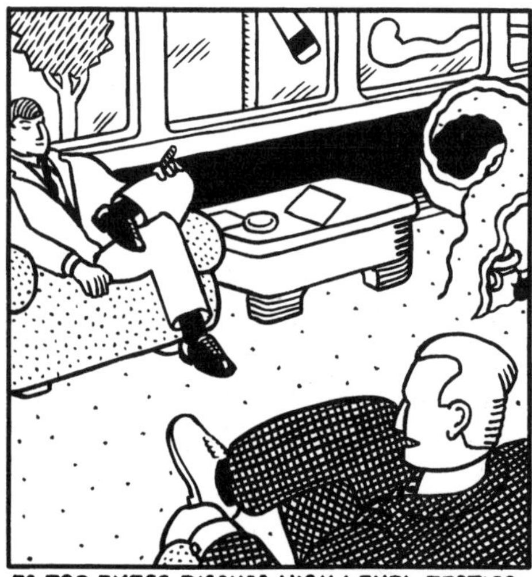
AS TOP EXECS DISCUSS HIGH LEVEL TACTICS

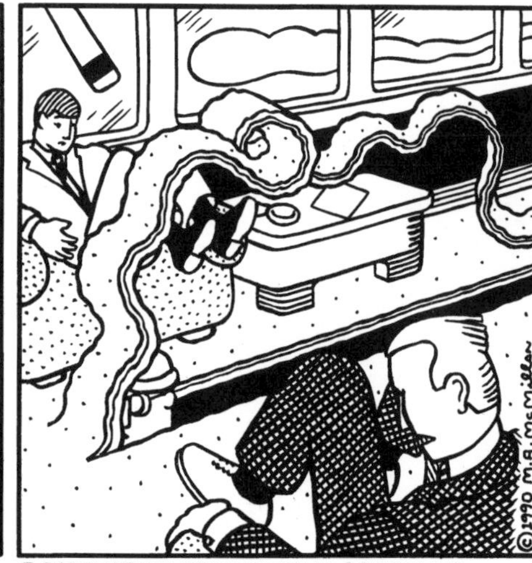

A DISRUPTIVE PRESENCE IS OBSERVED

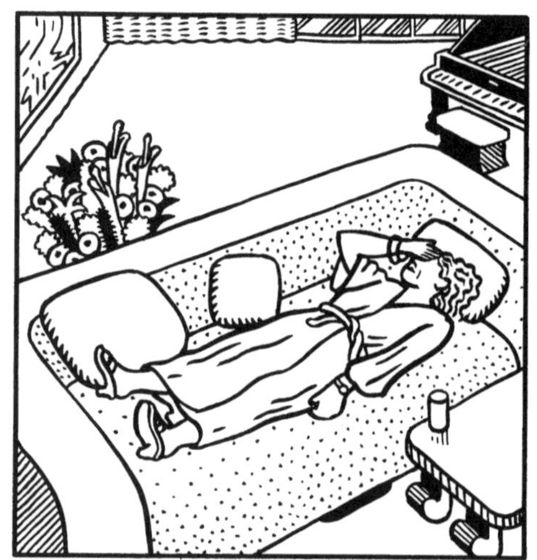
I KNOW I MUST BUT I JUST CANNOT GET UP!

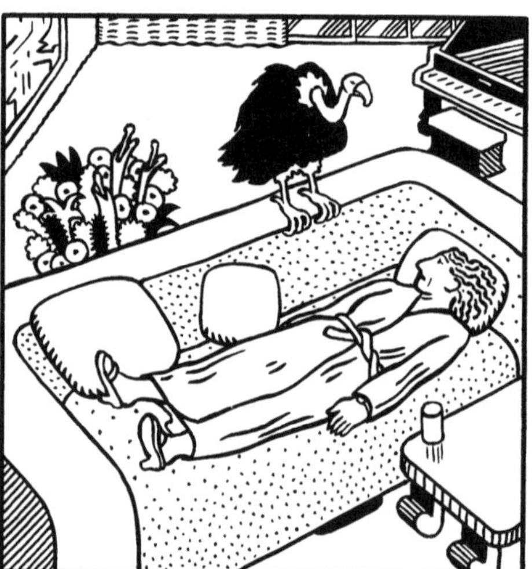
NOW WHAT AM I TO MAKE OF THIS?

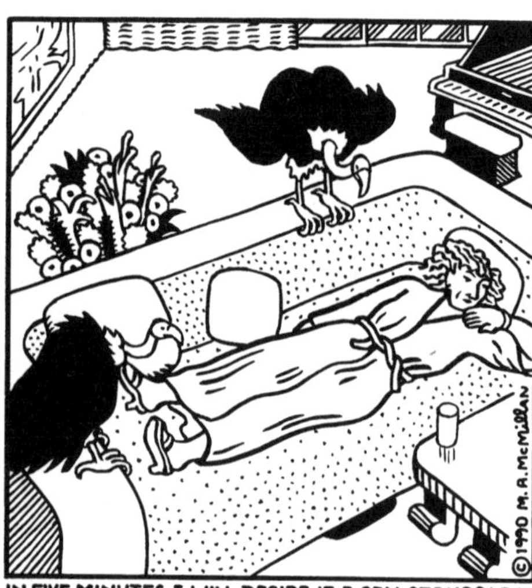

IN FIVE MINUTES I WILL DECIDE IF I CAN STRUGGLE!

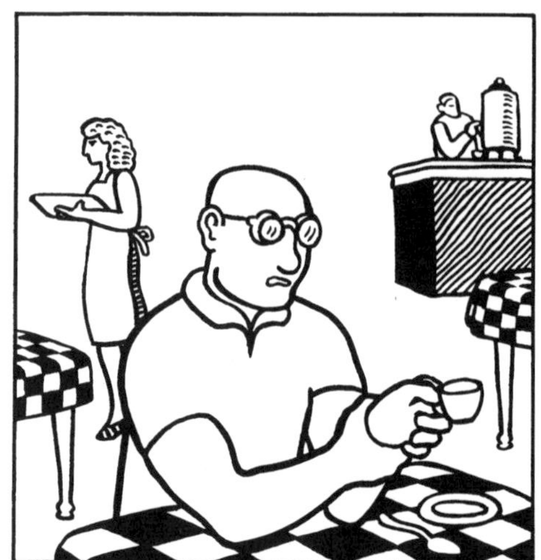
I AM ABNORMALLY AFFECTED BY GRAVITY

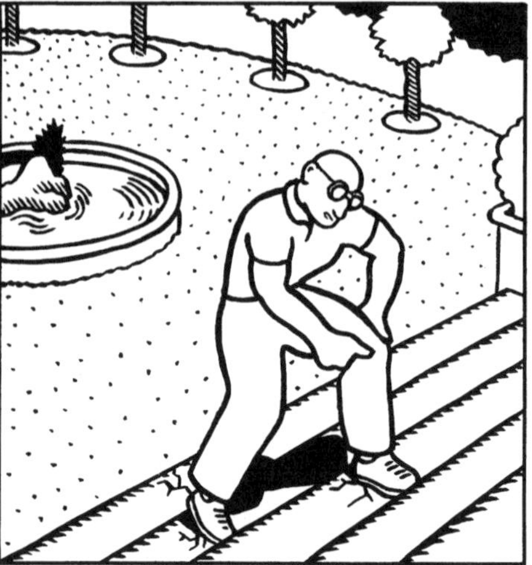
I HAVE TO BE VERY STRONG TO MOVE ABOUT

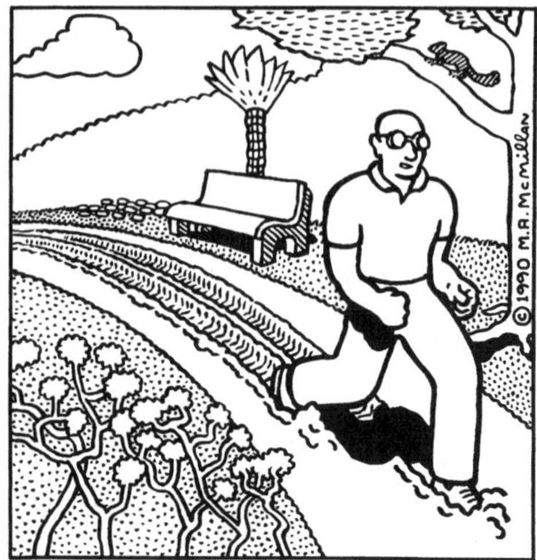

BUT I ENJOY THE SOLID ATTACHMENT TO EARTH

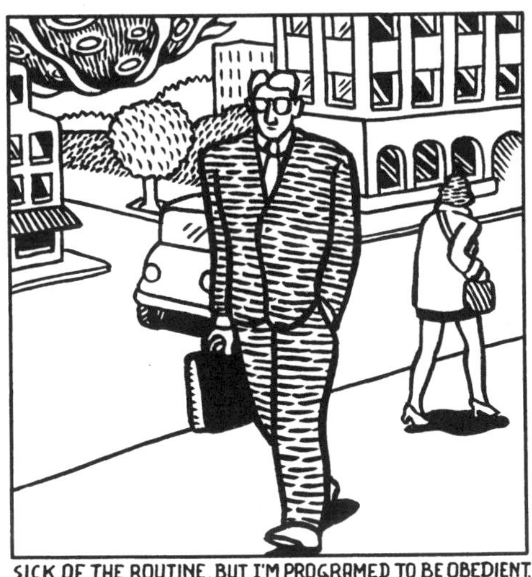

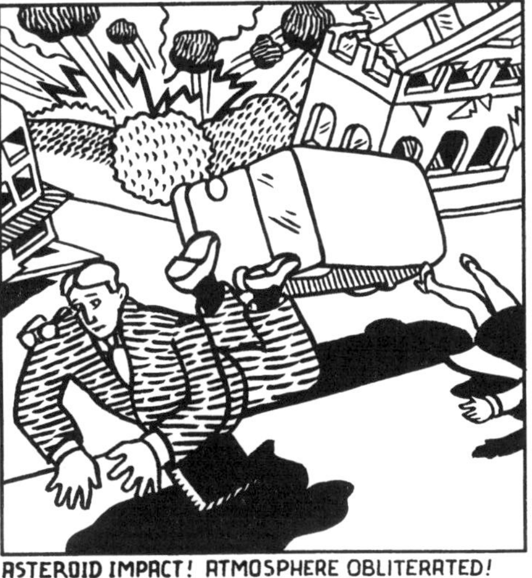

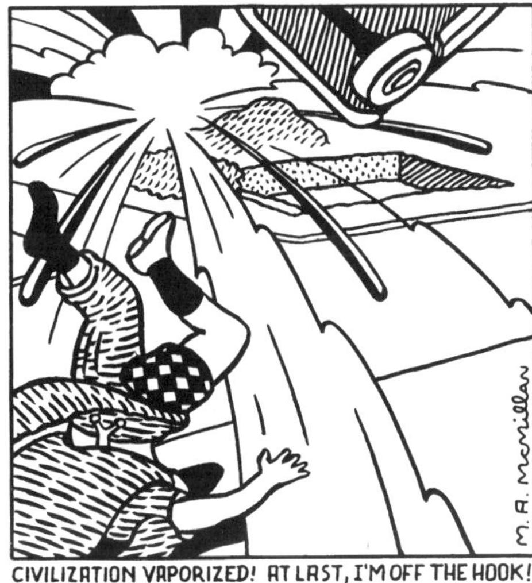

SICK OF THE ROUTINE, BUT I'M PROGRAMED TO BE OBEDIENT. ASTEROID IMPACT! ATMOSPHERE OBLITERATED! CIVILIZATION VAPORIZED! AT LAST, I'M OFF THE HOOK!

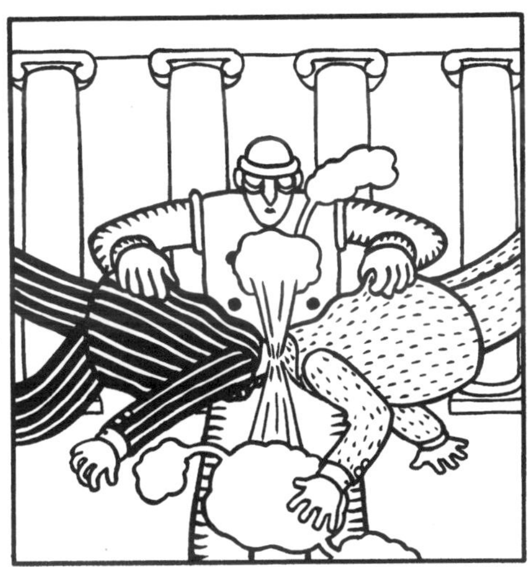

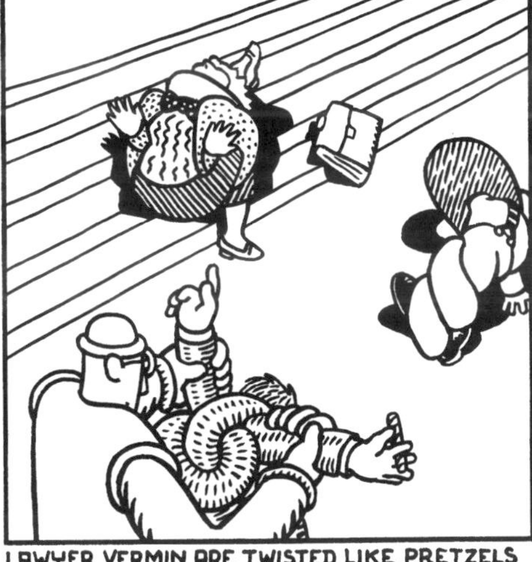

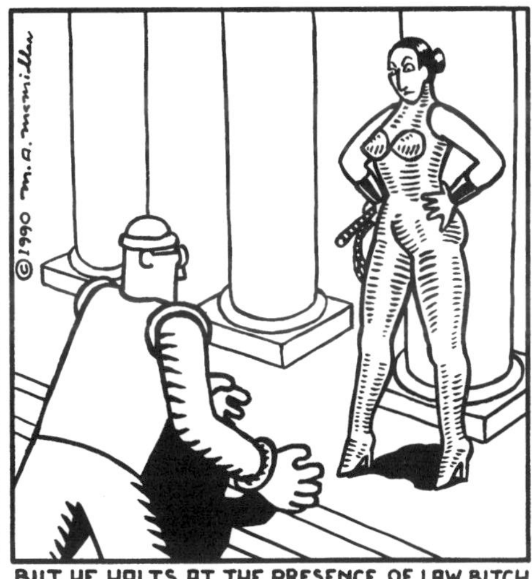

ZOMO THREATENED WITH LIBEL RUNS AMUCK LAWYER VERMIN ARE TWISTED LIKE PRETZELS BUT HE HALTS AT THE PRESENCE OF LAW BITCH

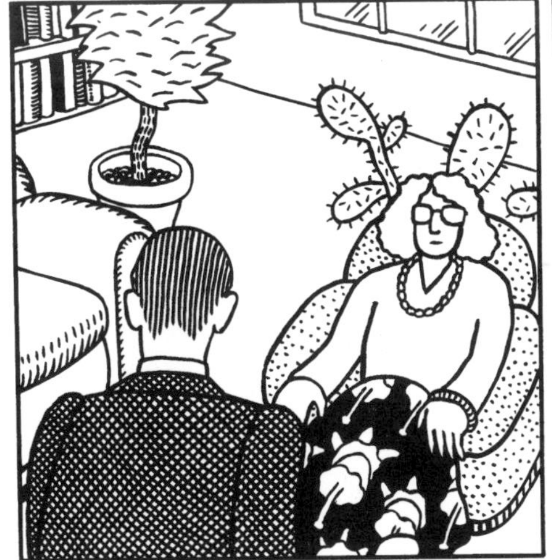

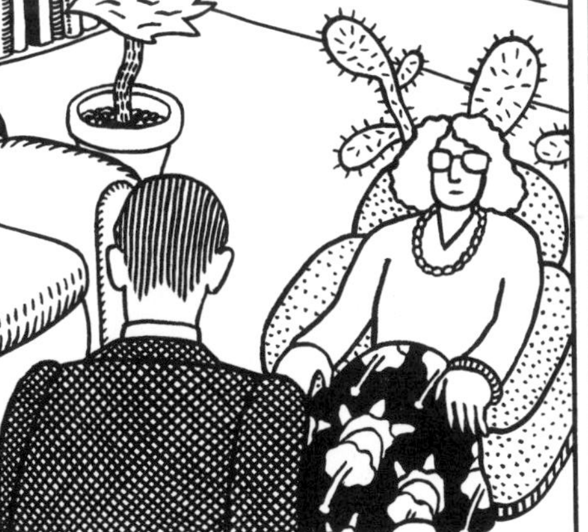

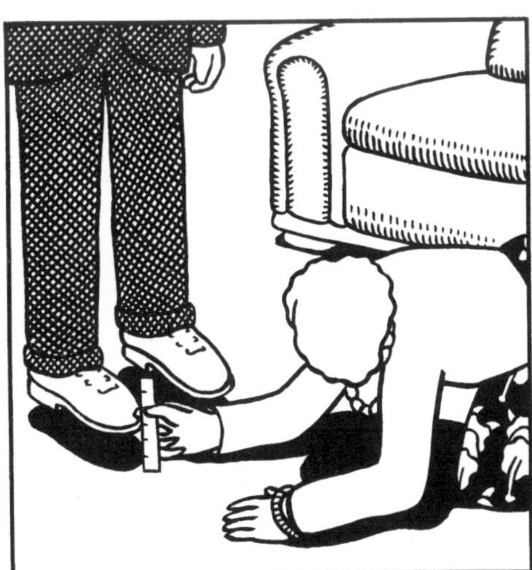

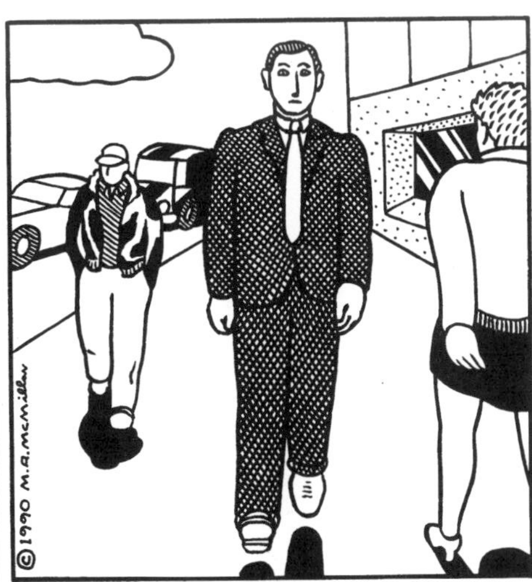

AT THE USUAL APPOINTMENT WITH MY THERAPIST SHE FOUND THE CONDITION UNCHANGED BUT SHE ASSURED ME I AM MAKING PROGRESS

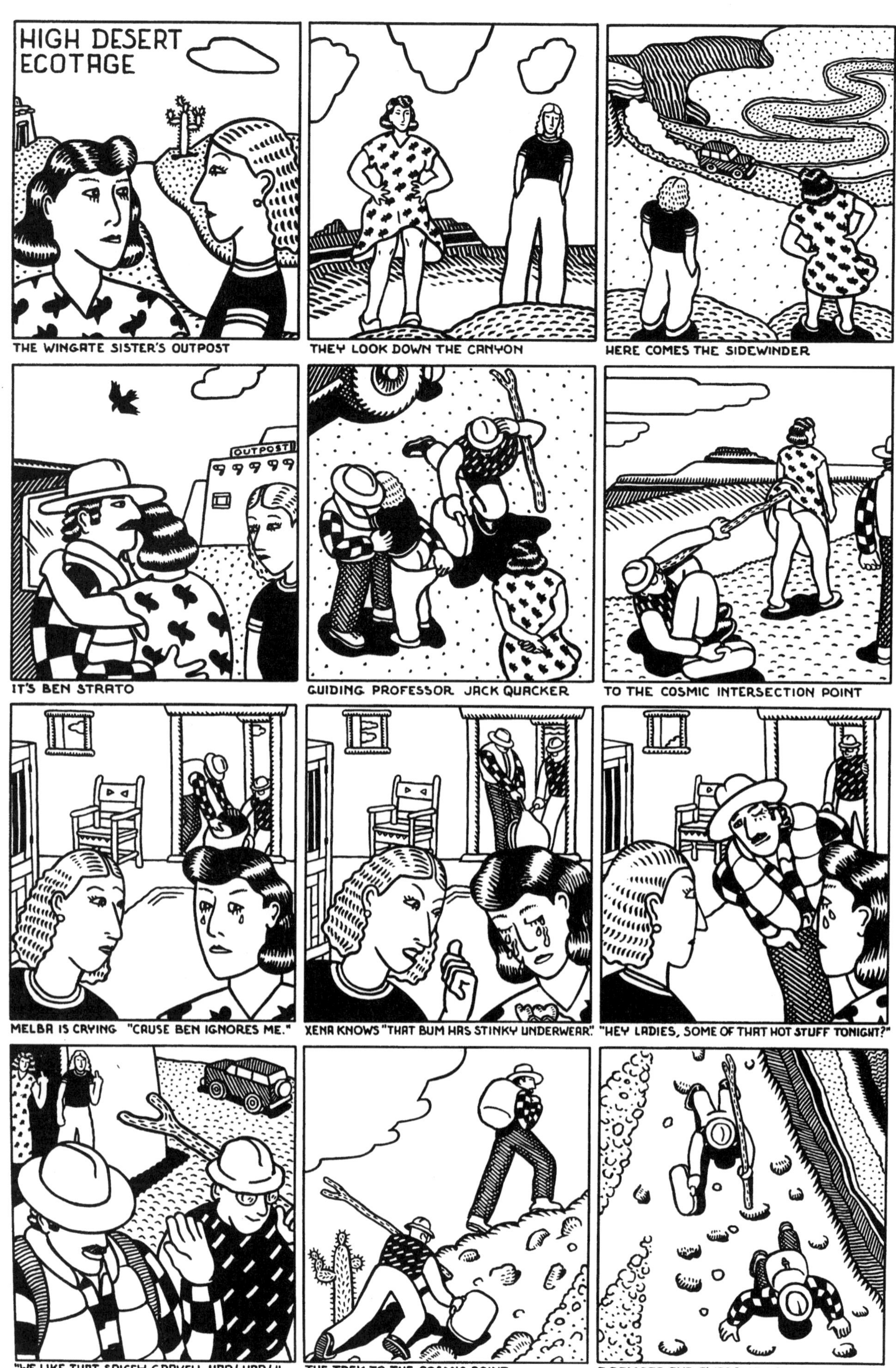

HIGH DESERT ECOTAGE
THE WINGATE SISTER'S OUTPOST
THEY LOOK DOWN THE CANYON
HERE COMES THE SIDEWINDER
OUTPOST
IT'S BEN STRATO
GUIDING PROFESSOR JACK QUACKER
TO THE COSMIC INTERSECTION POINT
MELBA IS CRYING "CAUSE BEN IGNORES ME."
XENA KNOWS "THAT BUM HAS STINKY UNDERWEAR."
"HEY LADIES, SOME OF THAT HOT STUFF TONIGHT?"
"WE LIKE THAT SPICEY GRAVEY. HAR! HAR!"
THE TREK TO THE COSMIC POINT
A REMOTE AND AWESOME LOCALE

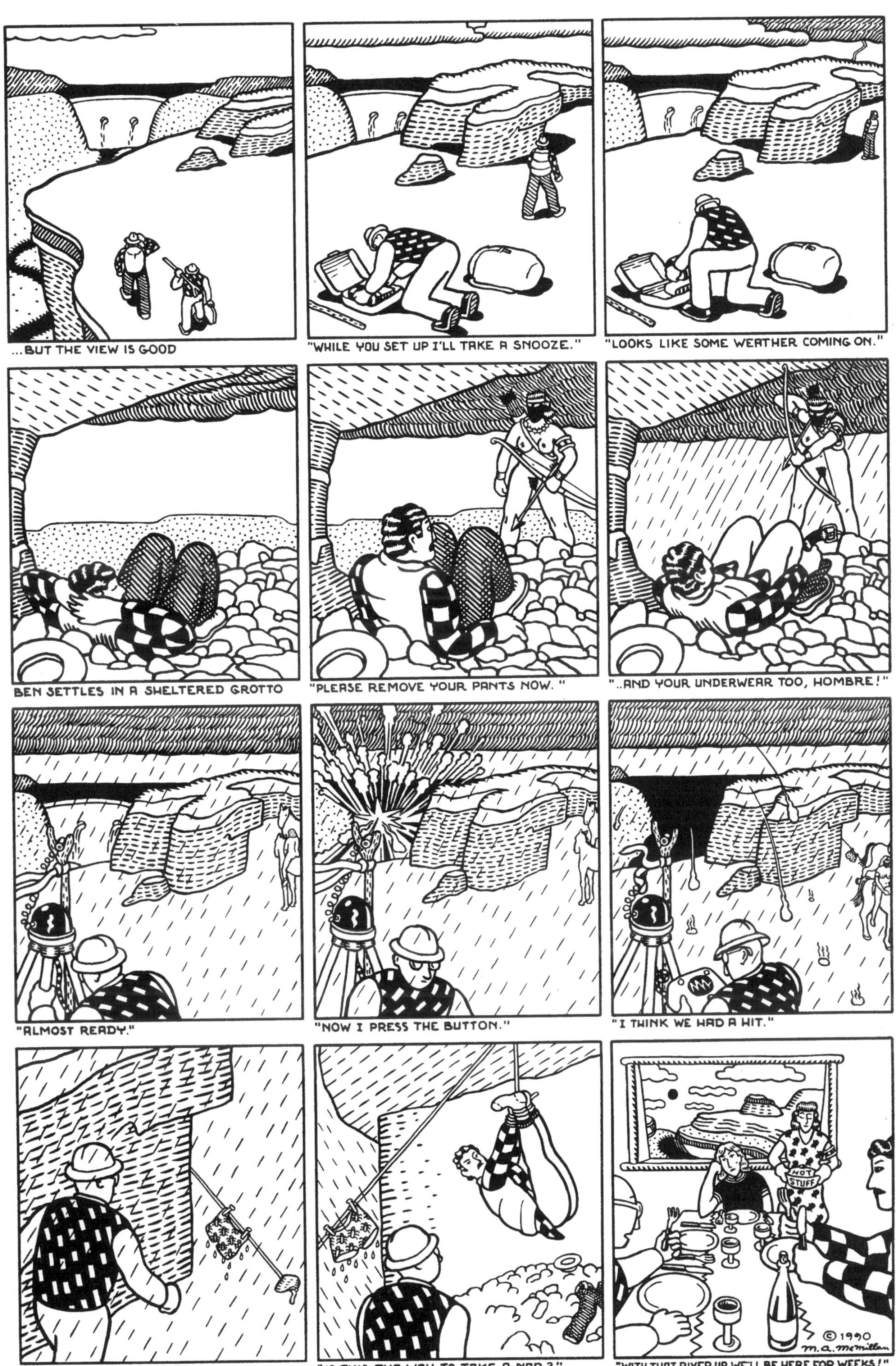
...BUT THE VIEW IS GOOD
"WHILE YOU SET UP I'LL TAKE A SNOOZE."
"LOOKS LIKE SOME WEATHER COMING ON."
BEN SETTLES IN A SHELTERED GROTTO
"PLEASE REMOVE YOUR PANTS NOW."
"..AND YOUR UNDERWEAR TOO, HOMBRE!"
"ALMOST READY."
"NOW I PRESS THE BUTTON."
"I THINK WE HAD A HIT."
"OKEY, LET'S PACK IT!"
"IS THIS THE WAY TO TAKE A NAP?"
HOT STUFF
©1990 M.A. McMillan
"WITH THAT RIVER UP WE'LL BE HERE FOR WEEKS!"

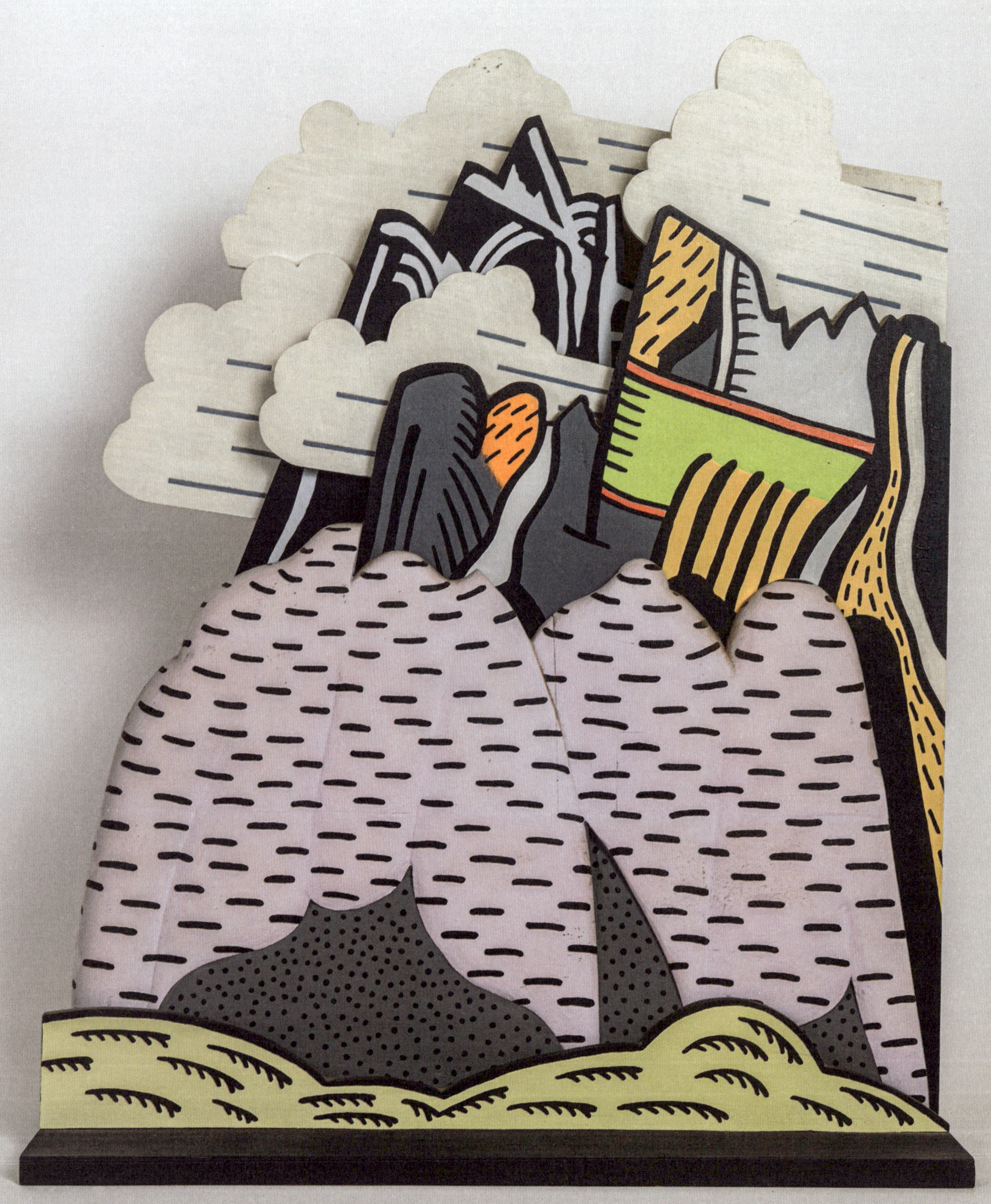

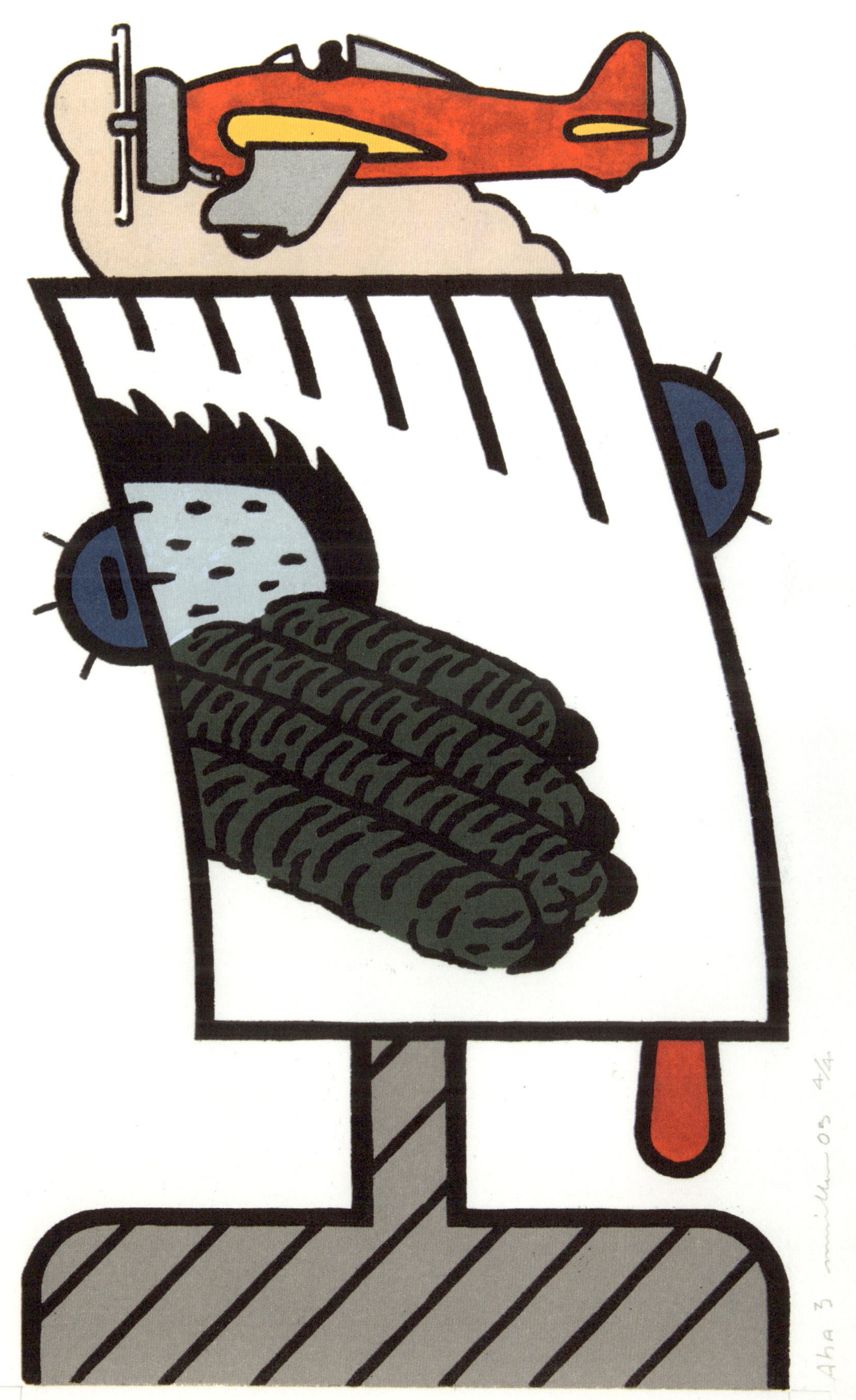

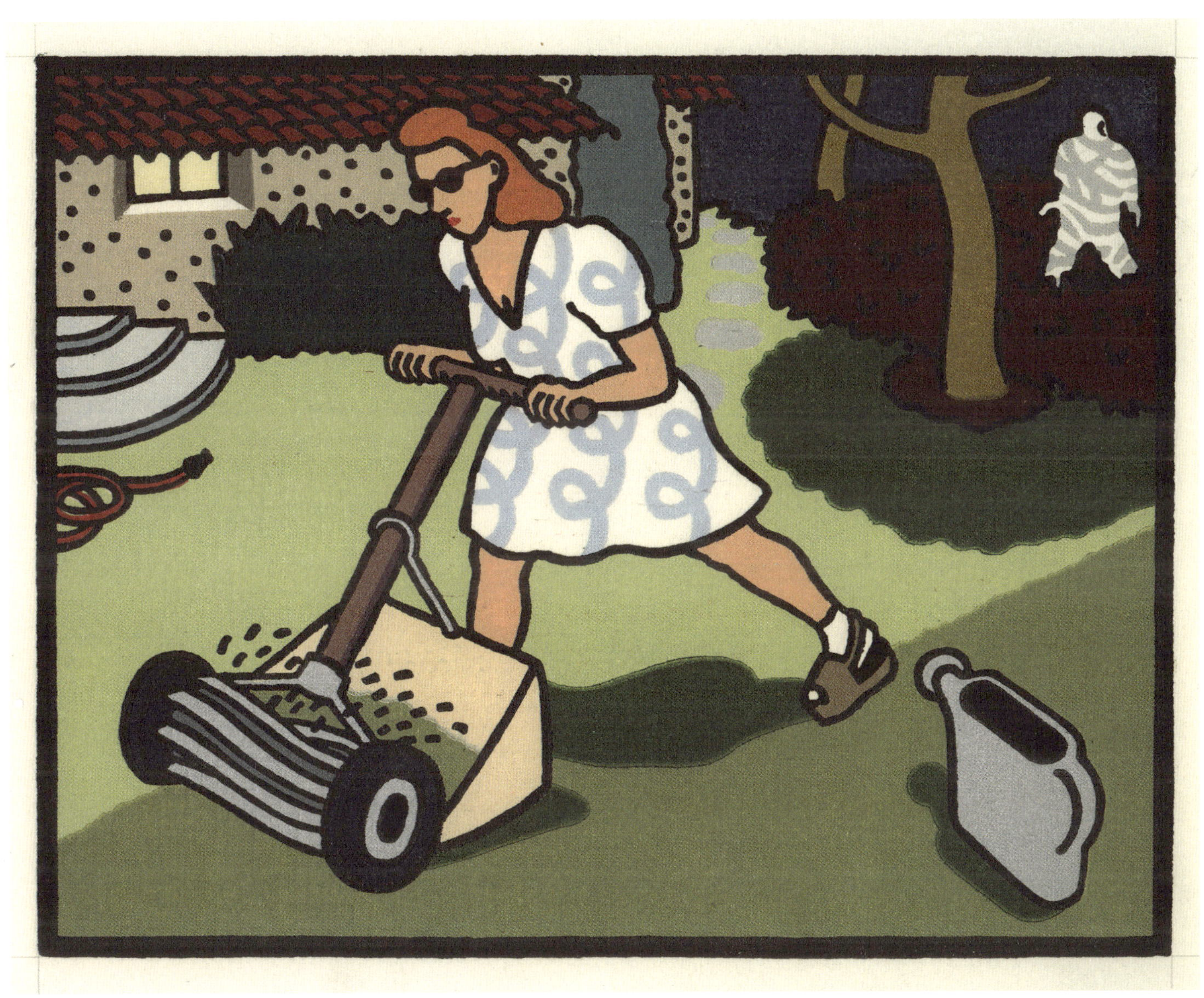

Yard Work

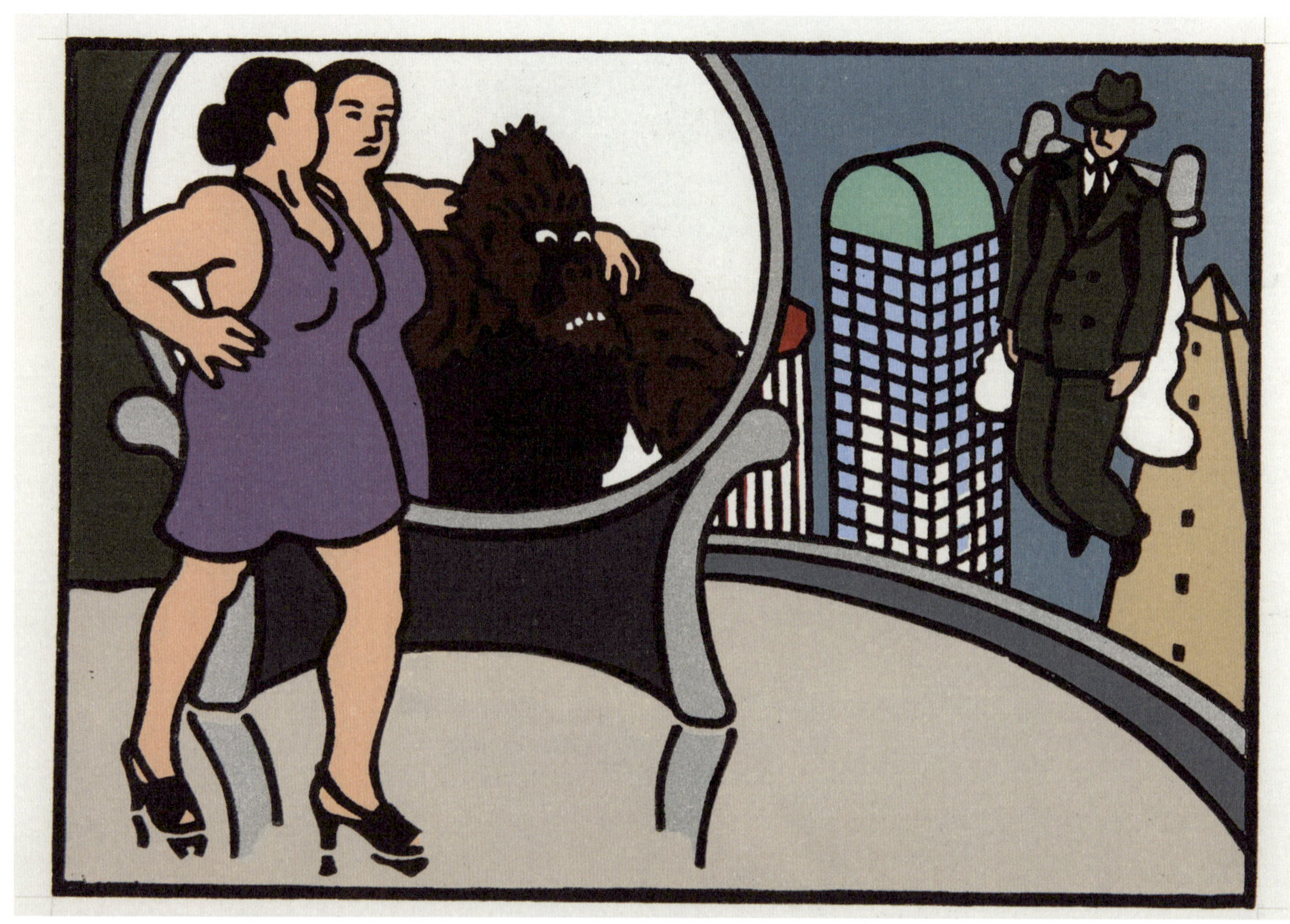

Law of the Jungle

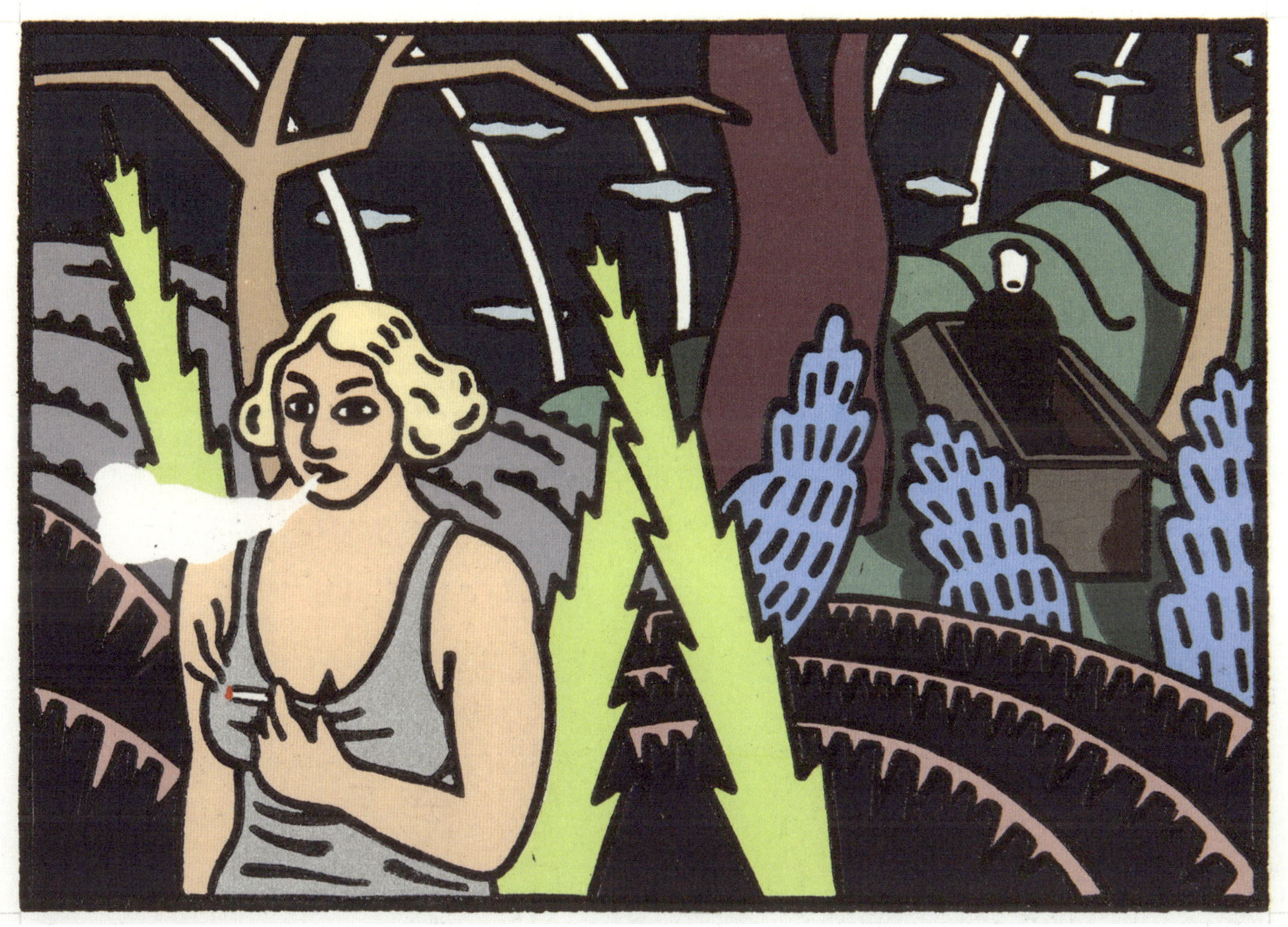

Evening Interlude

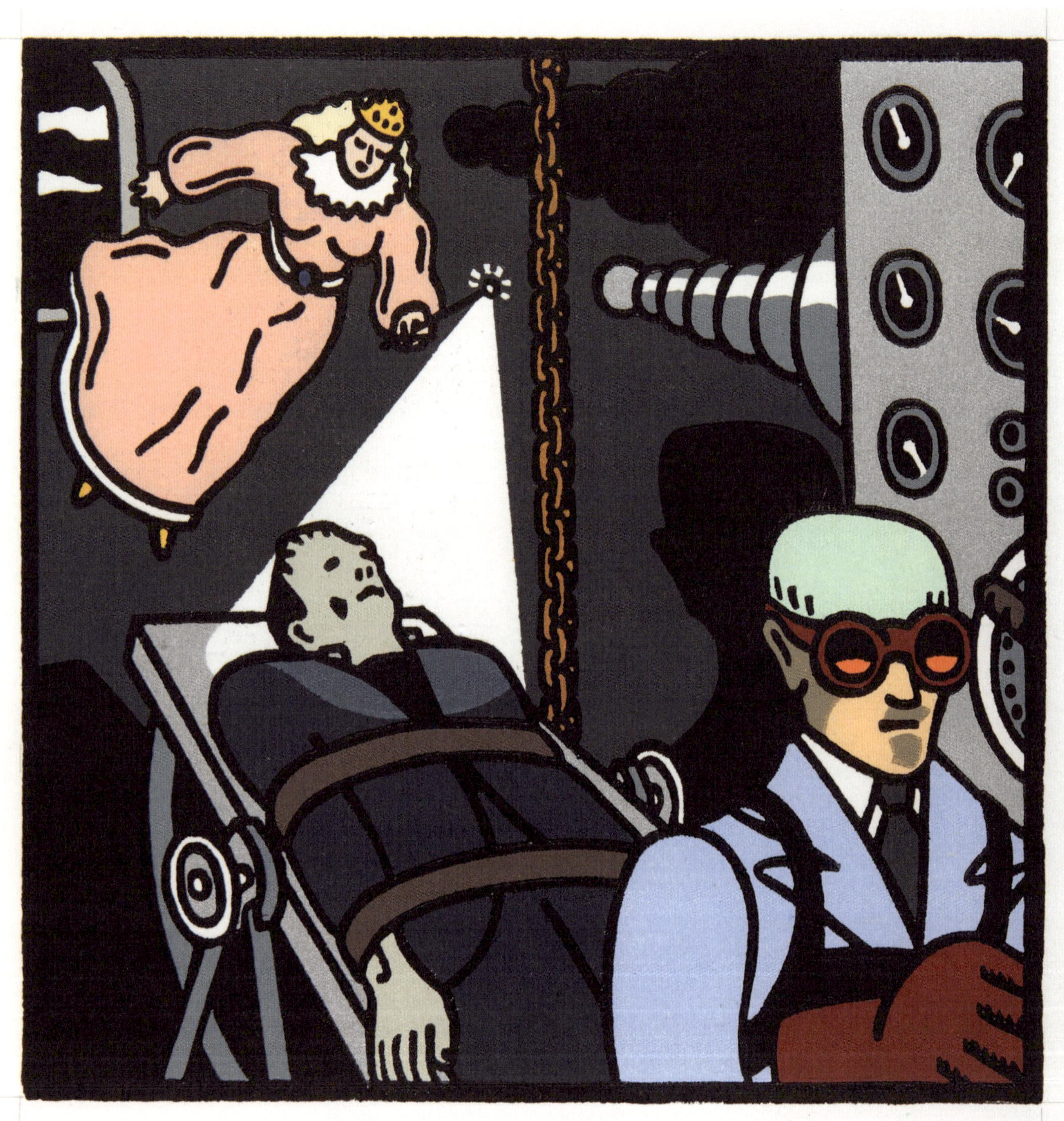

My Funny Valentine

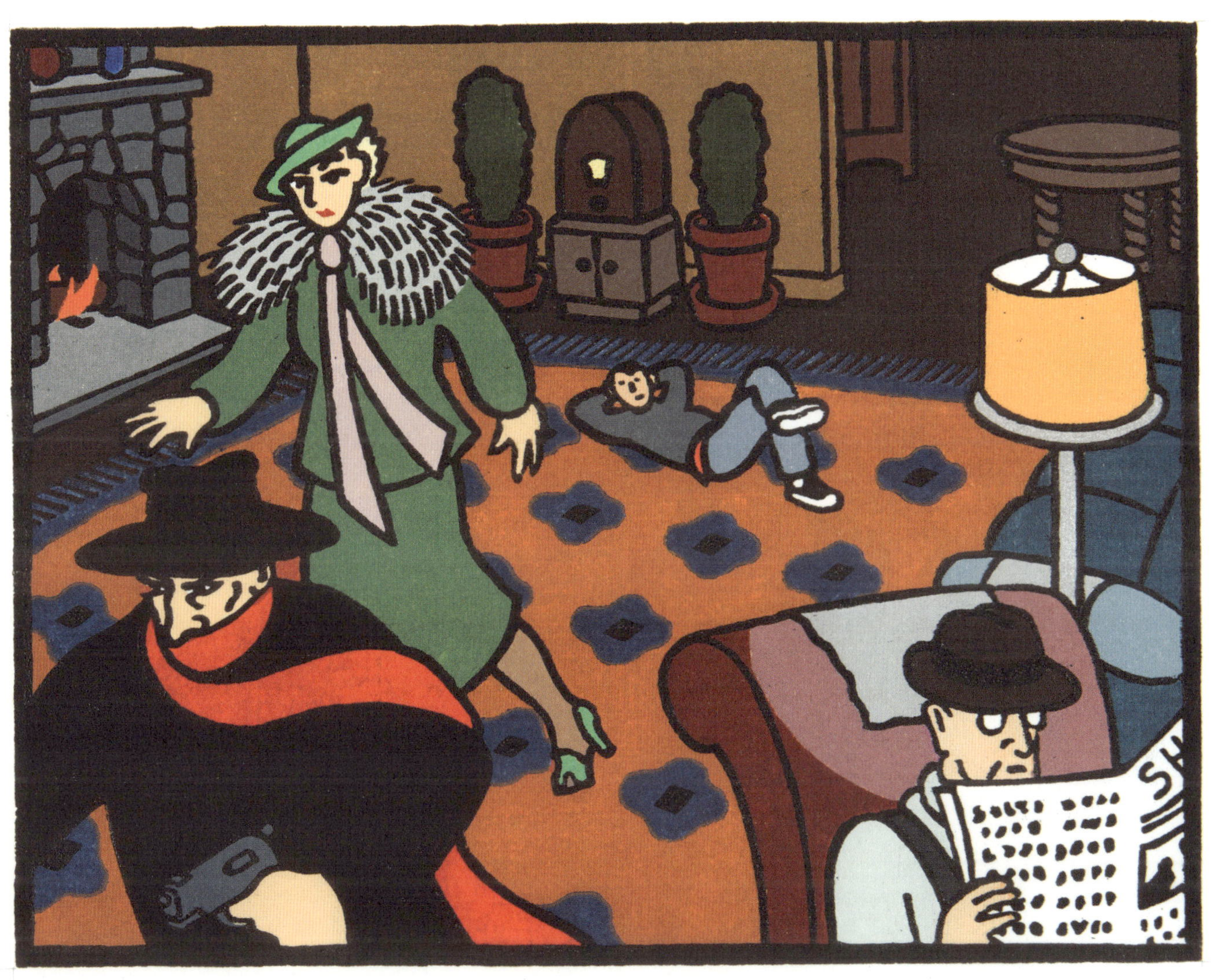

Our Big Living Room 1940

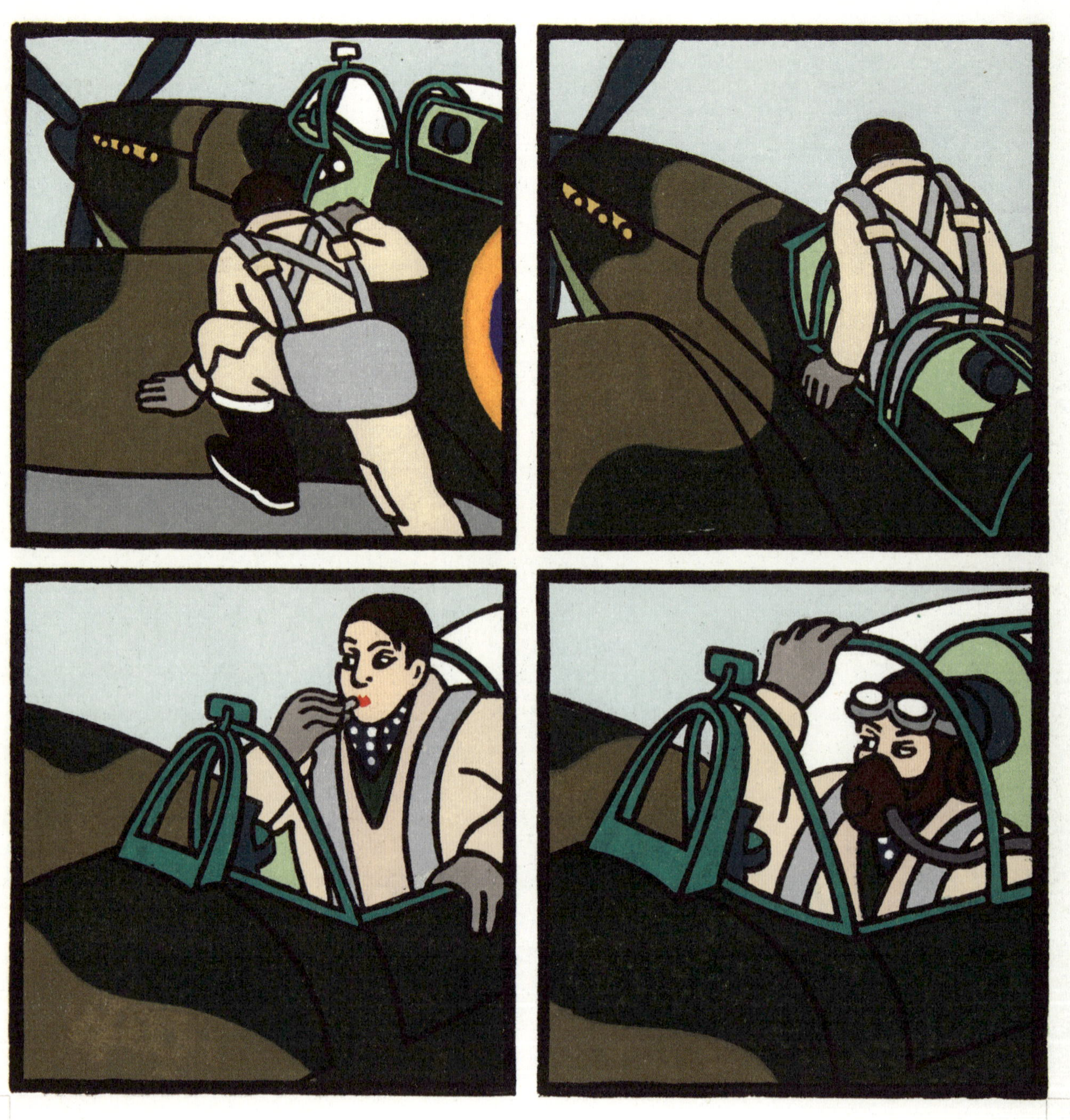

Spitfire MKIA Rolls Royce Merlin III 1940

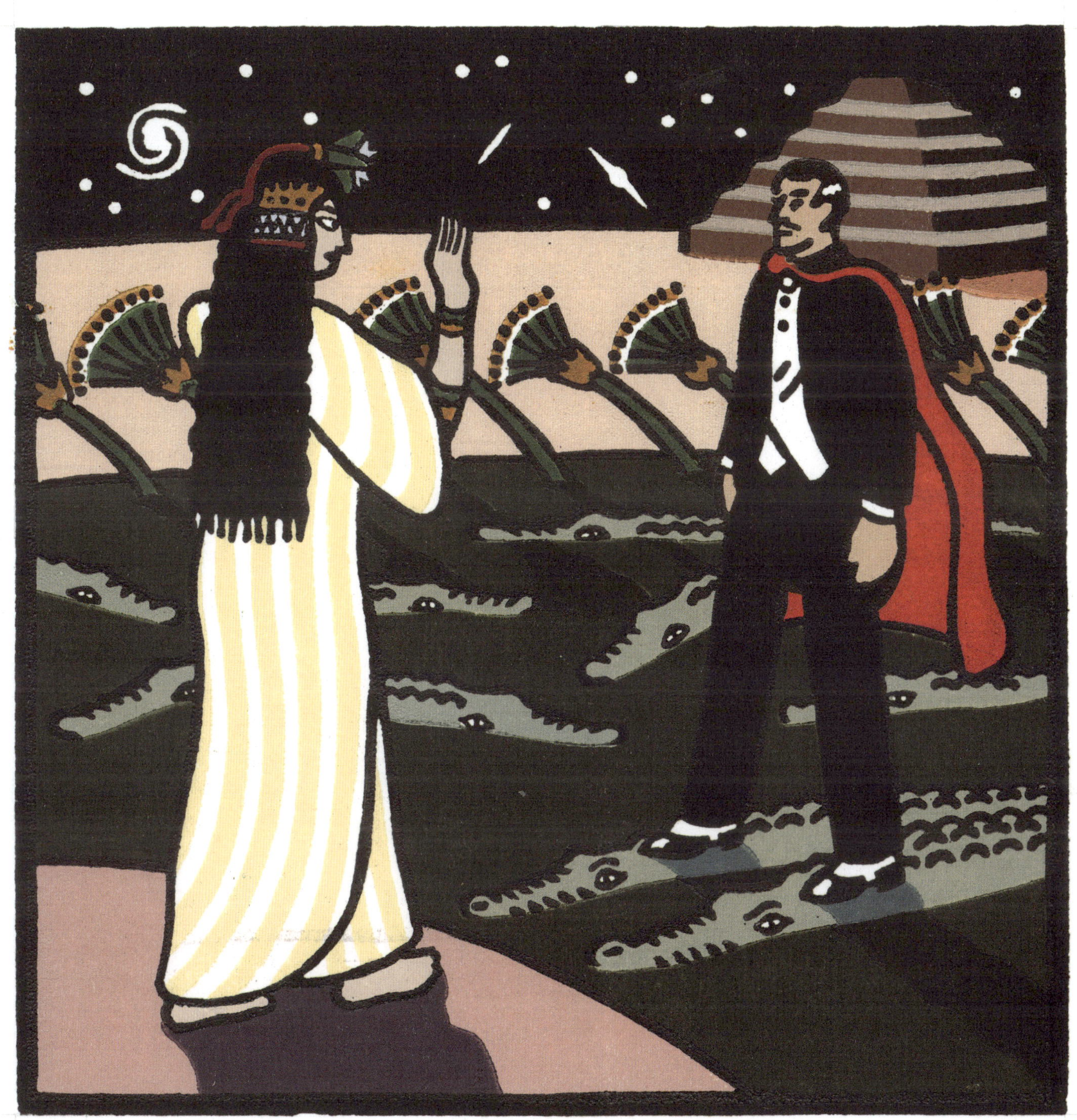

Long Time No See

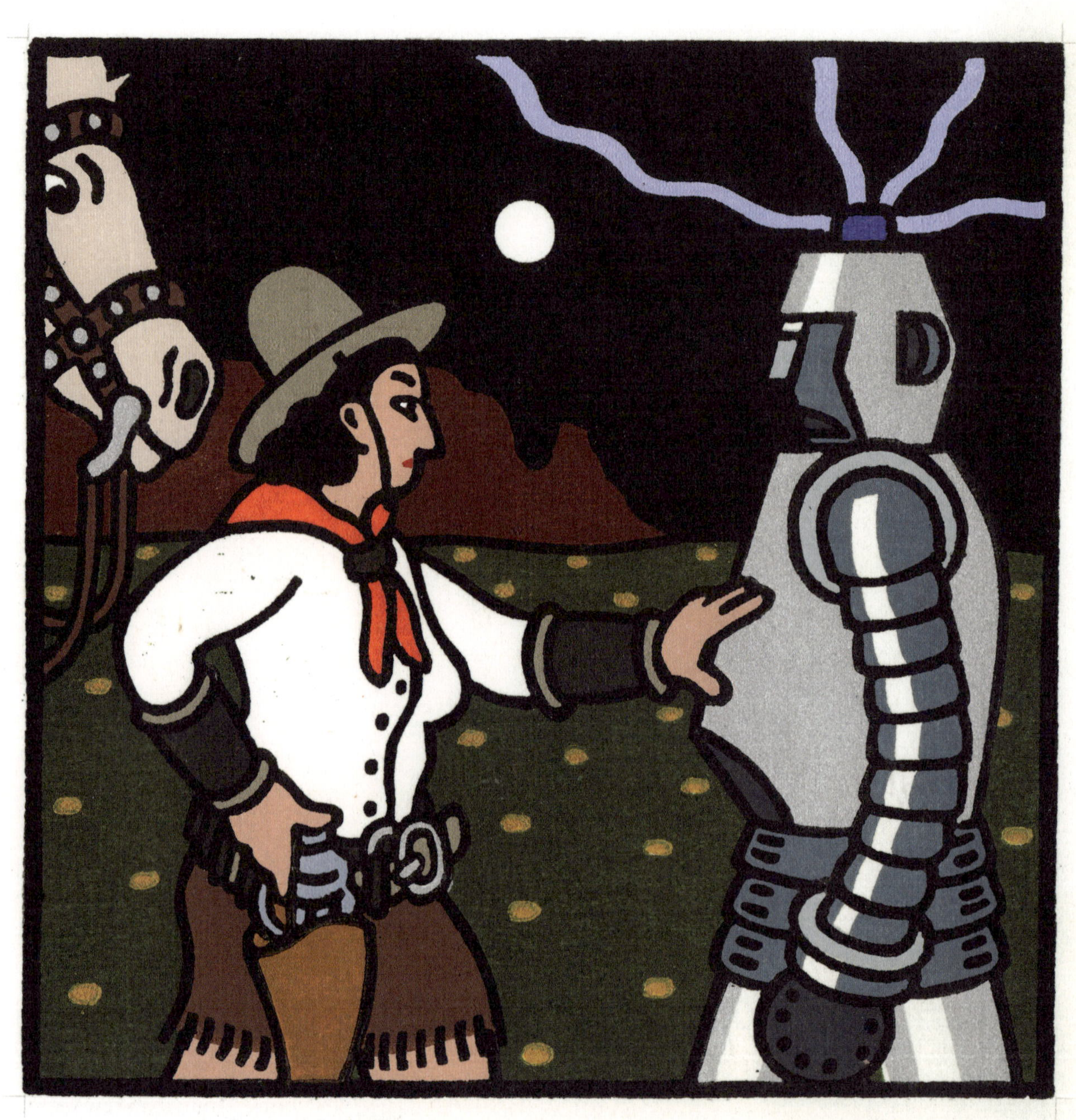

Home on the Range

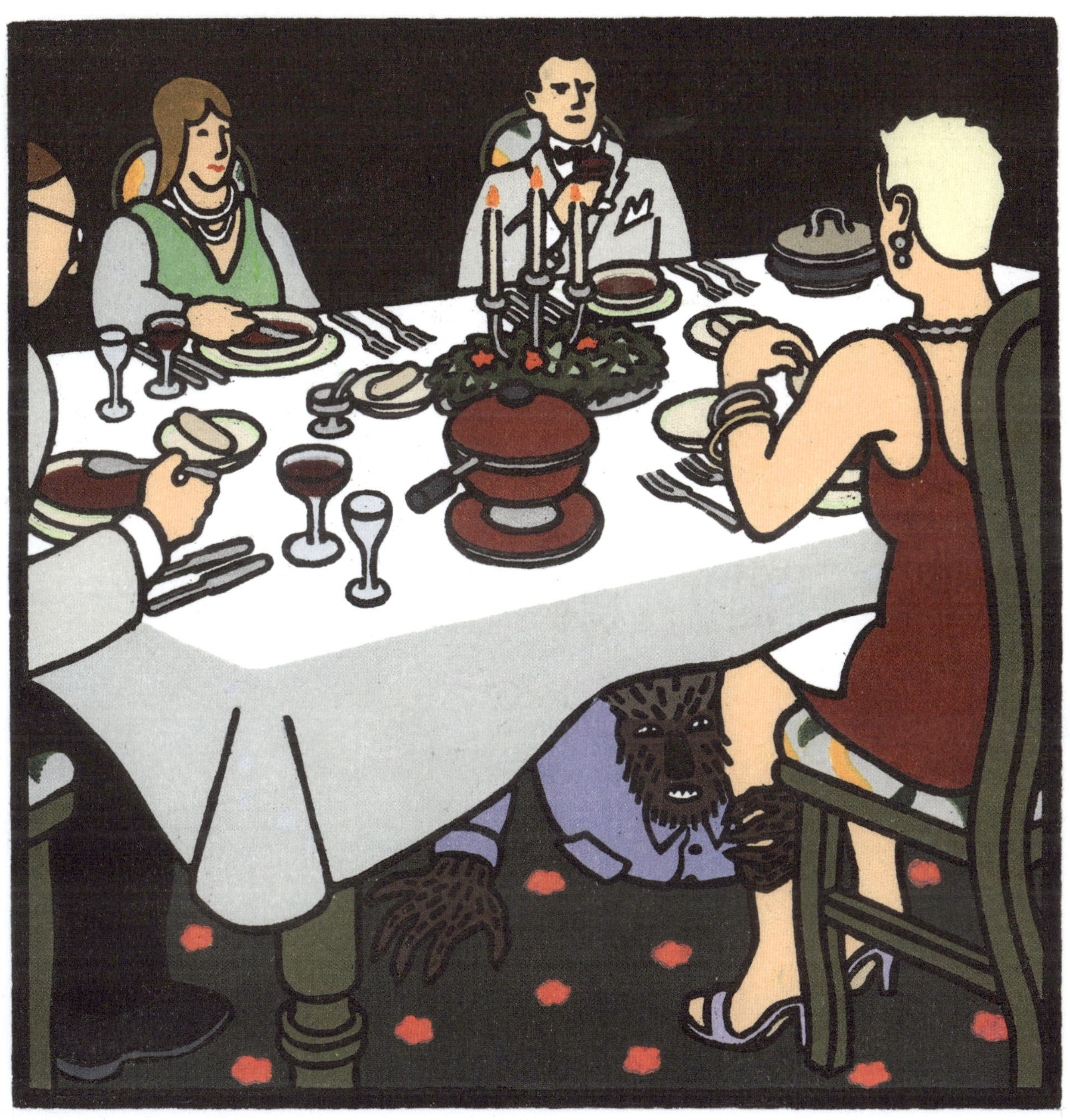

When The Moon Is Full Cuisine

2/6 04

When the Moon Is Full Cuisine

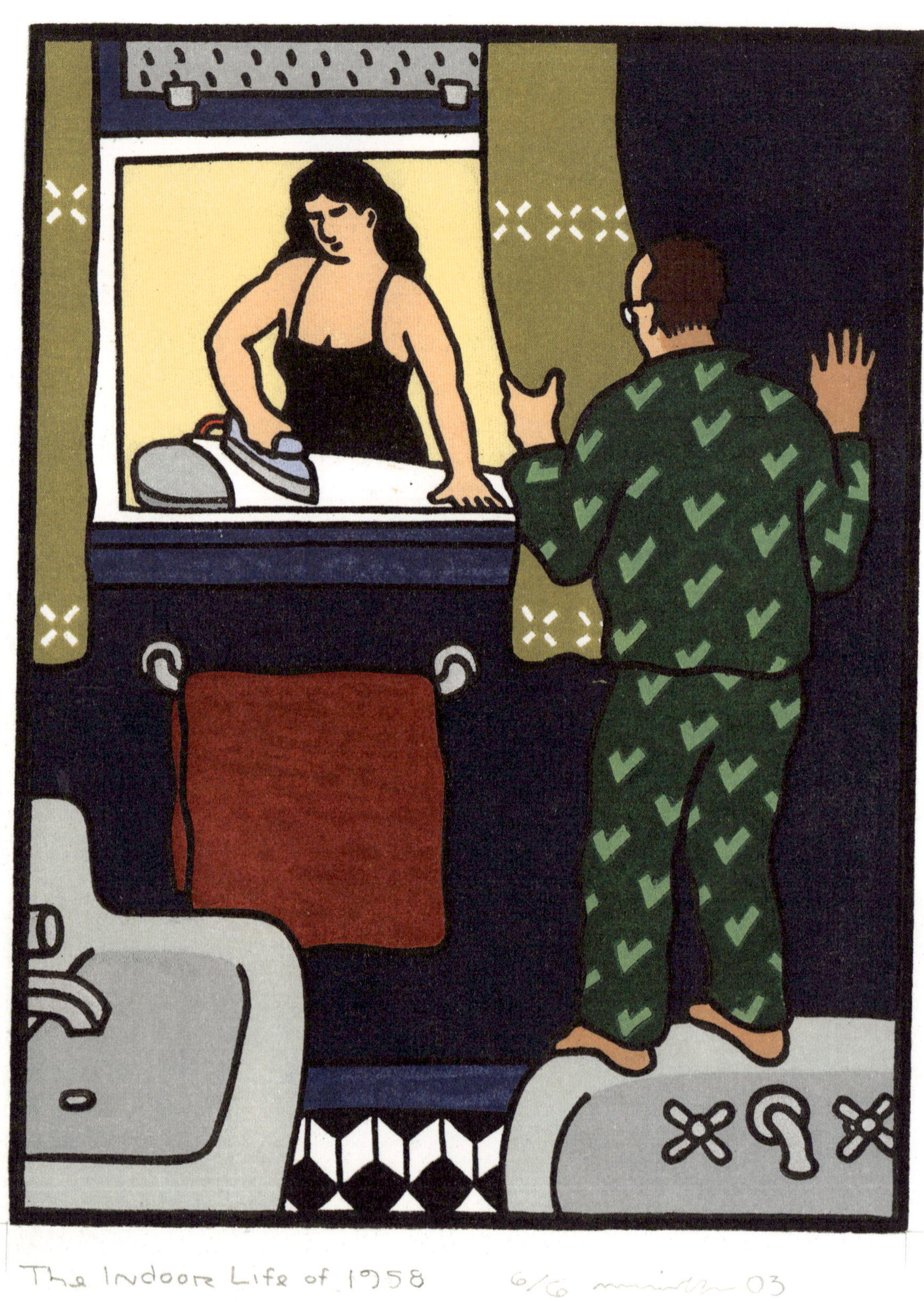

The Indoor Life of 1958

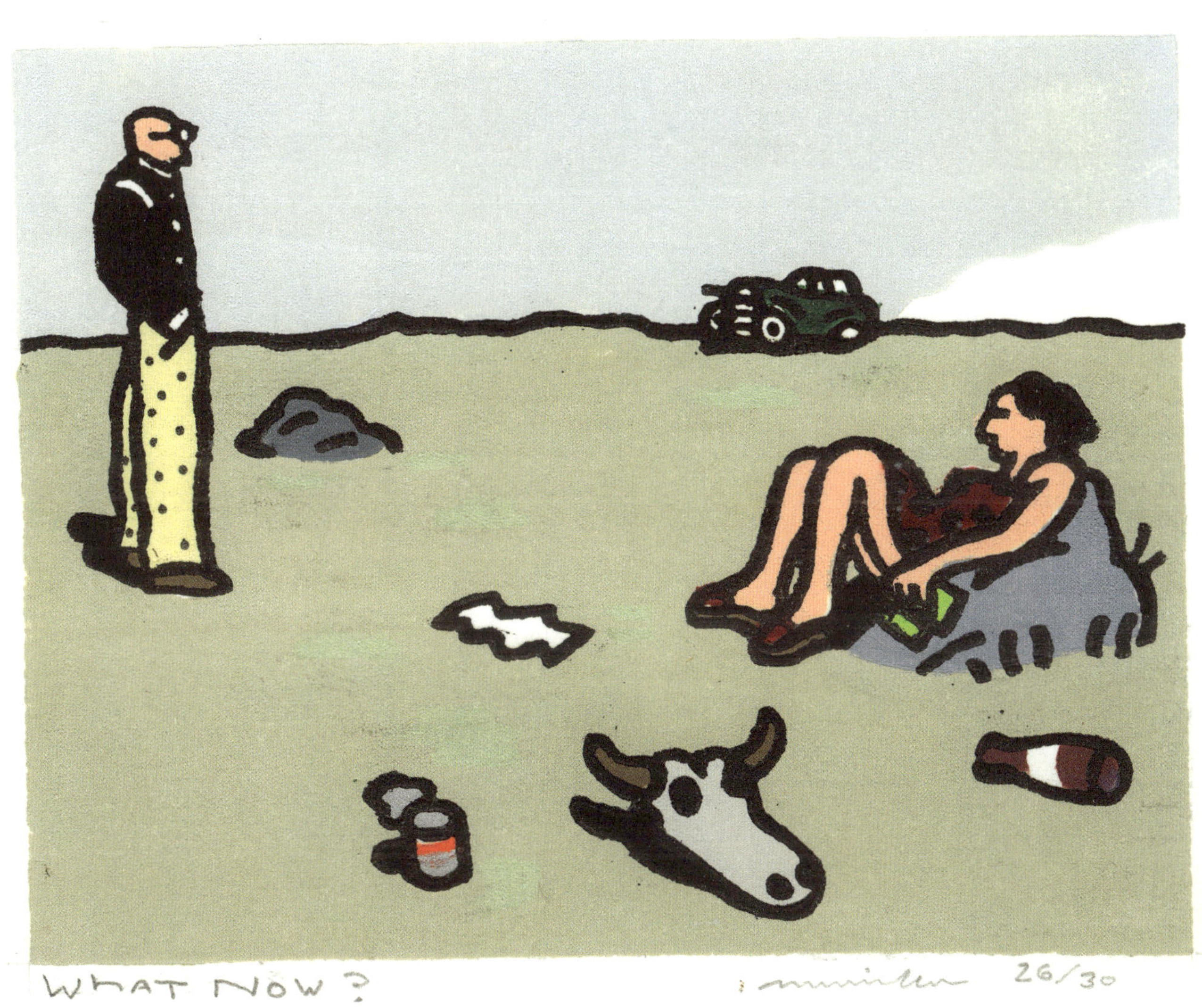

What Now?

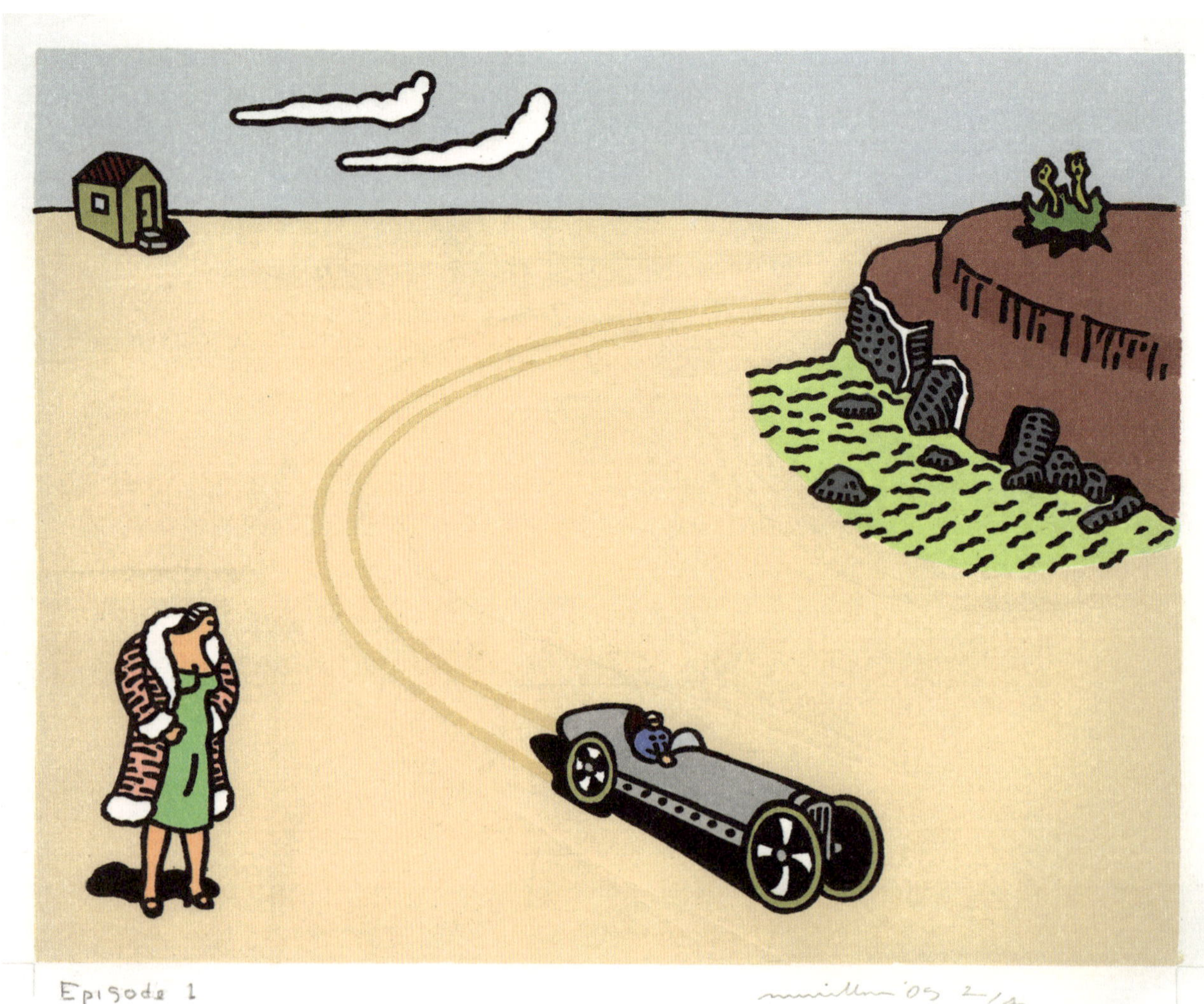

Episode 1

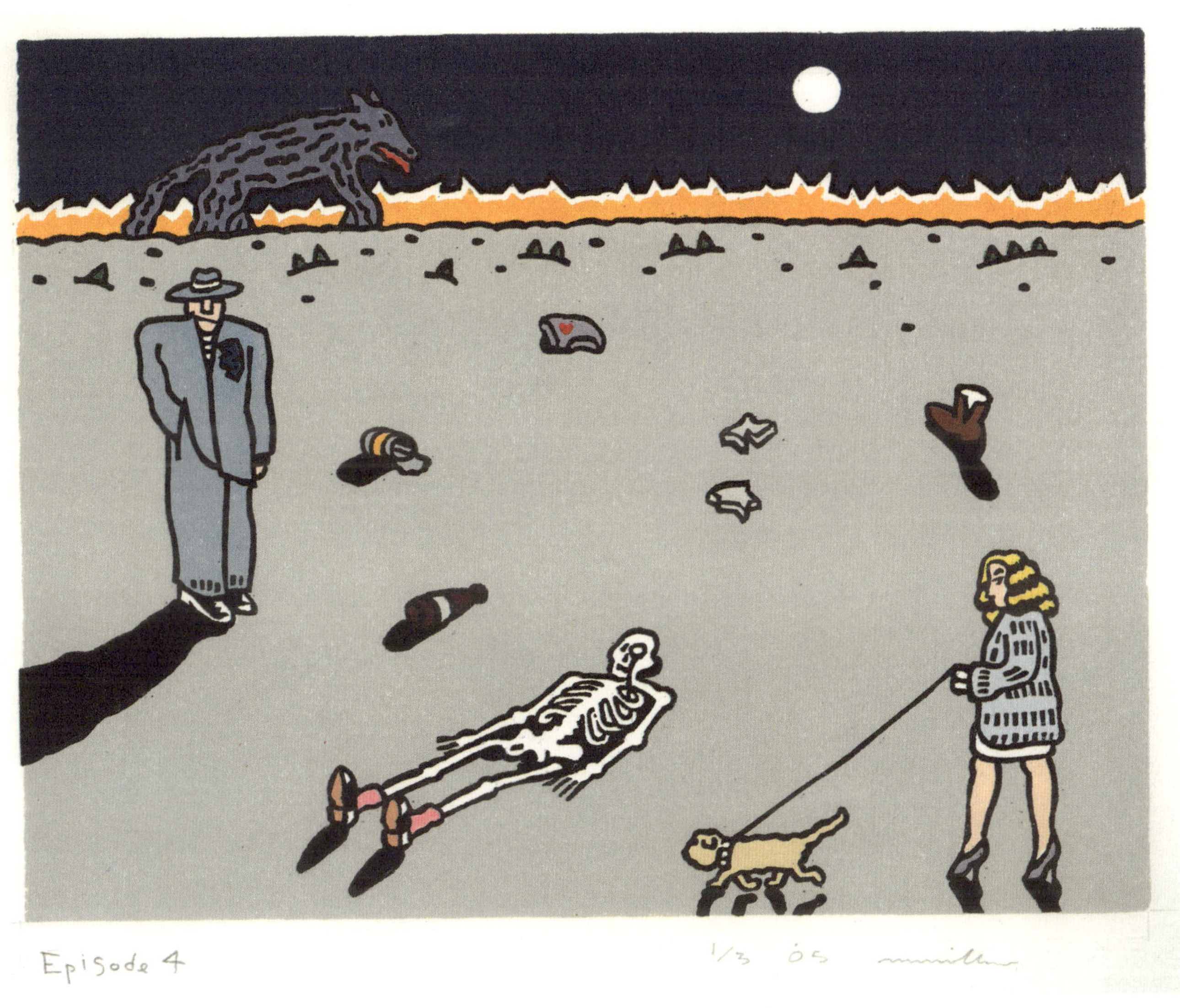

Episode 4

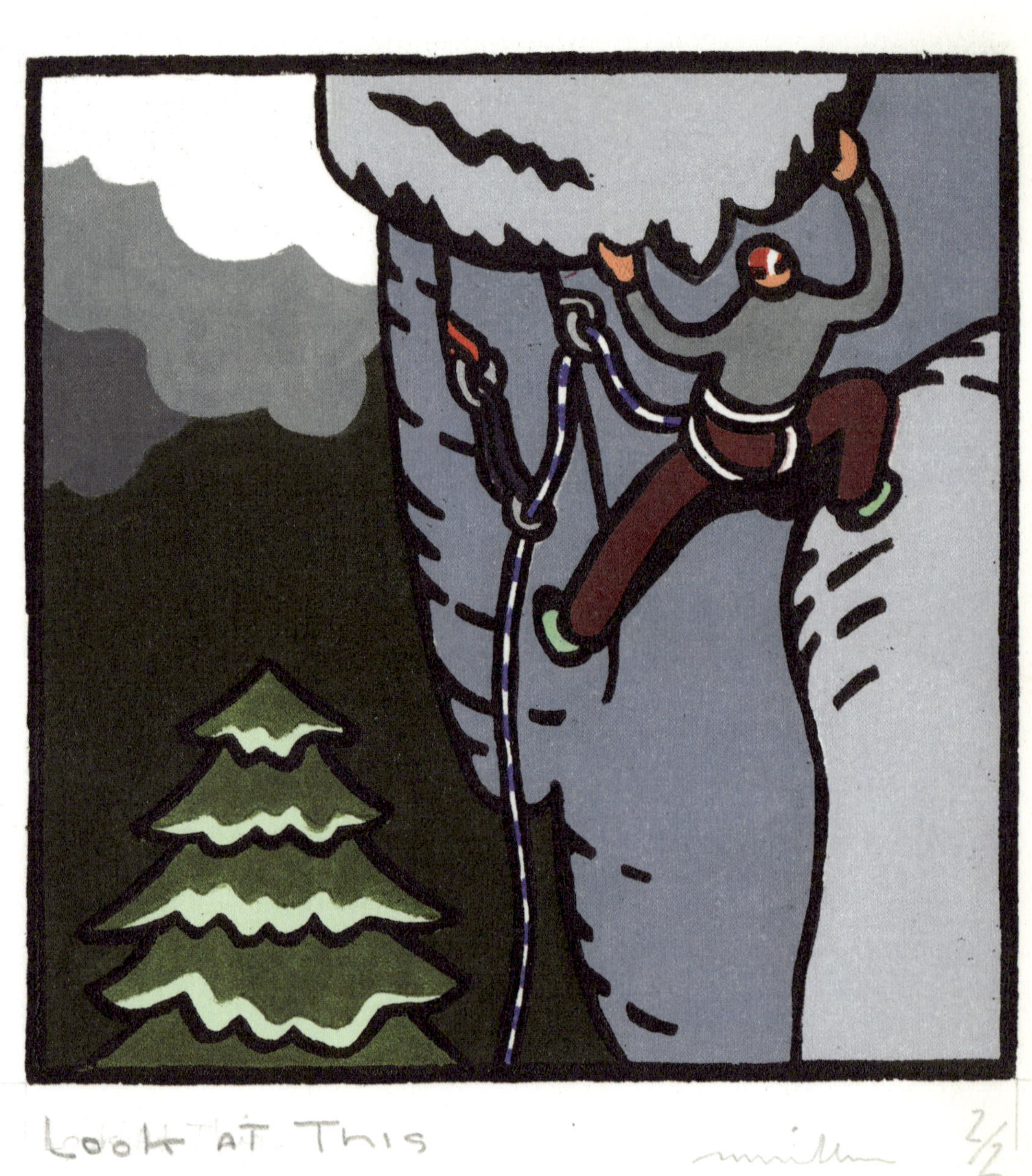

Look at This

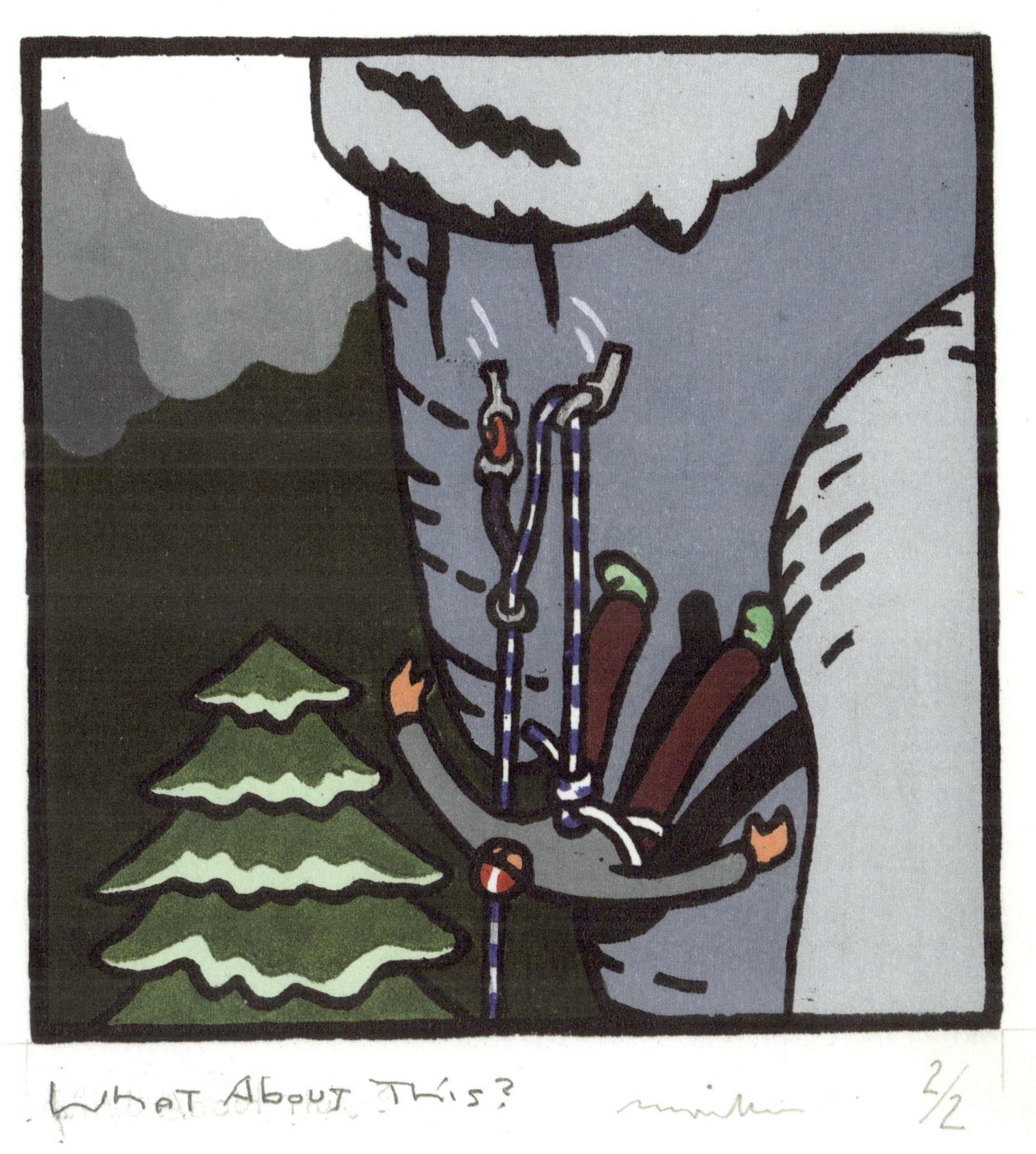

What About This?

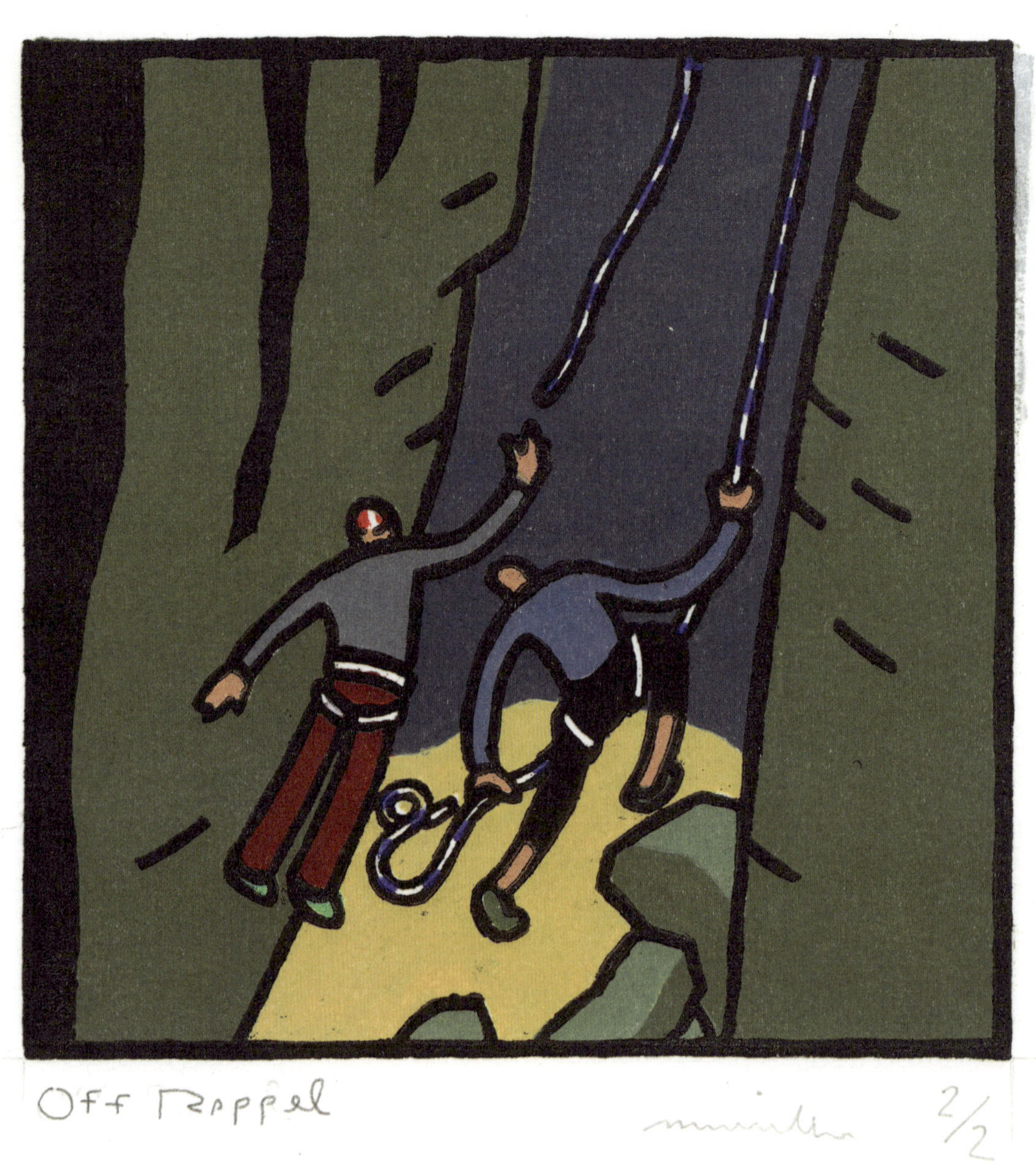

Off Rappel

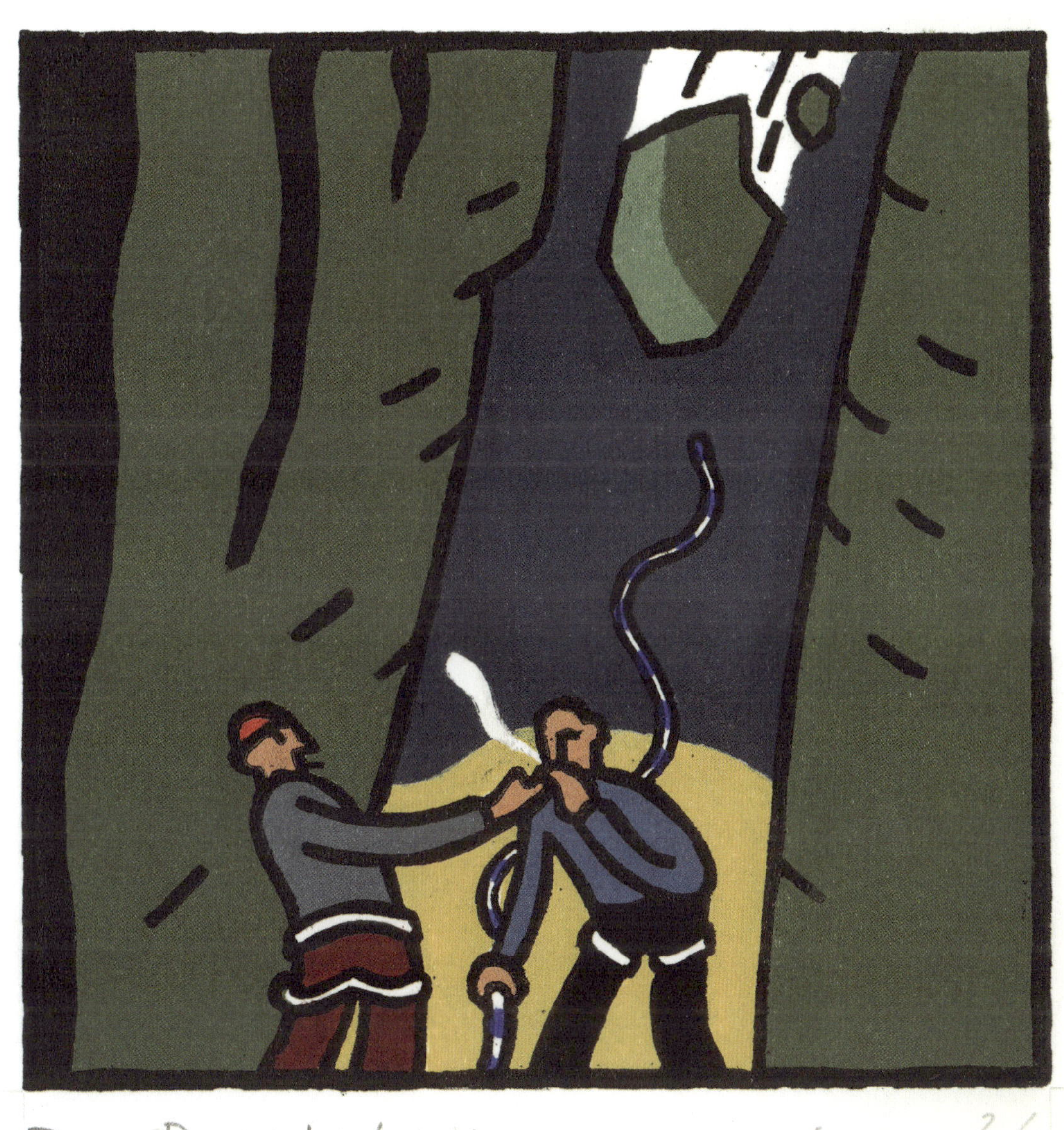

Rope Down, Light Up

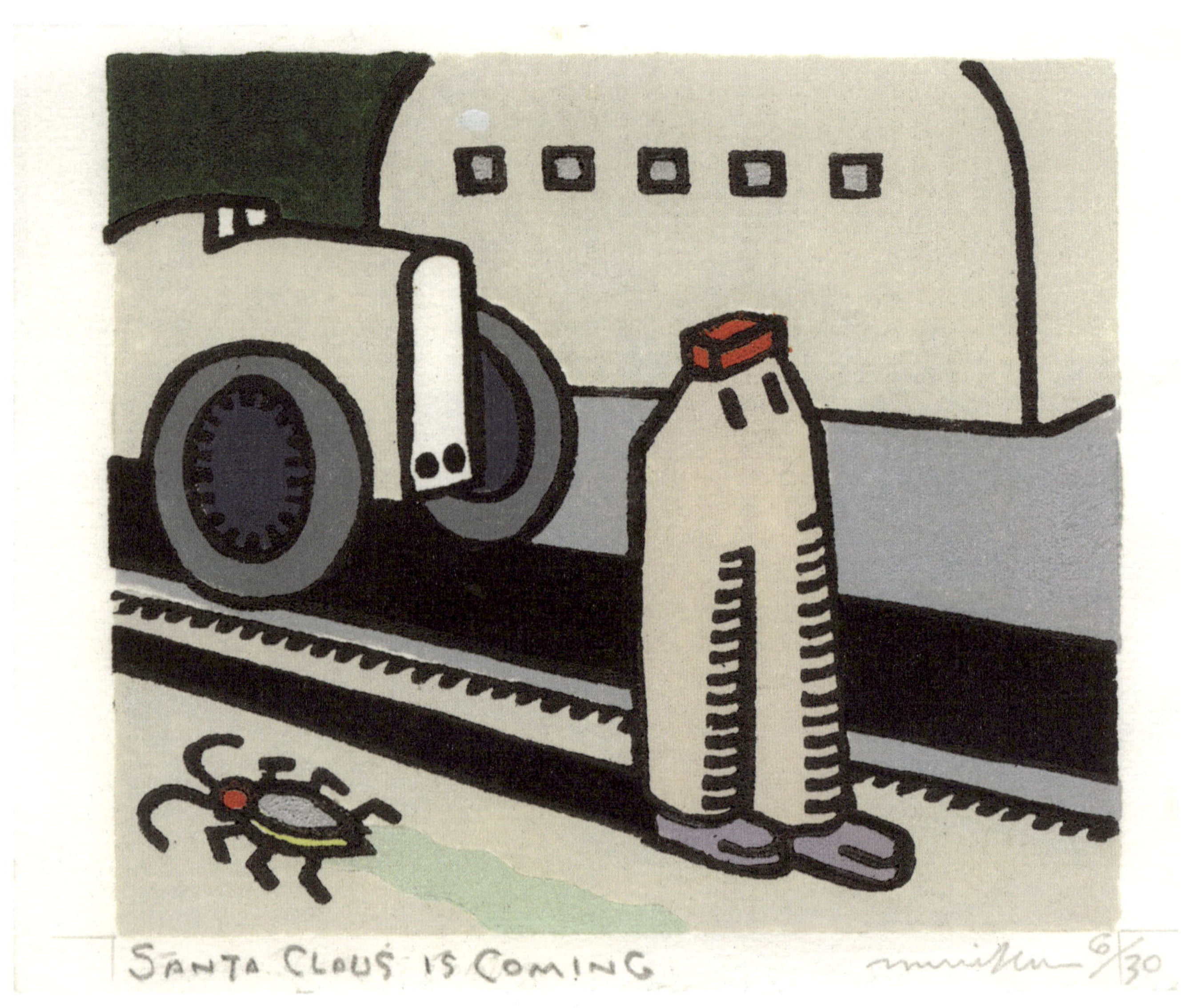

Santa Claus Is Coming

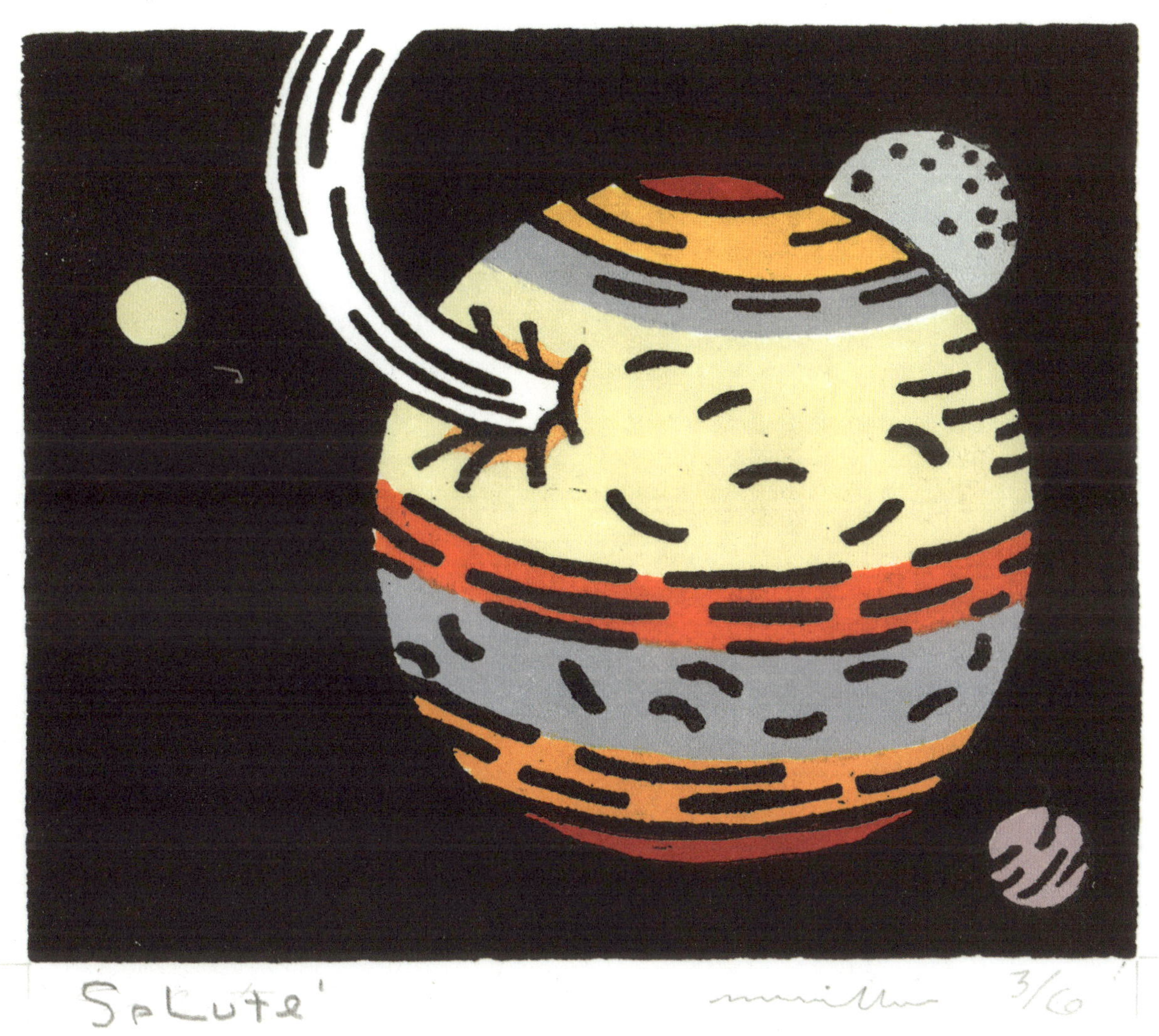

Salute

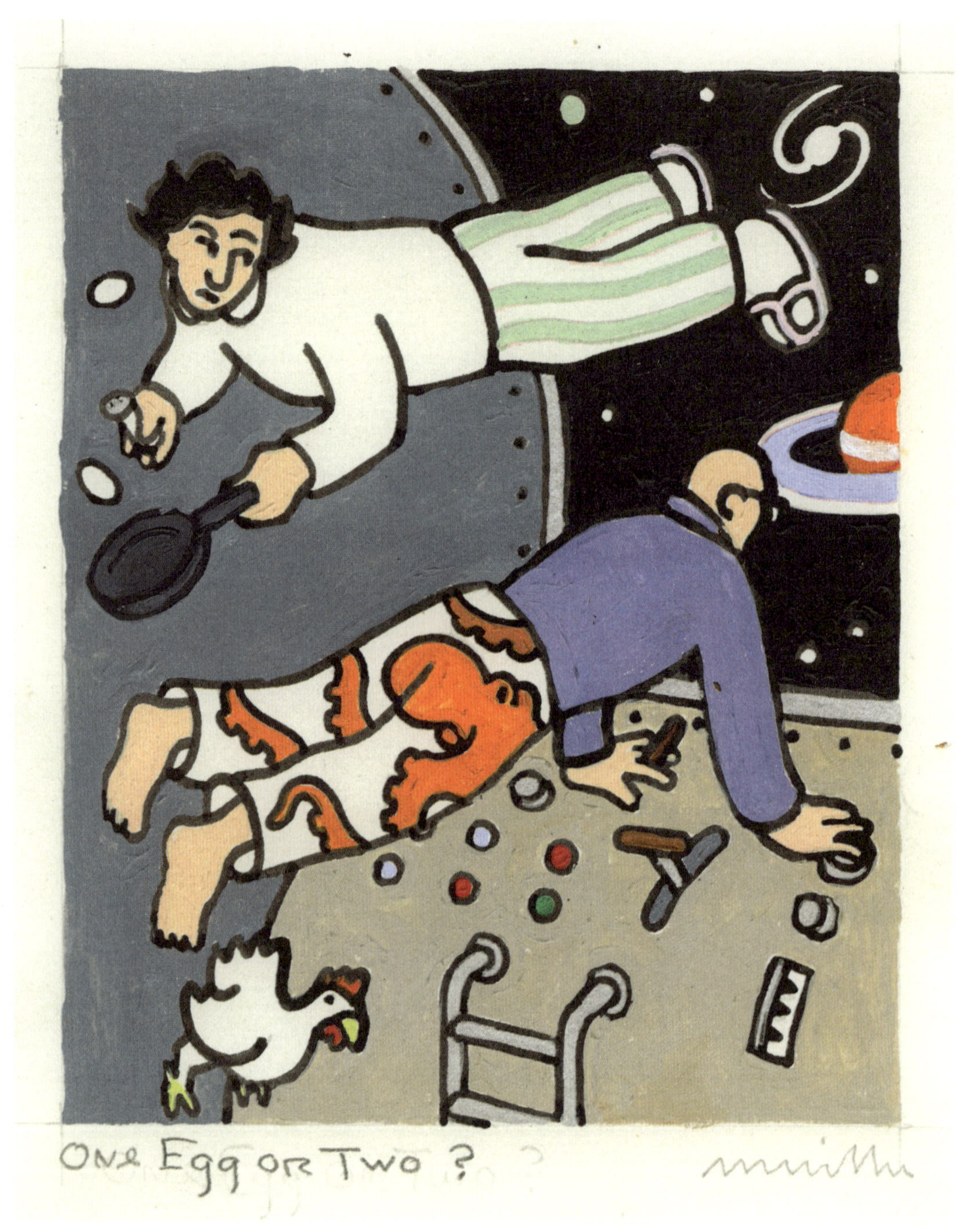

One Egg or Two?

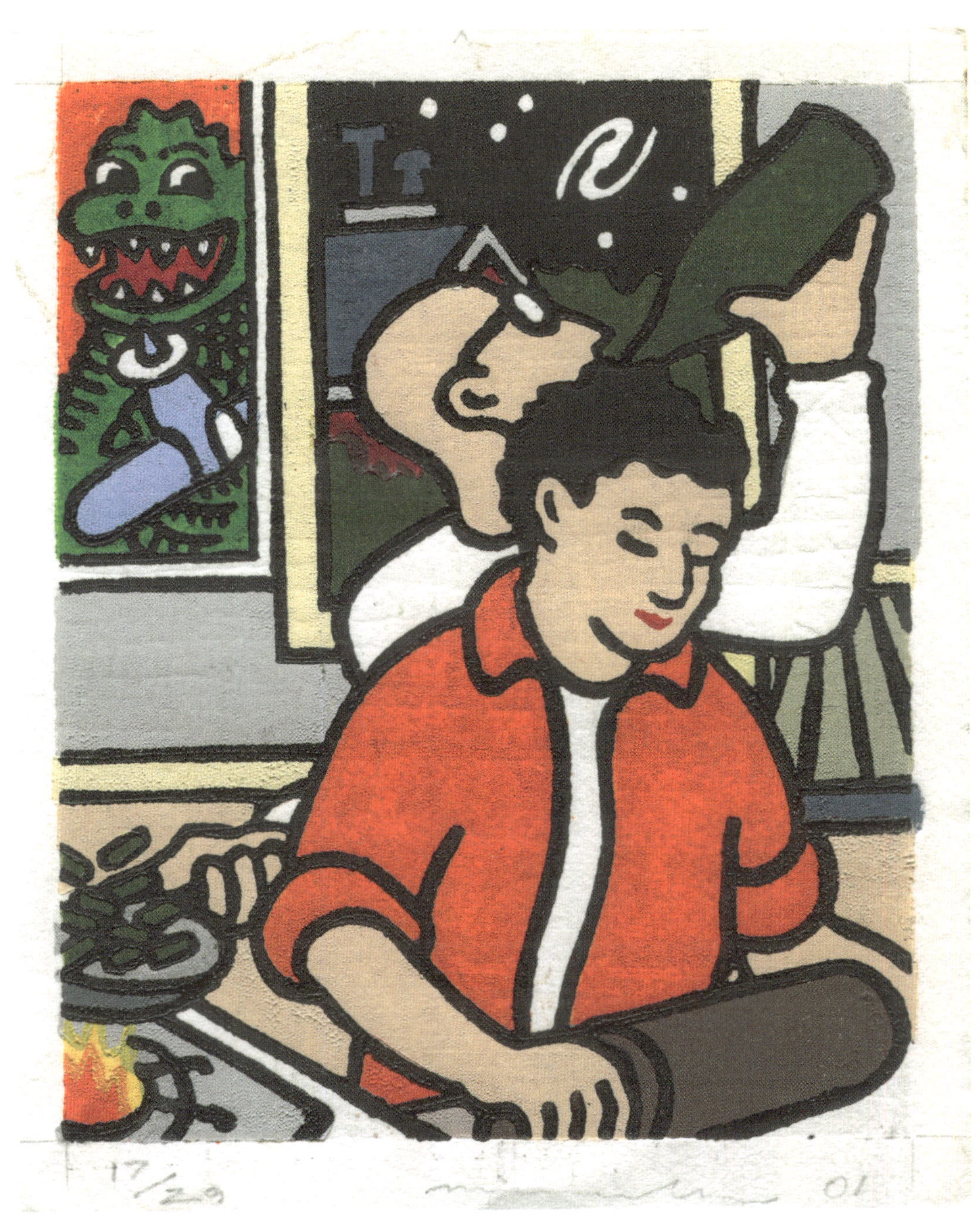

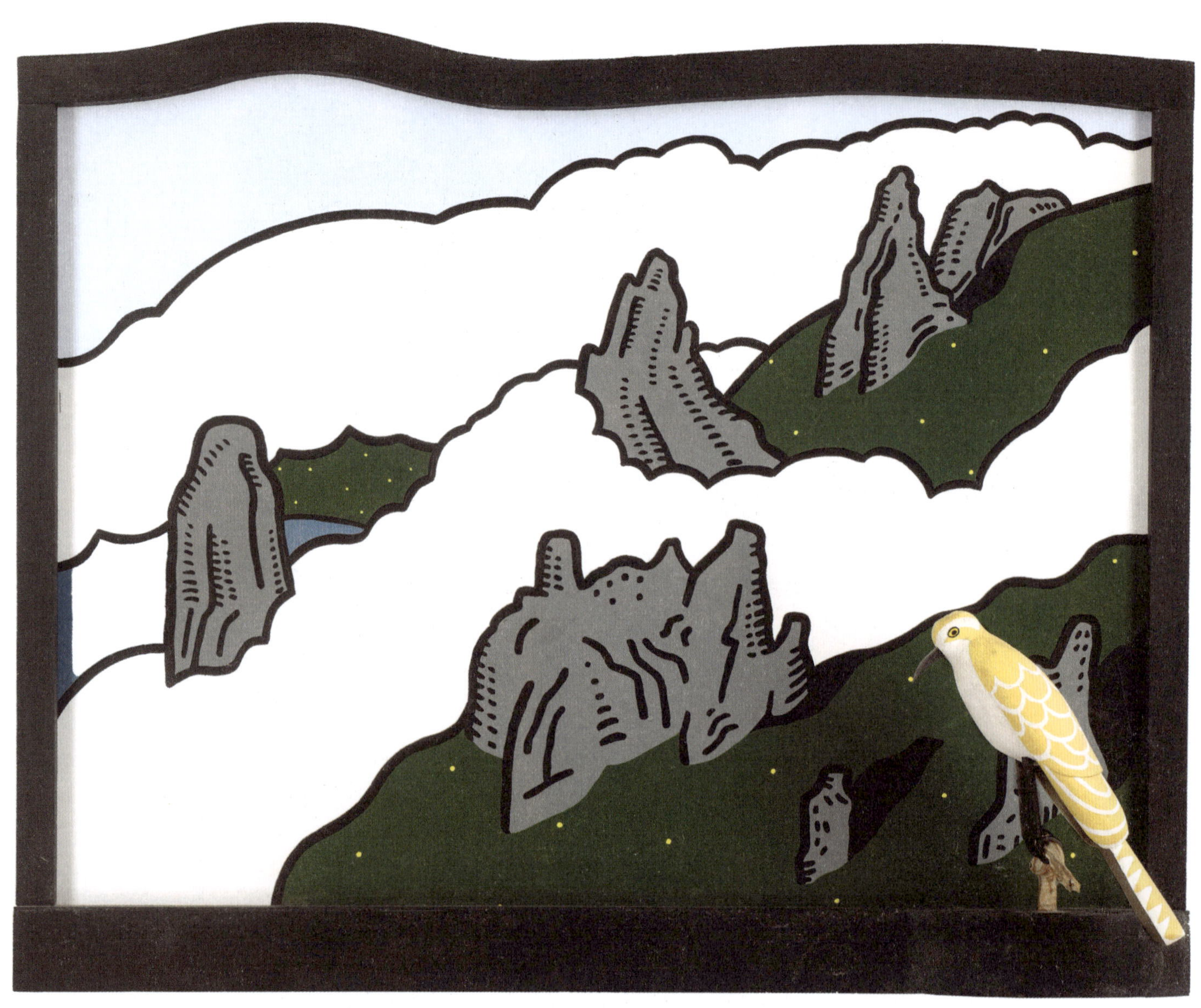

In the Grigna area of Northern Italy, we hiked in the forest among the impressive pinnacles to the persistent call of the cuckoo birds. Many cuckoos make those pinnacles and that forest their home.

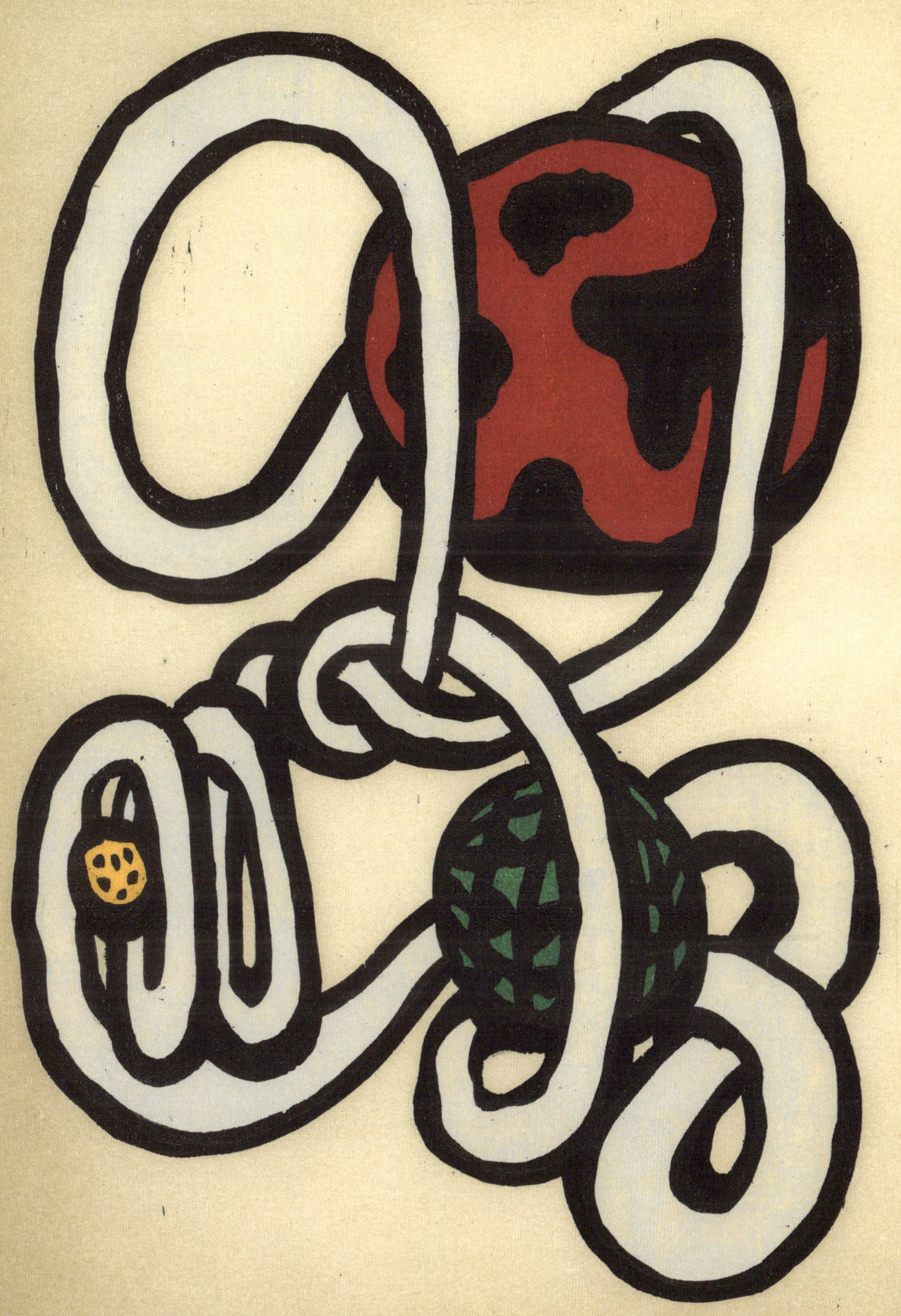

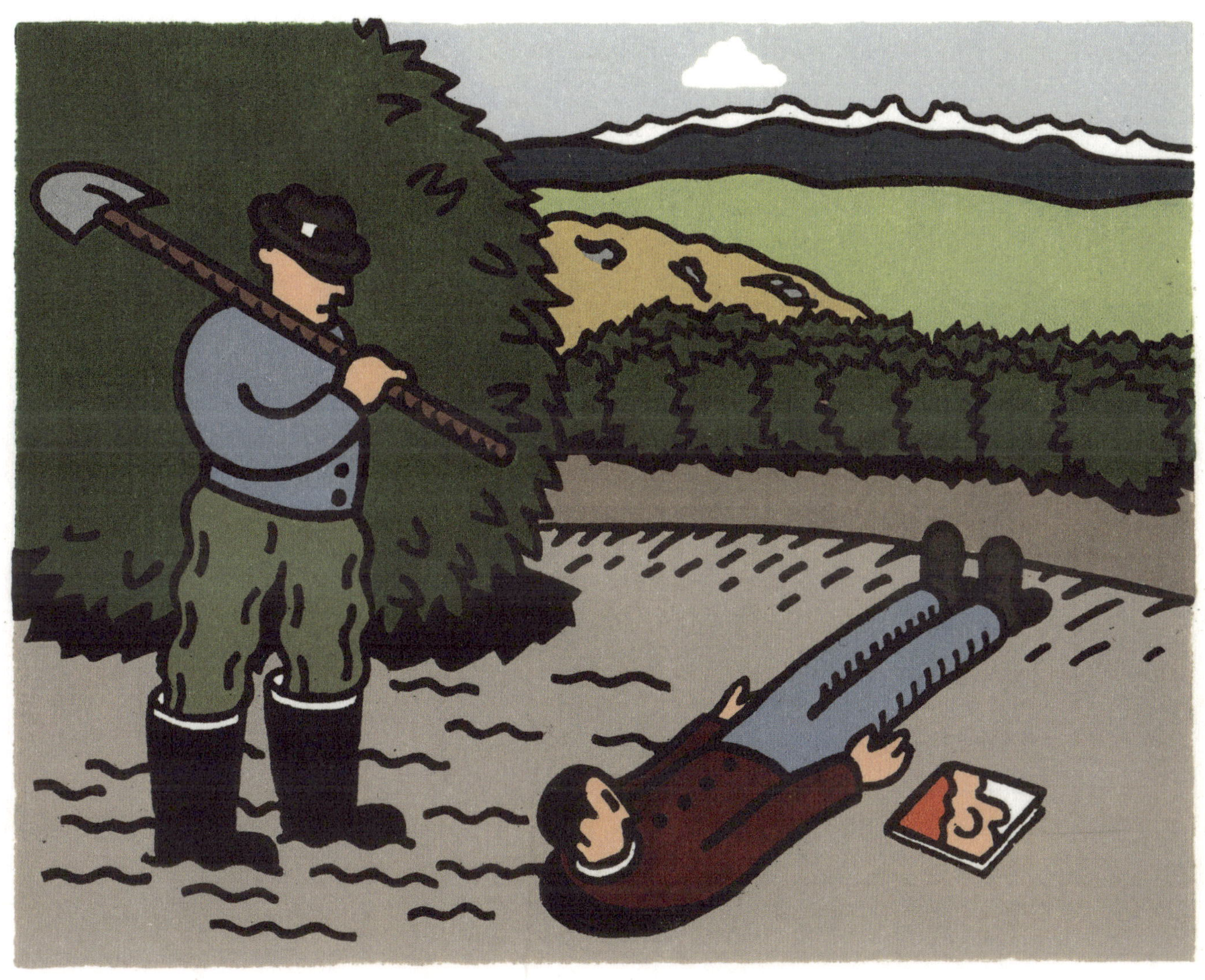

1. 1951 : Laying about in a straightforward reclining position

My stepfather owned an orange orchard near the foothills of the western Sierra. He was an advocate of the Puritanical work ethic.

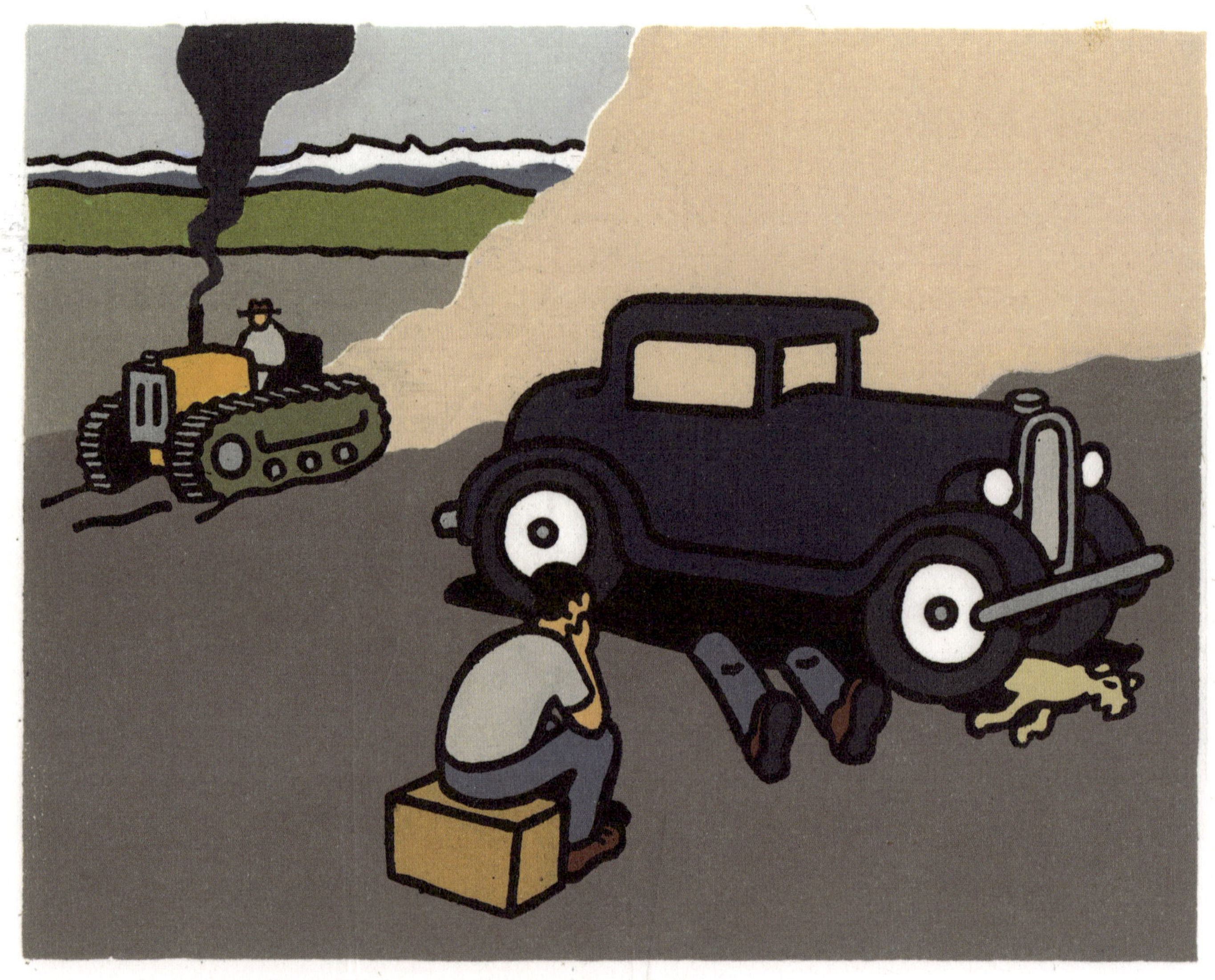

2. Unengaged and unindentured to the prevailing indentured servitudes

My pals were all involved with their family farms or slaving away in fruit packing houses to support their cars or girlfriends.

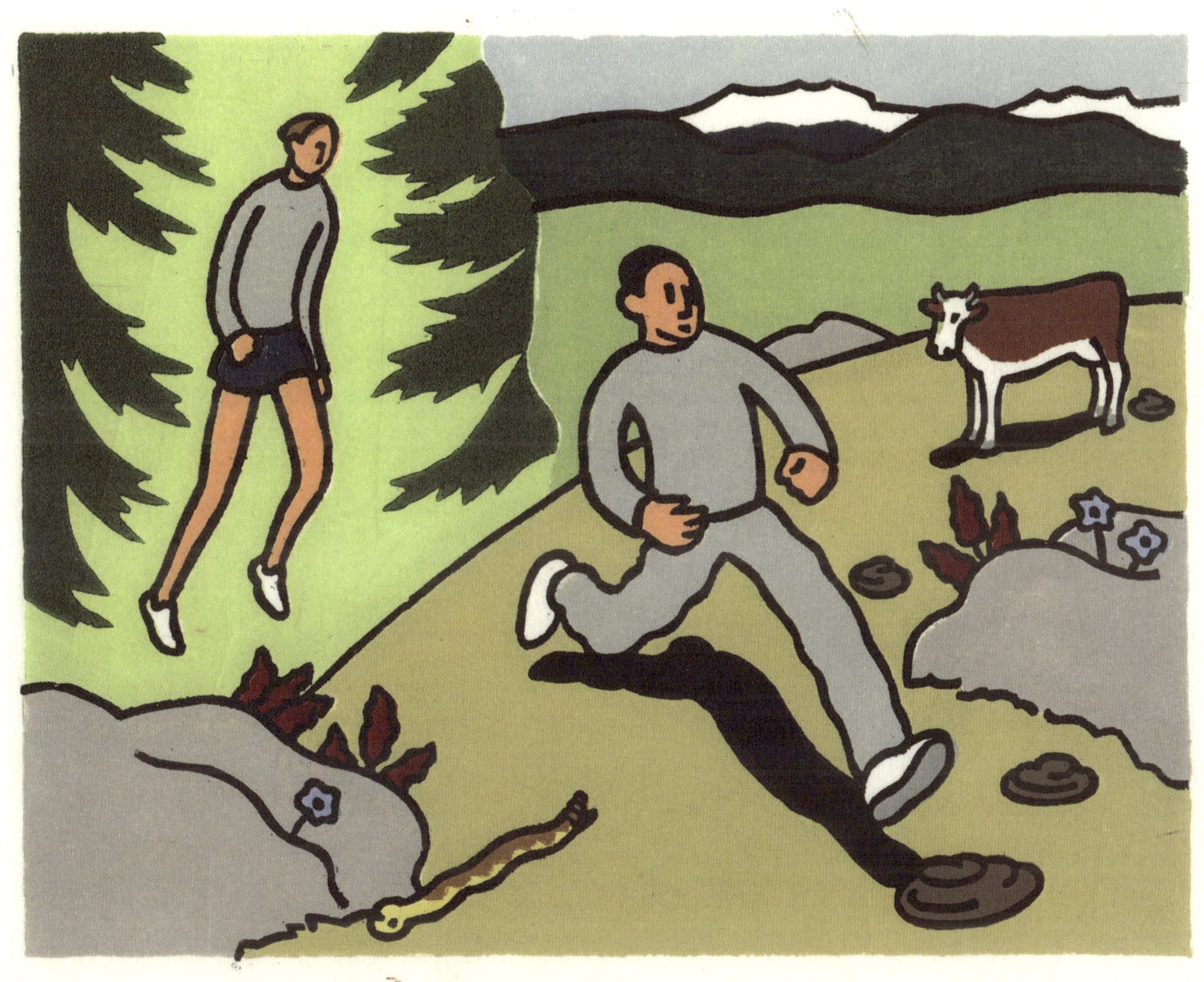

3. Running with Hägg in the imaginary Swedish forest

In high school, track was my only sport. I often trained in the foothills, emulating my role model Gunder Hägg, who held the mile and 5,000-meter records at the time. Nobody just ran in those days.

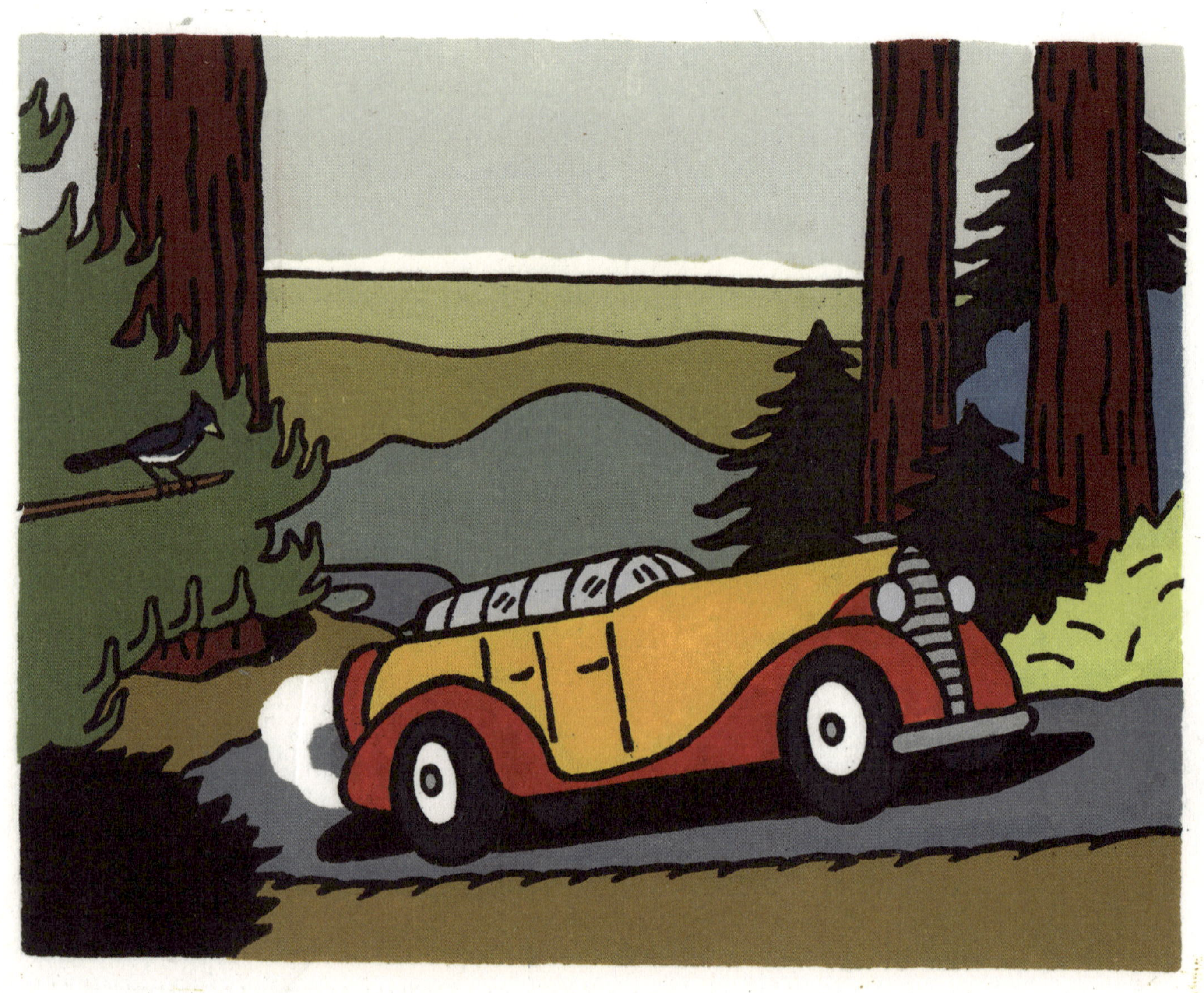

4. Leaving the valley work ethic for a mountain work ethic

Saved from the flatlands by finagling a job for the summer at the Giant Forest Concession in Sequoia National Park.

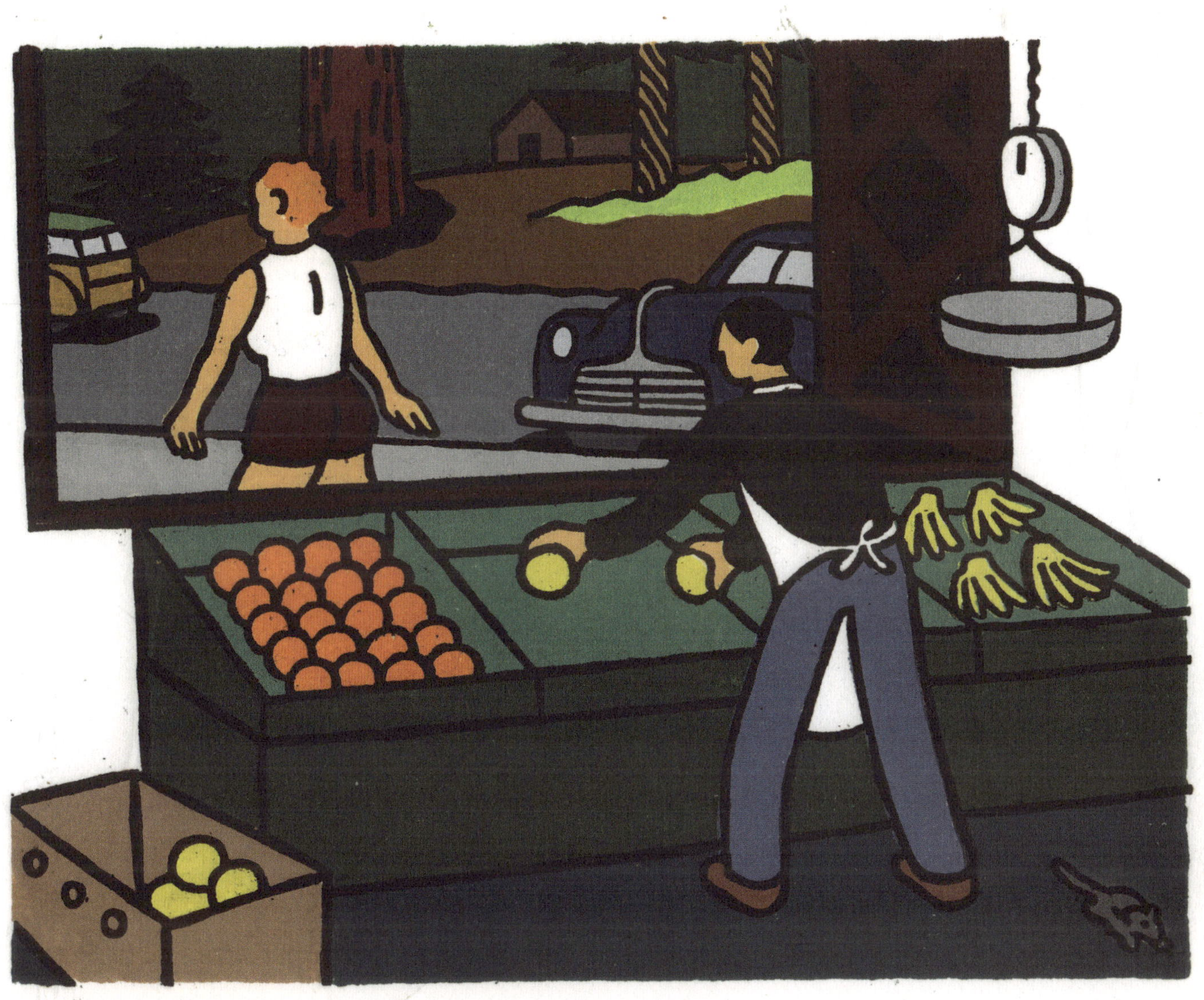

5. The fruit stand with the view

Assigned to be in charge of the fruit stand at the Market.

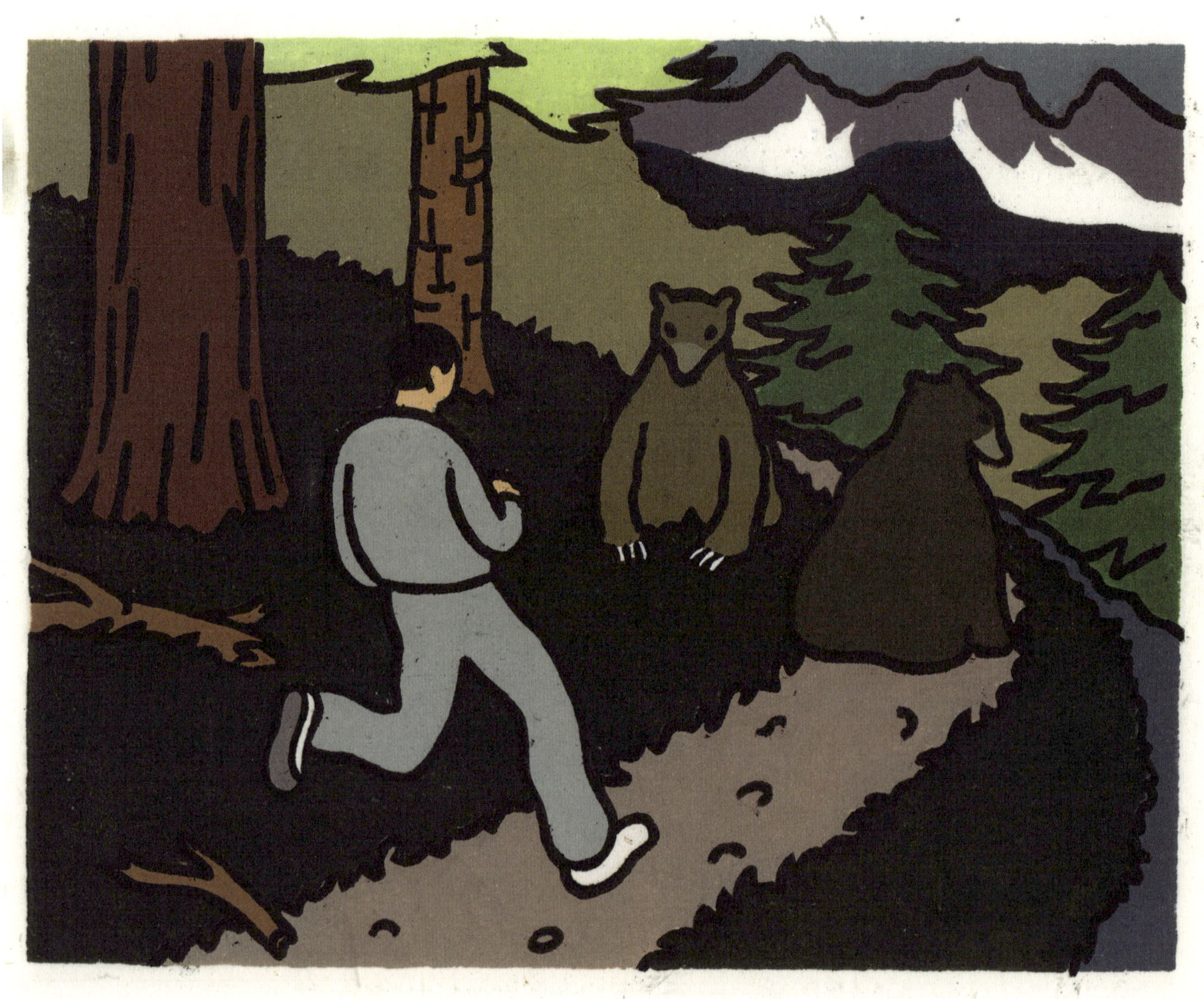

Continued with running in the evenings after work.

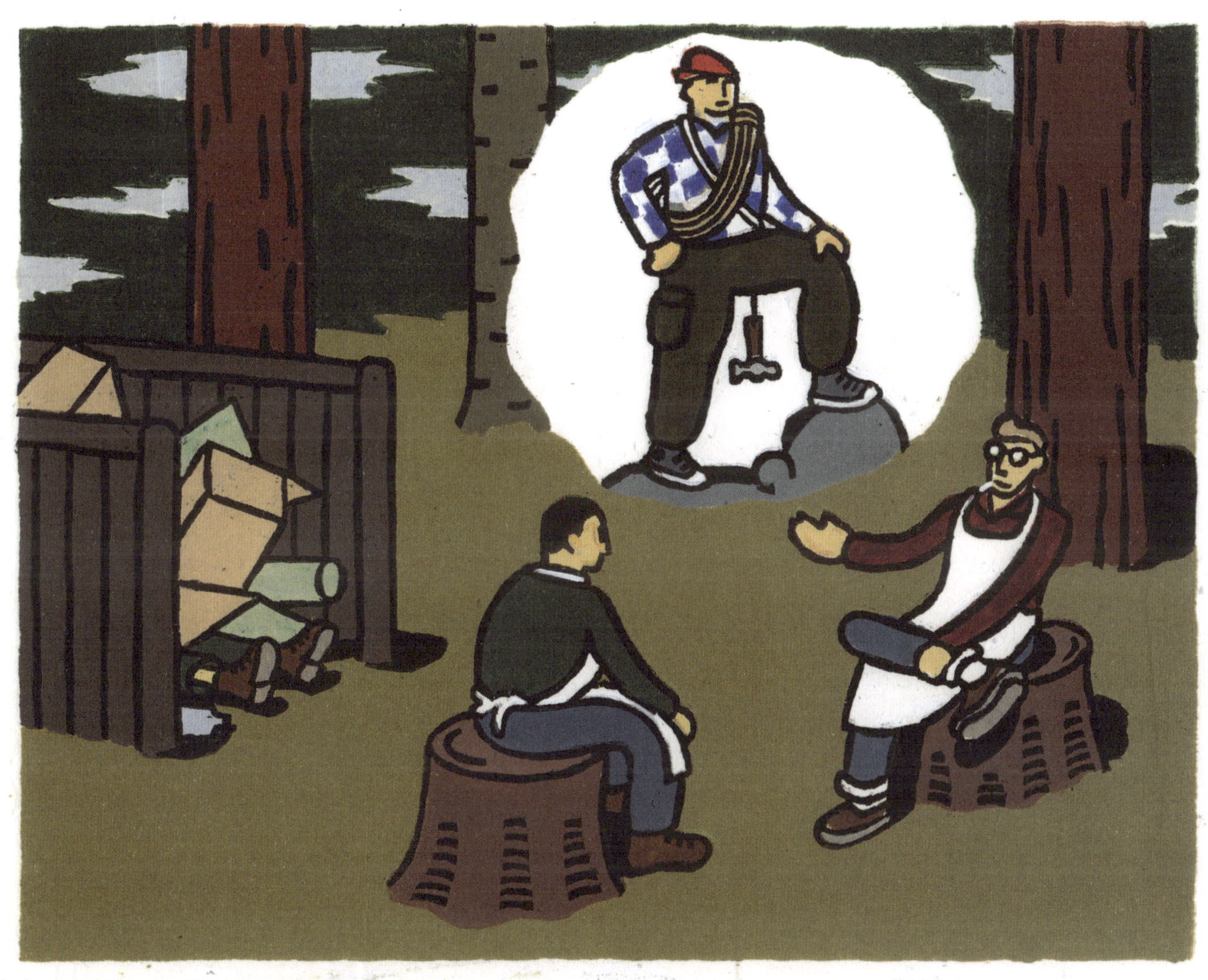

7. An associate proposes the novel idea of mountain climbing

At the Market I became friends with Allen, who worked at the meat counter. He was from Florida and came west to climb mountains. The guy in the rubbish bin was a four-season employee sleeping one off.

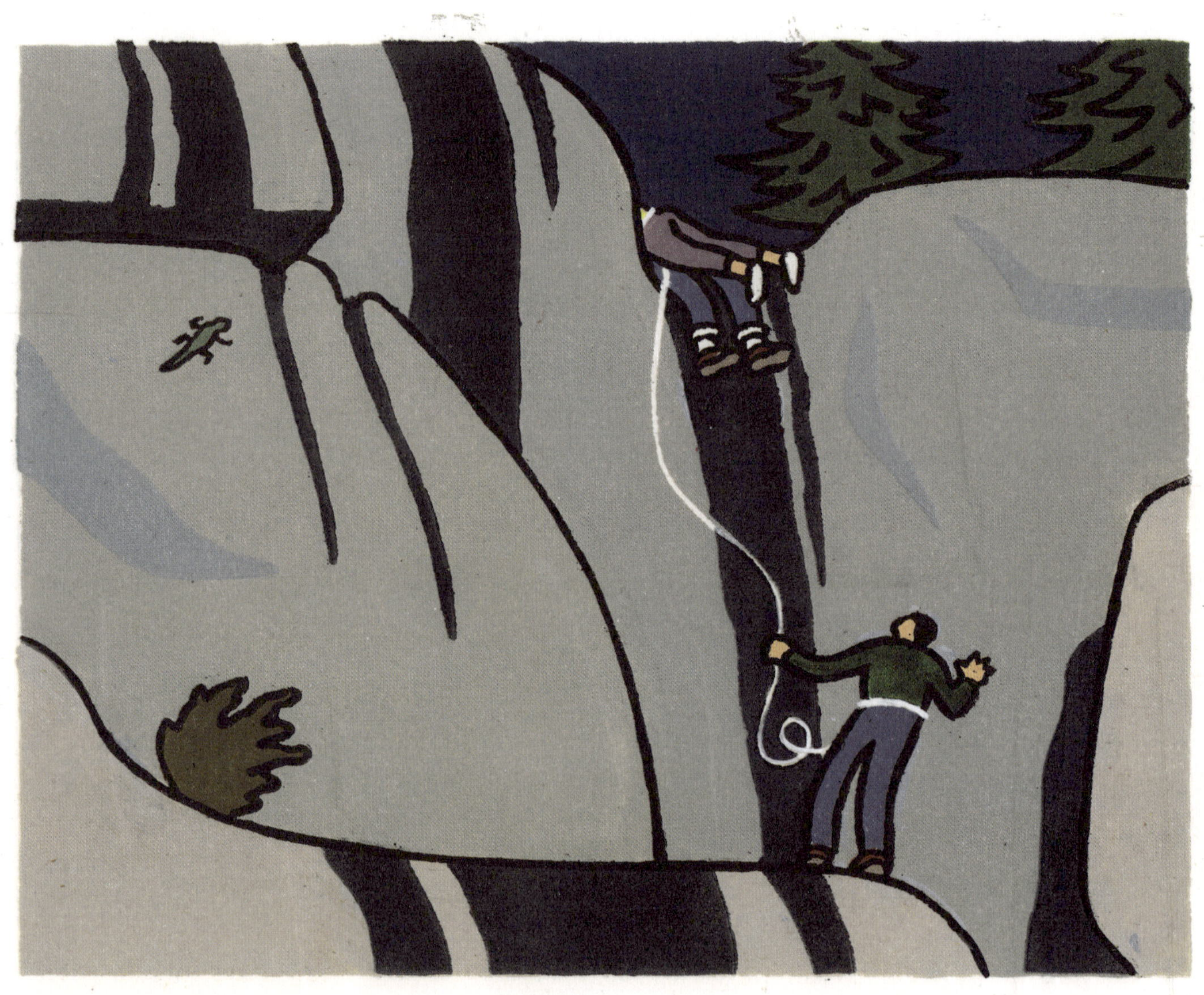

8. A training session fully equipped with clothesline and girlfriend

We actually bought ourselves a clothesline and made regular visits to a nearby slab. Allen enlisted girlfriends, who rarely lasted more than one session.

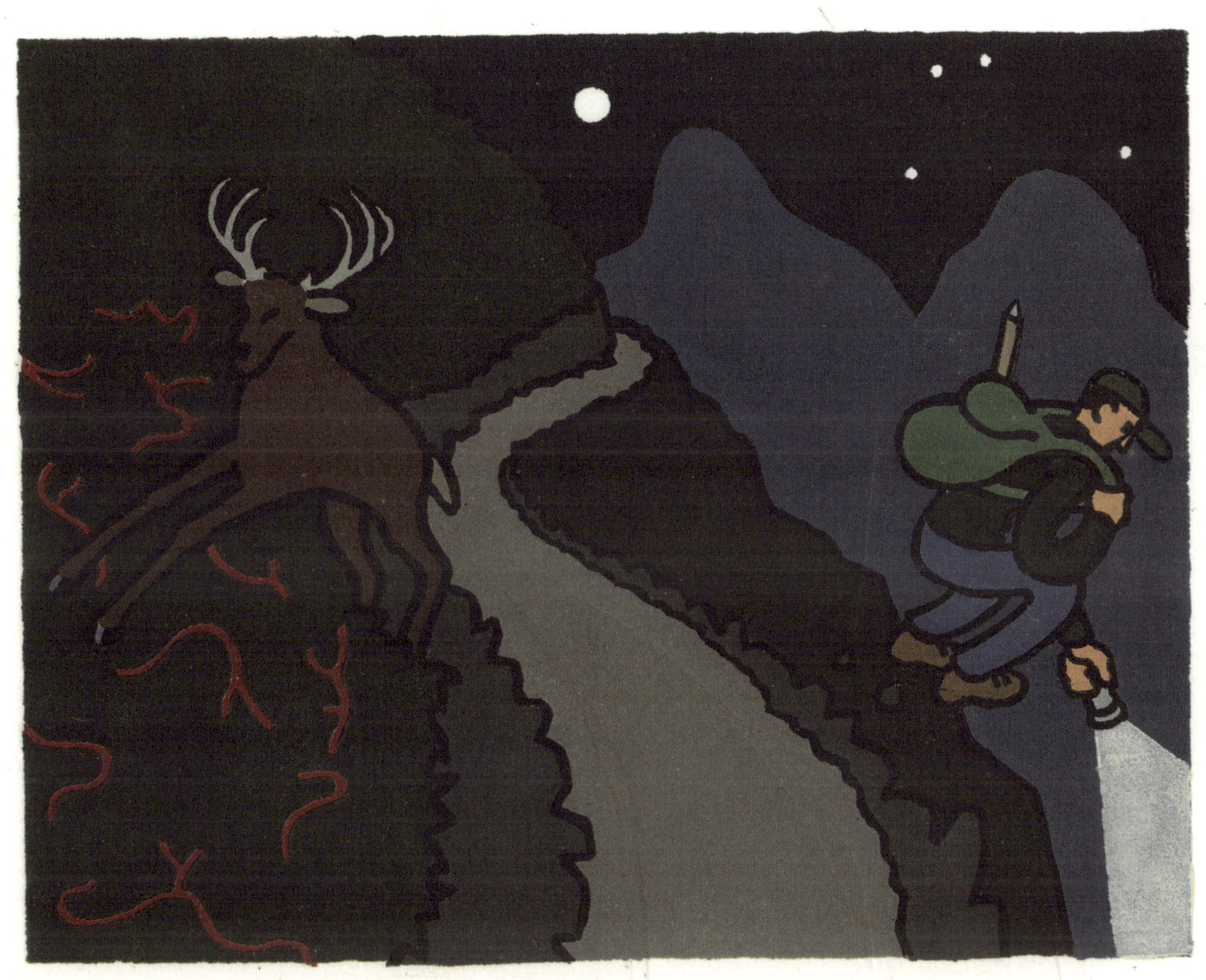

A night before my day off, I was determined to get to the real Sierra. Hiking at night with a dimming flash led to an almost-collision with a panicky mule deer.

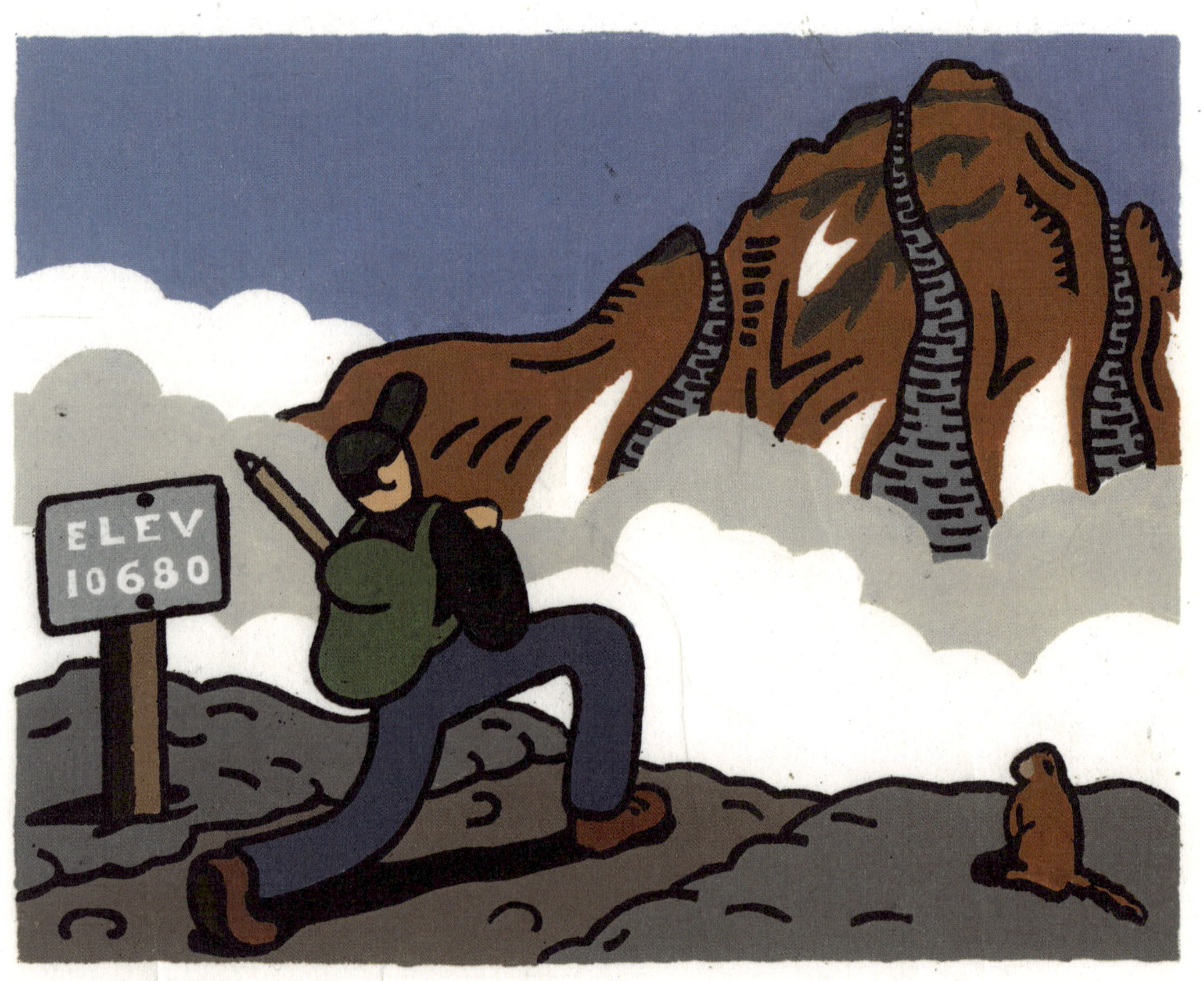

10. Twenty miles out and up: Behold the overwhelming presence

The next day I reached a pass called Kaweah Gap, and there was the peak I had selected from a topo map: Black Kaweah (13,680′).

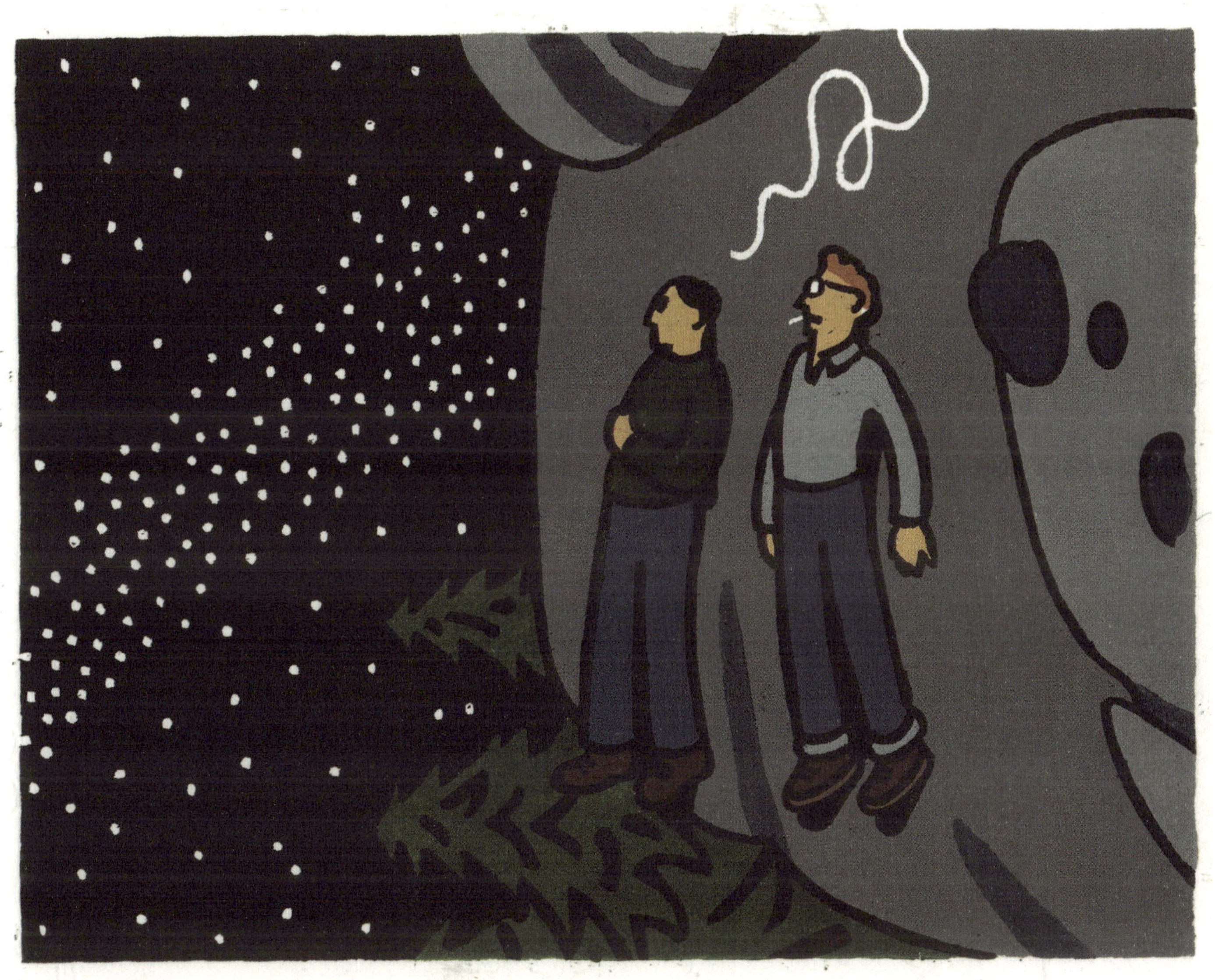

11. Back to laying about while laying plans... as the earth turns

During the next few weeks, Allen and I planned our assault—a stretch with only one day off, but a "piece of cake" from Kaweah Gap.

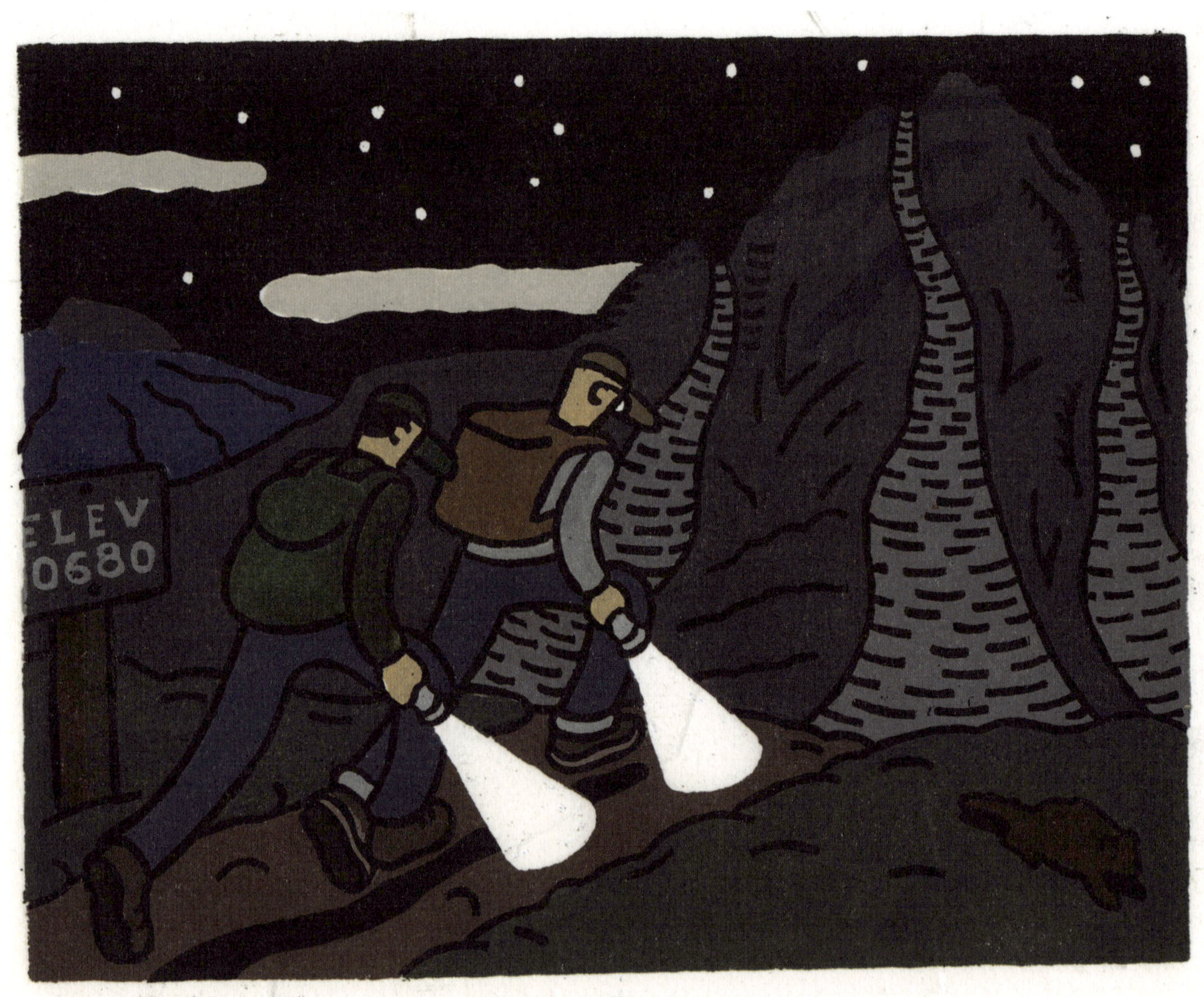

12. A nine hour trot puts the aspirants into position

Toward the end of summer we were in superb condition. We arrived at the base of the peak at 2 A.M.

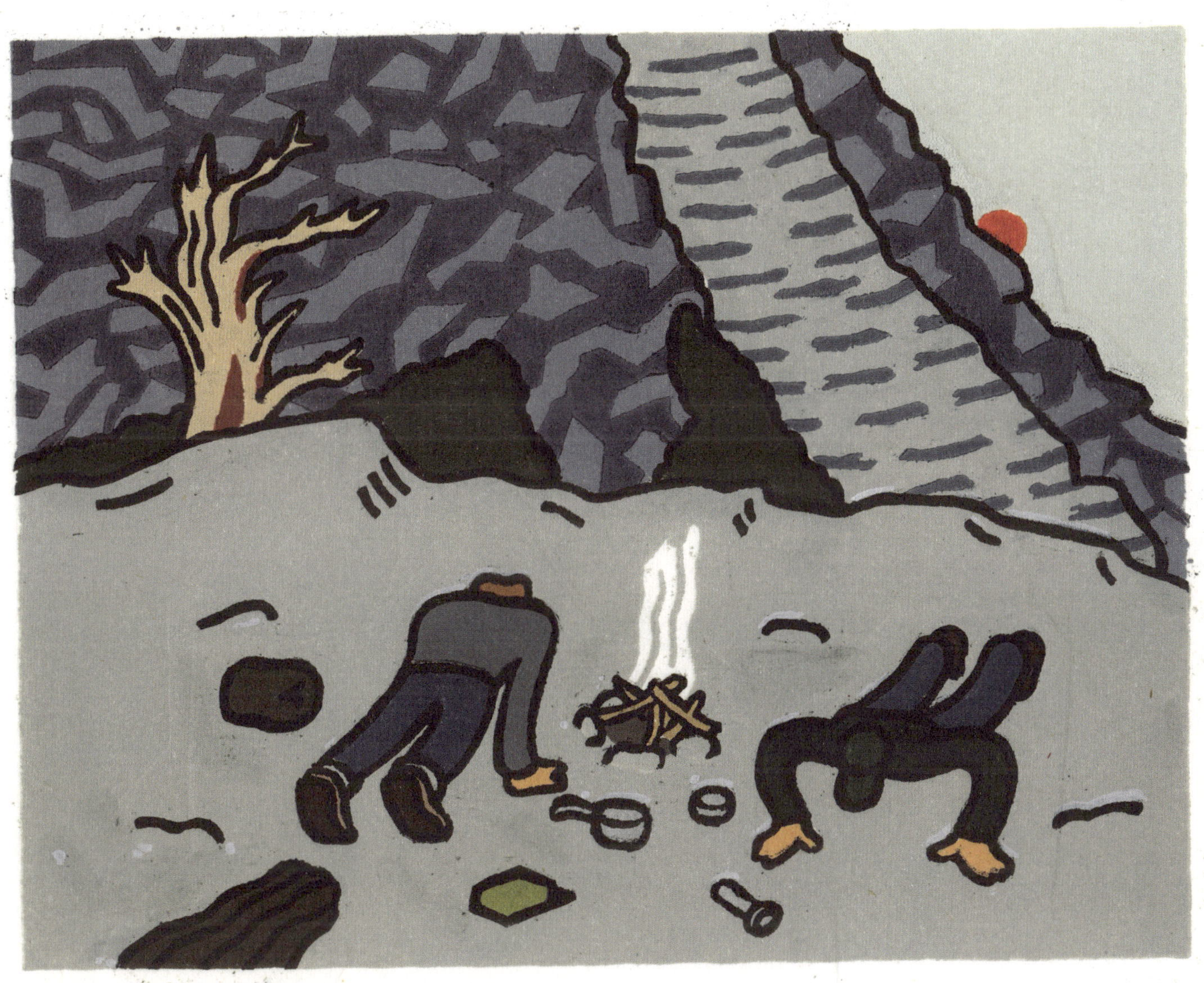

13. Preparatory push ups at base camp

At daybreak we put on our boots, scraped up some oatmeal, and began climbing.

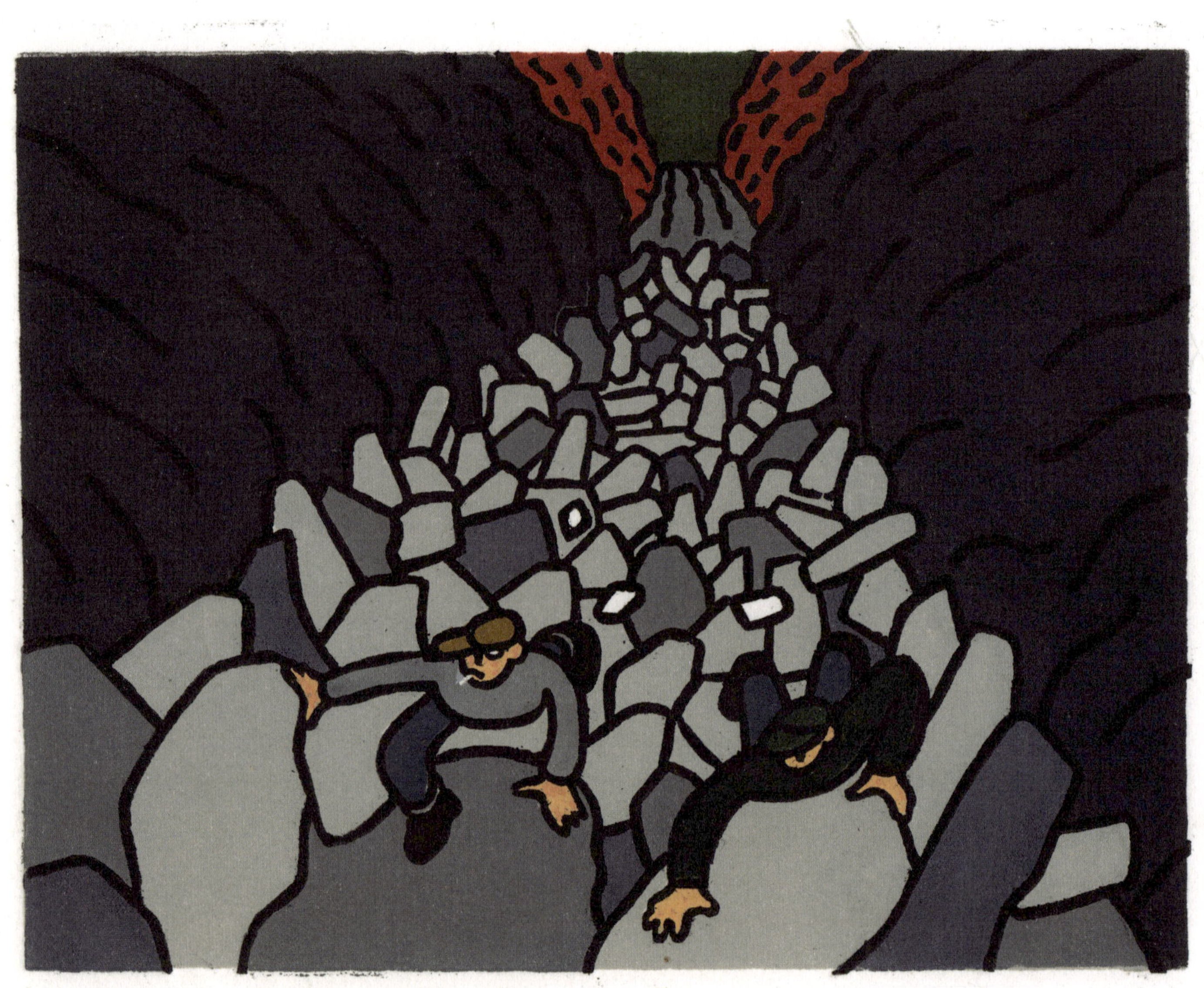

14. A three thousand foot slide and stumble upward

The talus slopes on the western spur of Black Kaweah are interminable.

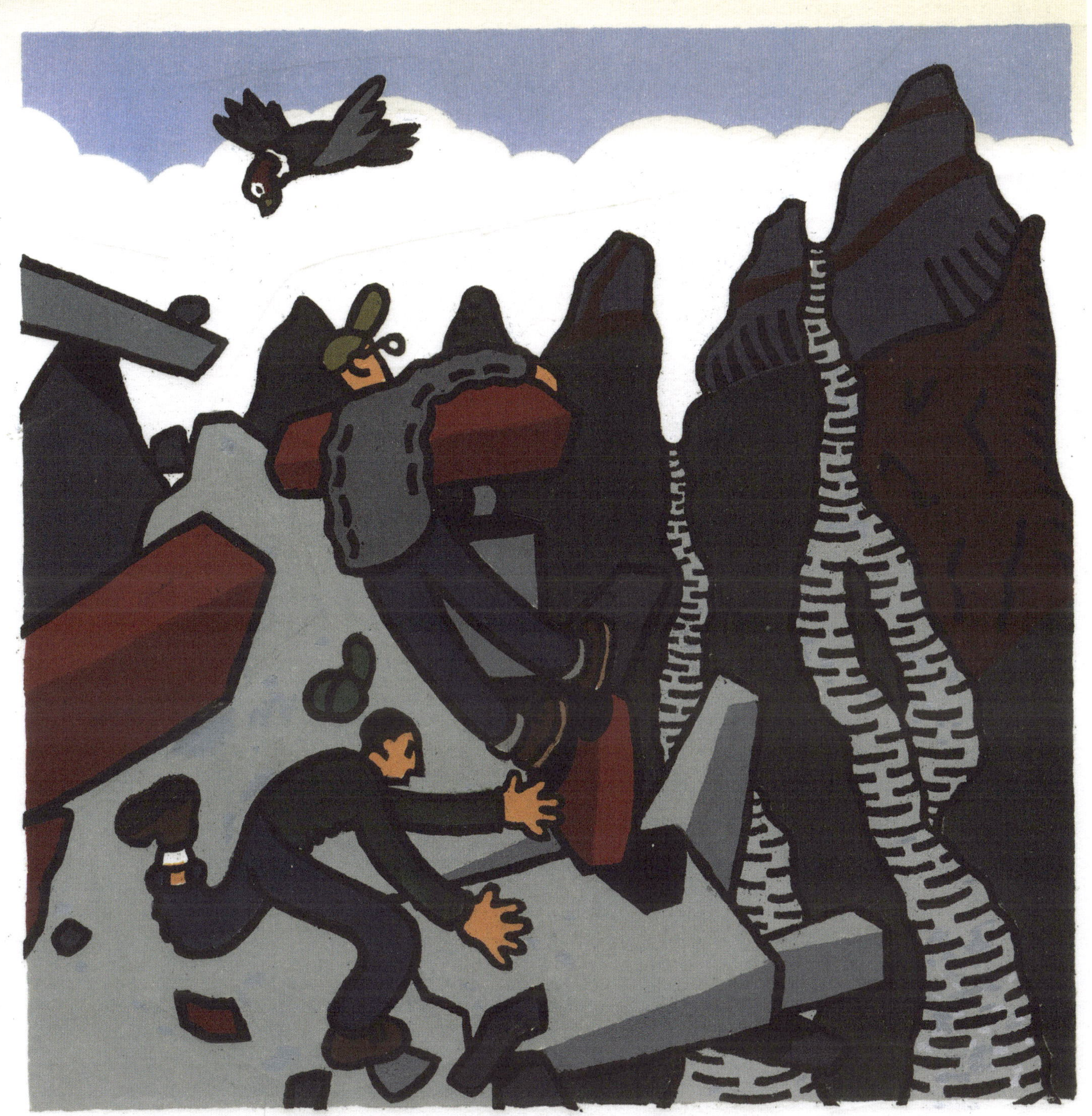

15. At the top of the overwhelming presence: Behold the distant summit

And here is the surprise the mountain held for these young upstarts. The "summit" visible from Kaweah Gap was not the summit at all! Innumerable towers and steep chutes of unstable rock were the name of the game here. It was turnaround time at 2 P.M. After all . . . we had to show up at the Market by 7 the next morning.

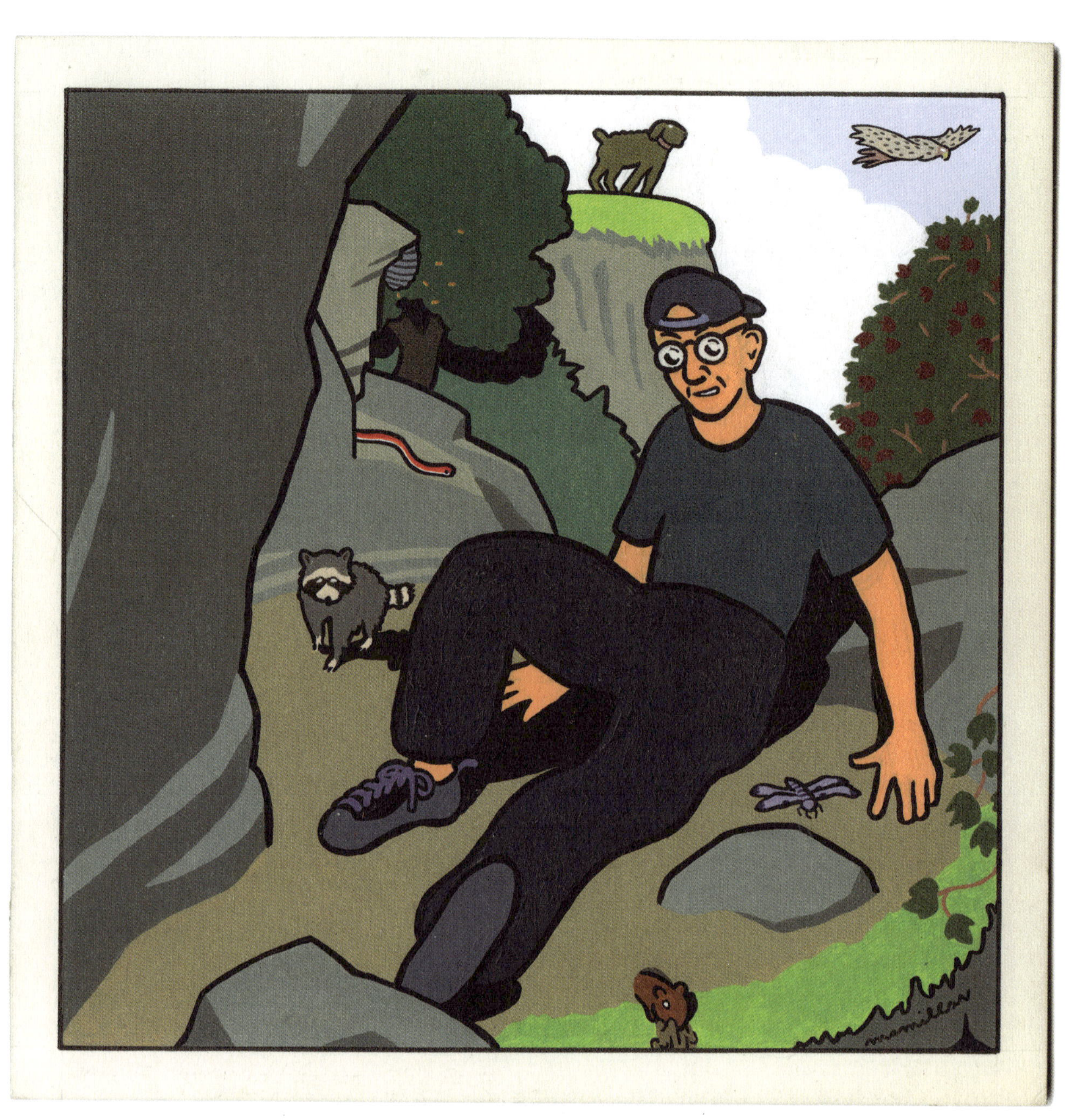

Adrenaline Junkie pays dues: a broken femur at Glen Park, San Francisco.

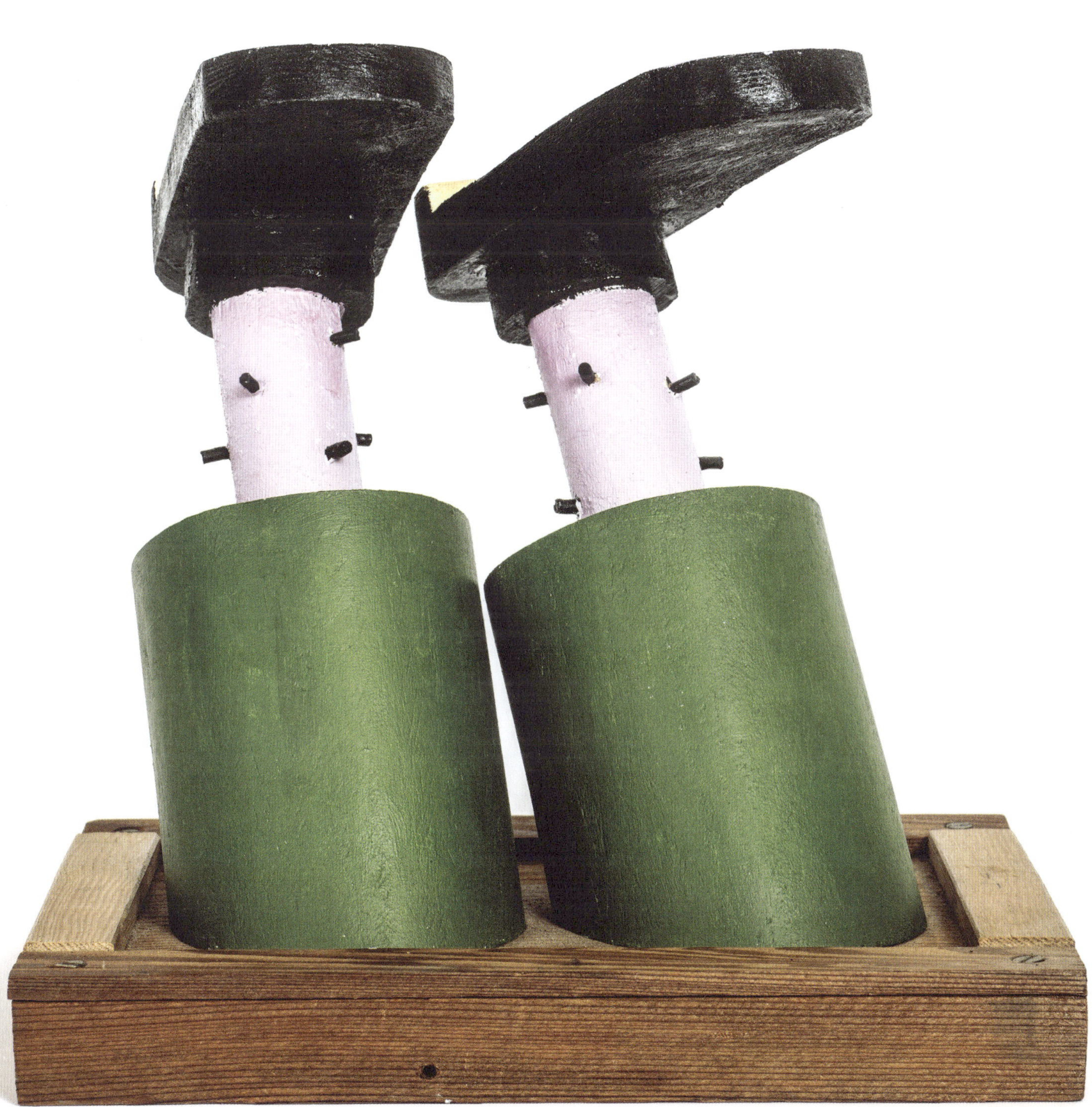

series ZZZZZ no.1 Thank You For Not Smoking © 1999

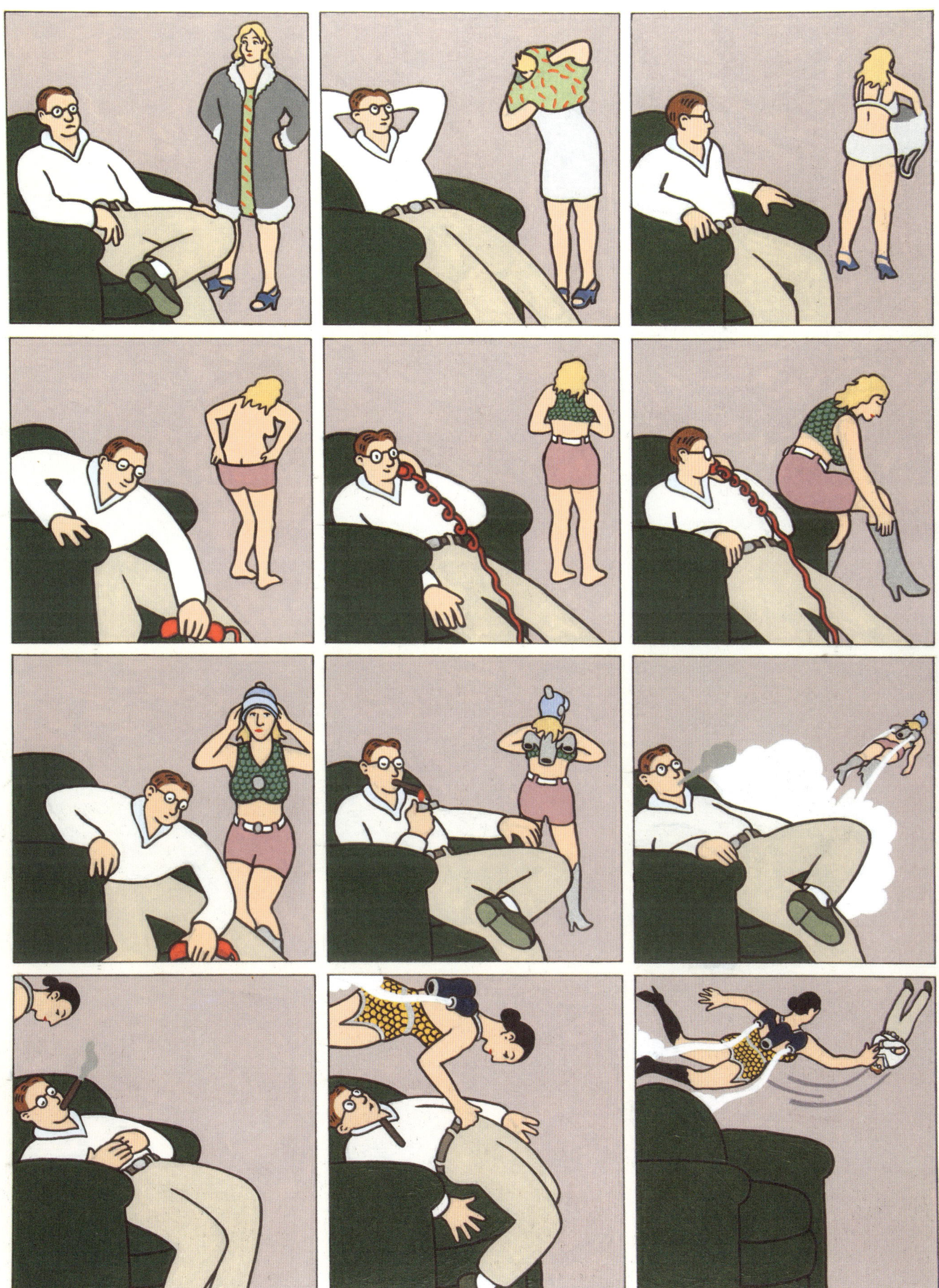

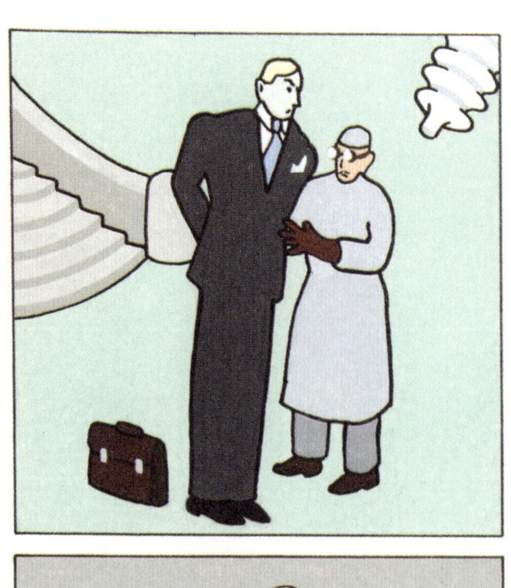
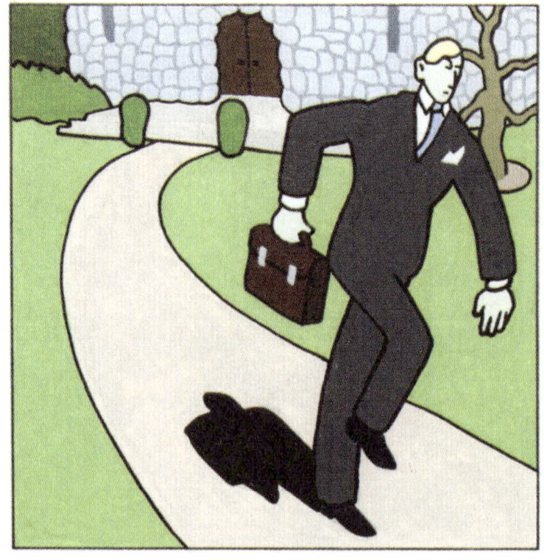
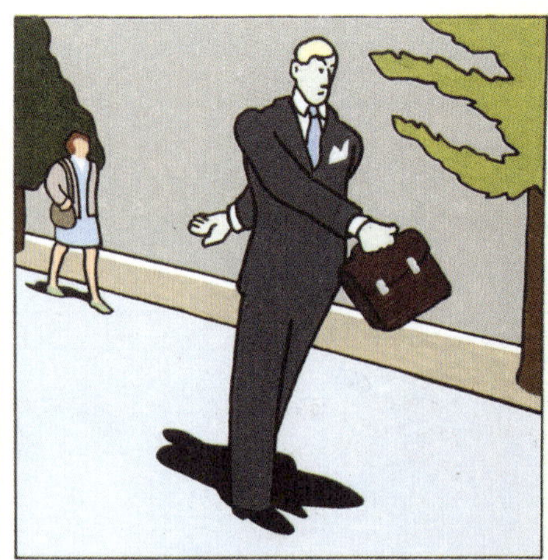
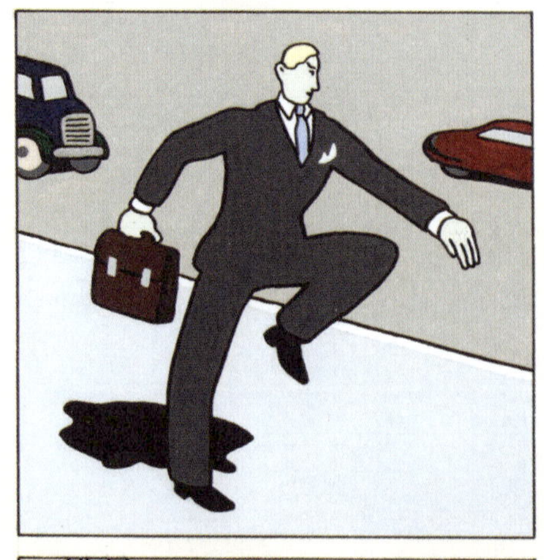
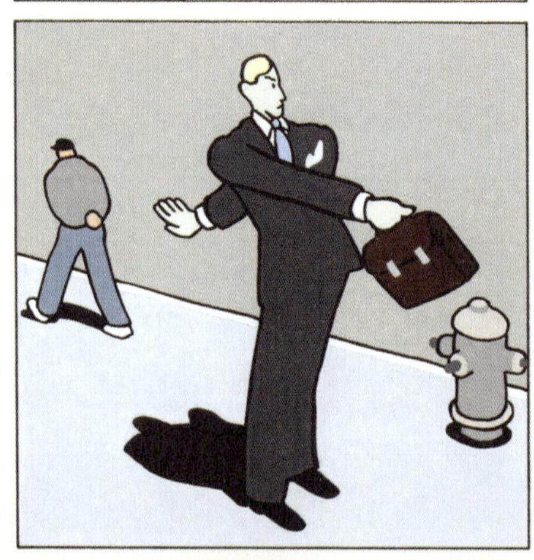
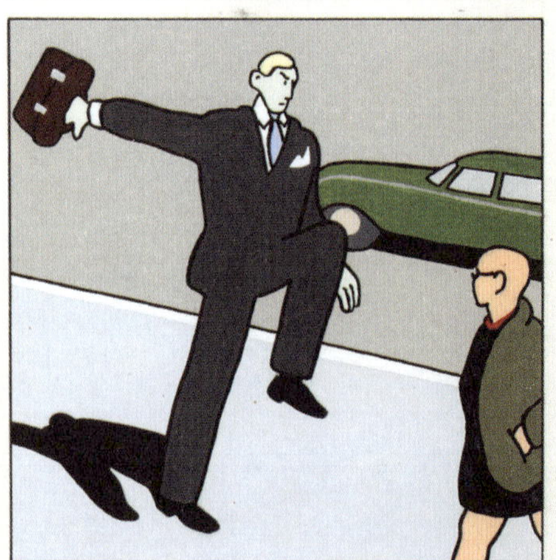
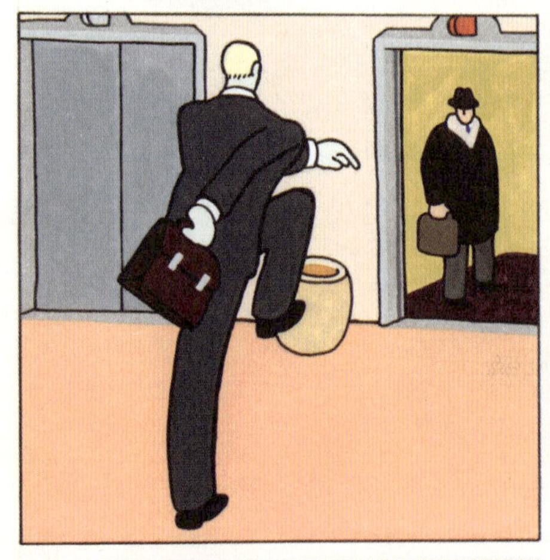
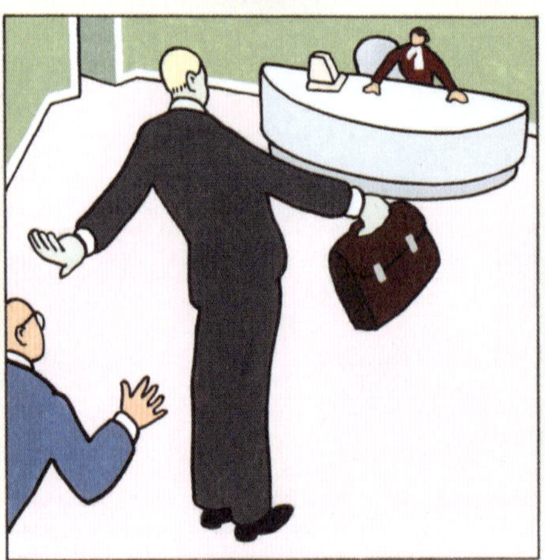
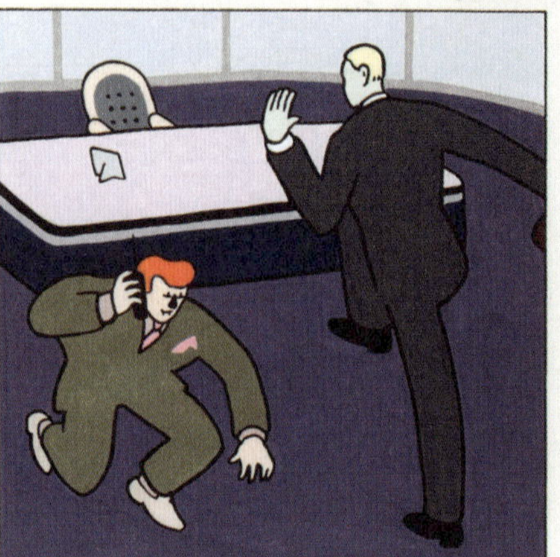
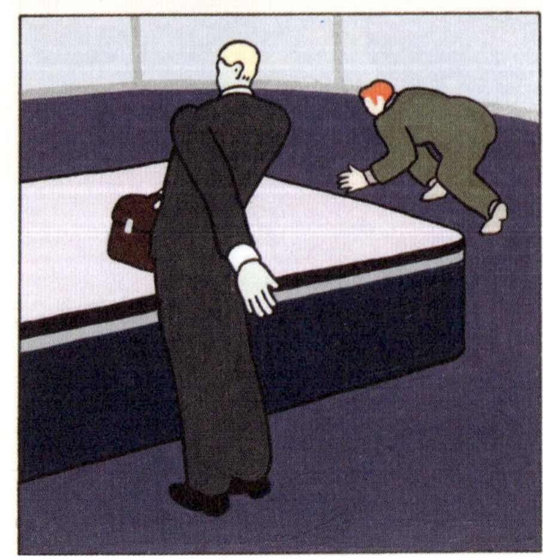
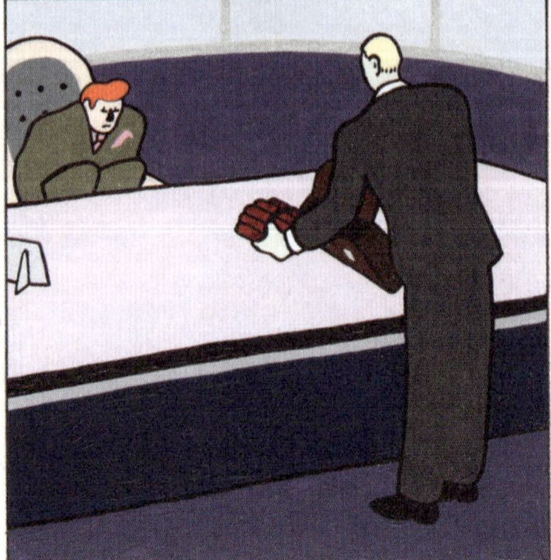
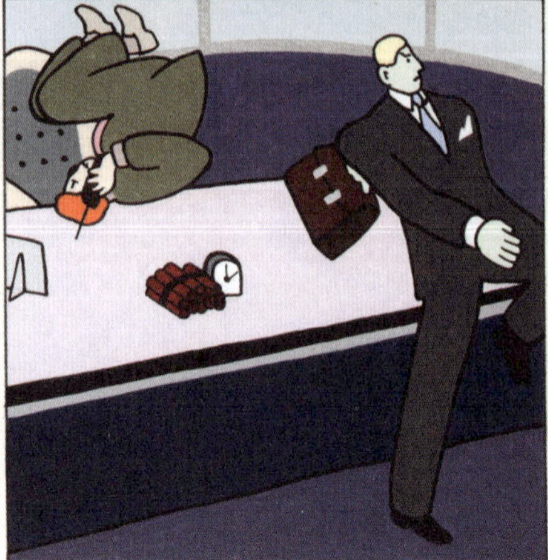

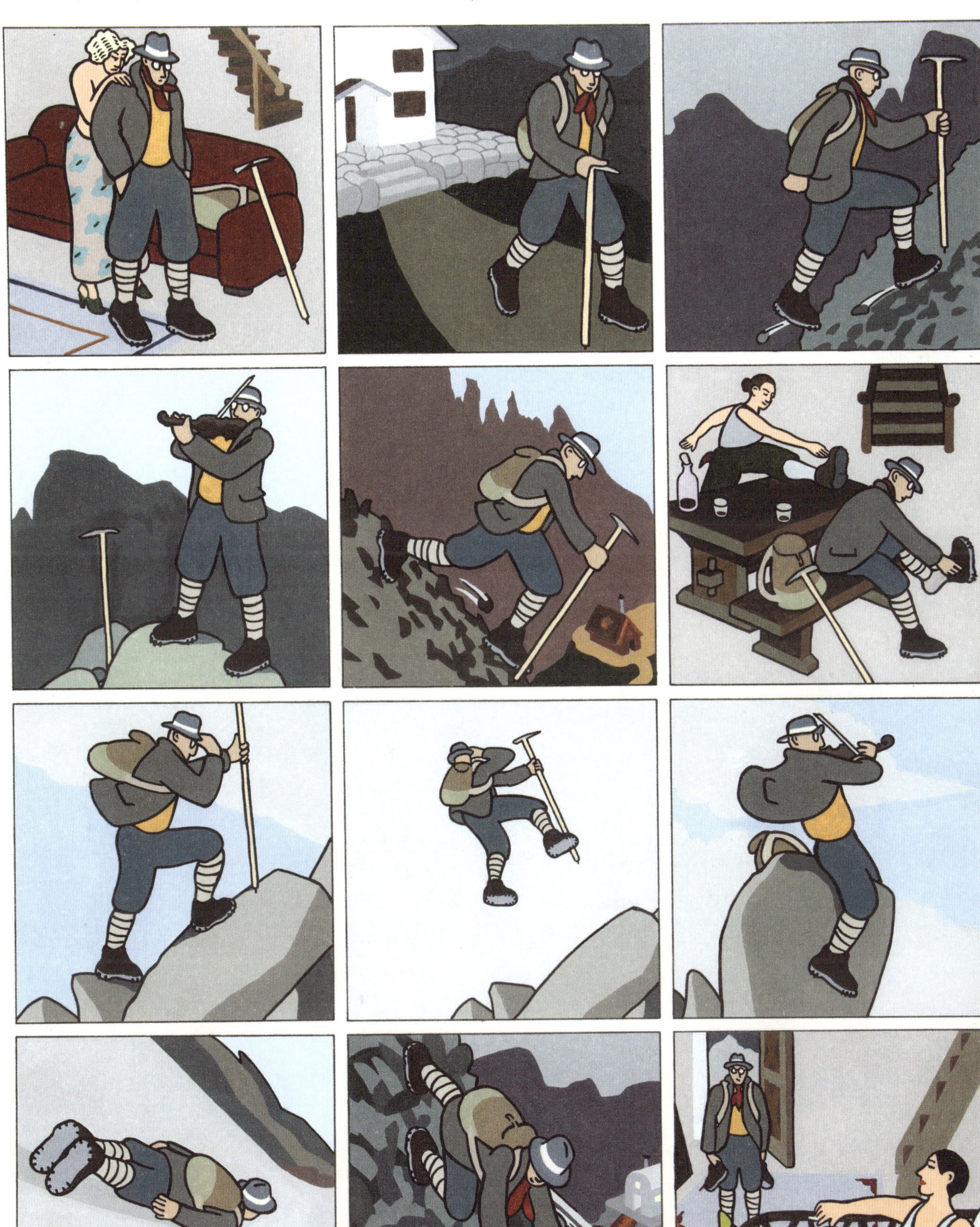

series ZZZZZ no.4 Domestic Ballet ©1999

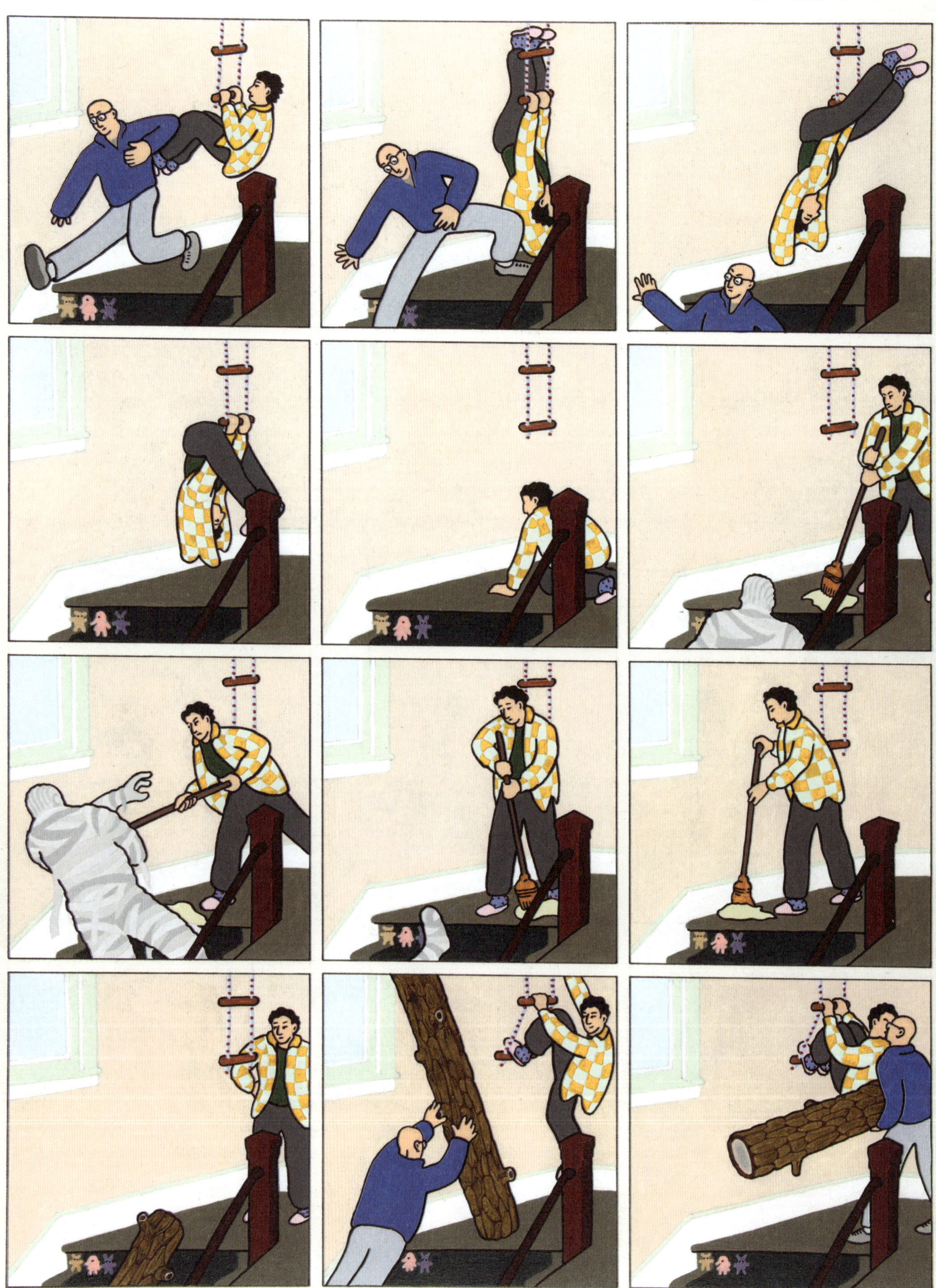

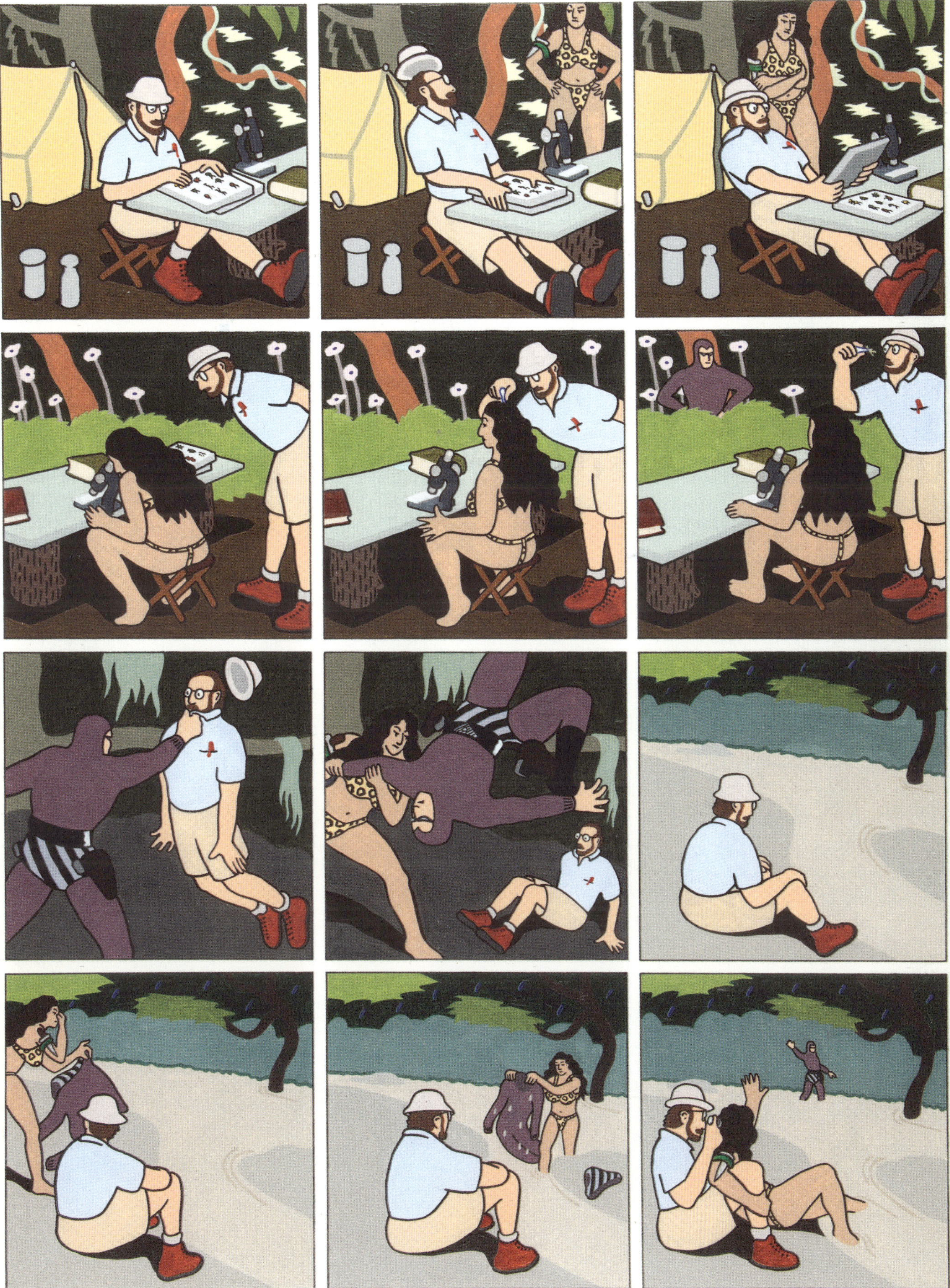

series ZZZZZ no. 6 Ballet Moderne' © 1999

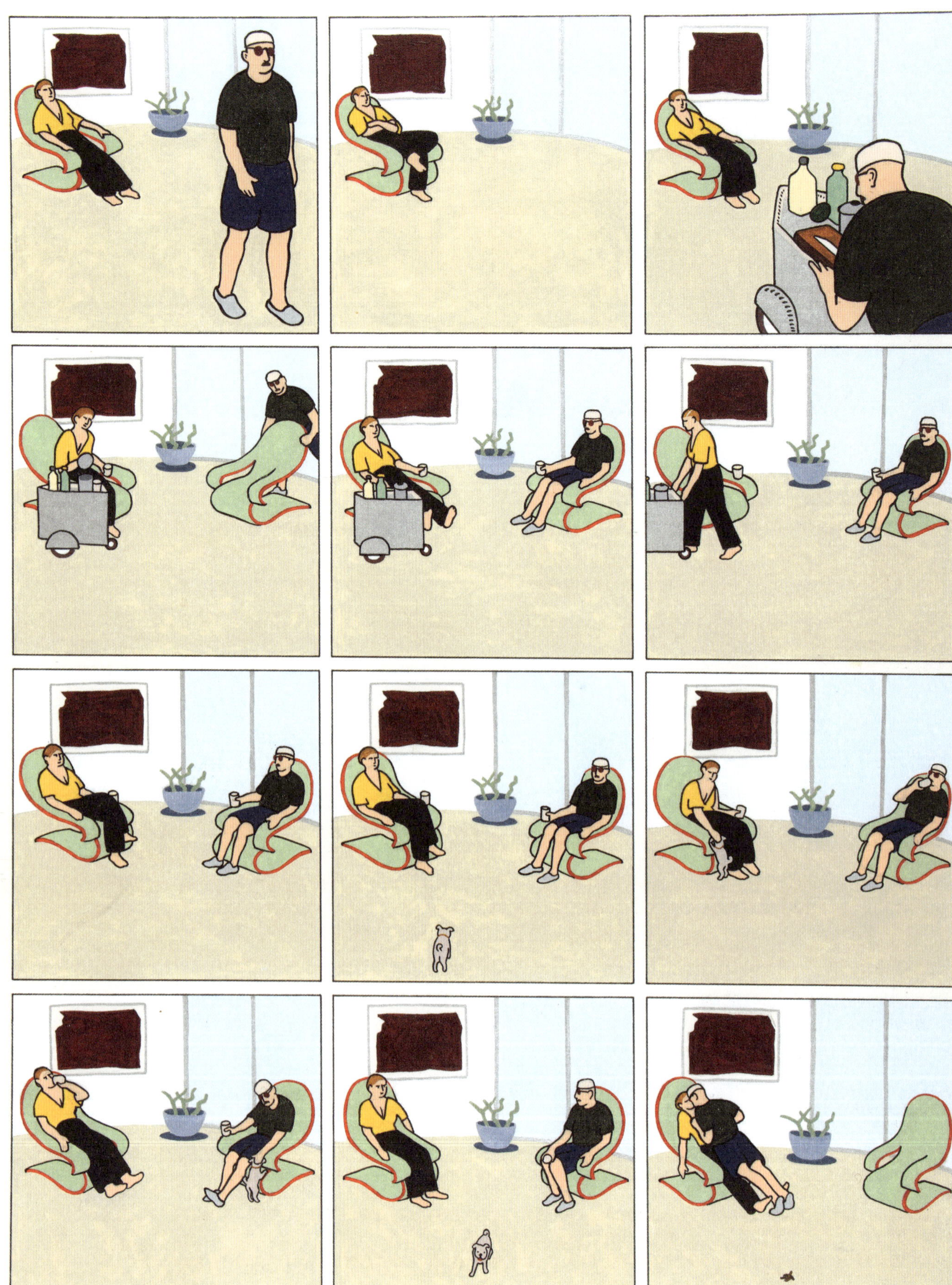

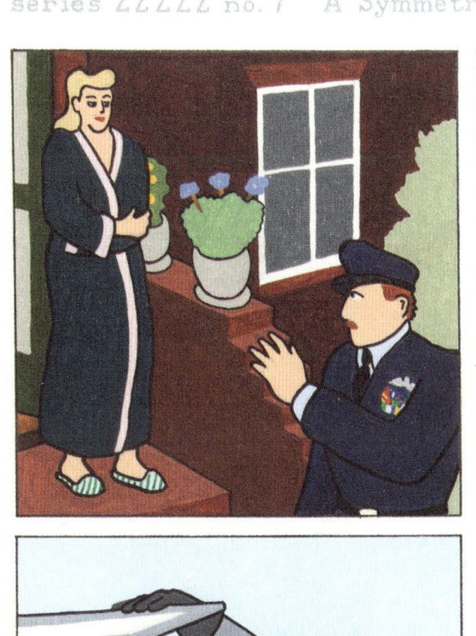
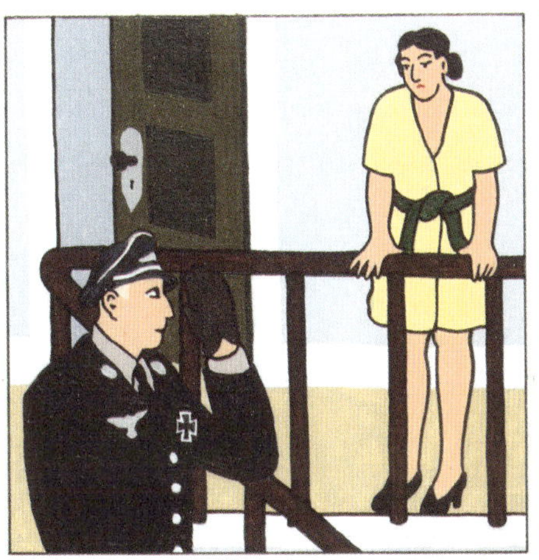
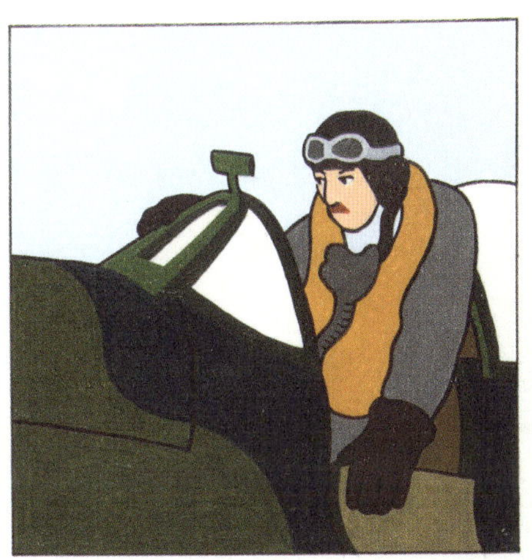
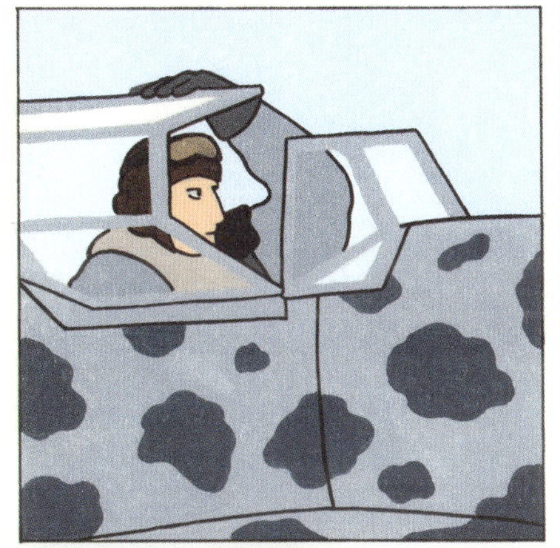
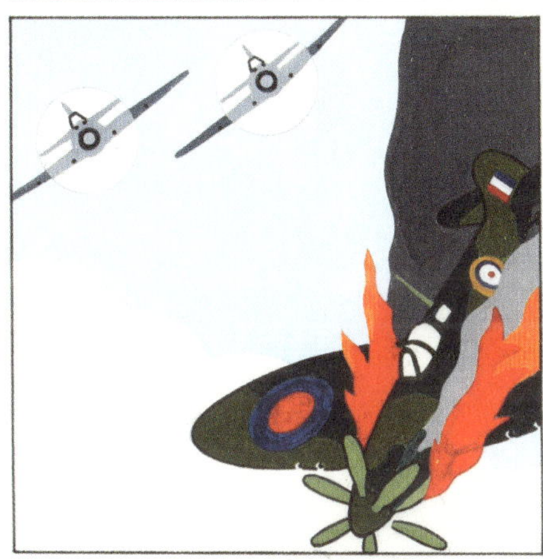
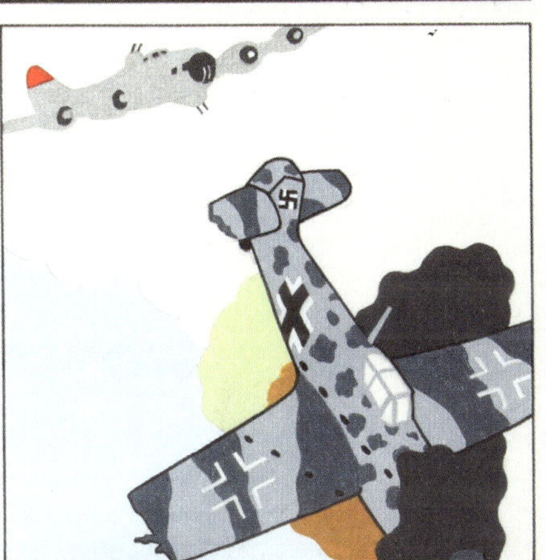
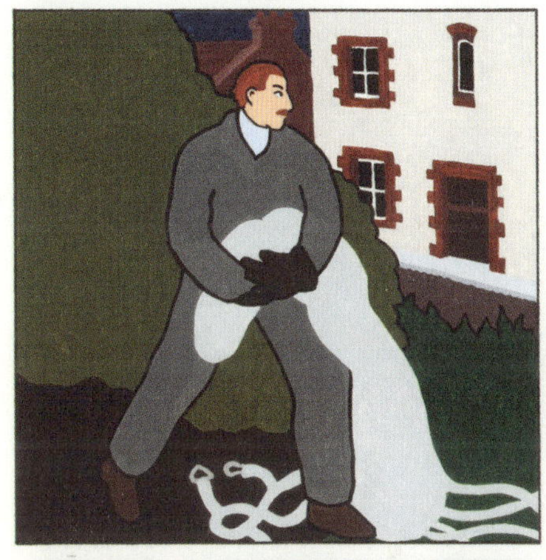
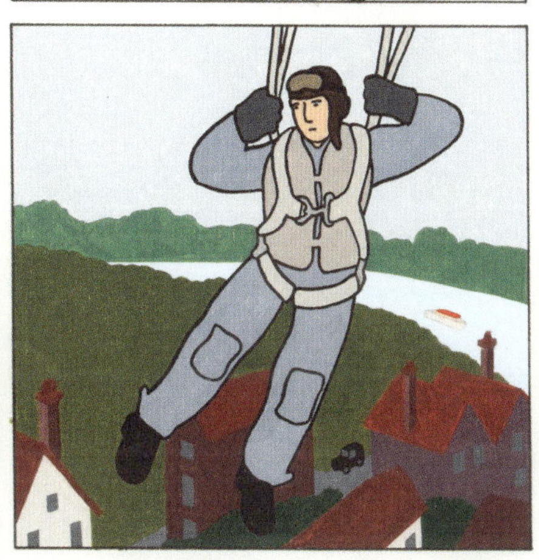
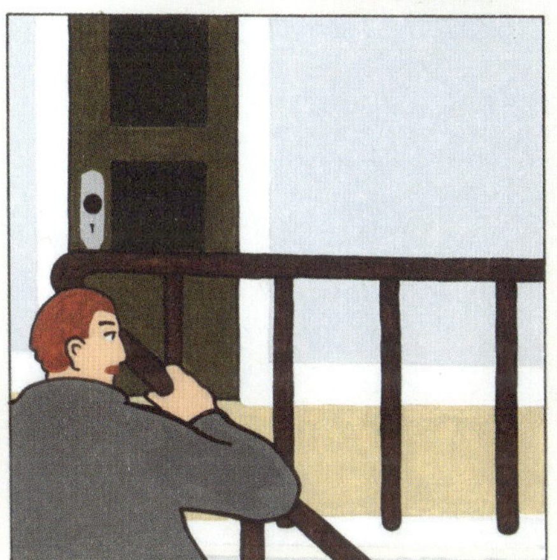
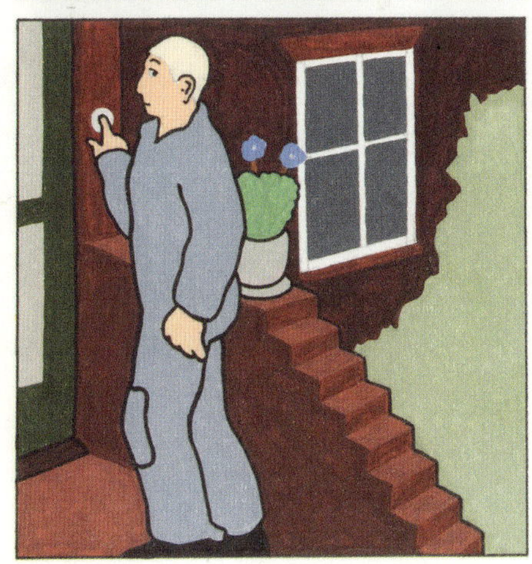
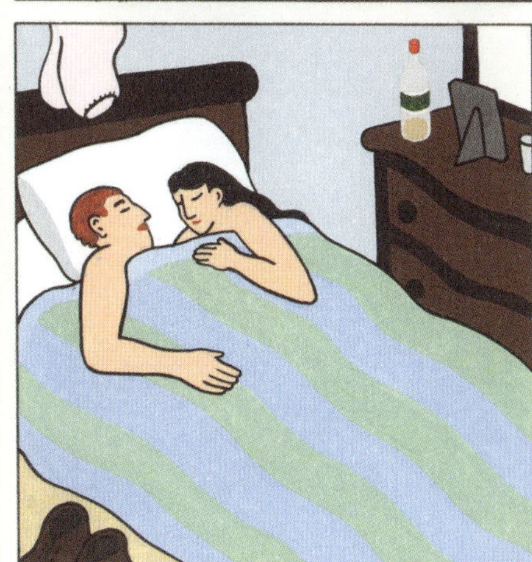
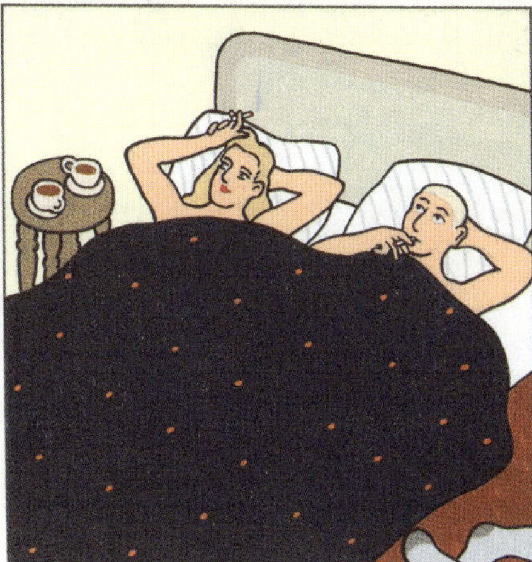

series ZZZZZ no 8 Ham on Rye © 1999

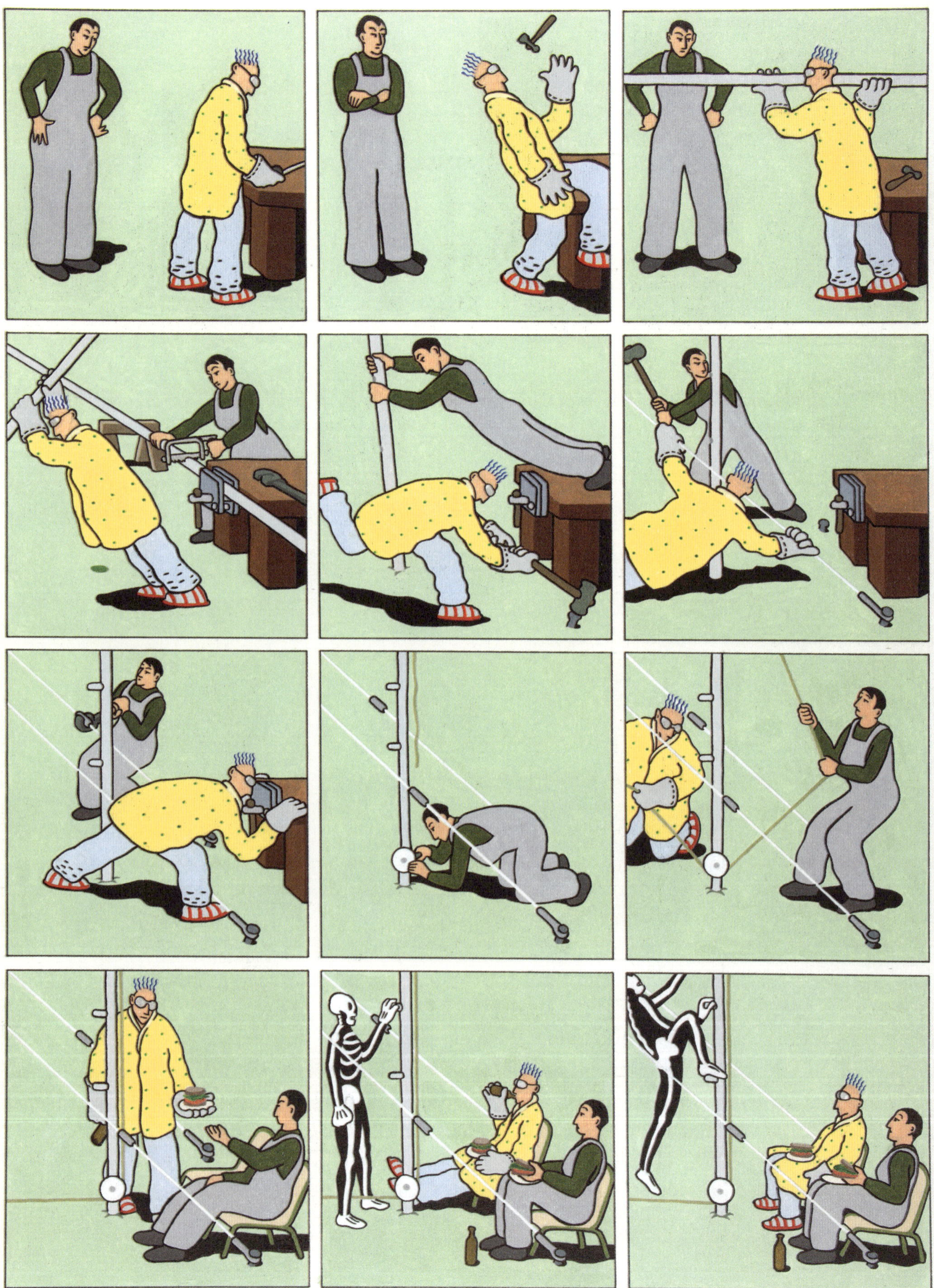

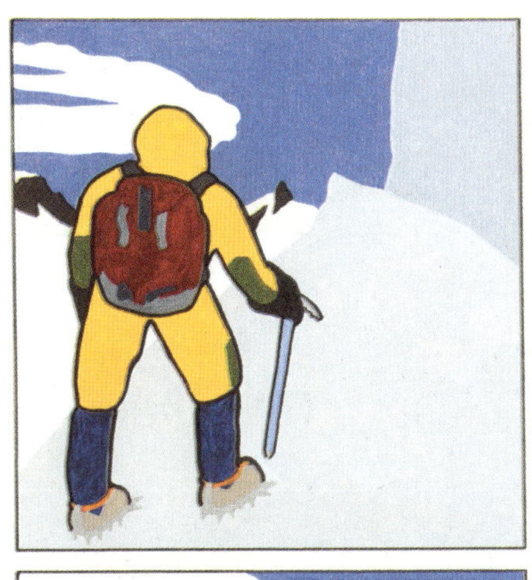
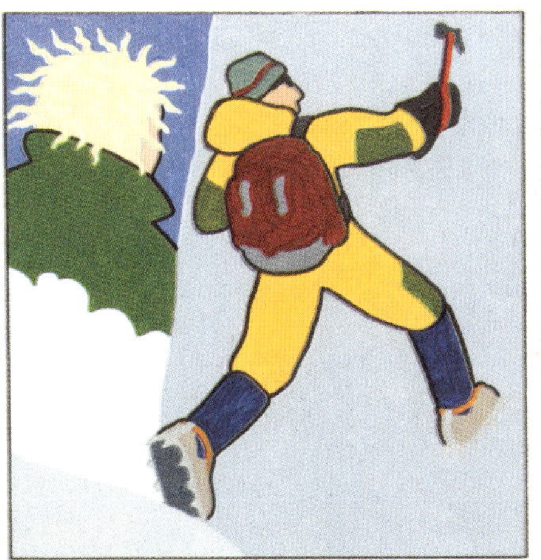
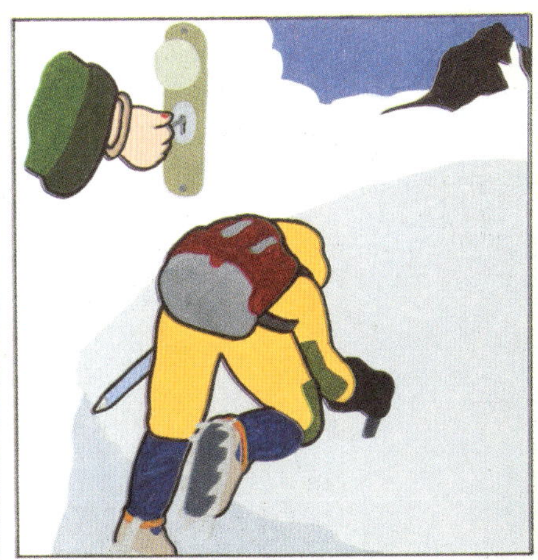
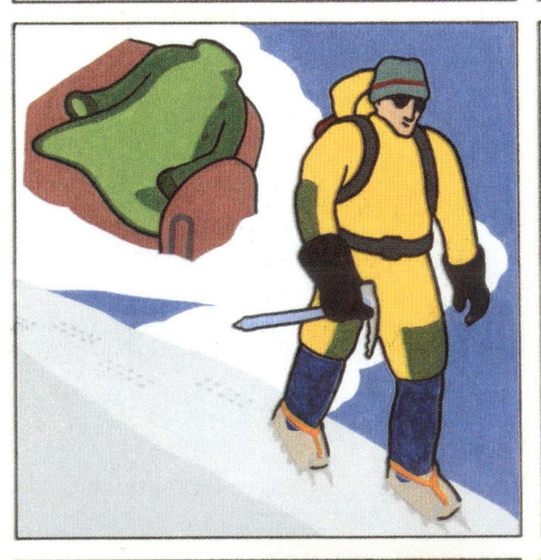
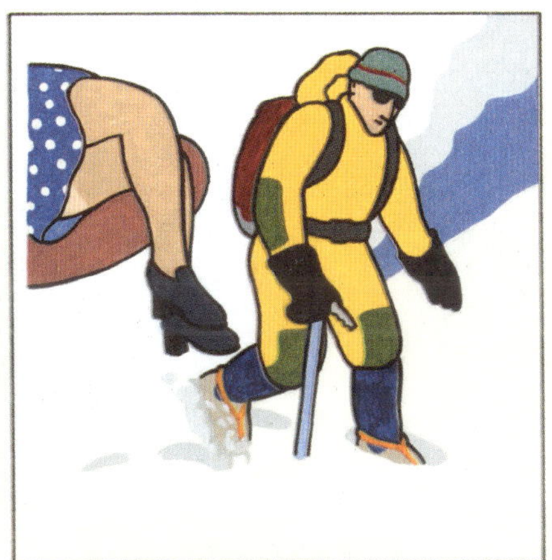
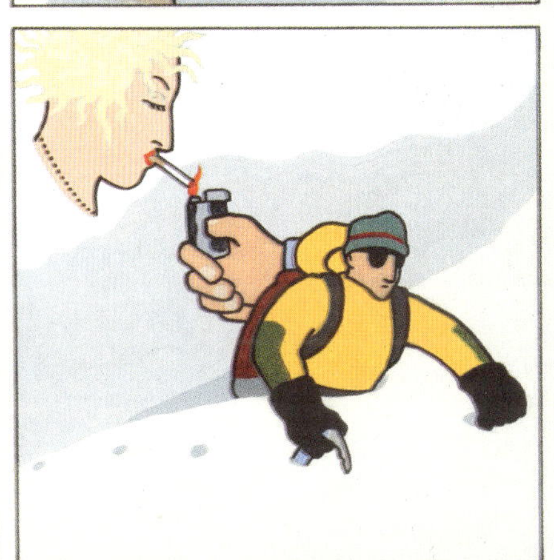
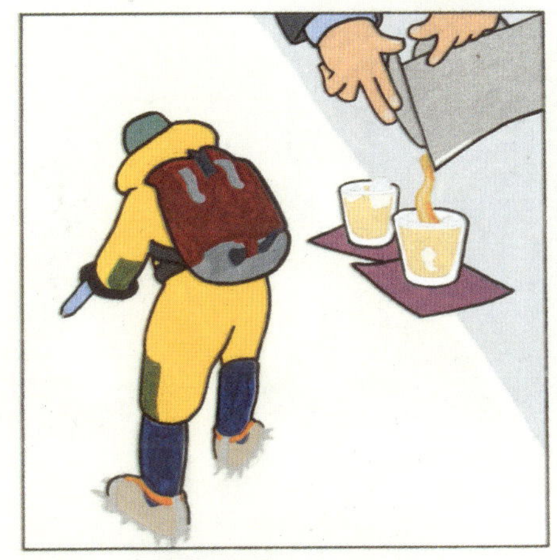
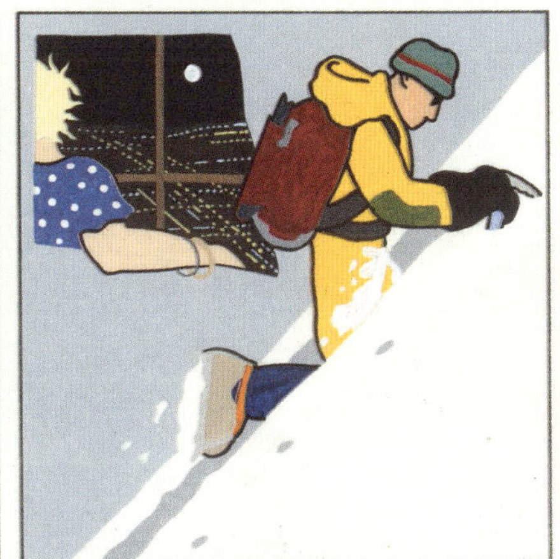
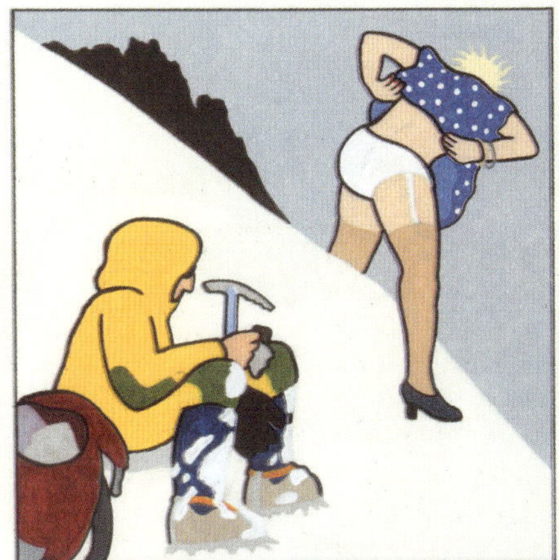
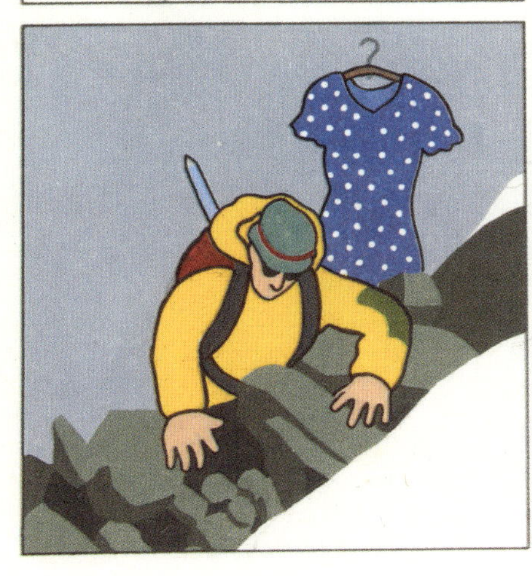
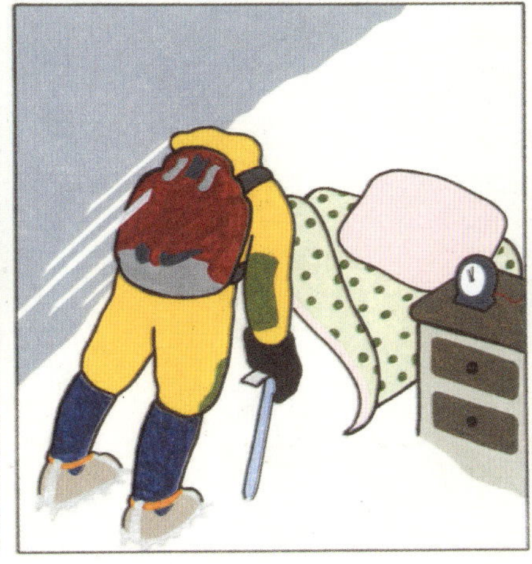
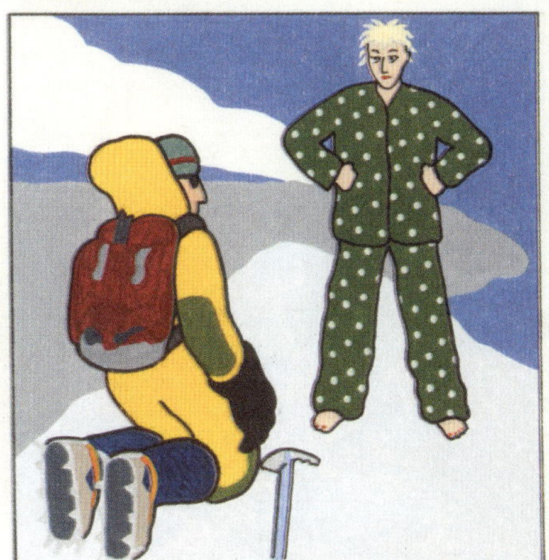

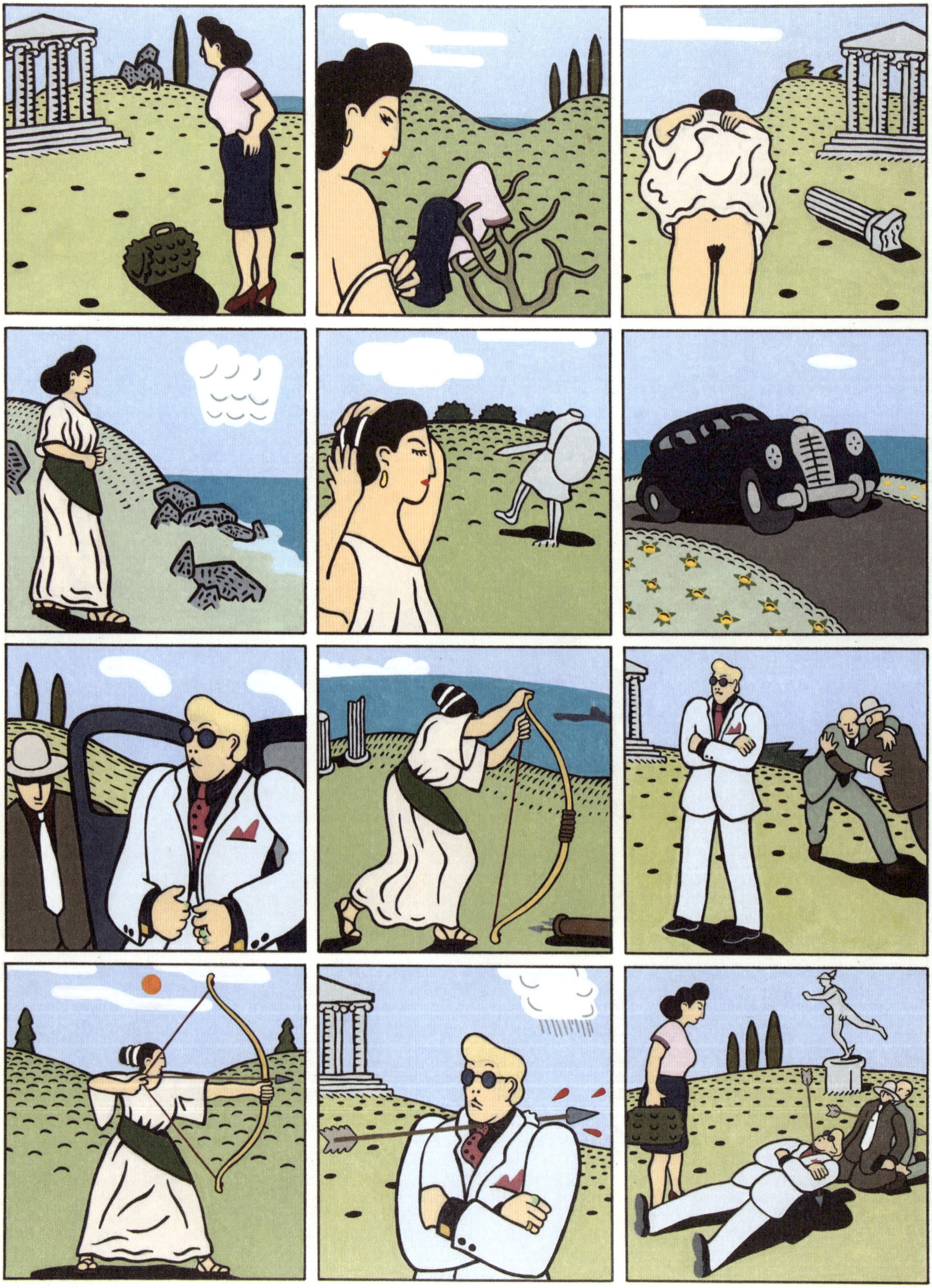

series ZZZZZ no. 10 Showdown at the Elysian Field

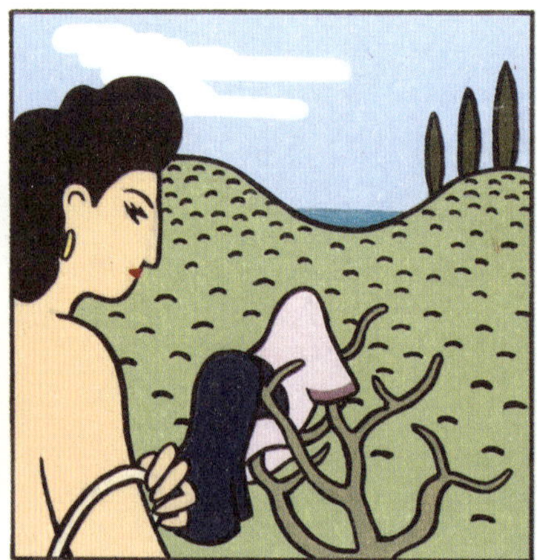

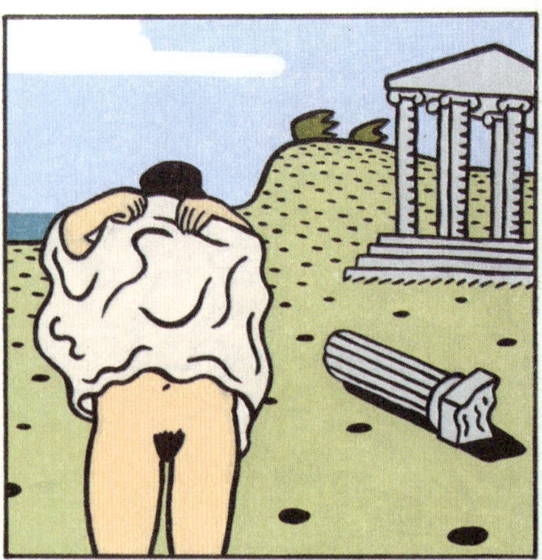

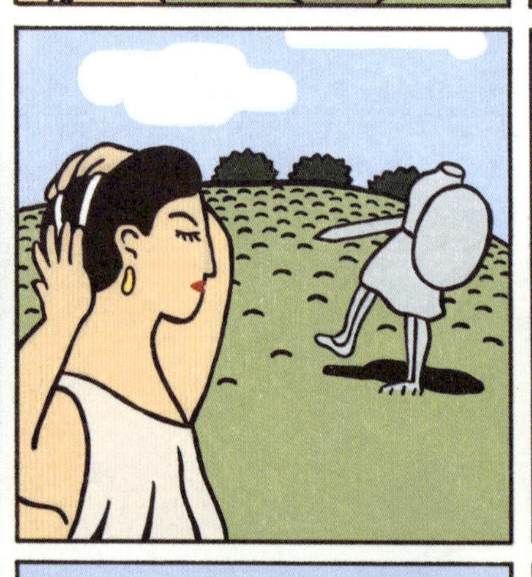

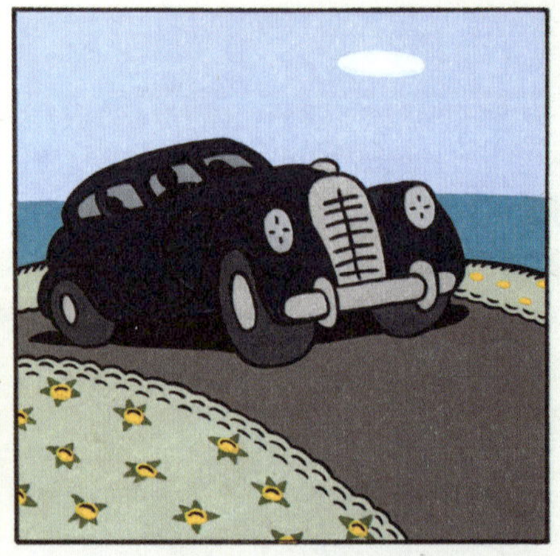

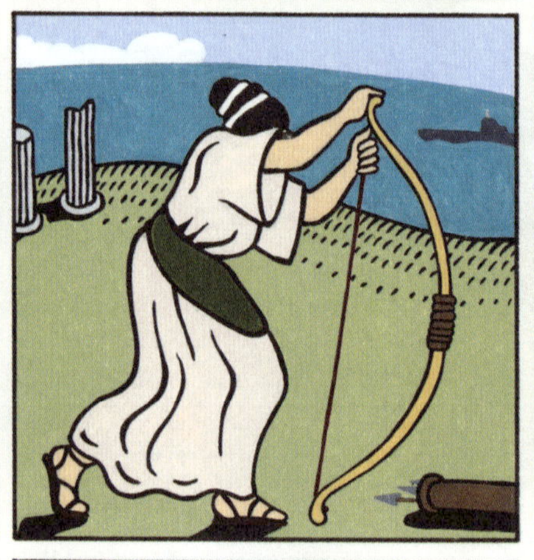

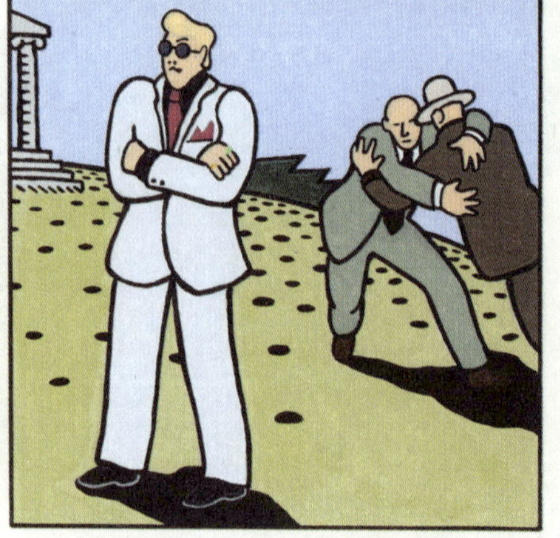

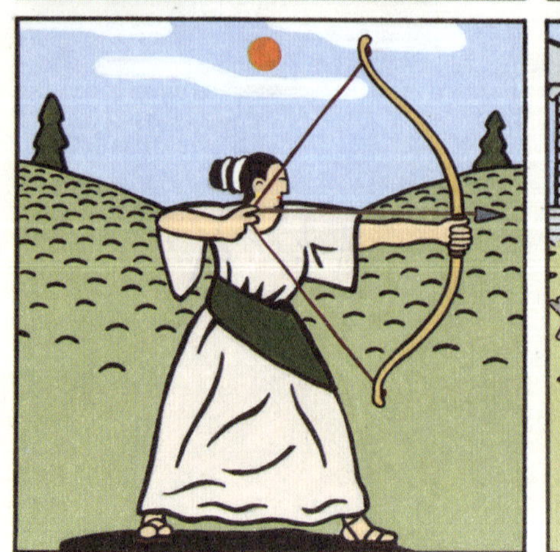

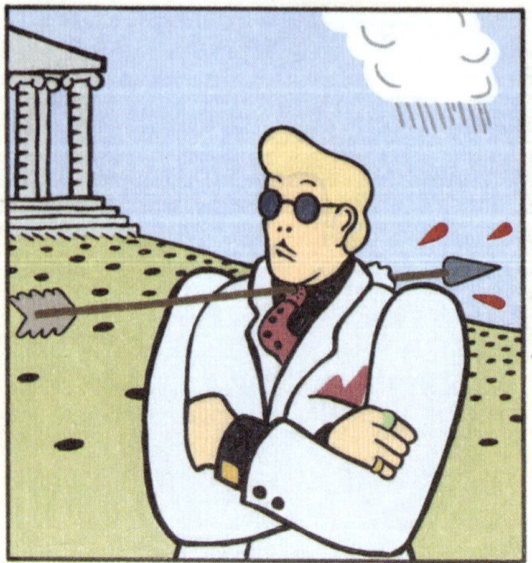

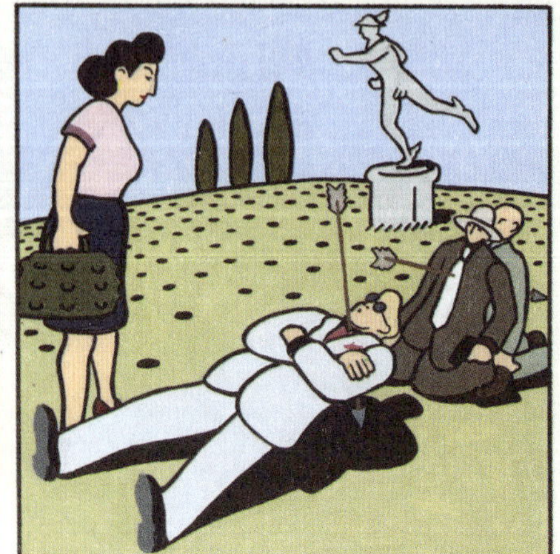

series ZZZZZ no. 11 A Discussion of String Theory as the South Face of Chingow Spills Forth

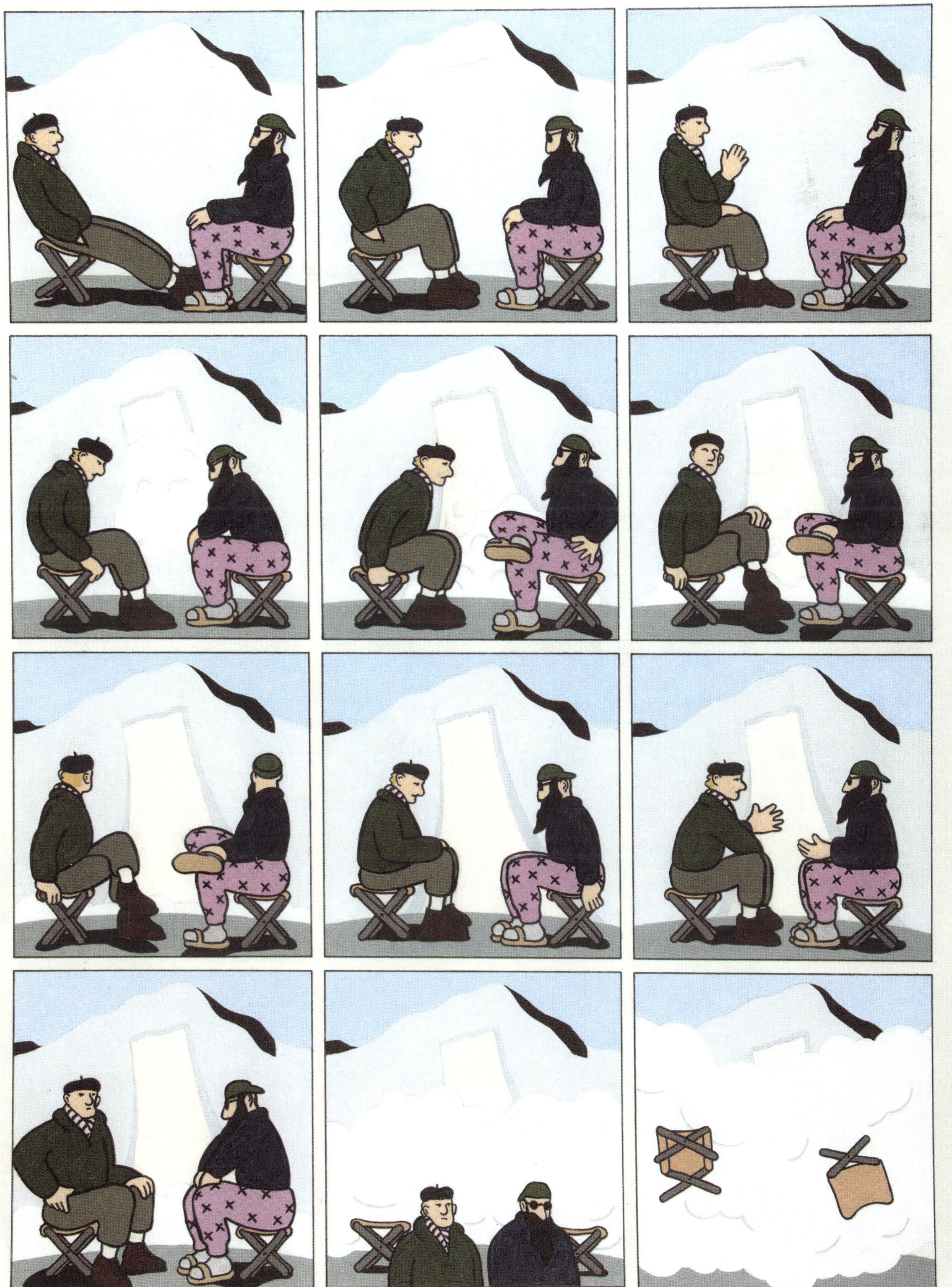

series ZZZZZ no. 12 What Music They Make

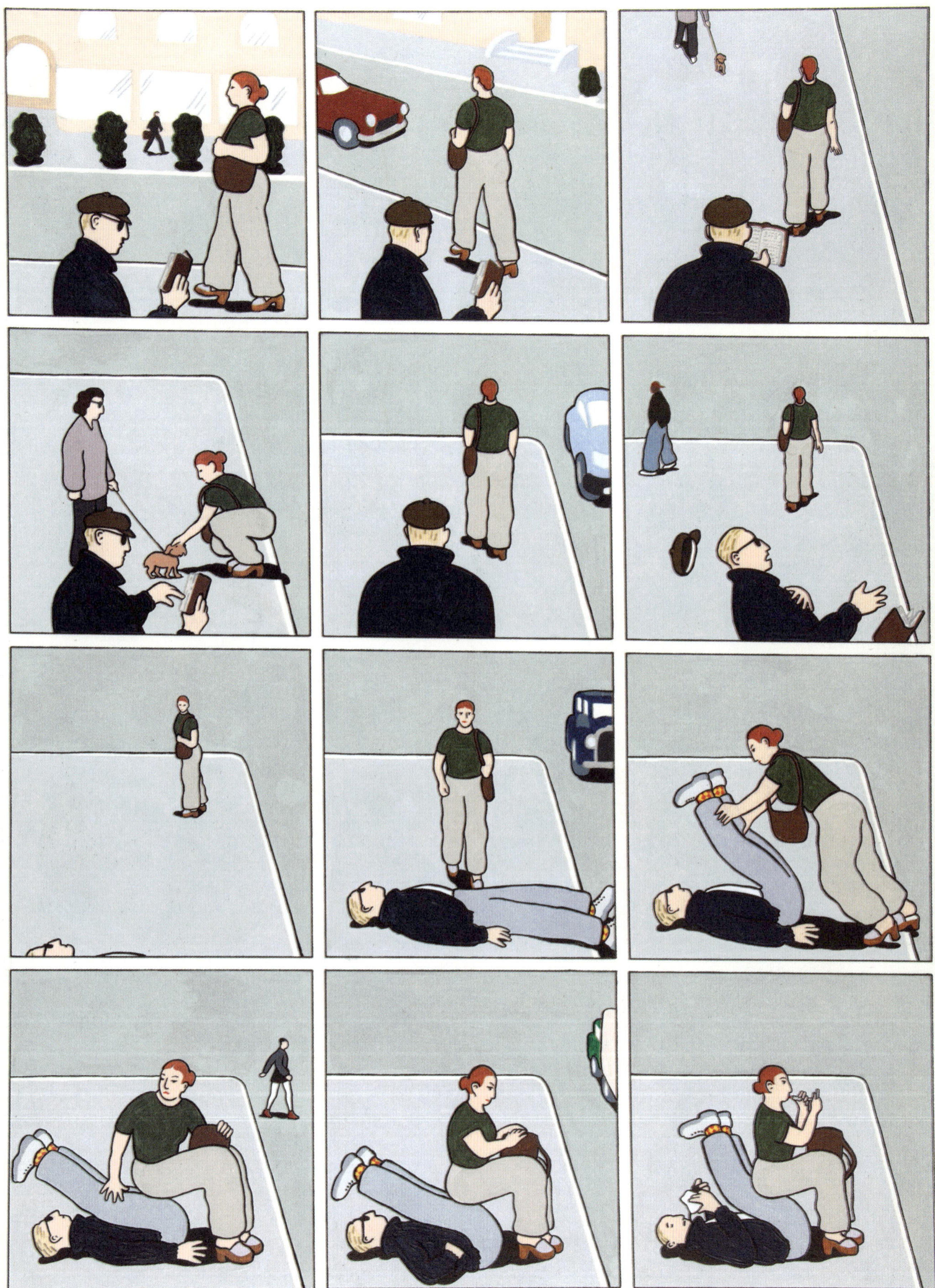

 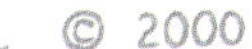

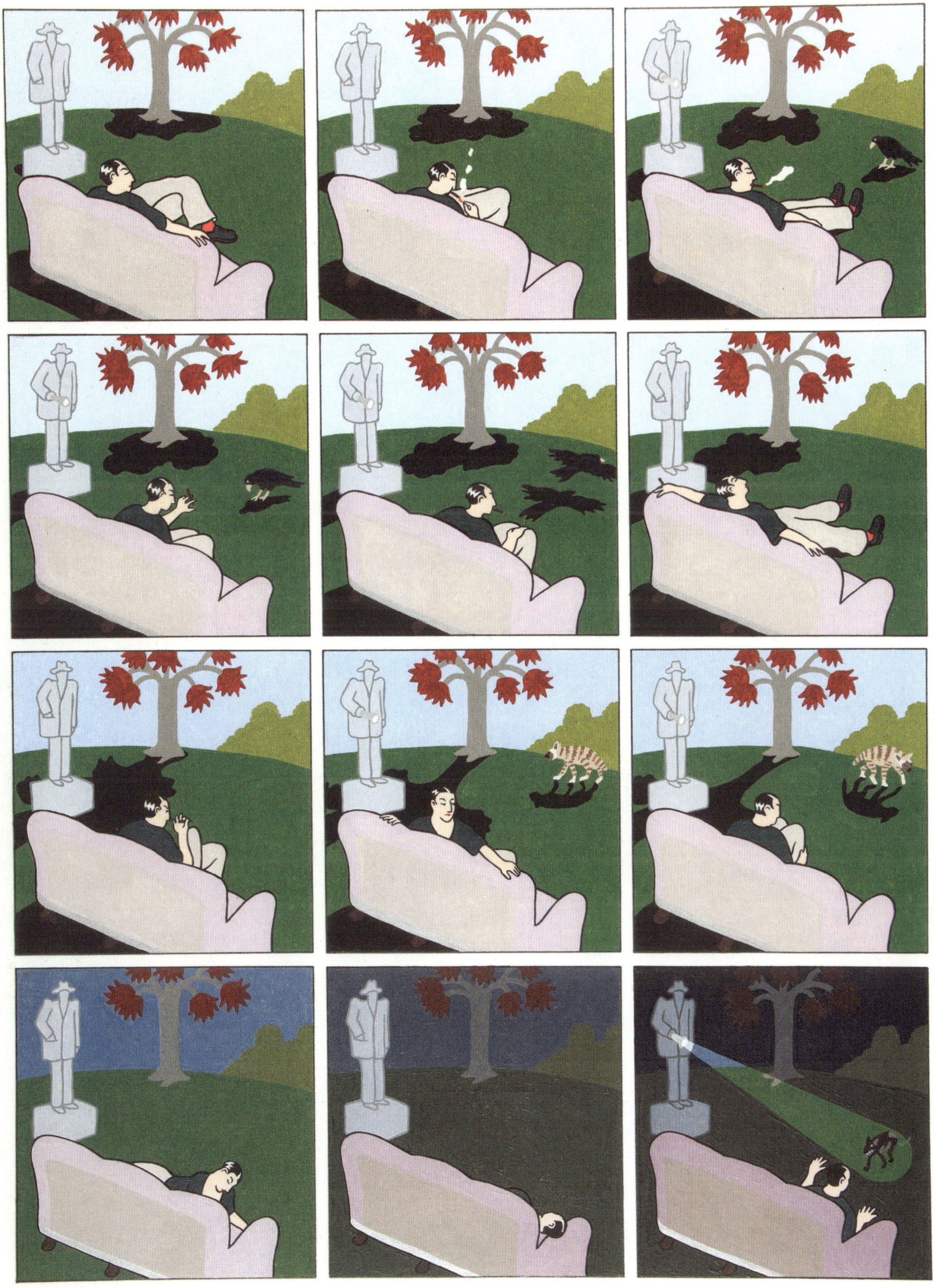

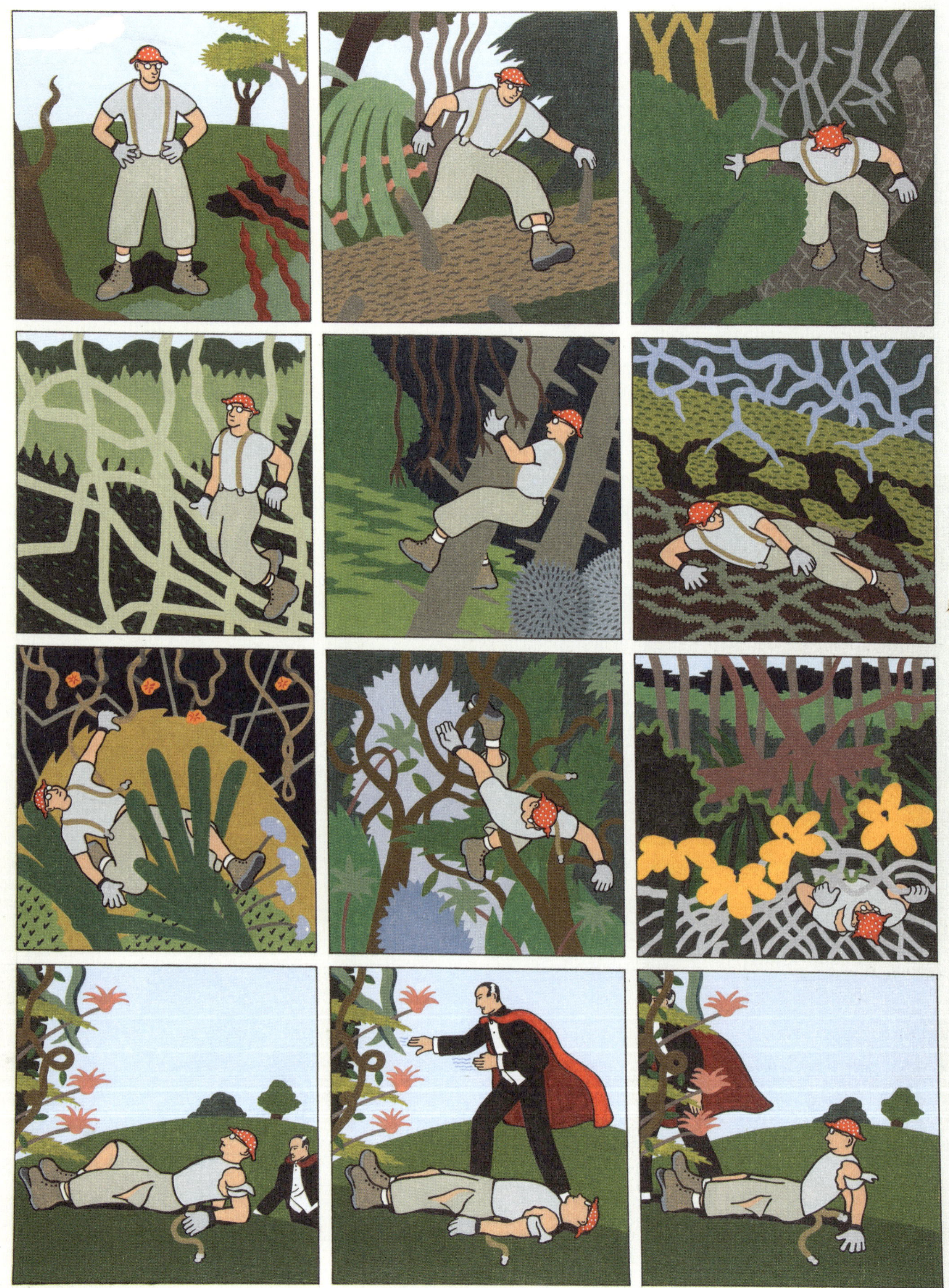

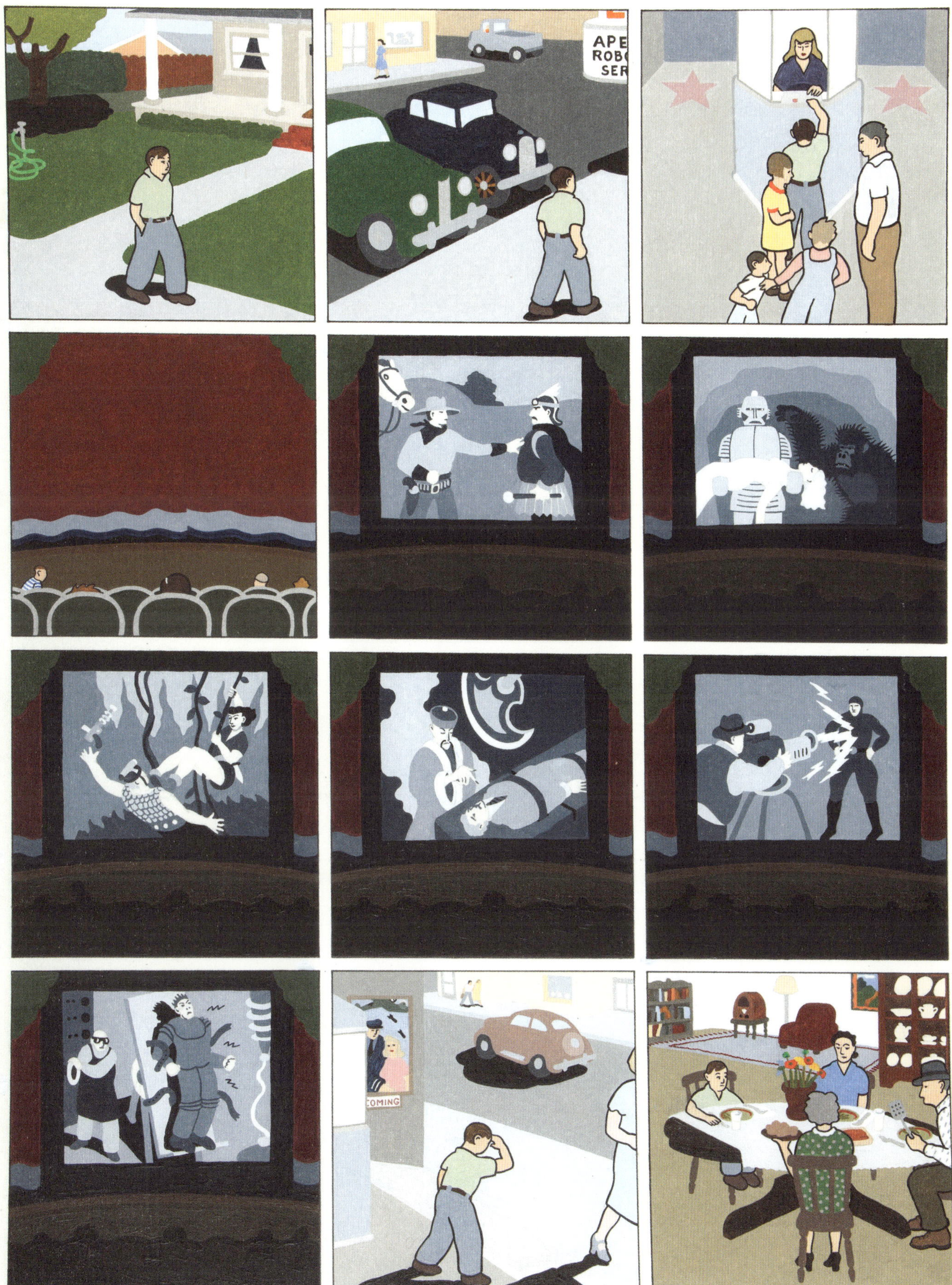
APE
ROBO
SER
COMING

ACKNOWLEDGMENTS

This is a Note of Appreciation and Thanks to the following, who offered motivation, support, and association through the years of my career covered in this collection of work: Salvatore Merendino, Stephen De Staebler, Van Galligan, Elsa Cameron, Michael Learner, Don Donahue, Bob Armstrong, Al Dodge, Dennis Calabi, Laura and John Mattos, Dan Nadel, Patrick Kroboth, Bill Griffith, Victor Moscoso, Lucas Adams, and of course Diane Balter.

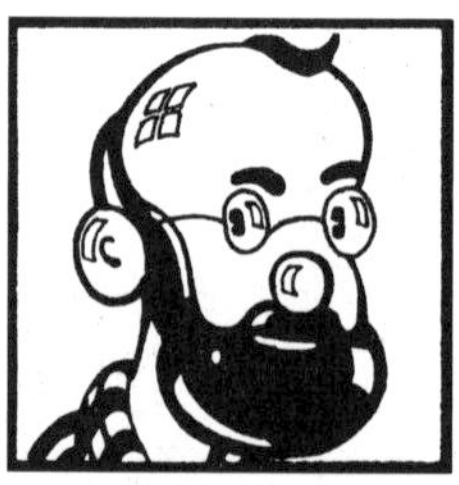
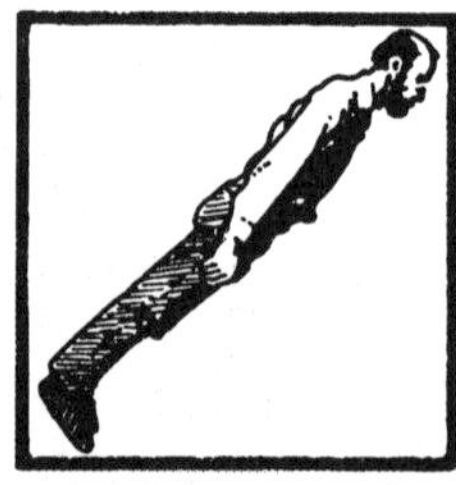
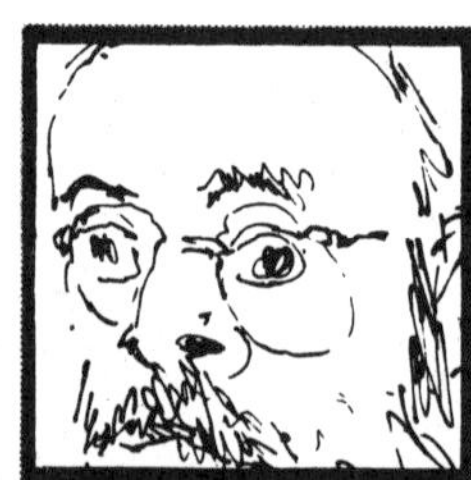
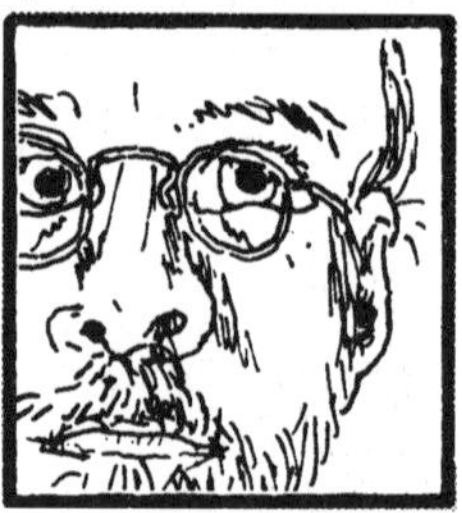
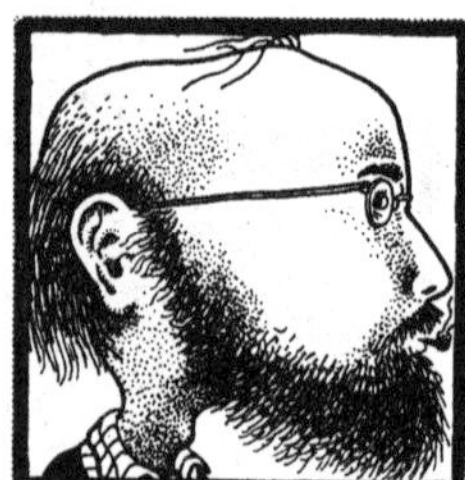
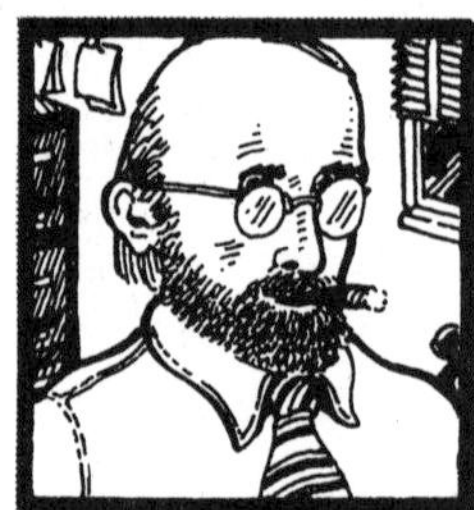

This is a completely collapsible sports facility made possible by high tech developments in structural materials. At full expansion the unit houses not only a football and baseball stadium, but an Olympic size swimming pool, a basketball court, a running track, a bicycle velodrome, and an ice skating rink, all with spectator seating.

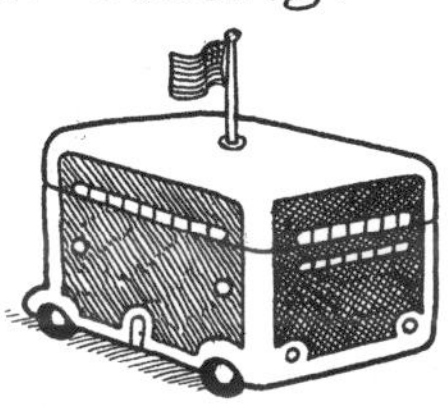

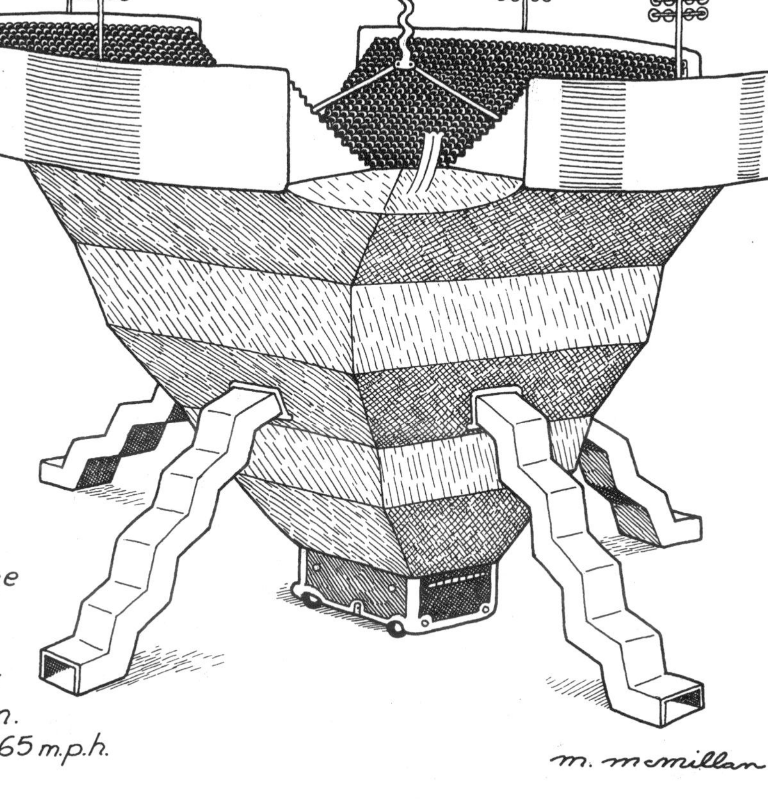

When collapsed the facility fits into a mobile unit the size of a large recreational vehicle. The vehicle is fully mobile thereby solving the 'stadium location' problem. It is capable of speeds up to 65 m.p.h.

m. mcmillan

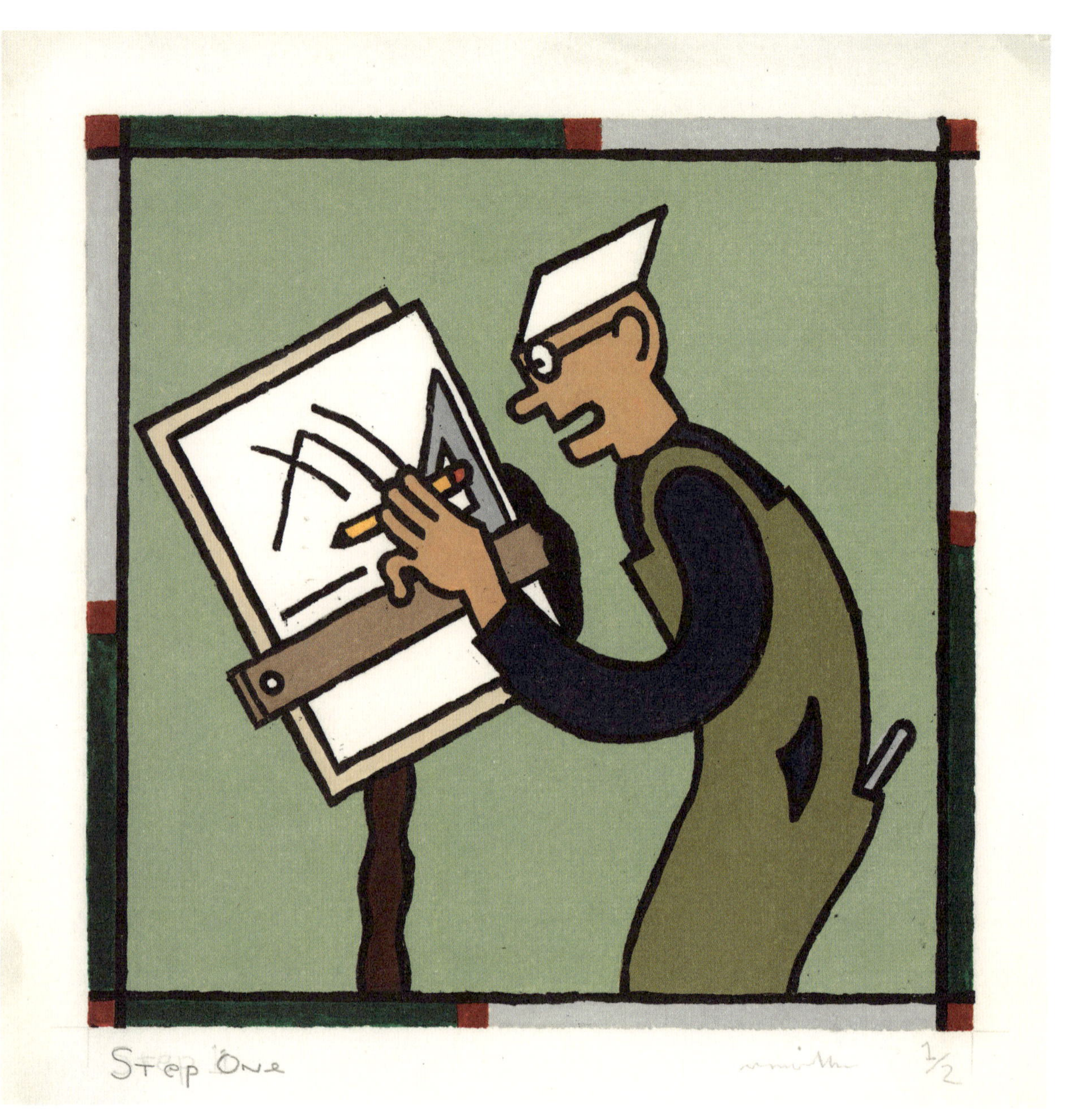
Step One
1/2

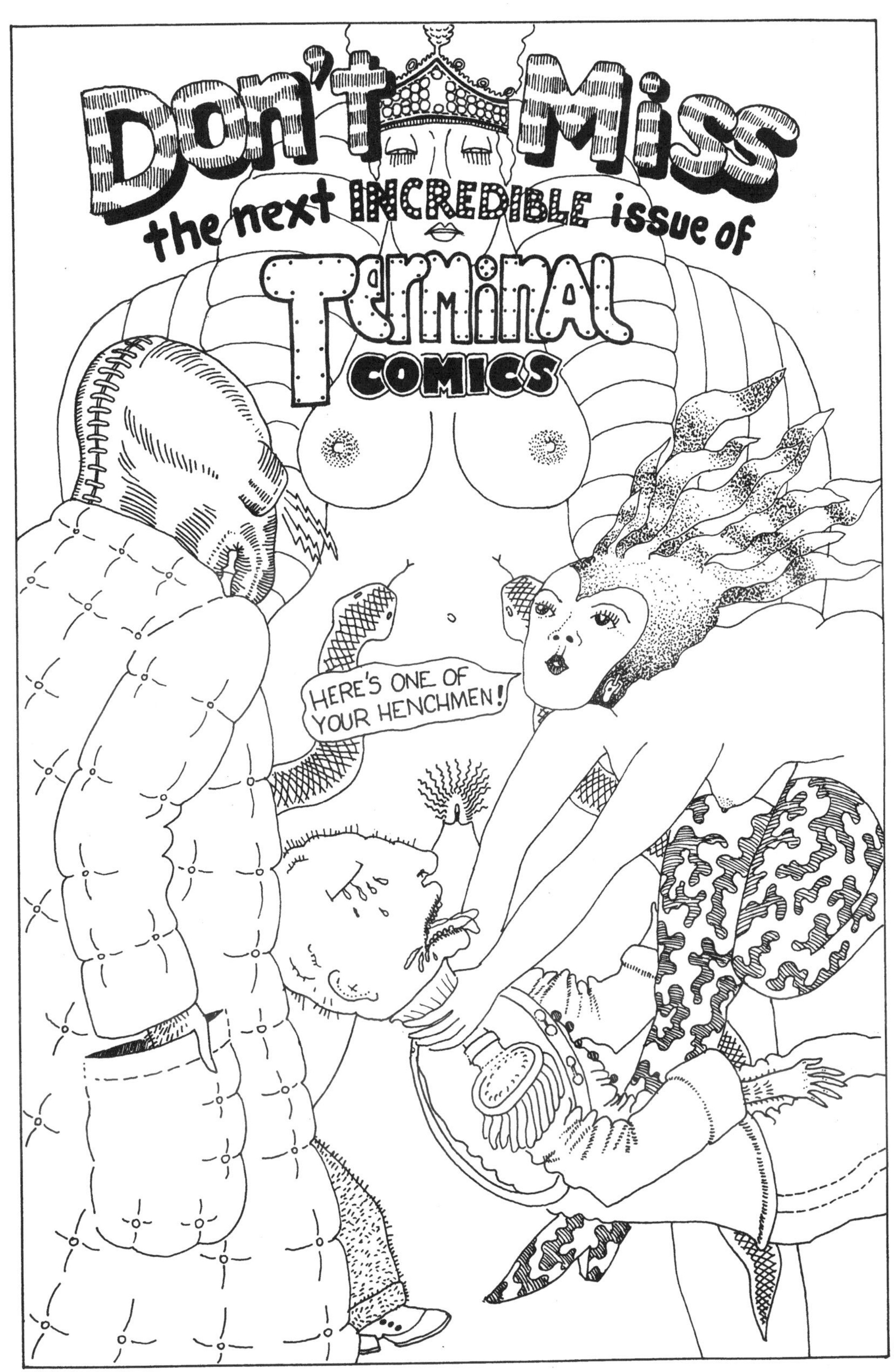
Don't Miss
the next INCREDIBLE issue of
Terminal
COMICS
HERE'S ONE OF YOUR HENCHMEN!

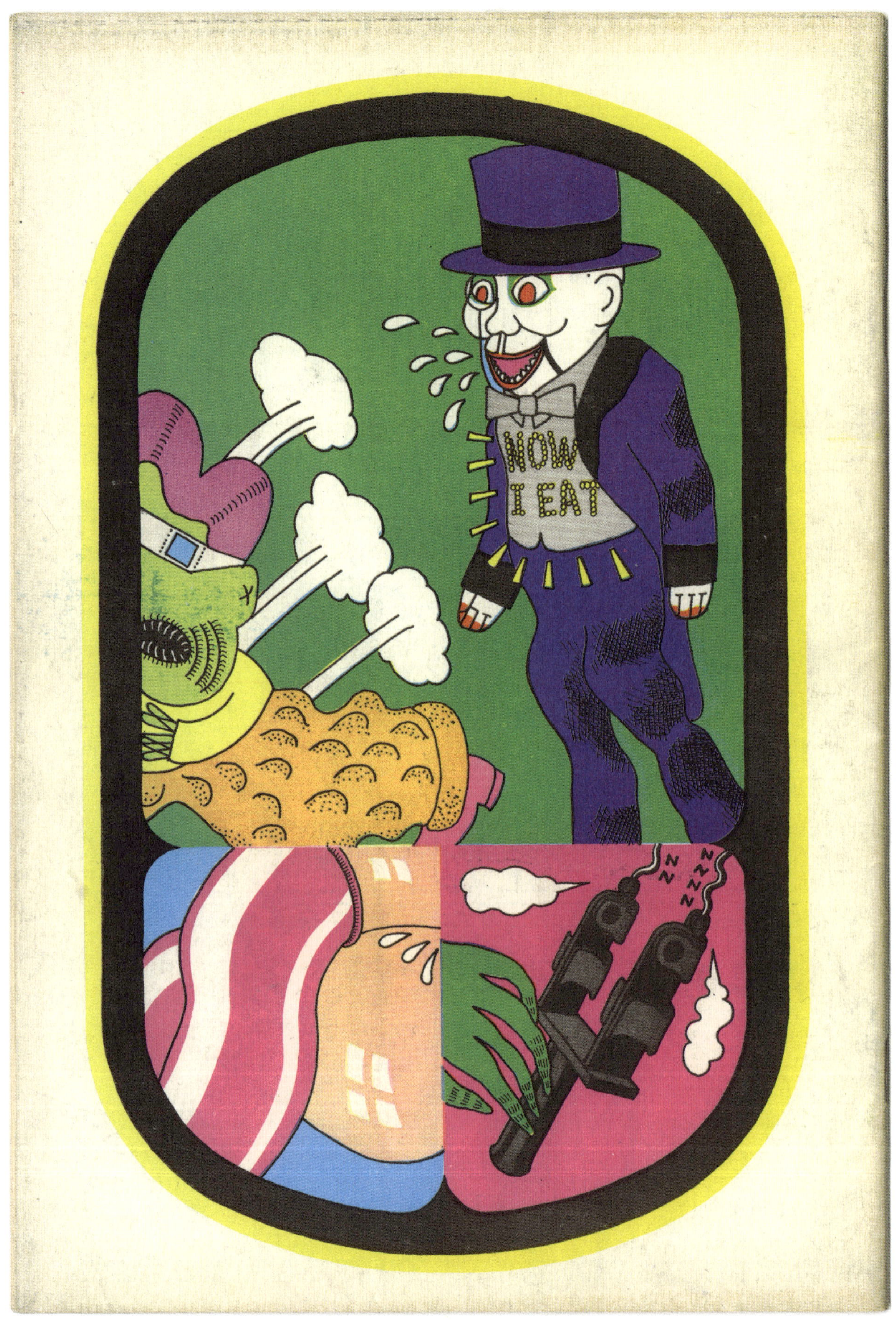
NOW
I EAT
ZZ
ZZZZ

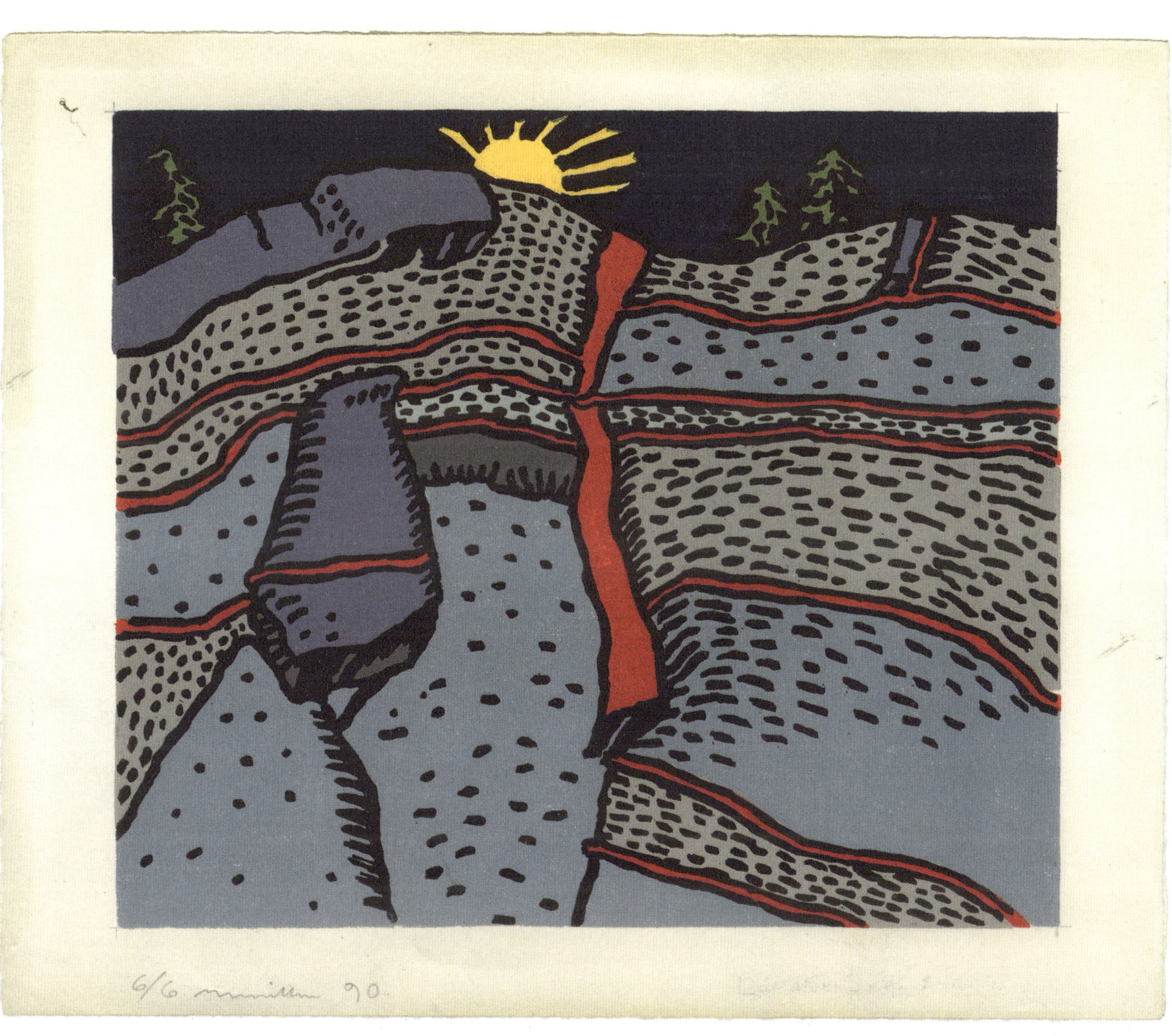

ALSO AVAILABLE FROM NEW YORK REVIEW COMICS

YELLOW NEGROES AND OTHER IMAGINARY CREATURES Yvan Alagbé
PIERO Edmond Baudoin
ALMOST COMPLETELY BAXTER Glen Baxter
AGONY Mark Beyer
MITCHUM Blutch
PEPLUM Blutch
NANCY AND SLUGGO'S GUIDE TO LIFE Ernie Bushmiller
DISTANT RUPTURES: A SELECTION OF COMICS, 2000-2010 C.F.
THE GREEN HAND AND OTHER STORIES Nicole Claveloux
WHAT AM I DOING HERE? Abner Dean
W THE WHORE Anke Feuchtenberger and Katrin de Vries
TROTS AND BONNIE Shary Flenniken
LETTER TO SURVIVORS Gébé
PRETENDING IS LYING Dominique Goblet
ALAY-OOP William Gropper
THE RULING CLAWSS Syd Hoff
BUNGLETON GREEN AND THE MYSTIC COMMANDOS Jay Jackson
ALL YOUR RACIAL PROBLEMS WILL SOON END Charles Johnson
THE GULL YETTIN Joe Kessler
SPIRAL AND OTHER STORIES Aidan Koch
VOICES IN THE DARK Ulli Lust
SOCIAL FICTION Chantal Montellier
IT'S LIFE AS I SEE IT: BLACK CARTOONISTS IN CHICAGO, 1940–1980
Edited by Dan Nadel
JIMBO: ADVENTURES IN PARADISE Gary Panter
FATHER AND SON E. O. Plauen
MASTERS OF THE NEFARIOUS: MOLLUSK RAMPAGE Pierre La Police
SOFT CITY Pushwagner
THE NEW WORLD: COMICS FROM MAURETANIA Chris Reynolds
PITTSBURGH Frank Santoro
BLURRY Dash Shaw
DISCIPLINE Dash Shaw
MACDOODLE ST. Mark Alan Stamaty
POOR HELPLESS COMICS! Ed Subitzky
NINJA SARUTOBI SASUKE Sugiura Shigeru
SLUM WOLF Tadao Tsuge
THE MAN WITHOUT TALENT Yoshiharu Tsuge
THE PROJECTOR AND ELEPHANT Martin Vaughn-James
RETURN TO ROMANCE Ogden Whitney

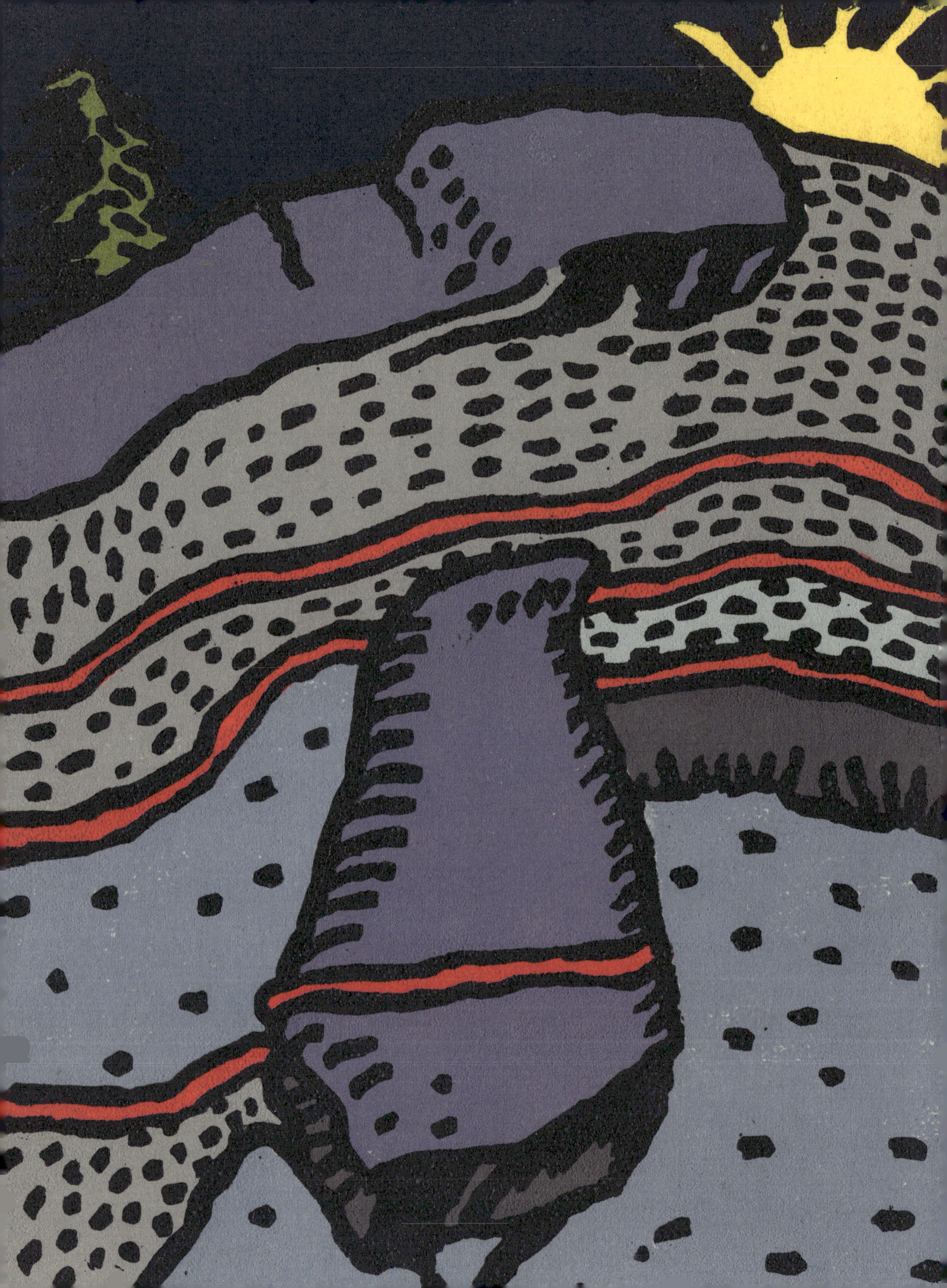